GODLY LEARNING

GODLY LEARNING

*Puritan Attitudes towards Reason, Learning,
and Education, 1560–1640*

JOHN MORGAN

Department of History, Ryerson Polytechnical Institute, Toronto

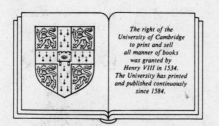

The right of the
University of Cambridge
to print and sell
all manner of books
was granted by
Henry VIII in 1534.
The University has printed
and published continuously
since 1584.

CAMBRIDGE UNIVERSITY PRESS

Cambridge

New York   New Rochelle   Melbourne   Sydney

124836

Published by the Press Syndicate of the University of Cambridge
The Pitt Building, Trumpington Street, Cambridge CB2 1RP
32 East 57th Street, New York, NY 10022, USA
10 Stamford Road, Oakleigh, Melbourne, 3166, Australia

First published 1986
First paperback edition 1988

Printed in Great Britain at the University Press, Cambridge

British Library cataloguing in publication data
Morgan, John Philip
Godly learning: Puritan attitudes towards
reason, learning, and education.
1. Education – Great Britain – History – 16th century   2. Education
– Great Britain – History – 17th century   3. Puritans – Great
Britain – Attitudes
I. Title
370′.941   LA663.4

Library of Congress cataloguing in publication data
Morgan, John, Ph.D.
Godly Learning.
Bibliography: p.
Includes index.
1. Puritans. 2. Learning and scholarship – History – 17th century.
3. Pastoral theology – History of doctrines – 17th century. I.
Title.
BX9322.M63   1986   285′.9   85-11026

ISBN 0 521 23511 1 hard covers
ISBN 0 521 35700 4 paperback

for Bronwen

Credit through writing bookes, is a thing of such dangerous hazard, by reason of the varietie of the censurers, that it is doubtfull whether a man shall winne or lose thereby: Gaine also is so slender, as that, for a booke of a yeeres paines and studie, it will be a verie hard matter to attaine, if it were set to sale in Pauls Church-yard, so much money as inck, paper, and light cost him that penned it: so as except a man should doate, hee must have better grounds of publishing his writings, than either *credit* or *gaine*: especially considering the plentifull harvest of bookes of all sorts, amongst which there appeareth variable contention. In some it is questionable, whether wit or learning getteth the victorie: in others the strife is betwixt wit and the truth . . .

    John Smyth, *A Paterne of True Prayer . . .*, Address to Edmund Lord Sheffield, President of the Council of the North.

You see, gentlemen, reason, gentlemen, is an excellent thing, there is no disputing that, but reason is only reason and can only satisfy man's rational faculty, while will is a manifestation of all life, that is, of all human life including reason as well as all impulses.

    Fyodor Dostoevsky, *Notes from Underground*

The final conclusion of absurdist reasoning is, in fact, . . . the acceptance of the desperate encounter between human inquiry and the silence of the universe.

    Albert Camus, *The Rebel*, Introduction.

CONTENTS

vii

PREFACE

Despite the usual fear and trembling which accompany the creative act, I have immensely enjoyed researching and writing this book. Part of the satisfaction – sometimes even the joy – that is the academic life comes from the camaraderie that occasions and accompanies the exchange of opinion and thoughtful interpretation. The journey from first interest in a topic to finished manuscript thus becomes a progress told in the accumulation of debts. My chief indebtedness is to my former supervisor at Cambridge, Roger Schofield, whose brilliance, lucidity, and patience were of immeasurable help to me in writing my Ph.D. Geoffrey Elton taught me much in his research seminar, and has acted as a kind guide since. Jack Lander first attracted me to the problems of education when he supervised my M.A. thesis on an earlier period. To Christopher Hill, John Dunn, and Joan Simon, I owe gratitude for very helpful advice during my research for the thesis. Earlier drafts of this present work were read, with much generosity of time and spirit, by Richard Greaves, Roger Schofield, Geoffrey Elton, Peter Lake, and Felicity Heal. All of these people have criticized – from various points of view – my interpretation of the puritans. The synthesis provided here, while a product of all these academic experiences, is of course my own responsibility.

Pursuit of the puritans has carried me to a great number of libraries. In all repositories of the nation's past, I have been met not only with professional efficiency, but also with kindness and interested inquiry. It is my real pleasure, therefore, to thank those who preserve and deliver our heritage: the workers of the British Library, the Bodleian, Lambeth Palace Library, the John Rylands Library, the Inner Temple Library, the Lincoln Record Office (Lincoln), the Essex Record Office (Chelmsford), Dr Williams's Library, the Public Record Office, and, above all for me, the Cambridge University Library.

The Social Sciences and Humanities Research Council of Canada has supported this project by means of two post-doctoral fellowships (No. 456–80–0067 for 1980–1 and No. 456–81–3471 for 1981–2) and a research grant (No. 410–80–0650). Queen's University, Kingston, Ontario, provided me with travel assistance to attend the History of Education Conference on Literacy held at Leicester in March 1980 (to which Joan Simon very generously invited me). Ryerson Polytechnical Institute of Toronto, where I currently teach, provided financial assistance for the typing and photocopying of the final draft.

Crucial, too, were those members of the supporting cast whose credits are always run too quickly at the end. Julianna O'Brien (assisted by Ann Maycock) typed the final drafts rapidly, efficiently, and with good cheer. Cambridge University Press, in the incarnation of Patricia Williams, and then Bill Davies and Jennifer Fellows, was always helpful, and also patient in putting up with the delays occasioned by my having annually to prepare new courses at different universities in this age of the peripatetic academic. Bob Malcolmson, David Booy, Deanne Bogdan, Sharon Bailin, and Doug Stoute offered very useful suggestions from radically different perspectives.

Always last: the person who most closely shares the burden with the author, whose cooperation is the *sine qua non* of completing the work. I thank Bronwen for her stalwart encouragement, and also for the gentle reminders that there could be existence beyond the puritans.

I have followed the usual convention of providing both years for dates between 1 January and 25 March. I have not altered any punctuation in quotations; the spelling, too, follows the original form.

Toronto
16.xii.84

INTRODUCTION

I

While it may well be current historical practice to require a sympathetic comprehension of the *mentalité* of any past society, in practice this dictum has frequently boiled down to an analysis of either the thought of the few savants or the cultural activities of the many folk. Far less common have been attempts to understand the general ideas and attitudes of the broad band of educated people 'below' the level of the leading intellectual lights of the age. In such a vein the ideas of the puritans are frequently taken by historians merely as a backdrop to the influence of puritans on their society. Patrick Collinson has recently noted that sociological influences have caused the modern historian of religion to ponder not only 'what people were supposed to believe, but what they in fact believed, and still more what they did with their belief, its meaning and function'.[1] Much recent work has examined the degree of proliferation of puritan attitudes, the social connexions of puritans, and the social, economic, and political impact of 'puritanism'. Beyond this, there has been serious scrutiny of the specific reforms which puritans wished to introduce into the church and, more generally, into social existence. Other scholars have investigated the degree to which 'puritan' views were adapted by contemporaries for their own private uses.

Few historians, on the other hand, have concentrated on a comprehension of what puritans were themselves trying to say to their contemporaries. Because there were no puritan intellects in the period 1560–1640 to rival Shakespeare or Bacon, or the greatest continental theologians and philosophers, historians have tended to write about a tight intellectual heritage called 'puritanism' rather than about individual puritans. This 'puritanism' has been accepted as a given, as an historical essence which could then be investigated as a catalyst and necessary groundwork to the pillars of an emerging modern society. 'Puritanism' was thus seen in the historical literature as one of the great factors of 'modernization'. While it is of course

---

[1] Collinson, *The Religion of Protestants*, p. 189.

legitimate to search for the origins of modern society, we must also be aware
of attempts at change that were unsuccessful, or only partly successful. One of
the chief themes of the present work is that puritans aimed at a radical alteration (*vis-à-vis* the legacy of the Renaissance) of the ways in which reason was
perceived and in which learning was used, and that their suggestions would
have carried the intellectual thrust of England in seriously different directions
from those which dominated by the end of the seventeenth century.

It is important to understand that while there was general unity of purpose,
on specific topics puritans could (and did) disagree among themselves even
while publicly offering a common front against those whom they perceived as
their foes. Part of the difficulty in studies of puritan thought has been the
paucity of opinions upon which historians have relied. Several hundred
puritan works are cited in the text here as a testament to a lively and broad
thought. They represent, I wish to make clear, not the product of feverish
source-mining and lumping, but rather the slow distillation over the years of a
wide search of puritan authors. I have constantly endeavoured not to use a
source to establish what I think puritans 'should' have said, or what they
'meant' to say while not quite bringing themselves to it.[2] I have rather
attempted to accumulate an understanding of the different puritan opinions
on many questions of reason, learning, and education. I have therefore not
attempted to draw a reinterpreted portrait of '*the* puritan mind'.

I have argued throughout that puritans did not have a fixed blueprint for
the reformation of society. Much as Lenin found himself in power in 1917
with an historical view of why socialism had to prove victorious, so the
authorities that puritans held dear – especially the apostle Paul – delineated
much that was unacceptable, against which puritans knew they would have to
contend in these latter days. But, like Lenin, puritans had no bequeathed
master-plan for the full erection of a reformed society. They conceived of an
end at which they were aiming, but the route was a matter of discovery, of
application of trial-and-error methods, of reaction to context. And as the context changed, so, too, did the visible puritan thrusts and pressures on the
various facets of contemporary society. The historian who looks for internal
consistency in the thought of a single man, let alone uniformity in a host, may
well be forcing an unnatural structure upon his evidence.

This raises another problem of historical methodology. Academics, partly
because of their own (self-)interest, tend to praise in the past the advancement
of learning as being self-evidently 'good'. Those who have opposed the
expansion of human reason or the corpus of humane learning have sometimes
been branded as the 'lunatic fringe'. This praise of reason, and of learning as its
visible product, would seem to be one of the greatest social and intellectual

<hr/>

[2] On this point see the warning in Schochet, 'Quentin Skinner's method', *Political Theory*, 2, pp.
265–6.

effects of the Cartesian world-view which dominated the West from the late seventeenth century to the late nineteenth or early twentieth century. Here, reason was the essence of human being. The Cartesian world turned Being upside down so that, philosophically, the very existence of the biological unit was established by the continuation of thought processes. Essence, in a strange reformulation of the Platonist position, again came before existence.

Even in a post-Nietzschean, post-Freudian, post-existentialist West, historians of ideas seem commonly to look for the advance of reason as the chief indication of man's 'progress' through the ages. Those factors in the past which have challenged the supremacy of the rational have therefore been seen as retrogressive. If they were aspects of a movement which was nonetheless held to be a catalyst of modernization, then they were downplayed. So Perry Miller, while acknowledging that puritans on occasion stressed enthusiasm in religion and criticized the contribution of reason, was forced by his desire to stress the development of a 'puritan *mind*', to downplay this aspect, and to slough it off as, really, no more than a theatrical gesture, almost an aberration in the puritan character. The attempt to redress this false emphasis has been one of the primary tasks of the present work

Part of the difficulty is that historians themselves are products of the stress on the rational. With questions of non-rational behaviour and belief in the past, however, the question immediately arises as to whether the historian's reason is sufficient to capture the past, or whether it will inevitably create a false picture of a continuum of thoughtful action and behaviour. Historians generally acknowledge the necessity of 'historical imagination' or the 'creative leap', but this is usually taken to mean merely filling in the gaps between the empirical data. The limitations of this approach may perhaps be made clearer by use of an illustration. If the historian of the coal industry totals the tonnage of coal, recounts the capitalist's profits, the geographical mobility of the labour force, the frequency of disruption of marriage in that labour force, the socio-economic effects of the industry in a region, and so on, then what will he have told us? From the point of view of an *objective* observer, who simply wanted to know *about* another universe, this information will present an accurate study. But it will tell us very little about the existence, the *Being*, of the coal worker, from the inside. Of course, experiencing the conditions about which one writes is often not fully possible. The historians of slavery and feudalism can hardly be expected to subjugate themselves to such conditions. The historian of religious ideas, who possesses no religious beliefs himself, and who writes in a secular age, faces similar problems. The great difficulty is to comprehend the religious fervency of the puritans which, as I shall argue, was the core of their Being. While the manifestations of this fervency can readily be catalogued, this act of compilation is hardly the same as having felt the drive oneself.

The difficulty, then, is to combine our 'objective' knowledge of 'what happened' with a comprehension of the meaning of having *been* that experience. To reconstruct this, as Dostoevsky and Henri Bergson informed us, we must go beyond the empirical, even beyond the rational, to the realm of the intuitive. It will be helpful to attempt to follow Bergson's idea of 'getting inside' something in order to have 'intellectual sympathy' with it. Bergson saw empirical, or quantitative knowledge as 'relative knowledge', since it was only an accumulation of knowledge concerning frozen moments in time. He emphasized, in the search for what he called 'absolute knowledge' as distinct from the 'relative', the power of human intuition. In order to transcend (*not* to abandon) the empirical and objective point of view, it is necessary to come to an empathic comprehension of the questions of the past, and the ways in which the inhabitants of the past addressed them. Instead of distancing ourselves, like Blind Justice, we should perhaps rather attempt to *become* the *experience* of the past, at least in so far as this effort would enable us to appreciate not just a different view of a single question, but a radically different *Weltanschauung*.

The prime message of puritan Reformed protestantism was irrational: the free grace of God made available to his chosen, dependent upon nothing that people did in their own lives. This gift was not based on a rational decision, and so could not be fully comprehended by analysis alone. Schoolchildren could attend sermons, and on Monday in school analyse the *explanation* of the gift, but only the elect could feel the blessing that was assurance, and thus come to 'absolute knowledge' of their bond with God. Perhaps a well-known illustration will help here. It was said of William Perkins that he could pronounce the word 'damn' with such effect in a sermon that the very walls of the church would shake. In order to be able to understand the experience of puritan existence, I think it is crucial to come to some comprehension of this 'fear and trembling', this existential search for meaning by (some of) the people in Perkins' audience. Doubtless there were social, economic, and political reasons for the rise and spread of such fervency. But we must also comprehend the non-rational causes and effects. Indeed, that relationship between the puritan believer and the only 'meaning' that mattered must be fully appreciated before one can understand the puritan attitude towards any social policy, and specifically towards learning and education.

II

English history of the early and mid-seventeenth century has frequently been interpreted as a series of divisions. In sum, most interpretations – though they differ radically in emphasis – have seen the end of the first half of the seventeenth century as a breakdown in consensus on the social, political, and religious affairs of England. It is possible, however, that not enough has been made of the growing self-confidence with which Charles' opponents approached the venture. I am concerned here to portray an aspect of the cultural history of the period 1560–1640 which contributed to that rise in individual confidence, not only by aggrandizing the view of the self, but also by developing a network so that such ideas could readily be distributed throughout the countryside and passed along to the next generation. Specifically, I am interested to know the means by which that set of people called 'puritans' came to grips with the great questions of existence, and the extent to which they did this by developing specific attitudes towards the human mind. I have attempted not to overlook the pragmatic aspect of puritan planning – indeed, the emphasis here on reaction to context may well go too far for those who hold that there was a fixed set of beliefs called 'purita*nism*'. At the same time I have operated throughout under the belief that in the *post*-conversion state, puritans did possess an essence. It is the delineation of that core as it applied to the central questions of reason, learning, and education in a Reformed society that forms the basis of this study.

In an extremely perceptive article, Quentin Skinner argued that there can be no timeless questions in a context that is forever changing. He further explained that realization of this requires the historian to be thoroughly aware of the context in which the ideas being studied are produced. As well, the historian of ideas must recognize the distinction between the intention to do something (which may be called a 'cause'), and the specific intention *in* doing something, which is not a 'cause' but rather a perception of one's own purpose at the time the action is being committed.[3] Skinner concluded that the essential question to ask of any text is what the author 'could in practice have been intending to communicate by the utterance of this given utterance', and that the specific aim of the historian of ideas is the recovery 'of this complex intention on the part of the author'.[4] This function is obviously related to, but distinguishable from, the assessment of the effect of a single tract or of an author's career upon the society around him and upon the longer-term interests of his civilization.

There is, obviously, a continuum of intellectual action, from first conceptions and intellectual influences all the way through to the commission of an act based (in part) upon one's principles or beliefs[5] While we now know much more about the material context and the *mentalité* of our period, little

[3]   Skinner, 'Meaning and understanding in the history of ideas', *History and Theory*, 8, *passim*.
[4]   *Ibid.*, pp. 48–9. For an expansion and slight modification of this argument, see Skinner, 'Some problems in the analysis of political thought and action', *Political Theory*, 2, pp. 277–303.
[5]   For an explanation of the way in which principle can serve as motivation, even when it is turned into *ex post facto* rationalization, see the comments on the connexion of protestantism and capitalism in Skinner, 'Some problems', pp. 295–301.

effort seems to have been expended on analysing the ideas of the puritans (beyond the purely theological and ecclesiological) and the ways in which these ideas could be connected to *intention* in social action: that is, not what did the puritan ministers accomplish, and not (as in so many recent studies) what did those lay men and women touched by derived puritan beliefs effect, but rather (one stage previous) what was at the core of puritan thought, and in what ways did this thought condition social action through a compromise of principle and context? One cannot comprehend puritan intentions from the acts alone (because of this compromise), nor can one hope to understand puritan thought without an awareness of the degree to which puritan ministers were ready to accept the requirements of the context and build them into their patterns of thought. I have therefore concentrated on what may loosely be termed the social history of ideas, that is, the connexion between principle and plan-for-action. This has necessitated taking account of the process of 'action' from theology to 'social act'. By this latter term I mean the connexion with society on a basis beyond writing or speaking: what is usually encompassed by the phrase 'doing something', such as (in our interest here) founding a school. But I have concentrated especially on that part of the process which, I hope, will explain the motivation which turned principle into the formulation stage of social action. As applied directly to the puritans, this approach is reflected in the general question which dogged puritan thought: how could the intellect and the will be blended to produce a meaningful Christian existence in a fallen world?

In specific terms I have attempted to evaluate the theological, ecclesiological, and (certain) social causes for views on learning and education; the limits placed on reason, and the degree to which these limits may have affected educational pronouncements; specific educational plans for the training of ministers; views of the role of householders, schoolmasters and tutors – that is, the function of the individual teacher in the building of a Reformed society; the degree to which educational views either affected or reflected attitudes towards the relationship of the laity and the clergy; the contribution to curriculum, to text-book reform, and to the development of pedagogical theory in general; the innovations necessary in education, as in the church, to promote reform within an occasionally hostile environment.

III

The completion of a book brings with it an awareness of the compromises that have been fashioned between prior intention and the degree of actualization. Constraints of time and space, of energy, of materials looked at, as well as the limitations of the author, mean that tasks originally believed possible cannot be fitted between the covers. I regret, for example, that I have not been able to present a broader European context for the puritan attitudes and proposals for reform discussed below. I have occasionally supplied examples of continental precedents for puritan action, but my knowledge does not permit me to comment more fully on the degree to which European ideas were taken directly as the basis for English development. I have also not been able to offer a comparison between the puritan and English Romanist attitudes towards learning and education. I am not persuaded, however, that this is necessarily a worthwhile venture. My research has led me to the opinion, which seems to be becoming the current orthodoxy, that puritans were always at the stage of becoming part of a general synthesis of English protestantism. Any parallels might well therefore better be sought between more radical English protestants and the Romanists. It would no longer seem possible to view puritans and papists as similar groups (at opposite ends of the spectrum) fighting under the constant oppression of a rigid administration of the 'middle'. Every book thus leaves much undone; one can only hope to return to some of the questions at a later date.

Another form of compromise is perhaps more important, since less commonly commented upon by the historian. This is the compromise made between the historian and his material. I do not mean here the preconceptions, biases, and opinions which the human agent brings to the archive. Rather, I intend here what we may call the 'bias of creation', of which historians perhaps do not frequently enough inform their readers. Evidently, scholars of the works of Kafka were not sure of the precise order in which the chapters of *The Trial* should appear, since the manuscript was left in disarray. It may well be that the following material could have been arranged in a way which some readers would have found superior. I do not offer this as an *apologia pro libro suo*, but rather as a conscious reminder that, as all historians know, a book becomes a collection of changes as the historian investigates his subject. That is, it is a frozen instant of the historian's perception, the point in his ascending knowledge at which he reaches print. It is a static where what is truly needed is a canvas to portray the whole. Thus, the linear medium of print itself is perhaps insufficent to portray the experience, except as recourse is had to those devices of language such as metaphor which defy the bounds of analysis. For that reason I have constantly attempted to employ, and occasionally even to imitate, puritan language.

More specifically, the constant reshuffling of information means that we come to perceive the past as a series of connexions which may well *not* have occurred to the people actually living in the era we are studying. In so linking what was not perceptibly linked in the past, we are perhaps not so much recapturing the past as creating it to suit our own structure and perceptions. In that sense, we become the active authors of the past. Richard Reinitz commented on the work of Perry Miller that 'there is no way in which the overall accuracy of such a basic structural recreation of the underlying mental geology of a past period can be judged, short of the creation of an equally basic alternative structure'.[6] In offering an analysis of what I judge to be the puritan *mentalité*, especially concerning the relationship of salvation and humane learning, I do not claim to have re-written Miller, who still towers over all approaches to the puritan use of reason. I have merely been aware that the highest standard of accuracy by which this present work can be appraised is whether I have been able to recreate, to transport to the present, the terrible search for meaning which drove such a torment into the heart of puritan existence.

[6]   Reinitz, 'Perry Miller and recent American historiography', *Bulletin of the British Association for American Studies*, 1964, p. 34.

1

>->

THE PROBLEM OF DEFINITION

I

Few facets of English society of the late sixteenth and early seventeenth century have received as much attention as the problem of the definition of what, precisely, constituted a 'puritan' or, in its generic form, the collection of beliefs known as 'puritanism'. Over the last forty years great effort has been expended on the attempt to devise a universally acceptable definition of 'puritan' or 'puritanism'.[1] From those such as John New,[2] who found puritans diametrically opposed to the 'orthodox' members of the Church of England, to those such as Charles George,[3] who could find little distinctive in puritan attitudes and actions, there is a very wide spectrum. There have been atttempts to demonstrate the social and economic impact of 'puritanism', as well as investigations of the social background of puritans. But, by and large, approaches to the history of the puritans have been most concerned with theology and ecclesiology. While some historians have noted real differences of religious belief,[4] the greater part of historical opinion has argued that the theological differences between puritans and non-puritans were minimal before the rise of the Laudian–Arminian group. In terms of ecclesiology, however, there has been a longer historiographical tradition of portraying puritans as an opposition group.[5] There has been a long-standing dispute, too, over the matter of whether 'puritanism' was an imported or a domestic

---

[1] For different approaches to the historiography of the question of definition, see especially Hill, *Society and Puritanism*, Ch. 1; B. Hall, 'Puritanism: the problem of definition', in Cuming, ed., *Studies in Church History*, II, pp. 283–96; Christianson, 'Reformers and the Church of England', *Journal of Ecclesiastical History*, 31, pp. 463–82; Collinson, 'A comment: concerning the name puritan', *ibid.*, pp. 483–8.

[2] New, *Anglican and Puritan*.

[3] George & George, *The Protestant Mind of the English Reformation 1570–1640*.

[4] Coolidge, *Pauline Renaissance*; McGee, *The Godly Man in Stuart England*.

[5] See especially Haller, *Rise of Puritanism*; Knappen, *Tudor Puritanism*; Seaver, *Puritan Lectureships*; Maclure, *Paul's Cross Sermons*.

specimen.[6] More recently, some historians have taken to discussing 'puritanism' without offering substantive definitions.[7]

After some earlier battles,[8] most historians now seem willing to omit the separatists from any definition of 'puritan', a contemporary practice which has been followed here. On the other hand, certain historians have recently portrayed the characteristics of puritans as pervasive in the Jacobean church.[9] Attention has been drawn especially to the minimal effort offered by puritans, particularly during the first twenty years of the seventeenth century, to alter the structure of the Church of England.[10] This re-interpretation has involved, too, a minimization of the change from political to pastoral puritanism in the 1590s. The battles of the Elizabethan presbyterians against the church administration, it is argued, should not blind historians to the fundamentally pastoral nature of 'puritanism' from its (English) beginnings.[11] However, recent calls for stricter definitional limits of the term 'puritan', and the revivification of the broader term 'Anglican',[12] would seem destined to return historians to oppositional paradigms.

The term 'puritan' was evidently first used as an insult,[13] and it was used as such throughout our period. In an age of general concern among the educated for the condition of the national church, it is natural that terms of social abuse should arise from ecclesiological matters. Reformers, however, almost unanimously objected to the label: 'these names we Abhore & detest'.[14] Martin Marprelate employed the term as self-description,[15] but this did not mean a conversion to general acceptance. Perkins still referred to the 'vile termes of Puritans and Presitians', and Josias Nichols curiously thought that such a contemptible slander should be applied only to papists, and not to the godly of England.[16] Thomas Adams, on the other hand, preferred to use the term to describe religious radicals; again, the godly, conforming ministers were not to be included.[17] Even as late as 1641 the name was a slur: there was 'nothing [which] is so monstrous, which is not branded upon Puritans, and no man is so

---

[6] See, for example, Trinterud, 'Origins of puritanism', *Church History*, 20, pp. 37–57; Brauer, 'Reflections on the nature of English puritanism', *Church History*, 23, pp. 99–108.
[7] See, for example, Cross, *Church and People 1450–1660*; J. Simon, *Education and Society in Tudor England*; Collinson, *Elizabethan Puritan Movement*.
[8] B. Hall, 'Puritanism: the problem of definition', pp. 283–96; Hill, *Society and Puritanism*, Ch. 1.
[9] On the latter group, see, for example, Tyacke, 'Puritanism, Arminianism and Counter-Revolution', in Russell, ed., *The Origins of the English Civil War*, pp. 119–43; Collinson, 'A comment: concerning the name puritan', pp. 483–8.
[10] Collinson, 'Lectures by combination', *Bulletin of the Institute of Historical Research*, 48, esp. pp. 184, 209; Lake, 'Matthew Hutton – a puritan bishop?', *History*, 64, esp. pp. 202–3.
[11] Collinson, *Mirror of Elizabethan Puritanism*, esp. p. 28.
[12] Especially by Christianson, 'Reformers and the church of England', esp. pp. 464–76, and by Greaves, *Society and Religion, passim*.   [13] Collinson, *Elizabethan Puritan Movement*, pp. 86–7.
[14] Morrice MSS, Vol. B, II, fol. 196ᵛ.   [15] Knappen, *Tudor Puritanism*, pp. 488–9.
[16] Perkins, *Workes*, III, p. 15; Nichols, *Plea of the Innocent*, pp. 2–4.   [17] Adams, *Workes*, p. 561.

innocent as to escape that brand'[18] Most puritans, then, described themselves as 'protestants', and attempted to dissociate themselves from the radicals, whom they blamed for the opprobrium cast upon reformers.[19]

Throughout the period puritans fought especially hard against the common charge that they were oppositionists. King James warned his son Henry that puritans were a scourge 'breathing nothing but sedition and calumnies, aspiring without measure, railing without reason, and making their own imaginations (without any warrant of the word) the square of their conscience'.[20] This was a continuing theme. In 1626 John Knight, a prisoner in the Gatehouse, petitioned for a pardon for a sermon which had raised the question of resisting the monarch. He explained that he had not acted from 'puritanic' disloyalty.[21] Even John Foxe, the martyrologist, was disturbed by the 'factius' sort.[22] Puritans understandably sought to restrict use of the name, where opponents such as Oliver Ormerod and Thomas Cooper sought its widest employment by refusing to distinguish clearly between seditious sectaries and more moderate reformers.[23] Few puritans would have disagreed with Richard Hooker that no one could be a member of either the church or the commonwealth without also belonging to the other jurisdiction.[24] William Perkins stood vehemently opposed to 'the schismatical and undesired company' who would 'sever themselves from our church . . .'.[25] As late as the Revolution, Calamy could sum up the 'orthodox' puritan tradition by noting 'We are all of one nation, of one body, one flesh, one Church. There is a National Communion, a Morall Communion, a Politicall Communion, a Spirituall Communion amongst us.'[26] For puritans, then, it was a constant struggle to set the record right.[27]

Definitions were so varied that it is difficult to assimilate them into one coherent understanding of contemporary opinion on the subject; indeed, such

---

[18] Parker/Ley, *Discourse*, p. 2. Thomas Fuller, too, admitted that the word was little more than a common slur (Olsen, *John Foxe*, p. 9).

[19] See, for example, Josias Nichols' condemnation of Marprelate as a 'filthie Sycophant' who had 'slanderously abused manye persons of reverend place and note . . .' (Nichols, *Plea of the innocent*, pp. 33–5). The radical's opinion of the puritans is also interesting. Henry Barrow explained that the difference between the Brownists and the puritans 'is layd downe in few words. The former doe both hold and practise the truth, and separate themselves from the contrarie. The latter have the trueth in speculation onely, and either dare not or at least doe not practise it. Neither dare or doe they leave off all the unrighteous ordinances of Antichrist, but daily do bend and stoupe unto many of them.' ([Henry Barrow?], *Mr. Barrow's Platform*, sig. K3).

[20] Quoted in Sensabaugh, *That Grand Whig Milton*, p. 11.

[21] *C.S.P.D. 1619–1623*, p. 44.   [22] Olsen, *John Foxe*, p. 158.

[23] Ormerod, *Picture of a Puritane*; Cooper, *Admonition*, esp. p. 46.

[24] Collinson, *Elizabethan Puritan Movement*, p. 22.

[25] Quoted in Breward, 'Significance of William Perkins', *Journal of Religious History*, 4, p. 117.

[26] Calamy, *Englands Looking Glasse*, p. 31.

[27] For typical defences, see Morrice MSS, Vol. B, I, p. 40; Nichols, *Plea of the Innocent*, pp. 11–12; Wilcox, *Unfouldyng*, sig. F^v.

a singular comprehension probably did not exist. Job Throckmorton, in a speech to the Commons in 1586/7, summed up the common puritan understanding of the term: it was simply 'to bewail the distresses of God's children' and to struggle for a learned ministry.[28] It was a good, if general, starting-point. Other contemporary commentators defined puritans in terms of a struggle for freedom of opinion,[29] or of a desire to order society according to extremely rigid and restrictive rules of conduct.[30] William Bradshaw, who wore the label 'puritan' as a badge of pride,[31] defined puritans in terms of devotion to Scripture and obedience to the ecclesiastical prescripts of the Word, including the equality of congregations, the power and duty of civil magistrates to reform, and the restriction of the minister's role to purely spiritual functions.[32] In a general sense, though from a different perspective, Giles Widdowes, the anti-puritan controversialist, agreed:

This Puritan is a Non-Conformist. For he is oppositely set, a Contradictist to the Scriptures deduceable sence in three things. The first is the 39 Articles of our Churches Reformed faith. The second is our Common Praier-booke. The third is the Canons of our Church.[33]

Widdowes managed to list ten kinds of puritans in an attempt to define the spectrum of reformist opposition to the established church. Along with 'precisians' and 'sabbatarians', however, he included 'Brownists' and 'separatists'.[34] Another common contemporary association was of puritanism with presbyterianism, especially in the period following the university and parliamentary struggles of Thomas Cartwright, John Field, and Thomas Wilcox.[35] Indeed, a belief in the Reformed church polity was still regarded as a significant badge of identification thirty years later by John Robinson, pastor of the congregation which filled the Mayflower.[36]

Such expressions of puritan opposition to the practices and (sometimes) to the structures of the established church, but at the same time of affinity with its basic theology, became the standard note of Elizabethan and Jacobean definitions. Archbishop Hutton, at the turn of the century, replied to an inquiry from the Council concerning nonconformity that, while he found the puritans very zealous, he did not understand them to differ substantially from the doctrines of the established church.[37] Only with the rise of the Laudian–Arminian

[28] Quoted in Neale, *Elizabeth I and her Parliaments, 1584–1601*, p. 151.
[29] See the anonymous verse cited in Hill, *Society and Puritanism*, p. 23.
[30] See, for example, the 1618 complaint of John Tabor, quoted in Hart, *Country Clergy*, p. 64. See also Wrightson, 'Puritan reformation of manners', unpub. Ph.D. thesis, Univ. of Cambridge, 1974, *passim.*   [31] Lake, *Moderate Puritans*, pp. 268–9.
[32] Bradshaw, *English Puritanisme*, sig. A2, pp. 5, 7, 17.   [33] Widdowes, *Schismatical Puritan*, sig. A3ᵛ.
[34] *Ibid.*,sigs. B2–C3ᵛ.   [35] See, for example, B.C., *Puritanisme*, pp. 38–9.
[36] B. Hall, 'Puritanism: the problem of definition', p. 292.
[37] Hutton to Viscount Cranborne, 18 Dec. 1604 (*C.S.P.D. 1603–1610*, p. 177).

group did theology become an open point of hostile differentiation. Then even the belief in predestination, which had been a staple of Grindal as much as of Cartwright and Perkins, became to opponents a mark of puritan belief. Katherine, Duchess of Buckingham, wrote imploringly to an acquaintance not to become a 'puritan', 'to believe in predestination'.[38] Some observers managed something approaching analysis, though it was almost always tempered by political considerations. Sir Francis Hastings explained his understanding of the term (which was Laurence Humphrey's old definition) to the 1601 Parliament. He saw four types of religious opinion:

first the Catholic which holds that a man cannot sin after baptism, secondly the papist, which is such a merit-monger, that he would not only save himself by his own merits, but by the merits of others also, a third sort are the Brownists or Family of Love, a sect too well known in England, I would they had never so been, the fourth and last sort are your evangelical Puritans, which insist wholly upon scriptures as upon a sure ground; and of these I would we had more than we now have.[39]

It was a valiant attempt to delineate the puritan cause, distinct from both reaction and social revolution.

By sifting the contemporary literature, historians have concluded that the puritan characteristics most commonly noted were a dedication to preaching; an exceptional hatred of popery; an emphasis on the propagation of the Word even above obedience to the rules of the church and, occasionally, to those of the state; a growing dedication to the sanctity of the Sabbath; an abiding despair, beyond that of other moralists of the age, at the level of licentious behaviour; a passionate willingness to attack any theological innovations that detracted from English Calvinist orthodoxy; a greater emphasis on the pastoral activities of the minister, and therefore also on the purity of the minister's conversation (which led to contemporary accusations of Donatism); a general unwillingness, born of the doctrine of non-separation, to push disagreement with the hierarchy beyond suspension to the point of ministerial deprivation; and a close alliance between ministers and their lay patrons or protectors.

The problem with relying completely on contemporary assessment is that much depended on whether the author of the definition was friend or foe. By the end of our period, the term 'puritan' was even being used defensively against the 'Arminians'.[40] Are we therefore to acknowledge as accurate Samuel Clarke's descriptions of the godly and peaceable lives of the 'saints', or instead the accusation of Samuel Brooke, Master of Trinity College, Cambridge, who in a letter to Laud, written in 1630, described the puritans as

---

[38] *C.S.P.D. 1627–1628*, p. 400.   [39] Quoted in Cross, *Puritan Earl*, pp. 36–7.
[40] But see also C.U.L. MS Mm.v.1(c), No. 10, fol. 29, Proceedings in Parliament, 1628: the remark of a Mr Sherland, who said that the Arminian party had 'involved all true hearted Englishmen, and Christians under the name of Puritanes'.

'the root of all rebellious and disobedient intractableness in Parliament, etc., and all the schism and sauciness in the country, nay in the Church itself'?[41]

Historians have also detected certain other traits which they have taken to be characteristic of puritans. Among these are a dedication to the social and political hierarchy (which clashes with contemporaries' attempts to paint the puritans as politically subversive); a close affinity with continental Reformed beliefs; an extremely strong 'brotherhood' of ministers; a close connexion to the scholarship and the civic (as well as family) attitudes of humanism; a pronounced apocalypticism; and, finally, a general dedication to covenant theology. All stemmed from a belief that the English church had not progressed far enough in its separation from Rome, and that the present task was both to win the administration to further institutional reform, and to propagandize the Word in the country pulpits so that the laity would understand the evil of Rome and also the necessity for a reformed personal existence. In this scheme, political presbyterianism, covenant theology, and pastoral advice were not disparates, but simply different modes of reform, dependent for their course and emphasis on the context.

This listing is not intended to be exhaustive. Other 'characteristics' have also been the subject of much debate among both contemporaries and historians. In searches for 'the emergence of the modern world', puritans have variously been linked with capitalism, science, charity, social mobility, individuality, and, of course, learning and education. It is this last possibility which primarily concerns us here. As we shall see in more detail below, while it was by no means uncommon for puritans to be accused of over-reliance on learning, by and large contemporary critics preferred to accuse puritans of ignorance and a desire to destroy England's educational institutions so that in future there would be no learned men to see through the fallacies of the precisians' arguments. A papist priest, for example, dedicated his tract to the 'Unlearned (but well meaning) Puritans'; he explained that he had not supplied references for his citations since they would have been of no use to the uneducated.[42] Peter Studley regarded the ignorance of scholastic terminology as a common characteristic of the 'silly, ignorant and downe-right English Puritans'.[43] An undated poem on the problem of definition recorded the common view of puritans as unlearned; a puritan was he

> That at his belt a buffe clad Bible weares
> Stampt with the new Geneva characters:

---

[41] Brooke to Laud, 15 Dec. 1630 (*C.S.P.D. 1629–1631*, p. 411). Against Brooke's charge of factionalism, puritans also had a ready defence. Jeremiah Burroughes relied on Tertullian to argue that the truly godly could never accurately be described as a 'faction' (*Excellency of Gracious Spirit*, p. 140).

[42] B.C., *Puritanisme*, sigs. *3, *3ᵛ–*4.   [43] Studley, *Looking-Glasse of Schisme*, p. 160.

Whose thin beat volume scorneth to admitt
The bastard monuments of humane witt.[44]

Richard Montagu, finally, in defending his *Appello Caesarem*, accused the puritans of being too unlearned to comprehend his arguments, and so promised that if 'I have any occasion hereafter to speak of *learned* and moderate men, I will ever except and exempt you and yours.'[45]

Historians, however, have traditionally linked puritans with a highly favourable attitude towards learning: puritans built schools and colleges in England, and did the same very shortly after their arrival in New England. Puritans, too, always demanded learned preachers and a Bible-reading public. Despite this emphasis on the connexion of 'puritanism' and education, the question of a particular attitude towards reason, learning, and education has rarely been considered a criterion of categorization in the debate over the definition of 'puritanism'. Seldom, too, in analyses of educational thought, have the great debates of the 1640s and 1650s been shown to possess a genealogy.[46] Indeed, the weight of opinion has been that educational changes in our period do not reflect directly any specifically 'puritan' qualities. Knappen, for example, denied that puritans were able to develop a curriculum specific to their desires,[47] and Morison, on balance, saw the New England educational system as not 'in any peculiar sense religious or puritanical'.[48] More recent work on the early American context has debated the question of the trans-

---

[44] Bod. Lib. MS Tanner 465, fol. 82.   [45] Quoted in Austen-Legh, *King's College*, p. 117.

[46] Watson, *English Grammar Schools*, pp. 61, 63, 174, 181, 535ff. W. K. Jordan found 'no really significant distinction' between 'puritan' and pre-Laudian 'Anglican' theory (*Philanthropy in England, 1480–1660*, p. 155 and *passim*). H. C. Porter's understanding of puritan reliance on godly tutors, and his brief mention of the training of future ministers in the homes of clerics, are crucial points that have scarcely been examined (*Reformation and Reaction in Tudor Cambridge*, esp. pp. 222–3, 237ff., 269ff.). Kocher, *Science and Religion in Elizabethan England*, pp. 15, 23, asserted that only the radicals attempted to establish 'strictly religious patterns' of education. Greaves, *Puritan Revolution*, p. 125, argues that the 'apologists for a learned ministry dealt mostly with the sectaries, *though as early as 1637* the accusation of an ignorant clergy was levelled by one Puritan against the Anglican ministry.' (My italics.) The unsuspecting reader might draw the conclusion that such accusations were not made before 1637. For an adjustment of this earlier view, see Greaves, *Society and Religion*, Ch. 8. Cf. Short, 'Theory of common education', *The Journal of Ecclesiastical History*, 23, pp. 31–48; Curtis, *Oxford and Cambridge*; Curtis, 'The alienated intellectuals of early Stuart England', *Past and Present*, 23, pp. 25–43 (for criticisms of Curtis' view of the universities as adaptable institutions, see Hill, *Intellectual Origins of the English Revolution*, Appendix); Wood, *The Reformation and English Education*, esp. pp. 311–12ff., 320ff., 325–32, 334–5, 339; Kearney, *Scholars and Gentlemen*; Green, *Religion at Oxford and Cambridge*, pp. 106–7, 138f.; Prest, 'Legal education of the gentry at the Inns of Court', *Past and Present*, 38, pp. 20–39; Costello, *The Scholastic Curriculum at Early Seventeenth-Century Cambridge*. Even Joan Simon dealt only relatively briefly with puritan influence, but she forcefully supported Foster Watson's conclusion of its great impact (Simon, *Education and Society in Tudor England*, pp. 397–8). See also Stone, 'Educational revolution in England', *Past and Present*, 28, p. 77.   [47] Knappen, *Tudor Puritanism*, Ch. 26.

[48] Morison, *Puritan Pronaos*, p. 87; Morison, *Founding of Harvard*, pp. 247, 45, 148, 149, 157–8; Morison, *Harvard in the Seventeenth Century*, I, pp. 175 n. 4, 200.

mission by puritans of a specific culture from England to the New World.[49]
Whether puritan attitudes to learning and education of the period 1560–1640
in fact constituted a distinct approach is therefore one of the prime questions
of this present study.

II

Much of the difficulty in comprehending the nature of the puritan imperative
has been due to definitions and methodologies which have encumbered rather
than enlightened. Such definitions can too easily become tautological. Even if
the historian approaches his research without a firm definition of the term
'puritan', his work may well soon bring him to an understanding of that
category (however he defines it). At what point, however, does his definition
change from a collection of existences (the nominalist position) to that of
essence (the realist view)? At what stage of his thinking does he stop meeting
'individual puritans' who are added to his definitional list to explain the
generic term, and start categorizing according to a now-fixed essence, so that
new variations are not added to the definitional characteristics, but are rather
rejected as being outside the fully formed term? Even those historians who
scrupulously avoid offering a definition in an introductory chapter, contending that the 'definition' can arise only as the book 'progresses', are perhaps
hiding the fact that the finished form of the text is a distillation of conclusions
reflecting lengthy analyses of relatively fixed bodies of knowledge. The continuing debate over definition reveals not only a blind affinity for settling a
problem through greater refinement of the definition, but also an evident
feeling that definitions must have firm boundaries in order to encompass
essence.

The solution, for two related reasons, lies in abandoning the term
'puritanism'. First, any 'ism' is likely to connote a fixed entity, definable
because it accords with a collection of beliefs or actions laid down by certain
theorists (as in the case of Marxism). A view of a fully formed 'puritanism' as
essence distorts the changing balances *within* the spectrum of what can
legitimately be called 'puritan' activity in the eighty years before the Revolution. Secondly, the abandonment of 'puritanism' will allow historians to
view the past not as a collection of contending 'essences', but rather as a
collection of 'existences', so that there will be less difficulty in coming to grips
with the empirical evidence that 'puritans' at one end of the spectrum blended
into the ideas of the administration (also, of course, flexible and changeable
over time), and at the other end shared certain views (though not in such radical

[49]   Bailyn, *Education in the Forming of American Society*, esp. pp. 14, 27; Cremin, *American Education: The
       Colonial Experience*, esp. p. 16; Axtell, *School upon a Hill*, esp. pp. 282–3.

measure) with the separatists. It will, in short, enable them to stop seeing the era as a dichotomy of 'administration' and 'opposition'.[50] Historical definitions should not be written in terms of this-and-not-that (the law of the excluded middle). One must see such themes as always in flux.

The difficulty of giving a definition, then, is that it must be precise. A definition is not only a matter of description of something that is either constant or 'frozen' for a moment of time; it is also a way of excluding other characteristics. To define is, I think, necessarily to put essence before existence. If we approach puritans from a nominalist position, conceding that existence precedes essence, then we can still collect characteristics (which will vary, to a degree, over time with the changing context), but we shall have to recognize that the sum of these characteristics is a 'composite', and that not all of the characteristics were displayed, or even expected by opponents to be present, in all 'puritans' all of the time. Individual contemporaneous examples differed in emphasis, and, of course, within each life there were modifications of thought and practice as new crises produced the necessity for different responses.

Puritans were presbyterians and congregationalists, covenanters and stricter predestinarians, conformists and nonconformists. They were fellow-travellers to an idea rather than the disciplined members of a party. Puritans included Thomas Adams as well as John Field and William Fulke; conformists numbered in their ranks Bancroft as well as Grindal, and, of course, in the seventeenth century, also the 'Arminian' coterie in a changed pattern of 'conformity'. The very act of associating people under a general heading unfortunately tends to give them a monolithic appearance, or at least tends to minimize the differences, so that they can be distinguished from other groups. The term 'puritan' must be retained as reflecting contemporary perception of a stream of the church. For the authorities of the church, who sometimes tolerated and sometimes persecuted the precise wing, a unifying label is more difficult because so much of the thrust depended on the single figure of the Archbishop of Canterbury. I have chosen the term 'administration', though I am fully aware of its deficiencies. Its advantage is that it reflects the sense of authority without requiring like-mindedness; it thus permits serious changes of position over time and under the rubric of power. It is a political rather than theological or even ecclesiological term.

But in tearing down the structure of a monolithic 'puritanism', we must perhaps not become so concerned with discrete individuals that we forget that there was some form of group mentality. Puritans did form associations of interest, did communicate their ideas to each other, and did organise (to a degree) for ecclesiastical action. The great difficulty, then, is to find the

---

[50] For recent re-emphasis of this point, see Collinson, *Godly People*, pp. 534–5.

proper balance between talking about 'puritan' opinion as though it were single and undivided, and, on the other hand, talking about individual puritan attitudes as though they existed *in vacuo*. Perhaps the guiding principle might be that which motivated many of the more temperate churchmen (puritan and non-puritan alike) of our period: we should look for unity without trying to find (or, even worse, trying to impose) uniformity where it did not exist. In this perspective, the touchstone would be the degree to which a person shared in the set of common experiences leading to the same conceived end. For a puritan throughout our period these 'ends' and 'experiences' would be dominated by the fervent quest for salvation and the concomitant subordination of all other considerations. That is to say, the puritan image was a religious *experience*. It was the ways in which this fervency was manifested in attitudes and actions that delineate the puritan, and distinguish him from contemporaries.

All who contributed to the call for drastic internal alteration of the operation of the church, the purification of the household, and an immediate dedication to active faith have therefore found a place in this collection of experiences. In large measure puritans represented simply the common expression of basic protestant opinions, especially concerning the individuality of faith and the all-sufficiency of Scripture. Puritans took the common heritage of the Reformation and adapted it to the various needs of university, pulpit, and household so that in each sphere it was no longer simply a matter of belief, but rather a doctrine of daily practice. As John Downame explained, the good puritan life consisted 'in our walking before him in the duties of piety, righteousness and sobriety, with faith, a pure heart, and good conscience all the dayes of our lives'.[51] Here again, puritans did not contradict the theology of the administration but only, through their evangelical zeal, questioned the slowness of application. In this sense, as the puritans themselves claimed, they were both the strongest proponents of a more reformed church and the firmest defenders of the Church of England, now freed from the Romanist stain. Puritans were loyal to the English church because they saw the true seed in it and perceived what it could grow to be.[52] From the beginning, then, puritans existed in a dialectic: critical yet overwhelmingly supportive of the church.

Much recent work, perhaps especially that of Cross, Shipps, Sheils, and Zaret, has concentrated on the part played by the godly laity in reforming the daily operations of both church and state. Collinson, too, has recently emphasized the importance of seeing 'puritanism' as the effect of a set of ideas

---

[51]   Downame, *Guide to Godliness*, p. 18.
[52]   For a recent, similar suggestion, see Lake, *Moderate Puritans*, p. 3.

upon the lives of godly laymen.[53] Doubtless, puritan ministers could not have withstood the periodic attacks of the administration without the strong support (and counter-attacks in parliament) of influential lay people. Expressions of lay gratitude to ministers for showing them the light that led to assurance were matched by notes of thanks for the protection which permitted God's mediators to continue their labours.[54] And it is without doubt true that the laity influenced the course of religious events, and even, on occasion, the response of their own clerics. Zaret has recently demonstrated the close parallels between secular contractual language and the terms in which puritan ministers drafted the propagandization of the religious covenant. Nonetheless, his contention that 'lay initiative' was '*the* central feature of puritan nonconformity'[55] seems exaggerated, especially in the field of thought. Against this, I should like to reiterate the old contention that at the heart of the puritan effort in re-drafting certain English ideas stood the godly ministers. One of the arguments of the present work is that even the godly laity still recognized the elucidation of intellectual responses and broad social attitudes as one of the aspects of the prerogative and specific vocation of ministers. This does not mean that the ministers held the stage alone. Exceptions to this rule, such as Thomas Norton, have received strong play in this book, but they were a small minority.

Another common problem for historians of the pre-revolutionary English church is the sub-division of the eighty years before the Revolution. Change in one field is often painted against a static 'backdrop of the age'. The difficulty in such a work as this is to fit a useful scheme of periodization into a thematic approach, which tends to deal with long periods as static wholes. Recent revisionists have rather downplayed the old notion of a significant break in the 1590s. Puritans were always interested in practical divinity, and in the practical employment of the intellect as an aspect of this approach to the people. This, indeed, is one of the points of coherence and unity in puritan thought over the whole period: the ecclesiastical uproar has often been overstated as being central to 'puritanism', to the exclusion of matters of greater import to the individual. The 1590s remain important, perhaps because of a dramatic growth in the use of covenant theology in this decade. But here again we must suggest that it was not the essence of puritans that was changing, but perhaps only their way of proselytizing, given changes in their

---

[53] Collinson, *Religion of Protestants*, esp. Chs. 4, 6; idem, *Godly People*, esp. pp. 541–9.
[54] For one example of a plentiful form, see the address by Thomas Gataker to Sir Henry Hobart, Lord Chief Justice of the Common Pleas, in the printed version of a sermon originally delivered at Serjeants Inn in Fleet Street. Gataker noted his 'thankfull acknowledgement of that undeserved favour and countenance that your Lo: hath beene pleased from time to time to vouchsafe me, as well before, as since I came under the wing of your Honourable protection' (*Gods Parley with Princes*, sig. A4ᵛ.)
[55] Zaret, 'Ideology and organization in puritanism', *Arch. europ. sociol.*, 21, p. 91. (My italics.)

context. When the stimuli were repeated, so, often, were the responses. So puritans established household seminaries in the 1620s for the same reasons that they had defended prophesyings in the 1570s: to train a godly pastoral ministry when the other structures of society failed in this responsibility.

If we accept this notion of fluidity over time, the manifestation of different characteristics should cease to cause definitional problems. Richard Greenham at Dry Drayton, and John Field at Westminster, obviously were in different environments, with different obstacles to their achievement of godliness about them. Field's oft-quoted remark after the failure of parliamentary reform, that puritans would have to look to the multitude if the magistrate stood firmly in the way, is perhaps overemphasized as reflecting a changed essence of 'puritanism'. The problem recurs at the end of our period. William Haller's 'brotherhood' has traditionally been seen as the dominant mood of 'puritanism' in the early seventeenth century. But by the 1630s many of the leaders in this group were dead.[56] They were replaced by younger men educated in the 1620s and 1630s, when the universities were far less given to English Calvinism, though of course puritan tutors still abounded at both Oxford and Cambridge. They came to represent a 'new phase' primarily because of changed context rather than because of radical alteration within any 'essence' of 'puritanism'. Puritans were thus always in a state of flux, that is, they were always in the process of 'becoming'. Covenant theology and an emphasis on the pastoral side of the puritan thrust were thus not innovations after 1590, but rather continuing adjustments to the requirements of a modified context. Periodization should therefore be seen as marking the ebb and flow of puritan reaction to environment.

Thus far, I have concentrated on distinguishing between a 'realist' approach to definition, based on a belief in a distinct 'essence' of 'puritanism', and a 'nominalist' method, proceeding from the collection of a spectrum of 'existences', all of which, though not identical and occasionally even contradictory on certain matters, may be called 'puritan'. There is also a second way in which we may illustrate the dichotomy of essence–existence in puritan experience. Those characteristics, mentioned above, which are usually taken to be 'puritan' should be seen only as the most obvious manifestations of puritan belief. These factors we may see as existence at what I should term the second, or 'immediate', level. Here, response, while a reflection of inner belief (though of course never its pure actualization), is also a reaction to non-agreeable aspects of environment. Below this, as we work towards the core, is the first, or 'contemplative' level of existence.

[56] Among those chief lights who died in this period were Paul Baynes (1617), Richard Rogers (1618), John Preston (1628), Arthur Hildersam (1632), John Carter (1635), and Richard Sibbes (1635). On the spiritual brotherhood, see Haller, *Rise of Puritanism*, Ch. 2.

It was in the puritan diaries and spiritual autobiographies, as well as in the biographical 'lives', that the central qualities of puritan existence were most readily demonstrated: the introspection concerning sin, regeneration, and the relationship with God which marked the Augustinian facet of the puritan, and the externalization which denoted the Pauline aspect of the drive for edification. Questions of assurance, and of the possible loss of grace, dominated the puritans' deep quests into their own souls. But the diaries and spiritual autobiographies served not only as the puritan confessionals; they were intended as well for public consumption, to aid the edification of other seekers of the covenant. The stress on conscience in the diaries served puritans as a way of defining themselves in terms of their own (corrupt) will, which they constantly struggled to control. This externalization helped the puritan to judge the visibility of his own grace also in terms of that of others.[57]

The dialectical activity of these two levels of existence, including the struggle for a new synthesis, constituted the essence of puritans, that godly fervency that, as Miller noted, is a continuing aspect of human existence. It was, in large part, the cry of the existential being for meaning in a universe which itself could provide him with none. For puritans, the earth did not prove a firmament, but rather a perilous island which could stand strong against the ravaging storms of spiritual desolation only as it was protected by a meaning which stood outside time and space, and was the only unchanging Essence. This is not to argue that the puritan world-view was pessimistic. Everlasting glory – for some – would follow the progress through earthly existence, which was a necessary precondition as it afforded the opportunity for conversion. At the same time, the outlook can hardly be described as optimistic. The world would always be populated chiefly by reprobates; the puritan could therefore never conceive of an earthly Utopia. The ideal life was a function of a higher plane. This world was always portrayed as a battleground. The corruption of the world was ineradicable. Puritans such as Arthur Dent incessantly reminded their readers of the dangers, challenges, and temptations of earthly existence:

The worlde is a sea of glasse: a pageant of fond delight, a Theatre of vanitie, a labrynth of error, a gulfe of griefe, a stie of filthinesse, a vale of misery, a spectacle of woe, a river of teares, a stage of deceit, a cage ful of Divles, a denne of Scorpions, a wildernesse of Wolves, a cabbin of Beares, a whirlewind of passions, a fained Comedie, a delectable phrenzie: where is false delight, assured griefe: certain sorrow, uncertain pleasure: lasting woe, fickle wealth: long heavinesse, short ioy.[58]

This spiritual fervency was not primarily a product of socio-economic existence, but rather one of the conditions of the soul which came out of an

---

[57] Wolff, 'Literary reflections of the puritan character', *Journal of the History of Ideas*, 29, pp. 20, 21ff.
[58] Dent, *Plaine Mans Path-way*, p. 97.

irrational experience of conversion. Our task here, then, is to proceed from a comprehension of this core of fervency to an assessment of the puritan 'contemplative' response to the questions of the use of reason and the purpose of learning. In tracing these connexions I shall proceed from belief to reason to learning to education. That, I believe, parallels the puritan approach. Though, for many puritans, formal education was almost completed before the seizure of the soul by godliness (that is to say, before they actually became puritans), once that eruption had taken place, all other levels of existence, all other responses, were immediately reconditioned in accordance with it. I wish to illuminate that process as it moved from the core of lively faith through the first to the second level of existence. Such an examination may bring us to an understanding of the structure as well as the content of the distinct puritan response to the existential problems of reason-and-learning-in-action.

So far, I have attempted to provide only a framework for approaching the problem of definition in more accurate historical terms. Much of the rest of the book will be an exercise in expanding and investigating the general statements of this chapter. First, we must look at the patterns which puritans established for Reformed existence: how to be saved and how to conduct oneself in the city of man. It was the answers to these questions that defined puritans, and that thus differentiated them from their contemporaries. Against the heritage of Christian reason, with which they were well imbued by the universities, they placed, as it erupted forcibly from within their converted souls, the fervency of their faith in the God who had made a contract with them. The puritan thus arrived at a chasm in his confrontation of faith and reason; from this dire struggle emerged his response to the external world. He concluded that if one had faith, then the question of 'meaning' could not be divorced from it, since Providence was designed rather for God's purposes than for the satisfaction of man's curiosity. If one did not have faith, then the timeless question of 'meaning', as applied to the general context of human life, became irrelevant, since without that faith in a Superior, there could be no meaning, but only existence. That rending struggle for assurance becomes our starting-point.

2

>>>

RELIGION AND THE GODLY LIFE

I

The prophet of Geneva had made it abundantly clear that salvation was no longer a prize to be won. No paltry act of man, in his fleeting passage on earth, could possibly atone for the moral catastrophe of the Fall. The humanist concept of the dignity of man was shattered; no son of Adam could ever please God by his own design or inspiration. For the mass of humanity the just penalties of reprobation awaited. The Lord's bountiful mercy, however, moved him to save some of his forlorn creatures: they were the few, the elect, chosen freely by God from before time.[1] Calvin had argued that faith lay in the direct apprehension of the sacrifice which Jesus had made; understanding of this deed constituted assurance of election. To Calvin, then, assurance was a function of the mind. Since man had been utterly degraded by the Fall, the supernatural injection of faith had to precede the repentance which caused visible changes in human existence.[2]

The history of the puritan side of English 'Calvinism' is the story of a preference for the blended tradition of the Heidelberg theologians and Beza, Calvin's successor at Geneva. This stream, as it was modified by the 'experimental predestinarians', decreased the emphasis placed on the role of the understanding in gaining salvation, and stressed instead the changes fashioned by grace in the human will. Perkins emphasized the understanding; his followers generally split the task between understanding and will. William Ames, at the end of our period, realized the difficulties of dividing the undertaking, but unified the task under will alone. The effect of this was to place the onus on man to work towards the realization of his own election through the achievement of good works. The will *could* desire the good because of the effect of the infusion of grace. But the process of repentence depended for its strength and vitality upon the force of the human effort.[3]

---

[1] Indeed, Calvin argued that it was the 'very inequality' of the distribution of God's grace which proved that it was free: (*Institutes of the Christian Religion*, ed. McNeill, II, p. 929).
[2] Kendall, *Calvin and English Calvinism*, Ch. 1.
[3] This paragraph depends heavily on Kendall, *Calvin and English Calvinism*, *passim*.

Until its diminution in the early seventeenth century, the doctrine of 'temporary faith' (the idea that reprobates could for a time share the perceptions and the effort at repentance of the elect) must have upset the progress towards the solution of the central and most troubling problem of all – achieving certain assurance of salvation. This stumbling block did not, however, stand in the way of the distribution of the idea that there were recognizable differences between the states of reprobation and grace, and that it was possible to move from the former to the lattter state.[4] That recognition was the cornerstone of both puritan popular religious belief and social theory. It was this concept that *all* of society should be reformed – not only by government or church edict, but chiefly by inner repentance and continual instruction – that separated the fervent puritan social attitudes from those of their immediate predecessors and their contemporaries. While puritans taught the utter necessity of class differentiation on earth, the Reformed idea that all souls were equal (and needed equal preparation for a godly life) prevented the decay of the puritan thrust into class-restricted courtesy education.

The idea that faith could be infused at any time during the life of the elect allowed Calvinists, and especially the English puritans, to use the *pursuit* of salvation as the basis for a coherent religious and social ethic. In practice, almost from the beginning, puritan preachers reversed the order laid down by Calvin, and stressed that repentance, which was acclaimed as the 'very substance of all religion, and the whole sum of Christianitie',[5] would lead to faith. On the other hand, it was abundantly clear that those who did not repent, regardless of station, 'shall perishe and bee damned in hell fire for ever'.[6] The doctrine that repentance removed the penalty of damnation for the sins unavoidably committed was propounded from the start.[7] It was a practical instigator of the softening of the central notion of predestination, a change that was progressive throughout the Elizabethan period, and became dramatic with the full flowering of covenant theology.[8] Like so many puritans, Edward Dering, having emphasized how horrible the fate of most people would be (and deservedly so), concentrated on telling his readers how they might seek to attain the faith which alone could save them.[9] Similarly, the sub-title of

---

[4]   McKee, 'Idea of covenant', p. 143, commented that there is a discernible difference between the early covenant theologians (Perkins, Greenham, Ames) and the later exemplars (Sibbes, Preston, Goodwin, Ball): 'The outlook of these latter men tended away from emphasizing the sovereignty and rule of God to stressing God's faithfulness, his reasonableness, and his mercy to men.'

[5]   Udall, *Certaine Sermons* ('Amendment of Life', part 2), sigs. H.iii[v], I.ii[v].

[6]   Dent, *A Sermon of Repentaunce*, sig. A4[v]. See also Gifford, *Catechisme*, sig. K2.

[7]   *Geneva Bible*, marginal comments to Romans 10.4 and 11.29; Holme, *The Burthen of the Ministerie*, sig. C; Troeltsch, *Social Teaching*, p. 498; H. Smith, *Trumpet of the Soule*, sig. A4 and *passim*.

[8]   Miller, *New England Mind*, p. 17. Haller, *Foxe's Book of Martyrs and the Elect Nation*, p. 75, argued that this English watering down of the strictness of Calvin's theories began as early as the reign of Edward VI with the Regius Professorships of Bucer at Cambridge and Martyr at Oxford.

[9]   Dering, *A Briefe and Necessarie Catechisme, passim*.

George Gifford's catechism, referring to those who 'seek to enter the path-way to salvation' implied that such a voluntary venture was indeed possible.[10] William Perkins, the most influential of Elizabethan puritans, offered his readers a detailed plan of the path to the state of salvation from the depths of reprobation.[11] English 'Calvinism' thus provided a revolutionary cultural prospect: instruction for all, designed primarily not for daily labour, but for the personal reformation and continuing struggle which would lead to salvation.

It was therefore the duty 'not only of the ministers publickly, but also of all men privately, to instruct those that be ignorant, and bring them from error . . .'.[12] Even those who might never be saved were to be instructed so that their lives would in some small way reflect the glory of God. Separation from the Church of England was forbidden by the majority of puritans for a variety of theological and political reasons, including that it would deny the educative role of God's elect.[13] In the late sixteenth century the most immediate way of bringing others into the presence of the Lord – even while some stormed the walls of Westminster – was recognized by puritans such as the pastoral Richard Greenham of Dry Drayton to be the propagation of the Word by both private reading and public sermons. Though it is of course impossible to determine the exact nature of sermons which were not printed, it would seem that from the start puritans sought to reform England more by spreading encouragement than by offering the dread of Calvinist double predestination. They argued, as I noted above, that it was possible to recognize the states of faith and lack of faith; secondly, they contended that the path to salvation was much broader and thus of greater capacity than had at first been assumed. Together, by leading to a concentration on the problem of assurance, these changes permitted much more liberal interpretation of specific cases of practical

[10] Gifford, *Catechisme*, title-page. See also Perkins, *Foundation of Christian Religion*, sig. A2^{r-v}; Olsen, *John Foxe*, p. 103, quoting Foxe.
[11] Perkins, *A treatise tending unto a declaration whether a man be in the estate of damnation . . . or of grace*, pp. 28–9; Hall, 'Calvin against the Calvinists', *Proceedings of the Huguenot Society of London*, 20, p. 295.
[12] Udall, *Certaine Sermons* ('Obedience to Gospel', part 1), sig. Ii.ii^v, also sig. Kk.v^{r-v}; Gybson, *Fruitful Sermon*, sig. E3^{r-v}. See also John Winthrop's 'Christian Experience', *Winthrop Papers*, 1, p. 156. This proselytizing urge also took the form of a missionary drive. For a very different point of view, to the effect that among 'the Puritans of seventeenth-century England not only any missionary enterprise but any missionary concern was almost entirely absent', see Nuttall, *Puritan Spirit*, p. 77. A fine refutation of Nuttall's argument can be found in Crashawe, *Sermon Preached in London*, sig. C.3, where the author talks of the necessity of sending preachers to convert the Amerindians. See also the section on evangelizing the Indians in *New Englands First Fruits*, reprinted in Morison, *Founding of Harvard*, pp. 420–47; and also the example of John Eliot, who translated the Bible into Mohican, prepared a Mohican grammar and established schools for Indians (Jarman, 'Education', in Morpurgo, ed., *Life Under the Stuarts*, p. 71). See also Edward Howes' remark, in a letter of 20 Apr. 1632 to John Winthrop Junior, that he hoped a suitable grammar text would quickly bring the 'indians to the perfect understanding of our tonge and writinge truly, and speaking elegantly . . .' (*Winthrop Papers*, III, p. 77).
[13] Udall, *Certaine Sermons* ('Amendment of Life', part 3), sig. M. iii; Gifford, *Catechisme*, sig. K3^{r-v}.

divinity, a branch of Christian thought for which puritans became famous over the course of our period.[14]

In the late sixteenth, and especially in the seventeenth, century, these changes metamorphosed into a mature form of covenant theology, which generally held that God had made two specific covenants: first with Adam ('of works'), abrogated and rendered ineffective by the Fall; secondly, with mankind ('of grace') in which agreement man's salvation was assured on the basis of faith.[15] Though there were doubtless continental origins to the formulation of the theological structure of the covenant, the method of its presentation and the timing of its development in England were likely due to local conditions.[16] Theorizing about Calvinist double predestination produced a search for knowledge of election which could not easily be satisfied by a passive confidence, or by the reassurances of a minister. Knowledge of election could come only from the *experience* of true faith. In this, the role of the individual as a voluntary receptor of faith, and as the builder of grace, was increasingly emphasized from Edward Dering onwards. The development of voluntarism into the covenant idea in England resulted from the interaction of the evangelical demands of a populist pulpit and the puritans' theological position; the demands of the former gradually and haltingly modified the latter.[17] Before the 1590s, the notion of the individual arrangement with God as an agreement which had duties and responsibilities on both sides was not fully formalized. After this rough dividing line, however, the search for knowledge of salvation became ever more pressing as the evangelical thrust grew apace.

The fundamental tenet of the agreement was the recognition that God's bargain with Jesus (who acted on man's behalf) removed the *necessity* for man to live by the Law in order to achieve salvation.[18] Man was still bound to *attempt* to conform to the Law, but his inevitable failure would no longer doom him, as long as he lived in faith in Jesus Christ. The Law had served as a command of what not to do, whereas the Gospel, the doctrine of the covenant, was a positive blueprint for life.[19] But, though the Law had been abrogated as a

---

[14] Collinson, *Mirror of Elizabethan Puritanism*, p. 28, suggested that practical divinity was the prime concern of puritans in Elizabethan times, though he did not specifically link it with covenant theology.

[15] Brown, 'Covenant theology', in Hastings, ed., *Encyclopaedia of Religion and Ethics*, IV, p. 216.

[16] For a variety of interpretations concerning those chiefly responsible for the origins and growth of covenant theology, see Møller, 'Beginnings of puritan covenant theology', *Journal of Ecclesiastical History*, 14, p. 49; Little, *Religion, Order, and Law*, p. 257; McKee, 'Idea of Covenant', pp. 14–19, 239–45; Miller, *New England Mind*, p. 374; Emerson, 'Calvin and covenant theology', *Church History*, 25, p. 136; De Jong, *The Covenant Idea*, pp. 19–22, 68–71; Greaves, 'The origins and early development of English covenant thought', *The Historian*, 31, esp. pp. 21–4, 27–8; Pettit, *The Heart Prepared*, pp. 38–9, 119.   [17] I am very grateful to Peter Lake for help with this point.

[18] See, for example, Bulkeley, *The Gospel-Covenant; Or The Covenant of Grace Opened*, pp. 29–30; see also Miller, *New England Mind*, pp. 405–6.   [19] Perkins, *Workes*, III, p. 752.

standard for salvation, it still served, in a negative sense, as 'a scholemaster to bring us into Christ. . .'.[20] The covenant, explained a host of puritan authors,[21] was entered into voluntarily, though naturally not equally, by both parties. It was everlasting and assured, since invented by a perfect God. The sacraments were the seals by which man confirmed his agreement. The covenant was not universal, but offered only to those who had been elected.[22] As an illustration of the terms of the contract, and of the fervency it aroused, we may cite the case of John Winthrop, later governor of Massachusetts. His diary reveals that he was sure that on 20 April 1606 – such was the certainty of the awareness of the change – I made a new Covenant with the Lorde', the terms of which were:

Of my part, that I would reforme thesse sinnes by his grace, pride, covetousnesse, love of this worlde, vanitie of minde, unthankfulnesse, slouth, both in his service and in my callinge, not preparinge myselfe with reverence and uprightnesse to come to his word: Of the Lords part that he would give me a new heart, joy in his spirit, that he would dwell with me, that he would strengthen me against the World, the fleshe, and the Divell, that he would forgive my sinnes and increase my faith.[23]

David Zaret has recently demonstrated the use that puritan ministers made of earthly parallels in explaining the nature of the covenant with God. The use of such analogies to common experience permeated puritan writings and, along with their 'plain style' of rhetoric, may well account in large part for the popularity of puritan preacher–authors. Zaret argues that the covenant was propagandized through a general comparison to the nature of earthly con-tracts, in the sense both of creating a binding relationship, and of offering the individual a proprietorship in God.[24] This may, as Zaret argues, lend a greater credence to Hill's notion that puritan preachers addressed themselves par-ticularly to the 'middling sort', who would be familiar with mercantile or land law, though his point that contemporary relations of production provided the '*sources* of puritan theology'[25] seems to underestimate the degree to which puritan preachers were intent on proselytizing an older, Pauline–Augustinian strain of pious faith.

Puritan preachers did not aim at a fully rational approach to religion, as the

20 Dent, *Pastime for Parents*, unpaginated; Perkins, *Workes*, II, p. 250; Gifford, *Catechisme*, sig. D.8. See also the marginal comment to Galatians 3.25 in the Geneva Bible, which noted, 'Not that the doctrine of the Law is abolished, but the condemnation thereof is taken away by faith.'
21 The vast majority of puritan divines publishing in the period 1590–1640 made some mention of the covenant. The short description here is based primarily on the works of Perkins, Ames, Sibbes, Ball, and Bulkeley. For further explanation, see McKee, 'Idea of Covenant', pp. 103–15; Trinterud, 'Origins of puritanism', *passim*.
22 Taylor, *Davids Learning*, pp. 163–4; Emerson, 'Calvin and covenant theology', pp. 137–8.
23 *Winthrop Papers*, I, pp. 162–3.
24 Zaret, 'Ideology and organization in puritanism', esp. pp. 96–111, where he cites many interesting examples.   25 *Ibid.*, pp. 112, 104.

seventeenth-century bourgeois grew accustomed to rationalized business and legal practices. Contracts, it should be clear, did not provide the source of covenant thought: the inspiration came directly from Scripture. Contracts, however, did provide a useful analogy, a parallel for those whose minds dwelt most of the week on bargains struck between men. That puritan ministers chose the particular language of contracts reveals something about their ability to respond to what they perceived as the interests of some of their audiences. But in order to comprehend the core of the puritan plan for reform, we must examine not only the public language, but also the duties, of the covenant, and the way in which it clarified both the balance in English puritan protestantism of reason and faith, and the puritan concept of experiential learning.

The argument that man's relationship with God now lay in the form of a contract soon prompted the question of whether man had to be totally passive in the matter of salvation, or whether he could actively pursue heavenly glory by suitably preparing himself in case the Spirit did offer him grace. This, in turn, depended on the dominant view of the manner in which faith came to the individual. Though clerics did not seek to limit God's ways, the Elizabethan era saw a significant increase among puritans of those who believed that God no longer suddenly plucked sinners from their seeming destiny, as he had saved Paul on the road to Damascus. Rather, God now led his elect along a more gradual path to redemption. The human role was to be prepared to engage in the contract. Elianor Stockton, penning her 'diary' in the later seventeenth century, recalled her own younger awareness of the covenant, and of the respective parts played by the deity and the penitent: 'if thou wilt be my God and make me one of thine and put thy spirit with in me to cause me to walk in thy statutes and keep thy Judgements and due them and put thy feare in to my heart that I shall not depart from the[m]. . . '.[26] Awareness, however, was not sufficient motivation for a thorough change; it was acceptance of the covenant by the human that transformed the will.[27]

This notion of an *agreement* quickly spawned the idea that man could help by 'predisposing' himself to accept God's free gift.[28] Typical of the process was Simonds D'Ewes' recollection of how reading a godly tract had moved him to resolve to improve both his knowledge of grace and his style of life, that is, both levels of his existence.[29] This concept of preparation was based on the ability to come first to a recognition of the condition of one's own soul.[30] Preserving the freedom of the Almighty to act as he saw fit in individual cases

[26] Dr Williams's Library, Modern MS 24.8, fol. 4ᵛ; see also fol. 5 for her acquiescence in the covenant when it was eventually offered to her.   [27] Dent, *Plaine Mans Path-way*, p. 14.

[28] ·For a further explanation of this involved problem, see Pettit, *Heart Prepared*, esp. pp. 2–8, 52–6.

[29] D'Ewes, *Autobiography*, I, pp. 249–50. The work was *The Life of Faith*, by Samuel Ward, the puritan lecturer of Ipswich.

[30] There were many explanations of how one might 'recognize the condition of one's own soul'. See, for example, Ames, *Conscience*, Bk II, Chs. 1 & 2.

while also encouraging their (as yet unregenerate) parishioners to courses of preparation involved puritan ministers in paradoxical offerings. A strong theme soon emerged to the effect that present doubt should not be interpreted to mean perpetual exclusion from the contract. God, it was argued, listened to those who asked for the covenant.[31] So Richard Sibbes argued that a man could not even desire a change in himself – that had to come from the Spirit – and yet he also offered his readers 'Directions to get the Spirit'.[32] The covenant was still not seen as universal, but stress was laid on the interpretation that 'salvation is offred to many, that do not offer themselves to salvation'.[33] So while he argued that grace was implanted by God without any preparation by man,[34] John Preston also put forward the proposition that fervent prayer, the result of prior repentance, could build up a 'stock' with God, that is, that God could be more attracted to an individual because of his actions.[35] He even listed seven conditions which had to be met before God would hear a man's prayer.[36] Indeed, the preparationist case soon developed to the point at which ministers such as Thomas Hooker saw preparation as a 'condition' of receiving God's grace, and Bulkeley argued that a man could *demand* that God take him into the covenant.[37] Not all preparationists were carried to this extreme. John Ball, even while arguing the value of preparation, readily admitted that it could not be held to be absolutely necessary, since this would impose a condition upon God, and thereby restrict his freedom.[38] Extreme preparationist ideas may thus perhaps not have had a wide following in pre-revolutionary England, but they were only the working out of a doctrine at which English covenant theologians had made broad hints, especially concerning the question of whether man could reject, as well as accept, the heavenly contract.[39] Richard

[31] Harris, *Gods Goodnes and Mercie*, pp. 19–23. See also Hill, *The World Turned Upside Down*, p. 128.
[32] Sibbes, *The Excellencie of the Gospell*, pp. 58–9, 70ff., 625–32. Pettit, *Heart Prepared*, pp. 70–1, views Sibbes as 'by far the most extreme [of the covenanters] in terms of the abilities he assigned to natural man' in the preparationist debate. See also Whately, *New Birth*, pp. 104–13; Adams, *Workes*, p. 1066.
[33] Adams, *Workes*, pp. 1193–5. See also Downame, *Christian Warfare*, p. 340.
[34] Preston, *Breastplate*, p. 34. See also McKee, 'Idea of covenant', pp. 161–2, for similar contradictions in the thought of William Ames.
[35] Preston, *Saints Daily Exercise*, p. 71. Miller, ' "Preparation for salvation" in seventeenth-century New England', *Journal of the History of Ideas*, 4, p. 261, explains that this preparation was not meant by puritans in the sense of any meritorious work (as with the Arminians), but rather just as a declaration of inclination to accept faith should the Spirit ever offer it.   [36] Preston, *Saints Daily Exercise*, pp. 102 ff.
[37] Miller, 'Preparation', pp. 278–9. Miller also notes (*ibid.*, p. 265) that there was some opposition to Thomas Hooker from those who regarded him as a sort of 'sophisticated Arminian'. See also McKee, 'Idea of covenant', pp. 158–9.   [38] Ball, *Treatise of the Covenant of Grace*, pp. 337ff.
[39] See, for example, Ames, *Marrow*, p. 113; Perkins, *Workes*, I, p. 125; Ball, *Treatise of the Covenant of Grace*, pp. 154–5. This is an extremely involved topic, of which only a summary has been attempted here. The problem is discussed more fully, though not without serious differences of opinion, in the following works: Pettit, *Heart Prepared, passim*; McKee, 'Idea of covenant', esp. pp. 158–9; Coolidge, *Pauline Renaissance in England*, p. 72 and *passim*; Emerson, 'Calvin and covenant theology', pp. 140–2; Holden, *Anti-Puritan Satire 1572–1642*, pp. 36–8; Miller, *New England Mind*, pp. 27–8, 200, 289; Miller, 'Preparation', *passim*; Simpson, *Puritanism in Old and New England*, p. 4; Kendall, *Calvin and English Calvinism, passim*.

Sibbes, after all, had argued that God and Jesus 'begged' man to accept the offer of the covenant.[40] William Ames had hinted that the individual had final say over entering the covenant,[41] and had conveniently provided a step-by-step progress towards grace.[42]

Since covenant theologians taught that people were brought to an understanding of their relationship to the eternal through a gradual process, it became extremely important for theologians to offer signs to their readers by which they could, on the basis of their experiences, effectively categorize themselves as members or non-members of the covenant.[43] And so there arose a massive puritan corpus which explained in very simple terms the workings of faith that could be recognized as full assurance. At its climax this self-confidence could serve not only to effect an Augustinian inner struggle to develop a mystical love for God, but also to encourage the desire for similar assurance in other members of the household.

At the same time, the doubt that prevailed in most hearts led puritan preachers to direct their efforts especially towards those who were in the formative stage of their struggle, who did not yet feel assured. So William Burton, towards the end of Elizabeth's reign, outlined a full course of preparation:

if thou feele not as yet the gracious presence of Gods spirit in thee as thou wouldest, yet use the holy means that God hath appointed for the conversion and confirmation of his children; frequent the word preached, read in the scriptures, & labours of the godly learned, use praier, & Conference & meditation & so wait on God, who is thy present helpe and thy God, but thou saist thou canst not heare with delight, thou canst take no pleasure in reading of good books, nor hearing of them redd unto thee, thou canst not brooke conference and praier, thou doest distast them all, yet I say use them still, as a good man taketh meate and drinke, and phisicke thou it be against the stomacke, and cast up all againe, yet he desireth to digest it, and so often by taking, at last doth gather strength, and take that willingly with hope, which before hee received against his will with a kind of loathing. So thy sick soule by often using the holy means that God hath appointed, at last through his blessing will strengthen thee, and make them to use them of love & desire. . .[44]

The very act of engaging in these practices with an honest hope would bring a metamorphosis from loathing to love in the searcher that would be indicative of his changing inner state. So Nicholas Byfield, one of simplest and most lucid expositors, concluded his explanation of the covenant with a section

[40] Sibbes, *Light From Heaven*, pp. 119–20. The basis for this argument was Romans 10.13: 'For whosoever shal cal upon the Name of the Lord, shalbe saved.'
[41] Ames, *Conscience*, esp. Bk II, Ch. 3.   [42] *Ibid.*, Bk II, Ch. 4.
[43] The literature on this point is truly extensive. For a sampling, see Sibbes, *Complete Works*, I, pp. 270, 266, 268; IV, pp. 16, 182, 214; V, pp. 103, 319, 350; VI, pp. 12, 87; Bulkeley, *The Gospel-Covenant*, p. 87; Perkins, *Workes*, I, pp. 117, 290, 392, 410; Whately, *New Birth*, pp. 101, 117; Ames, *Marrow*, p. 132; Preston, *Breastplate*, pp. 251, 249; Ball, *Treatise of Covenant*, pp. 85, 113, 153; Byfield, *The Principles Or, The Patterne of wholesome Words*, pp. 125, 138ff.   [44] Burton, *Davids Thanksgiving*, pp. 27–8.

entitled'What wee must doe that wee may goe to heaven'. Arthur Hildersam listed a confidence that assurance was possible, use of God's ordinances to get and increase grace, humility over one's own wretchedness, a constant care to please God, and a dependence on Christ as the means by which a believer could come to assurance of election.[45] A strong element of opinion arose which also advised the Christian petitioners not to forsake the quest simply for lack of early assurance. Henry Scudder, for example, strongly opposed any suggestions of universal salvation, but also cautioned people not to be too pessimistic about their chances, not to believe too soon that they might be reprobate stock. He told his readers that if only they would try, 'you shall reade your Election written in golden and great letters'.[46] Simonds D'Ewes, in 1641, went so far as to suggest that mere 'desire of assurance, and complaint of the want of assurance' amounted to assurance itself,[47] for God could not reject the seeker of the covenant.

This need for assurance understandably encouraged a strong awareness of conversion. It was still held that there was 'a certaine appointed time of every mans conversion' which one could recognize.[48] Thus John Preston could later recall the moment of his conversion during a sermon by John Cotton. For others he publicized five signs of assurance which Christ had laid down.[49] Parallels were still occasionally drawn with the model of Christian earthly existence. So we are told of Robert Bolton, future godly minister, that, after narrowly missing an appointment to be enrolled in a papist seminary, he returned to Brasenose College, where he was soon converted

by such a way of working as the LORD seldome useth but upon such strong vessels which in his singular wisdome he intendeth afterward for strong incounters and rare imployments. The first newes he heard of GOD was not by any soft and still voice, but in terrible tempests and thunder, the LORD running upon him as a gyant, taking him by the necke and shaking him to peeces, as he did *Iob*; beating him to the very ground, as he did *Paul*. . .[50]

But far more common was the lengthy internal struggle. John Winthrop, governor of Massachusetts, recorded at great length his own progress to Christian existence.[51] One of his great worries was that someone who fell

---

[45] Byfield, *Principles*, pp. 448ff; Hildersam, *CLII Lectures*, pp. 406–11.

[46] Scudder, *Christians Daily Walke*, p. 518; also p. 462. See also Hildersam, *CLII Lectures*, p. 495; Airay, *Lectures upon Philippians*, pp. 183ff., 195; Smith, *Davids Repentance*, pp. 283–4, 282; Greenham, *Workes*, p. 122; Dod & Cleaver, *Ten Commandements*, p. 24; Taylor, *Christs Combate*, p. 277. Non-covenant puritans also took an interest in this point: Richard Rogers (probably not a covenanter) listed 'Eight infallible signes of Regeneration (Rogers *et al.*, *Garden of Spirituall Flowers*, sig. D2).

[47] Quoted in Hill, *World Turned Upside Down*, p. 128. At times, even the efficacy of baptism was brought into the debate over assurance. See Pettit, *Heart Prepared*, pp. 74–7, 92–6, 123–4.

[48] Crashawe, *Sermon Preached in London*, sig. B4ᵛ.   [49] Preston, *Saints Infirmities*, pp. 151–2.

[50] Bolton, *Last & Learned Worke*, to which is appended the 'Life of Bolton', sig. b5.

[51] *Winthrop Papers*, I, pp. 154–61 ('John Winthrop's Christian Experience'), 161–238 ('Experiencia').

away from the 'heavenly gift' would not get it again. Assurance – and this is
crucial to an understanding of puritan social existence – was thus not only a
matter of moment of recognition; rather, it was a continual struggle which
could have no ending, know no resting places.[52] Winthrop went through the
common doubts that his conversion was only the sham of the hypocrite, enjoying 'temporary faith', and then melancholy as he temporarily shunned his
'wordly businesse' and 'lawfull recreations' while he pursued inner comfort.
Winthrop recounted that he had been labouring under the burden of the Law
until, when he was about thrity, 'it pleased the Lord in my family exercise to
manifest unto mee the difference between the Covenant of grace, and the
Covenant of workes. . .'.[53] The actual conversion followed, and exemplified
the pattern of pain resulting from the prerequisite awareness of man's sunken
state: the Lord, Winthrop recounted, laid

[me] lower in myne owne eyes then at any time before, and showed me the emptiness
of all my guifts, and parts; left mee neither power nor will . . . I knew I was worthy of
nothing for I knew I could doe nothing for him or for my selfe. I could only mourn,
and weep to think of free mercy to such a vile wretch as I was.[54]

From this state of utter desolation, which perforce had to precede the
experience of conversion, Winthrop was moved to exclaim that he 'was filled
with joy unspeakable, and glorious and with a spirit of Adoption'.[55] Indeed,
once the doctrine of temporary faith had been largely abandoned, puritans
could even suggest that the honest, heartfelt awareness of degradation could
legitimately be seen as the first step towards repentance, the first link in the
chain of salvation.[56]

Puritan ministers constantly warned their flocks that one's own assurance
was a difficult enough matter, but that the eternity of others – no matter their
earthly station – could not finally be judged. Hence one of the arguments
against separation. But it can scarcely be doubted that in practice outward acts
were taken to be manifestations of the condition of others, as well as of oneself. Thus Margaret Winthrop, writing to John Winthrop Junior in 1630 concerning the death of Forth, noted that Forth's *actions* 'gave us assurance that he
was the child of god. . .'.[57] Each action was truly understood as reflecting the
individual's progress to heaven or to hell. Thus Margaret Hoby's declaration
in her diary, on a certain Sunday, that 'this day, as ever, the divell laboureth to

---

[52] For one of Winthrop's more optimistic statements on assurance, see *ibid.*, i, p. 413. Even Cromwell
     knew doubt as he faced death (Hill, *God's Englishman*, p. 213). See also Scudder, *Christians Daily Walke*,
     pp. 684–6.   [53] *Winthrop Papers*, i, p. 158.   [54] *Ibid.*, pp. 158–9.
[55] *Ibid.*, p. 159. See also p. 183 for a statement of contrast between Winthrop's condition before and after
     conversion. Winthrop also gives witness to the Augustinian weakness in man. Even as the 'Covenant of
     Grace began to take great impression in mee', he recalled, 'I thought I had now enough . . . [and] rather
     took occasion to be more remisse in my spirituall watch, and so more loose in my Conversation' (*ibid.*,
     iii, p. 342).   [56] Kendall, *Calvin and English Calvinism, passim*.   [57] *Winthrop Papers*, ii, p. 321.

hinder my profittable hearinge of the word and callinge upon god, but the Lord, for his mercies sach strengten, his children to rissist and over Come'.[58] William Ames, among others, offered his readers a list of the 'signes of true Repentance'.[59] The importance which the keeping of diaries and spiritual autobiographies assumed is further testimony to the depth of this concern in the puritan soul.[60]

Patrick Collinson has recently suggested parallels between Samuel Clarke's view of a godly life, the ethics of Aristotle, and Erasmus' view of Christ's philosophy as the 'restoration of human nature, originally well formed. . .'.[61] Even if Collinson's portrayal of Clarke as downplaying the centrality of conversion were to be accepted, Clarke would not seem, here at least, to reflect the common puritan experiences of the previous seventy years. In this case, my theory of puritans at a second, or 'immediate', level of existence may perhaps be usefully applied. Clarke was writing in the 1640s, when both formalized religion and the relevance of learning to religion were under strong attack. He may well have been more concerned in his character sketches to support the contemporary defenders of learned religion than to give an accurate portrayal of the importance of conversion in recent puritan experience. The moment of conversion, even if it came after a long course of preparation, was a non-rational occurrence, an adoption into the soul and conscience of a supra-rational truth. It was one of the few pieces of obvious 'enthusiasm' which puritans still permitted in their experience. Writing at a time of apocalyptic revolt by the forces of enthusiasm, Clarke perhaps found it necessary to strike a balance by emphasizing the learned qualities of his subjects and their common civic 'virtues', rather than the eruption of assurance.

To comprehend the true importance of conversion, we should therefore look to pre-revolutionary comment. At bottom rested the fervour of a love of the Lord, and the desire (if not the full capability) to perform his will. Neither of these emanated from an Aristotelian civic virtue; neither, after all, was rational. So Jeremiah Burroughes, in painting the change which came with conversion, settled on its supernatural and anti-rational qualities:

The wayes of God are not onely above nature, but contrary to nature, and therefore there must bee needs, some speciall choicenesse of spirit, to carry a man on in them . . .

---

[58] *Diary of Lady Margaret Hoby*, ed. Mead, pp. 66–7.
[59] Ames, *Conscience*, Bk. II, Ch. 8, p. 20. See also *ibid.*, p. 32, for 'The signes of Gods love to us', and *ibid.*, Bk. II, Ch. 14, on 'the hope of eternall life', which encouraged an optimism.
[60] On spiritual autobiographies, see Spufford, 'First steps in literacy', *Social History*, 4, pp. 407–35, and, more generally, Watkins, *Puritan Experience*.
[61] Collinson, ' "A Magazine of religious patterns" ', in Baker, ed., *Renaissance and Renewal in Christian History, passim*, esp. pp. 235, 238–39, 248. In this article, Collinson downplays the importance of conversion in puritan experience (*ibid.*, esp. pp. 240–1).

In following after the Lord, all natural abilities, and common grace will doe no more but stop the streame of corrupt nature, they cannot so overpower it, as to carry the soule another way, but the worke of grace in this choicenesse of spirit will doe it.[62]

Conversion was thus the time of the infusion of personal meaning. This necessitated, understandably, a strong *experience* of conversion. So Simonds D'Ewes, even after he had 'gained an exact *knowledge*' of the workings of salvation, could still remark later that 'at this time I knew nothing *experimentally* touching the assurance of salvation'.[63]

Quite simply, man, by offering God his due, could work at his own salvation. That the Almighty had reached out again to humans and offered them a strand, a thin filament, that would connect them to a fixed meaning outside a natural universe always in a state of flux provided protestant man with a purpose beyond himself, an answer to his search. The outward appurtenances of belief were the steps by which man ascended from his own dark irrationalism – his deep 'fear and trembling' in such a chaotic existence – to the realm of meaning. The visible church could not provide this internal meaning. Only the establishment of an individual bond between man and his Maker could solve the sublunary quest for meaning, and thus provide peace and stability. The puritan thrust can therefore be seen, in one way, as a statement of the existential quest following the rejection of the theological bases of the pre-Reformation church. The lifeline was woven of faith; for reason, this implied, as we shall see, a serious restriction of capacity, for if meaning was extra-terrestrial, and discoverable only by faith, then man's rational capacity, by itself, could answer only the questions of earthly existence.

Puritans were nonetheless wary of being too lenient on the question of preparation, lest they appear to intimate that man could aid in his own salvation by his works.[64] Indeed, not all puritans subscribed to a notion of a covenant which involved preparation; certain strict predestinarians such as John Cotton feared a weakening of the majesty of God.[65] This in turn reflected the difference over the duration of the actual 'time of conversion', Cotton arguing that it was a sudden predestined moment rather than a gradual process.[66] It

---

[62] Burroughes, *Excellency of Gracious Spirit*, pp. 415–16.
[63] D'Ewes, *Autobiography*, I, pp. 249, 276.
[64] See, for example, the opinion of Thomas Hooker (Miller, *New England Mind*, p. 28). On the importance, however, of godly works, see below, pp. 35–40.
[65] See Pettit, *Heart Prepared*, pp. 139–40, for a brief summary of Cotton's position. See also Greenham, *Workes*, p. 589.
[66] Crashawe, *Sermon Preached in London*, sig. B4ᵛ. For a good explanation of the gradualness of regeneration, see Miller, 'Preparation', *passim*, and Miller, *New England Mind*, pp. 25, 51, 200, 289. Miller seems to go too far, however, in his argument that God was willing to 'treat with men in a rational negotiation' ('Preparation', p. 260). I could find no evidence of a belief in a human ability to negotiate the covenant. See also Pettit, *Heart Prepared*, pp. 219–20.

might be surmised that this difference would have led also to a division over the dependence on human reason, the preparationists allowing a greater measure of reliance on the human intellect, while the others relied more heavily on an enthusiastic faith. In practice, no such neat dichotomy can be drawn within the ranks of the puritans. Even after his conversion, John Cotton's published works reveal great learning, and the seminary he ran in his household did not shun the humane arts. Conversely, John Preston, a preparationist, issued dire warnings about the necessity of restricting human reason (though he also made great use of humane learning). English puritans broadly conceded that some inward struggle had to occur, and that without this education and other favourable activities could not bring men to God. Preparationists attempted to circumvent the objections of the stricter predestinarians by insisting that God was still responsible for faith and grace; man merely responded to God's initiative, though of course he could still deny God and choose reprobation.

II

The Christian, like all men of 'good will', had always been bound by a charitable duty to the less fortunate. But, with the propagation of solafideism, believers might well come to question whether 'good works' were possible from fallen creatures, and whether in any case they were relevant when God had decreed another path to salvation. Much of puritan thought, therefore, had to be directed to establishing a pattern for Reformed Christian living, to telling the faithful how, first, they should improve their own being, and how, secondly, they might better display their faith in their actions. Against the perceived evils of pure contemplation and Antinomianism, puritans reacted swiftly with a casuistry which even in the sixteenth century was very much based on the covenant. As Coolidge has pointed out, this agreement was 'conditional' not in the sense that man could negotiate changes, but rather in that the contract created a 'condition' in man,[67] namely a willingness to struggle to maintain his faith and obedience. This clarified a puzzling aspect of double predestination. William Perkins, the 'prime man of the precise faction',[68] shattered the idea that the elect would be saved even if they did not lead godly lives by pointing out that this was a contradiction of the condition imposed by membership in the covenant. The saved, by their faithful attempts to follow the injunctions of the Gospel, as well as the terms of the Law, were bound to lead eminently (though of course not perfectly) godly lives. Simonds D'Ewes

---

[67] Coolidge, *Pauline Renaissance*, esp. pp. 112 ff.
[68] The description was John Chamberlain's. See his letter to Dudley Carleton, dated 4 Nov. 1602, noting Perkins' death (*C.S.P.D. 1601–1603 and Addenda 1547–1565*, p. 259).

argued in the same vein against the 'profane atheistical men, who say that assurance brings forth presumption and a careless wicked life'.[69]

Godly conversation – the social expression of one's faith – was thus seen to be a visible seal of membership in the covenant.[70] As Thomas Taylor succinctly put it, 'Doctrine is but the laying of a ground. Application is the building up of a Christian.'[71] Richard Rogers divided the Christian's struggle into three stages: 'first, they must have a cleare knowledge of their salvation. Secondly, they must make account of it as of their chiefe and principall treasure. Thirdly, they must take some good course of life. . .'[72] It was, however, the last act which provided a sure basis for the first. This was not a development which awaited the full flowering of covenant theology. Right at the beginning of the puritan thrust Edward Dering, in informing his catechetical readers of their proper response, asserted his opposition to a determinist-inspired passivity:[73]

We must doe good works not to deserve our salvation by them, but by our works to glorifie God, in walking as becometh Gods children, declaring thereby our thankfulness to God for our redemption. Secondly by our workes to make our election more certaine unto our selves. Thirdly, to win others to Christ by our holy life and conversation.[74]

The added incentive to the performance of the duties of obedience and struggle was the immediate assurance it could give. And, as John Downame put it, once the covenant had been more clearly drawn, 'who would not courageously fight, that is beforehand assured of victory?'.[75] John Preston, in a similar vein, noted that the covenant was 'a very comfortable doctrine, if it be well considered'.[76] At the end simple desire to remain faithful was the guarantee of election. 'Temporary faith' had been abandoned as a doctrine. The covenant was now the perfect message to take to the countryside.

For the purpose of this study, the necessity of good works, preached without rest by the puritans as an obligation on the part of man to fulfil his side of the contract, is of the utmost import. Good works came to be defined as an

[69] Perkins, *Workes*, I, p. 709; D'Ewes, *Autobiography*, I, p. 369. See, similarly, Corderoy, *Short Dialogue*, pp. 3–4, 31.
[70] See, for example, Chaderton, *Excellent and Godly Sermon*, sig. Cvii'; Dering, *Briefe Catechisme*, sig. B6; Wilcox, *Large Letters*, pp. 48, 95–6; Smith, *Trumpet of the Soule*, sigs. B2'–3; Egerton, *Briefe Methode of Catechizing*, p. 10.
[71] Taylor, *Davids Learning*, p. 309. See also Becon, *Sicke Mans Salve*, pp. 83–4.
[72] Rogers, *Practice of Christianitie*, p. 136; also pp. 538–43. See also Bolton, *Discourse . . . True Happiness*, pp. 67–8.
[73] For a comparison with the Lutheran response, see Strauss, *Luther's House*, Ch. 8, *passim*.
[74] Dering, *Briefe Catechisme*, sig. B6. See also Perkins, *Workes*, II, p. 323, quoted in Breward, 'Significance of William Perkins', p. 125; *Gods Goodnes*, pp. 6–7ff.
[75] Quoted in Huehns, *Antinomianism in English History*, p. 59 n. 5.
[76] Quoted in Miller, *New England Mind*, p. 390.

integral part of the earthly existence of the regenerate, in that they were necessary to the living of a godly life, which was indeed the lot of the elect.[77] Good works, in short, were the effect, and not the cause, of faith. Quite simply, the individual was bound to apply Christ's doctrines to the greatest use of all God's people.[78] They were the due which man owed his Creator.[79]

Thus John Udall could insist that it was not enough simply to espouse godly sayings; one had also to perform good (godly) works.[80] Good works even reached the level of recognition as an integral part of the process of moving to salvation. Jeremy Corderoy argued that salvation would not come without 'sanctification & good works', and that death-bed repentances (so beloved of the puritan view of religiosity in the Roman church) could not bring salvation for the very reason that they did not allow of time for the performance of good works.[81] William Whately summed up that 'it behoveth every man to have firme and evident proofes of his being a true and not a false Christian . . .'.[82] Puritans had to beware, however; such explanations could easily trespass upon the dangerous territory of meritorious works. An earlier, safer outline of the orthodoxy was presented in a sermon by Laurence Chaderton which included a clarification of the doctrine of 'temporary faith'. He reminded his audience that good works could be 'pledges and seales of our salvation', if performed from a godly conscience; but, from hypocrites, they were 'rather the subtile sleyghts of Satan, and the deceites of sinne'[83] and marked the reason for which at the Day of Judgement 'they shalbe eternallye condemned'.[84]

One of the specific duties was charity. Always fearful that Reformed religion would turn inward, concentrate exclusively on the spiritual bond of God and man, to the grave neglect of earthly society, puritans insisted on outward charitable works as a manifestation of true belief.[85] Especially was there a great duty towards the poor, to set them upon the path to Christian living.[86]

---

[77] See, for example, Downame, *Summe of Sacred Divinitie*, pp. 506–10. In this, of course, they were not alone. See, for example, Cooper, *Certaine Sermons*, p. 15. But Cooper does not seem to have adopted the extreme puritan position that only the regenerate could perform good works, and that all the actions of the unregenerate were reprehensible to God.

[78] Sibbes, *Light from Heaven*, pp. 58–9, 117–18; see also Taylor, *Davids Learning*, pp. 31–2; Bernard, *Ready Way to Good Works*, pp. 300–1, 87ff., 252–3; Preston, *Breastplate*, p. 207; Dod & Cleaver, *Ten Commandements*, p. 276; Potter, 'To the Christian Reader', sig. A2r–v, in Airay, *Lectures Upon Phillippians*.

[79] See, for example, Egerton, *Briefe Methode of Catechizing*, pp. 10, 14; Downame, *Summe of Sacred Divinitie*, pp. 509–10; Cliffe, *Puritan Gentry*, p. 119.

[80] Udall, *Certaine Sermons* ('Amendment of Life', part 3), sigs. Lv, L.ij. See also Harris, *Gods Goodnes*, pp. 5ff. [81] Corderoy, *Short Dialogue*, pp. 4, 31, 57, 63.

[82] Whately, *Poore Mans Advocate*, pp. 20–1.

[83] Chaderton, *Excellent and Godly Sermon*, sig. B.viv. Chaderton recalled (*ibid.*, sig. C.i) that the Epistle of James commanded the necessity of works as well as faith.

[84] *Ibid.*, sig. H.iv. [85] See, for example, Gataker, *Davids Instructer*, sig. A3.

[86] See, for example, Bernard, *Ready Way to Good Works*, pp. 91–2, citing Robert Bolton; also pp. 252–3.

While in practice class interests conditioned the content and universality of charitable foundations, the theory was that in their donations, the truly godly aimed only at the glory of God, while the unregenerate crassly sought earthly reputation.[87] One of the increasingly common forms of charity in this age, for puritans as for others, was educational provision.[88] But this presented a conundrum: why was it, Laurence Chaderton asked, as he urged his countrymen onwards to both public and private responsibilities, that protestant charity did not, seemingly, far exceed that of the papists?[89] Indeed, the degree to which puritans censured other Englishmen for their tardiness in promoting education is a continuing theme of the Elizabethan and early Stuart period.

The task of fulfilling the requirements of the covenant might well have seemed impossible to many believers had there been no record of human success. Quite simply, it was necessary to have not only abstract advice but also a model of proper Christian behaviour for the context of an ungodly world.[90] The imitation of Christ incarnate was an unrealistic standard for those who still bore the sin of Adam.[91] Rather, puritans settled on the figure of Paul as their role model – Paul the epitome of assured conversion; Paul the chief proselytizer of the true religion in hostile circumstances; Paul who had a covenant with the Lord; Paul who demonstrated the strength of the individual mediator between God and those who sought proof of their election. Reliance on individual action became, as we shall see, the mark of the puritan 'programme' for the household, school, college, and, most important, for the pulpit. This reflected not simply the lack of puritan control of circumstances, but also the belief that it took godly people to build a godly city. Paul, through his remarkable combination of faith and good works, provided an example above suspicion of the godly individual in an imperfect world. This urge to proselytize and to edify the church – what I have chosen to call the *imitatio Pauli* – enabled puritans to condition their Augustinian sense of inner struggle into a programme for simultaneous existence in both the external city of man and the internalized City of God of the elect.

The specific tasks and attitudes which this externalization of assurance entailed formed the basis of much puritan thought concerning reason, learning, and education. It may be helpful to emphasize here as a starting-point the degree to which the *imitatio Pauli* permeated puritan biographies. All facets of Paul's existence – as unregenerate then converted, as proselytizer, as bedrock of the community's faith – were examined and elaborated upon in these

---

[87]   *Ibid.*, p. 285. See also *Winthrop Papers*, I, pp. 159–60; Cliffe, *Puritan Gentry*, pp. 120–24.
[88]   See especially Jordan, *Philanthropy in England;* Jordan, *Charities of London*; Jordan, *Charities of Rural England*.   [89]Chaderton, *Excellent and Godly sermon*, sig. C.v.
[90]   Udall, *Certaine Sermons* ('Obedience to Gospell', No. 1), sigs. Hh.viii^v, Ii.i^{r–v}.
[91]   See, for example, Laurence Chaderton's comment that God did not expect Christians to be 'perfect' followers of his will (*Excellent and Godly Sermon*, sigs. B.vii^v–viii).

sketches. As with Paul, it was not so much the consideration of the faith as the daily living of it that set the godly apart as Christian models. Thomas Cawton's biographer not only recorded the great learning and efficacious preaching of his subject, but also noted that his whole life was a testament to Christian assurance, a mixture of knowledge and practice that was at the core of lively protestantism:

Neither did he only delight in God's law, but was very clear and plain in expounding it also, he could fit his discourses on it to every necessity and capacity; but which was most, he interpreted Scripture (as one speaks in *Solomons* words) with his feet, and taught it with his fingers, his walking and working were Scripture explications: his life was a lively effigies [*sic*] and transcript of the word of life, and he cast into the mould of it, there was a sweet and harmonious concord and correspondence between the originall and the copy, the Bible and his conversation.[92]

A letter Cawton sent to his son stressed the necessity of the humane arts in providing an 'outward grace' in later preaching, but also twice reminded the young man that such commitment to learning should be tempered by a dedication to the way of St Paul.[93] Robert Bolton, also a puritan minister, was described by his lay biographer as a man of piety, gravity, zeal for God, wisdom, discretion, and charity. Like Paul, he did not desert the cause of proselytizing, even when greater position was offered him; he 'divers times refused preferment from some of the Nobility and Prelates of this Kingdome, and for no other cause in the world, but that hee might not be divorced from that countrey where his Ministery was so much embraced and wrought so good effects'.[94]

Nor was the portrait of godliness in puritan literature confined to ministers. Especially was the occasion of a funeral sermon used to recall the godly equality of women. John Mayer, portraying the life of the late Lucy Thornton of Suffolk, entitled his work *A Patterne for Women*, and proceeded to detail Thornton's insistence on attending 'everie occasion of preaching' and on maintaining a scrupulous routine of godly study and practice in her household.[95] Attention was also directly drawn in this biographical literature to the magnitude of the gulf between unregenerate and converted states, often by comparing contemporary and scriptural role models. Mistress Jane Ratcliffe, 'widow and citizen of Chester', was addicted to the light pleasures of youth; her biographer's stress upon the evident appearance of Ratcliffe's changed state following her conversion is commonplace. More important for our purposes here is that Ley, immediately after recounting Ratcliffe's conversion,

[92] Cawton, *Life and Death*, p. 57. See *D.N.B.* for the details of Cawton's later conformity.
[93] *Ibid.*, pp. 71, 73.
[94] Bolton, *Last & Learned Worke*, including 'Life' by Edward Bagshaw, sigs. C2^v–3.
[95] Mayer, *Patterne for Women*, pp. 9–10. See, similarly, Gataker, *Two Funerall Sermons*, sig. A3^v.

recalled the story of St Paul's rescue from darkness.[96] It would thus seem that the lesson of *imitatio Pauli* was offered to the godly laity, as well as to young ministers, as the pattern for godly modern external existence.[97]

There was also another aspect of the image of Paul and the godly life which concerns us here. In this and the preceding chapter I have attempted to outline the ways in which we might usefully approach the problem of categorizing puritans and the core of puritan existence at the first level. The basis of the puritans' approach to existence at both the extra-terrestrial and sublunary levels – that they were in covenant with the Lord – brought them to a full realization of their own limitations. The perceived necessity for assurance of conversion, and the growth of a huge literature dedicated to the manner of the concrete observance of this phenomenon, lay at the bottom of the puritans' desire and ability to function in indifferent, and sometimes actively hostile, circumstances. But the continuing struggle for faith brought man's soul into conflict with its own earthly frame. It was the infusion of an external power that brought the Light to man, and that empowered him to know grace. This cast furious doubt on man himself. Fallen from almost the beginning of time, he had nonetheless managed to create wondrous spheres of knowledge from his own reason. And yet election came only to those whom God had chosen, who could not necessarily be equated with the most intelligent. The insistence that Christian existence did not depend solely upon enthusiasm, but also required a sound basis of knowledge, so that present action could accord with scriptural precedent, meant that puritans were inexorably drawn to a consideration of the proper function and content of education, as earthly preparation for adult Christian life. First, however, as they stressed the singular role of faith, puritans had to comprehend the remaining abilities of human reason and its connexion with the dominant question of the search for salvation. Only when they had come to an understanding of their own intellectual capacities could they judge rightly the utility of various forms of learning and education.

[96] Ley, *A Patterne of Pietie*, esp. pp. 21, 22ff.
[97] For a similar example of a godly woman, whose life included the composition of prayers as well as the study of Scripture, see Nicholas Guy, *Pieties Pillar*, esp. p. 48.

3

>-

THE LIMITS AND PROPER USES OF
HUMAN REASON

I

The history of Christianity has always contained the dialectic of reason and faith. Though Augustine contributed greatly to a tradition of piety, he was also largely responsible for the early Christian approval of the employment of humane learning to scourge the enemies of 'orthodox' Catholicism. Against this stood the spectre of Tertullian, who had called for the abandonment of humane learning since it represented a threat to faith in God. At the apex of mediaeval Christian philosophy, Thomas Aquinas had posited that reason, if functioning correctly, would produce no conclusions contrary to those of revelation. But Thomism did not hold the field alone, and was subjected to much contemporary criticism. Under the influence of Duns Scotus greater emphasis was laid on belief than on knowledge as the basis of Christian existence. Chief among Thomism's university opponents, however, stood Ockham, who argued that knowledge of God was properly the endeavour of faith alone, that is, of a direct acceptance of the truths which God chose to *reveal* to man. Even the very existence of God was not demonstrable by reason. By the later Middle Ages this nominalist attack had led to a stream of thought that the tenets of faith were not merely non-rational, but inherently irrational. This, in turn, meant that God became *less* intelligible, since everything in this world was contingent upon God's will, that is to say, could have been different. The universe thus became less of a rational structure and its mysteries less open to solution by human reason. Here, then, in a binding together of Tertullian, Ockham, and popular fideism, were the roots of the attacks by Luther and Calvin on the power of human reason to decipher God's mysteries, and of the Reformation promotion of faith as the only pathway to comprehension of the Infinite.[1]

Yet the thrust of protestantism was not only against the Schoolmen. Humanists seemed to aim away from later mediaeval fideism and towards a civic moral virtue based on rational deduction combined with imitation of the

---

[1] This paragraph owes much to Haydn, *Counter-Renaissance*, Ch. 3, and to Gilson, *Reason and Revelation, passim*.

41

virtues of Christ and the Christian saints. The mediaeval concentration on
knowing God, that is, on the contemplative, had been replaced by a belief that
man's central purpose was his justification through his existence, through
what he himself had *chosen* to make of his own life.[2] The moral life – action
based on learning – entailed a merging of the realms of reason and faith. Stress
was on the *life* of Christ, rather than on the mystery of his essence or the non-
rational bases of belief.[3] The stress that some Italian humanists had placed on
ancient wisdom had involved a circumvention of orthodox Christianity in
favour of the glorification of the ability of man's intellect, far beyond the
ultimate limits of reason always conceded by the Schoolmen. Classical wisdom became, until the advent of Baconianism, very much the measure for
modern behaviour and beliefs.[4] Learning was seen as a positive good, following Plutarch's insistence that 'truely the thynge that in us is divyne and immortall
is lernynge . . .'.[5] Roger Ascham reflected the typical combination of
humanist and protestant educational impulses in Elizabethan England by arguing that anyone who did not favour Aristotle and Cicero in learning was likely
soon to rise either to dissension in religion or to faction in politics.[6] This
reflected the stress on rationality as the highest attribute of man, and led to a
suffusion of religion with the rational ethics of the ancients.[7] Even Juan Luis
Vives, who stressed the superiority of Scripture, and the occasional danger
that the vanity of learning might pose, insisted that generally, 'where there is a
lack of knowledge [of the arts], there true and sincere piety does not flourish
at all'.[8] The 'use' which humanists demanded as evidence of 'virtue' did not
have to be oriented towards the dissemination of godly religion.[9] At the centre
of the humanist thrust, therefore, stood what has been described as the
Renaissance's patient attempt to separate 'wisdom' from Christianity and to
restore the former to 'its old autonomy and its purely human dignities'.[10] Thus
one of the very important aspects of the Renaissance was this development of
non-religious (as distinct from anti-religious) intellectual interests, even
though the greater thrust remained Christian.[11]

[2]   Haydn, *Counter-Renaissance*, esp. pp. 37–8, 51–2.
[3]   *Ibid.*, esp. pp. 59–60.
[4]   Bush, *Renaissance and English Humanism*, pp. 71, 78, 79.
[5]   Plutarch, *Education*, transl. Thomas Elyot, sig. C.ii, and his further remark that there were two things 'in
      the nature of manne/whiche be good, . . . knowledge and reasone' (*ibid.*, sig. C.ii').
[6]   Bush, *Renaissance and English Humanism*, p. 89.
[7]   Kristeller, *Renaissance Thought*, pp. 72, 73–5, 78–9.
[8]   *Vives on Education*, ed. Watson, pp. 29, 31.
[9]   See, for example, Sadoleto, *On Education*, esp. pp. 67–8, 69–71, 74. See also *Vives on Education*, ed.
      Watson, pp. 283, 286, 288.
[10] Rice, *Renaissance Idea of Wisdom*, p. 3.   [11]   Kristeller, *Renaissance Thought*, p. 72.

II

One of the themes of this book is that puritans were neither unique nor extreme in the context of the protestantism of the late sixteenth and early seventeenth centuries. In many ways, puritans may well have been the best representatives in England of the dominant strains of continental thought. The problem of reason provides an example. Luther's attitude to reason ranged from 'extravagant praise' to 'unqualified opprobrium', but it settled primarily on the idea that reason could not comprehend God's message of free forgiveness by grace alone.[12] Reason's value in the sublunary world Luther did not doubt, but he was extremely sceptical about its application to matters divine:

In temporal affairs and those which have to do with men, the rational man is self-sufficient: here he needs no other light than reason's . . . But in godly affairs . . . where man must do what is acceptable to God . . . nature is absolutely stone-blind, so that it cannot even catch a glimpse of what those things are. It is presumptuous enough to bluster and plunge into them, like a blind horse; *but all its conclusions are utterly false*, as surely as God lives.[13]

His argument that reason was indeed largely uncorrupted by the Fall, but was still of no use for salvation, indicated that it had always been incapable in the spiritual sphere.[14] Luther divided man's intellectual capacity into three types of reason: natural, which ruled the earthly existence as its proper domain; arrogant, which trespassed on the domain of faith; and regenerate, which served faith, but always in a subordinate capacity, subject to the Word of God.[15] In establishing this division, Luther initiated a pattern which puritans also, as a distinct thrust of the Counter-Renaissance, were to follow throughout their existence. And in emphasizing the arrogance of reason, Luther established the bedrock of fervent protestant doubt of the intellect.

John Calvin, though less given than Luther to outbursts of anti-reason, nonetheless at times also took an extremely critical stance. Before the Fall, man's reason aided him to mount up 'even to God and eternal bliss'.[16] But the Fall, argued Calvin, following Augustine's interpretation, had stripped away man's supernatural gifts, and severely impaired his natural abilities. Reason still had a desire for truth and was still able to detect parts of it. But reason's corruption led it into vanity and absurd curiosity.[17] Reason was still competent in the 'earthly' sphere, which he separated distinctly from the 'heavenly'.[18]

---

[12] Gerrish, *Grace and Reason*, esp. p. 71ff.
[13] Quoted in *ibid.*, p. 12 (my italics.) See also *ibid.*, p. 26.
[14] *Ibid.*, pp. 73, 147.   [15] *Ibid.*, pp. 26, 85, 90–1.   [16] Calvin, *Institutes*, ed. McNeill, I.15.8.
[17] *Ibid.*, II,2.12. This section was based especially on Ecclesiastes.   [18] *Ibid.*, II.2.13.

For Calvin, the full knowledge of God's kingdom consisted in three things: knowing God himself; knowing his favour – including salvation – in our behalf; and knowing how to live according to his rules. He argued that reason was thoroughly incompetent – 'the greatest geniuses are blinder than moles!' – in the first two categories, but especially in the second. Man had some basis in natural law for the third, though even here natural capacity would not prove entirely satisfactory.[19] Man's own restrictions always stood in his own way:

I maintain that the wisest men are blinded by their own pride, and never even taste the heavenly doctrine, til such time as they become fools, and commanding their own notions to be gone, devote themselves in meek simplicity to the obedience of Christ. For human reason is utterly undiscerning, and human acuteness stupid, in the mysteries of God.[20]

In pointing out, with Paul, that it was the understanding of reason's *limits* that became the point of departure for the comprehension of the Lord,[21] Calvin prepared the argument which puritans so forcefully developed.

III

In England, possibly because of such a heavy dependence on the theology of the continental Reformation and the later native emphasis on casuistical divinity, systematic theologians remained scarce. Few historians, therefore, even among those who label the collected ideas of the puritans as 'puritanism', have described this reformist thrust as an intellectual *system.*[22] Nonetheless, there have been some attempts to analyse the puritan vision of the role of reason. Foremost was the work of Perry Miller. While he admitted the fundamental importance of the 'piety' of the puritans,[23] Miller argued that it had been emphasized to the detriment of appreciating that puritans always understood that 'the life of the elect was the life of reason . . . .'.[24] According to Miller, puritan Ramists argued that, despite the Fall, man's intellect was still, in principle, 'divine', since it had been given to him especially of the creatures

[19] *Ibid.*, II.2.18.
[20] Quoted in Armstrong, *Calvinism and the Amyraut Heresy*, p. 33 n. 90, from *On Secret Providence*. See also Calvin, *Institutes*, ed. McNeill, II.2.18. [21] Calvin, *Institutes*, ed. McNeill, II.2.20.
[22] Indeed, Knappen specifically argued that it could not accurately be described as such (*Tudor Puritanism*, esp. pp. 466–7).
[23] Miller, *New England Mind: The Seventeenth Century*, p. 187. George Marsden, in criticizing this aspect of Miller's emphasis, has commented that Miller's readers might well be drawn to think that 'the most important characteristics of the Puritan intellect were reverence for reason and particularly Ramist logic' (Marsden, 'Perry Miller's rehabilitation of the puritans: a critique', *Church History*, 39, p. 94). [24] Miller, *New England Mind*, p. 202.

by God.[25] Reason's reach might well not be quite as long as before the Fall, but its manner of functioning was basically unchanged.[26] Miller also contended that as the seventeenth century wore on, the argument gathered force that grace was merely a restoration of natural capacities which had survived the Fall and which still existed in the soul.[27]

Miller's understanding of the puritan approach to the use of reason in religion seems split between his occasional admissions that the doctrine of Christianity was not built into the cosmos, and therefore remained 'incomprehensible to human reason',[28] and his espousal of the view that the adoption of Ramist logic meant, in fact, that puritans could explain by reason all but the most basic mysteries of a Platonist world.[29] Ramist logic provided not only a method of knowledge, but also a means of security against the undue aggrandizement of reason.[30] Reason could be trusted to help faith by providing it with an intellectual base, but it could not discover the means to salvation, would realize this, and would be content not to try.[31] Miller explained that the puritan Alexander Richardson grounded his logic not on the *ens primum*, since God was unfathomable, but rather on the *ens a primo*, that is, on the visible form which had proceeded from the 'secret essence'. By this tactic, argued Miller, puritans could remain 'men of piety, . . . but proceed as logicians to establish durable bases for scientific knowledge . . .'.[32] Miller constantly disregarded or minimized puritan warnings about the danger of reason, noting them only in infrequent asides.[33] He referred to puritan criticism of rhetoric, for example, as the 'occasional ridicule of carnal eloquence'.[34] Part of the misconception may have derived from Miller's reliance on a very few puritans who were especially attached to the universities and to higher learning; he made little of the puritan struggles to decide what practical use they could legitimately make of reason away from the epistemological discourses of the university.

As Miller noted, puritans found that they could not readily analyse the methods by which grace assumed command of the individual without also de-

---

[25] Miller, *New England Mind*, p. 159. Even one of Miller's critics, John Coolidge (*Pauline Renaissance*, p. 3) agreed that in the realms of natural essence, prudence, civil policy and morality, 'there is no evidence that the Puritan is any less confident of natural reason and the evidence of the senses than the Conformist'. [26] Miller, *New England Mind*, pp. 155–6.

[27] *Ibid.*, pp. 184–6; Miller & Johnson, eds., *Puritans*, p. 39. But see *ibid.*, pp. 53–5, for the seeming corrective that regeneration was more than the raising of capacities already existing within each person.

[28] Miller, *New England Mind*, p. 188.

[29] *Ibid., passim*, but esp. p. 162 on Alexander Richardson. On a 'Platonist' world in the sense that it was a pale copy of a more perfect vision (i.e., God's ideal), see Miller & Johnson, eds., *Puritans*, pp. 38–9. [30] Miller, *New England Mind*, p. 189; see also p. 194. [31] *Ibid.*, p. 201.

[32] *Ibid.*, p. 163. That puritans, *qua* religious beings, were not interested in furthering 'scientific' knowledge I have argued elsewhere (Morgan, 'Puritanism and science: a reinterpretation', *The Historical Journal*, 22, esp. pp. 551–60. [33] Miller, *New England Mind*, for example, p. 187. [34] *Ibid.*, p. 303.

scribing the structures of the human soul.[35] The psychology of the period was an eclectic product based chiefly on Aristotle's *de anima*, though refined by the intermixture of notions from Plato, Augustine, Albertus Magnus, and Aquinas. The retention of this primarily Aristotelian scheme by puritans – permissible, as Miller notes, because it had classified the acts of the soul without explaining them – forced the puritans to describe regeneration in terms of psychological theory as well as theology. Much of the psychology evident in puritan tracts is simply the common coin of the age.[36] The soul of man, it was held, was divided into three parts: vegetable, sensible, and rational.[37] Of these, the first controlled the basic processes of life, and was common to all levels of being; the second involved the five senses, and included the faculties of common sense, imagination, and memory. Under the sensible soul also came the three appetites: the natural, which governed movement, according to the nature of the objects (heavy things fall); the sensitive or animal, which controlled the life functions; and the voluntary or intellective, which, unlike the other two, was supposed to be controlled by reason. In this theory the voluntary appetite contained the desire to seek pleasure and avoid pain, but it could easily disturb the mind by the passions it aroused.[38]

The rational soul itself was composed of the passive power of wit (reason), and the active power of will (desire). Wit was the power of intellectual perception; it embraced all rational faculties and was known by its various headings of knowledge, understanding and wisdom. Wit served to separate man from the irrational beasts; it contained the power of logic and possessed innate ideas. The object of wit was knowledge of the 'good' (the highest 'good' of course being God) and the choice of this 'good' as the proper end of existence. Will, also known as the 'rational appetite', provided the desire to carry out what the wit had decreed. That is, once the wit had determined that something was 'good', the will proceeded to pursue it. In particular, the imagination, which provided pictures for both memory and reason, had to be controlled; if distorted, then the judgement of reason would likewise be askew. But even if the passions and imagination could be controlled, and the will properly subordinated, all would still depend, in this scheme, on the ability of reason to identify the 'good'. The enormous corruption of the will in fallen man was

[35] This paragraph is based on Miller, *New England Mind*, esp. pp. 239–45.
[36] For two puritan works which explain the common divisions of the soul, and yet which also explain the role of reason vis-à-vis grace, see Burroughes, *Excellency of Gracious Spirit*, esp. pp. 8–10, and Preston, *Saints Qualification*, esp. pp. 48–70. For a good, straightforward summary of the psychology of the age, see Bamborough, *Little World of Man*, esp. pp. 20–4, 29–33, 41–3.
[37] These were divisions, and not separate souls. Calvin specifically rejected Plato's argument that each person had two souls: rational and sensitive (*Institutes*, ed. McNeill, I.15.6).
[38] This clash of 'reason' and 'desire' was a standard theme of Renaissance psychology (see, for example, Sadoleto, *On Education*, pp. 19ff.)

'passed along' from the understanding.[39] Human will now suffered from deep maladies: it opposed God's will in all matters; it was proud and vainglorious; it was weak in 'good things' and inconstant of purpose; and, finally, it was disobedient in regard to the Law.[40] Even conscience, which should serve as the last bastion of the connexion with God, and as a reminder that all of our faculties were 'dead, disordered, and corrupted',[41] no longer even restrained man from evil, let alone persuaded him to the 'good'.[42]

More than other Englishmen puritans emphasized that the Fall had impaired the free ability of the rational soul to follow the right path to salvation. John Preston referred to the 'incredulity' of the understanding concerning the progress of faith, and even to its 'enmity' because it 'is not subject to the law of God, neither indeed can it be . . .'.[43] But it was perhaps Robert Bolton who best clarified the present state of man's soul:

the whole speculative power of the higher and nobler part of the Soule, which wee call the Understanding, as it is naturally and originally corrupted, and utterly destitute of all Divine Light; and doth afterward, through its owne sinfull working and sensuall discourse, grow wise in the World and earthie affaires, but disconceitfull and opposite to the wayes of God, and heavenly wisedome, by concluding and commending to it selfe false Principles, from deluded sence, and deducing false Conclusions from true Principles, and by a continued exercise and experience in contemplation of Earth and passages of worldly pollicie.[44]

Puritans thus adopted, by and large, a slightly modified view of the common form of contemporary psychology.[45] With the various divisions of the soul, they found no serious quarrel. But whenever they came upon the question of the devastating effects of the Fall upon the efficient operations of man's 'soul', they amplified above all the dissonance and turmoil which rang in corrupted man.[46] As a starting point, then, puritans strove not to glorify the remaining

---

[39] Preston, *Saints Qualification*, pp. 48–9. For Calvin's view of the division of tasks, see *Institutes*, I.15.7; I.15.8; I.2.12.   [40] Preston, *Saints Qualification*, pp. 49–53.   [41] *Ibid.*, p. 55.

[42] *Ibid.*, esp. pp. 55–8. According to Costello (*Scholastic Curriculum*, pp. 65–9), puritans were greatly influenced by Aristotelian ethics, which had held that 'ethical virtue' was the necessary state of mind which held 'free will' to the course dictated by reason.

[43] Preston, *Saints Qualification*, pp. 45, 46–7.

[44] Bolton, *Saints Sure and Perpetuall Guide*, in *Workes*, p. 247.

[45] Perhaps the best contemporary summary of the state of psychology is Robert Burton's *Anatomy of Melancholy*. This work was first published in 1621; it ran to five editions before 1640.

[46] The greatest statement of this devastation came from Milton's pen:

> high Passions, Anger, Hate
> Mistrust, Suspicion, Discord, and shook sore
> Thir inward State of Mind, calm Region once
> And full of Peace, now tost and turbulent:
> For Understanding rul'd not, and the Will
> Heard not her lore, both in subjection now
> To sensual Appetite, who from beneath
> Usurping over sovran Reason claimed
> Superior sway.   (*Paradise Lost*, IX, 1122–31).

abilities of human reason, but rather to emphasize its present degradation. Above all they sought a means of guarding against its fulsome excesses by imposing the efficient restrictions which only faith could provide.

IV

In practical terms, that is, in sermons and religious tracts, puritans seem to have used the term 'reason' in a variety of ways. For them (as for us), the word could mean 'cause', 'need', or 'argument', as well, of course, as 'whatever the individual conscience might decree'. Generally, however, the word meant simply an ability to apply the formulas of logic to an intellectual problem. This in turn meant, despite the modifications introduced by Ramus, the syllogistic forms of deductive thought. Despite the catastrophe of the Fall, puritans, like their contemporaries, were adamant that, in its earthly vocation, reason was still highly competent. John Robinson could insist in general terms that 'Reason is that wherein man goes before all other earthly creatures and comes after God only, and the angels in heaven.'[47] Jeremiah Burroughes was quite willing to accord heathen philosophers such as Socrates, Seneca, and Cicero a certain praise for the civil and moral application of their reason.[48] But these more specific terms brought caution. John Winthrop emphasized that reason's success against lust in fallen man would prove only temporary; only grace could bring final control.[49] William Ames, too, stressed the separate benefits of reason, but checked any enthusiasm for its moral value:

it is a thing good in regard of nature: and so to be commended and labour'd for: although in respect of any morall goodnesse, it is a thing of an indifferent nature, neither good nor evill, as all other naturall perfections also are. Civill wisdom therefore considered in it selfe, is not opposed to spirituall wisdom, but only as a disparate.[50]

In short, puritans joined with their contemporaries in recognizing that there was a sphere in which natural reason was fully competent – 'the knowledge of civill and humane things', as Richard Greenham put it.[51] Indeed, the early seventeenth century took great pains, in general, to argue that man's knowledge of his world and of himself was increasing, as was his capacity to understand. In these areas puritans were ever willing to learn from the accomplishments of classical, as well as Christian, scholars. But reason, puritans

---

[47] Robinson, *New Essays*, Ch. 10, p. 67.
[48] Burroughes, *Excellency of Gracious Spirit*, p. 25. But Burroughes also remarked that, if reason could do this for man, how much higher could grace raise him (*ibid.*, p. 26).
[49] *Winthrop Papers*, I, p. 237 (John Winthrop's 'Experiencia', entry for 1619). See also *ibid.*, I, p. 84 (Winthrop to his wife, 28 Apr. 1629); also *ibid.*, I, p. 136.
[50] Ames, *Conscience*, Bk III, p. 66; see also Rogers, *Seven Treatises*, p. 149.
[51] Greenham, *Workes*, p. 757.

feared, was not content to be master of that which it could rule so easily. It sought a role – indeed, a leading part – in the drama of the relationship of God and man. That it was bluntly denied any such role in the search for salvation by both Lutheran and Reformed theology barely interfered with what puritans envisioned as reason's campaign for due recognition.

Imbued as they were with scholastic education, it is little wonder that puritans did not wholeheartedly reject reason, or abandon it to their enemies. If reason could interpret the concrete evidence of God – the Scriptures and the natural world – then could it not also, on the basis of this knowledge, build a bridge to the Lord? Richard Hooker emphasized the role of reason in deducing saving knowledge from the body of Scripture. He stressed, too, the religious side of the Law of Reason as equal to the especial laws of religion revealed in the Bible, and so argued that at no time was man 'wholly lawless', since his natural reason always influenced his decisions and actions. Hooker's rationalism, as John New has noted, lessened the certainty of 'Anglicans' about their assurance of faith, but also reduced the gap (as they perceived it) between God and man.[52] In some ways the willingness of Bishop Fotherby of Salisbury to overwhelm atheists 'with the testimony of Heathen-writers and not of holy Scripture' was a logical conclusion of the propensity for mixing reason with religion.[53] It was an attempt to push the limits of reason back from the position enunciated by the founders of the Reformation. For puritans, this quickly became a sign that reason, as ever, had attempted to defy the limits of the Fall and usurp the role for which it was not qualified; it was against this that puritans, most fervently of Englishmen, asserted the fullness of faith. Only faith, they argued, could drive out the Trojan horse that was reason. Reason, in its earthly sphere, was the supreme carnal weapon, and only man, of all God's creatures, possessed it. It made him natural master of the land and water, of the valley and mountain, of the wheatfield and of the beasts. It could solve limitless problems of a worldly nature. But it could not find God. If only it would be content with such power . . .

But of course it had not been. It had insisted on straying, on trying to assert its earthly magnificence in a realm for which it had no natural capacity. Robbed by the Fall of its original immortal closeness to God, reason still expected to solve mysteries that God preferred to keep clouded. It was in defining the limits of man's intellect that puritans both best exemplified Reformed theology and differed from their English contemporaries. Against

---

[52] New, *Anglican and Puritan*, pp. 20–1, 26. For a useful discussion of the place of reason in Hooker's thought, see Grislis, 'Hermeneutical problem in Richard Hooker', in W. S. Hill, ed., *Studies in Richard Hooker, passim*; Haydn, *Counter-Renaissance*, pp. 38–40; Allen, *Doubt's Boundless Sea*, pp. 117–19, 132–3; Sykes, 'Richard Hooker', *Social and Political Ideas*, ed. Hearnshaw, pp. 64, 73.

[53] Quoted in Allen, *Doubt's Boundless Sea*, p. 111. See also Schultz, *Milton and Forbidden Knowledge*, p. 190.

the humanist glorification of man's reason and learning, puritans responded
with the vision of a shattered humanity. Even at the end of our period, the
puritan mystic Francis Rous made it clear that, while reason might see the
shadows, it could not perceive the Forms. This clash of man's two highest
capacities was elucidated for the public by puritans in two ways: in direct comments on the differences in the purposes of reason and faith as human abilities
and, arising from this tension, in the involvement of the seekers of salvation in
the covenant of grace. Puritan concern with reason was not aimed at bridling it
at all in philosophical or utilitarian ways as it related to 'secular' activities.
Rather, puritans sought a new equilibrium (to replace the decayed Thomist
model) that would recognize the different areas of expertise for reason and
faith, and would confine reason to the status of an 'aid' in the achievement and
propagation of belief.

Puritans hammered at those who (they believed) had attempted to reduce
religion to mere intellectual endeavour; thus they excoriated the Schoolmen
who had supposedly used their logic to comprehend the Gospel only in 'a
meere metaphysicall and carnall manner . . .'.[54] Though in this approach
puritans mirrored contemporary continental protestant theologians, they also
depended heavily, here again, directly on Paul's message, or at least on the
common mediaeval and sixteenth-century interpretation of it.[55] In spreading
the Word in a society permeated by classical learning, Paul had had to address
himself directly to the question of the relationship of man's reason and learning to his ability to hold unquestioning faith in the *mysteries* (i.e., non-rational
aspects) of an all-powerful deity. Puritans seem to have seen their own context
as similar. They existed in a world newly interested in the glories of classical
learning. The period between the Reformation and the Restoration can
readily be seen as the working out of many dialectics. One of the less
emphasized is the struggle between 'enthusiasm' and 'reason' for dominance
in religion (as, indeed, in magic and medicine). The Reformation was not, in
many of its *impulses*, a rational revolt. Luther himself, though he started by
offering theses for debate, sustained his revolt by proclaiming the supremacy
of the Spirit, and by decrying the strength of reason. Puritans always wished to
control what historians might call 'mindless enthusiasm', partly because of
their concern with the proper status of the godly ministry. But equally they
wished to place very strict limits on the liberties of human reason.

The great ambiguity about learning, and yet the insistence upon a ministry
fully practised in the heights of human learning, spanned the protestant spectrum. The all-sufficiency of Scripture as a source of religious truth, and its
autonomy from all human commentary as a source of religious authority, pro-

[54] Sibbes, *Light from Heaven*, pp. 20–1.
[55] On the possible misunderstanding of Paul, see below, p. 66–7.

duced concern from Thomas Grindal to Richard Hooker to John Donne over
the ministerial use of reason to demonstrate religion. This central question was
also at the heart of differences over the 'plain style' of sermonizing. As with
ecclesiology and soteriology, it was not barriers, but rather shades of opinion,
that distinguished English 'Calvinists'. Throughout our period, however,
puritans did generally take a more emphatic line than their English contemporaries in insisting on the clarification of the differences between reason and
faith. The puritan William Burton did concede that some of the things 'plainly
proved' by Scripture could also be detected by the 'light of naturall reason'.[56]
Reason could not be faulted at every turn. But puritans usually concentrated
on the proposition from the opposite end of the telescope; their creed was
always that 'there are many things to be learned, which we cannot attaine unto
by naturall reason onely, without spirituall revelation'.[57] Across its spectrum,
puritan consideration of the application of reason to faith therefore
emphasized first and foremost the distortions which reason would undoubtedly produce in reaching beyond its capacity. Robert Bolton noted that people
could see things only with a 'natural eye'. And if

a man looke upon GODS wayes onely with the eye of Reason they are *foolishnesse* to
him; and sure if a man looke upon GODS Word and Workes through the false glasse
of worldly wisedome, he cannot but imagine the thing promised in the one and in
agitation in the other impossible to be effected as promised for his childrens
good.[58]

John Winthrop added a more personal note from his own experience, pleading that man's 'owne corrupt reason' could not 'enioye the comforte of livinge
by faithe . . .'.[59]

This was not to argue, as John Preston stressed, that God's prescripts were
*un*reasonable; it was rather that natural reason could not see through the
gloom of its own corruption. The light remained as bright as ever, but the fog
which now clouded man hid such truth.[60] Now, this was only the staple of the
age. Godfrey Goodman, later a bishop, also argued that the mysteries of grace,
necessary for salvation, were 'beyond the apprehension of nature . . .'.[61] But,
having said that, he did not proceed to denigrate reason for this incapacity. It
was rather the puritans who, perceiving this grave limitation of natural reason,
set out to ensure that it did not stray from its appointed path. Thus Thomas

---

[56] Burton, *Certaine Questions and Answeres*, Preface.   [57] Greenham, *Workes*, p. 757.
[58] Bolton, *Cordiall for Christians*, 'To the Reader', referring to Acts 28.26.
[59] *Winthrop Papers*, I, p. 215.   [60] Preston, *Profitable Sermon at Lincolnes Inne*, p. 22.
[61] Goodman, *Creatures*, p. 30. Again, we must beware of picturing (by force of their absence from this discussion of the imperatives of fervency) the non-puritan English protestants as basing their faith
primarily on reason. My purpose here is to analyse puritan belief, but the reader should understand that
while non-puritans allowed a greater say to reason, they did not question the supremacy of revelation in
the central mysteries of Christianity.

Adams, though he strongly favoured the use of humane learning in scriptural exegesis, nevertheless emphasized that reason perpetually even asked the wrong questions in the cause of spiritual advance: 'There are two lights in man as in heaven, Reason and Faith: Reason, like *Sarah*, is still asking; *How can* this be? Faith, like *Abraham*, not disputes, but beleeves. There is no validity in Morall vertues: Civill mans good workes are a meere carkase, without the soule of Faith.'[62] Reason could not confirm God's wisdom, since man was so inferior, and also because God's wisdom, as perfection, could admit of no need of confirmation.

At the same time, puritans did not subscribe to the Thomist notion that while reason's horizons were ultimately limited, its propositions and those of faith were in accord. Puritans concluded instead that 'there is no greater ods in the world than betweene our owne reason and Gods wisedome'.[63] It was not simply a case of applying the wrong tool to the job. Richard Capel pointed out that frustrated reason could itself indeed become a barrier to salvation:

And as our reason is carnall, it is a secret friend to Satan, takes part with him against us, good stuffe for a man to thinke to conquer the divell, with a wisdom which the Apostle saith is *divelish*: How divelish? Because it hath the Divell for its dam; we must not then consult with flesh and bloud; downe with reason, away with our owne wit, let faith doe all, else faith will do nothing . . .[64]

Time and again, because of its blindness, reason had exceeded its proper limits; in so doing its vanity had led it to become an agent of ungodliness. Perhaps Jeremiah Burroughes best emphasized this distinction which separated the 'fervency' of the puritans from the 'humane vertue' of many humanists:

where there are onely naturall & morall excellencies, they do not raise the soule to a love of the strictest wayes of God; they thinke of accuratenesse and exactnesse in Gods ways to be but nicenesse and too much precisenesse; lukewarmenesse is the onely temper suitable to them; they thinke wisedome consists in the remission of godlinesse, not in the improvement of it; and what is beyond their temper, they judge as weak-nesse and folly . . .[65]

John Preston, ever in the forefront of exploring the role of reason, also handily explained in a list the complete incapacity of 'the best of the heathen' to lead to dedication to Jesus, and reminded his readers that it was but equity that God should have condemned mankind for putting the promptings of his own reason above true obedience.[66] Thomas Adams similarly reminded his

---

[62] Adams, *Workes*, p. 406.
[63] Greenham, *Workes*, p. 646. See also Adams, *Workes*, p. 406; Rogers, *Seven Treatises*, p. 4.
[64] Capel, *Tentations*, pp. 106–7.   [65] Burroughes, *Excellency of Gracious Spirit*, pp. 234–35.
[66] Preston, *Doctrine of the Saints Infirmities*, pp. 56–60; Preston, *Saints Qualification*, pp. 38–9. See also Sibbes, *Light from Heaven*, p. 49; Perkins, *Workes*, I, p. 633.

readers that God had used reason as the temptation in Eden; it was human knowledge that the serpent offered as the spur to disobedience, the knowledge of evil. Adam and Eve were already possessed of God's free grace and eternal life. They lost both through presumption.[67] The salvation of man depended to a large extent, therefore, on the struggle which was bound to ensue between faith and reason.

By blocking the required emphasis on faith alone, reason could actually come to stand directly in the way of the efficacy of the offer of the covenant. Christopher Potter, in the Preface which he wrote for Henry Airay's lectures on Philippians, noted this precise problem, that no age 'was ever blessed with such a light of knowledge, and yet none [had been] more fruitful of the workes of darknesse'.[68] Henry Airay himself explained that his contemporaries were all too often contented by superficial knowledge, with the gloss of reason. Too often they became 'like unto little children, which if they see faire and great and coloured letters in a booke, are in great love with the letters, but care not for the sense and understanding of the words'.[69] The answer to this problem, insisted puritans, lay not in greater emphasis on the possibilities of natural reason, but rather in propagandizing its inefficacy in entering, and fulfilling the terms of, the covenant of grace. Thus John Downame insisted that 'we must not content our selves with such a knowledge as swims in the braine, but labour after such a saving and effectuall knowledge if we are to be saved'.[70] William Perkins had earlier argued that he who wished to be truly wise, that is, to have knowledge of God, 'must reject his owne naturall reason, and stoppe up the eyes of his naturall minde, like a blinde man, and suffer himselfe wholly to be guided by Gods spirit in the things of God, that thereby he may be made wise unto salvation'.[71] The puritan mystic Francis Rous, in an attempt to turn his readers to the study of God, 'brought forth patternes of some, who have taught and professed a deniall of their own wits and reasons, though acute and excellent; and have ... quenched their owne naturall lamps, that they might get them kindled above by the Father of lights'.[72] He specifically noted that the 'heart of man, that is, the naturall reason of a naturall man, doth not rightly discern' the principles of saving divinity.[73] Indeed, greater intelligence could prove a barrier to godliness: 'the admission of humane wit, against Gods wisedome, by some great wits, ... hath beene the cause of many dangerous errours in the Church'.[74] Richard Capel later insisted in this vein that reason could not even

[67] Adams, *Workes*, pp. 1130–1, 1170.
[68] Christopher Potter, 'To the Christian Reader', sig. A2, in Airay, *Lectures Upon Philippians*.
[69] Airay, *Lectures Upon Philippians*, p. 119.   [70] Downame, *Guide to Godliness*, p. 38.
[71] Perkins, *Workes*, II, p. 464; see also *ibid.*, I, pp. 626–8 and II, p. 211. For later puritan statements to the same effect, see Hooker, *Soules Vocation*, pp. 108–9; Wright, *Godly and Learned Sermons*, pp. 194–5. Taylor, *Principles*, p. 432; Preston, *Sinnes Overthrow*, pp. 49–50.
[72] Rous, *Heavenly Academie*, sigs. A7ᵛ–8.   [73] *Ibid.*, pp. 13–14, 17.   [74] *Ibid.*, pp. 110–11.

dispel atheism, for it could not fully establish the dimensions of the Irrational that was God.[75]

A crucial question in the determination of the relationship of reason to the covenant was the consideration of how the Spirit first took hold of the individual, and the actual method by which conversion (as a process over time) took place. Of the nature of the workings of the covenant, Preston wrote:

Faith is but the lifting up of the understanding, by adding a new light to them [God's truths] and it [man's understanding]: and therefore they are said to be *revealed*, not because they were not before, as if the revealing of them gave a being unto them; but even as a new light in the night discovers to us that which we did not see before, and as a prospective glasse reveales to the eye, that which we could not see before, and by its owne power, the eye could not reach unto.[76]

Miller argued that this passage meant that puritans saw the infusion of faith as the 'reinvigoration of capacity already existing' in man, that is, the rectifying of fallen reason. Conversion was the 'sight of existing truths, exactly as a telescope is the revelation of new stars'.[77] Now, Preston was arguing here, I think, that some innate knowledge of God exists in man, but that the illumination (which is analogous to faith and grace) has to come from outside. Both the 'light' and the 'glasse' – external agents – are needed since man could not see without them. Preston's analogy certainly concedes that the external truths already existed, since God the Creator existed, but a telescope is also an outside agent which is used when man's own capacities, no matter how finely honed, prove incapable. True, the telescope aids a natural capacity of man (the eye), as grace similarly aids the soul. But without the addition of something (telescope or grace) which is external to man's being, the greatest efforts of both the eye and soul would prove barren. Man is thus forced to admit his own inability and look outside himself. In this sense, Miller's analogy of the telescope proves what Preston was saying. It does not, however, establish what Miller evidently thought it would, that is, that grace was solely the development of internal capabilities in man. Preston further clarified the suggestion of grace as merely the amplification of some 'humane vertue':

This is a common Truth, but men consider not of it, they thinke there is some goodnesse in them, they will not be persuaded of this Truth in good earnest. And therefore when a man comes into the state of Grace, it is not mending two or three things that are amisse, it is not repairing of an old house, but all must be taken downe, and be built anew, you must be New Creatures.[78]

[75]   Capel, *Tentations*, pp. 269–70.
[76]   Quoted in Miller, *New England Mind*, pp. 200–1.   [77]   Miller, *New England Mind*, p. 200.
[78]   Preston, *Saints Qualification*, pp. 39–40. See, similarly, Robinson, *New Essays*, Ch. 10, p. 61.

The term 'light' was an obvious and common metaphor for the instilling of faith. Richard Bernard, for example, who founded a covenanted congregation, spoke in terms very similar to those of Preston. In explaining that the 'obscurity' of certain texts of Scripture really meant the deficiency of humans, he, too, relied on the heavens for an analogy. 'The Sunne is ever cleere, though we cannot ever see it shining, by reason that either wee want eyes to behold it, or for that it is so be-clowded, that our sight is thereby hindered, and so wee cannot see the light, till these clouds be removed.'[79] Preston himself further explained that while unregenerate and regenerate people were similar in 'natural' capacities, the regenerate man 'hath a new light *put into* his heart'. The puritan Francis Rous similarly commented on the necessity for an infusion of 'light' by the Spirit, such as would radically alter the human ability to perceive. 'But before this light and sight bee *created* in us, let that Infinite light shine right into the eyes of blindnesse and darknesse, the darknesse will never comprehend it . . .'[80] In short, the highest human faculty could obtain no reward by its own merits, while simple faith, a free gift of the Spirit, gained heaven.[81]

Nothing of this world could finally act as a bridge to the next. Reason could teach its followers only the rational. As far as salvation was concerned, it could require only a civil, good life, the peaceful carrying out of the duties of earthly existence. But this 'blind Divinitie', because rational, led only to good reputation among men: 'in a life acceptable to God, faith is required, the light of reason will not serve the turne'.[82] God did not allow rational behaviour as the basis for salvation because the wicked reprobate could excel as easily as the godly man.[83] But if entry into the covenant did not depend upon intellectual capacity, and if all that was needed within the covenant was continuing faith (and that was the staple of the hundreds of popular religious manuals), then to intrude reason was to argue implicitly that God's offer was inadequate, that man did not believe God would save him without the use of his (man's) reason. Puritans at no time sought to deny the utility of reason in the sphere for which God had granted it. As muscle dealt with toil, so should reason struggle with questions of intellect. But only faith could comprehend grace. Reason should look down to earth, and around at other men and their society. Puritans sought to demonstrate that when reason looked upwards, towards God, it superseded its proper calling and became a reprehensible enemy, indeed an ally of Satan, which then stood between man and the fulfilment of his covenant with the Lord.

---

[79] Bernard, *Faithfull Shepheard* (1621), pp. 176–7.
[80] Preston, *Saints Infirmities*, p. 75; Rous, *Diseases of the Time*, pp. 155–7; also pp. 164–6. (My italics in the two quotations.) [81] On this point, see, for example, Taylor, *Davids Learning*, p. 2.
[82] Perkins, *Workes*, I, p. 482.
[83] This was an extremely common theme. See, for example, Dent, *Plaine Mans Path-way*, pp. 17–18.

V

Since the truth about God and his requirements could not emanate from the mind, the only way for man to avoid making a paradise out of his mind's creation was to concentrate diligently on the prescripts of the Word, the offices of one's specific calling, and the covenant duties of faith and obedience.[84] Faith had not only to lead man to God; it had also to fight a rearguard action against the hostility of reason to its own exclusion from the terms of the covenant and against its infernal curiosity.[85] Fully appreciating that reason would have to be abandoned as the architect of the preparation for salvation, puritans also came to ponder the manner in which membership in the covenant might affect the working properties of natural reason. The infusion of the Spirit which came with entry into the covenant of grace, as it offered regeneration of the 'soul' of man, included the raising of its rational aspect to the level that was termed 'regenerate reason'. 'Regenerate reason', to puritans, meant the restoration of 'right reason', that is, reason in proper control over erratic and perverted will. It was crucial that the first step had to be taken by the Spirit, in instilling the first ounce of faith. But then, once man had been first invigorated (though not, of course, fully restored), he could apply his reason to the search for greater assurance through discerning and fulfilling the tasks as laid down in Scripture. Thus could puritans of 'obvious salvation', such as the learned divines of the universities, both rely increasingly in practice on their own reason for particular casuistical problems, and yet denounce in the very strongest terms any general reliance by the (probably largely unsaved) commonalty on the supernatural powers of reason. The paradoxical halves of this one doctrine at once protected both the irrational core of a Pauline view of Christian existence and the status of ministers as rational interpreters of the Word. In this doctrine one can perceive that the ancestry of puritan thought lay rather in the Reformation than in the Renaissance. Erasmus, too, had argued that the 'philosophy' of Christ could be seen as a 'restoration of human nature originally well formed', but had added that much of this 'philosophy' was available, through reason, in 'the books of the pagans . . .'.[86] Luther had rather argued that it was only regeneration that could save reason, and set it on a path of assistance to faith.[87]

Of puritans, John Preston spoke most clearly on the question of the degree to which reason might prove helpful in the stage following the first infusion of grace by the Spirit. Even he, however, did not delineate the specific step-by-step changes in reason which accompanied the individual's progress from a

---

[84]   Goodwin, *Vanity of Thoughts*, pp. 5–6, 20–4, 64–5, 95–96, 118ff. See also Taylor, *Davids Learning*, pp. 3–4; Granger, *Exposition on Ecclesiastes*, p. 183; Featley *et al.*, *House of Mourning*, pp. 372–3.

[85]   Granger, *Exposition on Ecclesiastes*, p. 183.   [86] Erasmus, *Paraclesis*, ed. Olin, p. 100.

[87]   Gerrish, *Grace and Reason*, pp. 81–2.

natural condition through preparation to the moment of conversion and then growing assurance of a regenerate condition. Preston at first warned his audience that education, which appealed to reason, could not *cure* the deficiencies now inherent in fallen man. But the infusion of faith produced a 'super-reason' which, now better guided, could perceive godliness where before all was hidden.[88] In addition, the regeneration of reason in turn invigorated the rest of natural man, for it 'flows by a redundancy unto the other faculties, and thereupon may take away those lets and impediments unto good'. Preston explained that with the aid of the Spirit, man's natural incapacity to comprehend the mysteries of salvation, his inability to 'bring his will and affections to embrace the truth . . . is now taken away by that light that is communicated unto him by the understanding' as it was now illuminated by grace.[89] But, as John Winthrop recorded in his diary of 'Christian Experience', the victory was never complete. Winthrop noted, perhaps reminiscent of Augustine, that he could still 'as occasion required write letters etc. of meer vanity; and if occasion were . . . others of savory and godly counsell'.[90] Reason did not become pristine once again – the stain could never be wholly excised – but it could, under the guidance of the Spirit, act as a dramatic aid in determining the proper earthly course under the covenant. It could also employ learning to persuade the unconverted of the logic inherent in protestant Christianity, and of the rational necessity for internal reform.[91]

But, even in its regenerate state, reason's function remained the defence of the truths of faith against detractors of religion.[92] Reason was subordinate also because the Spirit could in fact effect valuable change even where the reason was still distracted:

Yea, this teaching of the affection is sometimes so pregnant and powerful, that though the head being captivated by humane reason subject to errour, or by the prejudice of education, doe hold and maintaine an evill tenet, yet the heart shall even then, by the Spirit, endite a good matter, contrarie to that evill errour which the head maintaineth.[93]

The head might well become, in its regenerate state, the normal channel for communication from the Almighty, but where it resisted, it could temporarily be bypassed. The increased allowance of a sphere of competence to reason only in its regenerate state meant that establishing the proper *limits* of natural reason was always the puritan priority.

---

[88] See also Rous, *Heavenly Academie*, pp. 44–5; Ames, *Conscience*, Bk III, pp. 49–50ff.; Rainolds, *Excellent Oration*, p. 97. [89] Preston, *Sinnes Overthrow*, pp. 51–6.
[90] *Winthrop Papers*, I, p. 154. [91] *Work of Perkins*, ed. Breward, p. 39.
[92] Sibbes, *Light from Heaven*, pp. 22–3. [93] Rous, *Heavenly Academie*, pp. 44–5.

VI

This determination to set limits to the power of natural reason was further emphasized by the growing doctrine that experience was also an important source of knowledge. It is well known that certain separatist congregations argued at great length over the question of whether new candidates for admission had to be able to prove their conversion and regeneration.[94] Natural reason was increasingly held to be insufficient not only as an independent method for finding salvation, but also as a *source* of heavenly truths. Puritans favoured, rather, an individual approach to conversion and regeneration. Neither the lessons of others, nor the logic of human reason, could beforehand do more than suggest possible courses of action. Only *after* the experience of religion could reason be used to interpret and to suggest personal meaning. Reading the Word was important not so much because it presented 'knowledge' to the reader as because it involved the reader in the first level of *experiencing* the true religion. Knowledge *of* would perhaps be the first step towards participation *in*, that is, the catalyst which sparked a desire to experience faith. So John Cotton (like so many others), trained in the linear explanation of the Word as a printed statement of existence, came to certain comprehension of the Word as a *lively* message of salvation only through an intuition which he grasped while in the middle of an experience (a sermon) which was, in part, non-rational, in the way in which the theatre, oral poetry, or any *spectacle* is non-rational.

The doctrine of favouring experience over rationalism served as a way of attacking both the corrupt Schoolmen, whose Aristotelian logic had been seen as a way of creating truth out of the mind, and the heathen philosophers, who had paid little court to the importance of experiential faith as opposed to contemplative reason. But at the popular level at which the idea was promoted, the concentration was on drawing parallels between spiritual and secular existence. We have already noted David Zaret's illustrations of legal contractual language in explaining the specific terms of the covenant of grace. Richard Rogers explained in more widely comprehensible terms that the greater importance of experiential faith over rationalism was similar to that of the craftsman who obtained all his knowledge from books; he would not be able to conduct his business as well as the man who had direct experience, even though he (the book learner) might actually have greater knowledge of the formal principles of the trade.

Even so it is in the spirituall trade. For a man that hath bin taught soundly and plainly out of the work of God, & catechized in the principall points of Christian religion, is able by the helpe thereof to make a confession of his faith, and *give an account of the hope*

---

[94]   See Hall, *Faithful Shepherd*, Ch. 5 and sources cited there, for a variety of interpretations.

that is in him . . . But all this is but knowledge of the letter, if hee go no further . . . But the Christian who hath had the proofe of this knowledge, that is, how it hath been effectuall to him: how it hath assured him of his own salvation . . . he . . . that hath experience of this, hath received another manner of blessing then the other, and is likely daily to receive much more.[95]

That is, the Word (especially as it was preached) was efficacious, but he to whom the Spirit had granted some knowledge of grace was twice blessed.[96]

The knowledge of the reprobate is like the knowledge which a mathematicall geographer hath of the earth and all the places in it, which is but a generall notion, and a speculative comprehension of them. But the knowledge of the elect is like the knowledge of a traveller which can speake of experience and feeling, and hath beene there and seene and knowen the particulars.[97]

Similar, too, was Samuel Bird's use of the popular interest in geography to point his readers to the 'mappe' which led to true faith.[98] In the same vein Francis Rous noted: 'There is great oddes betweene an experienced, and a meerely-contemplative Captaine.'[99] The frequent parallel with the empirical knowledge of travellers was intended not to promote empirical research strategies, but rather, in the context of devotional manuals, to demonstrate to the household reader the necessity of a lively *expression* of one's faith.

Experimental knowledge, as John Preston clearly explained, referred to the attribute of those 'that heare the voyce of the sonne of God'; it had nothing to do with the efforts of man's own thought processes, which brought him but a 'meere inlightening and informing knowledge.'[100] As a good Ramist, Preston sought to give his readers a clear explanation of the 'use' of experience; as a good Christian covenanter, he explained the 'use' in terms of overcoming the hardships of faithful struggle. John Downame, too, in his extremely lengthy and explicit work on the leading of a godly life argued that no knowledge, but especially not the speculative type, could be compared to that attained through experience, though the experience did not in all cases have to be personal.[101] He, too, offered a parallel with earthly knowledge as an incentive to greater active faith: 'For as in civill affaires, that knowledge which is gotten by reading and mentall discourse, is of little use or worth, untill it be perfected by practice and experience: so is it much more true in the knowledge of Christianity.[102] That is, knowledge of the existence of God, and of his prescriptions

[95] Rogers, *Seven Treatises*, p. 279; also pp. 281, 148–9.
[96] Taylor, *Davids Learning*, p. 65; Downame, *Guide to Godliness*, p. 787; Thomas Hooker, quoted in Levy, *Preaching in New England*, p. 15. [97] Dent, *Pastime for Parents*, unpaginated.
[98] Bird, *Lectures*, sigs. A2ᵛ–3. [99] Rous, *Heavenly Academie*, pp. 32–3.
[100] Preston, *Four Godly and Learned Treatises*, p. 153; see also Hieron, *Workes*, pp. 157–8. See also Gerrish, *Grace and Reason*, p. 141, for Luther's similar view. [101] Downame, *Guide to Godliness*, p. 624.
[102] *Ibid.*, p. 626. See also Rous, *Heavenlie Academie*, pp. 32–3, 68, 93, on this point.

for this world which came to man by the efforts of reason would remain a dead letter until revivified by the force of experience of the Lord.

In solely human spheres of knowledge some puritans did encourage the use of experimental learning. Thomas Granger, for example, condemned physicians who 'learned' simply by reading Galen or Hippocrates, and praised those who possessed practical experience of the application of the theories. In similar fashion to the analogy of the earthly traveller, a parallel was drawn here by Granger between curing the body and easing the ills of the soul.[103] In this puritans reflected the growing intellectual unease of their age with continued reliance either on reason itself or on classical authority as a source of final truth, and might be seen to parallel the efforts of the Baconians.[104] But there was a firm line across which puritans would not allow the testimony of new experience to step. No human discovery from the collected 'experience' of empirical investigation would be allowed to challenge the supreme authority of Scripture. This was perhaps the fullest sense in which puritans were 'people of the Book'. For the puritans themselves (and here we must be careful to separate eventual impact from desired effect) the doctrine of experience simply announced the superiority of the individual's relationship with God – as suitably refined and explained by the godly minister – to all human authority. Here, then, was no alliance with empirical 'science',[105] but merely the terms of the covenant laid bare for popular audiences: experience thy faith, act upon it, reflect God's glory and thine own salvation in good works. The connexion between empiricism and religious experience undoubtedly existed in puritan minds, but in popular rendition it was always constructed so that 'empiricism', already accepted in daily affairs by practical people (as indeed it must always have been), was used to promote belief in the importance of religious experience too.

Puritans thus made it clear to their readers that, with the passing of the first covenant (of works), any ability of natural reason to find the path to grace had also vanished. God's new covenant was totally dependent on faith; natural reason might still serve, in 'cold' fashion, to analyse and explain objectively this restructured bond, but intelligence itself counted for nothing with the Spirit. Only regenerate reason, which followed the religious experience of

[103] Granger, *Application of Scripture*, pp. 5ff.
[104] Comenius declared that 'we do not trust a conclusion derived from reasoning unless it can be verified by a display of examples (the trustworthiness of which depends on sensuous perception)' (*Great Didactic*, p. 337).
[105] On this question, see Morgan, 'Puritanism and science', pp. 535–60. The puritan doctrine of experience in religion has frequently been propounded as evidence of a dependence on reason and a spur to the advancement of learning, especially as it related to the development of empirical methods in scientific research. Richard Greaves has pointed out the striking deficiencies of the parallel by noting that personal religious experience is frequently a unique occurrence, while the empirical affairs of the laboratory must, by definition, be repeatable under the same conditions, (Greaves, 'Puritanism and science', *Journal of the History of Ideas*, 30, p. 354).

conversion, could serve as a reliable handmaid in the comprehension of God and the performance of the duties of the covenant. In the intervening stage of preparation, there was also the possibility of assistance from reason which had not yet been fully regenerated. Indeed, the rise of the doctrine of preparation, since it allowed a certain, though indeterminate, contribution to natural man in his own search for salvation, may well have proved, over time, the great crack in the edifice of English Calvinism. But reason, in the guise of humane learning, was also a product, an ever-growing corpus available to more and more people. Puritans therefore found it necessary not only to concentrate on what man's mind could do, but also to turn to what it had produced, to sift the wheat from the chaff. In an era of growing emphasis on the glory of the ancients, of expanding school facilities, and of the publication of cheap print, puritans found that humane learning, too, threatened man's obedience to God within the terms of the covenant.

4

THE DANGERS OF LEARNING

I

Between the humanist flowering of reason applied to the knowledge of man, and the later application of reason to the secrets of nature, there bloomed also a reaction against both the Thomist alliance of faith and reason, and the humanist congruence of the Christian and rational lives of moral virtue.[1] The questioning of the power of man's reason and humane learning as absolute standards is what Hiram Haydn, under the rubric 'Counter-Renaissance', termed the 'revolt against intellectualism and systematization' and a return to 'first principles'.[2] It stood in the middle of a tripartite (though not fully sequential) development of the early modern age, between the Renaissance and the Scientific Revolution. This latter era again established the ability of man's reason (though now combined with an empirical base) to decode the mysteries of an external world, from which God was then progressively removed as anything more than a First Cause. Within this widespread opposition to reason's universal ability to solve man's problems, there were great divisions. Cornelius Agrippa's scepticism can hardly be said to be based in fervent religious belief. Yet his withering attacks on the ability of man to know external reality as a solid base for comprehension of the meaning of his own existence again promoted themes akin to puritan concerns. Montaigne came even closer, for at the end of the 'Apology for Raymond Sebond', he turned to faith as the only form of certain knowledge, though it is with learning that the essay is concerned.[3] Within Elizabethan and Jacobean literature, too, the question of humane learning loomed large, even outside strictly religious bounds. Spenser, Sidney, Greville, and Samuel Daniel all regarded learning as a source of doubt rather than certainty. The Calvinist Fulke Greville specifically stressed the vanity of corrupted man seeking to comprehend divine mysteries:

---

[1]   Haydn, *Counter-Renaissance*, p. 83. My schematic interpretation owes much to Haydn's appraisal of the sixteenth and seventeenth centuries. On only one occasion, however, did Haydn specifically mention that puritans fitted the patterns of the 'Counter-Renaissance'.

[2]   *Ibid.*, pp. 84–5.   [3]   *Ibid.*, p. 119.

Whence all Mans fleshly idols being built
As humane Wisedome, Science, Power, and Arts,
Upon the false foundation of his Guilt;
Confusedly doe weave within our hearts,
    Their own advancement, state and declination,
    As things whose beings are but transmutation.[4]

At the end of the spectrum, Henry Niclas, founder of the Family of Love, argued that humans should not set up their own learning against that of God and thereby become 'bewitched in their Understanding and Thoughts . . .'[5]

Throughout a broad strain of English literature in our period, then, there was serious discontent with formal learning. Much of the search for the proper uses of learning was based on Pauline anti-rationalism. But it also followed the more 'human' struggle of Augustine. Augustine's passion for learning, and yet, after his protracted conversion, his stated willingness to abandon any aspect of the classics not in accord with Scripture, established not only the supremacy of the Bible as an authority, but also the dialectic between humane learning and faith. Puritans should thus be seen not as unique, but rather as one aspect of a broad front of sixteenth- and seventeenth-century groups that proposed a working relationship for faith and learning based on a certain Pauline–Augustinian–Ockhamist view, rather than upon the Aristotelian–Thomist synthesis. This is not, of course, to suggest rigid boundaries. John Donne, for example, anti-puritan, non-Calvinist, and a believer in the importance of the beauty of sermons, at times exhibited the same quest for the exaltation of faith above reason. Though Donne on occasion portrayed an extremely close identification of faith and reason,[6] nonetheless, in a sermon preached at The Hague, he exhibited the force which was at the core of the fideist branch of the Counter-Renaissance:

The Scriptures will be out of thy reach, and out of thy use, if thou cast and scatter them upon reason, upon philosophy, upon morality, to try how the Scriptures will fit them, and believe them but so far as they agree with thy reason; but draw the Scripture to thine own heart, and to thine own actions, and thou shalt find it made for that.[7]

I have used Donne as an illustration of Christian fervency precisely because he can never be mistaken for a puritan. The purpose here is not to paint the puritans a different primary colour from all other sixteenth-century thought,

---

[4] Greville, *Treatie of Humane Learning*, quoted in Haydn, *Counter-Renaissance*, p. 111; also p. 81, for the similar approach of Samuel Daniel. See, similarly, Lyly, *Euphues*, fol. 65ᵛ.

[5] Niclas, *Introduction to holy Understanding*, sigs. C.7ᵛ, C.3.

[6] Bredvold, 'Religious thought of Donne', *Studies in Shakespeare, Milton and Donne*, p. 215.

[7] Quoted in *ibid.*, p. 216.

but rather to show the difference in their hue, which was not quite duplicated anywhere else.

II

Before the religious reformation had even begun in England, Thomas Müntzer had posed the problem which would plague the puritans. 'The man who has not received the living witness of God', explained Müntzer, 'knows really nothing about God, though he may have swallowed 100,000 Bibles'.[8] Thus, from the beginning, experience of the godly life was placed above an external knowledge of its content. Godliness was the dynamic of action, not the static of understanding. Eventually this theme, which was the core of the puritan paradox, would erupt under radical pressure. At first, however, it was employed by reformers to emphasize the commitment to a method of life. Thus John Foxe, in pointing out that 'we should search for a righteousness, which is no moral, humane vertue, but which is a Spiritual Grace and gift of God', summed up the difference between Reformed theology and the optimistic, anthropocentric stress of contemporary humanism.[9] With the Reformation came a greater stress on the individual's relationship with God as the central aspect of Christianity. And with that, understandably, came a questioning of the role of the human intellect in matters of faith.

As heirs of the Reformation doctrine of justification by faith alone, and, at the same time, of the humanist glorification of learning, puritans developed a schizoid attitude to human learning. Enthusiasm – the idea that faith had fundamentally non-rational and even irrational bases – was inherent in Christianity. But also ever present was that side of religion which relied on reason rather than on the 'direct apprehension' of intuition. Puritans admired Augustine's neo-Platonism as well as his piety, and, while they excoriated the academic hair-splitting of the later Schoolmen, they also acknowledged the breadth of Aquinas' achievement, and the textual improvements of the humanists.

This struggle of enthusiasm and learning was a constant of puritan being, regardless of changes in external emphasis. Against those whom they saw as leaning too heavily on the pillars of reason and learning, puritans hammered on the anvil of faith. But against those who would destroy all learning for the sake of the inner light, puritans stressed the necessity of learning to comprehend the full meaning of the Word and to launch counter-offensives against Antichrist. Man had fallen far, to the bottom of the abyss, so that only God's mercy could make for him a lifeline. And yet, he still had his reason and his learning, which could be applied to the comprehension of what God had

[8] Quoted in Harbison, *Christian Scholar*, p. 168.
[9] Foxe, *Of Free Justification*, p. 112, quoted in Olsen, *John Foxe*, p. 124. See also Granger, *Exposition on Ecclesiastes*, p. 175.

chosen to reveal. In the Revolution, when puritans finally sided with the universities against the enthusiasts, they were thus not reversing the course of their historical development. Rather, they had arrived at a solution towards which they had been edging for their whole existence. The radicalism of the Revolution simply proved the final catalyst which drove puritans to a scarcely tempered defence of humane learning.

Perhaps the most formative aspect of the development of puritan views of learning was their understanding of the manner of Paul's conversion: an irrational imposition of the Spirit upon Paul's will. Learning had played no part in it. In his letters to the new Christian communities of the Mediterranean, Paul constantly stressed the dangers of confusing the humane power of Athens and the spiritual force of Christianity. He warned of the vanity of humane learning, of the temptations and distractions it offered to those seeking salvation rather than human reputation, and of the inapplicability of humane learning to the roots of the greater search of mankind. Puritans, finding themselves in a world which (like Paul's) glorified the abilities of humane learning, turned to the Apostle for a Christian remedy which reached new heights in the Counter-Renaissance. So, in the earliest puritan scholarly effort, the Geneva Bible of 1560, Paul's own admonitions were joined by the dire warnings of the famous marginalia, the severity of which may partly be explained by the harsher dialectic of Christ and Antichrist which existed in the sixteenth century. So, while Paul asked simply, of the Corinthians 'Where is the wise? where is the Scribe? where is the disputer of this worlde? hathe not God made the wisdome of this worlde foolishnes?' the Geneva marginal comment portrayed more specifically the limitations of learning for a Renaissance world abounding in humane wisdom: 'herein Paul reprocheth even the best learned, as thogh not one of them colde perceive by his owne wisdome this mysterie of Christ reveiled in the Gospel'.[10]

Paul continually emphasized the purity of Scripture, and the improvement it produced in the true believer; the Geneva Bible gloss clarified that only Scripture 'sufficeth to lead us to perfection.'[11] Paul stressed the sermon as the central means of spreading the force of the Spirit,[12] and the consequent necessity to offer it in plain language; the Geneva edition noted that Paul reproved the Corinthians 'not as false apostles, but as curious teachers of humaine sciences, as they which lothing at the simplicitie of Gods worde, preache philosophical speculacions'.[13] Paul was also closely concerned with

---

[10] I Corinthians 1.20 and marginal comment of 1560 Geneva Bible. (The phrase 'marginal comment' in subsequent footnotes refers to this edition of the Bible, unless specifically noted to be the 'Tomson' gloss.)

[11] II Timothy 3.16 and 3.17 and the 1560 marginal comments. The Laurence Tomson gloss (translated from Theodore Beza) added that a 'Pastour must be wise by the word of God only . . .', thereby emphasizing the proper hierarchy of knowledge.   [12] Galatians 3.2 and 3.3.

[13] Marginal comment to I Corinthians 3.15. The Tomson gloss added that they would have to 'abide the losse of their vaine labours'. See also the comments to II Corinthians 11.6.

the effect that too-close reliance on humane learning could have on the Christian believer himself. Solomon, after all, had warned that 'there is none end in making manie bokes: and much reading is a wearines of the flesh,'[14] to which the Geneva Bible added the clear explanation that faith 'can not be comprehended in bokes, or learned by studie' but had to be instilled by God himself. In this tradition came Paul's greatest admonition to the Colossians to 'beware lest there be anie man that spoile you through philosophie, and vaine deceit, through the traditions of men, according to the rudiments of the worlde, and not after Christ'.[15] The Tomson Geneva gloss clarified this problem by distinguishing between the types of difficulty:

He bringeth all corruptions to three kindes: The first is that, which resteth of vaine an [sic] curious speculations, and yet beareth a shew of a certaine subtill wisedome . . . The second which is manifestly superstitious and vaine, and standeth onely upon custome and fained inspirations. The third kinde was of them which joyned the rudiments of the world (that is to say, the ceremonies of the Law) with the Gospel.

Here, then, in the insight of Calvin's great successor, lay the core of fervent protestant fear of humane learning. In expanding this fear puritans made their contribution to Reformed (and Counter-Renaissance) thought. Indeed, throughout this continuing stress on the necessity to know and teach the pure Christ runs the message that learning could avail man of no heavenly reward. It was a proposition propounded throughout our era by the reformers of the church against especially those who would place learning in competition with faith, against those, that is, who 'more estemed the outwarde shewe of wisdome and eloquence, then true godliness'.[16]

Carlo Ginzburg has recently suggested that Paul's warning in Romans 11.20 ('Be not highminded, but fear') was interpreted incorrectly after the fourth century in a 'collective slip' as being a 'warning against intellectual curiosity' rather than against moral perfidy[17] and that this misinterpretation was not corrected until Erasmus and Lorenzo Valla pointed out the error.[18] The Reformation, including the puritan thrust, seems nonetheless to have chosen to perpetuate the earlier (mis-)comprehension of Paul's admonition.[19] In commenting on Acts 26 and 27, Thomas Adams, who stood at the lenient end of the puritan spectrum regarding learning, noted the opinion of the procurator Festus, concerning Paul, that *much learning had made him madde*. He continued, noting the crucial juxtaposition of pride with learning, that 'Indeed, it might have done, if *Paul* had beene as proud of his learning, as *Festus* was of his

---

[14] Ecclesiastes 12.12 and marginal comment.   [15] Colossians 2.8.
[16] Marginal comment to II Corinthians 5.12.   [17] Ginzburg, 'High and low', pp. 28, 30.
[18] *Ibid.*, p. 29. Ginzburg argues that Pelagius had seen the moral aim of Paul's admonition.
[19] See, for example, at the beginning of our period, Thomas Lever, *Sermon at Pauls Crosse*, sig. B.vi[v]: 'Paule dyd dispose the secretes of God by the preachinge of the Gospel, which was ever secretly hydde from the wyttye, wise, and learned in the worlde.'

honour.'[20] And finally, to demonstrate that Paul's warnings entered even the innermost precincts of learning, we may note a sermon delivered by Nicholas Preston of Emmanuel at Great St Mary's in Cambridge. Using as his text I Corinthians 2.2,[21] Preston opened for his audience the theme of the Christian purity of Paul's learning, which, he insisted

desires noe other Geometry but to know the height, depth of the love of Christ . . . Noe other Astronomy than to know the bright morning starre, noe other Astrology but to know the vertues, & influences of the sunne of righteousness, as Christ is called . . . Noe Rhetorick but what he tooke from the bleeding wounds of his Saviour . . .[22]

Preston was of course not recommending the termination of all humane studies. Rather, he was simply issuing a reminder that all knowledge was arid compared to the comprehension of Christ, and that learning, of itself, was not godly. Indeed, even in their refusal to abandon learning, puritans modelled themselves on Paul. So Clement Cotton, in his concordance to the New Testament, included twenty-five entries on the subject of learning; seventeen of them referred to the Pauline epistles.[23] For puritans 'knowledge puffeth up' thus meant not simply that any knowledge is bound to be vanity, but rather that even knowledge of God, unless it is put to work to edify (that is, to build a community of believers) is not being used properly, and will therefore lead to dire results.

III

In the contemporary struggles at the universities and in the countryside, learning often served as a point of polemical self-justification and attack for the puritans' opponents. Antagonists tended to seize on puritan wariness of learning and present this as the whole puritan view. In a time of increased upper-class interest in the liberal arts, this form of propaganda could prove most damaging to the precisians' public reputation. That individual puritans were themselves very learned, and engaged in teaching the humane arts, did not detract from the vehemence of this attack. Robert Shelford, for example, criticized puritans for being, at the same time, both ignorant and overly dependent on learning, though the stress, as usual, was on the dearth rather than the surfeit of knowledge.[24] More common, however, was the rancour which saw Whitgift and Cartwright challenge each other's knowledge of logic, and Bishop Parkhurst of Norwich seek to deny a teaching licence to

---

[20] Adams, *Workes*, p. 773.
[21] 'For I determined not to know anything among you save Jesus Christ, and him crucified.'
[22] Bod. Lib. MS Tanner 88, No. 1(g), fol. 6.   [23] Cotton, *Christians Concordance, passim*.
[24] Shelford, *Five Pious and Learned Discourses*, p. 59.

Robert Harrison partly because he believed that Harrison would not teach the
'heathens' to young boys.[25] John Bridges' lengthy defence of the structure and
practices of the Elizabethan church offered the plea that puritans would not
'thinke and vaunt too much of their learning', which was, he argued, severely
limited.[26] Doubtless the height of the charge that puritans were opposed to
learning, however, came from the virulent pen of Richard Hooker, who
sought to paint puritans as the darkness of fervour which would blot out the
light of learning:

> But so it is, the name of the light of Nature is made hateful with men; the star of
> Reason and learning, and all other such helps, beginneth no otherwise to be thought of
> than if it were an unlucky comet; or as if God had so accursed it, that it should never
> shine or give light in things concerning our duty any way towards Him, but be
> esteemed as that star in Revelation called Wormwood: which being fallen from
> Heaven maketh rivers and waters in which it falleth so bitter, that men tasting them
> die thereof. A number there are who think they cannot admire as they ought the
> power and authority of the Word of God if in things divine they should attribute any
> force to man's Reason: for which cause they never use Reason so willingly as to dis-
> grace Reason.[27]

Hooker thus saw directly through the puritan dilemma of desiring the use of
learning, but only on terms of strict subordination to the demands of
faith.

Another frequent ploy in the struggle was the attempt to paint all puritan
reformers the same colour as the radicals. It was commonly said that they 'will
abide no degrees in Schooles, all humane Learning must be layd by,
Academies are to them abominable . . .'.[28] Indeed, in an attempt to protect
themselves against being lumped with such 'Brownists' (an umbrella term for
radicals), puritans often turned to join the common assault on the radicals, and
insist on their own dedication to learning. Thus, against Whitgift's criticisms
of the precisians as unlearned, Thomas Cartwright, himself a former Lady
Margaret Professor of Divinity, pointed out that the bishop's opponents were
'neyther voyde of the knowledge of the tongues nor of the liberall Artes . . .'.[29]
But while inviting Whitgift, D.D. and Master of Trinity, to the learned forum
of a public disputation, Cartwright also noted:

> Well/what we reade/and howe unlearned we are/is not the matter whyche we strive
> for. The iudgements thereof is firste wyth God/and then wyth the churches/and in

[25] C.U.L. MS Ee.ii.34, No. 152, fol. 128.
[26] Bridges, *Defence*, p. 20, also pp. 44, 45. At another point (p. 31) Bridges admitted that puritans might
   very well be learned, but even this would be no basis on which to interfere with the authorized forms
   and practices of church government.
[27] Hooker, *Laws of Ecclesiastical Polity*, in *Works*, ed. Keble, III. 8. 4.
[28] Anon., *Brownists Synagogue*, p. 1. See also Mason, *Authoritie*, p. 68.
[29] Cartwright, *Replye to answere*, sig. C.j, also sig. B.iij[v].

their iudgements we are content to rest. But if you be so greatly learned/and we so unlearned/and smally red/then the truthe of oure cause shall more appeare/that is maintained with so small learning and reading/against men of suche profounde knowledge and great reading.[30]

Cartwright was not merely hedging his bets. Rather, he was again proclaiming the puritan belief that, if on the one hand learning was indeed equal to godliness, then why was England's church, led by learned men, such a Laodicean institution; but, on the other, if learning did not automatically lead to godliness, then why should the establishment bother to criticize the puritans on this ground? This argument was a trap from which the authorities of the church found it difficult to extricate themselves; in the Revolution, the same question would be asked directly of the 'puritans' by the radicals, with the same confused answer.

IV

In the previous chapter, I argued that puritans sought to restrict the free run of unrepentant and unbowed reason. This temptation to aim too high was also carried over from the potential to the actual, that is, to humane learning. Above all loomed the vanity attached to humane learning. The first step in delineating this vanity was the recognition of the inferiority of humane to divine learning. In a household manual, John Downame stressed, in Pauline fashion, that we should not spend our labour trying to comprehend 'above that which is meete', but rather

bend our studies unto the attaining of such knowledge as is most profitable and necessary, wherein we shall find such plenty and variety, such high contemplations and divine Mysteries, that we shall have little leasure or pleasure, in looking after idle speculations, and fruitless curiosities.[31]

No matter how great the level of humane learning attained, argued William Perkins, the human capacity for rational understanding was limited:

In particular, wisedome is not to bee glorified in, seeing it is very defective, whether we speake of speculative wisedome, standing in contemplation, or practicall, consisting in action: For in arts and sciences, as also in the secrets of nature, our ignorance is greater than our knowledge . . . And as for practicall wisedome, standing in policy, it is not demonstrative, but mearely conjecturall, and therefore wee cannot build upon it, considering in it there is the concurrence of so many causes that are casuall, and of so many mindes which are mutable.[32]

---

[30] *Ibid.*, sig. L.ij.   [31] Downame, *Guide to Godliness*, p. 787.
[32] Perkins, *Workes*, II, pp. 416–17. It is perhaps significant that Perkins should use the occasion of a commentary on Paul's Epistle to the Galatians to make this point.

The highest form of learning's vanity was that it might tempt the educated to rely on their humane abilities alone, to scoff at the necessity for revelation too.[33] Vanity could make Christianity seem 'too obvious and common for our sublimated and subtle wits' and so lead man into 'heresies and foolish fancies . . .'.[34] Thomas Taylor asked his readers, in a fashion reminiscent of Jesus' warning,[35] about the purpose of rising to the heights of human endeavour when emptiness was its only final reward:

What were a man better if he were able to comprehend the frame of the World, measure the parts of the Earth, to discourse of the course and motions of the Starres, if the sense of unpardoned sinne proclayme himselfe a damned wretch, and a guiltie Conscience tell him to his face, that Heaven is ashamed of him, the Earth is weary of him, and his owne sinfull burthen beares him downe to Hell?

What profit were it to be able to discerne all diseases, and all remedies, and attayne all the skill of physicke to cure the body, when a mans owne soule is wounded to death without remedie?[36]

The invocation here is evidently not against humane learning, but rather in the Augustinian tradition of 'believing in order that one may know'.[37] Against the Romanist stress on contemplation, puritans advised that even self-knowledge, while valuable as leading to a comprehension of the burning need for repentance, could also easily lead to vanity, since it was static, and thus opposed to their concept of human existence as a struggle (which by definition is not static) towards salvation. Hence their insistence that all learning was laudable only as it conduced to, and aided, the living of a godly existence.

This fear of vanity also led puritans to argue that little emphasis should be placed on the possession of learning, once one had attained it. So William Bedell's son praised his father, B.D. of Cambridge and later provost of Trinity College, Dublin, not for the possession of his learning, but rather for conveying his knowledge in plain terms to the people, and specifically for his *lack* of vanity in such knowledge.[38] For our purposes here, the historical accuracy of the son's comment is less important than the indication of what he regarded as praiseworthy. In this tradition also stood Robert Bolton, who warned more directly that knowledge without evident reformation of life conduced only to 'many base bastard and degenerate ends', to wit: 'pleasure of curiosity, quiet resolution; refining and raising of the spirit; victory of wit; faculty of dis-

---

[33] See, for example, Hieron, *Helpe unto Devotion*, p. 751; Nicols, *Plea of the Innocent*, p. 88.
[34] Downame, *Guide to Godliness*, p. 787. See also Granger, *Exposition on Ecclesiastes*, p. 183.
[35] Matthew 16.26: 'For what is a man profited, if he shall gain the whole world, and lose his own soul?'
[36] Taylor, *Davids Learning*, p. 4. Taylor also reminded his readers that King David had accounted as 'knowledge' only that learning which instructed in godliness (*ibid.*, pp. 3–4). See also Greenham, *Two Learned and Godly Sermons*, sig. D.2.
[37] On this point, see Gilson, *Reason and Revelation*, esp. Ch. 1.
[38] Bod. Lib. MS Tanner 278, fols. 22ᵛ–3. See, similarly, Bird, *Lectures*, sigs. B8ᵛ–C1.

course; gaine of profession; ambition of honour and fame; inablement for businesse and imployment'.[39] One can also find similar touches in personal recollections and comments. Forth Winthrop, writing to John Winthrop Junior, after singing the praises of books and of the pursuit of learning, stopped himself short: 'but, abandoning such *trifling*, let us turn to something *serious*'. He then described the guidance God had offered for human existence.[40] Similarly, Samuel Ward, in his diary, condemned himself for his 'prid in doyng things in geometry', even though he was a recent university graduate.[41] Henry Smith warned that the 'wisedome which men gather more than *Sobrietie* doth no good, but puffe them and corrupt them; and turne them either into pride, or into envie, or into wiles, or into strife, or one contagion or other . . .'.[42] The greatest danger of learning, then, was that it would become an end in itself, the focus of the scholar's endeavour, not subordinated to godly utility.

As an extension of the theme of vanity, puritan preachers also harped on the grave moral dangers associated with humane knowledge. Thomas Adams recalled at length that God had used the Tree of Knowledge in Eden as a sign that man should not transgress God's Law.[43] It was thus the quality of the use of human abilities that determined the level of moral worth; of itself, learning was morally neutral:

it is a thing good in regard of nature: and so to be commended and labour'd for: although in respect of any morall goodnesse, it is a thing of an indifferent nature, neither good nor evill, as all other naturall perfections also are. Civill wisdom therefore considered in it selfe, is not opposed to spirituall wisdom, but only as a disparate.[44]

Ames' emphasis that humane learning was not opposed to spiritual may seem a long way from Richard Capel's fear that reason could only interfere with salvation.[45] Yet even Ames would not proclaim any 'goodness' inherent in learning; nor would he allow its free demonstration from the popular pulpit, even though in theoretical terms it was not of itself evil. Learning was simply a human tool, like any other, useful if properly applied, damaging if set to the wrong tasks.

Another aspect of the Counter-Renaissance claim made against learning was that it became a paean to the wrong authorities, either ancient or contemporary. Especially did this seem true of certain humanists who claimed learn-

[39] Bolton, *Workes*, pp. 46–7.   [40] *Winthrop Papers*, I, p. 394. (My italics.)
[41] Knappen, ed., *Two Tudor Diaries*, p. 111, entry for 6 Nov. 1595. Ward had just become a fellow of Emmanuel; he took his M.A. in 1596.
[42] H. Smith, *13 Sermons*, sig S4^{r-v}; see also Graham, *Workes*, p. 68.
[43] Adams, *Workes*, pp. 1130–1, 1170.   [44] Ames, *Conscience*, Bk III, pp. 67, 66.
[45] See above, p. 52.

ing as 'the onely precious jewel of immortality . . .'.[46] There were, against the
humanist predilection for the superiority of ancient minds, two responses in
our period. One was the beginning of a search for experimental knowledge,
urged on by Bacon and his followers. The other reaction (which included
puritans) stressed the fideist fear that the complicated learning of the
philosophers would be magnified above the simple truths of the Apostles and
other prophets of God.[47]

For Calvin, learning was one of the many gifts which God 'left to human
nature even after it was despoiled of its true good'.[48] So Calvin and his successor, Beza, incorporated humane learning into their own theological system
and into the Academy at Geneva. But, since Scripture was superior to all
human wisdom, Calvin reiterated the Pauline rubric that it was 'vain' to
attempt to fortify Scripture by human helps. Calvin was not averse to the joys
and allurement of Plato, Demosthenes, Cicero, and Aristotle,[49] but he stressed
that these giants were testimony not so much to the ability of the human mind,
as to the great superiority of God's Word in a hierarchy of wisdom.[50] He
noted, for example, that some parts of Scripture – he mentioned especially
David and Isaiah – possessed great eloquence of language.[51] But he insisted
that the inclusion of such passages served only to demonstrate that no skill was
beyond the Spirit. It was far more important to emphasize that the Spirit in
most cases chose the course of plain language, thus asserting the primacy of the
message over the beauty of the medium. Calvin's principle of accepting support from almost any source helped to join the classics to Christian service,
though in a regulated and subordinate role.[52] Thus the central doctrine of the
authority of the Word was maintained as the standard against which all human
actions could be judged.

At the same time, this created the atmosphere in which the ambivalent
puritan attitude towards learning would grow – that fear of human adum-
bration of the Word combined with the perceived need to marshal humane
wisdom in the ranks of Christ's army against the learned forces of Babylon.
The Pauline attempt to assimilate the Greek and Jewish heritages into Christianity posed some problems for puritans over the question of the supremacy
of the Old (Jewish) Law to Greek rational thought, with Scripture, on occasion, having to serve the purposes of the latter.[53] At the centre of the problem
lay the unchallenged belief of all Christians that a core of revealed knowledge
was of a higher order than anything man could discern by his own reason:

[46]   Chamberlain, *Nocturnall Lucubrations*, pp. 11–12; Terry, *Triall of Truth*, sig. C.
[47]   Agrippa, *Of Vanitie*, sig. A.iiii^{r-v}; Chaderton, *Excellent and Godly Sermon*, sig. E.ii^v.
[48]   Calvin, *Institutes*, ed. McNeill, II.2.16.
[49]   *Ibid.*, I.8.1. For Calvin's early scholarship, see McNeill, *History and Character of Calvinism*, p. 105.
[50]   Calvin, *Institutes*, ed. McNeill, I.8.1.   [51]   *Ibid.*, I.8.2.   [52]   *Ibid.*, II.2.15.
[53]   Coolidge, *Pauline Renaissance*, Ch. 2.

Christians, which are taught and have learned Christ, according as the truth is in Christ Iesus, doe by many degrees excell all Philosophers and wisemen of the world whatsoever: for their learning was naturall, earthly, sensuall; but the learning of Christians, is supernaturall, heavenly, and spirituall.[54]

At the opposite extreme, and especially for rhetorical purposes, this argument could be taken to show that ignorance of humane learning could be a blessing if replaced by God's saving grace.[55] At the very least, puritans urged a better balance of the earthly and the divine.

To any reader of puritan tracts, the debt owed to the Fathers, and especially to Augustine, soon becomes clear.[56] At the same time puritans were not willing simply to regard the Fathers as the fount of all knowledge, and to denigrate contemporary protestant writers. Robert Bolton made this point clear in a striking analogy:

> I say, I will suppose them to be as it were Gyants, and wee Dwarfes: Yet set a Dwarfe upon a Gyants shoulders, and he will see further, and so might certainly wee, but for Slouth, Idlenesse, Worldlinesse, Ambition, and other such base and vile degenerations of these later Times.[57]

There was, then, some contention about the relative contemporary importance of the early and post-Reformation Christian authors. Generally, some attempt was made to achieve a balance. A typical puritan paper on reform of the discipline of the church thus included proofs taken from, in order, Scripture, the Fathers, and 'late writers', including Bucer, Calvin, Beza, and Zanchius.[58] But even the purest humane sources, present or past, always had limits for puritans. Nicholas Bownde, in treating of the sabbath, noted that he had indeed checked the supporting arguments of the thesis against the writings of the Fathers (Latin and Greek) and had found agreement. But he made it clear that he had done this only after he had extracted 'the bare proofes out of the scriptures . . .'.[59] That is, the testimony of other godly authors was but an elaboration and explication of the clear truth of Scripture. There was to be no confusion of the relative authority of humane and divine wisdom. As Nicholas Preston of Emmanuel College neatly put it,

> Doe not take this, which I have said, as simply spoken against knowledge . . . Lett Leah, humane knowledge, have roome within doores; but lett Rachell, the sacred knowledge of Christ, have cheife roome amongst us. If other sciences will come bring their myrrh, & frankincense, and lay them at Christs feet, lett them come, & wellcome

---

[54] Anon., *Office of Christian Parents*, p. 14.
[55] Thomas Hooker, *Comment upon Christs Last Prayer*, p. 404. Hooker had voiced the same opinion in very similar terms in his *Soules Vocation*, pp. 108–9.
[56] On this point, see especially Miller, *New England Mind*, Ch. I.   [57] Bolton, *Workes*, pp. 212–13.
[58] B.L. MS Sloane 271, fols. 66–8: 'The Discipline of the Church taught in the Worde of God. Reasons grounded upon the Scriptures which prove this Doctrine.'
[59] Bownde, *Doctrine of Sabbath*, sig. A3ᵛ.

. . . All Humane arts, & sciences are Artes ancillarie, handmaids, have respect to them.
Take a greater care for Leah the speculative knowledge of Theology: But lett thy
strongest, & most affectionate care be for Joseph & Rachel, for practical
knowledge of Christ.[60]

In stressing constantly the magnitude of the gap between humane and divine,
puritans diverged from the dominant themes of the Renaissance and became
part of the Counter-Renaissance struggle to restrict the application of reason
and learning.

The puritan willingness to test humane authority by the light of Scripture
was not confined to pre-Christian heathen literature, or to those who wrote in
defence of the Roman church. Thomas Cartwright criticized Whitgift for
claiming that 'all the godliest and best-learned men' agreed with his interpretation. Cartwright insisted that, in a quarrel over the requirements of
Scripture, the summoning of other humane testimonies (even if they were
godly), in place of deeper exegesis, constituted a vain reliance on a form of
authority that did not have an adequately solid base. He therefore criticized
Whitgift for relying even on the godly Martin Bucer, especially as Bucer was
sometimes guilty of offering opinions unsubstantiated by 'evidence' from
Scripture, or even from examples of the primitive churches or from human
reason itself, which to Cartwright represented a declining order of proofs.[61]
Here, too, the puritan emphasis on the individuality of interpretation – at least
for the learned – was evident.

An over-concentration on humane texts could also lead the casual reader to
imagine that Scripture provided only 'cold' knowledge. William Pemble pronounced against this dangerous practice:

Prophane studie of sacred things, to know onely, not to doe, to satisfie curiositie, or
give contentment to an all searching and comprehending wit; who study Divinitie as
they would doe other arts, looking for no further aide than Nature's ability, or as men
doe trades and occupations meerely to make a living by it, who reade the Scriptures, as
wee doe morall authors, collecting what pleaseth their fancy, to bee scattered as flowres
of Rhetoricke, here and there for the garnish of their discourse, but no whit for
sanctification of the heart.[62]

Humane learning was malleable, changing, open to challenge. Knowledge of
the divine made clear that humane learning was truly 'blindnesse, vanity,
inward filthinesse, and naturall corruption . . .'. Humane learning thus
became greater as it managed to approach the lessons of Scripture by imitation

---

[60]   Bod. Lib. MS Tanner 88, No. 1(g), fol. 6ᵛ.
[61]   Cartwright, *Replye to Answere*, sigs. L.iiij–v, X.iijᵛ. See also Taylor, *Christs Combate*, p. 253; Dering,
XXVII Lectures, sig. L.iᵛ: 'All counsels, all doctours, all examples, all decrees, all what you will, they are
not our schoolemasters, but our fellowe scholars, that we may learne together out of the worde
of God . . .'.   [62]   Pemble, *Plea for Grace*, p. 18.

of purpose; it became dangerous when it forgot its place, and aspired to be an *alternate focus* for man's being. Only Scripture, after all, contained the key to salvation, and represented a constant, fixed essence of truth which man could only absorb, not legitimately alter.[63] Puritans, then, were wholly people of the Book.

Another reason for wariness concerning humane learning was the confusion that certain sources might cause in readers. The simplicity of the Gospel, readily comprehensible by the masses, stood in stark contrast to the labyrinth of learning's structures, which could not easily be explained. An extreme example of such concern was the response to Richard Hooker's *Laws of Ecclesiastical Polity*. Puritans subjected it to a good deal of criticism for its ornate language and involved allusions, which, they argued, blinded rather than aided the seeker of godly knowledge. Where the puritan, of course, saw the Bible as containing *all* necessary knowledge, Hooker viewed it as a 'doctrinal statement' from which 'saving knowledge' was to be deduced by the 'industry of right discourse'. An anonymous reply to Hooker charged that the defenders of the church confused the populace by making the learning which came from reason equal to revelation.[64] The attack on Hooker's style and his use of learning was merciless:

your bookes bee so long and tedious, in a stile not usuall, and (as wee verelie thinke) the like harde to be found; farre differing from the simplicitie of holie Scripture, and nothing after the frame of the writinges of the Reverend and learned Fathers of our church, as of Crammer [*sic*], Ridley, Latimer, Iewell, Whitgeeft, Fox, Fulke, etc. And that your Prefaces and discourses before you come to the question are so longe, & mingled with all kinde of matters and sutes of learning and doctrine: whether your meaning bee to shewe your selfe to bee some rare Demosthenes, or extraordinarie Rabbi, or some great Pythagoras, that enioyne your schollars or your adversaries to five yeares silence, before they can be perfect in your meaning or able to replye: or that these men you write against, bee not sounde in matters of fayth; and therefore you handle all thinges, or else you had no better way to make doubtfull the chief groundes of our faith and religion, and that you would have men better seene in Philosophie and schoolmens divinitie, and namelie in Aristotle: or that were afearde, that if you had no handled it with so grave, heroicall and loftie a maiestie, you should have bene reputed like some other man, and so your fame should have bene but small . . . or that you would shew your selfe another Aristotle by a certaine metaphisicall and crupticall method to bring men into a maze, that they should rather wonder at your learning, the[n] be able to understand what you teach in your writinge.[65]

---

[63] Bolton, *Workes*, pp. 44–5. See also Thomas Granger's illustration that even Solomon had been wise only because he possessed a 'special illumination of the Spirit of God' (*Exposition on Ecclesiastes*, p. 39); in like fashion, Rous, *Arte of Happiness*, pp. 29–31; Rous, *Diseases of the Time*, pp. 25, 27, 155.

[64] Anon., *Christian Letter . . . unto . . . R. Hoo.*, p. 43.

[65] *Ibid.*, p. 45. It is worthy of note that Whitgift is included in the list of wise authorities; his doctrine was not at issue.

So harshly were the combined dangers of vanity, of confusion, and of forgetting the proper role of the minister painted by those who sought a purity of religion.

This theme of the confusion caused by learning permeated puritan thought throughout our period. Thomas Granger warned that only faith could prevent the Bedlam-like disorientation which learning naturally caused:

if a man be not guided by the Spirit, his observations are but superstitious, and false rules, his readings erroneous, yea, though he hath read all Bookes, and hath not roote or seede in himselfe, he is but in a maze tossed too and fro, hearing and seeing as in a dreame: In a word, he wants wisedome, he hath no learning.[66]

John Northbrooke even reiterated Ambrose's warning that the learned had indeed had (and here the implication was, always would have) a professional stake in maintaining the confusion of humane learning.[67] By the 1640s the awareness had crystalized among radicals that the 'confusion' caused by advanced learning was to a large extent class-oriented.[68] Originally, however, puritans centred on the fear that the involved techniques of learning could easily subvert progress towards godliness among the less well-educated.

This confusion also had another inherent danger: as it muddled both the learned and the multitude, it served to foster irreligion. The examples of both ancient heathens and contemporary papists established firmly that learning did not necessarily lead to godliness. It seemed a telling comment on the perversity of learning that quite often the most learned people were the hardest to convert. Samuel Wright emphasized that Christ had favoured 'the contemptible, the base and despised ones of the world; the simple and unlettered multitude are for him . . .; The great clerkes, the famous doctours, they stand against him.'[69] John Udall insisted that the delights of learning could interfere with 'the power of the spirit to cast downe mans pride . . .'.[70] William Pemble warned of 'this leprosie of Atheisticall contempt of Gods wisedome'.[71] William Ames himself listed eight ways in which humane wisdom could be carnal. First came the occasions on which it directly opposed God; also included were its refusal to subordinate itself to God's wisdom, and its argument that its own methods were superior to those of heavenly wisdom.[72]

---

[66] Granger, *Exposition on Ecclesiastes*, pp. 40–1.   [67] Northbrooke, *Poore Mans Garden*, fol. 54ᵛ.
[68] See, for example, Greaves, 'Early Quakers and educational reform', esp. p. 30; Hill, *Change and Continuity in Seventeenth-Century England*, Ch. 5: 'The radical critics of Oxford and Cambridge in the 1650s'.   [69] Wright, *Divers Godly and Learned Sermons*, pp. 194–5.
[70] Udall, *Certaine Sermons*, sig. H.iiᵛ. Wright, *Divers Godly and Learned Sermons*, p. 195. See also the phrase of Dod and Cleaver: 'the many have beene fooles, and yet learned Philosophers . . .' (Dod & Cleaver, *Exposition of Eleventh and Twelfth Chapters of Proverbs*, p. 115).   [71] Pemble, *Plea for Grace*, p. 18.
[72] Ames, *Conscience*, Bk III, p. 67. The other five represented occasions on which 1) learning condemned the wisdom of God; 2) it made a man incapable of 'those things which are of the spirit of God'; 3) it was a matter of boasting; 4) trust and confidence were (wrongly) placed in it; 5) it was separated from innocence and sincerity.

Thomas Adams attacked the achievements of the high Middle Ages by noting that 'use', so important a part of religion to those concerned with individual repentance and conversion to a godly existence, had ranked at the bottom of mediaeval successes.[73] Again, puritan writers used biographical description for emphasis. The life of Robert Bolton noted the common juxtaposition of advanced learning and retarded godliness in so many learned university men:

But all this while though he was very learned, yet he was not good, he was a very meane scholler in the schoole of CHRIST, he drew no religious breath from the soyle he came, and his master like an ill seedsman sowed the tares of Popery in most of his schollers: this manner of education made him more apt to tread in any path than that which was holy; he loved Stage-playes, cards and dice, he was a horrible swearer and sabbath-breaker, and boone-companion . . . he loved not goodnesse nor good men, and of all sorts of people could not abide their company that were of a strict and holy conversation, such he would fetch within the compasse of *Puritans*, thinking that by the lawlesse name he had deprived them *ipso facto* both of learning and good religion.[74]

The question of most immediate concern for most puritans was therefore not the degree to which reason offered the same conclusions as faith, but rather the degree to which humane learning, with its different interests, could serve as a temptation to confuse and seduce Christian scholars.[75] Praise of knowledge by puritans thus intended primarily 'the precepts revealed by God concerning the path to salvation'.[76] Those who attempted to make an academic pursuit out of a free gift were in grievous error.[77] At the end of our period, in the cataclysm of the Revolution, many radical groups turned away from formal learning, and relied instead on Scripture and the light of inspiration.[78] Puritans, however, traditionally attempted the more difficult task of scrupulously maintaining a delicate balance of spirit and philosophy. This had ever been their desire. Henry Smith, for example, had encapsulated this approach with his prayer that the 'Lorde Jesus so moderate our learning with his bold feare, that wee may directe al our studies to the enlarging of his glorie and kingdome here on earth.'[79]

For puritans, the central fact of human existence was thus the relationship, in all its intricacies, of the individual and God, not the free being in control of his own destiny. Intellectually, the pre-revolutionary puritan reaction to

[73] Adams, *Workes*, p. 903.
[74] Bolton, *Last & Learned Worke*, 'Life', sig.b3^{r-v}. See also Burroughes, *Excellency of Gracious Spirit*, pp. 342–5, for the similar story of Julian the Apostate, whose great learning had not prevented him from becoming 'a vile cursed Monster'.   [75] See, for example, Sibbes, *Christians Portion*, pp. 128–33.
[76] Burroughes, *Excellency of Gracious Spirit*, pp. 225–6. See also Hildersam, *CLII Lectures*, pp. 495, 496.   [77] Preston, *Saints Qualification*, pp. 43–5.
[78] See Hill, *World Turned Upside Down*, *passim*, and esp. pp. 210–15, for those who questioned even the authority of printed Scripture.   [79] Smith, *Lawiers Question*, sig. B2.

learning was based on the premise that fallen man, equipped only with corrupted reason, could never discover *arcana Dei* by his rational powers alone. And yet, despite learning's inferiority and dangers, foremost of which was the vanity that could deny the supremacy of grace over reason, puritans did not deny learning any role whatsoever on the long march to the New Jerusalem. All the citations above and the argument which developed from them, had been for the purpose of criticism rather than utter condemnation. At times, the puritan espousal of the sufficiency of pure, divine wisdom seems to contradict the requirement that humane learning (and especially its methods) be mastered by the clerical mediators of godliness. And yet, the point is that puritans *did* stress (and practise) the importance of this mixing of earthly and heavenly. The puritan road to Jerusalem *did*, in spite of questions raised during construction, detour through Athens. It is, then, now time to examine the reasons why Athens aroused such interest, and the methods by which a seemingly unnecessary stopover was explained to be a required pause.

5

>>

THE ROLE AND STATUS
OF MINISTERS

I

Rosemary O'Day has recently argued that it is possible to trace in the eighty years before the Revolution the emergence of what may fruitfully be termed a 'profession' in the ministry, in the modern sense of a group possessing a corporate structure, with a complement of personnel especially trained for the particular vocation, and a system of regulation.[1] First, and most important in her interpretation, is the broad trend she sees towards a laicization in the church – that is, towards greater lay control of the structure of the church and against the functional separation of a distinct clerical caste. Secondly, she notes increasing pressures for the purification of religious life in both individuals and the Church. Thirdly, she emphasizes the general application of much more rigorous standards for entry into this ministerial 'profession'.[2] Central to this 'professionalization' was the changing function of the minister: 'The Reformation in England undermined the clerical position. Now that the priest was no longer necessary as a mediator between the individual soul and God, a new *raison d'être* had to be sought, either consciously or unconsciously.'[3] O'Day immediately suggests that this 'was to be found in the pastoral function of the Reformed ministry',[4] which she regards as the real key to 'professionalization'. She also emphasizes the advent of the notion that ministers should be given special training for their various functions.

---

[1] O'Day, *English Clergy, passim.*

[2] In raising the question of 'professionalization', O'Day leans to a certain degree on the categories earlier suggested by Charlton, 'The professions in sixteenth-century England', *Univ. of Birmingham Historical Journal*, 12, pp. 21–3. Charlton's criteria of a profession were: 1) a professional relationship with a client; 2) the offering of a *public* service to the community; 3) the possession of theoretical knowledge, as distinct from practical knowledge gained from experience; 4) a period of training which involves higher education in a specialized institution; 5) a special organization which 'qualifies' its members; 6) existence as a social group with its own hierarchy and social life; 7) a particular status, though there may well be a difference between what the profession claims and what the society confers. Charlton was careful to note, however, that historians would not be likely to find all his criteria collected together in any early modern setting. Charlton also concluded (*ibid.*, p. 41) that professionalization was aided by (and contributed to) a growing division of labour in the sixteenth century, and also a growing secularization – the belief that human effort could cure earthly evils.

[3] O'Day, *English Clergy*, p. 126.   [4] *Ibid.*

It must be granted that there is much evidence to support this view of professionalization, to wit: the rapidly improving standard of education of ministerial entrants; the organization of the 'self-help' groups (prophesyings,
exercises, household seminaries) aimed at sharing education and scriptural
exegesis; and the development of what may be termed a 'community feeling'
among ministers which is fairly taken as a mark of any modern profession. But
there are also immediate objections to this view. Though O'Day notes the difficulty of including the ministry with earth-bound professions, there is little
real concession to the problem of dealing with an occupation which stretched
beyond the sublunary realm. The Reformation produced a great debate over
the nature of ministerial vocation, a question which distinguished ministers
from all other 'professionals' in this period.

At the core of puritan being, I have argued, lay 'enthusiasm', a quality
which at the second level of existence puritans attempted to restrain severely,
though certainly not to eliminate. This continuing paradox, this eternal clash
between 'enthusiasm' and learning which forms one of the major themes here,
led puritans to push for what we might call professional attitudes and standards, while at the same time they refused to rely on these standards alone. In
this sense, perhaps a closer parallel to the minister than the other (secular) professions was the Head of State, the monarch who was also to be trained (as
especially the humanists asserted), but who also was first, *ex officio*, the Lord's
anointed. Training might well make a superior monarch, but the crown did
not depend on learning. So it was, argued puritans, with ministers. Knowledge
of Scripture, of the arts, and of the forms of religion could not alone make a
godly minister – the Jesuits were living proof of that. Only God's special calling, which provided the core of enthusiasm, could accomplish this feat. So
Samuel Ward agonized and sought counsel on this very question before he
could bring himself to practise the ministry for which, by earthly standards, he
was eminently qualified.[5] This may, in part, explain the popularity of the
puritan household seminaries of the early seventeenth century which took
university graduates and trained them not only in the practical tasks of a pastoral ministry, but also in developing a sense of a calling by God.[6] Human
training was therefore to be combined with the mystery of God's selection.
Only after the emphasis on the dramatic struggle for conversion – which was
at the heart of the puritan version of religious experience – had been
downplayed could the 'profession' emerge. Conversion was a non-rational, in
a sense even an *ir*rational, experience. When learning became the prime
requirement in a minister, then the non-rational core of lively faith was sub-
verted as the primary mode of existence. Puritans consciously resisted the
realization of this goal, though they did not reject all its aspects.

[5]   Knappen, ed., *Two Puritan Diaries*, p. 128.
[6]   On puritan household seminaries, see below, pp. 292–300.

While recent research has provided us with a great deal of knowledge about the socio-economic conditions of ministers, and to that extent suggests that many of the outward marks of professionalization had been accomplished by 1642, a due consideration of the ministers' own perception of the non-rational aspects of their purposeful existence points to a set of powerful beliefs which inhibited the growth of a modern profession established on a rational basis. If the ministry was not fully professionalized in the modern sense, what then can be said about the role and status of ministers? This is a matter of great importance in the present study since, as I argued above, ministers largely determined methods and content of education. Puritans of course desired special training for ministers, but their view of the ministry extended far beyond this to a group separated by God's calling, which was to serve as the nation's moral and intellectual elite. They perhaps did not hope to be an 'estate', in the mediaeval or *ancien régime* sense, but they did aim (though the word has certain difficulties) to elevate the ministry to the level of a special caste, which operated within society, but which in a sense stood outside its hierarchy.

O'Day has contended that ministers after the Reformation no longer played the crucial role, traditional in the Christian church, of mediators between man and God, that is, to some degree acting as mediums or agencies of salvation. Certainly, ministers could no longer perform the central miracle of the Roman mass, nor could they absolve people of responsibility and punishment for their sins. Nor could it be said categorically that God would not save any who were deprived of a minister. But far more frequent was the cry that 'thousands of souls' were lost because of insufficient or negligent ministers.[7] But how could this be, if they were not needed as 'mediators'? Puritans (and English protestants generally) stressed that God no longer often wrenched sinners from the mire, as he had Paul. Now he was content to allow his ministers to act for him as mediators, to spread the Word, to urge repentance, to comfort struggling and doubting souls. So Richard Greenham stated baldly that as God had appointed magistrates to rule, and schoolmasters to teach, so had he provided ministers to save souls and act as agents of grace. Richard Bernard was even more succinct: 'Who ever by an ordinary course were won to God but by the Ministery'? And John Brinsley Junior, son of the famous educational writer, noted specifically that ministers were 'agents betwixt God and his people', and added that they should preach to the people 'as Heralds, in the name, in the authority of him that sendeth them . . .'.[8] Arthur Hildersam explained that the *public* ministry, by which he meant especially sermons, was crucial to salvation. Only ministers had the ability to interpret and apply the

---

[7]   See, for example, the many statements and petitions to this effect in the Morrice MSS, partly printed in Peel, ed., *Seconde Parte of a Register*.
[8]   Greenham, *Workes*, pp. 340, 342, 735; Bernard, *Faithfull Shepheard* (1621), p. 7; Brinsley, Jr, *Preachers Charge*, pp. 4, 7.

Word; but, more important, God used the spoken sermon as 'the meanes whereby hee will worke all saving grace . . . in the hearts of his elect . . .'.[9]

There are, indeed, logical difficulties with this position. Puritans held, along with other English protestants, that the elect had been chosen from before time. The implication of Hildersam's message, however (and it was commonplace), is that those who did not attend sermons would likely not be saved. Protestants, including puritans, were hesitant to say that one *could not* be saved without sermons, since this was to lay the blame for damnation on the failings of the non-preaching minister; after all, even where there was a preaching minister, most protestants expected most people to be damned. Rather, the sense is that while the elect were chosen by God before time, they had both a dormant quality within them (which the force of a godly sermon awoke) and the need for the interpretation of Scripture which the minister brought in his sermon for application to specific cases. It might be the case, as Perkins argued, that the godly would lead godly lives, but they would not do so without instruction; the will of the godly needed guidance for correct participation in the fallen world.

In seeing the office of the minister as an ordinance of God, puritans stood squarely in the Reformed tradition. Indeed, Calvin himself had seen ministers as dispensers of salvation, standing in place of Jesus as mediators between man and God.[10] Luther, too, at times had seen the office as a 'distinct, a divine institution'.[11] Nor was this opinion simply the self-defence of a 'profession'. Puritan ministers possessed a 'populist' as well as a clericalist strain.[12] They were concerned as much to shape their message for effect as to establish the formal structure of a true ministry. These two aims, sometimes divergent, and occasionally contradictory in popular effect, are a crucial aspect of the impact of puritan preaching in the period before the Revolution. But in terms specifically of developing attitudes towards learning and education, the mediating role of ministers in the drive to assurance of salvation took pride of place.

Ministers existed to preach obedience to the lower orders and the obligation of a just rule to the powerful of society. In this they reflected the continuation of the Christian tradition that the commonwealth was required by natural law (as well as by the pursuit of godly standards) to be hierarchical, moral, and interdependent. The juxtaposition and interrelationship of the monarch, the ministry, social order and salvation with learning were by no means coincidental: learning and the concomitant ability to teach all levels of

[9] Hildersam, *CLII Lectures*, pp. 499–501.   [10] Hall, *Faithful Shepherd*, p. 6.
[11] Gerrish, 'Priesthood and ministry', p. 415. Gerrish notes that Luther could not always easily correlate this view with the doctrine of the priesthood of all believers.
[12] I am indebted to Peter Lake for emphasizing this point in private correspondence.

society their duty was the basis of the continued status of ministers. In return, godly gentlemen recognized the unique role of the ministry, upon which educational attitudes in this age were still heavily, though of course not exclusively, based.[13] It is almost unknown in the godly biographies for conversion to occur except as the direct result of ministerial action, specifically of the workings of grace caused in the hearts of those who listened to sermons. Even future ministers were turned to godliness by the mediation of those whom God had called; the conversion of Richard Sibbes by Paul Baynes, of John Cotton by Sibbes, and of John Preston by Cotton is only the best-known example of this godly succession.

But though the centrality of the minister had been preserved, his necessary credentials underwent a metamorphosis during and following the Reformation. Though puritans still accepted the importance of the sacraments, these were now seen as the seals of a pre-existing relationship between the individual and God. In practice and thought puritans exchanged altars for pulpits as the proper method of bringing God and the elect together. Sound had thus been added to the dramatic mime of the pre-Reformation priest. But though the Reformation brought the minister closer to the people – both during the vernacular service and as a married member of the community – the cleric was not 'just like' anyone else in the community, nor was he expected to be. He was expected, especially in rural parishes, to be the most learned man, for both religious and secular reasons.

As the leader in the ever-present struggle against ungodliness, he was also not bound by the usual limits of the social hierarchy. Occasional criticism of the well-born and the powerful became an important feature of the ministers' social function. In this, puritans were in agreement with continental Reformed beliefs. Peter Gerard insisted that preachers should be able to speak openly 'not onely to Artizans and labourers, but also to kings and great Lordes, so that they keepe themselves within the compasse of their dutie'. Edward Dering's intemperate critique of Elizabeth's policy may have cost him dearly, but it is testament to his view of his calling that he would not shirk his godly responsibility wherever he saw it. Thomas Wood's criticism of the Earl of Leicester's conduct becomes much more understandable in this light.[14] But Leicester's detailed defence also tells us much. That he even bothered to reply (as he surely would not have replied to a *lay* inferior) is indicative, but that his retort was a *defence*, rather than a reminder that inferiors did not rightly criticize superiors, is crucial. Wood's action could be given legitimacy within the bounds of social conceptualization only by placing the vocation of the minister outside that group described solely by earthly criteria. Indeed, puritan ministers seem to

---

[13] See, for example, Hastings, *Watch-Word*, pp. 21–2. Francis Hastings was a Leicestershire M.P. and the younger brother of the third Earl of Huntingdon.

[14] Gerard, *Preparation for Ministerie*, p. 19; *Letters of Thomas Wood*, ed. Collinson.

have considered the willingness of the gentry to accept criticism (and appropriately reform their conduct) as a mark of godliness.[15] In this sense the minister possessed the privilege of a special caste rather than the mere outward characteristics of a 'professional'. As long as the fervent core – the 'enthusiasm' – remained a central aspect of the leaders of the godly, they existed on a special plane of their own.

It would not be a great exaggeration to say that puritan schemes of education for the ministry were oriented largely towards preparing the minister for the ascent of the steps which took him above the congregation. The sermon, after all, was the prime means by which God moved his elect to repentance and faith. It was the dedication to the necessity of frequent sermons that caused puritans to oppose unequivocally non-residence, reading ministers, and unlearned clerics incapable of expounding the Word.[16] Preaching was to be extended to 'all the dark corners of this Kingdom . . . to those people that sit in darkness and in the shadow of death'.[17] The hierarchy of the English church was, of course, not opposed to preaching. Whitgift himself admitted that, all other things being equal, 'the oftner a man dothe preache . . . the better it is'.[18] Nonetheless, puritans constantly accused bishops of temporizing over the implementation of a spiritual necessity by supporting the reading of homilies.[19] Whitgift's argument that sermons should come only from the well-learned, and then only infrequently, convinced his opponents that the institution of a fully preaching ministry took a distant second place to the establishment of proper order.[20] And while he protested his desire for a preaching ministry, he maintained that reading could be as efficacious as preaching in leading some of the flock to salvation.[21] At the end of our period,

[15] For other examples of this phenomenon, see Cliffe, *Puritan Gentry*, esp. pp. 10–11, 126, 133–4, 166–7. Not all magnates were willing to be corrected. Burghley, a friend of the puritans, and quite often their supplicant with Whitgift, replied in a rather acerbic tone to a correcting letter from Dering which had suggested that Burghley should provide Thomas Cartwright with a public lectureship in Cambridge. Burghley replied with a defence of his activities, and signed the letter 'Yours to be taught, but not to be condemned, W. B.' (B.L. MS Lansdowne 102, No. 86 (3 April 1572)). For a general rationale of the minister's duty in performing such a function, see Gataker, *Abraham's Decease*, sig. C2.
[16] But for cases of puritans guilty of non-residence and pluralism, see Greaves, *Society and Religion*, pp. 59, 60–1; Haigh, 'Puritan evangelism', *E.H.R.*, 92, pp. 33ff.
[17] Sibbes, *Saints Safety*, p. 331, in *Complete Works of Richard Sibbes*, ed. Grosart. This plea was ubiquitous in the puritan literature; see Hill, *Society and puritanism*, Ch. 2.
[18] Whitgift, *Answere to the Admonition*, in *Works*, ed. Ayre, I, 83.
[19] For examples of the defence of homilies, see Cosin, *Answer,* sig. D.viff.; Bridges, *Defence*, pp. 495–7.
[20] Whitgift argued that 'four godly, learned, pithy, diligent and discreet preachers might do more good in London than forty contentious, unlearned, verbal and rash preachers'; quoted in Herr, *Elizabethan Sermon*, p. 17. See also B.L. MS Lansdowne 64, No. 32, fol. 86, Knollys to Burghley, 31 Mar. 1590, expressing the opinion that both men knew 'how vyolent the Archebysshoppe [Whitgift] hathe often bene agaunst the request of the parlement' for a learned, preaching ministry.
[21] Whitgift, *Answere to Admonition*, pp. 159, 163; *idem, Defence of Answer*, pp. 539, 542.

the efforts of the administration seemed to be directed more at the restriction than at the provision of sermons.[22]

Much of the learned puritan insistence on sermons derived from Paul's admonitions to the early Christian settlements.[23] But the ground-level emphasis on preaching also continued a pre-Marian tradition based on observation of the still-unreformed context.[24] Common were the outcries that maintained that preaching was 'most necessarie for the welfare of the soule'[25] and that the poor people were 'vexed with the want of the word preached'.[26] Fear was expressed that 'for want of faith by preaching, wee bee condemned with the Divel and his angels into hell fire . . .'.[27] Puritans argued for ever more frequent sermons, but at bottom it was more a question of expounding the Word *whenever* an assembly for worship occurred, than simply a debate over a minimum number of sermons to be preached in a year. God's command to preach thus took precedence over the attempts of the authorities to limit exposition of the Word.[28] Nor should mere 'reading' ministers be allowed to substitute the leaner fare of homilies for the richer diet of sermons.[29] Those who could not preach, it was frequently argued, were not true ministers, and should be removed.[30] Even to read the sermon of another minister was to reduce one's role as special intermediary between God and penitents. Proper preaching therefore served as the central task of the ministry, even above the administration of the sacraments and the establishment of a proper discipline within the church.

[22] See, for example, the Orders issued at the primary visitation of Matthew Hutton in the diocese of Norwich, 1636, esp. No. 23: 'Whereas Sermons are required by the Church of Englande, only upon Sondayes and holy dayes in the Forenoones, and are permitted at funneralls, that none presume to take upon them to use any preachinge or expowndinge (or to holde any such lecturinge) at any othe [sic] tyme, withowte expresse lycence from the Byshoppe' (*Winthrop Papers*, III, pp. 374–5).

[23] For example, Romans 10.17; I Corinthians 1.17; II Timothy 4.2, and the Geneva Bible marginal comments.   [24] Greaves, *Society and Religion*, p. 79.

[25] Morrice MSS, Vol. B, I, p. 465. See also *Aunswere to the Complaint*, p. 131, in *A Parte of a Register*; Becon, *Catechisme,* pp. 307, 566; More, *Three Godly Sermons*, pp. 66–7; Babbage, *Bancroft*, p. 16; Stockwood, *Sermon at Paules Crosse*, sig. Avj.

[26] Morrice MSS, *passim*, for example, Vol. B, I, pp. 135–6, 144–5, 163, 177, 191, 326–7.

[27] *Petition of Communalitie*, p. 326, in *A Parte of a Register*; *Dialogue Concerning strife of Churche*, 'To the Christian Reader', *passim*.

[28] Coolidge, *Pauline Renaissance*, p. 57; also p. 26. See also Goodman, *Superior Powers*, pp. 29–31, 40–1; *Copie of a Letrer [sic]*, pp. 154–6ff. in *A Parte of a Register*; Craig, Jr, 'Geneva Bible as political document', *The Pacific Historical Review*, 7, pp. 43–4, for the implications of the marginal comments to I Kings 18.17–18 and II Kings 9.37.

[29] See Morrice MSS, Vol. B, II, fol. 198; C.U. Archives, Guard Book 6(i), No. 39; H. Smith, *Thirteene Sermons*, sigs. D4, V5; Gilpin, *Godly Sermon*, p. 23; Davies, *Worship of English Puritans*, p. 188. At the same time, Thomas Lever argued that in the absence of a minister, an honest layman might read Christian lessons to the congregation (I.T.L. MS Petyt 538, vol. 38, fol. 71^v).

[30] Morrice MSS, Vol. B, II, fols. 119, 219; Anon., *Learned Discourse*, p. 60; Bradshaw, *Briefe Forme of Examination*, p. 103; Dering, *Sermon before Queenes Maiesty*, sig. C.ii^v; Northbrooke, *Poore Mans Garden*, p. 228; Fenner, *Counter-poyson*, p. 55; B.L. MS Harley 6849, fol. 231^v; B.L. MS Harley 419, fol. 140^v.

Ignorance of religion was also transposed to other fields closer to the concerns of authority. Far more likely to appeal to the magistrate than reminders of divine law was the sound political tactic of suggesting that 'where there is a preaching pastor, the people, for the most part, are very well given.'[31] The causal connexion of preaching and social control seems to have been especially popular with important laymen whose specific vocation included the pacification of the general populace, and would include the military reduction of any papist uprising or invasion. So the 'gentry of Suffolk', in a petition of 1592 to the Council, commented on the daily decline of the church, due, they argued, to the harassment of godly preachers for minor offences. The petitioners were careful to point out that they had favoured no relaxation of doctrinal conformity; as magistrates they had proceeded harshly, they noted, against papists, Familists, Brownists, and Anabaptists, all described as 'the overthrowers of Church and common weal'.[32] A plea from the countryside went so far as to pose a close relationship between lower-class unrest and a dearth of preaching; the paucity of sermons meant that 'even our Servants and Apprentices are . . . so rude and unreformed as we are not able to keep them in any good Government, but cleane against our minds they also are ready to run headlong to all desperate attempts for wante of the feare of God . . .'.[33] Even secular authorities unmoved by the religious appeal of preaching might have felt uneasy about forsaking such a valuable method of social control.[34]

Within the English church in the late sixteenth century there also grew an emphasis on the pastoral aspect of the ministry that reflected the strong protestant concern that theology should not be separated from daily existence.[35] This concern with the flock was the staple of the presbyterian argument (likely derived from Calvin) in favour of the separate office of the pastor, who was to be concerned with the specific application of doctrine to members of the congregation.[36] Perhaps chief in importance among these extra-pulpit duties was catechizing, a venture which the minister led but which bound household

---

[31] *C.S.P.D. Addenda, 1580–1625*, p. 129, Earl of Huntingdon to Walsingham, 22 Nov. 1584. See also Neale, *Elizabeth I and her Parliaments*, II, p. 154, quoting Francis Hastings in the Commons; Nichols, *Plea of the Innocent*, pp. 224ff.; Granger, *Application of Scripture*, p. 4; Morrice MSS, Vol. B, I, pp. 160, 170, 181, 191; Gonville & Caius MS 197/103, p. 528. For reminders of divine law, see *Abstract Of Certain Acts*, p. 39; Hildersam, *Treatise of Ministery*, p. 102; Morrice MSS, Vol. B, I, p. 197.

[32] *C.S.P.D. 1591–1594*, p. 277. See also Morrice MSS, Vol. B, I, pp. 133–4, 211–12; Vol. B, II, fols. 121–3; *C.S.P.D. 1601–1603 & Addenda*, pp. 213–14; Hastings, *Watch-Word*, pp. 21–2.

[33] Morrice MSS, Vol. A, N.L.P., p. 118. See also *ibid.*, Vol. B, I, p. 170; B.L. MS Lansdowne 109, No. 11, fol. 11.

[34] Not all authorities placed order before the Christian duty of evangelization. Francis Knollys, in a 1584 letter to Whitgift, suggested giving more liberty to 'diligent zealous preachers of the ghospell' even if 'they have otherwyse infirmytyes as well in discretion, as in deepnes of judgement concerning matters poletyke and thynges Indifferent . . .' (B.L. MS Lansdowne 43, No. 9, fol. 17).

[35] For a prime example, see Crooke, *Ministeriall Husbandry*, Epistle Dedicatory.

[36] See, for example, Travers, *Defence of Ecclesiasticall Discipline*, p. 63, which acknowledges derivation of the idea from Calvin.

and ministerial office together. William Bradshaw explained that the presbyterian office of 'doctor' was specifically dedicated to giving instruction 'by
way of Catechizing the Ignorant of the Congregation ... in the maine
grounds & principles of Religion'.[37] The purpose was to balance the
ubiquitous threat of damnation with a frequent encouragement to godly practices. Richard Greenham, that paragon of the Elizabethan ministry, required
ministerial visits to the household on a more frequent basis than the church
was willing to legislate even for sermons. The example of Robert Bolton
recorded this conjunction of threat and encouragement that constituted the
approach of the puritan minister:

And though in his manner of preaching he was a Sonne of thunder, yet unto bruised
reeds and those that mourned in spirit, hee was so sweete a sonne of Consolation as
ever I heard, and with a very tender and pitifull heart powred the oyle of mercy into
their bleeding wounds.[38]

The vast number of domestic manuals which dealt seriously and yet
encouragingly with 'cases of conscience' is testimony to the importance of the
pastoral bond which grew after the Reformation. This accorded with Thomas
Cartwright's injunction that non-residents were bound to be ignorant of the
spiritual ills of their parishioners: 'it is as muche as if eyther the surgeon
shoulde applye hys plaister/or the Physition hys medicine/when they neyther
knowe of the wounde or disease of their pacients'.[39]

But post-Reformation ministers were also acutely aware that they were
judged not solely on the basis of their professional duties of preaching and
counselling. Ever more stress was laid by the vocation itself on the conduct, or
'conversation', of its members.[40] Puritans, too, emphasized the need for this
separate caste, as God's chosen mediators, to provide especial examples of
godly conversation.[41] There was a populist basis for this concern. Thomas
Tuke noted that congregations 'respect the life more then preaching . . .'.[42]
They were hardly likely to take correction from corrupt ministers, or to

---

[37] Bradshaw, *English Puritanisme*, p. 21.
[38] Bolton, *Last and Learned Worke*, fol. 107ᵛ ('Life', by Edward Bagshaw). See also Bod. Lib. MS Tanner 75,
      No. 60, fol. 318.
[39] Cartwright, *Replye to Answere*, sigs. G.iiij–vj; cf. Greenham, *Workes*, pp. 344–5; John Rogers, 'Sixty
      memorials for a godly life', in Cotton Mather, *Magnalia Christi Americana*, I, p. 424.
[40] Richard Greaves has recently noted that this emphasis was not unique to protestants. The Rheims New
      Testament annotations also insisted that bishops should conduct a thorough examination of the faith,
      learning and life of candidates for the priesthood (*Society and Religion*, p. 73).
[41] The well-known puritan surveys of the ministry in the various countries reflect this concern. A 1604(?)
      survey of Essex included mention of 94 preachers who were accounted 'diligent & of honest life' and
      106 ministers 'of scandulous life', as well as other categories (B.L. MS Add. 38,492, fol. 89. See also
      Greaves, *Society and Religion*, pp. 94ff.).
[42] Tuke, *True Protestant*, p. 35. See also Taylor, *Commentarie on Titus*, p. 111; Gilby, *Pleasaunt Dialogue*, sig.
      D3ᵛ; Bernard, *Faithfull Shepheard* (1621), pp. 75–6; Haller, *Rise of Puritanism*, p. 116.

believe an obvious sinner when he attempted to tell them of the struggle
needed to progress along the pathway to salvation. Puritans, aware of the difficulty of removing insufficient or corrupt ministers, therefore pressed very
hard to allow only the pure into the vocation. Thus Elizabethan presbyterians
recommended investigation of the personal conduct of those candidates
deemed suitable for the ministry on their other merits.[43] Indeed, so adamant
were puritans that the office alone could not effectively reform the man that
they fell victim on occasion to accusations of Donatism, which they adamantly
denied.[44] Perhaps this was one reason why the Dedham *classis*, in a meeting of
July 1584, decided to conduct a survey of ministers to find out not only who
was unlearned (and therefore insufficient), but also who was 'notoriouslye
offensyve in Liffe'.[45] Puritans were of course not alone in this concentration
on a moral behaviour,[46] but they provided a fuller and more emphatic version
of the same stress. Richard Bernard, in his manual for young divines, listed an
unreprovable and blameless life at the head of the requisite 'properties' of a
minister: 'A Ministers carriage should bee such as the well disposed should
love him, the indifferent should stand in awe, and the worst should bee kept
more in than perhaps they would, and not commit daily such outrages, as they
in their hearts desire.'[47] Richard Greenham supplied the reciprocal obligation
of ministers, that they should be willing to die for their flocks.[48]

O'Day concedes that the views of the reformers were 'in a very real sense,
less conducive to further professionalization of the clergy'.[49] This she puts
down to the congregational model pursued by most puritans in the period.
Congregationalism tended to tighten the local bonds between minister and
laity, while loosening those among the clergy, since they tended in this polity
to lack institutionalized forms of association.[50] The suggestion seems clear that
the puritans, with their close connexions to the lay godly, were less driven to
professionalization than were the Laudians and their regal ally, who strove to

---

[43] Even letters of reference, which invariably mentioned purity of conversation, were not to be trusted;
the investigation was evidently to be conducted independently (*Booke of Forme of Common Prayers*, pp.
17–18.   [44] See, for example, Taylor, *Davids Learning*, pp. 171–2.

[45] Usher, ed., *Presbyterian Movement*, p. 36.

[46] See, for example, Laud's lengthy denunciation of the 'excessive drunkenness' of the Lincolnshire clergy
(Hart, *Country Clergy*, p. 123).

[47] Bernard, *Faithfull Shepheard* (1621), pp. 75, 76, 77. Bernard actually listed the twelve 'properties' of a
good shepherd, and seven vices which should be avoided. The minister was to be of unreprovable and
blameless life; not a young scholar; watchful; temperate; modest; 'harborous'; apt to teach; gentle; a
lover of good things and good men; righteous; holy; and continent. He was not to be 'froward' (per-
verse); covetous; given to filthy lucre; given to wine; a quarreller; a fighter; of lewd life (*Faithfull
Shepheard* (1621), pp. 80–9. See also Ames, *Conscience*, Bk IV, Ch. 25, p. 65; *ibid.*, Bk V, Ch. 24.)

[48] Greenham, *Workes*, p. 342.

[49] O'Day, *English Clergy*, p. 239. She adds that there can be no doubt that the 'process of professionalization would have been more efficiently accomplished had the bishops held all the Church patronage'
(*ibid.*, p. 245).   [50] *Ibid.*, p. 241.

build a distinct group within society.[51] The congregational polity was not only a reaction to interference by the administration in the proper duties of the mediators, but also the simplest way in which a minister could establish a close bond with the people whose shepherd he was to be. Puritans did not reject the social hierarchy of the sublunary world, but they did insist that no earthly structure should come between God's mediators and the appointed tasks of their vocation.

II

Before the Reformation even the secular clergy had been accorded a special social status based on their peculiar role in society. The change of religion did not alter the general perception that ministers fitted into the social hierarchy just below gentlemen. The particular socio-economic background of puritan ministers occupied a wide spectrum, though there was an increasing number of entrants from the upper classes into the ministry as our period progresses. It should also be noted that sons of clergy provided a new post-Reformation source of ministers.[52] Although openings for lower-class entrants may have become fewer in Elizabethan and early Stuart Oxford and Cambridge, there was still a great desire for education as a step to a career. A degree did not level, but it could at times polish the edges of an otherwise rough background.[53]

A great concern within the church, perhaps especially among puritans, was to establish adequate provision to attract learned candidates (who, it was thought, could reasonably expect a higher income) without having to resort to pluralism.[54] Any economic lure attached to the ministry as a career is difficult to pinpoint. Despite Green's recent portrayal of a surfeit of positions in the church until perhaps the 1630s,[55] the average income can have brought limited financial comfort.[56] The ordinary clergy, with the exception of some well-paid town lecturers, continued generally to have to find its comforts in the spiritual rather than in the material sphere. The Reformation, it soon became clear, had produced a call for an improved ministry, but no system for

[51] *Ibid.*, pp. 238–9, on Elizabeth and Charles I.

[52] Green, 'Career prospects and clerical conformity', *Past and Present*, 90, p. 73.

[53] Christophers, 'Social and educational background of the Surrey clergy, 1520–1620', unpub. Ph.D. thesis, Univ. of London, 1975, pp. 46–7.

[54] Blench, *Preaching in England*, pp. 301–2; Hill, 'Plebeian irreligion', in Kossok, ed., *Studien über die Revolution*, pp. 50–1; *Winthrop Papers*, I, p. 304, 'Common Grievances', No. 14.

[55] Green, 'Career prospects and clerical conformity', pp. 93–103.

[56] Whitgift told Elizabeth that £30 per year was the accepted minimum for a minister with a degree, but that not 1 in 20 livings (i.e., under 500 in the whole country) measured up to this standard. Cited in Hill, *Economic Problems*, p. 205; see also *ibid.*, p. 204.

its financial amelioration.[57] Robert Harris voiced the common complaint that the costs invested in becoming a minister were seldom repaid: 'after you have spent your time, and your patrimony (two or three hundred pound it may be) for learnings sake to fit you for the ministry, a small meanes shall bee thought too much for you'.[58] Until the populace would pay, he warned his readers, it could expect no better than it was getting.[59]

There was evidently also strong feeling that the ministry was a full-time occupation. A minister demeaned his own status by taking an additional job; he also used time that could have been spent to the profit of his parishioners' souls. In an age in which few ministers below the level of rector could have lived comfortably on their church incomes, this was obviously a plea for enhanced salaries. This was a continuing problem throughout our period: in 1642 Nathaniel Fiennes was still complaining that 'in the clergy, some are so poor that they *cannot* attend their ministry, but are fain to keep schools, nay ale-houses some of them . . .'.[60] It was an old and popular cry. Thomas Cartwright had argued that the inequitable distribution of the church's wealth, as well as the flagrant use of power by the High Commission, had driven many ministers to quit their vocation and 'live by Phisicke and other suche meanes . . .'.[61] The purpose of the ministerial arguments against a 'labouring' ministry was, at least partly, defence of the status claimed as the specially chosen mediators of the Lord. So, while puritans favoured a choice of vocation based on talent rather than heredity, they tended to agree with contemporaries that, once an adult had made a choice, there should seldom be a change. So, not only did most of them frown upon the holding of an additional post; most also heartily opposed the entry into the ministry of those with previous secular callings.[62] Generally, however, there were two exceptions to this rule. Teaching was permitted because of the proximity of purpose of the two

---

[57] On this general question, see especially Hill, *Economic Problems*; Heal, 'Economic problems', in Heal & O'Day, eds., *Church and Society*, pp. 99–118; O'Day, *English Clergy*, esp. Ch. 13. However, there is some indication that the general standard of living of the clergy rose in the later sixteenth century Brooks, 'Social position', p. 37; Tyler, 'Status', in Cuming, ed., *Studies in Church History*, 4, pp. 76–97.

[58] Harris, *True Happinesse*, p. 185. See also Howson, *Sermon*, pp. 30–2, for a non-puritan statement of this common ministerial complaint.

[59] Harris, *Workes*, p. 246. See also Holme, *Burthen of the Ministerie*, sig. C.3ᵛ.

[60] Comment in the House of Commons, 1 Feb. 1641/2, quoted in Hill, *Economic Problems*, p. 39. See also Prynne, *Survay and Censure*, pp. 42–3.

[61] Cartwright, *Second Admonition*, pp. 22–6. See also *Winthrop Papers*, I, pp. 306–7, a statement against ministers with a cure of souls practising medicine for money.

[62] Morrice MSS, Vol. B, I, pp. 143–4. See also Travers, *Defence of Ecclesiasticall Discipline*, p. 132; *Winthrop Papers*, I, pp. 306–7; *Certaine Forme of Ecclesiastical Government*, p. 457, in *A Parte of a Register*. The corollary of this was Bishop Cooper's warning that ministers should not meddle in 'artificers' occupations' (Hart, *Country Clergy*, p. 33). At the end of our period, however, the radical Samuel How condemned ministers because they did *not* work for their own maintenance with their hands, as Christ had instructed the apostles (*Sufficiency*, p. 34). See also Hill, *Economic Problems*, pp. 208–9.

callings, and farming (as a minor, concurrent occupation) was not loudly objected to, presumably because of its ubiquity and necessity among poorly paid rural ministers. As well, the attitude towards former employments, if they had been entered merely as a stop-gap while awaiting a church living, was in practice frequently quite tolerant.[63]

It was this emphasis on vocation that became the most visible support of the status claimed by ministers within their communities. 'Whatsoever thou art', Thomas Adams told his readers, 'God hath honoured the poorest Minister above thee . . .'.[64] William Perkins counselled that 'the parents first and prin-cipall care must bee for the Church; that those of their children which have the most pregnant wit, and be imbued with the best gifts, be consecrated unto God, and brought up in the studie of Scriptures, to serve afterward in the Ministery of the Church'.[65] Against the background of a certain degree of economic deprivation, and occasional public ridicule, ministers such as George Gifford stressed the proper status due to God's intercessors. The populace, he argued, 'are bounde to esteeme them, as the Messengers of the Lorde of hosts, and *disposers of Gods graces*, they ought to submitte themselves unto them, to bee taught and guyded, and to obeye them in the doctrince [*sic*] whiche they teache: And to follow theyr steppes'.[66] This, as Greenham could have testified after his long years at Dry Drayton, was rampant optimism, though Greenham himself insisted that the people owed obedience to their ministers, since to disobey them was to 'despise the word and him that sent them . . .'. In order to emphasize the special rank of the minister as God's chosen mediator, Greenham required obedience only to doctrines which the minister delivered from the pure Word. Parishioners were not bound to follow the minister's 'owne devises'.[67] Though this restriction may have clarified the cleric's vocation, it may also have served to suggest to congregations that they test their own minister against the published Word.

As well as commenting on the obedience due to godly ministers, puritans expressed their fears that the ministry would not be able to attract suitable can-didates. Thomas Gataker noted that the callings – he included teaching – of which God thought most highly 'are commonly most disgraced and contemned in the World'.[68] Though Dorothy Leigh hoped that some of her sons would enter the ministry because it was such a 'high' calling,[69] Richard Bernard feared that the well-born would avoid the ministry because of low economic

---

[63] See, for example, the testimonial for John Fiske, sent by Robert Ryece to John Winthrop in 1637 (*Winthrop Papers*, III, p. 394).
[64] Adams, *Workes*, p. 76. See also Harris, *Samuels Funerall*, sig. A4ᵛ. [65] Perkins, *Workes*, III, p. 694.
[66] Gifford, *Catechisme*, sig. G.5ᵛ. (My italics.) [67] Greenham, *Workes*, pp. 350, 351.
[68] Gataker, *Davids Instructer*, p. 18. See also Gifford, *Catechisme*, sig. G.5ᵛ; C.U.L. MS Baker 38.9, p. 74, a letter from Toby Matthew to the Earl of Leicester; Hill, *Economic Problems*, pp. 208–11; Blench, *Preaching in England*, pp. 301–2. [69] Leigh, *Mothers Blessing*, p. 238.

reward and fear of harassment by the oppressive machinery of the church.[70] Also common was the belief that suspension for trivial offences and the little regard commonly paid ministers would mean that in future 'few will set their sonnes to learning, and thei which shall be set to it will rather turne their studies anie waie then to serve in the ministerie . . .'.[71] Indeed, despite modern historians' indications of a rising social background in the ministry, the period was rife with complaints of a lack of sons of gentry and noblemen in the vocation.[72] Bartimeus Andrewes insisted in 1583 that the people admitted were popularly thought to comprise 'ruffians, gamesters, fornicators, idolaters, popish prelates, idol ministers . . . dumb dogges, belly Gods, lovers of filthy lucre . . .'.[73] In turn, however, puritans reacted harshly against those who considered the ministry a base calling or who abused its members.[74] Indeed, in a conscious effort to raise the status of the ministry, they either pursued upper-class candidates or sought at least a close association of future ministers with the gentry.[75]

, That clergy continued to be ranked just below the gentry in contemporary social analyses seems to indicate success in the maintaining of status, despite the reduction of the church's independent power in the Reformation. As well as a doctrine of calling, it was the appropriation of, and the ability to maintain as secluded from the general population, a specific type and body of learning, that set off the godly ministers even from godly laymen.[76] Laymen, armed with the Reformation doctrine of the priesthood of all believers, might well require their minister to lay aside the surplice, and offer him protection in case of trouble with church authorities; conversely, they might influence him against open nonconformity for the sake of pastoral peace. Laymen exhorted in Parliament, and wrote their own way to salvation in diaries, but few of them, comparatively, counselled the reading public as to the true path of godliness. Save on the radical fringes, lay people seldom *formulated* new ideas concerning the structure of the church, the importance of the sacraments, or the proper role of the minister. They rather took sides in already-opened

---

[70]   See, for example, Bernard, *Faithfull Shepheard* (1621), pp. 5–6; Andrewes, *Certaine Verie Worthie Sermons*, p. 121.

[71]   Morrice MSS, Vol. B, I, pp. 168–9. See also Nichols, *Plea of the Innocent*, p. 145; B.L. MS Landsowne 64, No. 13.

[72]   See, for example, Nichols, *Plea of the Innocent*, p. 145; Stockwood, quoted in Haweis, *Sketches of the Reformation*, p. 71; Cooper, *Admonition*, pp. 29, 31. For other examples, Greaves, *Society and Religion*, pp. 73ff.

[73]   Andrewes, *Certaine Verie Worthie Sermons*, p. 120.

[74]   Wright, *Godly and Learned Sermons*, p. 264; Broughton, *Require of Agreement*, sigs. A2–3ᵛ; Harris, *Way to True Happinesse*, p. 185; Hill, *Economic Problems*, p. 209, quoting Thomas Adams.

[75]   On Emmanuel College as an illustration of this practice, see below, Ch. 12.

[76]   Schwarz, 'Religious thought of the protestant laity', unpub. Ph.D. thesis, U.C.L.A. 1965, p. 54, notes that Robert Bolton was the only divine he found whose works were edited by a layman (Edward Bagshaw, one of Bolton's former pupils).

debates, and supported ministers, financially and politically, as best they could.[77]

Especially when they turned their pens to theology, or even matters of practical divinity, laymen of impeccably godly qualifications sought advice from ministers. The presbyterian Francis Hastings had been Thomas Cartwright's patron. When Hastings finished writing his *Watchword*, a tract on the simplicity of true religion, he sent it to his former protégé for correction and, one surmises, approbation. In an interesting example of lay–clerical reciprocity among the godly, Cartwright wrote back deprecating his own ability to criticize the work of others – Whitgift would have appreciated this! – but noted at the same time that he had 'obeyed your desire in setting down wherein I thowght yowr judgement (folowing others ether in their writinges or speakinges) might seem somewhat to swarve'.[78] It was Cartwright's vocation, as well as his great learning, which made him Hastings' tutor in this matter. Thus Hastings saw his own godly duty as bringing together a 'longing people' and a 'labouring, speaking minister to teach them . . . .'.[79] When a minister was retrograde in his duties, Hastings would scold and encourage him, not because he held the ministry in low esteem but rather because 'they that labour in the worde are worthie of doble honor . . . .'.[80] The layman might well – *should* well – be the catalyst of proselytization, but he remained an outsider in the act of mediation.

While separated from laymen by vocation, puritan ministers may well also have seen a way, through their learning as well as through the increasing assumption of a connexion of class and godliness, to link their own fortune to the rising star of the gentry in the late sixteenth century. For ministers, the gentry represented a group which could comprehend godliness, and which had the local political influence to protect the godly evangelists from the inquisitions of the High Commission. On the other side of the balance, it was in the interest of the possessing classes to have ministers who offered a continuing vehement lesson for the lower classes that earthly hierarchy was married to heavenly equality, and that who would reject the former could not

---

[77] For an example of the supportive activities of a powerful godly layman, see Cross, *Puritan Earl*, esp. Chs. 4 & 5, on Huntingdon's 'planting of preachers' in his home county (Leicestershire) and in the north. The Corporation of Leicester's 'Booke of Actes' for the town also regulated the lecture for Wednesdays as well as Sundays, on the advice of Huntingdon (*H.M.C. Eighth Rep., App., Pt I*, p. 427. [78] *H.M.C. MSS Hastings*, II, p. 37. [79] Quoted in Cross, *Puritan Earl*, pp. 43–4.

[80] Hastings to his cousin, Sir Richard Grenville, 1583, quoted in Cross, 'Example of lay intervention', in Cuming, ed., *Studies in Church History*, 2, p. 278. Hastings, the godly younger brother of the third Earl of Huntingdon, appointed puritan ministers wherever he could, and 'mixed [with them] not as a superior but as an equal' (*ibid.*, esp. p. 279). For another look at a close personal relationship between godly laity and puritan ministers, see the portrayal of patronage in East Anglia, and especially Ch. 2 on Samuel Fairclough and Nathaniel Barnardiston, in Shipps, 'Lay patronage of East Anglian puritan clerics', unpub. Ph.D. thesis, Yale Univ., 1971.

expect the latter.[81] It was this alliance, based on symbiotic social necessity, that tied ministers and gentry together.[82] As well, a mutually dependent relationship with 'obviously' godly clerics must have served to assure certain gentlemen that they were indeed of the elect.

We still need to know more about the social composition of the English ministry and specifically of its puritan members. We know that in the century between the Reformation and the Revolution the clergy became increasingly an hereditary occupation. But there is no broad statistical evidence, as yet, concerning whether puritan ministers came more frequently than was the norm from clerical families. It would also be helpful to know whether they came more often, too, from the 'merchant/tradesman' group which was increasingly thrusting its way into the universities.[83] If a disproportionate number of puritan ministers were of bourgeois origin, it may be that economic background – rather than any conscious decision to seek an external alliance with a different group – conditioned the language in which these puritan ministers explained the covenant.[84] If such was the case, then it may also be necessary to see the aspirations of a particular socio-economic group as a factor which contributed to the eventual dominance of learning over enthusiasm. Adjustments in interpretation may well therefore be necessary, but the prior need is for more ground-level knowledge of the puritan clergy.

As yet, however, before the Revolution, the true minister for puritans was the man who *felt* the Spirit in him, who by the power of his preaching and comforting (when supported by an organized course of learning) could demonstrate his own calling. Ministerial status therefore derived not just from income or from independent social position but at a more basic level from the function which ministers were perceived to fill in society. It depended largely upon the importance popularly ascribed to the task of mediation between God and the repentant sinner. At the core of the connexion between vocation and this ability to move others to participation in the covenant stood the spectre of humane learning. The next task, then, is to outline why, in a vocational sense, puritans held learning to be necessary for God's mediators, and to determine the kinds of humane studies of which they approved.

---

[81] Note John Cotton's famous comment to the effect that if all would be governors, who should be the governed? Quoted in Morgan, *Puritan Family*, p. 25.

[82] This carried on into the Revolution. Richard Greaves has noted that the 'participants in the ordination controversy tended to be divided along class lines. Advocates of the necessity of ordination, with a prerequisite of higher education, came from higher socio-economic backgrounds than those who championed the cause of lay preaching' ('Ordination controversy', *Journal of Ecclesiastical History*, 21, p. 232).

[83] Again, see especially Cressy, 'Social composition', *Past and Present*, 47, p. 114, on Gonville and Caius College, Cambridge.

[84] Zaret, 'Ideology and organization in puritanism', esp. pp. 103–11.

6

>>

A LEARNED MINISTRY

I

From the beginning, puritans distinguished clearly between the role of learning in the heavenly and sublunary spheres. They were usually content to encourage vocational arts and certify them as acceptable. Thus Richard Greenham insisted that heresy was the likely end of those who 'under the pretence of knowing nothing but Christ, condemne all humane learning, arts, and sciences, all manuall professions . . . as though a man were the more holie for not using these outward meanes'.[1] Training in manners and in specific vocation – from the craftsman to the statesman – was encouraged by puritans since it contributed to the carrying out of Providence in secular affairs. Puritans, then, as we noted earlier, exhibited no especial concern over the extension of the mind for the solution of problems of earthly existence.

It was rather the application of reason and learning to matters divine that caused puritans grave concern. And yet, paradoxically, it was the assertion of a particular mediating function for Reformed ministers which brought them to accept the necessity of humane learning. This, as well, was shaped by the pressures of their late sixteenth-century context. First, puritans grew up in an age of school foundations and university expansion, and amid the proliferation of the humanists' revivification of ancient wisdom and glorification of the place of learning in human existence. Their youthful years were spent in Latin grammar, logic, rhetoric, and philosophy. By the time conversion grasped them, therefore, they were commonly imbued with a favourable attitude towards scholarship. As preachers, secondly, they had to react to audiences which, ever more learned themselves, demanded visibly higher standards in their ministers. In turn, puritans hoped to use learning as a bond with the influential. It was in this spirit that John Brinsley suggested that learning be made more palatable so that the ruling classes would avail themselves of it.[2] Thirdly, it would hardly help the Reformed cause if the Romanists possessed

[1] Quoted in Kocher, *Science and Religion*, p. 14.
[2] Brinsley, *Consolation*, intro. Pollock, p. 150; Hill, *Economic Problems*, p. 46.

the upper hand in learned and polemical battles over interpretation of the Word. Fourthly, as I have already suggested, the increasingly popular preparationist view of conversion also encouraged a (restricted) application of humane learning.

In driving puritan ministers to an acceptance of the necessity of humane learning, their own context and, specifically, their relations with the laity were of enormous importance. It has been argued that in this period 'the gap between the educated clerk and the illiterate layman was considerably reduced'.[3] But starting from what must have been almost universal vocational literacy, the ministry raised itself to the point, just before the outbreak of the Revolution, of admitting almost no one but university graduates. While lay illiteracy rates declined in this period, they did so unevenly, and only to a small degree for some groups such as husbandmen and women of all classes.[4] Certainly more laymen were attending school, and a small percentage a university or an Inn, but the gap between the 'illiterate' and the ministers grew immeasurably after the Reformation. Even between literate laymen and the ministers it grew 'laterally', in that specific knowledge and vocational experience allowed the minister to erect the barrier of specialization against his well-educated lay parishioners. Ministers engaged, in colleges and in exercises, in sermons preached in Latin. The continuation of the pre-Reformation distinction between popular sermons and those given *ad clerum* helped to support the claim to an independence and special status by virtue of the combination of learning and vocation.[5] In the new medium of print they reinforced their status by displaying their Latin and Greek. 'Professional' works, such as William Perkins' *Arte of Prophecying*, a manual on preaching, were still commonly issued first in the learned tongue of Latin,[6] serious knowledge of which was confined to graduates of (at least) the grammar school, that is to say, by and large to the gentry and to those intended for the ministry.[7]

As well, puritans argued in the heritage of the Christian Aristotelian belief in the necessity of retaining the natural or divine order in the building of *societas christiana*. Not only were reason and learning themselves part of this

[3]   Charlton, *Education in Renaissance England*, p. 298.   [4]   Cressy, *Literacy*, esp. Chs. 6 & 7.
[5]   Note the example of William Clarke, expelled from Peterhouse and Cambridge in 1572 for an attack
       on the hierarchical nature of the church. He appealed to Burghley (as Chancellor of the University),
       excusing his actions on the grounds that he had not spoken in front of the common people, but rather to
       a learned assembly, and that he had spoken in Latin (Cooper, *Annals of Cambridge*, II, pp. 312–
       13).
[6]   Perkins' *Arte of Prophecying* was first published in Latin in 1592; it was not published in English until
       1607, and then by Thomas Tuke. Similarly, Ames' *Marrow of Sacred Divinity* was issued first in Latin, in
       1630, in English only in 1638.
[7]   This is not to deny the education afforded sons of merchants, who had little effective claim on gentle
       status, and who remained in secular pursuits. But they were a small (though increasing) minority in the
       universities (Simon, 'Social origins', *Past and Present*, 26 p. 61; Cressy, 'Social composition', *ibid.*,
       47, p. 114).

divine order; the structure also was susceptible to rational analysis. One of the special functions of the minister was to apprehend this divine order and communicate it to the rest of society as the basis for patterns of right living. Learning thus served not only to ally the ministry socially with the increasingly well-educated gentry; it also provided protection against the assaults of radical 'enthusiasm' by functioning as a method of entry (which ignorance could not attain) into the divine plan. Protestant ministers may thus have downplayed miracles at least in part because by introducing an element of the irrational into human existence miracles reduced reliance on the humane learning of the minister as the interpreter and arbiter of the divine order. As I have already argued, puritan ministers did not abandon the concept of 'enthusiasm' (as fervency); faith was to them always a non-rational aspect of human existence. At the same time, they also insisted that the universe was not a chaos merely to be experienced by the sensations. Their psychology taught them that reason could categorize and interpret these sense perceptions. The conjunction of a general belief in an understandable divine order and the assertion that the present social hierarchy was an instance of the natural order conduced to enhance the ministers' own role as the godly *intellectual* elite of Reformed society.

It was an old Reformation theme that allowing ministers to be as unlearned as their congregations would lead to 'ignorancy', the decay of good letters, and the destruction of learning.[8] As to this last, specific complaints were made that divinity, and thus the universities, would suffer enormously if learned students were not hurriedly offered preferment.[9] It was similarly argued that it was better to have a few good (learned) ministers than a 'great many evil' (unlearned).[10] In this defence of their status, the puritans made common front not only with continental reformers, but also to a degree with their non-puritan confrères.[11] Control of the means of communication, of which the pulpit was a vital part, was seen by the powerful classes as one of the foundations upon which their future rested.[12] As the plea had been made that only preaching could pacify the populace, so was the claim made that the ministers would be effective 'for the common peace and securitie of Prince and people'

---

[8] Becon, *Early Works*, pp. 8–9. See also Morrice MSS, Vol. A, NLP, pp. 118–21; *ibid.*, Vol. B, i, pp. 43, 435; *ibid.*, Vol. A, OLP., fols. 152-3ᵛ; *Thomas Wotton's Letter Book*, ed. Eland, pp. 24–5.

[9] See, for example, Morrice MSS, Vol. B, i, pp. 138–9, a 1586 supplication from some Cambridge students to Parliament; anon., *Short Dialogue*, p. 64.

[10] *Abstract, of Certain Acts*, p. 5. This was not, of course, uniquely an English theme. Andrew Gerardus (Hyperius) argued that if unlearned men were allowed to expound the Word, they would surely lead the congregation into great error (*Practise of Preaching*, sig. C.iiiᵛ).

[11] For example, Askew, *Brotherly Reconcilement*, pp. 278–9.

[12] To this end, see the 1586 petition to the queen from the Mayor and Aldermen of London, complaining that unlearned ministers did not instruct the populace in their proper duty to the prince (Peel, *Seconde Parte of a Register*, ii, Item 208.)

only if learned.[13] Thus again did puritan ministers seek to make learning and divine order interdependent.

Puritans came to be as captivated by the possibilities as they were perplexed by the dangers of learning. Of learning solely for the sake of human knowledge they showed no appreciation, or rather exhibited disdain; in learning for the sake of material improvement of earthly existence they displayed little particular interest; but by learning as a catalyst to godliness they were enthralled, whether for or against. For puritans Scripture, as the *Word*, was literally an objective truth in the sense that it was the incarnation of God's will, both as desire for the world and as his plan for the establishment of a proper order. The pattern of human society remained a partial (or rather, corrupted) actualization of God's plan. Puritans argued also that certain inklings of the original design could be inferred from the natural world, though this, too, was a level of imperfection.[14] Only the Word remained an attainable perfect reflection of the Almighty's intentions. Not in its latter-day form however. It, too, had suffered from the accretions and deletions of the Roman supremacy. The key to restoration of the exact corpus of truth was the application of purified humane learning. Since Wyclyffe the process of cleansing and restoration had battled against the papists' love of darkness. In this last age knowledge of the ancient and oriental languages had now reached a level at which one could reasonably expect to attain the purity of the original message. The successes of humane learning, rightly applied, were the foundation on which mankind (and thus, in effect, each individual, by the percolation of knowledge) built salvation.

From this view followed the main objections to unlearned ('mechanick') ministers: that they could not fully understand the Word and that consequently they could not preach efficaciously.[15] God no longer spoke directly to the common people or appointed the unlearned as his apostles; lengthy training was now required.[16] Walter Travers, at times a biting critic of the structure of the church, nonetheless downgraded the power of the Light in one person to illuminate, by itself, another man's pathway.[17] Much of the vehemence was directed against the radicals' cry for reliance on enthusiasm alone, which arose

---

[13] Anon., *Petition of Communaltie*, p. 313, in *A Parte of a Register*. See also *Complaint of Commonalitie*, p. 239, in *ibid*.; Greenham, *Workes*, p. 24.

[14] On the limitations of the study of nature as a guide towards salvation, or even towards proper standards for earthly behaviour, see my 'Puritanism and science', pp. 535–60.

[15] *Abstract, of Certain Acts*, p. 71. See also Travers, *Full and Plaine Declaration*, p. 99.

[16] Crooke, *Ministeriall Husbandry*, pp. 122–3. See also Hieron, *Preachers Plea*, pp. 530–1; Harris, *True Blessednesse*, p. 246; Richardson, *Workeman*, p. 12; Bernard, *Faithfull Shepheard* (1607), pp. 12–13, 27–37; *ibid*. (1621), pp. 40, 43; Greenham, *Workes*, p. 24; Adams, *Workes*, p. 69.

[17] Travers, *Full and Plaine Declaration*, pp. 96, 65. See also Fenner, *Defence Of the Godlie Ministers*, pp. 57ff., 126; *Abstract, of certain Acts*, pp. 17–18, 70–1; Morrice MSS, Vol. A, OLP., fol. 158ᵛ; B.L. MS Add. 48064, fols. 191ᵛ–2ᵛ; Udall, *State of Church, passim*; Nichols, *Plea of the Innocent*, pp. 217–18.

in part perhaps from the socio-economic restrictions on attaining education. It was commonly reported of the radicals that they 'will abide no degrees in Schooles, all humane learning must be layd by, Academies are to them abominable . . .'.[18] Against this eruption puritans fought staunchly. George Gifford, himself once a Brownist, carried John Greenwood's criticism of the mixing of humane effort with the purity of Scripture to the extreme of arguing that Greenwood's final conclusion must be that even the English Bible would have to be abandoned as an inevitably corrupt translation effected by human powers, a position which Greenwood, of course, did not himself espouse.[19] Gifford ridiculed the Brownist argument that set prayers were an interference of learning with the spirit,[20] cited Augustine's approval of logic, and concluded that the Brownist charges against the universities constituted 'a barbarous . . . error'.[21]

William Perkins, doyen of puritans at late Elizabethan Cambridge, tempered his criticism of the vanity of learning with the insistence that learned knowledge of the Word could not be replaced by enthusiastic imagining:

Let no man thinke I here give the least allowance to Anabaptisticall fancies, and revelations; which are nothing but either dreames of their owne, or illusions of the Devill; for they contemne both humane learning, and the study of the Scripture, and trust wholly to revelations of the spirit . . .[22]

He therefore urged students with an eye to the ministry to 'hasten to furnish themselves with all good helps and meanes, that they may become *true Ministers and able Interpreters* . . .'.[23] There was some indication in the petitions to the Council and to Parliament for learned ministers and the exclusion of 'hedge-priests, and caterpillers, as are spread over the land in great number', that the puritans were having some success in degrading the public image of the radicals.[24]

In a private person the inability to comprehend would likely affect only his own chances of salvation (unless he was a householder). But in a minister this deficiency *created* the failing of ineffective preaching, and thus affected the eternity of the whole congregation: 'a Minister without learning, is a meere Cypher, which fills up a place, and increaseth the number, but signifies

---

[18] Anon., *Brownists Synagogue*, p. 1. See also Gifford, *Plaine Declaration*, sig. K3, for the same charge.
[19] Gifford, *Plaine Declaration*, sigs. M2^v–3^v.
[20] Gifford, *Treatise against Brownists*, p. 18.
[21] Gifford, *Plaine Declaration*, sig. K3; Gifford, *Short reply unto Barrow and Greenwood*, p. 83. See also Lawne, *Brownisme Turned*, pp. 16–17.
[22] Perkins, *Workes*, III, p. 431 ('Duties of Ministerie'); see also Hieron, *Preachers Plea*, pp. 530–1; Becon, *Early Works*, p. 8.   [23] Perkins, *Workes*, III, p. 431 ('Duties of Ministerie').
[24] *Complaint of commonalitie*, p. 210, in *A Parte of a Register*. There is, however, always the suspicion that those most likely to petition the ruling powers were those who shared at least some aspirations and beliefs, perhaps about the proper status of learning. Those already alienated would likely have seen no purpose in the exercise.

nothing'.[25] Adam Martindale was at first pessimistic about the likely quality of his ministry because of his 'utter insufficiency for want of university learning . . .'.[26] In New England, as we shall see, Harvard was founded to avoid the dreaded fear of leaving an 'illiterate Ministry to the Churches . . .'.[27]

In this, however, puritans had to be careful lest they impute to the Lord an inability or unwillingness to impart his clear meaning in the body of the Word, which protestants had insisted be offered in the vernacular for popular consumption. The difficulty was thus to avoid delegating all power to the minister yet at the same time to prove his necessity as a learned interpreter. Richard Bernard rose to the occasion by noting that protestants meant of the Word not that it was 'to be so taken as if it were obscure in it selfe, being light, and enlightening the eyes of the blinde; but it is so sayd in respect of us, which want eye-sight to see into it'.[28] Since the deficiency lay in man's ability, those trained to the highest point of human refinement, if they also possessed a calling, would obviously make the most efficacious ministers. And since calling was often difficult to detect immediately, formal learning and an ability to preach were accepted in combination as the marks of God's chosen mediators. Conversely, those who were ignorant or did not preach were unfit and ought to be removed from the ministry.[29]

This commitment to learning-in-action seems to have pervaded puritan thought in our period, rather than built to a climax at any particular time. Against what they saw as episcopal temporizing on the issue of a learned ministry, puritans rather argued that a learned minister was 'a thing necessarily required at our hands by God almighty, and therefore we must object no impossibilitie, especially when our own negligence, is the cause of all the difficultie, or if you will so call it, impossibilitie'.[30] In spirit, the authorities of the church seemed to be in wholehearted agreement.[31] Time and again, however, the church's spokesmen infuriated those dedicated to the achievement of a learned ministry. Bishop Cooper's rejection of the possibility of the decentralization of education from the universities, Covell's insistence that lack of learning was not the fault of the governors of the church, and the continued

[25]   Adams, *Workes*, p. 69. See, similarly, Penry, *Defence of Questions*, p. 44.
[26]   Martindale, *Life*, ed. Parkinson, p. 49.
[27]   *New Englands First Fruits*, p. 432, in Morison, *Founding of Harvard*.
[28]   Bernard, *Faithfull Shepheard* (1621), pp. 176–7.
[29]   See, for example, Anon., *Learned Discourse*, p. 35; Adams, *Workes*, pp. 296, 69; Travers, *Full and Plaine Declaration*, p. 99.
[30]   *Learned Discourse*, p. 37. See also *A Petition Made to Convocation*, pp. 328–9, in *A Parte of a Register*; Penry, *Treatise Proved Reformation*, sig. E3; Morrice MSS, Vol. B, i, pp. 220–2.
[31]   At the end of the century, for example, John Howson regretted that past policy had hindered preaching, and admitted at Paul's Cross that 'it cannot stand either with the pollicie of any Christian Church or Common-wealth, to have ignorant teachers, ignorant Priests, ignorant Preachers' (Howson, *Sermon*, pp. 36, 37.) Howson became a notorious puritan-beater after his appointment in 1602 as Vice-Chancellor of Oxford (Maclure, *Paul's Cross Sermons*, p. 76).

allowance of reading ministers demonstrated what puritans considered to be the basic unwillingness of the hierarchy to forge advances. John Bridges went so far as to argue that, even if puritans were the best interpreters of Scripture, they should not be allowed to circumvent any of the rules laid down by the established government of the church – an interesting example of placing order before edification, a hierarchy which puritans found execrable.[32]

It may well seem to a modern that these 'opposition' spokesmen were exaggerating the problem, but to them, we must comprehend, any hesitancy was ungodliness, an aid to Antichrist. The prodigality of puritan rhetoric may well have sprung from their sense of urgency concerning the continued practice of sending 'unlearned ministers as Locusts, into the vineyarde of the Lorde . . .'.[33] This did not mean, of course, that puritans expected all ten thousand parishes to be served by equally learned ministers. Richard Bernard was pragmatic enough to realize that different gifts suited different congregations: 'to a more learned Congregation is needfull a better Clarke, and one of lesse note to a ruder sort'.[34] The thrust of the puritan complaint was rather that a certain minimum was required which had not yet been attained. The proposition was therefore put forward that all pre-Reformation legislation commanding a learned ministry was still in effect, and indeed had been strengthened by Elizabethan statutes.[35] Backed by their allies in Parliament, puritan ministers commonly argued for the supremacy of statute law to other forms of authority, specifically to the Book of Common Prayer, which they felt condoned an unlearned ministry.[36] Thus did the status of ministerial learning conjoin with political (and perhaps even constitutional) battles of the period.

Even as they attacked what they (inaccurately) painted as the radicals' complete opposition to the use of humane learning in the minister's vocation, puritans also had to defend themselves against similar accusations of a lack of learning. John Bridges expressed the hope that the puritans would not vaunt

---

[32] Cooper, *Admonition*, p. 90; Bridges, *Defence*, pp. 31, 131; Covell, *Modest Examination*, p. 141; Sutcliffe, *Treatise*, pp. 69–70; Hill, *Society and Puritanism*, p. 35. See John Udall's attack on administrative temporizing (*State of Church*, p. 347, in *A Parte of a Register*).

[33] *Petition to Convocation*, p. 330, in *A Parte of a Register*.

[34] Bernard, *Faithfull Shepheard* (1621), p. 97. John Bridges used this same principle to argue that serving ministers should not be dismissed if inadequate (*Defence*, pp. 476ff., 504).

[35] See, for example, B.L. MS Add. 38, 492, fol. 4, an argument on the legal aspects of the question of unlearned ministers. See also *Abstract of Certain acts*, pp. 1–2, 13, 17–18, 62–3; *Short Dialogue*, p. 56. Most frequent reference was made to 13 Eliz. Cap. 12, which required a Latin statement of basic knowledge of the faith from all prospective ministers. In 1603/4, a committee of the House of Commons recommended that new ministerial candidates possess at least a B.A. and references from their college as to their ability to preach (Babbage, *Bancroft*, p. 238).

[36] See, for example, Morris MSS, Vol. B, i, p. 322–34, esp. p. 323; also p. 365; *ibid.*, Vol. A, OLP., fols. 158–9, a petition of 1585 to the House of Commons, questioning whether in fact 13 Eliz. Cap. 12 was being enforced.

what was not there,[37] and Thomas Nashe criticized them for having 'no wit to moove, no passion to urge, but onlye an ordinarie forme of preaching, blowne up by the use of often hearing and speaking . . .'.[38] Similarly, the Parnassus plays, performed at St John's College, Cambridge, in 1598–1601, contain a character called Stupido (possibly William Gouge, the puritan Ramist), who argues that students should 'follow noe longer these profane artes, that are the raggs and parings of learning, sell all these books, and buye a good Martin [Marprelate], and twoo or three hundreth of chatechismes of Ienevas printe, and I warrant you will have learning enoughe'.[39] Against the charge that puritans would in fact open the floodgates to enthusiasm and eliminate the role of humane learning, Dudley Fenner replied heatedly: 'O unspeakeable untrueth! Who be these some? They can not be such as seeke a sufficient Ministerie, they can not be such as denie to subscribe: for the Canonicall Scriptures can not well be studied without other helpes . . .'.[40] The carping exchange early in our period between Cartwright and Whitgift, in which each criticized the other's learning, quickly indicated that puritans, as much as the administration, were unwilling to abandon such a useful ally.

II

As I have already argued, one should not approach this subject solely from a paradigm of dichotomy between puritans and the defenders of established church and state. Perhaps it would help to think of puritans and non-puritans as being on wavelengths of different amplitudes, so that at certain points the crests and troughs coincide almost precisely. Puritans recognized that they could not rid England of extra-scriptural knowledge. Nor is there any reason to conclude that they could not make their peace with much of the classical heritage. Richard Sibbes, that influential covenanter, reminded his readers that 'Truth comes from God, wheresoever we finde it . . . wee may take it from heathen authors as a just possession . . .'.[41] Thomas Gataker similarly expostulated, of the Psalms, that where the Holy Ghost 'useth more Art, we may well expect more excellence . . .'.[42] Learning could be pursued almost relentlessly if the intent and result were the transmission of saving knowledge to the populace. Richard Rogers, Thomas Adams, and John Brinsley thus all praised learning – Brinsley called it 'the heavenly light, the truest honour, the best riches, the sweetest pleasure'[43] – but also added caveats that it was useful

[37] Bridges, *Defence*, p. 20.   [38] Nashe, *Pierce Penilesse*, quoted in Herr, *Elizabethan Sermon*, p. 106.
[39] Leishmann, ed., *Parnassus Plays*, p. 70 (lines 343–52). The identification of 'Stupido' with William Gouge is Leishmann's.   [40] Fenner, *Defence of the Godlie Ministers*, p. 126; see also p. 127.
[41] Sibbes, *Christians Portion*, pp. 68–9.   [42] Gataker, *Davids Instructer*, pp. 1–2.
[43] Rogers, *Seven Treatises*, p. 149; Brinsley, *Consolation*, ed. Pollock, p. 3; Adams, *Workes*, p. 296; Clement, *Petie Schole*, ed. Pepper, pp. 95–6.

only as long as it served the cause of edification.[44] So Seneca was especially revered as a moralist, but his stature, for protestants, flowed from the recognition that his standards agreed in large part with those of the Word. Thus, as Miller noted, William Ames could reveal Platonist influences in his doctrine of 'conscience', because Platonism and Christianity had frequently blended on this question.[45] When puritans perceived learning as overemphasized, then, as we have seen, the fear and loathing of the intellect, which were always fundamental in the Pauline outlook, would erupt with a vengeance. William Pemble, for example, strongly criticized ministers who

stiffely and truely maintaining against the Papists the all-sufficiencie of Scriptures for heavenly instruction, do yet intheir [sic] private studies condemne them of insufficiency, bestowing, to say the least, three parts of their times and paines in the wearisome reading of those huge volumes of Fathers, Schoole-men, and other Writers, for one part which they spend in the meditation of the Scriptures.[46]

The puritan support of learning as an aid to religion was thus still a long way removed from Roger Ascham's belief that, where learning suffered, religion would necessarily decay,[47] though the similar sound of the protests is not to be denied.

The basic educational norm for a minister in the puritan scheme quickly became a bachelor's degree.[48] It should be noted, however, that, in addition to concern over the lack of formal vocational training for ministers at the undergraduate level, there was also some apprehension about the absence of subjects regarded as necessary for a Christian education, and specifically for future mediators. History, a fringe subject at Oxford and Cambridge for most of our period, provides a good illustration. The study of the past, and especially of the ancient world, had been encouraged by the early humanists. For puritans, too, a record of the past was crucial, but for the radically different reason that it would chart the progress towards the building of the New Jerusalem. In personal terms, this need motivated the puritan autobiography and diary as a new form of written spiritual recollection *cum* admonition. At a national level, the same imperative of use governed the academic discipline. William Gouge, D.D., fellow of King's College, Cambridge, minister in London and, later, member of the Westminster Assembly of Divines, stressed the importance of keeping a written record of events, not for social necessity,

---

[44] The caveats are linked directly to the praise: see the references in the previous note. See also Smith, *Davids Repentance*, 'To the Reader'; Rainolds, *Letter*, sig. Z3.

[45] Miller, *New England Mind*, pp. 30, 177.

[46] Pemble, *Plea for Grace*, p. 25. See also *Diary of Thomas Crosfield*, ed. Boas, p. 18; Cartwright, *Replye to answere*, sig. Ciij; Northbrooke, *Poore Mans Garden*, fols. 76ᵛ–7; Rainolds, *Excellent Oration*, pp. 96–7; also pp. 122–3, for further criticism of the 'obstinate, and pertinacious Patrons of Philosophy'; Gouge, *Learned and Useful Commentary*, Ch. 11, section 244; Davenport, *Apologeticall Reply*, pp. 171–2.

[47] Ascham, *The Scholemaster*, fol. 46ᵛ.   [48] See, for example, *Abstract, of Certain Acts*, pp. 13, 30, 71.

but rather because he believed that God had commanded it in Scripture. The Lord's intent, as Gouge saw it, was that 'not the present age onely, but also all succeeding ages . . . reape benefit by the evidences of his wisdome, power, mercy, justice, and other his divine properties . . .'.[49] Gouge argued that Christian history, with a belief in a determined end (the apocalypse) differed from the commonly cyclical view of classical historians. The written past was not to be a record of man's own efforts against environment, but rather the story of God's willingness to aid man, a modern continuation of the record of Scripture. Indeed, he specifically suggested that history could be viewed as an imitation of the preserving of the Ten Commandments in the Ark.[50] It is unlikely that Gouge desired 'objective' reconstruction of the past; he rather judged 'history' by its utility for edification. Gouge's standpoint thus clashed irreconcilably with the view of Francis Bacon that 'it is the true office of History to represent the events themselves, together with the counsels, and to leave the observations, and conclusions, thereupon, to the liberty and facultie of every mans judgement'.[51] Gouge's argument presented a thorough indictment of previous (especially classical) historical writing. Even the most 'admirable' events of the past were not to be interpreted as successes of man's natural abilities – here, again, we see the pervasive fear of vainglory – but rather as the reflection of God's power through regeneration. In this sense, history was to be redirected and restructured so that the serving of Christian Providence became the central function of the written recall and analysis of the past.[52]

For the most part, puritans concentrated their efforts at reform of the undergraduate curriculum, on the redirection of those subjects which would prove most helpful in comprehending Scripture, and in supplying efficacious exegesis to the congregation: the learned languages, logic, and rhetoric. Grammar, since it was a school subject, was taken virtually for granted. The trilingual ideal had long been promoted by both Romanist and protestant humanist scholars.[53] Across north-west Europe the religious eruptions

---

[49] Gouge, *Gods Three Arrowes*, pp. 297–8, 301–2.   [50] *Ibid.*, p. 303.
[51] Bacon, *Twoo Bookes . . . Learning*, p. 15.
[52] The notion of 'building' a 'predetermined' future is not self-contradictory. The general outlines of Providence, and the specific fates of individual souls, were already determined by God, but the course of the specifics of earthly affairs, and the rapidity of the development of man's relationship with God, depended to some extent on man's own actions. For an example of an attempt at this kind of history, see Governor Bradford's 'of Plimmoth Plantation', ed. J. A. Doyle; the manuscript dates from *c.* 1650.
[53] At the turn of the century in Spain, Cardinal Jiminez, in the constitutions for his new college at San Ildefonso, offered priority to the learned languages (Hall, 'Trilingual college', in Cuming, ed., *Studies in Church History*, 5, pp. 122–3). Jiminez's grand scheme for a new Bible, based on the best scholarship of languages as well as theology, thus closely paralleled the production, almost a half-century later, of the 'puritan' Geneva Bible. Latin, Greek and Hebrew studies were incorporated into St John's College, Cambridge at the beginning of the sixteenth century; into St Mary's college of St Andrews in the 1530s.

brought concrete proposals for colleges of the arts based on language study.[54] The Marian exiles, too, carried back with them experience of contact with a Reformed curriculum as well as with Reformed theology.[55] The learned languages provided an avenue to the 'original' Scriptures, the Fathers, and contemporary European protestantism, as well, of course, as a powerful weapon for the confrontation with the learned forces of the Romish Antichrist. William Crashawe, a noted puritan warrior against Rome, was able, on the basis of his learning, to accuse his opponents of 'altering the bookes of learned men after they are dead . . . so that the crime is no lesse then corruption and forgerie in the highest degree'.[56] John Field noted a hierarchy within humane learning which corresponded to a clear movement towards God's truth. He supported trilingual knowledge for preachers, since 'if any question arise amongst the lattines concerning the New Testament, or if the copies vary, we must go to the Fountaines of the Greeke, or if any doubts occure with the Greekes, we must to the Hebrue . . .'.[57] At the same time, familiarity with the learned languages also produced a purer knowledge for distillation into casuistical divinity. Because translations were 'meerely humane', and the vernacular changed so rapidly, there was need for constant improvement through increased learning.[58]

Chief among the academic weapons which puritans sought to bend to their use was logic. Logic, though rather downgraded by humanists, nonetheless retained an immense importance in its own right, and also served as the foundation of the revived art of rhetoric. Given their devotion to the idea of the simplicity of the Word, and also the small proportion of the population that ever studied logic, puritans had to deny that logic was absolutely necessary for comprehension of the Bible.[59] But it was nonetheless logic that could drain the last drop of meaning from the Word. John Penry, radical enough in other

In England, the last decade of Henry VIII's reign saw the establishment of the regius professorships, which supported Greek and Hebrew, as well as divinity, law and medicine. For a recent account, see Logan, 'Origins of so-called regius professorships', in Baker, ed., *Studies in Church History*, 14, pp. 271–8.

[54] Cameron, 'Renaissance tradition in Scotland', in Baker, ed., *Studies in Church History*, 14, p. 254, mentions the primacy of Zwingli's work at Zurich. He also notes the college proposals in Bern, Bordeaux, Strasbourg, Nimes, Basel, Heidelberg, Lausanne and Geneva, all between 1533 and 1559.

[55] For an example of an important member of this group, see Danner, 'Anthony Gilby', *Church History*, 40, pp. 412–22.

[56] Crashawe, *Romish Forgeries*, sig. ¶3ᵛ. In the same vein came the defence – not confined to puritans – against Jesuit attacks on the English as unlearned. See, for example, the remarks by Dove, *Advertisement*, p. 2; Drant, *Three Godly Sermons*, sig. Ciij; Rous, *Diseases of the Time*, Ch. 8. The Jesuits' learning was generally admired, at least for its efficiency.

[57] Field, *Caveat for Howlet*, sig. C.vᵛ; Broughton, *Principall Positions*, esp. sigs. A2–4. That puritans did in practice stress Greek and Hebrew more than their contemporaries was suggested even by Richard Bancroft (*Dangerous Positions*, p. 113).

[58] Yates, *Modell of Divinitie*, p. 263–4.   [59] Northbrooke, *Poore Mans Garden*, fols. 55ᵛ–56.

ways, insisted that 'the Lord doth not ordinarily bestowe [full comprehension of the Word] upon any in these our dayes, without the knowledge of the artes, especially the two handmaydes of all learninge, Rhetoricke and Logick, and the two originall tongues wherein the worde was written'.[60] Logic was also the skill that allowed puritans to prepare such skilful defences against English bishops.[61] So important was it, indeed, that John Eliot translated a treatise on logic into Algonkian in order to teach the Indians 'the knowledge of the Rule of Reason'.[62]

The process of reasoning employed in the academies at the beginning of our period was, by and large, Aristotelian and highly systematized.[63] In this scheme, theology was considered a 'science', part of the body of knowledge concerned more with 'knowing' than with 'doing'.[64] Aristotelian reasoning 'knew' things by assigning them to specific mental compartments, based on the philosopher's five classifications ('predicables') and ten categories ('predicaments'). The comprehension of the 'thing' in question came from its fine distinction from all other 'things' as they appeared to the observer by this process of cataloguing. The method of demonstration in Aristotelian logic was the syllogism, which flourished in the pre-revolutionary universities, and is therefore prominent in puritan proof in both popular and learned tracts. Aristotelianism proved a hardy plant. Adapted first by the humanists to the end of teaching a 'good life', and then by such Oxford puritans as John Rainolds to serve the comprehension and exegesis of more godly knowledge, it flourished throughout our period.[65]

Against this system arose the challenge of Peter Ramus. Ramus' chief objection to the Aristotelian system was that it had no real application to living *experience*. His specific changes to the actual practice of logic were not particularly severe: he sought to banish the predicables, to reorganize the categories, and to reduce dependence on the syllogism, which he argued proved only what had been conceded in the major premise.[66] Perhaps more important than criticism of the categories in arousing the ire of the Aristotelians was

---

[60] Penry, *Defence of Questions*, p. 44. Even John Smith, the Se-Baptist, stressed the importance of minis-
        terial training in logic: Smith, *Paterne of True Prayer*, p. 169.
[61] See the logical bantering between Francis Marbury and the bishop of London, during the latter's
        examination of Marbury: *H.M.C. Rep. on MSS in Various Collections*, III, pp. 3–4.
[62] Miller, *New England Mind*, p. 114.
[63] Costello, *Scholastic Curriculum*, p. 8. I am heavily indebted to this source, and to the works of Miller,
        Ong, and Howell (cited separately, below). For the applicability of Ramism to puritan needs, I have
        assimilated the arguments of these scholars to my own interpretation.
[64] Costello, *Scholastic Curriculum*, pp. 37–8.
[65] On John Rainolds and protestant Aristotelianism at Oxford, see especially McConica, 'Humanism and
        Aristotle', *English Historical Review*, 94, pp. 291–317, *passim*.
[66] Miller, *New England Mind*, esp. pp. 122–4. The brilliance of Ramus' method is now held in severe
        doubt; see, for example, Nelson, *Peter Ramus*, University of Michigan Contributions in Modern Philol-
        ogy, ii, *passim*; Ong, *Ramus*, esp. pp. 174–5. For contemporary doubts, see McConica, 'Humanism and
        Aristotle', p. 314, n. 1.

Ramus' division of arguments into 'artificial' and 'inartificial'. The former were demonstrable to the observer by the plain facts of the question at hand, while 'inartificial' arguments, such as the resurrection of Christ, had to be taken on trust. Aristotelians evidently feared that the doctrine of inartificial argument would challenge all authority, including reason itself, by placing belief on a higher plane.[67] At the core of Ramist logic stood the three general laws of truth, justice, and wisdom.[68] But Ramus became best known for his scheme of 'method', which sought to arrange various things 'down from universal and general principles to the underlying singular parts, by which arrangement the whole matter could be more easily taught and apprehended'.[69] 'Prudence' (part of 'method') reminded the student that explanations had to take account of the time, place, audience, and so on.[70] The attraction of 'natural method', Ramus claimed, was that it was 'not solely applicable to the material of the arts and doctrines, but to all things which we intend to teach easily and clearly'.[71] Of great assistance here were the well-known schematic diagrams of the argument (which always moved from the general to the particular) that introduced so many Ramist works.[72]

Ramus, following Plato, argued that logic could draw upon the 'real' world of human existence for its illustrations because the world was to be understood as a 'material counterpart of an ordered hierarchy of ideas existing in the mind of God'.[73] Thus the principles of 'art' were not, as the Aristotelians held, categories of the human mind, but rather statements of a reality beyond human existence. The connexion between this order in the external world and comprehension in the human mind is reason, and its chief tool logic. Logic's propositions would be both true and useful, since they would correspond to the true and eternal laws of nature. Ramus also concluded, again possibly from Plato, that all logical possibilities could be arranged in pairs, some forming

[67] Miller, *New England Mind*, pp. 129–30. Ramus' own logic consisted of a tripartite scheme: 'invention' (the arrangement of individual terms), 'judgement' or 'disposition' (the methods for putting these terms together), and 'method' (the manner of arranging the terms in order) (*ibid*., pp. 128–33; Howell, *Logic and Rhetoric*, p. 155).

[68] Howell, *Logic and Rhetoric*, p. 151 ff. Very simply, the law of 'truth' allowed the student to separate propositions that were true only at certain times, and thus approach the drawing of the 'universal and necessary affirmations' that Ramus favoured. 'Justice' allowed the separation from one art of any propositions which properly belonged to another; it was on this basis that Ramus assigned invention and disposition to logic rather than to rhetoric, which had traditionally claimed them. The final law, of 'wisdom', was the basis of organization of the subject matter of the liberal arts into a hierarchy of statements from 'most general' to 'least general'. Ramus did not invent these laws, but rather lifted them from Aristotle's *Posterior Analytics*, and modified them in light of Melanchthon and Sturm.

[69] Quoted in Ong, *Ramus*, p. 245; Howell, *Logic and Rhetoric*, p. 160.   [70] Ong, *Ramus*, p. 246.

[71] Quoted in Howell, *Logic and Rhetoric*, p. 163.

[72] Ong goes so far as to conclude that the 'origins of Ramism are tied up with the increased use of spatial models in dealing with the processes of thought and communication' (Ong, *Ramus*, p. 314; also pp. 247, 260).   [73] Miller & Johnson, eds., *Puritans*, Introduction, p. 31; also p. 31, n. 1.

dichotomies. The task of the Ramist logician thus became largely the arrangement of all options into choices.[74]

Ramus, working with Omer Talon, stripped rhetoric of all but style and delivery, that is, the ornamenting of speech and the expressing of that which logic had revealed.[75] By reducing rhetoric to this subservient position, Ramus managed to turn delivery into a reproduction of a 'natural' method established in the external world. Rhetoric, which had won the favour of the humanists, and which dominated the undergraduate curriculum in our period, thus also became a fierce weapon in the puritan arsenal against both Antichrist and English temporizing:

Rhetorick is an Art sanctified by Gods Spirit, and may be lawfully used in handling of Gods word: there may bee given, and are already by learned men set downe instances of all the parts of Rhetoricke out of the Scripture. And therefore the Art is to be approved, and only the abuse thereof is to be condemned.[76]

Rhetoric was the means by which the logical analysis of the Word was brought home to the common congregation to spur repentance and conversion. As subjects of the university, logic and rhetoric also served to separate the future minister from the people, and ally his professional status with the increasingly well-educated gentry.

The especial significance of Ramus' work, first translated into English in 1574, came from two sources: Ramus' biography, and the application made of his work by English translators and admirers. Brought up in the Roman church, Ramus had nonetheless won his M.A. by a scathing attack on the Aristotelians. Even better, he had been converted to the Reformed faith. In his own outline of a 'confession of French protestantism', Ramus cited Biblical texts but, interestingly, also added classical citations which he believed had analogous meaning.[77] In one of their learned champions puritans thus confronted the juxtaposition of classical and scriptural learning which they found so troubling. Ramus' 'martyrdom' in the Bartholomew massacre of 1572 made him personally unassailable.

But perhaps even more important than the spectre of Ramus himself was the treatment accorded his work by his first two British translators, the Scot Roland MacIlmaine and the English puritan Dudley Fenner.[78] MacIlmaine

---

[74] In practical terms this system often relied as heavily on the commonsense denial of one of the possibilities as on a tight logical proof. On this question, see Miller & Johnson, eds., *Puritans*, Introduction, pp. 34–5.

[75] It would seem, therefore, that in a Ramist educational scheme, rhetoric would follow logic, and indeed this was usually the case. But Ramus himself taught rhetoric before logic (Ong, *Ramus*, pp. 276, 290–2; Miller, *New England Mind*, pp. 315–16, 326).   [76] Bernard, *Faithfull Shepheard* (1621), p. 44.

[77] Miller, *New England Mind*, p. 146.

[78] MacIlmaine published the first translation in 1574 as *The Logike*. Fenner's *Artes of Logike* was first published in 1584.

stressed the general utility of the work for Christians in performing their duties to God and to commonwealth.[79] More important, however, were his suggestions concerning the application of Ramism to a protestant sermon.[80] He emphasized the inclusion of scriptural allusions, and condemned those who sought to keep the liberal arts in the learned tongues and the people thus in ignorance.[81] Dudley Fenner, in England, made Ramism the cornerstone of much (but certainly not all) future puritan thought by the extremely significant step of changing all Ramus' examples from classical to scriptural texts. The logic was in no way affected, but the book immediately became more acceptable to those afraid of contamination by humane learning.[82]

There was, among puritans, an immediate desire to co-opt such a purified system of reason and apply it to all levels of human activity. The degree of repudiation of the past, true to puritan form in other matters, depended on the context. At Oxford, John Rainolds, though a staunch supporter of Ramus' criticisms of the errors of Aristotle and of the applicability of Ramism to the tasks of the preacher, nonetheless protested against the Frenchman's immoderate approach, and attempted himself to blend this protestant logic with the extremely influential strain of humanism at his university.[83] The adoption of Ramism as a weapon against the administration, and as a method for popular sermons, fell primarily to Cambridge puritans. Dudley Fenner, having presented the purified Ramus to Englishmen, also sought to apply him to their lives in his *Methode in the Government of the Familie* (1590), a Ramist explanation of the proper ordering of a godly household. Thomas Gataker, in a sermon at Tunbridge school, noted that the psalm upon which he would speak was 'artificially framed', that is, taken from 'real life'.[84] The development, too, out of Ramism of technometria – 'the scrupulous delineation of each art or discipline within the context of the entire field of knowledge' – by puritans such as Alexander Richardson, John Yates, and William Ames, helped to separate useful knowledge from the unhelpful, and to lay the foundations for a modified and godly curriculum.[85] Especially did this tend towards the subordination of natural reason to a reason guided by faith ('right reason'), since technometria saw theology as an 'all-inclusive guide to life'.[86]

Thomas Granger, in issuing a Ramist logic text, noted that he had composed the work from his own readings and from his own experience as a preacher in Lincolnshire. He stressed that logic, since it now conformed to human reason, was to be seen as a help to both preachers and auditors.[87] It could immediately serve two complementary purposes: 'inwardly', to give 'true direction to our

[79] Ramus, *Logike*, transl. MacIlmaine, sigs. A.ii[v], A.iiii.
[80] *Ibid.*, sigs. A.vi–vij[v]. [81] *Ibid.*, sigs. A.vi[v]–vij, A.viii[r–v]. [82] Fenner, *Artes of Logike*.
[83] McConica, 'Humanism and Aristotle', esp. pp. 302–9. [84] Gataker, *Davids Instructer*, p. 2.
[85] On this question, see Sprunger, 'John Yates', *Journal of the History of Ideas*, 37, esp. pp. 700–1.
[86] *Ibid.*, p. 701. [87] Granger, *Divine Logike*, sigs. a.2, a.2[v], a.6.

reason' and, 'outwardly', to direct man's aim to 'the obtaining of truth science, and knowledge of all things'.[88] He then offered a detailed explanation of the various parts and structures of reformed logic, together with their use, illustrated by pithy sayings which ministers could easily lift for their own sermons. Granger's purpose, then, was to channel reason into 'right action' by providing a basic, standardized structure for a plain, Ramist sermon.[89] That man had now to rely not solely on the ability of his own thought, but on the concordance of his ideas with the external world, was also one of the themes of the 1638 attempt by Thomas Spencer to bring the systems of Ramus and Aristotle into agreement.[90]

Yet there were also gainsayers of logic on the fringes of the puritan spectrum. Here, as in so many other matters, there was a wariness inherent in the puritan approach. Walter Travers, the presbyterian, warned all Christians that 'th'argumentes of Logike are as common to good and badde, as are the rules of grammar'.[91] An anonymous puritan paper similarly commented: 'the ignorance of logicke a shame to schollers. The knowledge no great commendacion.'[92] For the more severe critics, this willingness of learned method to serve any master precluded its dependability for divinity. Robert Browne, for example, stressed the superfluity of such arts to the comprehension of Scripture. The common people – so plain was the Word – could easily understand the message without the addition of involved 'Syllogismes, . . . Predicables and Predicamentes, and your argumentes of Invention'. Indeed, Browne went so far as to challenge both Beza's and Calvin's support for the vain art, and vilified even the Ramist system. Any *system* of knowledge, he claimed, was bound to develop involved rules and expressions which inevitably became the prized possessions of the 'learned', and the tools by which understanding was hidden from the congregation, which then easily fell into error.[93] This attempted rejection of logic continued in the seventeenth century. John Lilburne, for example, criticized an opponent for his reliance on such learning, warning that the supreme authority of Scripture should not be subjected to the ratification of logic, an invention of the '*Divell* and *Antichrist*, with which they mainly and principally have upheld and maintained their black, darke, and wicked kingdome . . .'.[94] The puritan search for a purer logic may well have been at least in part a response to radical insistence on simplicity in the analysis and diffusion of Scripture.

Perry Miller argued that New England puritans paid such court to reason

---

[88]   *Ibid.*, pp. 1–2.   [89]   *Ibid.*, sig. a.2ᵛ.   [90]   Spencer, *Art of Logick*.
[91]   Travers, *Defence of Ecclesiasticall Discipline*, p. 180.   [92]   B.L. MS Lansdowne 120, No. 3, fol. 52.
[93]   Browne, *23. of Matthewe*, pp. 175, 182–9, 192, 197. For a European parallel, see the remark of the sceptic Cornelius Agrippa that logic could best be defined as a process 'by the whiche al other sciences are made more obscure, and harder to learne . . .' (Agrippa, *Of Vanitie*, fols. 17–20ᵛ). Agrippa offered similar accusations against Ciceronian rhetoric.   [94]   Lilburne, *Answer to Nine Arguments*, pp. 2–3.

because they were Ramists.[95] He contended that Alexander Richardson's view that the natural world could reveal God's wisdom was the epitome of the puritan mind, in which the dialectic of Ramus blended perfectly with the theology of Augustine and Calvin.[96] But Ramism may perhaps have been overestimated by historians of ideas who concentrate more on structures of thought than on contemporary practical necessity. Puritan ideas about the use of the intellect were not *determined* by Ramism. Puritan preachers used Ramism not because it removed blockages to the free use of reason, but rather because it was so constructed that it allowed only one direction for man's reason. Ramus offered a guide to puritans in the attempt to explain the coordination of the human individual struggle with the external universe. That is, the revisions to the Aristotelian system made the correspondences of microcosm and macrocosm more readily comprehensible to an audience. The Ramist stress on general laws also satisfied the puritans' intellectual desire for a system which would encompass a synthesis of the fervent drive of enthusiasm and the mental curiosity which they had absorbed from their humanistic training.

As Miller himself noted, puritan ministers found Ramist logic especially suited to the exposition of the Bible because, as a deductive system, it was a method of discovering rather than inventing meaning.[97] For the saints, a logic that was warranted to produce 'objective truths', not merely statements that satisfied its own structures, could be accepted as keeping far enough away from the brink of the chasm represented by a full reliance on the independent powers of free reason. As well, by confining itself to the deductive explanation of knowledge 'already known', Ramism might indeed have proved a deterrent to the adoption by puritans of any appreciation of the advancement of learning in a Baconian sense. On the other hand, Ramus' insistence that logic should agree with nature may have meant that puritan educators conditioned an era of students to see 'truth' in an empirically approached natural world, even though the puritans themselves had no such intention of diverting scholarly attention, or of shifting the bedrock of 'reality', from the Word to the world.

Certainly the form affected the content, but puritans were already fervent believers with a duty to proselytize. When John Field decided that it might be necessary to 'go to the people' in the 1580s, it was because of the failure of political reform at the centre, not because Ramus' logic emphasized 'use'. The works of William Perkins, as Miller pointed out, demonstrate only a borrowing from, and not a slavish following of, Ramus.[98] 'Plainness' devolved from

95 Miller, *New England Mind*, p. 203.
96 *Ibid.*, p. 162. See also Sprunger, 'John Yates', pp. 705–6.
97 Miller, *New England Mind*, *passim*, but for example, esp. pp. 141, 144, 150–1.
98 *Ibid.*, pp. 313, 338; Howell, *Logic and Rhetoric*, pp. 206–7. Perkins' *Arte of Prophecying*, a text on sermonizing, was heavily influenced by Ramism.

the puritan imperative to bring the 'meaning' of the Word to Christian congregations. The emphasis on the 'natural meaning' of the text in turn derived
from a Pauline view of the self-evident nature of the truths of the Lord.

The adoption of Ramism thus did not mean a yielding to reason, but rather
its specifically utilitarian employment for two different audiences. First, those
who were learned but who had not yet been converted could be brought to an
'external' (or preparationist) appreciation of the procedures of Christianity;
secondly, for those whom faith had already made regenerate, the structures of
reason, familiar from secular existence, could be shown to be compatible now
with the truths of revelation. While Ramism did not overwhelm its opposition
in the universities – Aristotelianism always dominated Oxford, and was
resurgent at Cambridge by the 1620s[99] – it became extremely popular among
those who sought to explain their knowledge to a wider audience. These
included puritan preachers and schoolmasters. These people, it should be
remembered, were the puritan conduits to the English populace.

III

But puritans did not confine themselves to occasional comments on the quality
and types of humane learning for ministers; throughout our period there were
attempts at the elucidation of more precise courses of study for God's
mediators.[100] In 1577 John Rainolds, leading Oxford puritan, later President
of Corpus Christi, and an important spokesman at the Hampton Court conference, outlined a plan of study for divinity students.[101] In his 'Letter'
Rainolds sought a way to direct the labour of his unnamed friend 'to the
advancement of God's glory, the profit of his Church, & your own comfort'.[102] He was careful to explain that godliness was a matter of faith, prayer
and grace, as well as proper study, insisting that 'without the grace of the holy
spirit, all study, especially in divinity, is vaine . . .'.[103] Divinity, he
emphasized, aimed not simply at knowing, but also at converting others to
become 'godly livers'.[104] Rainolds advised those who would become wise in
the Scriptures to become, first of all, scholars in the necessary aids of learning:

[99] Howell, *Logic and Rhetoric*, p. 364; Kearney, *Scholars and Gentlemen*, p. 82; Costello, *Scholastic Curriculum*, pp. 45–6; McConica, 'Humanism and Aristotle', *passim*; Schmitt, 'Renaissance Aristotelianism', pp. 178–9.

[100] Some of these courses of study appeared in preaching manuals – Richard Bernard's suggestions are an example. Where that is the case, I have separated the recommendations on the pulpit *use* of such learn-ing and discussed them in the next chapter.

[101] Rainolds' *Letter . . . Concerning his Advice for the Studie of Divinitie* was not published until 1613, but it was written in 1577, and therefore can be taken as indicative of views of the earlier period. I have sup-plemented the outline offered in this work with statements from Rainolds, *Excellent Oration*.

[102] Rainolds, *Letter*, sigs. A2ᵛ–3.

[103] *Ibid.*, sigs. A4ᵛ–5ᵛ. I think that the term 'vaine' is used in both its senses here.

[104] *Ibid.*, sig. A4ʳ⁻ᵛ.

logic and the languages of Biblical study.[105] The student trained in Greek and Hebrew would be able to search the 'original' Scriptures for himself, and would subsequently be able 'to discern the craftinesse of interpreters, which is too frequent in prophane writings, but chiefly in the Scriptures'.[106]

At the same time, these studies were to be pursued only to the extent that they would profit religious pursuits. Rainolds specifically noted the probably disappointing results in store for those who held that it was possible to train fully in the humane arts, and then *consciously* decide to turn to God.[107] Rainolds stressed the usual puritan caveats against impure heathen learning, and offered a lengthy list of authors who had agreed concerning the dangers of philosophy. Pico, Savonarola, and Vives were among the more recent authorities. True to the puritan paradox, Rainolds did not, however, execrate learning to the point of its expulsion from the Christian community. Rather he offered that

it may be lawfull for Christians to use Philosophers, and books of Secular Learning, but with this condition, that whatsoever they finde in them, that is profitable and usefull, they convert it to Christian doctrine, and do, as it were, shave off, and pare away all superfluous stuffe.[108]

To guide his friend better, Rainolds added specific recommendations of what a divinity student should read. Greatest emphasis, of course, was placed on the Word itself, to be studied in the original Hebrew and Greek, since translations were often inaccurate.[109] As a guard against the dangers of overmuch individual interpretation, Rainolds suggested that the future preacher acquaint himself with 'some learned interpreter' such as Calvin or Martyr to help, but certainly not to replace, his own study of the most difficult passages of Scripture.[110] He recommended especial concentration on the Gospel of St John, the Epistle to the Romans, Isaiah and the Psalms, which he thought represented the sum of the scriptural message.[111] Rather than rely on printed commonplace books (presumably because they represented another fallible interpretation) the student should instead note points in the margins of his own books, or even compose his own paper book of especially important matters, using as a model perhaps Bunny's work on Calvin.[112] This type of exercise would also help the student to develop his own sense of fulfilling his vocation. He con-

[105] Rainolds, *Excellent Oration*, pp. 58–60; Rainolds, *Letter*, sig. A5^{r-v}.

[106] Rainolds, *Excellent Oration*, pp. 58–60.

[107] He recalled the example of Richard Fox, who had founded Corpus Christi for the training of divines, but who had allowed (in Rainolds' opinion) far too great an emphasis on ungodly authors (*ibid.*, pp. 126ff., 138; McConica, 'Scholars and commoners', in Stone, ed., *University in Society*, I, pp. 153–4).   [108] Rainolds, *Excellent Oration*, pp. 96–7.   [109] Rainolds, *Letter*, sig. A5^{r-v}.   [110] *Ibid.*, sig. A7.

[111] *Ibid.*, sig. A6^{v}.   [112] *Ibid.*, sig. A8.

cluded his work with an exhortation to pursue godly knowledge, and to avoid the carnal pleasures of university life.[113]

A paper in the Morrice Manuscripts, almost certainly by Laurence Chaderton,[114] illustrates the same approach. Chaderton emphasized the advantages of group learning, in the form of a conference, so familiar to contemporary in-service training.[115] The types of knowledge he recommended were similar to those suggested by Rainolds for more solitary study. Indeed, Chaderton seems to have been in full agreement with Rainolds' view that the purpose of learning was the application of the 'guiftes . . . which God hath promised and given to his Churche' to searching out the 'the trewe sense and meaning of the text appointed'.[116] Chaderton stressed the importance of Greek and Latin, rhetoric, logic, familiarity with learned commentaries on Scripture, and, finally, in a practical vein for the public explanation of texts (at which, of course, this whole plan was aimed), 'knowledge of Greke and Lattin Histories, and Chronologies, for the better understanding of the Historyes in the scriptures, and the reconciling of many places, which otherwyse myght seeme doubtfull'.[117] In a sermon Chaderton, at the centre of Cambridge theology and college politics for half a century, and thus a powerful mentor of the godly, explained the puritan view of the necessary conjunction of learning with personal reformation. He complained bitterly of those improperly trained people who entered the ministry 'not onely voide of all skill in the Hebrue, Greeke, and Latin tongues, in Logicke, Rhetorick, and other Artes: but also (which I am ashamed to speake,) both voyde of the knowledge of the Doctrine of repentaunce, and also wicked and lewde in life . . .'.[118]

In 1583 Thomas Cartwright wrote to Arthur Hildersam, then a young man of twenty with a B.A., who had petitioned Cartwright for advice on the study of divinity.[119] Cartwright hesitated to take upon himself the burden of suggesting a course of study, and had evidently delayed his reply to the young student.[120] Paramount, he said, was the necessity of studying the Bible daily; the student should apply 'aequal study' to Old and New Testaments.[121] But

---

[113] *Ibid.*, sig. A8ᵛff. See also Rainolds, *Excellent Oration*, pp. 125, 109–10, for an exhortation to even greater vigilance in Christian supervision of philosophy.

[114] The document, 'An order to be used for the trayning upp and exercising of Students in Divinitye, whereby they may be made fitt and meete to dyscharge the dewtyes belonging to that profession' is in Vol. A, OLP, fols. 191ff. It was reprinted, in part, by Peel, *Seconde Parte of a Register*, I, pp. 133–4. The document is unfortunately not dated.

[115] For aspects of this plan which were employed in Emmanuel College, see below, pp. 250–2.

[116] Morrice MSS, Vol. A, OLP, fol. 191ʳ⁻ᵛ.   [117] *Ibid.*, fol. 191ᵛ.

[118] Chaderton, *Fruitfull Sermon*, pp. 33–4.

[119] *Cartwrightiana*, ed. Peel & Carlson, 'Letter to Arthur Hildersham', pp. 109–15. Hildersam later became one of Cartwright's executors. He was of Romanist parents.

[120] *Ibid.*, pp. 110, 115. Cartwright noted that he had replied only after intercession by (probably) John Field, and he asked Hildersam either to keep the letter secret 'or els let it smell of the fyre'.

[121] *Ibid.*, p. 110.

within the Word, Cartwright made it clear that there were certain books which were of especial value.[122] He also stressed that mere reading would not be adequate to the task; he advised Hildersam that there had to be a *will* to comprehend. Most of the letter details the later writers of greatest advantage to a divinity student, though Cartwright reminded his correspondent that human interpretation was not to be taken as equal in force to the revealed Word.[123] He suggested the reading of recent writers before ancient, so that one could more easily get an overview of the present state of the struggle, and of the 'friends and Patrons of the Truth' before the 'Adversaries', so that one met good doctrine before error.[124] Cartwright was adamant that the divinity student should read the history of a period before delving into its writers; knowledge of context would aid comprehension of argument.[125]

After this introduction, Cartwright felt, Hildersam would be ready for commentaries which, because they more familiarized the reader with Scripture, were to be approached before commonplaces. He suggested that one could generally avoid the Romanist efforts, and concentrate on Calvin, Oecolampadius, and Peter Martyr. Of all the Greeks Chrysostom was easily the most important.[126] Of commonplaces, which were useful to the divinity student for explaining the body of doctrine, he stressed Calvin's *Institutes* and Beza's *Confession*, and of the 'Adversaries' noted the importance of Lombard, Aquinas, Hosius, and Caninius.[127] From here, Cartwright turned to the councils and canons, with the general rule that the older they were, the less corrupt they were likely to be. From the Greeks he suggested Gregory Nazianzus, and from the Latin doctors Tertullian (though with some reservations), Cyprian, and Hilary.[128] He advised Ambrose, Augustine, and Jerome for their epistles, but only the former two for their arguments against adversaries.[129] Cartwright finished the outline of his course with a recommendation to read Luther, Bucer and Calvin.[130]

Cartwright's proposed course for his correspondent was in no way controversial. It was basic and brief, and specifically avoided the temptation to delve into recent English disputes, which might have been important to a student preparing to meet not only theological intricacies, but also perhaps a congregation alert to contemporary divisions. Cartwright was offering here

---

[122] For their general matter, the first five books of Moses (especially Deuteronomy), Joshua, the 'stories' of the Old Testament, Chronicles. Because of their difficulty, Daniel, Ezekiel, Zachariah, Revelation. Because packed with matter, Proverbs (Ch. 10 on), the prophecy of Ozias (Uzziah), Ecclesiastes and, from the New Testament, Romans. Because especially important for doctrine, Psalms, Proverbs, Romans (*ibid.*, pp. 111–12). [123] *Ibid.*, p. 112. [124] *Ibid.*, p. 113. [125] *Ibid.*, p. 113.
[126] *Ibid.*, pp. 113–14. Cartwright noted, however, that Martyr's 'Commentaries are rather Commonplaces then Commentaries' and should be treated as such. [127] *Ibid.*, p. 114. [128] *Ibid.*, p. 114.
[129] Jerome, he felt, became too hot in his polemic, which suffered from the presence of such anger (*ibid.*, p. 115). [130] *Ibid.*, p. 114.

not a revision of the undergraduate curriculum – Hildersam already possessed his B.A. – but rather a reading course for a student who had decided to enter the ministry. Though Cartwright rejected divinity degrees on the grounds that they represented a distortion of the proper offices of the church, he questioned neither the validity of university learning in a future minister, nor the application of these subjects to the preparation for pastoral tasks.

Some twenty-five years later Richard Bernard offered perhaps the most detailed godly course of studies for future ministers in our period. He condemned outright that 'brain-sicke opinion to deny the use of the Arts to the Scripture' which he found even in his day, and rather commended what he saw as the 'great necessitie of upholding Schooles of learning for the attainment' of knowledge useful for ministers. And so Bernard recommended daily reading of two chapters of the Bible, accompanied by a useful aid such as Gerardus' *de oratione studii*.[131] He also stressed the value of taking detailed notes on the Scriptures, to which the student could refer in his ministerial career. As a reminder that this course of study, though published in English, was indeed for the very learned, Bernard noted that to these exercises could profitably be joined the reading over once a day of a chapter of Scripture, alternately in Greek and Hebrew, with reference where necessary to the Latin and English translations.[132] To ensure a sufficient learned base for the future preacher, he required the usual university subjects, but added the study of 'Christian Ethicks, Politicks, Oeconomicks, naturall Philosophy, such as have written of Trees, Herbes, Beasts, of Husbandry, Geography, Histories of jewish customes, of their Weights and Measures . . .'.[133] On top of this substantial background of professional knowledge came the learned paraphernalia which accompanied Bible study: dictionaries, concordances, analytical expositions, annotations, reconciliations, catechisms, commonplaces, commentaries, ecclesiastical histories, acts of the councils, and, finally, summaries of controversy, for all of which Bernard made some studious recommendations.[134] Such a list was necessary to prepare the godly novice against the forces of learning evilly used.[135]

In setting out this course of studies for young ministers, Bernard was reflecting the wisdom of continental protestants such as Gerardus and Hemmingsen, who had also praised the study of logic, rhetoric and the three languages.[136] As our period wore on, and the godly scholarship of England grew, puritan divines were able to lean rather less heavily on continental scholarship. Robert Harris, though he did not expound a curriculum as full as that of Bernard, is a useful case in point. Well known himself for his

---

[131] Bernard, *Faithfull Shepheard* (1621), pp. 59–65. This was an expanded version of the first edition of 1607. [132] *Ibid.*, pp. 65, 71. [133] *Ibid.*, pp. 147–8. [134] *Ibid.*, pp. 148ff. [135] *Ibid.*, p. 157.
[136] Gerard, *Preparation to Ministerie*, esp. pp. 169ff., 261–2, 264–6; Hemmingsen, *Preacher*, fol. 7v; Ferrarius, *A Woorke*, fol. 77.

knowledge of Hebrew, case-divinity, chronology, and church history,[137] he also left a sketch of what divinity students should study. He regarded the Schoolmen as too obscure; he commended, within limits, the Lutherans; and he allowed Arminius himself while abhorring all Arminians. Pareus, Calvin, and Cartwright deserved attention. He recommended Aquinas and even contemporary papists (presumably for purposes of controversy), but in the main encouraged the reading of other puritans such as Ames, Baynes, Sibbes, Ball, Capel, Preston, Hildersam, Whately, Whitaker, Downame, Perkins, and Rainolds.[138] The generations of puritan stress on the interconnexion of learning and enthusiasm had by now established a solid enough corpus of knowledge both to inspire and train the future godly proselytizers.

Such exhortations about the necessity for specific kinds of learning in ministers, and the contemporary pressure among colleagues and congregations not to lag behind, may well account, along, of course, with simply the increased availability of printed books, for the increase in book ownership among ministers after the Reformation. By the end of the sixteenth century, it has been reported, few clerical inventories do not mention a 'study' in the home, whereas before the Reformation only about 14–15% of a sample of ministers possessed books.[139] Ministers were evidently reading increasingly widely within their field of expertise.[140] Though probably few aspired to (or could have afforded) the collection advised by Richard Bernard, which ran to several score titles in twelve categories,[141] many, especially as our period wears on, would at least have retained their university texts, their lecture notes and their indispensable commonplace books, which no doubt long served as the basis of many a learned sermon in the countryside. Those most devoted to learned godliness would have continued their studies in their ministerial posts, but for many the degree would have marked the end of any serious pursuit of scholarship. It was therefore imperative for puritans that they compose these lists of mandatory and suggested books; the correctness of future proselytizing lay in the proper guidance offered in the universities.

IV

Statements concerning the types of learning that future ministers should possess were complemented by sketches in diaries, in autobiographies, and especially in the 'lives' of puritan saints. By the end of our period, virtually all

---

[137] Clarke, *Ten Eminent Divines*, pp. 309–10. [138] *Ibid.*, pp. 314–16.
[139] Brooks, 'Social position', pp. 29, 32. For examples of books owned, and the size of clerical libraries, see also O'Day, *English Clergy*, esp. pp. 185–6; Clark, 'Ownership of books', pp. 95–111, in Stone, ed., *Schooling and Society*.
[140] On the late Tudor clergy in Yorkshire, see Purvis, 'Literacy of later Tudor clergy', in Cuming, ed., *Studies in Church History*, 5, pp. 149–55. [141] Bernard, *Faithfull Shepheard* (1621), pp. 146–58.

entrants into the ministry were graduates. The learned quality of the subjects in contemporary 'biographies' (including funeral sermons) is therefore interesting for delineating the achievement *vis-à-vis* the subjects recommended by the early puritans in their manuals. Perhaps consciously attempting a modern Christian hagiography, puritan biographers made the contrast between youthful adoration of learning and its later utilitarian employment into a central theme. The degree of praise in this type of sketch is of course to be expected, but we may at least draw from what is lauded those characteristics deemed most praiseworthy. The case of Bernard Gilpin is particularly interesting, because Gilpin had disputed on the Romanist side against John Hooper and Peter Martyr, making full use of his humane learning. In his Romanist days, Gilpin evidently

profited wonderfully in Humane Learning. He was very conversant also in the writings of *Erasmus*, which were in much esteem at that time: And to the study of *Logick*, and *Philosophy*, he added that of *Greek* and *Hebrew*; yea, after some few years spent in these studies, he grew so Famous, that there was no place of preferment for a Scholar whereof the eminency of his Virtues had not rendered him worthy . . .[142]

Gilpin's pre-conversion learning could thus serve both as a lesson in the possible utility of humane learning, and yet also as a warning that of itself it did not advance godliness; the will, too, had to be purified. After his conversion, Gilpin's learning had not been affected in its ability, but rather in its use: the scholar metamorphosed into the 'Apostle of the North', known for his widespread preaching.

The same course of studies and high achievement was recorded for the several generations of puritans before the Revolution. So John Carter, upon being asked at his ordination whether he had read the Bible through, replied that he had indeed 'read the Old Testament twice through in the *Hebrew*, and the New Testament often through in the *Greek* . . .'.[143] Samuel Crooke was reputed to be very knowledgeable in Greek, Hebrew, and also Arabic; he was, as well, fluent in modern European languages.[144] He had also studied history, politics, and 'physick', which he later used for the 'amplification' of divine subjects.[145] Richard Blackerby, of Trinity College, Cambridge, a future shining light in the training of yet another godly phalanx, was evidently known for his learning, 'especially in his great skill in the Hebrew, Greek and Latine tongues, being reckoned one of the best *Hebritians in Cambridge* in those days'.[146] Of Samuel Fairclough, finally, Clarke recorded that at Queens'

---

[142] Clarke, *Marrow of Ecclesiastical History*, I, p. 362. See the similar description of the vanity of Thomas Goodwin before his conversion (Goodwin, *Workes*, p. v).
[143] Clarke, *Ten Eminent Divines*, p. 3. The 'life' of Carter was written by his son, John.
[144] *Ibid.*, p. 27.   [145] *Ibid.*, p. 27.
[146] Clarke, *Eminent Persons*, p. 57. For Blackerby's seminary, see below, pp. 296–7.

College, Cambridge, he was soon recognized as a very able student by no less a scholar than John Preston. Fairclough indeed refused to take his B.A. at the usual time, because he had come to Cambridge 'to *study* and gain Learning and Knowledge, and not to *Commence* or take Degrees'. He therefore took another year to 'read what *kind* of Authors he *pleased* . . .': 'all the *Arts* and *Sciences* of *Logic, Rhetorick,* of *Ethicks, Physicks* and *Metaphysicks* . . .'.[147]

Biographers were careful, however, even while praising the learning of their subjects, to emphasize that their scholarship did not *cause* the later conversion. Born and educated in Blackburn, and then trained at Lincoln College, Oxford, under the puritan divine John Randall, Robert Bolton became a fellow of Brasenose. He then proceeded to fortify his academic knowledge of natural philosophy, metaphysics, mathematics, and school divinity, but was described as having as yet 'nothing in him for Religion . . .'.[148] Indeed, he evidently indulged his love of stage plays, cards, dice, swearing and sabbath-breaking.[149] Learning thus stood in Bolton on its neutrality; it could hardly be said to cause these vices, but, more important, it did not of its own curb them. Bolton's pre-conversion learning was examined in great detail; after receiving his M.A. he became Reader in, successively, logic, moral philosophy, and natural philosophy. He was even chosen to dispute before the king. His biographer also acknowledged Bolton's excellent skills in 'Schoole-Divinity', especially the works of Aquinas.[150] Despite this abundance of learning, when Bolton, as an unregenerate, went to hear the preaching of the eminent William Perkins, he was thoroughly disappointed (presumably because of his desire for a demonstration of humane learning from the pulpit), and concluded that Perkins was '*a barren empty fellow, and a passing meane scholler*'.[151] Such an effect did the plain truth have on the learned but unconverted. But when God had changed Bolton's heart, then Bolton in turn 'changed his opinion of Mr. *Perkins*, and thought him as learned and godly a Divine as our Church hath for many yeares enjoyed in so young a man . . .'.[152] The visible blending of such advanced learning with an emphatic experience of conversion epitomized the saints' use of humane knowledge.

In the sermon at the funeral of Richard Stock, Thomas Gataker stressed not only the deceased's learning, but even more his godly application of it. Stock was evidently

of eminent note in the Colledge he lived in, both for his unweariable industry, and his singular proficiency in those studies of humanitie, that are as handmaids to Divinity,

---

[147] *Ibid.,* pp. 155, 158. Fairclough took his degree at the end of this extra year.
[148] Clarke, *Marrow of Ecclesiastical History,* p. 457. [149] *Ibid.,* p. 457.
[150] Bolton, *Last & Learned Worke,* 'Life', sigs. b2ᵛ–3. [151] *Ibid.,* sigs. b3ᵛ–4.
[152] *Ibid.,* sig. b4ᵛ. See the similar description of the vanity of Thomas Goodwin before his conversion (Goodwin, *Workes,* p. v).

and helpe to lay a good ground for any future profession. So his care was to entertwine pietie and humanitie the one with the other, that as web and woofe they ranne on ever along together through the whole course of his studies . . .[153]

Stock's 'humanitie' was thus made acceptable – was cleansed – by being interwoven with his own 'pietie'. The usage of such learning by the obviously regenerate was tantamount to saying that it had received the Lord's sanction. That such paragons as Perkins, Fenner, Chaderton, and Preston *all* excelled in humane learning, and its application, doubtless created in the hearts and minds of the aspiring young repentants an awareness that learning did not have to be cast off even after conversion.

It should thus be clear that the puritan scheme of the allowable types of knowledge was heavily indebted to the humanist refinement of classical learning,[154] and to the humanists' desire for a 'vigorous, ethical Christianity'.[155] Erasmus especially, in his *Paraclesis* (the preface to the 1516 edition of his Latin and Greek Testaments), accorded particular importance to the application of humane learning to produce a purer Gospel. Advanced learning, obtainable in general only at the universities, became a virtual *sine qua non* for puritan ministers. In these darker days, the purer Light was to be assisted by the flickerings of humane scholarship. This was the basis of the enduring compromise which puritan fervency struck with the intellect. At the same time, the extent to which puritans adopted the learning of the age should not blind us to the very different purpose they envisaged for such learning. Perry Miller called puritans 'disciples' of Erasmus and Colet.[156] This, I think, confuses the relationship. Puritans used humanists for their scholarship and pedagogy, as they also used the ancients, the Schoolmen, even their Romanist opponents whose schools they admired – that is, as aids to the task of extracting from the Word all that humane learning could recover. But they also fell back on the simplicity of Scripture and the fundamental irrelevance of learning to salvation. The fastest and most useful route to Jerusalem might well run through Athens; so much the puritans were willing to concede. But the intrinsic pleasures of that city were to be an experience for use, never a refuge or sanctuary, as puritans sought constantly to remind themselves and their society. The goal at which puritans aimed was rather the accurate and efficacious public propagation of the Word. The minister had been called as a mediator, as a proselytizer. He had therefore not only to discover, but also to publicize, and that took a special application of this dichotomous union of learning and fervency.

---

[153] Gataker, *Abrahams Decease*, sig. B2.
[154] This notion permeates Miller's *New England Mind*. In short (but concentrated) form it can be found in Miller & Johnson, eds., *Puritans*, pp. 19ff.   [155] Haydn, *Counter-Renaissance*, p. 59.
[156] Miller & Johnson, eds., *Puritans*, p. 21.

7

THE USE OF LEARNING
IN THE PULPIT

I

At the core of the Reformation was not only the idea that the dogma, hierarchy and services of the church universal should be cleansed, but also the proposition that the undefiled truth of Scripture should be propagated in the clear vernacular to the people. Recent scholarship has reinforced the picture of the centrality of preaching in puritan views of the ministry, and demonstrated the importance of Ramist structure and plainer style in puritan sermons.[1] This perhaps helps to explain the lack of first-rate theologians, but on the other hand the huge pulpit literature of the eighty years before the Revolution. Especially has Blench elucidated the divisions within protestant preaching: the ancient (or traditional) style, the new Reformed method, and the modern (based on imitation of the classical oration). Puritans generally employed the first two structures, and especially the new Reformed style, which emphasized the parallel importance of 'doctrine' and 'use', so necessary to instruction in the existential living of the faith at the core of the puritan thrust.[2] Blench has also divided contemporary rhetorical forms into three main styles: plain but uncolloquial, colloquial, and ornate. The first of these, to which most puritans belonged, itself can be broken down into three subdivisions: extremely bare and austere, then a somewhat less colourless style, and, finally, a moderately decorated delivery.[3]

One of the questions around which debate centred (both within the puritan camp and against opponents without) encompassed the dilemma of whether the godly preacher was to limit himself to his own comments on a scriptural

---

[1] For a good basic summary, see Haller, *Rise of Puritanism*; Knappen, *Tudor Puritanism*: Hill, *Society and Puritanism*, esp. Ch. 2; Horton Davies, *Worship and Theology*, I, esp. Ch. 8; II, pp. 161–77; Blench, *Preaching in England*, esp. pp. 168ff.; Herr, *Elizabethan Sermon, passim*.

[2] Blench, *Preaching in England*, pp. 100–2.

[3] *Ibid.*, pp. 168ff. Blench says that, while the first subdivision allowed neither tropes nor schemata, the second allowed tropes but still not schemata; the third subdivision allowed tropes and occasional schemata. He also notes that Ramist (Talonist) rhetoric, which was so influential with puritans, allowed tropes (because they aided clarity of meaning) but not schemes (which savoured of 'mere oratorical display').

text, or whether he could legitimately rely upon – even include – the conclusions of other learned exegetes. On top of this, could heathen learning which advanced a rational ethical system, or which illustrated scriptural lessons, be used in the preparation or delivery of the popular sermon? Obviously, the minister did not study simply to forget; the consciousness which he carried from college to congregation was bound to be infused with human thought. The practical difficulty, then, was to establish a force somewhere between 'an unlearned ministerie [and] . . . a pontificall Hierarchie'[4] which could bring the clear and efficacious Word to the people.

Puritans had not only to apply theological belief and intellectual theory to a text of Scripture; they had always also to keep in mind that they were guiding people who were conducting a search for assurance. The employment of different modes of preaching by single preachers thus may be explained at least in part by variations in both the composition of the audience and the difficulty of the sermon topic. In a society in which ministers were increasingly expected to possess higher levels of humane learning, there was likely increased pressure to explain the more intricate aspects of salvation by demonstration of this learning. The occasional rhetorical flourish could also serve as a defence against establishment charges of 'ignorance', and as a point of distinction from the truly radical enthusiasts who demanded the sole conjunction of the Scripture and inner light in pulpit explanations. As well, the university experience meant that for most puritans their writing would almost naturally tend to an involved regimen of arguments and proofs. The attempts to keep sermons rigorously plain must have involved a self-conscious struggle against a constant temptation to demonstrate one's academic worth.

Our purpose here is to work beyond an analysis of what the sermons actually contained in terms of structure and rhetorical devices, to the question of the degree to which puritans' sermons and their specific advice on sermonizing reflected the whole pattern of their coming to grips with reason and humane learning. It may perhaps be most useful to approach this first by looking at the general attitudes of puritans towards the question of the proper content of sermons, and then by examining several more detailed puritan analyses.

The starting-point for all puritans in the question of what a sermon should contain was the scriptural condemnation of those who 'hid & toke away the pure doctrine & true understanding of the Scriptures'.[5] Again it was Paul who provided the basic lessons – but also the confusion. In an era in which the fledgeling religion was struggling to find its own intellectual ethos, Paul could not permit admiration for the classics, which might all too easily lead to the

4   Travers, *Defence of Ecclesiasticall Discipline*, p. 25.
5   1560 Geneva Bible, marginal comment to Luke 11.52, Jesus' condemnation of the 'interpreters of the Law'.

submersion of the basically non-intellectual message of the Saviour.[6] So he noted to the Corinthians that '[n]either stode my worde, & my preaching in the entising speache of mans wisdome, but in the plaine evidence of the Spirit and of power'.[7] The whole purpose of preaching – to Paul this was at the core of lively Christianity – was to edify, not to display knowledge.[8] And so the Geneva commentators condemned those false preachers who 'more esteemed the outwarde shewe of wisdome and eloquence, then true godliness'.[9] Had not Paul himself certified to the Galatians that 'the Gospel which was preached of me, was not after man', and to the Corinthians that his task was to 'preache the Gospel, not with wisdome of wordes . . .'?[10]

And yet, just when a Christian might be on the verge of concluding that, indeed, humane learning could have no part in religion, Paul had refused to utter the final condemnation. Edification did not, in the end, deny a lesser, supportive role to learning.[11] Indeed, the pressures from audience expectation and individual familiarity with logic, rhetoric, and the arts were almost bound to ensure that demonstration of learning could not in practice be totally excluded from the pulpit. Puritans clamoured for learned preachers, and insisted that ministers make use of their college studies in the involved preparation of sermons. The famous story of John Dod delivering a sermon at a moment's notice might well testify to his great learning, ability, and experience, but puritans would have been extremely wary of proposing it as the usual manner of preparation. Those who delivered *ex tempore* might well do more damage than good. This did not necessarily mean a full longhand draft, however. When Daniel Featley requested a copy of one of Thomas Gataker's sermons, Gataker replied that originally, all he had left was 'no more than some generall heads and brief notes scribled in a loose paper before . . .'. Robert Harris, on the other hand, noted that he had produced a draft of a sermon before delivery.[12] The difference in method likely depended on the familiarity of the subject, and the quality of the preacher's memory. Nonetheless, the different approach hid a general agreement concerning the considerable planning that each sermon entailed. Before the pulpit oration could prove helpful to the congregation, it had to be constructed as a clear exposition of the doctrine

---

6   For example, the Geneva Bible explained I Corinthians 1.20: 'herein Paul reprocheth even the best learned, as thogh not one of them colde perceive by his owne wisdome this mysterie of Christ reveiled in the Gospel'.
7   I Corinthians 2.4. The Tomson version of the Geneva marginalia on this verse expressed in even clearer terms the advantage of keeping pure the Word: 'for his vertue and power which they knewe well enough, was so much the more excellent, because it had no worldly helpe joyned with it'.
8   See, for example, the admonitions in I Corinthians 8.1; *ibid.,* 14.4,5. See Coolidge, *Pauline Renaissance,* esp. Ch. 2, on the puritan understanding of 'edification'.
9   1560 Geneva Bible, marginal comment to II Corinthians 5.12.
10 Galatians 1.11; I Corinthians 1.17. See also the Geneva gloss by Laurence Tomson on the latter verse.   11 I Corinthians 14.5.
12 Gataker, *St Stevens Last Will,* sig. Z2; Harris, *Samuels Funerall,* sig. A4.

contained in a scriptural text.[13] Preparation was recognized as the proper province of the handmaids of learning, for 'the finding it out is by Logick Analysis, unto which Retoricke also and Grammar serveth'.[14]

This was also the stage for application of moral and philosophical lessons culled from the sources imbibed at university, in a puritan 'seminary', or at a prophesying or exercise. Emphasis was always on personal guidance: Henry Smith advised that it was far more valuable for ministers to listen to other preachers than to try to improve their craft by searching in books.[15] Private correspondence between members of the brotherhood, and the lending of books, likely also promoted a wider range of ideas in England's several pulpits. Preaching manuals, too, encouraged a higher degree of expertise, and offered illustrations of different styles.[16] Commonplace books listed useful phrases and references to classical sources and scriptural commentaries alike. Finally, puritan divines themselves soon became a source of great help, if not actually of 'authority', to younger ministers. Thus a preface to Robert Bolton's collected works praised the late divine for his careful approach to, and valuable use of, the Fathers, and offered his method as a lesson to those who had still to find a satisfactory balance.[17]

But if in requiring learned preparation puritans did not differ noticeably as a group from other English preachers of this period, in response to the second problem – deciding what part of this learning the congregation could be permitted to see – puritans clearly parted company with their fellow churchmen. Indeed, the puritan spectrum stretched as far as the radical John Rudd, who was suspended from his ministry early in 1597 for 'errors' which reportedly included the belief that 'the use of humanity, humane Arte, and prophane Authors in sermons was and is altogether unprofitable and unlawfull'.[18] Edward Dering, whose credentials of forthrightness were impeccable, if hard-won, was known at Cambridge for his immense scholarship. Nonetheless, he argued that a preacher could not publicly rely on the Fathers, nor even on the oft-cited Augustine, not because they spoke untruly, but rather because the congregation might come to think of them, rather than of Scripture, as the

[13] H. Smith, *Sermons*, sig. D4. [14] Ames, *Marrow of Sacred Divinity*, p. 157.
[15] Smith, *13 Sermons*, sig. D2.
[16] In 1646 John Wilkins' preaching manual recommended 14 fairly recent predecessors, and mentioned that there were 'above forty other Authors' available (Wilkins, *Ecclesiastes*, pp. 2–3). William Chappell, in his manual, offered a list of works for preachers which is almost an index of English protestantism (with heavy emphasis on puritan writers) (Chappell, *Preacher*, at end of text following p. 204).
[17] Bolton, *Workes*, 'To the Reader', by 'C.C.', sig. a5.
[18] C.U.L. MS Baker B.8 (Mm.ii.23), pp. 193–4. Rudd promised to recant publicly in order to keep his licence to preach, but on 6 Mar. 1596/7, at St Mary's, Cambridge, he evidently confirmed his radical opinions. He was again suspended and threatened with an appearance before the High Commission if he did not recant fully and properly.

source of truth. He praised the Old Testament prophets for excluding humane wisdom, and concluded that 'only God must speke in the mouth of all ministers' in the present age, too.[19] This became the puritan pattern: the attainment of great learning followed by close restriction on its demonstration to the populace. Richard Rogers similarly reminded his readers that it was the 'sound plaine, and powerful preaching of the Gospell' that God had chosen as the especial means of transmitting grace, and so heartily complained of those who do 'stuffe their sermons with authorities of men . . .'.[20] Even the lenient Thomas Adams, who stressed the importance of humane learning in a minister, and would not utterly condemn the appearance of 'the morall Sayes of a Poet, or a Philosopher, or perhaps some golden sentence of a Father', nonetheless protested against radical criticism, that 'we make not the Pulpit a Philosophy, Logicke, Poetry-Schoole: but all these so many Staires to the Pulpit. . .'.[21] Adams' image of learning as the stairs to pulpit eloquence is very helpful, for, as we shall see, most puritans stressed that once they had reached the top step, only Scripture should pour forth.

There were, within the ranks of 'non-puritans', also a great variety of approaches to sermonizing, and specifically to the use of humane learning within sermons. I have already argued the infelicities of a dichotomous model for puritan/non-puritan relations. Reformist-minded bishops such as Grindal and Thomas Morton elicited little opposition or criticism from puritans, for in many ways they seem to have represented the ecclesiological and evangelical idea of reformers who comprehended the possibilities and likely limits of immediate change. William Evans, a strong supporter of the administration, wrote that after years of preaching he had learned the necessity of simple language and basic reasoning if one hoped to reach an unlearned auditory. Joseph Hall, an Emmanuel-trained 'Calvinist', but hardly a puritan, worried concerning pulpits that 'much ornament is no good sign: painting of the face argues an ill complexion of the body, a worse mind'.[22]

But puritans also found within the church, and sometimes in positions of authority, those who overvalued the contribution which humane learning could make to the clarification of religion. John King, who was later Bishop of London, stated plainly that he was 'not of opinion with those men who thinke that all secular & prophane learning should be abandoned from the lips of the preacher, & whither he teach or exhort, he is of the necssity [*sic*] to tie himselfe to the

---

[19] Dering, *XXVII Lectures*. sigs. A.v^v–vi^v. See also Airay, *Lectures Upon Philippians*, p. 173; Gybson, *Fruitful Sermon*, sig. D.3; Bolton, *Last & Learned Worke*, 'Life' by Edward Bagshaw, sigs. b.2, b8^v.

[20] Rogers, *Certaine Sermons*, p. 131; Preston, *Sinnes Overthrow*, pp. 103, 102; Whately, *New Birth*, p. 113.　　[21] Adams, *Workes*, p. 69; see also Rainolds, *Excellent Oration*, pp. 58–60.

[22] Evans, *Translation of the Booke of Nature*, 'Epistle', pp. 48–9; Fisch, 'Puritan prose style', *ELH*, 19, p. 238. In Hall's case, this was perhaps a strange remark, given that he was not known for his own virtuous shunning of all the embellishments of prose.

sentence and phrase of onely scripture. Good is good wheresoever I finde it.'[23]
Similarly, Egeon Askew, who was writing shortly after the conflict with the
Barrowists had brought much of puritan concern with learning into the open,
argued that the three main objections to the inclusion of humane learning
were the necessary emphasis on Christ in the pulpit, the sufficiency of the
Word alone, and the proper separation of theology and philosophy.[24] Against
these objections he laid out the answers, respectively, that: Christ had not
spoken against truth emanating from any source; that one should not deny the
support of such figures as, say, Zanchius and Aristotle, who provided good
arguments for the existence of God; and, finally, that secular learning in truth
is not oppposed to the ends of theology, but, in fact, might well contribute
towards their achievement.[25] Indeed, if only pure Scripture could be used in
church, then godly knowledge devised later, by such stalwarts as John Calvin,
could not be used in sermons.[26] God might originally have chosen the
unlearned to carry the message, but the present age required altered methods
for different circumstances.[27] Askew similarly argued that since Christ and
Paul had used foreign tongues in their speech to the populace, no objection
could be raised against that practice, provided it did not comprise the bulk of
the sermon. He even cited Calvin's own opinion that the contemporary objection to eloquence, based on Corinthians, was a misinterpretation of the
Apostle.[28] Against the third objection – that philosophy and theology should
be kept separate – Askew produced a counterargument that must have
touched puritan sensibilities as well as logic. On the basis that humane learning was a 'thing indifferent', he contended that any denial of its use in the
preparation and delivery of the sermon was also a refusal to respond to the
wishes and needs of the auditory, and a continuation of the 'divellish policie'
of the past.[29]

Insistence on the banishment of humane sources from the public orations
concerned two objections which, as we have seen, were at the core of puritan
difficulties with learning in general: the vanity such sources might well cause
in the preachers themselves, and the 'insult' that inclusion would offer to God
by intimating that the pure Word was not sufficient for the exposition of faith.
Concerning the first charge, puritans constantly warned of the temptation of
exhibiting university learning at the expense of the plainer exegesis of the
Word. 'Some' there were, who would, after enjoying this status of
knowledge, 'refuse to joyne with Christ, because they are wedded to their
pleasures and profits, and are loth to be weaned from them'.[30] John Udall

[23] King, *Lectures Upon Jonas*, p. 541.   [24] Askew, *Brotherly Reconcilement*, pp. 259–61.
[25] Ibid., pp. 259–62.   [26] Ibid., pp. 262–4.   [27] Ibid., pp. 267, 270–1, 279.
[28] Ibid., pp. 286–7, 296–7, 262–4.   [29] Ibid., pp. 305–6, 311, 327, 335–41ff.
[30] Andrewes, *Certaine Verie Worthy Sermons*, pp. 31, 28; see also Dyke, *Sermon Dedicatory*, C2ᵛ–3;
Cartwright, *Second Admonition*, p. 32.

regarded puffed-up ministers as 'the greatest foes to mans soule', for their 'painted eloquence' was intended rather 'to delight the sences' than to humble the believer.[31] Lost in their own 'wisdom' and eloquence, these 'selfe-preaching men, that make preaching little else, but an ostentation of wit and reading, doe put this sword of the Spirit into a velvet scabbard, that it cannot pricke and wound the heart; it cannot worke life, by working death first . . .'.[32] Those preachers who dug so deeply in the poets and philosophers for wisdom and the enhancement of their own reputation could hardly have spent enough time in the garden of the Word.[33] Learning, in practice, even in the hands of God's chosen messengers, could thus prove a most dangerous tool.

But human learning in the pulpit was not only proud; it was also, quite simply, superfluous, given the clarity of the message itself. Paul had warned that the arts could detract from the simplicity of the message if they became the central feature of the pulpit exercise. John Preston was insistent that preparation required learning – 'we had need to use all the Arts, Sciences, and Knowledges that we can' – but that the *public* use of humane learning could easily hide the plain truth: 'humane Wit and Eloquence is so farre from setting forth the excellencie of the Word, as it obscures the excellencie of it. . . '.[34] A further refinement of this argument as to the superfluity of humane learning in preaching was the awareness that God might take it amiss that his special servants thought his Word insufficient to be presented naked to their congregations. So Walter Travers insisted that it was also '*impertinent* to speake with strange tongue' in the church.[35] Bartimeus Andrewes expanded on the insult to the Lord offered by those who hid his saving message behind the effusions of their own puny wit: they

thinke Christe too base to bee preached simply in him selfe . . . and thinke that Christe commeth nakedly, unlesse cloathed with vaine ostentation of wordes. Others esteeme him too homely, simple and unlearned, unlesse he bee beautified and blazed over with store of Greeke or Laten sentences in the pulpits . . . or els he must be glosed out and printed with the frooth of Philosophi, Poetry or such like.[36]

So far I have outlined what one might term the duties which the preacher owed to God (who had called him) to preach the Word plainly. But the sermon was also the chief medium for the instillation of faith, and for the

---

[31] Udall, *Certaine Sermons*, sig. H.ii^v; see also Gilpin, *Godly Sermon*, p. 23.

[32] Whately, *New Birth*, p. 113. For very similar opinions, see also Taylor, *Davids Learning*, p. 4; Dyke, *Sermon Dedicatory*, sig. C2^v.

[33] Francis Johnson and Henry Ainsworth, the radicals, took this idea to the extreme by arguing that *any* study of the heathens wasted the time that a preacher might have applied to further schooling in the Word (Johnson & Ainsworth, *Apologie for true Christians*, pp. 78–9.)

[34] Preston, *Sinnes Overthrow*, pp. 104, 102. See also Northbrooke, *Poore Mans Garden*, p. 55.

[35] Travers, *Defence of Ecclesiasticall Discipline*, p. 67. (My italics). It was perhaps an extension of this argument that moved the separatist Robert Browne to argue that the scaffolding of Ramist or Aristotelian logic should similarly not be visible (*Writings of Browne and Harrison*, ed. Peel & Carlson, p. 17).

[36] Andrewes, *Certain Verie Worthie Sermons*, pp. 26–7.

proclamation of how assurance might be attained; this required that all in the congregation be able to understand the abstruse points of divinity raised by the sermon text. Here puritans faced the twin problems of those who wanted a demonstration of humane learning and those (the great majority of country congregations) who would likely not have been able to wade through involved structure and complicated rhetorical flourishes. The fervency and level of attention of congregations should not be over-estimated; visitation books are rife with accusations of 'disorderly conduct' during the service.[37]

Preaching of course had first to be comprehensible.[38] John Stockwood therefore insisted that preachers not 'make of the pulpet a schoole of philosophie, nor of the Churche the desk of an Oratour'.[39] Dod and Cleaver, in their highly popular exposition of the Commandments, pursued the same point, noting that the minister's duty was '*to speake to the capacitie and conscience of his hearers*, in all diligence and faithfulnesse'.[40] Dod was evidently of the opinion that 'most Ministers in *England* usually shoot over the heads of their hearers', and so suggested that the preacher should 'stoope to the lowest capacity'.[41] Indeed, he insisted that 'till men be perswaded that God is their God, they count it bootlesse to pray . . .'.[42] The greater stress placed by puritans on the function of the sermon necessitated plainness of style. Puritan preachers might especially seek the aid and conversion of the well-born, but they did not confine their efforts to this increasingly well-educated group. In order to reach below the ranks of the gentle, puritans (and those non-puritans who addressed the evangelical problem) had perforce to use simple language.

Thomas Gataker, in a funeral sermon, cast the point in a personal light through the remembrance of a conversation he had had with Daniel Featley in the presence of the woman who was the subject of his oration:

when he and my selfe were in her presence talking together, of the occurrents of the time, and some points of Schoole-learning, somewhat out of her element, and above her sphease, she strooke in with us, and requested us to discourse rather of somewhat, that she might also receive some benefit by, that we might be useful as well to her as to us.[43]

---

[37] Granger, *Exposition on Ecclesiastes*, sig. A4; Drant, *Three Godly Sermons*, sig. Lvi. This was not only a puritan complaint; see also John Jewel's caustic comment, quoted in Herr, *Elizabethan Sermon*, p. 18, to the effect that 'Many are so ignorant, they know not what the scriptures are, they know not that there are any scriptures.' On disorder in churches, see Wrightson, 'Puritan reformation of manners', unpub. Ph.D. thesis, Univ. of Cambridge, 1974, pp. 122–3.

[38] See, for example, the citation of this point from Corinthians by Dering, *XXVII Lectures*, sig. C.iiii[v].   [39] Quoted in Greaves, *Society and Religion*, p. 85.

[40] Dod & Cleaver, *Ten Commandements*, pp. 239–40. (My italics).

[41] Clarke, *Thirty-two English Divines*, p. 176.   [42] Dod & Cleaver, *Ten Commandements*, p. 18.

[43] Gataker, *St Stevens Last Will*, p. 15.

Puritan ministers were ever ready to use their learning as protection against the radical enthusiasts and 'mechanick' preachers. But, in the presence of those who seemed dedicated to the puritan view of the godly struggle, they displayed a remarkable sensitivity to the popular need for a simplified yet authoritative and efficacious gospel. Gataker illustrated the balance by noting for his readers that he had put quotations from Scripture 'and such shreds or parcels of exotike Language, as might be some rub to an English Reader' into the margin.[44] Samuel Clarke was insistent that such an approach was successful: 'It mightily affected poor creatures to hear the Mysteries of God, (by his excellent skill that way) brought down to their own language and dialect.'[45] In this context one might remember that regional dialects were still spoken by the learned. Difficulties arising from this are seldom commented upon in the contemporary literature, possibly because a high percentage of university graduates who entered the ministry seem to have returned to the county of their birth. For the more difficult task of reading, but in the same vein of approaching scantily educated parishioners, the printed sermons commonly included a Ramist diagram which clearly delineated the structure. In the pulpit, where the listener could not 're-hear' the words as he might re-read them, the language had to be at the same time simple and powerful enough to yield both comprehension and repentance. Here, a further aspect of the all-sufficiency of the Word – its rhetoric – was drawn forth.

Popular preaching could also not afford to address the reason alone. Many puritans, with their doctrine of voluntaristic faith, held that the will, as much as the understanding, was the seat of faith. The will was moved rather by an appeal to the heart and to the 'affections'. Thus the dialectic of learning and enthusiasm existed not only within the preacher himself, but also externally, in the appeal he launched to the congregation as their means of salvation. Richard Sibbes, in prefaces to tracts by other puritans, stressed the importance of stirring the emotions in readers, as indeed the Bible similarly moved them.[46] Thomas Hooker warned that ministers should beware of scantily educated or even illiterate congregations which affected a love for classical allusions, foreign phrases, and even the wisdom of the Fathers. Too often, he lamented, this reflected simply a desire to avoid a more fervent exposition of Scripture which would awaken them and 'sting' their hearts.[47] Of Richard Greenham's pulpit style Clarke noted: 'He was so earnest, and took such extraordinary pains in his preaching, that his shirt would usually be as wet with

---

[44] *Ibid.*, sig. A2ᵛ.   [45] Clarke, *Thirty-two English Divines*, p. 177.

[46] *Complete Works of Richard Sibbes*, ed. Grosart, pp. ciff., Prefaces to works by John Smith, John Ball, and Richard Capel. As Grosart notes (p. cx n.), Sibbes' recommendation of a text was a useful advertisement.

[47] Hooker, *Soules Preparation*, p. 66.

sweating, as if it had been drenched in water. . .'[48] Learning, especially at the grass-roots level of proselytizing, far away from the measured debates of university scholasticism, was not to be permitted to drown protestant 'enthusiasm'. The message of the covenant was that the sinner had to *work* at his faith. The mediator with the Almighty should be seen to struggle alongside him. The visible act of wrestling with sin might well produce a greater sense of solidarity between preacher and people. One did not debate Antichrist in the countryside; one fought him from the battlement of the pulpit.

The common opposition to rhetorical devices such as tropes and schemes, though not always followed in practice, can perhaps be better understood in this light. Those puritans who did allow tropes had to correlate them with the call for 'Christ plainly preached', which produced an even higher state of paradox regarding the role of visible learning. Finally, one can unfortunately only muse concerning the degree to which a greater part of the congregation may have been alienated by preachers who brought their learning to bear too heavily from the pulpit. While visible learning may have bred a desire to possess education among the upper classes, who had an economically realistic chance of attaining it, it may well have fostered among lower orders who were, by and large, effectively excluded from more than a few years' schooling a hatred of the universities and the social status they conferred. Throughout our period the separatists evidently received some support for their emphasis on the rigorous extirpation of visible humane learning.[49] Their radical stance can be seen as an attempt at full application of the implications of certain of the puritan attitudes. The hostility to the universities which exploded in the freer atmosphere of the 1640s may have been just as important a product of the 'educational revolution' as a more literate populace.

In practice, though they became renowned for their 'plain style', puritans could not bring themselves to break their bond with learning, and thus possibly jeopardize their elevated status. As a key, we may take the view of Richard Rogers, a preacher of renowned sensibility towards his pastoral requirements, who argued that, although 'the people have many infirmities, much dulnes, slipperie memories, and sundrie other pullbackes', preachers should not lower themselves completely to the level of their charges.[50] Thomas Taylor openly criticized preachers who cited few scriptural texts, and rather relied on 'Doctors, Fathers, Councels, nay profane Poets and

[48] Clarke, *Thirty-two English Divines*, p. 12. See also John Rylands Library Eng. MS 524, fols. 1–72, Arthur Hildersam's record of Richard Greenham's ministry, which may perhaps have been Clarke's source: 'Hee being put in mind of his great zeal and fervency of speakinge, that hee should leav it, said hee would not have any use it with constraint, but when the weightines of the thing provoked therunto and gods spirit should move unto it . . .' (fols. 5ᵛ–6).   [49] Greaves, *Society and Religion*, pp. 84–5.
[50] Rogers, *Seven Treatises*, pp. 26, 27. On Rogers see Haller, *Rise of Puritanism*, pp. 36–7. See also Drant, *Three Godly Sermons*, sig. Lvi.

heathens . . .'.[51] And yet – *imitatio Pauli* – Taylor would not betray his humane learning for the banner of enthusiasm alone. I quote him at length as a clear example of the dialectic that has been a theme throughout this study:

> I am not so nice, as that I thinke not there may be a sparing and sober use of humane testimonies in Sermons; sometimes in cases of Grammar; sometimes in matters of great controversie, to show the consent of the ancient Church, especially dealing with an adversarie that will claime all antiquitie for him; sometime by way of conviction, to shame Christians by the heathen, as the Lord did the Iewes by *Chittim* and *Kedar*, and the sluggard by pismire. Neither am I an enemie to learning, but would have a man well seene in naturall *Philosophy*, in humane literature, in the writings of Fathers and Schoolemen, and be as a good housholder stored with *things new and olde*. But needlesly, and for ostentation, to give tongues unto dead men; and in the message of God, to put to silence the voice of God, speaking in the Scripture, to set up Hagar the handmaid above *Sarah* her mistresse, is a fearful sinne of these dayes; wherein for a man to tie himselfe close to the Scripture without such flourishes, and to scorne to send a rich Iewell to the painter, is to bring a blot on himself, that he is a man of no learning.[52]

Here, then, encapsulated, are not only the conclusions, but also the *order*, of puritan thought. First came Taylor's proscription of relying for proofs and textual sources on anything save Scripture; then followed the allowance that godly human authors and past Christian practices could help illuminate the point at hand, and, also, that even the morality of the heathen might be alluded to; and finally, the stern reminder that all this was dross and ungodliness if set up as an equal authority with the Word, or as a source of pride in the preacher.[53]

The degree of learning in the sermon seems to have depended very much upon the context. Sermons delivered *ad clerum* bore far fewer restrictions on humane allusions and structural devices than pulpit offerings for the laity. Such flexibility may well have heightened the status of ministers, for they could preach to the very learned (other ministers), the moderately learned (gentry, merchants, perhaps yeomen), and to the unlearned (the common auditory) as occasion demanded. Those who mistook the occasion, or lacked adequate flexibility, or who slipped into the temptation of vanity, were mocked by those puritans who had learned the lesson of matching their words to their listeners' capacity.[54]

This seeming confusion may possibly have reinforced the status of the minister by pointing out that full comprehension of the advantages and disadvantages of humane learning came only from the special abilities which God

---

[51] Taylor, *Christs Combate*, p. 252; see also Northbrooke, *Poore Mans Garden*, fols. 64–5^v.
[52] Taylor, *Christs Combate*, pp. 252–3.   [53] Harris, *Gods Goodnes*, sig. A5.
[54] See, for example, Taylor, *Christs Combate*, p. 103.

conferred on his mediators. The way in which a minister used learning might thus be taken as external evidence of his own progress in godliness. Thus Samuel Crooke, B.D., sometime Reader in rhetoric and then in philosophy, a man who added Arabic to his Greek and Hebrew, still never 'strove for vain glory, *nor of men sought he praise*, disclaiming to stoop to the lure of popular applaus: and therefore he ever shuned those more gay, and lighter flourishes of a luxuriant wit . . .'.[55] Nor did biographers forget the primary function of saints as messengers to the masses: 'Though he was a good Linguist, and well read, both in ancient and modern Authors, yet (ordinarily) he Preached, though always with evidence of Reason, yet still in a plain, and clear Stile, by Doctrine, Reason and Use, that so he might be understood by the meanest Capacity.'[56]

Since religion was more a matter of practice than of cold knowledge, puritan sermons were frequently directed to the end not only of proposing a detailed scholarly explanation of the text but also of detailing the application of the lesson. Thomas Gataker's description of William Bradshaw, lecturer at Christ Church, London, will suffice:

For he seldome made any Excursion into the handling of common places, or drew his subject matter out at length by any prolixly continued Discourse: But the main frame both of his publick Sermons and private Exercises, for the most part, if not wholly, consisted, after some brief and genuine Resolution of the context, and explication of the Terms, where need required, of Notes and Observations, with much variety and great Dexterity drawn immediately from the Text, and naturally, without constraint, issuing and flowing forth either from the main Body, or from the several Limbs of it, with some useful Application annexed thereunto . . .[57]

Puritan admonitions to guard against too-free use of humane learning in the pulpit thus, for the reasons we have seen, did not produce a monolithic preaching style. Much depended on reaction to context, which we have taken to be the defining characteristic of puritan existence at the second level.

II

Especially for young ministers, and for those who did not readily take to preaching, the construction and delivery of a sermon must have been a great burden. For them, however, the Reformation developed an improved form of vocational assistance – the preaching manual – which illustrated in detail these general patterns of the relationship between humane learning and godly preaching. First we should note in passing the variety of continental influences

---

[55] Clarke, *Ten Eminent Divines*, p. 35.
[56] Clarke, *Eminent Persons*, p. 34. This was said of Thomas Wilson, B.A. of Cambridge and later a member of the Westminster Assembly.   [57] Clarke, *Thirty-two English Divines*, p. 52.

which bore on English preaching styles.[58] Generally, they emphasized the importance of a learned background in ministers, and of learned preparation in a sermon, but stressed the importance of offering the pure Gospel to auditories who could not readily decide on the credence to lend to different kinds of authorities.[59] Most allowed an appeal to the emotions, though there were to be careful safeguards to ensure only seemly gestures and a proper purpose.[60] But while the English preachers were glad to add continental advice to their own experience, they could not rely wholly on the humane testimony of the continentals (as also not upon English homilies) and remain consistent in their belief that godly existence had to follow from one's own conversion, and not merely from the imitation of others.

Already by the middle of Elizabeth's reign puritans were drawing up extensive statements about the pulpit use of learning.[61] Laurence Chaderton, renowned as a preacher and as the bedrock upon which Walter Mildmay built his college, was one of the earliest to attack the heart of the matter. Chaderton concurred with contemporary wisdom that preachers should be trained in languages and in the arts, but he issued a scathing denunciation of weak-willed preachers who submitted to the demands of the auditory for a demonstration of humane learning:

many doe stuffe their sermons with newe devised words, and affected speaches of vanitie, not being content with the words which the holy Ghost teacheth. Many with unnecessary sentences, proverbes, similitudes, and stories collected out of the wrytings of prophane men: many with curious affected figures, with Latine, Greeke, and Hebrewe sentences without any just occasion offered by their texte, with multitudes of humane authorities, and divers opinions of men . . .[62]

Chaderton also addressed the question of the 'behaviour' of the minister in the pulpit. He protested against weird gesticulations and mannerisms, and noted the possibly evil origin of this corruption in stage-plays.[63] These were arguments also seized upon by Richard Greenham, who lamented that he lived in

---

[58] Restrictions of space unfortunately do not permit an analysis of these manuals. For a selection, see Hemmingsen, *Preacher*, transl. 1574 John Horsfall; Gerard, *Preparation to Ministerie*, transl. 1593 N. Becket; Serres, *Godlie and Learned Commentarie upon Solomon*, transl. 1585 John Stockwood; and also C.U.L. MS Dd.II.32: 'The Art of Preaching . . . from Mr. Claude Minister of Charanton in Paris. Translated by L.D.M.'. Gerard even noted the manual by William Perkins in his list of existing treatises (*Preparation to Ministerie*, sig. A3).

[59] The introduction to Gerard's work noted that the treatise was more suited to 'countrey Divines, which have pastoral charges' (*ibid.*, sig. A3).

[60] See, for example, *ibid.*, pp. 248–51; Gerardus, *Practise of Preaching*, sig. E.vij^{r-v}, F.j., F.iiij^{v}ff., G.j.ff.

[61] The following section is intended as an illustrative selection, rather than as an exhaustive treatment, of puritan preaching manuals. Thus such works as Thomas Granger's *Exposition on Ecclesiastes* and John Brinsley Junior's *The Preacher's Charge* have not been included. Especially have I neglected post-1640 sources such as William Chappell (1656) and John Wilkins (1646).

[62] Chaderton, *Excellent and Godly Sermon*, sigs. F.vi^v–vii, G.i.   [63] *Ibid.*, sigs. F.vi^v, F.vii.

an age of such vainglory, an age in which sermons had 'alreadie growne so cold and so humane, that the simple preaching of Christ doth greatly decay'.[64] He also condemned those ministers whose only real interest was scholarship, but who kept up a pretence of religion in an effort to attract patronage and promotion. The pretence quickly disappeared, he asserted, if the promotion was not forthcoming.[65]

It was, however, William Perkins who produced the most comprehensive Elizabethan puritan commentary on the difficult matter of constructing learned but not ostentatious sermons. In his emphasis on the distinction between the stages of preparation and delivery, and specifically with regard to the different place of learning in each, Perkins set the pattern for puritan manuals and practices. In *The Arte of Prophecying*, Perkins argued that preparation could readily be divided into two tasks: correct division and proper interpretation. He advised preachers to concentrate on a core of divinity: to wit, a grammatical, logical, and rhetorical analysis of Romans and the Gospel of St John, then the rest of the New Testament. He recommended taking notes of useful phrases and ideas on which ministers could expound in their own sermons.[66] For those preachers who might need additional aid in preparing their sermons, *The Arte of Prophecying* noted various ways of comparing and collating different verses of Scripture which concerned the same theological, historical or ecclesiological point. Perkins also specifically allowed the use of Latin and Greek concordances.[67] Perkins' analysis of the formal structure of a sermon indicated that there was to be no going back to spreading the light of the Gospel solely through recounting personal experiences of revelation.[68]

Since the ministry was an individual vocation, it was also evident that a minister could not rely wholly on the good offices of another member of the godly fraternity.[69] Printed sermons, though highly useful, could but tender godly advice; they could not transport the power of godliness through the medium of print from one of God's true servants to another. Perkins also even spoke against memorizing a sermon – this rule applied to one's own work as well as to the thought of others – since this turned the sermon into a piece of oratory and removed the force of exposition and application, which could be determined only by knowledge of the auditory and the immediate occasion.[70] The success of a sermon depended heavily on a close correspondence of pulpit and pew. It was crucial for the preacher to be able to recognize the level of preparedness of his audience. To this end, Perkins delineated six kinds of congregations. In order to bring his listeners together, and to leave them further along the road to repentance, Perkins stressed the fervency that could be

---

[64] Greenham, *Workes*, pp. 42, 20.   [65] Greenham, *Two Learned Sermons*, sig. E.7.
[66] Perkins, *Workes*, II, pp. 650–1.   [67] *Ibid.*, p. 653.   [68] *Ibid.*, pp. 655ff.
[69] *Ibid.*, p. 673. Perkins did, however, recommend the works of Erasmus, Hemmingsen, and Gerardus.   [70] *Ibid.*, p. 670.

aroused to produce an emotional experience in church. While the auditory had to be prepared by reading Scripture, the preacher could also take note of the frame of mind Perkins suggested was appropriate for the congregation:

> We must come unto it [the sermon] with hunger-bitten harts, having an appetite to the word, wee must marke it with attention, receive it by faith, submit ourselves unto it with feare and trembling, even then when our faultes are reproved: lastly we must hide it in the corner of our hearts, that we may frame our lives and conversations by it.[71]

The sermon was to be a vibrant personal lesson of conversion and reinforcement for the congregation.

To this end Perkins clearly enunciated the difficulties associated with the use of Latin and Greek phrases, and the terminology of learning, in the pulpit:

> 1. They disturbe the minds of the auditours, that they cannot fit those things which went afore with those that follow. 2. A strange word hindreth the understanding of those things that are spoken. 3. It drawes the minde away from the purpose to some other matter.[72]

It was enough of a Herculean struggle to prevent learning leading to vanity in godly ministers who had the advantage of a calling. To put such distraction in front of a popular congregation was simply to risk bewitching and confusing it. So, while Perkins stressed that a 'Minister may, yea & *must* privately use at his libertie the artes, philosophy, and varietie of reading, whilest he is in *framing* his sermon', he was equally adamant that in public the minister was absolutely bound 'to conceale all these from the people',[73] because

> the preaching of the word is the Testimony of God, and the profession of the knowledge of Christ, and not of humane skill: and againe, *because the hearers ought not to ascribe their faith to the gifts of man, but to the power of God's word.*[74]

To this end, too, he forbade ministers to use 'humane testimonies', even of the 'Philosopher, or of the Fathers' to establish doctrine.[75]

The notion that a preacher might use a heathen writer as an unidentified illustration, but not as source material, for a sermon amounted to what may perhaps best be termed a 'schizoid' attitude in puritan thought. That is, not only was there a deep cleft between the two approaches; there also existed an awareness of the benefits of what was, at any given time, the position *not* then

---

[71] Perkins, *Foundation of Christian Religion*, sig. C4^{r-v}. Perkins' six kinds of congregations were: 1. ignorant and unteachable; 2. ignorant but willing to be taught; 3. taught but unsanctified; 4. those who have knowledge and demonstrate the fruits of sanctification; 5. those 'declining', or falling back; 6. a mixed company. Most congregations, of course, were of this last sort.

[72] Perkins, *Workes*, II, pp. 670–1.   [73] *Ibid.*, p. 670 (my italics of the word 'framing'.)

[74] *Ibid.*, p. 670 (my italics); see also *Workes*, III, p. 430.   [75] Perkins, *Workes*, II, pp. 664, 670.

being espoused. Humane learning was good because helpful, but potentially harmful because non-scriptural. If they could be kept within strict bounds, then brief classical allusions might prove of immense help to the uneducated in understanding the Word and moral path which the Lord expected them to follow. At no time, however, did puritans try to explain the rather intricate question of why humane learning, infused through the consciousness of the minister who wrote and delivered the sermon, was less dangerous than an acknowledged quotation from a heathen source. It could be argued that the former was a type of subversion of the sole authority of Scripture. At least in the case of the suitably ascribed quotation the forewarned congregation would know to treat it with the utmost caution, and not as naturally edifying material. Perhaps ministers were sorely afraid of the temptations of Athens – if they gave in once to the delights of humane learning then the pure Word would no longer cascade through them like a surging, sanctifying torrent. Perhaps only by hiding this profane knowledge from the people could puritans hope to emphasize strongly enough the simplicity and availability of the covenant.

Perkins' final argument against the pulpit use of learning was the common theme of the age: the avoidance of self-adulation. Perkins regarded the advantages of intellect and (possibly) material means which accrued to university students as forms of temptation:

Now [in the university] we have many occasions to be puft up in selfe conceit: we see our selves grow in time, in degrees, in learning, in honour, in name and estimation: and to many of us God gives good portions of his gifts; what are all these, but so many baits to allure us to pride and vaine opinions of our owne worths? but let us remember the end we aime at, is not humane nor carnall; our purpose is to save soules . . .[76]

The stern reminder was intended to wrench them from the academic comfort of their college disputations and instil in them the abnegation of pride that should accompany a divine vocation.

In the final section of the *Arte of Prophecying*, Perkins indicated the proper structure of a sermon.[77] As a crucial last step the minister was to turn to 'use'; 'if he have the gift', he was to attempt to apply the points of doctrine he had just enunciated 'to the life and manners of men, in a simple and plaine speech'.[78] Although this part of the sermon would call for far less expertise in humane learning, it was here that the puritan preachers could display their prodigious ability for casuistical divinity. Perkins did not object to the use of 'pulpit mannerisms' if they were an integral part of the exhortation directed at

---

[76] Perkins, *Workes*, III, p. 442.
[77] The section is entitled, 'The Order and Summe of the sacred and onely methode of Preaching'.
[78] Perkins, *Workes*, II, p. 673.

the congregation. Interpretation of doctrine and exhortation were separate steps in the structure of the sermon; in the former, the minister should be 'more moderate', but in the latter he could profitably be 'more fervent and vehement'.[79] The heavenly strength which God granted his mediators was not to be shunned for politeness' sake: 'For though it be a worthy gift of God to speake mildely, & moderately, so that his speach shall fall like deawe upon the grasse: yet it is the *fierie tongue* that beates down sinne, & workes sound grace in the heart . . .'[80] It must have been this part of a sermon, far more than the demonstration of technical expertise in extracting doctrine from a short text, that impassioned those among the congregation who sought the godly path. Here, then, was the union of reason and enthusiasm.

Perkins thus included in his manual the four elements which constituted the puritan approach to the plain style: the necessity of learned preparation, the dangers of exposing the auditory to the direct rays of humane learning, the importance of a formal structure and a plain style of delivery, and the inclusion of a fervent exhortation to make 'application' of the particular lesson of the sermon. It would seem that not all these facets could easily blend together, and, indeed, the modern reader of the hundreds of extant sermons can soon detect the learned base struggling with the public restrictions. Perkins' contribution in this vein was that he managed to synthesize the various aspects of this dialectic over learning with such success that his recommendations became the pattern for puritan preaching at least to the end of our period.

In the early seventeenth century Richard Bernard, in his manual for young divines, managed to build on Perkins' base, especially in his emphasis on an imitation of the eloquence of Scripture. Indeed, Bernard noted that the Pauline story of partaking of the New Testament as the blood of Jesus had given him the 'first and chiefest occasion' for writing his manual. Bernard acknowledged the same sources (such as Erasmus and Gerardus) and also employed Perkins' sixfold division of the types of congregations.[81] He also expanded Perkins' initial interest in aiming at the simple level of most congregations.[82] Bernard suggested that the minister write down the heads of the sermon as they would be publicly related. This act would help the minister to note his own progress, to avoid the loss of original ideas, and to serve as an aid to other preachers who consulted him. The written heads would also provide the basis for meditation, which was to prepare the preacher for the exposition of the text. Such methodical preparation would also help the preacher to

---

[79] *Ibid.*, p. 672. [80] Perkins, *Workes*, III, p. 455.
[81] Bernard, *Faithfull Shepheard* (1621), sig. A.7 citing I Corinthians 11.23ff.; *ibid.* (1607), pp. 29, 99ff., on his sources. This work was first issued in 1607, the year after the appearance of the English edition of Perkins' *Arte of Prophecying*, and was offered in an expanded version in 1621.
[82] Bernard, *Faithfull Shepheard* (1607), pp. 32–3.

remember Bernard's definition of preaching, which, true to the puritan outlook, combined the unchangeable with the demands of context: 'a sound and plainely laying open of holy Scriptures, by a publike Minister before the people, to their understanding and capacity'.[83] For Bernard, learning and fervency were thus twin axles which drove the efficacious pulpit forward:

> Discreet understanding must goe with zeale, and gravity with sincerity: affection is heady without wisedome: this moderates as the other pricks forward: they must be linked inseparably. Knowledge alone delivereth remisly, and Zeale alone not respectively: Knowledge without zeale permitteth of more than is meete by distinction: and Zeale not according to knowledge breedeth but dissension.[84]

Thus were the ornate preachers reminded of the core of fervency, and the 'mechanicks' shut out of the specially trained caste of mediators.

At the same time, learning remained a subordinate capacity to fervent belief in God.[85] Worried about the confusion which learning could cause in congregations, Bernard suggested that pastoral advice take the place of contentious debates, which were suitable only for the learned auditories of the Schools.[86] And so that the congregation would depart with the proper assurance of the truth of the sermon, Bernard insisted that the minister should not simply 'deliver' the doctrine, but also 'prove it and confirm the same by reason'. The sermon was to make 'sense' to the auditory; that is, the preacher had to explain the doctrine in rational terms. Learning was thus to pervade the structure and even to determine the meaning (interpretation) of the sermon. This explanation could be based on a principle from either divinity or nature, on commonsense and experience, or on agreement with other places of Scripture.[87]

Like most puritans, Bernard stressed the importance of bringing out in the sermons both the four 'uses' (confutation, instruction, reprehension, and consolation)[88] and the 'application' of the text. Whereas 'use' was a general statement delivered in the third person, 'application', usually offered in either the second or first person, was designed as a 'neerer bringing of the use delivered',[89] a task which obviously necessitated the specific knowledge of the auditory which he had earlier commended. To maintain attention, the preacher should speak in plain English, though he was allowed the occasional 'allegation of an authenticall testimony in the originall language'.[90] Bernard also noted that an appropriate tone and volume were important, as were comely gestures. The conclusion of the sermon was thus to be a 'loving exhortation to moove affection and to quicken the hearers to understand' and 'to long after

---

[83] *Ibid.* (1607), pp. 22–3, 29; sig. A5^{r-v}.   [84] *Ibid.* (1621), sig. A6^{r-v}.   [85] *Ibid.* (1621), p. 204.
[86] *Ibid.* (1607), pp. 113ff.   [87] *Ibid.* (1607), pp. 136ff., 258–61.   [88] *Ibid.* (1621), pp. 274ff., 327ff.
[89] *Ibid.* (1607), p. 327.   [90] *Ibid.* (1621), pp. 350–1, 274, 141.

more'.[91] But, as had Perkins, he warned against too 'fine' a show; preachers were not to end up like those who, 'by having beene Actours upon a stage, . . . cannot but shew their vaine and fantasticall motions ridiculously in pulpit . . . '.[92] Rather, it was a 'methodicall' exposition that could best apply learning to 'this great and *miraculous* worke of converting soules'.[93]

William Ames possessed perhaps the greatest international reputation of any early seventeenth-century puritan; his works, like those of Perkins, traversed protestant Europe and New England.[94] His manual *Conscience* included a lengthy chapter on the construction and delivery of sermons. Ames insisted that the whole body of Scriptures – he laid especial emphasis on the Laws – be expounded in pure form according either to some order or to some immediate necessity.[95] Though of course he disallowed the public reading of other men's sermons, Ames emphasized the use of commentaries and printed sermons to ministers 'lesse exercised'.[96] He flatly opposed the use of Latin, Greek, and Hebrew phrases in popular sermons, since they tended to hinder the understanding, interrupt attention, and foster gross ostentation in ministers.[97] Excerpts from heathen writers were to be excluded, because they reduced the 'efficacy' of the sermon. Even the Fathers were not to be used openly in popular sermons, primarily because they did not possess the authority of divine Scripture, but also because such use might give rise to a belief in the insufficiency of the Word itself. Ames was quite willing to allow allegories, for the better understanding of the auditory, but only if presented as the opinions of men and their fallible wisdom, and not as the certainties of the Word.[98] 'The summe is', he insisted, 'that nothing is to be admitted which doth not make for the spirituall edification of the people, neither any thing to be omitted whereby we may in a sure way attaine to that end.'[99] For the similar reason of desiring to reach the level of the auditory, Ames adopted the common argument that both the choice of a particular text and the style had also to be 'directed according to the condition of the hearers, times, and places'.[100]

Preaching, for Ames, as for other puritans, was thus a combination, a duality of reason and an appeal to the heart. It should be stressed, however, that for Ames, perhaps alone of the pre-1640 puritans,[101] the seat of voluntaristic faith was in the will alone. This had to be reached and 'converted' by an awakening of conscience. All this, however, despite a belief in predesti-

---

[91] *Ibid.* (1621), pp. 352–3.
[92] *Ibid.* (1607), pp. 108–10, 36.   [93] *Ibid.* (1621), pp. 354–5. (My italics.)
[94] Miller & Johnson, eds., *Puritans*, p. 66, note that Ames' *Marrow of Sacred Divinity* was a standard theology text at Harvard and Yale until the mid-eighteenth century.
[95] Ames, *Conscience*, Bk IV, Ch. 29, pp. 71–2.   [96] *Ibid.*, pp. 72–3.
[97] *Ibid.*, pp. 74–5; Ames, *Marrow*, Bk I, p. 181.   [98] Ames, *Conscience*, pp. 74–5.
[99] Ames, *Marrow*, Bk I, p. 183.   [100] Ames, *Conscience*, pp. 76–7; Ames, *Marrow*, Bk I, p. 178.
[101] Kendall, *Calvin and English Calvinism*, pp. 152ff.

nation, depended on the individual's decision to search for godliness. To bring him to this favourable stage of preparation, he perforce had to be 'pricked to the quick'. The sermon therefore had to be 'lively and effectuall'; it was not merely an explanation, but also an encouragement, an exhortation, and an inspiration, so that an 'unbeliever' would be turned to God.[102] Therefore rhetorical devices which were 'repugnant to the powerfull demonstration of the Spirit' were to be forsaken.[103] Ames believed that most auditories could comprehend the rational meaning of the Word. More difficult was to convince them of application: 'The word of God is much more easily into the eares and understanding of men, then into their hearts and hands.' Since the 'principall worke of the Sermon . . . is in the use and application', Ames emphasized the direction of sermons to the instilling of a *desire* for improved existence in the auditory, to a *will* for repentance.[104]

The lyrical quality of Donne's sermons was anathema to puritans specifically because of its 'beauty', which they said hid the purpose of the pulpit offering and thus negated the function of the chosen mediator. This is not to deny that puritans had an aesthetic sense, but it was always linked to godly utility. Beauty lay not in the outward appurtenances of 'holines' (as Laud would have it) but rather, intrinsically, in those acts which were godly. The puritan sermon was thus not just a cold, dry, rational and academic explanation of a distant text. It was indeed that in part but, as I have tried to demonstrate, it was also sensuous, emotional, and fervent – a dramatic application of godly lesson to the immediate context of the auditory.

This paradox – which ran the length of our period – was ably summed up in the *Directory of Church-Government*, first published in 1644, but offered to the 1584 Parliament as part of the 'Bill and Book' intended to establish a presbyterian church system in England. It well illustrates the continuity of the dialectic on enthusiasm and learning in the pulpit, and so is worth quoting at some length:

He that Preacheth must performe two things, the first that his speech bee uncorrupt, which is to be considered both in regard of the Doctrine, that it be holy, sound, wholsome and profitable to edification, not divelish, hereticall, leavened, corrupt, fabulous, curious, or contentious; and also in respect of the manner of it, that it be proper to the place which is handled, that is, which either is contained plainly in the very words; or if it be gathered by consequent, that the same be fit and cleare and such as may rise upon the property of the word, grace of speech, and suit of the matter, and not be allegoricall, strange, wrested, or far fetched . . . and let the whole confirmation and proofe be made by arguments, testimonies and example taken only out of the holy

---

[102] Ames, *Marrow*, Bk I, p. 179.
[103] Ames, *Conscience*, p. 78. For this reason he staunchly opposed the inclusion of an *exordium*, or preamble, in a sermon, since it was a device suited only to 'an humane Oration' (*ibid.*, p. 78).
[104] *Ibid.*, pp. 77, 78.

Scriptures, applied fitly and according to the naturall meaning of the places that are alleadged. The second thing to be performed by him is that preaching is a reverend gravity; This is considered first in the stile, phrase and manner of speech, that it be spirituall, pure, proper, simple and applied to the capacity of the people, not such as humane wisdome teacheth, nor favoring of new fanglednesse, nor either so affectate as it may serve for pompe and ostentation or so carelesse, and base, as becommeth not Ministers of the Word of God. Secondly, it is also to be regarded aswell in ordering the voyce in which a care must be had that (avoyding the keeping alwayes of one tune) it may be equall, and both rise and fall by degrees; as also in ordering the whole body is to follow the voyce, there being avoyded in it all unseemely gestures of the head or other parts and often turning of the body to divers sides. Finally, let the gesture be grave, modest and seemly, not utterly none, nor too much neither like the gestures of Players or Fencers.[105]

'Spirituall' and yet obviously learned; 'a reverend gravity' and yet not 'so affectate as it may serve for pompe and ostentation'. The balance had been struck: use but not abuse; necessity but not superfluity. In 1646, finally, John Geree looked back in an attempt to sum up the movement for religious reform. He noted the paradoxes which we have seen to be characteristic of the puritan approach. The godly auditor, he recalled for his readers, 'esteemed that preaching best wherein was most of God, least of man, when vain flourishes of wit, and words were declined . . . yet could he distinguish between studied plainnesse, & negligent rudeness . . .'. Here, in the system of Ramist dichotomies – each force balanced by its opposite – puritans had found their approach to the public use of learning in the cause of godliness.[106]

In the previous two chapters I delineated the puritan view of the proper role and status of ministers and the types of learning they were to possess. Here I have concentrated on the ways in which that learning was to be applied to the pulpit aspect of the ministerial function as God's mediator. But, having emphasized the necessary use of learning, puritans realized that it was not sufficient to attempt to purify and control knowledge only at the end of long years of humane studies. They would also have to reform England's sources of learning so that they would produce first of all a ministry dedicated to learned preaching and, secondly, a laity geared to the appreciation of the Word above all other knowledge. The rest of this book will therefore investigate puritan critiques of England's educational institutions, and suggestions for their purification.

---

[105] *Directory of Church-Government*, sig. B^(r-v).
[106] Geree, *Character of an Old English Puritan*, quoted in Miller & Johnson, eds. *Puritans*, p. 65.

8

>▸▸

THE GODLY HOUSEHOLD

I

Much of the puritan attempt at reform, perhaps especially in Elizabethan times, concentrated on the chambers of power. But even from the beginning of our period puritans were also keen to proselytize at the lowest organizational levels; hence a new interest arose in the possibility of the household as a centre of godly instruction. At the bottom of all social analysis came the family rather than the individual.[1] Both Luther and Calvin set their seal of approval on the conjugal bond and the resultant family structure.[2] Almost all writers agreed, citing the fifth commandment, that the family could exist only as a hierarchy.[3] Democracy was considered to be as dangerous in the family as in the state.[4] Both religious and political parallels were commonly drawn between the head of the family and the head of state: as the magistrate promoted the church, so too did the patriarch guide his charges under the covenant.[5] All commentators stressed the socializing function of household education, but puritans especially saw the prime duty of the patriarchal household as the inculcating of godliness. John Downame illustrated the proposition that the family was the bedrock of instruction by comparing it, fittingly enough, to a school:

let us consider that the family is the Seminary of the Church and Common-wealth; and as a private schoole, wherein children and servants are fitted for the public assem-

---

[1]   John Field called God the 'householder of the whole world' (*Godly Prayers*, fol. 104ᵛ). Gregory King, in 1696, still considered the family the basic unit of society.
[2]   Calvin, *Institutes*, IV.17.1; Strauss, *Luther's House*, pp. 109–12.
[3]   See, for example, Dod & Cleaver, *Ten Commandements*, pp. 184ff., 221–6, 240–4, 372; Dent, *Plaine Mans Path-way*, p. 46; Downame, *Guide to Godlinesse*, p. 148; Perkins, *Workes*, I, p. 50; Gouge, *Domesticall Duties*, pp. 331–2; Dering, *Briefe Catechisme*, sig. A 8; *The Office of Christian Parents*, pp. 207ff., even suggested that parents retained residual duties of encouraging their children even after they were married. For the generally similar non-puritan point of view, see Ayrault, *Discourse for Parents*, p. 28; Brathwait, *English Gentleman, passim*; Shelford, *Lectures*, esp. pp. 105–6. Radicals, too, held to this point of view; see Browne, *Life and Manners of all Christians*, section 123.
[4]   See the injunction in the Geneva Bible: marginal comment to Titus 3.1. See also Norden, *Progresse of Pietie*, fols. 53, 61ᵛ.   [5]   On this, see especially Morgan, *Puritan Family*, pp. 135, 174, 182.

blies, as it were the Universities, to performe, when they meete together, all religious duties of Gods worship and service. And as it is a notable meanes to make Universities to flourish, and the Students in them to succeed and prosper in their studies, when as the masters of private schooles doe well fit and prepare them, teach and nurture them in learning and manners, before they send them thither: So if Masters of private families would carefully traine up all their household in the feare of God, and in the exercises of Christian Religion all the weeke, they would [be far better Christians].[6]

Though there was much continuity from the humanists in this approach,[7] there were also manifestations of Reformation ideas. An illustration of the principle of *cuius regio, eius religio*, at the level of the most basic unit of social organization, was the pursuit of the allegiance of the patriarch as the corner-stone of domestic reform.[8]

It was in the family that the child learned basic social skills such as duty, humility, sobriety, and self-denial. The first necessity, in a highly stratified society, was obedience, and here the child could learn not only from its own experiences, but also from observing the inferior status of its mother. Domestic manuals generally ranted against those women who failed to be feminine, that is to say, submissive in all aspects of their marital relationship.[9] Puritans, aware that a woman was as likely to be saved as a man, seem increasingly over the period to have adopted the generally growing view that marriage existed primarily not for procreation and the avoidance of fornication, but rather for mutual spiritual comfort and companionship.[10] The importance of household education may well have imparted a new status to women, who were increasingly expected to be counsellors and mentors of their children,[11] but the degree to which this new emphasis affected patriarchal authority in the

---

[6] Downame, *Guide to Godlinesse*, pp. 329–30; Short, 'Theory of common education', pp. 31–48, comments on this theme in the work of Richard Greenham.

[7] Gouge, *Domesticall Duties*, Epistle; Todd, 'Humanists, puritans', *Church History*. 49, esp. pp. 19–22. She also notes that Perkins cited Aristotle for the view that the family was the 'Seminarie of all other societies'.   [8] See, for example, B.P., *Prentises Practise*, fol. 38[r–v].

[9] So, while the husband was indeed duty bound to 'rejoyce' in his wife, look after her, and refrain from sexual relations with other women, the wife was required both to fear and obey her spouse. See Dod & Cleaver, *Ten Commandements*, pp. 221–6; Gataker, *Good Wife*, pp. 7–17; Thomas, 'Women and civil war sects', *Past and Present*, 13, esp. p. 51, citing John Brinsley. Denunciation of women was a norm of the age. Not only John Knox chanced his luck. Bishop Aylmer, that stalwart of the Elizabethan church, also had the temerity, in a sermon before the queen, to preach that women were 'in every way doltified with the dregs of the devil's dunghill'. Quoted in Powell, *English Domestic Relations*, p. 147.

[10] See, for example, Ames, *Conscience*, Bk v, Ch. 37. It should be noted that this idea did also appear in Catholic thought, as well as in Luther and pre-puritan English reformers such as William Tyndale. See Schnucker, 'Elizabethan birth control', *Journal of Interdisciplinary History*, 5, p. 661. For examples of the highly visible affection between puritan spouses, see the correspondence between John and Margaret Winthrop (*Winthrop Papers, passim*). Kathleen Davies notes, however, that some puritan writers (such as Cleaver, Smith, Perkins) put procreation as the first reason for marriage ('Continuity and change in literary advice on marriage', in Outhwaite, ed., *Marriage and Society*, pp. 61–3).

[11] Charlton, *Education in Renaissance England*, p. 205.

puritan home is still a matter of some debate. William Ames, that immensely influential puritan, argued for the primacy of affection between husband and wife, but insisted, following Paul, that 'neverthelesse, hee ought in all things to beare himselfe, as the head of his Wife . . .'. John Downame, too, still advised a woman to 'cherish her husband as the better part of her selfe'.[12] For puritans, the submission of the temporal body and the equality of the eternal soul were not contradictory. Thus William Gouge could emphasize the primacy of a woman's obligation to obey God, but imply that in practice her duty was first to her husband, regardless of his religious state. Indeed, the whole question of the degree to which puritans were at all innovative in terms of domestic relations – whether they were in fact prescriptive, or merely descriptive, of current standards – is still moot.[13]

Even those puritans who stressed the primacy of 'companionable society' emphasized the added duty of raising children.[14] Procreation meant assisting Providence by bringing God's elect into the earthly church and commonwealth. Birth-control was to be avoided since bearing children specifically helped women to overcome their burden of responsibility for human sin.[15] Life was commonly divided into six or seven stages, including, with variations from writer to writer, infancy (birth to seven years), childhood (seven to fourteen), and youth (fourteen to twenty-eight). Concern with childhood as a distinct phase of life came only slowly to the general population, though increasingly in our period writers on education noted the different perceptions and needs of the very young. There seems, too, to have been a greater appreciation of adolescence as a separate stage of personality development, connected as it was with the specific tasks of apprenticeship or service.[16]

The first problem for puritan educationalists to consider was the nature of the new-born child: was it a *tabula rasa* to be encouraged in its natural desire for knowledge (including awareness of God), or substantially corrupt, in which case it would have to be purged of its evil before it could be brought to godliness? The state of the new-born child affected the whole rationale for family

[12] Ames, *Conscience*, Bk v, Ch. 21; Downame, *Guide to Godlinesse*, p. 148; Davies, 'Continuity and change', pp. 63ff.
[13] See Davies, 'Continuity and change', *passim*, but esp. pp. 68ff., 76, for a recent assessment of this question.
[14] Schnucker, 'Elizabethan birth control', p. 660; J. J. Johnson, 'English puritan thought on marriage', *Church History*, 38, esp. pp. 430–2.
[15] Schnucker, 'Elizabethan birth control', pp. 663–5. Schnucker suggests that wives of puritan ministers bore unusually high numbers of children. See also his 'English puritans and pregnancy', *History of Childhood Quarterly*, 1, esp. p. 642, for the argument that puritans believed that labour pains had 'redemptive quality'.
[16] S.R. Smith, 'Religion and the conception of youth', *History of Childhood Quarterly*, 2, esp. pp. 493–5; deMause, 'Evolution of childhood', in deMause, ed., *History of Childhood*, pp. 5ff., 16ff. For a puritan account of the divisions of life, see Gouge, *Domesticall Duties*, pp. 525–6, who regarded 'childhood' as encompassing the first 15 years of life. See also Yarborough, 'Apprentices as adolescents', *Journal of Social History*, 13, esp. pp. 73f.; Kussmaul, *Servants in Husbandry, passim*.

(and, later, public) education, and also the methods to be used. The humanist perception was that the child, while 'fallen', nonetheless arrived in the world without a *personal* blot. By application of love and gentle encouragement, children could be drawn to proper obedience, to learning, and to a fully socialized condition.[17] Personal evil was something that was introduced into the young by wrong contacts, and thus could be avoided by scrupulous care.[18] This tradition saw children's wills as pliable, and therefore accorded much power to reason.

One of the greatest social effects of the Reformation was the utter denial that environment alone could cure 'evil'. For puritans, children were created in sin, and pervaded by sin from the moment of that creation. They could therefore be set upon the path to salvation only by the breaking of their will as soon as it appeared, and by the subsequent imposition of a severe code of conduct which restricted the disposition of the child to follow the path of temptation.[19] This necessitated a literature aimed specifically at children. Even those matters which seem to be dominantly social or economic may well have been pre-conditioned by soteriological belief. Hence the puritan support for spinning schools and other forms of order for orphans and homeless poor children.[20] Children were not considered to start developing reason until the age of six or seven. But will, the rebellious agent of man's waywardness, appeared within the first year of life.[21] Household manuals, and even some educational tracts, stressed that parental duties were so important because of the early evil wilfulness of their children. Indeed, Richard Greenham started with the maladies that might attend pregnancy, arguing that premature birth and the deformed were God's immediate punishment for sexual intercourse without 'cause to increase the Church of Christ and the number of the elect . . .'.[22] The sins of the parents were thus immediately visited, even before birth, upon their children. John Robinson took the point to its extreme: 'Children should not know, if it could be kept from them, that they have a will of their own, but in their parents' keeping . . .'.[23] For parents, raising godly

[17] John Earle wrote in 1628 that 'A child is a man in small letter, yet the best copy of Adam before he tasted of Eve or the apple . . . His soul is yet a white paper unscribbled with observations of the world . . . he knows no evil . . .' (*Microcosmography*, quoted in Illick, 'Child-rearing', in deMause, ed., *History of Childhood*, p. 317).

[18] Ascham, *Scholemaster*, ed. Giles, p. 122; Sadoleto, *On Education*, pp. 7–11, 22; Morrice, *Apologie for Schoolemasters*, sig. B8ᵛ.

[19] Much of the literature depended on Proverbs 22.6: 'Teach a child in the trade of his way, and when he is old he shall not depart from it.' Also frequently cited was Proverbs 22.15: 'Foolishness is tied in the heart of a child, but the rod of discipline shall drive it away.' Both of these verses, for example, can be found on the title page of Kempe, *Education of Children*. For a puritan example, see Gouge, *Domesticall Duties*, esp. pp. 551–8. On Luther, see Strauss, *Luther's House*, esp. Ch. 5.

[20] See below, p. 176.

[21] See Greven, *Protestant Temperament*, pp. 32ff., for highly interesting examples of New England parental response to the early demonstration of childhood will.

[22] Greenham, *Workes*, p. 277.   [23] *Works of John Robinson*, ed. Ashton, I, pp. 247, 246.

children was a test of ability to perform good works as a reflection of their own standing in grace. Children so brought up would be for their parents a 'fruitfull field, a pleasant spectacle, ioyfull tidings, a comfortable remembrance, blessed of God, and honourable among men . . .'.[24] The parent who raised a wilful child had perforce to question his own standing with the Lord.

While wilful students might well come to master humane learning, and perhaps even 'manners', only those whose will had been suitably curbed before the appearance of reason would be likely to prosper in the godly aspects of the curriculum. In this context, puritans, too, adopted the model of the child as the pliable instrument of its parents. Parental discipline was seen as the earliest training for an adult life of self-denial. The desire to crush the young child's will reveals, then, a paradox central to protestant Christianity.[25] At all levels of instruction, puritans insisted that only the Spirit could work regeneration. And yet they also regaled their readers with scores of ways in which they could bring their households, *against their will* (in the fullest sense of that term), to a form of godly existence. That this coerced behaviour was a 'generational' duty of parents to children reveals even more clearly the degree to which optimistic preparationist notions suffused puritan being.

One method of social discipline was the development by protestants of a stronger theory of vocation than had existed in the pre-Reformation world.[26] Puritans seem to have followed contemporary belief in dividing themselves between those who thought, in a reductionist way, that the complex social hierarchy and its various interrelationships existed as a function of God's will,[27] and those, on the other hand, who thought that specific calling – one's occupation – should be chosen with two considerations in mind: the aptitude and desires of the individual, and the socio-economic needs of society. Even this latter group subdivided, however. There were those, puritan and non-puritan alike, who believed in 'horizontal' social mobility of the individual, governed usually by career choices effected by parents; there were also those few commentators who argued that an individual should be free, within the bounds of the hierarchy, to choose his own occupation. Almost universally, however, writers condemned those who attempted to rise through the ranks.

[24] *Office of Christian Parents*, p. 17.
[25] On self-denial, see Cliffe, *Puritan Gentry*, esp. pp. 49–54; for a revealing comparison with Lutheran pedagogical theory, see Strauss, *Luther's House of Learning*, Chs. 2, 3, 5 and 6.
[26] On this mammoth question, see, most recently, the discussion in Greaves, *Society and Religion*, pp. 377–95.
[27] See, for example, the marginal comment in the Geneva Bible concerning duty to fulfil one's calling willingly. Of the preacher, the marginalia to I Corinthians 9.16 commented: 'Seing he is charged to preache, he must willingly and earnestly followe it: for if he do it by constrainte, he doeth not his duetie.'

Puritans do not seem to have held distinct attitudes to the selecting of a vocation; rather, their uniqueness lay in the emphasis they placed upon striving within one's calling, however chosen. Idleness and discontent were sins, puritans contended, because they were a denial of the function for which God had suited the individual.[28] Contentment with one's vocation became a measure of confidence in one's relationship with the Almighty, that is to say, a step towards assurance, that quicksilver of human existence. So the puritan Thomas Adams noted that 'God is wont to blesse men especially, when they are busied in their proper element . . .'.[29] Social peace could be promoted by suggesting the availability of a heavenly reward for those who accepted class differences in earthly society. Puritans and radicals alike therefore stressed the evil inherent in idleness. Henry Barrow, for example, argued that God did not place men in callings simply so that they might then seek to escape them; Robert Browne believed that idle people had ceased to be members of the true church.[30] William Perkins regarded rogues, beggars and vagabonds as a 'foule disorder' since they had no calling, and praised a law directed against them as 'an excellent Statute, and being in substance the very law of God . . .'. However, Perkins, in similar fashion to most puritans who commented on this question, did not find a surfeit of leisure only in the dispossessed. He denied the Christian hermetic tradition, arguing that the Scriptures had not approved as a worthwhile calling the separation from society in the name of religion. Rather more pointedly, he also condemned the idle rich who were 'not imploying themselves in service for Church or Common-wealth'. His intention was not to disturb the hierarchy, but rather to ensure that all fulfilled the demands of the task to which God, in his mysterious way, had assigned them. 'God looketh not at the excellency of the worke, but at the heart of the worker', he reminded his readers.[31] Those who lived without a calling were truly 'a burden to the earth, the bane of the common wealth, and the worse creatures in the world'. Even the unregenerate were called to a specific vocation.[32] The elect, it was plain, were not to be found among the idle.

The duty of parents to prepare their children for conversion thus also included the obligation to bring them 'up in some profitable and lawfull calling, by which they may live honestly and Christianly, and not . . . bee fruitlesse burthens of the earth, clogs to their friends, and drones that must live

[28] See, for example, Stockwood, *Sermon at Paules Crosse* (1579), fols. 18ᵛ–19; Udall, *Certaine Sermons*, sigs. L.1.viiiᵛ–M.m.; Greaves, *Society and Religion*, pp. 383–91.　[29] Adams, *Workes*, p. 293.
[30] Greaves, *Society and Religion*, p. 381; Hill, *Society and Puritanism*, pp. 126–7.
[31] Perkins, 'Treatise of vocations', *Workes*, I, esp. pp. 750, 755–6, 758.
[32] R. Hill, *Pathway*, p. 82; Preston, *Four Godly and Learned Treatises*, pp. 41–2; Dod & Cleaver, *Ten Commandements*, pp. 305–7; R. Bolton, *Some General Directions*, pp. 70, 157ff.; Cotton, *New Covenant*, p. 44.

on other mens sweat'.[33] Parents and schoolmasters were required to direct the
child along the paths which seemed most in accord with natural abilities.[34]
This did not mean a free choice of occupation. For many boys, adolescence
meant apprenticeship, a process which involved not only learning a trade, but
also moving away from home, usually from a rural to an urban setting.[35]
Various guidebooks set out the ideal master–apprentice relationship for the
enlightenment of both parties. Puritans added to this literature of vocational
training and socialization,[36] but do not seem to have been distinctive in the
content of their contribution. Most youths, however, both male and female,
entered service-in-husbandry in their mid- to late-teens, and stayed, through a
series of annual contracts, until their early- or mid-twenties.[37] The age at
which parents decided they could no longer afford to keep a son or daughter at
home – dependent on the labour market, the number of other offspring in the
home, family relations, the price of consumables, and so on[38] – and therefore
sent that youth into service, likely also represented the terminal date of formal
education for that individual. Religious instruction might still be forthcoming
in another household, but there can have been few masters who would con-
scientiously develop, or initiate, a servant's literacy and schooling. As well, the
great mobility of servants – most moved annually, though within a restricted
geographic area[39] – must have reduced the incentive for a master in terms of
his own gain to educate his servants.

   Within the puritan family (and school), correction was the precondition
which allowed the father/householder to inculcate in children and servants
the necessary knowledge and reconditioned will to conduct themselves
properly as both Christians and members of a civil society. In the numerous
examples of severe physical discipline among puritans, then, we see a further
example of the pervasive paradox: even as puritan fathers beat their children
to punish their wilfulness, they cherished them for the biological tie, and for

---

[33]   Dod & Cleaver, *Ten Commandements*, p. 202.
[34]   Cleaver, *Householde Government*, pp. 232–3, 329–30; *Office of Christian Parents*, pp. 75–6; Bayne, *Briefe
       Directions*, pp. 155–6; Brinsley, *True Watch*, pp. 70–1; Dod & Hinde, *Bathshebaes Instructions*, p. 3;
       Downame, *Guide to Godlinesse*, p. 148; Downame, *Summe of Sacred Divinitie*, p. 185; Gouge, *Domesticall
       Duties*, pp. 533, 535, 559–63; R. Hill, *Direction to Live Well*, pp. 89, 94.
[35]   Anne Yarborough has noted that of 3069 youths apprenticed in Bristol (1542–65), just over 78% came
       from outside Bristol ('Apprentices as adolescents', p. 68).
[36]   Smith, 'London apprentices', *Past & Present*, 61, p. 151, noting the contributions of Gouge, Cleaver,
       Whately and Ames.
[37]   Kussmaul, *Servants in Husbandry*, Ch. 2, *passim*. Servants constituted about 60% of the population aged
       15–24 (*ibid.*, p. 3).
[38]   Richard Wall has recently argued that there was no dominant reason why people left home; nor, he also
       notes, was there any set age (Wall, 'Age at leaving home', *Journal of Family History*, 3, pp. 181–202).
       Wall notes that at Swindon in 1697, 18% of children (aged 15+) of gentry lived with their parents; the
       comparable figure for tradesmen/craftsmen was 71%, and for labourers 42%.
[39]   Kussmaul, *Servants in Husbandry*, Ch. 4.

the knowledge that they might be raising God's elect.[40] Puritan discipline, severe as it was, was based on the premise that children were redeemable; correction had therefore to be imposed as a duty owed to God as part of the covenant. Resort to the rod was to be seen not as the best method of discipline, but rather as the failure of other methods. Correction, in this Christian age, was preferably to be by the encouraging lesson of the pulpit, and the proximity of the printed Word, the guide to eternal life.[41] The aim of correction was to make children desire, through the development of a strong conscience, to act out the external terms of the covenant, even before the experience of personal conversion. The method, however, was to be gentle, in appreciation of childhood limitations. So William Perkins commented that 'the first instruction of children in learning and religion must be so ordered that they may take it with delight. For which purpose they may be sometimes allowed in moderate manner to play and solace themselves in recreations fitting for their years.'[42] Repression was obviously not the spiritual equal of conversion. Puritan parents therefore bemoaned the temporary nature of much childhood contrition,[43] the slowness of the disappearance of self-will, and the tardy development of godly conscience.

At the same time, puritans did not see training in solely secular terms. So Grace Mildmay, daughter-in-law of the famous Sir Walter, complained that, while parents were wont to worry about the nature of their child's calling, they frequently took 'no care to furnish theyr minds with true religion and virtue ...'.[44] Thomas Gataker similarly warned his readers:

You are not to thinke it enough, that you have taught them some trade, that you have given them learning, (humane learning, I meane) that they may live by an other day; but you must withall, or else you come far short of that you should do, teach them also to feare God, and so to serve him here, as they may live with him eternally, when they go hence.[45]

Even providing a full training for a career for their offspring made parents no better than the 'Infidell', Gataker insisted.[46] Richard Greenham made the point explicit: 'Knowledge of the Word is as necessary an arte for Christians,

---

[40] On the question of parental love, one should read, for example, John Penry's last instructions for his daughters, written shortly before he was killed, to comprehend the familial tenderness that lay within the puritan breast: B.L. MS Add. 48,064, fols. 22ᵛff. See also the letter to his wife, dated four days earlier (*ibid.*, fols. 19ff.). One could also pause over the extended agony which Ralph Josselin felt and recorded while watching his daughter Mary die (*Diary*, ed. Macfarlane, pp. 201–4).

[41] See, for example, *Office of Christian Parents*, pp. 119–20. This tempering was common to the age: see Kempe, *Education of Children*, sig. H2. See also Greven, *Protestant Temperament*, pp. 49ff.

[42] Perkins, *Workes*, III, p. 694, quoted in Berry, 'First English pediatricians', *Journal of the History of Ideas*, 35, p. 564. See also Greenham, *Workes*, p. 277.

[43] See, for example, *Life of Thomas Cawton*, p. 64.

[44] Weigall, 'Elizabethan gentlewoman', *Quarterly Review*, 215, p. 127.

[45] Gataker, *Davids Instructer*, p. 30.   [46] *Ibid.*, p. 31.

as the arte of Husbandrie for Husbandmen.'[47] Education certainly had to provide basic instruction; in this requirement puritans did not differ from their contemporaries. It was rather in the greater insistence that even vocational humane learning could not be imbibed distinct from godly indoctrination that puritans made their immediate contribution to the training of England's young.

II

The specific duties of the late sixteenth- and early seventeenth-century household, and especially those of the godly family, are now reasonably well known.[48] William Ames explained the parental burden as: nourishing children until they could look after themselves; raising them in the fear, knowledge, and discipline of the Lord; deterring them from evil, and inciting them to good; providing training for an honest occupation and arranging an 'honest and fit marriage'.[49] 'Manners' were as important to puritans as to their contemporaries. What set puritans apart was the exceptional emphasis on church attendance, reading, prayers, self-examination, family instruction, and conference that formed the household curriculum to lead children and servants to faith.[50] The householder who did not instruct his wife, children, and servants denigrated their souls before God. John Winthrop, for instance, noted in his 'Experiencia' that in the instruction of his family he had found a way to 'please God and further their and mine own salvation . . .'.[51] Josias Nichols recommended a minimum of two hours per week for the household instruction of children and servants, in addition, of course, to attendance at church.[52] So important were these responsibilities that they could not be dependent even upon a parent's continued existence; frequently, wills included provisions to ensure that children be raised in godly fashion.[53]

Though the concentration was generally on blood ties, it is important to

---

[47] Greenham, *Two Learned Sermons*, sig. A3.
[48] See, for example, Hill, *Society and Puritanism*, Ch. 13; Knappen, *Tudor Puritanism*, Ch. 25; E. S. Morgan, *Puritan Family*, Ch. 3; Cremin, *American Education*, Ch. 4; Axtell, *School upon a Hill*, esp. Ch. 1. For a recent assessment of puritan lay households, see Cliffe, *Puritan Gentry*, esp. Ch. 2 and pp. 69–70.
[49] Ames, *Conscience*, Bk v, Ch. 22. See, similarly, *Office of Christian Parents*, pp. 53, 65–6.
[50] See, for example, *Office of Christian Parents*, 'To the Reader'; Leigh, *Mothers Blessing*, pp. 59–61; Perkins, *Workes*, III, pp. 669–70; II, pp. 105–12; Rogers, *Seven Treatises*, p. 205; Dod & Cleaver, *Ten Commandements*, pp. 141–4, 146–53, 179, 182–3; Brinsley, *True Watch*, pp. 70–1; F. Bunny, *Guide unto Godlinesse*, p. 156.
[51] *Winthrop Papers*, I, p. 213; Dod & Cleaver, *Ten Commandements*, pp. 197, 216, 372; Gouge, *Domesticall Duties*, pp. 501, 536–8; Greenham, *Workes*, p. 276; Udall, *Certaine Sermons*, sig. G.vi^v; Gataker, *Davids Instructer*, pp. 29–30.   [52] Cited in Charlton, *Education in Renaissance England*, p. 202.
[53] See, for example, the will of Thomas Fones, who died 15 Apr. 1629, who did 'earnestly desire these my loving friends to have a special care that [my sons] be brought up in learning and in the fear of God and knowledge of his ways . . .' (*Winthrop Papers*, II, p. 82).

note that this duty of proper unbringing was extended to the care of servants and apprentices, too. Edmund Coote suggested that his manual would enable 'Taylors, Shop-keepers, Seamsters and such other' who should teach their charges to do so while 'on thy shop-bord, at thy loomes, or at thy needle, and never hinder thy worke . . .'. Education might well be valuable, but it was evidently not to be a distraction from the normal regimen of work. Instruction in godliness, however, as John Dod noted, would beget loyalty and productivity in servants. In heaven and on earth, spreading the doctrine of the Word was profitable to those possessed of its strength.[54] A manual of proper conduct for apprentices condemned those masters who had no time for instructing their charges in true religion.[55] Most of the author's anger, however, was directed at the strongheadedness of the youthful apprentices themselves, whose 'irreligiousness . . . doth farre exceed the negligence of the masters' and who would prefer to spend the sabbath in idle recreation.[56] He therefore called for a Sunday which included catechizing and prayer in the household, attendance at an early morning lecture (even outside one's own parish), presence both morning and afternoon at the parish church, attendance at an afternoon lecture somewhere in the City, and finally, in the evening, examination by the master of what the servants had learned that day. The regimen was to end with the singing of psalms – over twelve hours after the godly routine had begun at 6 a.m.[57] The author insisted that there was also a need for religious instruction on week days though, perhaps recognizing economic necessity, he advised that the course would not have to be as full as on the sabbath, 'for the Lord doth not require it at our hands'.[58] In his domestic manual aimed at servants themselves, Abraham Jackson advised that they commence their service by praying for an honest and religious master, and by perusing the parts of Scripture 'touching servants'.[59] The apprentice was to fulfil all his labours, but if he had any leisure in the week, he was to read the Bible and other religious books, and to pray for his master and his business.[60] Godliness and respect for the established earthly hierarchy were thus inseparable in puritan advice to the young. The frequency of puritan exhortations to masters to educate servants reflects perhaps not only the inherent importance of the task, but also the fear that masters were recalcitrant in their duty. At the same time, it is worth noting that none of the common puritan household manuals detailed any academic instruction for the apprentices, though they all expected servants to read the Word.

Perhaps above all else, the householder's duty was to take his charges fre-

[54] Coote, *English Schoole-Maister*, sig. A3; Dod, *Three Godlie Sermons*, pp. 49–50.
[55] B.P., *Prentises Practise*, fol. 45.   [56] *Ibid.*, fols. 64ᵛ, 65ff.
[57] *Ibid.*, fols. 38ff.   [58] *Ibid.*, fol. 41.
[59] Jackson, *Pious Prentice*, p. 3.   [60] *Ibid.*, pp. 36–7, 39.

quently to the sermons.[61] For his own part, the householder attended in large measure to receive guidance and reinforcement for his private rule. Attendance also buttressed the status of ministers: heads of households were encouraged to teach only 'such doctrine as they have learned and received from the publike ministery'.[62] In 1562 Leicester town council, under the influence of the Earl of Huntingdon, required that at least one member of every household attend the Wednesday and Friday sermons, on pain of a fine.[63] The common absence of godliness in England was often said to be due not so much to a lack of preaching as to the negligent preparation for and hearing of sermons.[64] The delineation of the 'heads' of a sermon, and the Ramist scheme itself, were intended not only to assist the preacher in delivering a coherent explanation of a text, but also to break down the lecture into manageable portions for those scantily educated people who had to listen for an hour or so. As an aid to memory, Henry Smith recommended the same tactic as was enforced on so many schoolboys in our period: the taking of notes.[65] On occasion, women, too, were encouraged to participate in this process of written memory. John Rogers, the puritan minister of Chacombe, suggested in a letter to Anne Smith, a waiting woman to Lady Cope, that she should join the hearing of sermons to her reading. So that she would be able to record her progress in godliness, Rogers noted that she should 'know that so manie sermons thou hast well hard as thou hast the notes to shew in thy bookes & the fruits apparent in the reformation of thy life and increase of thy knowledge . . .'.[66] The sermon left unrecorded was too easily forgotten. At the same time, this function was not to stand in the way of the visible and aural effect of the preacher in his pulpit. Smith therefore suggested only the writing of brief notes right after the sermon.[67] The church service was not to be turned into a school lecture full of note-takers. Puritans also commonly recommended that the family returning from church should immediately 'conferre', under parental guidance, about the sermon, since everyone was likely to remember something different of the lesson.[68]

The primary form of household instruction was catechizing, a simple pro-

[61] Rogers, *Seven Treatises*, pp. 570–2; Taylor, *Christs Combate*, p. 104; Smith, *13 Sermons*, sig. B.6; Hildersam, *CLII Lectures*, p. 499; Wright, *Divers Sermons*, p. 265.
[62] Perkins, *Workes*, I, pp. 700, 715; III, p. 698. See also Bownde, *Holy Exercise of Fasting*, p. 243.
[63] Cross, *Puritan Earl*, p. 132.
[64] Smith, *13 Sermons*, sig. Bᵛ; Bolton, *Workes*, pp. 165, 177–8; Perkins, *Foundation of Christian Religion*, sig. C.4ʳ⁻ᵛ; Smith, *13 Sermons*, sigs. C.2ᵛ, C.5, D.2ᵛ; Bod. Lib. MS Rawlinson D.273, p. 265 (sermon by ?Laurence Humphrey).   [65] Smith, *13 Sermons*, sig. D.2ᵛ.
[66] Bod. Lib. MS Rawlinson D.273, p. 379. For other examples, see Cliffe, *Puritan Gentry*, p. 66.
[67] Smith, *13 Sermons*, sig. D.3.
[68] Udall, *Obedience to Gospel*, in *Certaine Sermons*, sig. I i iijʳ⁻ᵛ. See also Gifford, *Sermon on Parable of Sower*, sigs. A.viiff. Nicholas Bownde drew a direct parallel between household conferences and ministerial 'exercises' (*Doctrine of the Sabbath*, pp. 398–9).

cess emphasized by all protestants, but perhaps especially by puritans among Englishmen.[69] A member of the Dedham *classis* noted that the simple Q. and A. structure of catechisms was the 'easiest and best way to trayne up young ones and the ruder sort . . .'.[70] The English hierarchy commonly tried to institute catechizing for all by the parish minister and schoolmaster, but seemed to regret the household liberty (which might lead to conventicles) provided by the mass of printed catechisms.[71] For puritans, catechizing was the prime weapon against the ignorance on which popery purportedly thrived.[72] That the earliest method of catechizing was not 'discovery', but rather rote learning and verbatim repetition fitted in with the emphasis on breaking the will.[73] It was extremely important to bring the activist message to the very young – Thomas Gataker insisted that it was an 'idle concept' that 'Religion and Godlinesse is not for children', and noted that he had penned an offering for children 'that are not past the breast yet'.[74] Since catechisms emphasized the hierarchical order of heaven and earth by using examples from common existence, they also offered, as Strauss has demonstrated for Lutheran Germany, a strong 'cultural affirmation and rededication of the entire community to the established order'.[75] The plethora of puritan manuals ensured that England's households were flooded with the same message over and over, so that response became a matter not of thoughtful choice, but rather of conditioning. Indeed, ministers were to oversee household instruction,[76] partly because it was seen, in turn, as the basis which allowed public preaching to have more effect. As well, the common duty of instruction tied minister and householder together. John Winthrop commented that he found

---

[69] See, for example, Nichols, *Household Government*, sig. B; Gouge, *Domesticall Duties*, pp. 540–1. The puritan preparation for the Hampton Court conference included the call for a new catechism to be used by every congregation (*H.M.C. Rep. on MSS of Lord Montagu of Beaulieu*, p. 33).

[70] Quoted in Usher, *Presbyterian Movement*, p. 90.

[71] Frere, *Articles and Injunctions*, III, pp. 22, 82, 87, 211–13, 258–9, 276, 286–7, for examples of episcopal pressure for catechizing. See also B.L. MS Lansdowne 109, fol. 7^{r-v}; *An Examination of Certayne Londonners*, p. 23, in *A Parte of a Register*; B.L. MS Lansdowne 157, No. 74, fol. 186; MS Harley 7042, fol. 13^{r-v}; MS Lansdowne 68, No. 48, fol. 110.

[72] Taylor, *Commentarie on Titus*, p. 113; Widley, *Doctrine of Sabbath*, pp. 147–8, 142; *Winthrop Papers*, I, p. 234, a letter from E. Culverwell. Eisenstein notes that in Romanist jurisdictions catechizing was not practised by the head of the household (*Printing Press*, pp. 424, 426).

[73] See, for example, Bernard, *Faithfull Shepheard* (1621), p. 102; Ball, *Short Treatise . . . Christian Religion*, sig. A3^{r-v}; Dering, *Brief Catechisme*, sig. A3^v; Nichols, *Household Government*, sigs. G7^v–8. Richard Greenham illustrated the tedium of catechizing: 'The office of the Catechist is to make his doctrine easie to enter by giving it an edge in perspicuitie, methode, etc. and of the catechised often to goe over the same thing, as a knife doth the whetstone, and to repeate and iterate it, till he have made it his owne' (*Workes*, p. 664).

[74] Gataker, *Davids Instructer*, p. 32; Gataker, *Christian Mans Care*, sig. a2. See also Gouge, *Domesticall Duties*, pp. 544–5; *Office of Christian Parents*, p. 58; Woodward, *Childes Patrimony*, pp. 6–7.

[75] Strauss, *Luther's House*, p. 169; see Ch. 8, pp. 151–75.

[76] F. Bunny, *Guide unto Godlinesse*, pp. 144–5, 147; Stockwood, *Sermon at Paules Crosse*, p. 132; Stoughton, *Assertion*, p. 241; Nichols, *Household Government*, sig. B^v; Perkins, *Workes*, I, p. 700.

this obligation 'as sufficient incouragement to my study and labour therein as
if I were to teache a publick Congregation . . .'.[77]

The connexion of home and other instructional institutions was firmly constructed by puritan writers. Thus Edmund Bunney referred to the same
'domesticall' condition in 'evry good familie', 'whereby parentes governe
their children, Scholemasters their schollers, and masters their servauntes'.[78] It
was commonly emphasized that a parent who neglected the instruction of his
children made the task of both minister and schoolmaster more difficult. But
the growing emphasis on the importance of catechizing by schoolmasters and
ministers reveals another paradox. As ever greater pressure was placed on the
householder to discipline his children and servants, and raise them in godliness, his exclusivity of instruction was removed both by state decree requiring
such indoctrination by ministers and by the concurrent expansion of public
educational facilities.[79] However, catechizing could also be a mark of the continuing independence of the household. Catechizing at home could be used to
provide a counterweight of puritan interpretation when the local minister was
either not fully reformed or simply negligent.[80] It seems significant that
Richard Rogers was content to leave the academic teaching in his home/school
to others, but insisted on performing the catechizing himself.[81]

Since catechisms were generally intended for the young, emphasis was on
plainness and clarity. This also set the pattern for the audience of later plain
sermons. John Rudd explained: 'the method wee have followed is plaine and
naturall, the matter wholesome, but not adorned with flowers of eloquence'.[82] Puritan offerings frequently made use of classical allusions, but
they were usually employed to the end of inculcating an appreciation of the
greater importance of godly learning. A tutor at Christ Church reminded his
intended young readers that 'if Socrates sayeth the fayrest of all creatures is a
man bountyfied with knowledge lett us account our selves most deformed and
ugly in gods syghte if our hartes be not purified by faythe & our lives directed
by his truthe'.[83]

Catechizing also emphasized a combination of print with the oral tradition.
Josias Nichols admonished householders not to 'be amisse to cause the learner
to repeate without booke, the places where all the stories and sentences are
written', a practice that would aid both memory and voice.[84] The danger was
always that rote learning would replace comprehension and the *feeling* of faith.

[77] Bayly, *Practise of Pietie*, pp. 431, 434; *Winthrop Papers*, I, p. 213.
[78] E. Bunny, *Short Summe of Christian Religion*, fol. 23.
[79] Strauss has already commented on this paradox in the German Lutheran experience (*Luther's
House*, pp. 157ff.).   [80] Nichols, *Household Instruction*, sig. C.
[81] Knappen, ed., *Two Elizabethan Puritan Diaries*, p. 27.
[82] Ball, *Short Treatise . . . Christian Religion*, sig. A3.   [83] Bod. Lib. MS Rawlinson D.273, p. 150.
[84] Nichols, *Order of Household Government*, sigs. C^v–C2.

The first contact with book learning was thus consciously structured to yield not only specific knowlege, but also attitudes and approaches for the contemplative as well as the active level of existence.[85] Long before the appearance of reason, the child was thus to be encouraged in fervency. The basis of the lifelong dialectic was laid early.

All family instruction, at bottom, depended on making acquaintance with the only book which 'sufficeth to lead us to perfection'.[86] Puritans, above both humanists and non-puritan churchmen, advocated a 'gathered-circle' communal godliness in which the progress of one might serve as the catalyst for the others. The householder should therefore 'call every morning *all* thy familie to some *convenient* roome; and first, eyther reade thy selfe unto them a Chapter in the Word of *God*, or cause it to be read distinctly by some other'. If time permitted, from the reading would proceed the singing of psalms, and prayers as well as admonition.[87] Interpretation was still to be the function of God's mediators.[88] The common centralization of reading on Sunday, before and after the sermon, was intended to maintain the hierarchical aspects of the approach to conversion and subsequent godliness.[89] Independent prior reading of the Word also made for more critical sermon audiences; Scripture-reading was thus to be the basis for action as well as contemplation.[90] Lack of formal learning and pressure of earthly affairs were of course no excuse for lack of familiarity with the vernacular Word.[91] The practice of household religious instruction had of course been strongly recommended in earlier tracts,[92] but the great explosion of emphasis arrived with the victory of protestantism. In England the established church attempted to introduce Bible-reading as a common protestant habit by ensuring that the vernacular Scriptures were placed in every church for public use.[93] But puritans went much further in their emphasis. The *Office of Christian Parents* (?1616) insisted that a married couple should read catechisms and the New Testament

---

[85] Ball, *Short Treatise . . . Christian Religion*, sig. A5^{r-v}; Bernard, *Common Catechism*, sig. A4; Greenham, *Workes*, p. 664.

[86] Geneva Bible, Marginal Comment to II Timothy 3.1. See also Dod & Cleaver, *Ten Commandments*, pp. 110–11; Byfield, *Principles*, p. 19, on the necessity of owning a Bible; also Scudder, *Christians Daily Walke*, p. 54; Perkins, *Workes*, I, pp. 714–15.

[87] Bayly, *Practise of Piety*, p. 437; Bownde, *Sabbath*, pp. 235ff., Nichols, *Household Instruction*, 'To the Reader'; Fenner, *Certain Godly Treatises*, pp. 12–13, 14–15.

[88] See, for example, the comment by Henry Smith that the common people should be 'content to be instructed of us' [the ministers] (*13 Sermons*, sig. B.7).

[89] Scudder, *Christians Daily Walke*, pp. 193–4.

[90] See, for example, Smith, *Certaine Sermons*, sigs. C3^{v}–4; Sorocold, *Supplication of Saints*, p. 9; Taylor, *Christs Combate*, p. 124.

[91] See, for example, Udall, *Certaine Sermons*, sig. Ii.v; Pemble, *5 Godly Sermons*, p. 24; Northbrooke, *Poore Mans Garden*, pp. 54, 55; Bolton, *Workes*, pp. 224–5; Hildersam, *CLII Lectures*, p. 494.

[92] See, for example, Richard Whitford's *Werke for Householders* (1530).

[93] See, for examples of such orders, Frere, *Articles and Injunctions*, III, pp. 2, 10–11, 81 and II, pp. 11–12; Cardwell, ed., *Documentary Annals*, II, pp. 11–12.

together, and be diligent in attending sermons until they had laid up a good stock of knowledge with which to nourish future progeny.[94] The duties of parenthood thus began even before conception.[95] William Perkins gave as one of the reasons for his attack on the separatists their scant regard for household reading of the Word.[96] Herbert Palmer both composed catechisms and gave free Bibles to those who could read.[97] This was the forward defence against the execrable 'policie of popish times, to keep the people in ignorance' by denying them unrestricted access to the vernacular Scriptures.[98]

In an era in which the political nation was availing itself ever more of formal education and of print, puritans had to compete in the market place for reading hours beyond basic devotion to Scripture and catechism. The church Fathers, Biblical histories which stressed the scriptural lessons, and the scriptural commentaries and concordances comprised the usual recommendations.[99] Richard Rogers recommended Calvin's *Institutes*, Peter Martyr's *Commonplaces* and, among others, the works of Beza and Perkins because they contained the 'summe of many learned Authors, in a plaine and profitable manner . . .'.[100] Although it was a common fear that the volume of books would perhaps lead to a 'distaste of the necessary use of reading',[101] puritans were not willing to limit their own production in an era of growing demand. Soon they were able to recommend each other's works. John Downame's list included Perkins, Dent, Rogers, Dyke, and Greenham. So that his readers would not go astray even after they had selected an acceptable work, Rogers offered them ten steps to the 'greatest profit' to be had from reading. It was, in effect, a scheme for the integration of reading into a general pattern of instruction for godly existence.[102] Thomas Beard allowed the reading of the histories of profane writers as valuable for drawing moral lessons from the past. But he emphasized that 'the true and *principall* use of their writings ought to be, diligently to marke the effects of Gods providence and of his justice'.[103] Print and humane learning were thus to reinforce in the household the trauma

[94] *Office of Christian Parents*, p. 27.
[95] See a letter of 12 Mar. 1618/19 from Ezekiel Culverwell to John Winthrop (whose wife was pregnant), reminding him of his duties to the child (*Winthrop Papers*, I, pp. 234–5). See also Gifford, *Catechisme*, sig. G.3ᵛ; Stubbes, *Christall Glasse*, sig. A4ᵛ; Fenner, *Certain Godly and Learned Treatises*, pp. 2, 13, 14–15.
[96] Perkins, *Estate of Damnation*, pp. 261–2; see also Nichols, *Household Instruction*, sig. G7.
[97] Clarke, *General Martyrologie*, pp. 188–9.
[98] Widley, *Doctrine of Sabbath*, p. 142. See also Byfield, *Principles*, pp. 18–19; Haller, *Rise of Puritanism*, pp. 128–33.   [99] Becon, *Sicke Mans Salve*, pp. 83–4; Clarke, *Holy Oyle*, esp. 'Preface'.
[100] Rogers, *Practice of Christianitie*, pp. 334–5.
[101] Philips, *Certaine Godly and Learned Sermons*, 'Preface' by George Bard. See also Pemble, *5 Godly Sermons*, p. 23.   [102] Rogers, *Practice of Christianitie*, pp. 342–4.
[103] Beard, *Theatre*, sigs. A4ᵛ–5ᵛ. See also Tuke, *True Protestant*, sigs. a–a3ᵛ.

caused by lack of assurance, and the consequent need for individual repentance, that is, the same message that was passed in its highest force orally from the pulpit.[104]

Diaries and wills yield some indication of the effect that this course in godly indoctrination had on the countryside. John Hayne, a wool merchant of Exeter, at one time bailiff and then sheriff of the city, denoted his puritan beliefs in his diary. He also made an express attempt to bring others into the circle. In 1634 he gave away a copy of Hildersam's *Lectures*, a Bible, and two books of sermons. He also bought copies of two works by Adam Harsnet, a puritan preacher in Essex, and gave them to his future wife. As well, he owned copies of works by, among others, Perkins, Whately, Thomas Taylor, Preston, Lewis Bayly, Thomas Brightman, Greenham, and Junius; he also possessed works by Erasmus, and Philip de Commines' *History*.[105] Charles Parrett, a citizen and draper of London, left a Bible to each of his grandchildren, and also expressed his will that 'every old poore Cottager dwelling in the Parish of Boebrickhill in the Countrye of Buckingham shall have a Bible . . . for their better Instruction, whereby God may be glorifyed and their soules comforted'.[106] So that his gift would not fall to the incapable, he sensibly also bequeathed £5 per year for the 'instructing and teaching to reade in the English Tongue poore Children borne and bredd . . . of poore decayed housholders within the said Towne and parish . . .'.[107] William Norton, citizen and stationer of London, who died in late 1593, combined his belief in the necessity of Christian learning with his faith in the proper training inculcated by the universities. He therefore bequeathed to graduates of Christ's Hospital who had gone on to Oxford or Cambridge, but who had not yet been beneficed, 'bookes to the value of twentie shillinges a peece such as them selves shall best like of . . .'. Norton also left an endowment to provide for a petty master at Onibury.[108] The impetus to produce a nation of godly readers thus became not a lonely cry of puritan ministers, but, seemingly, a charitable obligation of each fervent believer as he struggled to fulfil his duty to God by bringing others into the brotherhood of conversion.

Puritans also generally sought seriously to discourage books which could not only waste time, labour, and precious funds, but which could also, by concentrating the mind on carnal pursuits, threaten the dedication to godly exist-

[104] Spufford notes the 'unabashed use of fear as a lever to conversion' in godly chapbooks (*Small Books*, p. 207).
[105] Brushfield, 'Financial diary', *Reps. & Trans. of Devons. Assoc. for Adv. of Science, Lit., and Art*, 33, pp. 187–269.
[106] P.R.O. P.C.C. 17 Sadler 1635. The will was dated 26 Feb. 1633/4 and proved 9 Feb. 1634/5.
[107] *Ibid.*   [108] P.R.O. P.C.C. 8 Dixy 1593: dated 27 Aug. 1593, proved 1 Jan. 1593/4.

ence.[109] John Stockwood condemned popular romances and love stories, or
'filthie books', as he preferred to call them.[110] Thomas Taylor stressed that
one of the useful functions of reading especially the psalms was that they
not only revealed God's wisdom, but also helped to 'confute such as set out
filthy, amorous, and lewd Ballads and Songs, Fictions, Love-books, etc. which
tend to the corrupting of Men and Youth especially'.[111] In this vein, William
Crashawe argued that, while he heartily opposed the Romanist fashion of
withholding or changing 'holy and auncient Writers', if papists had purged
only 'Machiavel, Rabelesse, Peter Aretine', then he would 'have given them
the hand of fellowship . . .'.[112] Lacking the power of censorship, puritans had
to try to dissuade people from paying attention to contemporary trash. Robert
Cleaver warned householders that since their children would one day hold
them accountable, it was a great folly 'to linger children in the learning of
vaine, trifling, and unprofitable things, which as they grow in yeares they will
contemne and forget . . .'.[113] Finally, perhaps, we can cite William Prynne, a
man familiar with the power and penalties associated with the press, who
advised strongly against giving 'open Hospitality, and free welcome to all
Popish, Arminian, and other seducing forraigne Writers, which have lately
turned our Faith, into meere doubting . . .'.[114] Prynne would have banned,
among other works, those of Ovid, Catullus, Tibullus, Propertius, Martial,
Plautus, and Terence.[115]

But above all other material, puritans reacted against plays. Their opposition may have been due in part to the fact that plays could be presented
visually in three dimensions as well as in linear fashion on the page, and thus
could pose a challenge to the spectacle of the pulpit. Plays were 'heathenish
and diabolicall'; even their appearance in the universities did not redeem
them, for it was accounted that only the lowest types at Oxford and
Cambridge took part in them.[116] Plays contravened the seventh commandment;[117] plays, a 'monstre horrible to beholde', could indeed 'metamorphize,
transfigure, deforme, pervert and alter the harts of their haunters'.[118] John
Stockwood, at the more severe end of the Elizabethan puritan spectrum,
accused plays of encouraging sexual licence. Plays imparted the fanciful

[109] Rogers, *Seven Treatises*, p. 288; Rogers, *Practice of Christianitie*, p. 336; Perkins, *Workes*, I, p. 450; Bayly,
Practise of Pietie, sig. *4. Puritans did not stand alone in this criticism, of course. See Ascham, *Scholemaster*,
ed. Giles, pp. 158, 160, and Felltham, *Resolves*, p. 173.
[110] Stockwood, *Sermon at Paules Crosse*, p. 147.   [111] Taylor, *Davids Learning*, p. 2
[112] Crashawe, *Romish Forgeries*, sigs. H^r, H^v. See also *A Copie of a Letrer*, p. 145, in *A Parte of a
Register*.   [113] Cleaver, *Household Government*, pp. 232–3.
[114] Prynne, *Antithesis to Arminianisme*, sigs. C2^v, C3. [115] Prynne, *Histrio-Mastix*, Pt 2, esp. pp. 915–16.
[116] Greene, *Refutation of Apology*, sigs. A2, C2.   [117] Dod & Cleaver, *Ten Commandements*, p. 297.
[118] Clement, *Petie Schole*, p. 88; Dod & Cleaver, *Ten Commandements*, p. 297; Crosse, *Vertues Commonwealth*, sigs. P2, N4; Goodwin, *Vanity of Thoughts Discovered*, pp. 65–6; Bayly, *Practice of Pietie*, sig.
A4^{r-v}.

message of the Devil rather than the hard truth of the Lord. They even deflected people from dedication to calling and religion alike by portraying an unreal existence.[119] John Rainolds raged against Terence and the lesser ancient playwrights.[120] In 1633, William Prynne charged that over 40,000 'playbooks' had been printed in the previous two years; what especially appalled him was the indication that plays were now 'more vendible than the choycest Sermons', hardly an indication of a nation marching to Jerusalem.[121] Prynne likely felt sensitive to popular opinion on this matter, so he noted the tradition in Christianity of condemning plays, and insisted that opposition was by no means a 'factious Novalty, or puritannical singularity . . .'.[122] Though the thrust of his argument has often been seen as simply an attack on licentious public behaviour, we may also perhaps comprehend it as a way of placing the concern about print within the puritan search for the proper uses of learning. It was a source of constant irony as well as sorrow that the recent opening up of much knowledge seemed to forestall rather than to promote the spread of godly religion.

III

By stressing familiarity not only with the content of the Word but also with Word-as-print, puritans helped to promote the cultural revolution of the early modern period. Print represented a new and different authority from the figure of the minister preaching from on high to the gathered multitude.[123] Both parallel to, and ensuing from, this protestant (and especially puritan) fervour to spread the book-of-the-Word to each household was the development of the English language. Thomas Becon, for example, attacked both Romanist ignorance and the humanist preference for classical learning by penning a tract in which Scripture spoke in the first person in favour of its own vernacular propagation.[124] The argument that those in possession of learning had a duty to instruct the lower orders soon proved more powerful than traditionalism. Indeed, Eisenstein has commented that possibly 'no social revolution in European history is as fundamental as that which saw book-learning (previously assigned to old men and monks) gradually become the focus of daily life during childhood, adolescence, and early manhood'.[125] The fervent desire to spread the saving, vernacular message to all households was successful to the

---

[119] Stockwood, *Sermon at Paules Crosse*, p. 133. See, similarly, White, *Sermon at Paules Crosse*, p. 46.
[120] Rainolds, *Th'overthrow of Stage-Plays*, esp. pp. 122–4.   [121] Prynne, *Histrio-Mastix*, sig. *3ʳ⁻ᵛ.
[122] *Ibid.*, 'To the . . . Young Gentlemen-Students of the . . . Innes of Court', and pp. 915ff. For a similar, though less vociferous, opinion, see Northbrooke, *Treatise . . . Dicing*, p. 75.
[123] Eisenstein, *The Printing Press, passim*, esp. pp. 131–2.   [124] Jones, *Triumph*, pp. 58–63.
[125] Eisenstein, 'Impact of printing', *Journal of Modern History*, 40, p. 41.

degree that the Bible became the most commonly owned book in England.

This stress on reading the Bible, catechisms, and other godly works leads us to the question of the connexion of puritans and the growth of literacy. Traditionally, historians have emphasized the thirst for the printed Word as the prime cause of the thrust towards literacy in protestant countries.[126] 'Puritanism', as a particularly reformist protestant faction, is viewed as regarding literacy as 'a universal prerequisite to spiritual preparedness, the central duty of the covenant'.[127] The empirical evidence is rather sketchy, however. Lockridge has argued that while literacy rates in New England were higher than those in England, the advantage was due primarily to the lack of illiterate labourers.[128] There are also grave difficulties in testing the statistical literacy of puritans in England. Lawrence Stone suggested that 'puritan' villages achieved significantly higher literacy rates, but the nature of his sample, and the degree of possible inaccuracy in such historical statistics, have brought his conclusions into question.[129] Studies have also so far not carefully defined what can legitimately be called a 'puritan village'.[130] David Cressy has recently illustrated for Essex the vagaries of attempting to connect causally villages with puritan/non-puritan incumbents and areas of high/low literacy. The mere presence of a forward minister alone was not sufficient, he concludes, to alter substantially patterns of literacy.[131] Book-buying cannot assist in the determination of puritan influence until the problem of identification of areas has been solved.[132] Nor can individual wills and inventories yet establish a correlation between religious fervency and book-buying.[133]

[126] Cressy concludes that by 1642 rural illiteracy figures for English adult males stood at approximately 70% (*Literacy*, p. 72). Houston, 'Aspects of Society', unpub. Ph.D. thesis, Univ. of Cambridge, 1981, pp. 169–70, generally agrees with Stone's figure of approximately 65% illiteracy in 1640.

[127] Axtell, *School upon a Hill*, p. 13, concerning New England. Richard Vann agreed with Stone's conclusion of the connexion of puritans and high literacy ('Literacy', *Journal of Interdisciplinary History*, 5, esp. p. 290). Cressy, *Literacy*, p. 3, quotes Axtell and transfers the belief to the English puritans, though on an earlier occasion Cressy suggested, against Lawrence Stone, that the assumption of a connexion between puritans and literacy 'is untested and may be wrong' ('A reply', *Journal of Interdisciplinary History*, 8, pp. 800–1).

[128] Lockridge, *Literacy*, pp. 87ff. Lockridge also did not find any major differences between a designated 'puritan' area (New England) and a designated 'non-puritan' region (Virginia) with regard to charitable donations, including schools, the source in general of an ability to read and write (*ibid.*, pp. 85–7, 94–6.) But see also Hall, 'Education and the social order', *Reviews in American History*, 3, p. 182.

[129] Schofield, 'Some dimensions of illiteracy in England, 1600–1800', p. 13 (unpub. paper). I am very grateful to Roger Schofield for permission to cite from this paper.

[130] Stone, 'Literacy 1640–1900', *Past & Present*, 42, pp. 100–2; Schofield, 'Some dimensions', pp. 13–14; Richardson, *Puritanism*, pp. 8, 13; Cressy, *Literacy*, pp. 81–8.

[131] Cressy, *Literacy*, pp. 86ff., argues that the presence of a school had a greater effect on patterns of literacy.

[132] For a discussion of the difficulties of assessing book ownership from wills and inventories, see Cressy, *Literacy*, pp. 48–53.

[133] Clark, 'Ownership of books', pp. 95–111, in Stone, ed., *Schooling and Society*.

The major difficulties in the historical study of literacy are the looseness of definition and the difficulty of applying a standard of measurement.[134] Despite Roger Schofield's warning that taking the ability to sign as reflecting also an ability to read fluently is based on nineteenth-century evidence,[135] this correlation has frequently been read back into the sixteenth and seventeenth centuries, with resultant confusion.[136] One serious consequence is that the great gulf which separated those who could only read the vernacular from those who could read and write is often underplayed.[137] Margaret Spufford has reminded us of the social separation of the two skills by detailing the time they took, *consecutively*, to learn.[138] Reading skills, she suggests, were distributed much more widely than writing, not only across the breadth of particular economic classes, but also down to the level of husbandmen and labourers.[139] The argument is of momentous importance for those who would seek to demonstrate the speed at which new ideas can be distributed in a preindustrial society. Egil Johansson has demonstrated that in post-Reformation Sweden the Lutheran church encouraged adult reading ability and insisted that children learn to read before being confirmed.[140] By the end of the seventeenth century this had produced areas of an overwhelming preponderance of 'readers' among the population.[141] Almost no emphasis, however, was placed upon cultivating a mass ability to write. The church, as an agent of indoctrination, needed only a population able to *receive* information through print.[142] Though there was no similar testing in England, it would appear likely that an

---

[134] I am indebted to Joan Simon for an invitation to the History of Education Society Conference on literacy, held at Leicester in Mar. 1980. The discussions there shaped much of what follows.

[135] Schofield, 'Some dimensions', pp. 3–5.

[136] Cressy, *Literacy*, pp. 3–5, uses the term 'literacy' interchangeably as 'reading and writing' and 'reading'.

[137] There is no real way that we can project how many people could read, simply from numbers of signatures. Schofield notes that in Bottesford, Leicestershire, around 1847, out of 32 women, 12 were able to read who could not sign. Only 3 of 32 men fell into the same category. That 37.5% of women here could receive, but not themselves independently send, messages over time and space is surely of the highest significance ('Some dimensions', p. 4).

[138] By correlating the age at which a child could contribute significantly to the household economy (between the 7th and 8th birthdays) with the age at which the child was likely first to attend some form of 'school' (just before or just after the 7th birthday), and the length of time taken to learn to read (8 to 12 months), and then to write (a further 12 months), Spufford is able to produce a forceful argument to the effect that those boys who did receive some formal education would have been able to read but not to write by the time economic pressures (especially at the lower end of the economic scale) either interrupted or concluded their studies ('First steps in literacy', *Social History*, 4, pp. 412–13). Someone who left school with a basic ability to read might also develop into a fluent reader. But if a lad left school before he could write, and his subsequent job did not require this ability, then he might well have remained a capable reader, but an 'illiterate' in the records.

[139] Spufford, 'First steps in literacy', *Social History*, 4, esp. pp. 409–17; Spufford, *Small Books*, p. 22. Cressy designated husbandmen as 21% 'literate' and labourers as 15% 'literate', that is, able to sign their name (*Literacy*, p. 119).   [140] Johansson, *History of Literacy in Sweden*, esp. pp. 12ff.

[141] In the parish of Tuna, in 1688–91, 96% of the age group 11–15 either could read or was learning to read (*ibid.*, p. 29).   [142] *Ibid.*, pp. 55–6.

increasing body of 'readers-only' existed, and that 'signers' do not represent all who could read with certain critical skills.[143]

If there was a contemporary appreciation of how widespread the ability to read the vernacular really was in the social scale – and the assortment of catechisms and domestic manuals indicates an attempt to reach groups of very different educational and social backgrounds – then we may possibly be able to say something about the sociological purposes behind such adaptations of knowledge as the famed puritan 'plain prose', eminently suitable for those who could read but who had little learning. It may well have been, then, that attitudes towards the need to distribute godly knowledge were theologically determined by the covenant insistence upon edification, but perhaps as to *method*, in both sermons and tracts, sociologically conditioned as much by the qualities of the audience/readership as by the imitation of the Pauline model of wariness of vain learning. Reading was such a volatile factor in the Revolution (and even before) perhaps at least partly because, for many, the process of learning to read, and then the application of the skill, had not been accompanied by thorough assimilation into the norms of hierarchical society.

While the structure and dynamics of signing have been much clarified by recent work, the social, economic, and cultural impulses to learn to read and to write are still debated, at least concerning their relative significance.[144] There can be no doubt, however, that one of the principal catalysts to learning to read, especially for preparationists, was independent access to Scripture, the saving Word and the ultimate source of protestant truth.[145] No other activity, apart from sermon attendance, could so readily bring the inspirational message to the individual conscience. Nicholas Bownde therefore insisted that parents should either read to their children or, even better, ensure that the children attained the skill.[146] Josias Nichols, in his popular domestic tract, urged a universal reading ability upon the English nation.[147] Even adults could learn; it was, noted Samuel Hieron, as easy 'as to be able to play at the Cardes, if men were as desirous of the one as of the other . . .'.[148] Reading provided knowledge for the instruction of others, and so was to become a habit for Christians, who would devote to it 'so much time as they can spare from other

[143] Lockridge, *Literacy*, p. 15. This in turn leads to a suggestive point made by Eisenstein that the skill of being able to write is not necessary to the ability to compose literature or argument ('Impact of printing', pp. 30–1).
[144] The various factors conducing to a desire to be able to read are discussed in Cressy, *Literacy*, Ch. 1 and pp. 186–7; see also Stone, 'Educational revolution', *Past and Present*, 28, 1964, esp. p. 42.
[145] Hence the importance placed in his autobiography by Adam Martindale on being given an ABC when he was six, 'a gift in itself exceeding small and contemptible, but in respect of the designe and event, worth more than its weight in gold' (Martindale, *Life*, p. 5). See also Eisenstein, 'Impact of printing', esp. pp. 33, 31.
[146] Bownde, *Sabbath*, p. 202; see also Greenham, *Workes*, p. 278; Adams, *Workes*, p. 318.
[147] Nichols, *Household Instruction*, sig. G.7.
[148] Hieron, *Preachers Plea*, p. 489. See also Downe, *Two Treatises*, p. 41.

necessary duties . . .'.[149] Such phrasing was likely intended to soothe the hirers of labour because it did not permit sloth in the name of the pursuit of the Word. Those who could not read, though they could listen to others, were 'like to fare the worse for want of that ability', he warned.[150]

As ever, puritans were willing to phrase their encouragement in an analogy with everyday life. 'Looke as those who can read their Fathers Wills, Evidences, and other writings have a great advantage to know them, over another hath who cannot read at all: so it is no small furtherance, when wee can read this Will and Testament which Christ hath left us.'[151] In Massachusetts, this social and religious urge (combined with the necessities of the frontier) was transformed into the 1644 law which bound masters of families to teach their children and apprentices to read. Long before, in the 1580s, in Dedham, Essex, the *classis* had similarly agreed that 'all yonge children of the towne [including the poor] be taught to reade Englishe . . .'.[152] Dorothy Leigh insisted that, if one were asked to serve as a witness at baptism, one should extract from the parent the promise that 'the child shall be taught to reade, so soone as it can conveniently learne, and that it shall so continue till it can reade the Bible'.[153] Given the likely different skills of the parents, this instruction would be a cooperative and yet hierarchical process. Thus William Bedell expected his wife to instruct their children in the catechism and teach them to read English before he 'took them under his own teaching'.[154]

Much of the difficulty in assessing the strength of the puritan push for literacy lies in deciding on those aspects which can legitimately be called 'puritan' actions. Puritans, along with their contemporaries, recognized and encouraged the increasing vocational pressures towards literacy, and yet also understood that not all householders would make the effort to instil these skills in their charges. Frequently, then, puritans insisted only that householders read the Scriptures to their gathered dependants. This introduces us directly to the puritan attempt to combine oral and print cultures: the stress on 'reading and hearing' the Word that pervaded all household manuals.[155] There can of course be no doubt that seekers of godliness were first to hear the Word preached, and secondly to read it if they could.[156] But while there are many admonitions to raise children exercised in 'letters',[157] even more common, in the household manuals, is simply the

---

[149] Rogers, *Practice of Christianitie*, pp. 337–8.   [150] *Ibid.*, p. 598.
[151] Baynes, *Helpe to Happinesse*, pp. 400–1.   [152] Quoted in Usher, *Presbyterian Movement*, p. 100.
[153] Leigh, *Mothers Blessing*, p. 26.
[154] Bod. Lib. MS Tanner 278, No. 2, fol. 22ᵛ: 'Life' of William Bedell.
[155] See, for example, Dent, *Plaine Mans Path-way*, p. 298; Fenner, *Certain Godly Treatises*, pp. 14–15.
[156] See John Penry's final instructions to his daughters. He left each of them a Bible, but reminded them that 'the lord regardeth loveth and blesseth the publique worship, more then any private exercise of Religion whatsoever' (B.L. MS Add. 48,064, fols. 23ᵛ–4, dated 10 Apr. 1593).
[157] See, for example, the admonition given to Philip Stubbes by his dying wife (Stubbes, *Christall Glasse*, sig. A4ᵛ).

injunction to raise children in knowledge and practice of Christianity via the gathered family engaging in patriarchal instruction.[158] It is also to be noted that puritans held back from stating clearly that non-readers could not be of the elect. Reading and hearing doubtless existed best in united state, but, even as separated skills, they could conduce to godliness. Temporarily, then, even as England's educational facilities expanded and the reading public grew, puritans had to propagandize their cause orally through the masters of households as transmitters, and to wives, children, and servants largely as receivers, of the message. Indeed, this may have been the safer route. Puritans, as well as contemporaries, had to be careful that the 'educational revolution' did not upset the accepted patriarchal organization of society. If the householder was not the first person in a family to become literate, then the power structure within that domain might well on occasion be challenged. Against the traditional authority of the master the new standardized truth of print could arise. The insistence that the householder read to his flock was perhaps motivated at least in part by a desire to see speech and print united in defence of the familial unit as the centre of earliest indoctrination.[159]

This also raises the question of the greater intellectual struggle between 'enthusiasm' as an inner truth of belief, and 'print' as, increasingly, the actualization of knowledge which can be analysed. Indeed, in the middle of the seventeenth century, radical proponents of a counterculture, who presumably appealed to the lower social classes, sought to propagandize their cause partly through print even as they attacked the printed page, including the Bible itself. If there were many people who could read but not write, then learning would come first to them (and for a fairly long time) as the *receiving* of the ideas of the learned, who were of a higher socio-economic level. These readers would continue to transmit knowledge only in the traditional, oral manner, save perhaps for hiring a scribe to draw up the occasional document. The Revolution witnessed a great battle over spoken and printed methods of the dissemination of knowledge: not only the encounter between the 'ancients' and the 'moderns', but also the methodological skirmish between 'speakers' and 'writers'.

This ongoing struggle may well be present in the puritan exhortation that ministers should take only the 'heads' of sermons into the pulpit with them.

---

[158] For such vague instructions, see Taylor, *Principles of Christian Practice*, p. 460; Gouge, *Domesticall Duties*, p. 655.

[159] There is one further problem to be raised in this vein. I have been unable to ascertain the period in which people learned to read silently, or indeed whether this is a 'natural progression' once one has learned to read at all. If most reading was done aloud, then was it done only with the permission of our illiterate householder, who perhaps by his presence maintained the force of control over printed knowledge? Or, if silent reading was widely practised, did the material read then become the subject of discussion only under the control of the householder, or did it lead to beliefs and stated opinions which he might have to struggle to regulate?

Though this was partly a guarantee against inefficacious reading, it may also have been a culturally necessary commitment to the popular norm of oral composition as the passing along of knowledge rather than its creation. Popular congregations may still have regarded print merely as a form of capturing oral wisdom, as it indeed in part was, given the number of printed sermons. For the fully literate and influential minority this was indeed becoming the age of print. Print soon caught on; by the Revolution, penny-pages cajoled the masses. But the earliest ages of the Reformation were the dawning first and foremost of a new age of intelligible public *sound*: hearing the preacher expound and exhort. The cultural revolution that was the victory of print had to be content with a coalition of forces for several crucial generations in this period. People accustomed to the authority of speech might well have taken some time to accept that the conclusions they drew from private reading had greater validity than those offered from the pulpit. In England, it may have taken the multiplicity of denominations, the far greater freedom of the press and of religious opinion, the threatened social upheaval, and the more direct questioning of institutionalized learning – all facets of the Revolution – to raise the authority of print to such a level.

Perhaps this practical decision to disseminate knowledge through householders also helps to explain the puritan attitude towards writing. The attractiveness of writing did increase for godly reasons. Schoolchildren could combine their writing ability and their religious indoctrination by taking notes at the Sunday sermon.[160] Writing also permitted the taking of notes as one read the Scriptures, so that one could recall the moral without again searching the printed page. It was the ability to write that allowed the godly to produce their daily testaments of struggle, and for separated relatives to encourage each other to labour for (and in) the covenant, an important aspect of puritan written communication.[161] But though household manuals did on occasion argue that puritans owed their children instruction in writing as well as in reading,[162] writing remained the skill of the few, correlated directly with one's sex, vocation, and social status.[163] Note-taking at sermons, which inevitably involved the act of interpretation fashioned by selection, could be encouraged at least partly because of the likely social exclusivity of those who could actually perform the task.

Religious fervency does not seem to have been directed at overcoming the social-structural and economic bias against full literacy for both women and

---

[160] See below, pp. 189, 198.

[161] It is mere conjecture to speculate concerning the degree to which an ability to write instilled in the individual the *idea* to record his spiritual conversion. Those who could not write may well have produced epic oral accounts of their own transformation for family and friends.

[162] See, for example, Whately, *Ten Commandments*, p. 115; *Office of Christian Parents*, p. 73; B.L. MS Add. 48,064, fol. 22^vff.   [163] Cressy, *Literacy*, esp. Chs. 6 and 7.

members of the lower orders. John Northbrooke's recognition of (old) women and husbandmen as the extreme of those unlikely to comprehend the Word for themselves accords with modern conclusions which place these groups at or near the bottom of the literacy scale.[164] Even those domestic manuals concerned with well-born females consistently placed greater stress on the education of boys than on that of girls. Literacy was something which females frequently did not attain (if at all) until adulthood. Edmund Coote, in his immensely popular self-education manual, included lessons on learning how to write, 'for which I have heard many gentlewomen offer much'. Girls farmed out to other households might, with luck, be provided with a private tutor for English, music, dancing, and a smattering of Latin. Mulcaster saw the value of some classical education, rhetoric, logic, and modern languages for girls, but even he viewed their socio-economic adulthood in a traditional light. Grace Sherrington remembered studying reading, writing, arithmetic, botany, singing, lute-playing, and needlecraft, as well, of course, as religion. But this regimen, beyond vernacular reading, did not penetrate very far down the social scale, especially for women. More common was Thomas Becon's praise of silence in women.[165] *The Office of Christian Parents* expected religious instruction for females, but it was couched in the passive phrases of the usual subservience which puritans, too, saw as the proper lot of women:

If from twelve til the day of marriage, she be taught to use the needle exquisitely, and to doe and understand all points of huswifery rightly and perfectly; and therewithall doe grow in custome to read, to heare, to love and delight in the wisedome of Gods word faithfully, she may be brought into her husbands house, with . . . great honour and joy . . .[166]

This view of women helped to contribute to the slowness of the improvement of female literacy rates, in New England as in England itself.[167]

    Women did teach elementary school, and thus occasionally joined in as public agents of the expansion of literacy.[168] Occasionally, too, funeral sermons recalled great efforts of literacy by women. Nicholas Guy, for example, paid tribute to the accomplishments of Elizabeth Gouge, wife of the famous puritan preacher William:

With her owne hand shee penned sundry devout Prayers, whereof some being for helps to humble her soule the more before God, were very large. She hath also left written by her selfe many divine directions for Devotions. She further tyed her selfe

[164] Northbrooke, *Poore Mans Garden*, fol. 55^{r-v}; Cressy, *Literacy*, esp. Ch. 6.
[165] Coote, *English Schoole-Maister*, sig. A2; Charlton, *Education*, pp. 209–10.
[166] *Office of Christian Parents*, p. 137.
[167] Lockridge noted that female literacy stagnated (at below 50%) in New England in the eighteenth century even as male literacy approached universality (*Literacy*, p. 38).
[168] Spufford, 'First steps', p. 435.

by a set dayly taske to reade the holy Scriptures, whereby she was able readily to answer any question propounded about the History and Doctrin of the Scriptures. Shee did also spend much time in reading English books of divinity, whereof shee had a pretty Library.[169]

Nonetheless, as a rule, writing remained extremely troublesome for women. The separation of skills, even when the godly impulse was present, is well illustrated by Oliver Heywood's mother, who got her sons to take sermon notes for her.[170] The problems attendant upon writing also plagued puritan women of reasonably high station. Anne Winthrop, writing to Emmanuel Downing, her son, in ?1623, apologized for the infrequency of her correspondence, pleading that she had 'hetherto bin ashamed . . . to trouble you with my dull head and scriblinge hand . . .'. Ursula Sherman similarly noted that part of the reason for her neglect in communicating with her brother was her 'want of skill and art in writing . . .'.[171] John Winthrop recorded in his 'Christian Experience' that his first wife had had some severe difficulty in her writing; he referred to 'the scriblinge hande, the meane congruitye, the false orthog; and broken sentences, etc. . . .'.[172] Inferior training and probably insufficient practice likely reduced the self-esteem of these women as writers, compared to their husbands, brothers, and sons – commonly university-trained men to whom the pen was a completely familiar instrument.

Women were frequently praised, in fact, for possessing only a simple love of Christianity rather than a thorough knowledge of it.[173] Governor Winthrop evidently believed that the wife of Governor Hopkins of Connecticut went mad *because* she did not confine her learning to that required of her female intellect.[174] Women, too, were commonly associated much more with the practice of the faith than with analysis. Simplicity frequently became a virtue in sketches of godly women. Thus Thomas Gataker, in a funeral sermon, could point out the generally believed characteristics of women by portraying an exception. God had blessed the dead woman, he concluded, with 'such graces as are not so ordinarily incident to that sex, sharpnes of apprehension, and soundnes of judgement'.[175] Part of the continuing subordination of women was effected by making females of virtually all classes heavily dependent on males for sources of information. Insistence upon full female literacy was perhaps not feasible given the number of schools; it might also have cost puritans much influential male support. In this question, then, social sub-

---

[169] Guy, *Pieties Pillar*, p. 48. Guy unfortunately does not tell us whether Elizabeth collected any of this 'library' independently of her husband. [170] Spufford, *Small Books*, pp. 34–5.

[171] *Winthrop Papers*, I, p. 294; II, p. 224. [172] *Ibid.*, I, p. 203.

[173] Even the humanist Mulcaster fitted into the customary pattern of the age by cautioning against allowing women to 'passe beyond the boundes both of their birth, and their best beseeming' (*Positions*, p. 179). For statistical evidence of female literacy, see Cressy, *Literacy*, esp. pp. 33, 144, 177.

[174] Morgan, *Puritan Family*, p. 44. [175] Gataker, *Two Funerall Sermons*, sig. B2, B^v.

ordination remained a greater motivating factor than the promotion of a female contribution to Christian proselytizing.

Instead of universal reading and writing, puritans thus emphasized a complementary system of tasks that would bring all within the sphere of knowledge of Scripture. 'Reading and hearing' were perhaps not two mandatory duties for each and every person to perform, but rather complementary duties which illustrated the Ramist system of 'relatives'. This notion would have been well known not only to university-trained preachers and laymen, but also to attentive members of congregations and readers of puritan tracts with their schematic diagrams. Some were thus to read, and others primarily to hear. Puritans recognized the dangers of the liberty of speech to their movement, decrying unprepared sermons and the hotheadedness (as they saw it) of the separatists. But, in their insistence on spreading wide among householders (and children as proto-householders) the ability to read, they extended their belief in the power of the educated few to dominate the thought and actions of the many, assisted by a self-control which emanated from the breaking of the individual will in an earlier stage of socialization.[176] Writing was an adjunctive skill which puritan preachers could praise and encourage, but which they seem to have been careful not to *require*, since it was beyond the likely achievement of most of their parishioners. Writing also made the parishioner far more independent of his minister in his ability to become a separate source of recorded opinions, a development which ministers cannot have regarded as a completely unmixed blessing.

The substance of print was doubtless also discussed second- or third-hand by people who themselves had no knowledge of books. Any attempt to draw a firm line between the social role of the literate and the non-literate therefore presents great hazards.[177] Puritans urged the development of a large pool of the 'partially literate', that is, those who could read simple texts and pass along the message to other members of the household and community. If only a single Bible and a single reader existed in the household, then the message of salvation (and social order) could be spread quite effectively. Reading led not to isolation, but perhaps to even greater social intercourse.[178] Print soon became a means of standardizing the message and of imparting to it greater authority through the learned power of black-on-white. As print could reach those not yet served by a godly preacher, and could reinforce the pulpit message where a godly mediator had already arrived, it was to be praised and

---

[176] For an interesting approach to this question, see Walzer, 'Revolutionary uses of repression', pp. 122–36, in Richter, ed., *Essays in Theory and History*.

[177] This point has recently been made by Harvey Graff in reference to the eighteenth century, of which he argues, reiterating E.P. Thompson's contention, that any 'simple distinction between literate and illiterate' is fuzzy at every point (*Literacy Myth*, p. 194).

[178] On this point, see Spufford, *Small Books*, p. 68.

encouraged. As it brought the true form of the saving Word to each seeker of the covenant, it became a bounden duty for those whose socio-economic status allowed them the time to learn the skill. Reading thus became another pathway to the Lord, and it therefore took its rank in the file of sermon attendance, contemplation, prayer, and catechizing as important duties of the committed Christian household.

IV

The household was thus one of the centres of the puritan revolution – that proposed radical change in the purposes of social existence to the end of constructing a New Jerusalem in England. The household served as the central refuge of puritan practice when pulpit, college, and school came under increasing pressure towards the end of our period. While the adult generation felt the strain of rising ungodliness, the future could well be brighter through the instruction given to the next cohort of godly workers and magistrates. Advice on how to run a household, however, was probably not enough to encourage repentance and dedication to a new course. Therefore puritan authors offered their readers not only theory but also, in funeral sermons and biographies, sketches of contemporary examples of such seminaries of godliness. Like early Christian saints, they served to urge onward those whose own will might otherwise have weakened in the face of adversity. Thus it was said of Thomas Cawton, minister of London and then of Rotterdam, not only that he always kept his love of learning in subordination to his dedication to divinity, but also that he fully lived his faith, so that 'there was a sweet and harmonious concord and correspondence between the originall and the copy, the Bible and his conversation'. His loving dedication to Christian virtue evidently also pervaded his relationship with his wife:

he chose a wife for her lovely vertues, and loved her with the greatest affection; he found not only his Rib, but his Heart when he found her; they wedded one anothers humours as well as persons, and so went the shortest way to perfection.

With his children, 'he took a great deal of pains to instruct and catechise . . . , to bring them up in the nurture and admonition of the Lord . . .'. When he had to correct or punish them, paternal affection was smitten by the anguish of superior duty to God:

He was often so moved with compassion, his fatherly bowels did so yearn over them, that the tears would trickle apace from his eies when he was correcting them: nothing ever wrought upon me like this sight, which did plainly convince his Children of his unwillingness to chastise, but that he was forced to it; his tears did sink so deep into their hearts, but that they could not but be softened at least for that time . . .[179]

The godly household could not exist in isolation, however. Extremely important also was the association in conference of the godly members of the congregation with their minister. The details in the puritan hagiography are fairly standardized, so I shall cite only a few examples. Of Thomas Taylor it was recorded that his private ministry matched the power of his public vocation:

Neither was he altogether for the publick, but pious in private; and not only in the course of his Family, but in keeping Fasts among the godly of the place, which in those daies was something a dangerous exercise. And, to make them solid Professors indeed, he put them upon a weekly way of handling Catecheticall points of Divinity; that is, every week to conferre of one of the heads of Religion, according to the Catechisme subjoyned to Master *Dods* Treatise on the Commandments, still proving the Doctrines by Testimonies of Scripture.[180]

Even at the lowest social level of the family, the proper structures of learning, and the correct hierarchy of learned authority, were to be observed. Samuel Clarke recalled that when he was minister at Shotwick, every three weeks 'all the Professors, both Men and Women' would assemble in a circuit of 'all the richer mens Houses' for a day of prayer, discussion of some particular question, and especially the instruction and testing of the younger sort. At the end of the day, Clarke gave the assembled godly three questions to prepare for the next session.[181] In such manner did the prophesyings of ministers become a common method of transmitting greater understanding to a non-separated, but gathered, circle within the established church.

Heavy emphasis was given to the example of indoctrination of faithful servants and the next generation of influential householders. Of the household John Carter maintained as a minister in Suffolk his biographer recorded

For his carriage and deportment in his Family, it was sober, grave, and very Religious. He there offered up the Morning and Evening Sacrifice of Prayer, and praise continually: so that his House was like a little Church. Thrice a day he had the Scriptures read, and after that the *Psalm*, or Chapter were ended, he used to ask all his children and servants what they remembered, and whatsoever Sentences they rehearsed, he would speak something out of them that might tend to their edification.[182]

---

[179] *Life of Thomas Cawton*, pp. 57, 62, 63, 65.
[180] Clarke, *32 Lives*, p. 126.   [181] Clarke, *Eminent Persons*, p. 4.
[182] Clarke, *Ten Eminent Divines*, pp. 7–8. For a very similar encomium of a layman, see John Davenport's letter to the widow of the recently deceased Lord Vere, Baron of Tilbury (B.L. MS Birch 4275, fol. 167^{r-v}. See, similarly, Weigall, ed., 'Elizabethan gentlewoman', p. 125.) For a very interesting comparison, see the record of the Romanist household of Lady Magdalen Viscountess Montague, written by the Romanist priest Richard Smith (A.C. Southern, ed., *Elizabethan Recusant House*).

Indeed, success with servants, who may not always have attended church, not only contributed to the general tenor of the household, but also gave further evidence of the assurance of the householder. Of Nathaniel Barnardiston, Samuel Fairclough commented:

He had at one time *ten or more* such servants of that eminency for *piety* and *sincerity*, that I never yet saw their like at one time, in any family in the nation; *whose obedience* joyned to their governours care, produced as rare an effect, that truely they made his house a spirituall church and temple, wherein were dayly offered up the spirituall sacrifices of reading the Word, and prayer, *morning and evening*, of singing Psalmes constantly after every meal, before any servant did rise from the table: the chiefest of them did usually, after every Sermon they heard, call the rest into (*that place of most disorder in other houses*) the Buttery, and there repeated the Sermon unto them, before they were called to the repetition of it in their masters presence.[183]

The ameliorative process of household education, despite the proximity of the Apocalypse, was thus stressed by puritans as the necessary beginning of religious and civil preparation for the *imitatio Pauli.*

The separate functions of the household, taken together, thus constituted a dynamic balance between thought and deed – that is, between the contemplative and active levels of existence. The practical basis of household instruction was not fabricated on a philosophical response to the question of the nature of evil, but rather simply on an existential response to a given aspect of human being: that within each person there was a wilful ungodliness that had to be devastated. Household instruction was thus the first level at which the belief in an essential providence of each individual (already determined by God) encountered the existential belief in a future constructed of will acting upon environment. The extent and quality of instruction offered in the household were obviously limited by the intelligence, education, material means, will and godly dedication of the parents or master. And so, even while stressing the role of the family, ministers sought to provide other avenues of godly indoctrination which could reinforce these first precious advances. Nothing, then, was more natural than the puritan argument that young sons, armed with incipient literacy and an elementary grasp of the basic notions of godly protestantism, should be sent to the local school. It was but another step along the road to godliness.

[183] Fairclough, *Saints Worthinesse*, p. 17.

9

REFORM OF THE SCHOOLS

I

The century before the English Revolution has frequently been described as an era of 'educational revolution'. Lawrence Stone has noted three types of schooling in this period: the instilling of basic, vernacular literacy; preparation for apprenticeship, consisting of training in English and arithmetic; preparation for the universities and Inns of Court through the classical curriculum of the grammar schools.[1] Beyond the desire to teach people to read and write, the particular motives behind schooling can be given as: vocational (including the hope for upward social mobility); the improvement of manners or public behaviour; the spread of humane learning; social control and the related aim of class separation; and, finally, the extirpation of popery and the promotion of godliness in the young. Schooling, quite simply, was to be the basis of the commonwealth and also of full participation in the Reformed religion.

The combination of Reformation spirituality and Renaissance scholarship quickly produced in England, as on the continent, a seemingly ubiquitous desire to found schools.[2] So Edwin Sandys, Archbishop of York, noted in 1580 that founding a school was, for all protestants, 'so good and godly a purpose'.[3] Scores of founders and benefactors whose lives evince no hint of puritan beliefs obviously thought it was somehow 'good' for society (as well, perhaps, as for their own standing in that society, and possibly also with the Almighty) to provide schooling.

Puritans, with an historical reputation as 'progressives', are frequently portrayed as being in the forefront of the 'educational revolution'. This, indeed, has some basis in contemporary opinion. Matthew Wren, Bishop of Ely, believed that in addition to their well-known university colleges, puritans had

---

[1] Stone, 'Educational revolution', pp. 42, 44.
[2] Stone, 'Size and composition', p. 18, in Stone, ed., *University in Society*, I, suggests that the period 1480–1660 may have seen the opening of 800 new schools. See also Brown, *Elizabethan Schooldays*, p. 7; Watson, 'State and education', *E.H.R.*, 15, pp. 58–9.
[3] B.L. MS Lansdowne 30, No. 46, fol. 139. See, similarly, Bishop Oldham's remarks in the statutes he composed for his foundation at Manchester: Haigh, *Reformation and Resistance*, pp. 41–2.

'erected schools in every corner' of the country.[4] Seldom, however, has any conclusion been based on a close examination of puritan attitudes towards schooling. In this chapter I wish to examine puritan responses to the pre-university process of learning, and also particular puritan schemes for both the pedagogical and godly reform of the nation's schools. Here, then, I shall deal primarily with puritan suggestions for reform of the structures of education; in the next chapter I shall address the question of the proper role of schoolmasters.[5]

There would immediately seem to be a correlation between the degree of religious fervency and the vehemence of the demand for schooling. Thomas Lever and Thomas Becon, in the reign of Edward VI, had already called for more grammar schools, and Hugh Latimer had echoed the cry with a dire prophesy concerning the posterity of a nation which did not offer a godly education to the non-gentle ranks.[6] He suggested that the bishops' lands, a common target of educational reformers, could bear the brunt of the huge expense.[7] Thomas Cartwright insisted that all children should be educated 'as farre as their owne ability will reach . . .'.[8] Richard Bernard claimed that it was a 'right honourable and religious worke to give liberally' to educational pro-vision.[9] The schoolmaster and educational writer John Brinsley urged the well-off to remember 'the things that may concerne your own blessed estate and posteritie, and your joyfull appearing before the high Tribunall of our Lord and Saviour . . .'.[10] Charles Chauncey explained that founding a school revealed appreciation of God's blessings, and understanding of the tasks ahead.[11] The famous school laws of Massachusetts may in part have reflected a fear that many of the godly would not emigrate because of the absence of educational provision.[12] Though the frontier required special effort, the con-tinuing puritan emphasis on school provision even in England contrasted sharply with the view of the humanist Richard Mulcaster that the miraculous improvement of the Elizabethan period amounted to satiety. Indeed, he sug-

[4] Quoted in Stone, 'Literacy and education', *Past and Present*, 42, p. 79. For examples of puritan founda-tions, see esp. Jordan, *Philanthropy in England; Charities of Rural England; Charities of London*.
[5] On the background questions of the general structure, curriculum, duration, cost and availability of education, see Simon, *Education and Society*; Charlton, *Education*; Cremin, *American Education*, esp. Chs. 3 & 6; Greaves, *Society and Religion*, Ch. 8; Cressy, *Literacy*, Chs. 2 & 4.
[6] Latimer, *Sermons*, I, pp. 102, 349; Lever, *Sermon Preached at Paules Crosse*, sig. Aiiii^{r-v}; Becon, *Early Works*, p. 260; Becon, 'Catechism', p. 306, in *The Catechism . . . With Other Pieces*.
[7] Latimer, *Sermons*, I, pp. 291–2, 349.   [8] Cartwright, *Treatise of Christian Religion*, p. 129.
[9] Bernard, *Ready Way to Good Works*, pp. 336–7, 344–5.
[10] Brinsley, *Consolation*, sig. A2^v, pp. 29–31. See also Downame, *Plea of the Poore*, p. 10; Allen, *Odorifferous Garden of Charitie*, p. 43.
[11] Chauncey, *Gods Mercy*, pp. 32–3. See also Webbe, *Gods Controversies*, p. 35.
[12] In Mar. 1636/7 Lucy Downing wrote to John Winthrop concerning the possibility of coming to the New World. She expressed her 'fear [that] the Journie would not be so prosperous for him [her child], as I could wish, in respect you have yet noe sosieties [*sic*] nor means in that kinde for the education of youths in learning . . .' (*Winthrop Papers*, III, p. 368).

gested that opportunities for education had become so widespread that entry into schools should henceforth be restricted on the basis of the number of new livings that the church had at its disposal.[13] Even Francis Bacon, in opposing the foundation of Charterhouse in James' reign, argued that there was already adequate provision for secondary education.[14]

It has recently been suggested that before the explosion of educational charity in the 1620s and 1630s, the period 1590–1610 saw an 'educational recession', during which efforts to establish new schools fell off after the Elizabethan 'educational revolution'.[15] It would not seem, however, that there was a decline in puritan emphasis on the necessity of educational provision as one of the foundations of a godly commonwealth. The joy at seeing so many more university-trained ministers must have been severely tempered by the memory of how many ungodly householders the generation contained and the fear that English Calvinism was starting to lose its theological grip at the universities. The thrust of their educational exhortations reflects the position that, having lost the battle to influence government, and feeling insecure concerning the arenas which trained ministers, puritans consciously sought greater influence in the schools, which now reached a mass audience. At no time during our period did puritans have enough influence in central government to propose the introduction of a reformed scheme of schooling; such experiments were confined to individual schools or the occasional town in which puritans dominated the power structure. When the opportunity for local control arose, puritans seized it, well aware of the contribution schooling could make to godly reform. It should be remembered that the feoffees for impropriation, in addition to the church livings they gathered, also came to control the nomination of schoolmasters in several locations.[16]

Elementary schooling was a comparatively neglected topic amidst the contemporary humanist-inspired enthusiasm for Latin education. Richard Mulcaster's *Elementarie*, which advocated placing the best masters in the lowest forms, was exceptional, and, understandably given the pittance awarded junior teachers, unheeded. John Stockwood, Thomas Norton, and John Brinsley, among other puritans, emphasized the value to the nation – both temporal and spiritual – of systematically educating the next generation from an early age.[17] Brinsley especially was interested in engaging young children in word play, in education by visual aids, and in encouraging enjoyment of the classroom pro-

[13] Mulcaster, *Positions*, Chs. 36 & 37.
[14] Bacon, 'Advice . . . touching Sutton's Estate', pp. 252–3, in *Letters and Life*, ed. Spedding, IV.
[15] Cressy, 'Levels of illiteracy in England, 1530–1730', *Historical Journal*, 20, pp. 12–13, 19–20.
[16] Calder, 'Seventeenth-century attempt', *American Historical Review*, 52, pp. 765–6, mentions Kinver, Staffordshire, and Aylesbury, Buckinghamshire. For some examples of puritan schools, see Cliffe, *Puritan Gentry*, p. 80.
[17] See, for example, Brinsley, *Consolation*, sig.*3ᵛ. Frances Clement hoped that students could begin their education even at age 4 (*Petie Schole*, pp. 55–6, in *4 Tudor books*, ed. Pepper).

cess.[18] Here, then, was a pedagogue sensitive to the playfulness and limited attention span of the very young. It is extremely difficult to ascertain, however, the degree to which all aspects of Brinsley's classroom theories were motivated by his religious fervency; much may simply have been the result of empirical truths gained from years spent in front of classes. Discussion of Brinsley's ideas has therefore been restricted to two main points: his attitude towards the vernacular, and his concentration on religious instruction. These will be analysed below.

At times, too, puritans sought to regulate junior schools so that the progress to grammar school would be smoother and more rapid. Elementary education – primarily the inculcation of literacy – likely took about two to three years,[19] and seems generally to have occurred sometime before the age of nine to twelve years.[20] At Elizabethan Leicester, a town under the control of the puritan Hastings family, the under-usher taught the 'petits' in a separate building.[21] Indeed, at many schools in our period the role of the usher was not only to instruct the lower levels of grammar, but also to ensure that entrants possessed the required level of vernacular literacy.[22] The diversity of forms of elementary training – and its chronic lack of endowment – led puritans as well as their contemporaries to rely heavily on the household for instruction in literacy at the same time as they encouraged the founding of schools to build a greater literate population. Most puritans seem to have regarded literacy and elementary instruction in religion – the staples of elementary training – simply as givens, as prerequisites for the beginning of a scholarly course.

Throughout our period certain of the well-born continued to have their children educated at home by domestic chaplains or private teachers.[23] However, the growing attractiveness of a college education may well have acted as a spur to public education at an earlier stage, too; sons of the gentry frequently enrolled in grammar schools. Doubtless aware of this influx, and concerned with the traditional function of grammar schools as training centres for the universities and therefore the ministry, puritans not surprisingly concentrated their efforts at reform on the public rather than the private arena.

Their first concern was with the inadequacy of existing facilities. Thomas

---

[18] Brinsley, *Ludus Literarius*, pp. 9–10. For a recent discussion of Brinsley's pedagogical methods, see O'Day, *Education and Society*, esp. pp. 47–53.   [19] Spufford, 'First steps in literacy', pp. 411–12.

[20] On the actual age at first attendance at grammar school and university, see Cressy, 'School and college admission ages', *History of Education*, 8, pp. 166–77, and sources cited there. Cressy ends by agreeing with De Molen that pupils were generally 11–12 years old when they first entered grammar school, and around 17 when they entered university.   [21] Simon, *Education and Society*, p. 377.

[22] See, for example, the regulations of Alford and St Albans schools (Carlisle, *Endowed Schools*, p. 780; Dudding, *History of Alford*, pp. 120–1; *V.C.H. Herts.*, II, pp. 59, 70–1).

[23] On private education, see below, Ch. 13.

Godly Learning

Lever early bemoaned the poor state of English schools, which 'founded of a godly intent to brynge up poore mennes sonnes in learnynge and vertue' had suffered because of the covetousness of the rich.[24] In one of the few examples of puritan organization of a non-endowed local education system, all the young children of Dedham were to be taught to read English.[25] Instruction was to be free for the poor, reflecting puritan interest in spreading at least access to scriptural godliness to the lower end of the socio-economic scale. The organizers of the scheme sought to enforce compliance by requiring all masters and 'governors' to take as apprentices only those who could read the vernacular.[26] While this provision was not unique, and of course operated in the masters' economic favour, the coordination of religious, educational and economic powers to produce a literate youth is indicative of the puritan thrust to spread widely at least basic education. So is puritan support for the combination of instruction and enforced labour. In 1584 Thomas Clarke, Mayor of Leicester, and the third Earl of Huntingdon corresponded concerning the establishment of a school to set the poor to work at spinning.[27] Some sixty years later, the puritan Samuel Harmar similarly suggested that poor children might be maintained at school by working at spinning before and after school hours.[28] With so much of their strength based in the protective hands of the possessing classes, it is hardly surprising that puritans used schools to argue that, while souls were doubtless equal, the lot which God had assigned to man's mortal capacities was sternly structured. The extension of schooling down the scale was designed to propagandize both halves of this unitary proposition.[29]

Training in 'manners', so popular in this age, was important to puritans as a contribution to the re-training of the will. This did not, however, encompass the full public education of girls, which helps to account for their deficient literacy. Even humanists balked at equal education for girls.[30] Doubtless girls attended petty schools, but we have no basis for quantification. On occasion they were specifically excluded from grammar schools; more commonly it

[24] Lever, *Sermon at Pauls Crosse*, sig. E.iv^{r-v}.
[25] Usher, ed., *Presbyterian Movement*, pp. 99, 100.   [26] *Ibid.*, p. 100.
[27] H.M.C. *Eighth Rep., App., Part 1*, pp. 430–2. See also P.R.O. S.P. 12/41/67, a treatise on the well-governing of the commonwealth, which treats idleness as a sickness, which might be alleviated by extending some education to the lower orders. Such education would also serve to extend order and discipline, as well as faith and concord in society.   [28] Harmar, *Vox Populi*, sig. A4^v.
[29] See, for example, Cleaver, *Godlie Forme of Householde Government*, pp. 332–3. See also John Brinsley's telling remark that by widening the educational net to include the lower orders, 'every one shall be the better enabled to pay that debt, which by his very birth he oweth unto the Lord, and to his native country' (Brinsley, *Consolation*, pp. 29–31, 16). See also Gainsford, *Rich Cabinet*, fol. 133^v.
[30] The humanist Mulcaster argued that the education of girls should depend on ability (and class), and should not be restricted to 'housewifery' but should rather include the subjects boys studied; at the same time, he noted that girls were not destined to become 'preachers and leaders', and so some reasonable curb on their learning might be applied (Mulcaster, *Positions*, pp. 132–3, 167, 179–81).

was simply expected that they would not attend. Even where they did attend, there were often limits, as at Bunbury, where they could stay in school only until they had reached the age of nine or could read English.[31] Even schools founded specifically for girls tended to offer only the skill of vernacular reading, beyond religious instruction and an 'apprenticeship' in the duties of the distaff side of a future household.[32] Puritans, of course, expected girls to become acquainted with Scripture, but they seem to have adopted the general expectations of the age that girls were to be trained privately in morality and for the duties of the household. Even at the end of our period, a serious puritan writer on the development and education of children could comment:

and for the daughter that she have generall instructions, all qualities the parent can bestow, which may set off, and yet stand with decency, and sobrietie; more specially, that she be accustomed to the essentials of huswifery: unto all that may make her *rejoyce in time to come* . . .[33]

Puritans may well have stressed the companionship of marriage, but they seem hardly to have emphasized the institutional preparation of women for the intellectual aspect of this relationship.

II

It was at this level also that the future heads of England's households received not only the reinforcement of their incipient literacy, but also the inculcation of the religious message explained on a simplified and perhaps individual basis. As in the pulpit and at the universities, the puritan aim in the grammar schools was to employ humane learning while proselytizing. Schools thus had to ensure not only that the laity were trained in arts and godliness, but also that those select few who would lead the pilgrimage would receive the first serious grounding in those forms of knowledge which puritans held to be so important for ministers. Concerned with a type of self-actualization that depended on repentance and conversion (in addition to learning), puritans were not disposed to separate social classes for the purpose of instruction. Nor did this guiding force allow them ever to seek to restrict schooling in order to establish a priestly monopoly over knowledge.

From the first, puritans built not only upon the institutional accomplishments of the humanists, but also upon humanist curriculum emphases. In

---

[31] Stowe, *English Grammar Schools*, p. 127 n. 14.

[32] At the Girls' School of Christ's Hospital in London, reading and needlework were evidently the only skills taught; catechizing and instruction from the Bible rounded out the curriculum (Lempriere, *Girls' School*, pp. 4–5). On girls' boarding schools, see also O'Day, *Education and Society*, pp. 186–9.

[33] Woodward, *Childes Patrimony*, p. 165.

many early protestants the humanist and Reformed impulses were combined. The work of John Sturm served as a model for virtually all protestant (as well as Jesuit) school statutes of the sixteenth century. Tyndale the ardent protestant was also the translator of Erasmus. Zwingli, Bucer, Calvin, Beza, and Knox could all fairly be described as 'humanists' in their youth.[34] As Simon has commented, the humanist effect became less visible in England as it became more pervasive.[35] Partly it was absorbed by puritans who spent years being educated in humanist-tinged schools and colleges.

In England, humanists emulated the continental thrust by variously advocating school instruction in logic, rhetoric, history, English, philosophy, law, arithmetic, geometry, music, astrology, poetry, and medicine, though almost all agreed that the inculcation of a Christian sense into the boys was the most important accomplishment.[36] Though early humanists had concentrated almost exclusively on a classical curriculum, Mulcaster was willing to challenge the authority of both ancients and contemporary humanists, preferring to mix empirical evidence with the 'known truths'.[37] The exceptional Vives had even recommended training in the 'inferior' arts of husbandry, architecture, transportation, and politics, and also stressed the empirical value of observing the skilled workman.[38] At most country schools, however, such variety was lacking; students were instead force-fed a diet of basic English literacy and Latin grammar, relieved only by occasional instruction in writing and, in the higher forms, by Greek and possibly some rhetoric. Hebrew was mentioned occasionally in statutes, but its actual appearance in many schools must be doubted.[39] Particular texts, of course, would also yield some understanding of statecraft, history, perhaps even law, but this was ancillary knowledge, likely not studied systematically. The status of arithmetic is not altogether clear, but in many schools the pupils' ability may not have progressed much beyond simple sums.

Puritans seem to have accepted without serious dissension the proposition

[34] Bolgar, 'Humanist education', p. 8, in Bolgar, *Changing Curriculum*; Cremin, *American Education*, pp. 35ff.; Cameron, 'Renaissance tradition in Scotland', in Baker, ed., *Studies in Church History*, 14, p. 253.   [35] Simon, *Education and Society*, p. 122.

[36] See, for example, Lyly, *Euphues*, fols. 55ᵛ, 64ᵛ; W.S., *Compendious or Briefe Examination*, fols. 9ᵛ, 149–50; Cleland, *Institution of a Young Noble Man*, pp. 79ff.; Ascham, *Scholemaster*, p. 100. Mulcaster, at Merchant Taylors in London, taught singing, dancing, play-acting and music, as well as Latin, Greek, Hebrew, and French, according to the testimony of one of his ex-pupils, James Whitelocke (father of Bulstrode) (Bruce, ed., *Liber Famelicus*, pp. vi, 6, 8–9, 12).

[37] Simon, *Education and Society*, p. 353. DeMolen especially emphasized the similarity between Mulcaster's ideas and those of the earlier Vives and the contemporary Montaigne ('Richard Mulcaster and the profession of teaching', *Journal of the History of Ideas*, 35, p. 128).

[38] Vives, *de tradendis disciplinis*, pp. 208–10. See also Woodward, ed., *Erasmus: Aim and Method of Education*, Introduction, p. 94.

[39] See, for example, the statutes of East Retford (Baldwin, *Small Latine and Lesse Greeke*, I, pp. 314ff.).

that the primary function of the grammar school was to train young scholars for the universities. In this, English reformers again emulated continental protestant educators such as Melanchthon, Sturm, and Calvin, who had all approved the classical curriculum. Sturm himself had commented that 'as Religion maketh holie the societie of men, so doth eloquence make it pleasant: and both joyned togither, cause it to be helthful'.[40] Here, then, was the bridge between humanist studies and godly fervency, upon which English humanists and Reformers alike could build. Ascham praised Sturm highly for his pedagogy; Thomas Becon could approve the study of Cicero for his writing style; and even John Knox voiced no objection to the properly supervised youthful study of human arts. Thomas Gataker mentioned the usual regimen of Cicero, Virgil, Homer, and the ubiquitous Lily's grammar.[41] John Stockwood insisted against charges of anti-learning that 'where it is blowen abroade that I shoulde saye, . . . that [the] Schoolemaister ought to reade nothing to their schollers but the Scriptures . . . I am most fowly abused . . .'.[42] Thomas Granger, who stressed grammar as the key to the arts, was severely critical of English grammar schools which produced graduates unprepared for university study.[43] Knowledge, properly applied, could be a defence against the ungodliness which was inherent in ignorance; the wider its diffusion, the more godly the nation was likely to be.

In puritan schools, too, the regimen was unreservedly classical in the humanist mould. Despite puritan stress on the service learning was to provide to godly study, puritan curricula do not seem to reveal an unusually heavy emphasis on Greek and Hebrew. At Wakefield, Latin was to be based on Lily and the usual authors; Greek on Isocrates, Demosthenes, Hesiod, Homer, and whichever grammar text most Cambridge colleges used.[44] At Ashby, a puritan school in Leicestershire, the statutes left all to the schoolmaster, who was commanded simply to read 'to the Chieftest fforme such Authors as hee shall think most meet for his Schollers, Greeke or Lattin'.[45] At Leicester, Cicero dominated, but was supported by the common cast which included Virgil, Caesar, Erasmus, Cato, and Ovid; the only surprise perhaps was the inclusion of Terence.[46] Only in 1651 did the Mayor and Master of the Hospital (the governing body) decree the expulsion of Cicero, Ovid, and Virgil in favour of Christian authors;[47] it was an important break, not least because it established

---

[40] Sturm, *Ritch Storehouse*, fol. 14. For the outline of the curriculum at Sturm's school in Strasbourg, see Bolgar, *Classical Heritage*, pp. 351–2.

[41] Gataker, *David's Instructer*, p. 33. For an exhaustive study of grammar school texts, see Baldwin, *Small Latine and Lesse Greeke, passim*.   [42] Stockwood, *Very Fruiteful Sermon*, sig. A6ᵛ.

[43] Granger, *Syntagma Logicum*, sig. A5ᵛ; Granger, *Syntagma Grammaticum*, sig. A7.

[44] B.L. MS Sloane 2204, fol. 30. See also Miller & Johnson, eds., *Puritans,* p. 698.

[45] Fox, *Ashby*, p. 126.

[46] The Leicester statutes are reprinted in Cross, *Free Grammar School of Leicester*, pp. 26–7.

[47] *Ibid.*, p. 33.

that anti-classicism was not to be equated in practice with anti-learning. But in our period examples of the educated offspring of puritans reveal no deviation in academic terms from the generally desired norm. Abraham Johnson, son of Robert (the Archdeacon of Leicester, and founder of Oakham and Uppingham schools), was evidently trained 'by choice Schoolmasters' in rhetoric, logic, natural philosophy, music, handwriting, and modern languages. He was educated, too, in Latin and Greek, and also in Hebrew, well enough that he could read the Bible. Possessed of this background supposedly by the age of thirteen, he was able to impress Walter Mildmay and be accepted shortly after into Emmanuel.[48]

In strictly curricular terms, this left the study of English in limbo. Original literacy, taught in a 'petty' school, or by an usher at the grammar school, was inculcated in the vernacular. The vernacular was not, however, a school subject of the rank of Latin or Greek in the higher forms. As has often been remarked, however, one cannot take school statutes as a sure reflection of classroom practice. The thrust of the humanists towards vernacular learning, the great expansion of non-scholarly vocational knowledge, and the desire of people who could read to use the skill for recreation likely pressed schoolmasters, even in grammar school, into giving some instruction concerning the English half of the translations at which schoolboys were ever labouring. The appearance, too, of annotated English–Latin and English–Greek texts, and of dictionaries, must have improved the schoolboy's vocabulary in his native language as well as in his formal studies.[49] School statutes came to recognize and incorporate the demand for vernacular, vocational education. The 1572 statutes of St Olave's school in London, a grammar school it should be noted, stated the school's purpose as, in part, to teach students 'to wright, reade and cast accomptes, and so to put them forth to prentice'.[50] Finally, attendance at sermons (required by law) provided the obvious lesson that the highest knowledge was to be obtained through the vernacular. This in itself (but combined with the growing body of English literature) must have given an incalculable boost to the supporters of the vernacular. The puritan thrust may well have accelerated the process. We noted above the requirement of the Dedham classis that youngsters be taught at least to the level of reading the vernacular. Thomas Norton, explaining in his Preface why he had undertaken an English translation of Nowell's Latin Catechism, argued that English was necessary not only for those who had no Latin, but also for that sizeable number whose Latin was deficient.[51] This, one imagines, would include most

48 Bingham, Our Founder, pp. 22–3. See also P. Thompson, 'The Johnson family', New England Historical and Genealogical Register, 8, pp. 358–62. 49 Simon, Education and Society, p. 400.
50 Schulz, 'Teaching of handwriting', Huntington Library Quarterly, 6, p. 402. For a suggestion that grammar schools encompassed two curricula – one for university entrants, one for those who would soon seek work – see O'Day, Education and Society, p. 61. 51 Nowell, Catechism, ed. Norton, sig. A.ij^{r-v}.

people after a few years away from grammar school, unless the language was in fairly frequent use. As well, puritan schoolmasters were noted for using the sermon for school lessons; that is, an oration in the vernacular was deemed worthy of treatment for the study of rhetoric, for translation exercises, for memorization, as well, of course, as for the patently godly lessons it contained.

Conversely, it must also be noted that practice, given the contextual pressures which condition it, does not always clearly reflect attitudes. For this side of the question, the written record of the desires of founders and educational writers must carry great weight. It is therefore important to note that puritan school statutes do not seem particularly to have contained a positive theme of promoting the vernacular. This may in part reflect the degree to which English had already claimed status as a language of explanation, particularly in religious matters. As well, however, the full puritan acceptance that Latin was the 'learned' language reflects conservatism in pedagogy. Even in those schools endowed by merchants – men who had applied practical, vernacular knowledge to financial success in their vocation, and who are frequently linked with puritan beliefs – there is no evidence of a trend towards vernacular 'new learning'. As yet, the feeling that other forms of knowledge might better suit a changing nation had not brought the variety of subjects available in London to an invasion of the country grammar schools, even those controlled by puritan founders or schoolmasters.

In their general willingness to accept the common curriculum, puritans revealed both their limited intentions and their lack of innovation in developing an alternative educational path. Except in their emphasis on reformed logic and classroom bibliocentricity, there seems no reason to perpetuate the belief that puritans stood in the forefront of 'progressive' theories of educational practice. The succession of Mulcaster–Bacon–Comenius, which represented various ideas more amenable to later generations, struck no completely harmonious chord among pre-revolutionary puritans. This is not to say that the two streams of thought were wholly antipathetic. Reformers of the 1640s leaned heavily on the Bacon–Comenius–Hartlib approach to the reform of learning generally and of schools particularly. Nonetheless, puritans aimed rather at a restriction of endeavour, attempting a purer vision of the past *societas christiana*. Even in the freer air of Massachusetts, which possessed at least nine schools even before the law of 1647 (and about twenty-three schools by 1689),[52] there seems to be no evidence that puritans introduced any pedagogical or school-religious innovations that the 'hostility' of Laudian England had denied them. Schools remained academic dispensers of Latin, Greek, and, with the entrance requirements of Harvard, Hebrew; they also

---

[52] Cremin, *American Education*, pp. 181, 183.

served as strong adjuncts of the godly ministry.[53] The key change seems to have been structural: the increasing degree of public concern with education which eventually placed control in the hands of a narrow band of secular authorities.[54] This, in turn, may well have been determined by the exigencies of founding a new society as much as by pre-existing notions.

But though puritans would allow the continuation of curriculum that was not ungodly, there were limits beyond which godliness would not compromise. In this they extended the desire of the Elizabethan Privy Council to bring a protestant and nationalistic edge to school studies. Thus in 1582 the Council wrote to High Commission prescribing a book of Latin verse by Christopher Ocland, the schoolmaster of St Olave's, Southwark. The Council noted the superiority of this work to the usual reading matter in schools, 'where divers Heathen Poets are ordinarily read and taught, from which the youth of the realm doth rather receive infection in manners than advancement in virtue'.[55] Purification was a theme in which puritans could wholeheartedly join. John Northbrooke demanded that comedies, though common in universities and schools, be banned from the educational process. He added what seems a notably illogical argument that if they had to be studied, they should be read only in Latin.[56] Perhaps he simply hoped that scholars would be reading such material under the guidance of a godly schoolmaster; publication in Latin alone would forbid wide distribution in the hands of a less-educated, and non-supervised, population. And of certain *forms* of education puritans were immediately critical: they argued that girls' boarding schools tended to be too light and frivolous.[57]

Puritans did not confine their activities to recommending a certain curriculum. A number of them, though not a great proportion, also produced texts for schoolchildren. John Stockwood, the puritan minister, and schoolmaster of Tunbridge from 1578 to 1585, published in 1590 a translation of the authorized grammar of William Lily; it was issued, in part, to aid sales of his own 'Accidence', a manual in English which sought to explain Latin constructions.[58] By the latter part of the century the colloquies of Erasmus and Vives had largely been replaced by those of Castellion and Corderius, both of which originated in Geneva.[59] Significantly, John Brinsley seems to have been the first English translator of Corderius, admiring the Genevan both for his profoundly protestant religious preferences and for his suitability to the 'common country schools' for which Brinsley wrote. Puritan schools such as Heath and Leicester used Corderius, but this reflected nothing more than protestant-

[53] *Ibid.*, pp. 184–5.   [54] *Ibid.*, pp. 192–3.   [55] Quoted in Simon, *Education and Society*, p. 324.
[56] Northbrooke, *Dicing, Dauncing*, p. 75.   [57] Gardiner, *English Girlhood at School*, p. 219.
[58] Stockwood, *English Accidence*, esp. 'To the Reader'; Simon, *Education and Society*, pp. 326–7.
[59] On colloquies, see Watson, *English Grammar Schools*, pp. 325–48.

ism; by the latter part of our period, he was standard classroom issue.

Imitation of Cicero remained the highest rule of rhetoric in classrooms, though the methods of the rhetoric varied. Many influential writers, such as Thomas Wilson, and a large number of schools, conformed to the Aristotelian pattern. Against this came the Ramists – often, though not always, puritans – who offered a simplified version of Aristotelian rhetoric and logic. Dudley Fenner's edition of Ramist logic and Talonist rhetoric, replete with scriptural rather than classical illustrations, provided schoolmasters with a text of suitable level, which at the same time reinforced fervent protestantism. In terms of reaching large numbers of readers, doubtless the most important Ramist text was that of Charles Butler, graduate of Magdalen, Oxford, and later master of Basingstoke school.[60] Other puritans, such as Alexander Richardson and Anthony Wotton, also produced commentaries in the seventeenth century, aimed probably at a wider audience than the university fellow or student.[61]

Ramism, with its close dependence on observable phenomena, also encouraged schoolmasters to train their pupils on a more empirical and objective basis. Thomas Granger, in his Ramist school text, asserted that the teacher was duty bound to make his instruction of the microcosm (man) conform to the 'light of the macrocosme, or the great world', that is, to 'ground his teaching on nature especially the true foundation, following her even in her stepps, without aberration, or extravagation, and not upon bare imaginations, uncertaine conjectures, and imitation of others'.[62] Puritans thus at times, as we saw earlier, sought to relate knowledge to the world around them. The use of Ramism at the grammar school level was doubtless meant to encourage observation in a changing social and economic context, which increasingly demanded adaptation and invention rather than reliance on moribund knowledge from classical times. At the same time, its most immediate function, in the classroom as in the pulpit, was to simplify the process of understanding for the audience. Here one must separate the possibly radical effects of Ramist influence (which remain to be determined) from the intention of puritan users of the system. Puritan ministers, writers, and schoolmasters have left no evidence that they planned a wholly new approach to knowledge. Given the limits to the intellectual achievement of most grammar school students, it would seem reasonable to conclude that Ramism at this level was intended to provide a proper outlook concerning the value of empirical knowledge for those who were soon to enter apprenticeship, easier comprehension of basic logic and rhetoric for the few who would continue to university, and greater access to comprehension of the Scriptures for all who sought salvation.

[60] Simon, *Education and Society*, pp. 320, 380; Baldwin, *Small Latine*, esp. vol. II; Howell, *Logic and Rhetoric*, esp. pp. 262–9.   [61] Richardson, *Logicians School-Master*; Wotton, *Art of Logick*.
[62] Granger, *Syntagma Grammaticum*, sig. B.

III

The early humanists' practice of blending the morality of pagan authors with the doctrine of Scripture and the Fathers contributed greatly to the blurring of the sharp mediaeval distinction between philosophy and theology.[63] At the same time it posed special problems for the connexion of schooling with the inculcation of religion. Vives concluded, however, that while caution had to be applied to some studies, as a general rule 'no knowledge of things can be a hindrance to piety . . .'.[64] Vives' piety was thus to emerge as almost a metamorphosis of the individual because of his study of Christian authors.[65] Even Erasmus saw the inculcation of religion as only part of the general notion of wisdom, which he described as '*virtus cum eruditione liberali coniuncta*'. He therefore specifically praised John Colet's school, in which, he believed, 'the youth of England . . . might . . . absorb Christian principles together with an excellent literary education . . .'.[66]

Religious instruction would have existed in post-Reformation schools even without the catalyst of puritan fervency. Children were encouraged to know the Lord's Prayer, the Articles of Faith, and the Ten Commandments before attending school.[67] By the canons of 1571 and 1604, schoolmasters were bound to accompany their students, *en masse*, to the Sunday church service. School statutes of the period frequently specify this duty.[68] The canons of 1571 required school use of Nowell's catechism, which emphasized that children ought 'much more, to be trayned with good lessons to godlinesse, than with good artes to humanitie'.[69] Some schools used the Bible for instruction, though most seem to have confined themselves to the approved catechism, protestant colloquies, and the mandatory primer.[70] The commands of the state and church were intended to ensure that schools generally would raise a protestant population.

The religious value of education was a platitude of the age. William Kempe typified the approach with his insistence that his scheme would teach youths

---

[63]   Kristeller, *Renaissance Thought*, pp. 76–9.

[64]   Vives, *de tradendis disciplinis*, pp. 48–9, 29, 31, 89, 125.   [65]   *Ibid.*, pp. 34–5, 47, 276, 282.

[66]   Rice, *Renaissance Idea*, pp. 213–14; Erasmus to Colet, from London, 29 Apr. 1512 in *Collected Works of Erasmus*, ed. Thompson, Vol. 24, p. 284.

[67]   See the various regulations of Henry VIII and Edward VI to this effect (Watson, *English Grammar Schools*, p. 29; O'Day, *Education and Society*, p. 44).

[68]   See, for example, the statutes of Feversham grammar school: Bod. Lib. MS Tanner 126, fol. 147^{r-v}.   [69]   Nowell, *Catechisme*, p. 1.

[70]   Examples are given in Stowe, *English Grammar Schools*, p. 152; Watson, *English Grammar Schools*, pp. 38ff., 72–4; Bolgar, 'Classical reading', *Durham Research Review*, 2, p. 25; Brown, *Elizabethan Schooldays*, p. 63. For an example of the law requiring instruction in the Scriptures, see the 1559 Royal Injunctions (Frere, *Articles and Injunctions*, III, p. 21). For typical episcopal inquiries into whether the approved texts were being used, see *ibid.*, pp. 132, 327, 371.

'how to worship God aright, how to avoyde the pestilent errors arising out of ignorance . . .'.[71] Wills leaving funds for the foundation of schools frequently saw no need to explain the obvious purposes of 'the teaching, instructing and bringing up of the children of the saide parrishe in the feare of God, vertue, and learninge . . .'.[72] Typical of the countless educational 'good works' of the age was the £10 annuity left by Henry Fawcett in 1619 to defray the expenses of the local clergymen in Littondale in teaching poor children.[73] Arguments about the growing secularization of control and purpose of schools must be careful not to overlook hundreds of wills in which the impulse was still to link religion and education – if not under the aegis of the episcopacy, at least in the person of the minister. All founders, regardless of denomination, insisted on the religious imperative of education. John Royce, in the ordinances which he wrote for the grammar school he founded at Abingdon in 1563, laid emphasis on 'godliness'. It, too, was a common word of the age; Royce was a papist.[74]

Beneath this standard religiosity, puritans regarded schools as seminaries which linked the godly functions of households and churches to provide a chain of lifelong instruction. In this stress, puritans were not unique in protestantism: Knox in Scotland and the Lutherans in Sweden required religious education of the young above the Western European norm.[75] The thrust, too, crossed the ocean to New England.[76] At Market Harborough, in Leicestershire, Robert Smith, a local man who had found a measure of success in the capital as Comptroller of the Chamber of London, provided a fund for the establishment of a lectureship, since he perceived preaching as the usual means of proselytizing.[77] He specified that £20 was to be set aside for the education of the 'children of the most godly honest & religious poore parents . . .'. An extra measure of enforced godliness was the requirement of constant attendance at church sermons and at Smith's lectures both by the children who received free education *and by their parents*.[78] Smith went beyond the usual social purposes of much charity; his 'dependants', and their familial overseers, had to demonstrate an *ongoing* commitment to godliness.

The preamble to the 1607 statutes of Wakefield grammar school provided

[71] Kempe, *Education*, sig. E[v].
[72] Murray, *Sebright School, Wolverley*, pp. 103–4, founded by will (Jan. 1618/19) of William Sebright, a Londoner transplanted from Wolverley.
[73] Boyd & Shelffrey, *Littondale: Past and Present*, p. 83. Fawcett's brother William increased the sum to £18 per year in 1630.   [74] Preston, *Church and Parish of St Nicholas, Abingdon*, p. 305.
[75] Knox, *Book of Discipline*, cited in Potter, ed., *Puritanism in Tudor England*, p. 198; Johansson, *History of Literacy in Sweden, passim*.
[76] See, for example, the 1645 rules of the free school of Dorchester, cited in Fleming, *Children and Puritanism*, p. 105.   [77] Stocks & Bragg, *Market Harborough Parish Records*, pp. 13–14, 17.
[78] *Ibid.*, pp. 472–5. A further lesson in godliness was the placing of scriptural quotations on the outer walls (Simon, 'Town estates and schools', pp. 16–17).

perhaps the most succinct statement of the puritan religious thrust at this level:

> For as much as this school is principally ordained a Seminarie for bringing up of Christian Children to become in time Ambassadors of Reconciliation from God to his Church, and generally is intended a School of Christian instruction for vertue, and manners therein to be learned of all the Scholars thereof . . .[79]

Instruction was thus to be linked with the three responsibilities of the Christian: the relationship of man to God (the reconciliation), of man to himself (virtue), and finally of man to other men (manners). Unless the first was right, it was unlikely that the other two would be correct in a *Christian* sense, or – here was a point of differentiation from the humanists – that it would even matter greatly if they *alone* were solved.

We noted earlier the great importance to puritans of personal religious *experience*. Their purpose in education, in addition to the usual secular concerns, was to provide the conditions under which it was likely that the greatest number of people could be brought to their *own* religious awareness. In this sense, the whole struggle of puritans to erect a purified educational framework was 'preparationist' in nature. Schools were to provide each person with instruction – Bible-reading, catechizing, sermon repetitions – so that eventually he could place his own individual 'fear and trembling' into a personal perspective through the development of membership in the covenant. This effort contained, and in a sense ran parallel to, the more specific use of schools to train the as yet unknown few who would become a caste of learned ministers.

The most basic form of public (as well as household) religious instruction was catechizing. Nowell's Catechism, the prescribed text for schools, was issued by authority only after the queen's objections to its radical Calvinism had been overcome.[80] As well, the Catechism was translated into English by the ardent puritan Thomas Norton, translator also of Calvin's *Institutes*. But puritans were dissatisfied with Nowell's Catechism, and in the decades before the Revolution, produced scores of alternatives. School statutes had to be circumspect, but the reaction to Nowell varied. Though some, as at Leicester, confined instruction to Nowell or Calvin,[81] others, such as John Lyon's statutes at Harrow, also allowed 'some such other booke at [the schoolmaster's] discretion . . .'.[82] At Wakefield the statutes prescribed simply that the master should teach his pupils 'the truth of Religion out of Gods Booke . . .'. [83] At Otley, the master was to avoid heresy and corruption by re-

[79] B.L. MS Sloane 2204, fol. 29.   [80] Simon, *Education and Society*, pp. 307–8.
[81] Cross, *Free Grammar School of Leicester*, p. 17.
[82] Bod. Lib. MS Tanner 121, fol. 6r–v.   [83] B.L. MS Sloane 2204, fol. 29.

stricting himself to 'godly Authors, for Christian religion'.[84] From the stress placed upon catechizing, it seems that some puritans pragmatically regarded the schoolmaster as the chief catechist of the young, even above the minister, who could confine his activity to Saturday afternoons. At Leicester's godly school, for example, catechizing occurred throughout the school week in Form I, and intermittently in the higher forms.[85]

This puritan desire for purity pervaded all recommendations of school material. Thomas Becon had earlier set the style with his argument that 'to teach them nothing but the doctrine of the heathen and profane writers is not to edify, but to destroy, not to correct, but to corrupt, the youth of the Christians'.[86] John Stockwood, who is illustrative of the puritan thrust, reminded schoolmasters that Cicero, Plato, and Aristotle had not among them 'ever yet made a godly and vertuous man'.[87] He was therefore insistent that the young should have heavier doses of Christ, for the memory was most keen while young.[88] Puritans constantly feared that schools were dominated by ungodly authors and uncaring teachers, to the effect that 'the teaching of the principles of religion for the use of children and other that be simple and ignorant is not regarded'.[89] Stockwood argued that, in the face of the condemnation of this material by both Scripture and heathens, the 'magistrate' should outlaw all 'filthy bookes' for the young, and should instead set down a full list of proper and approved texts.[90] Puritan statutes, too, insisted (in common with the moral theme of the age) that the schoolmaster 'shall not teach his schollars any unsavoury Authors which may either infect their younge witts with Heresie or Corrupt their lives with uncleanness'.[91]

One solution was the introduction of puritan-authored texts into the schoolroom. At Worsborough in Yorkshire John Rayney, in addition to bequeathing funds for the perpetual support of a schoolmaster, left three volumes of the *Workes* of William Perkins to the chapel, for the specific use of the schoolmaster as well as the preacher.[92] Charles Hoole, while a schoolmaster at Rotherham, used Perkins' catechism in the sessions held on Thursday afternoons.[93] Another obvious step towards increased classroom purity would have been increased dependence on the Scriptures as a working text. Nonetheless, there seems to be no firm evidence that puritan schools demanded that pupils purchase a Bible for use as a classroom text. Even the thoroughly puritan Wakefield statutes did not specify whether the Bible was actually to be used in the classroom, or whether reference was being made simply to the

[84] Padgett, ed., *Chronicles of . . . Otley*, p. 43.   [85] Cross, *Free Grammar School of Leicester*, pp. 26–7.
[86] Becon, *Catechism with Other Pieces*, p. 382.   [87] Stockwood, *Sermon at Paules Crosse*, p. 91.
[88] *Ibid.*, pp. 91–3.   [89] Morrice MSS, vol. B, i, p. 544.
[90] Stockwood, *Very Fruiteful Sermon*, sigs. A7–8.   [91] Padgett, ed., *Chronicles of . . . Otley*, p. 43.
[92] P.R.O. C/93/7/4: Charity Commissioners' Inquiries.
[93] Leach, ed., 'Early Yorkshire schools, vol. ii', *Yorkshire Arch. Soc. Rec. Ser.*, 33, p. 208. Hoole, *New Discovery*, recommended Perkins' catechism.

schoolmaster's knowledge of the Word.[94] Part of the reason may have been the cost of Bibles, which were substantially more expensive than the mass-produced catechisms and academic texts. It is more likely, however, that puritan sensibilities concerning the unique mediating role of the minister would have been upset by allowing schoolmasters (many of whom were *not* ministers) too great liberty to expound Scriptures to children of such impressionable age. Furthermore, church authorities would have taken a much closer interest in teachers had they employed such an 'independent' text (especially if in the Geneva edition), rather than the approved catechism.

Puritan statutes therefore usually mention that the master should read the Scriptures *to* the boys. But this, in terms of statutory prescription, did not really go beyond Grindal's requirements for St Bees that 'the New Testament is to be taught', or the canons of 1604 that the schoolmaster must teach 'such sentences of holy scripture as shall be most expedient to induce them to all godliness . . .'.[95] The degree of exposition and discussion entailed in any of these requirements is not clear. Occasionally, however, the puritan impulse for godliness bursts forth in the statutes. The statutes of Heath grammar school, written by the puritan vicar of Halifax, John Favour, phrased the inculcation of godliness as a responsibility not only of the master, but of the students themselves who, in addition to the usual attendance at church, also found that daily

they must join with the Master and Usher both morning and evening in prayer for remission of sins, acceptation in Christ, direction by the Spirit to illuminate their understanding, enlarge their capacities, certify their judgments, and confirm their memories; and hear some chapters daily out of the Old and New Testament read publicly in the school with all reverence and attention, that they may repeat the principal contents thereof, if they be called forth by the Master, and sing daily some place of David in metre to the praise of God for all his mercies with feeling understanding and spiritual rejoicing, with thanks unto God for the founder of the School, and the good benefactors.[96]

This was a lesson in godly practice far beyond the usual prayers at the start and end of the schoolday.[97] It was also, it should be noted, exclusively an aural/oral programme. The separate tasks of 'reading' and 'hearing' could be continued to great purpose where, for whatever reason, an inadequate supply of the printed text existed. Such a programme of delivering information to a

---

[94] B.L. MS Sloane 2204.
[95] On St Bees, see *Eng.: Parlt.: 4th Rep. from Select Comm. on Education* (1818), p. 349. For the canons, see Watson, *English Grammar Schools*, p. 57.   [96] Cox, *History of Heath*, pp. 50–1.
[97] James Pilkington's statutes for his school at Rivington give perhaps the most extensive list of school prayers (Kay, *History of Rivington*, Appendix II, pp. 170–2). There is in some of the prayers such a striking similarity to the standard opening of late Elizabethan and early Stuart wills that it may be suggested that will-making perhaps involved a throwback to phrasing first memorized so many years earlier in school.

passive audience would also help to maintain the hierarchy of learning by re-pressing, at least temporarily, the spirit of inquiry by a swaddling of the mind.

Given the law requiring attendance of scholars with their teacher at Sunday service, it is understandable that scriptural exegesis played an increasing part in the school regimen. Puritan devotion to the sermon reinforced this emphasis. The sermon of a learned, godly preacher would provide Biblical references for study, perhaps illustrations of rhetorical and logical devices, and perhaps also a lesson in the proper subservience of oratorical skills to Christian utility.[98] Here again, then, was the coordination of oral and written knowledge, with the spoken information taking precedence, allied as it was to the status of the minister as interpreter of the Word. Simonds D'Ewes remem-bered that, as a young man, even before his conversion, he had found that tak-ing notes on sermons changed his approach to religion by involving him more closely in the experience of the sermon.[99] In extreme cases, note-taking could prove a radical challenge to the church authorities. The schoolmaster David Blake was accused of travelling 'with diverse of his schollers of purpose to quarrel at the sermons of some and he . . . with his schollers haveinge conferred thier notes [of the sermons] have very unchristianly libelled against the saide sermon'.[100] It was, perhaps, another example of the puritan emphasis on plac-ing proper edification before 'due order'.

For puritans classroom godliness was always to be reinforced by the experience at church. At Beverley Minster, John Garthwaite, headmaster of the school, repeated the morning sermon in the chancel after morning prayers to a large group which included schoolboys, an esquire, and a gentleman.[101] At both Leicester and Ashby, Huntingdon's statutes required the scholars of the two highest forms to attend, with the schoolmaster, the local prophesy-ing.[102] Boys who had reached this level were likely destined for the university.

---

[98] The statutes of Wakefield required that 'upon the Sabboth dayes [the schoolmaster] shall cause [the scholars] diligently to repaire to Church, where his carefull eyes shall overview their carriage and behaviour, their Attention, also and diligence in noting the heads of instruction delivered by the Preacher. For will have him to give Order to all his Schollars (which by their capacity and skill in writ-ing are able) in writing to note the Sermons for the help of their memory, and more profitable hearing. Of which their profiting the Master shall take further knowledge by examining upon Munday morning either all his Schollars or such as in his discretion he shall think for the time most meet to be apposed, and their severall Absences, Negligences, and Misdemeanours at Church, either noted by himselfe, or given up by the Monitors in the Bills . . .' (B.L. MS Sloane 2204, fol. 30).

[99] D'Ewes, *Autobiography*, I, p. 95. Joan Simon has noted that, while on a visit to England in 1641, Com-enius was impressed by the large number of people who took notes at sermons (*Education and Society*, pp. 384–5). Half a century before, Edmund Coote had suggested, in a work that was to prove enormously successful, that taking notes at sermons was one of the reasons for becoming literate (Coote, *English Schoole-maister*, Preface). [100] L.P.L. Carte Misc., XII/15.

[101] Marchant, *Puritans and Church Courts*, p. 37.

[102] Cross, *Free Grammar School of Leicester*, p. 19; Chalmers, 'Puritanism in Leicestershire', unpub. M.A. thesis, Univ. of Leeds, 1962, p. 270. On prophesyings, see below, Ch. 11.

Such an intensive study of sermons was probably intended to produce that close relationship of lay and ministerial members of the university evident from contemporary sources, and also that driving interest in religion evidenced by lay diaries.

Though statutory injunctions to textual purity and godly practices were crucial, puritans also sought suitable external guidance for schools. At some places, such as Wakefield, the connexion was with the gentry. The arms of the Saviles hung over the door, and those of others of similar rank were glazed in the windows.[103] It was also the custom of the day to connect grammar schools not only with a university, but also with a particular college.[104] It is well known that many merchants who founded schools placed them in the care of their companies, though often also with an attachment to a particular college.[105] Puritans seem to have been quite adept in building a network to link the process of reform at the two levels; after 1584 the godly house of Emmanuel also required a supply of entrants. Sir Wolstan Dixie, for example, who founded a grammar school at Market Bosworth, also endowed four scholarships for its graduates at Emmanuel, as well as two fellowships.[106] Geographical preferences in the statutes of colleges could also lead to closer bonds with particular schools. Sidney Sussex especially benefited from a spate of early seventeenth-century foundations in the north. Geographical connexions could also reinforce a religious bias. Sidney's statutes expressed preference for Kent and Rutland.[107] Most of the students from Rutland had attended either Oakham or Uppingham, the foundations of the puritan Robert Johnson.[108] Colleges were frequently also involved in selecting new schoolmasters.[109] At puritan Wakefield, if the local governors could not agree on a candidate, then the appointment was to fall to Emmanuel.[110]

Another common practice was the involvement of a bishop in the governing process: Harsnet at Chigwell placed the nomination of the schoolmaster, failing a decision by the governors, in the hands of the bishop of London.[111] Puritans seem to have shied away from episcopal intervention or to have

[103] Simon, *Education and Society*, p. 361.
[104] Tyler examined the school origins of 1,090 entrants to four Cambridge colleges and found that 800 of these youths had attended schools with close links to Cambridge; of these, 606 came from schools with a specific connexion – whether institutional or personal – with the college they were attending. Tyler, 'Children of Disobedience', unpub. Ph.D. thesis, Univ. of California at Berkeley, 1976, pp. 40–1, 68, 75, 90–2, 301. For a particular example of this connexion (at Melton Mowbray), see Simon, 'Town estates and schools', pp. 18–19.
[105] Jordan, *Charities of London* and *Charities of Rural England, passim*.
[106] Carlisle, *Endowed Grammar Schools*, pp. 753–4.
[107] Morgan, 'Cambridge and "the country" ', in Stone, ed., *University in Society*, I, p. 202.
[108] *Ibid.*, p. 202.
[109] *Eng.: Parlt: 4th Rep. from Select Comm. on Education* (1818), p. 347; *V.C.H. Bedford*, II, p. 157.
[110] Peacock, *Wakefield*, p. 13.
[111] Stott, *Chigwell*, Appendix I, p. 152. Stott notes that the Bishop of London performed a similar duty at least for the schools at Highgate, Harrow, Felsted, and Colchester.

balanced it with other forms of godly influence. John Lyon, for Harrow, depended not only on the bishop of London, but also on requiring the governors to procure annually thirty 'good learned and godly Sermons' for the parish church (which the schoolboys would attend).[112] Other safeguards circumvented fixed authority altogether. At Ashby, Huntingdon put his school under the charge of persons whose godliness he could virtually ensure by right of appointment: the Master of Wigston Hospital in Leicester, the preacher of Ashby, and the vicar of Ashby.[113] Sir William Paston, at North Walsham, Norfolk, provided for a weekly lecture for the better religious instruction of the schoolchildren; he also required that both schoolchildren and teacher should be inspected each year by two 'godlie and learned preachers', who were to have final authority over selection of texts.[114] All of these safeguard systems were, however, fraught with the possibility of failure. Colleges might change their religious orientation; new bishops might be reactionary, or oppressive; governors might choose non-fervent preachers to investigate education. Connexion with a college was also of necessity a distant safeguard, and operated, in general, at best annually, and possibly only when the local governors could not agree on a choice of new schoolmaster. This might well have been an infrequent occurrence if the very low degree of mobility in Yorkshire teachers is representative of the country as a whole.[115]

Changing attitudes towards the raising of the next generation may also be illustrated by contemporary statements on recreation and punishment in school. Humanists seem generally to have comprehended more fully than their predecessors the need for young boys to have physical exercise.[116] Some newer grammar schools were even equipped with their own playing fields.[117] Activities were attuned to military and moral requirements. Wrestling and archery were therefore commonly praised; football, card games, dicing, and swimming were equally often condemned. On the other side of the coin, school hours were long and discipline was severe; flogging and expulsion commonly awaited the unruly student. The age also seemed to show a growing awareness that punishment could not be left completely unregulated. Ascham for private scholars, and Daniel Lupton and Mulcaster for public scholars, complained of the overuse of the rod,[118] and indeed schools seem to have tried

---

[112] Bod. Lib. MS Tanner 121, fol. 2ᵛ.

[113] Fox, *Ashby*, p. 15; Turpin, *Boston Grammar School 1555–1955*, p. 13.

[114] Forder, *History of Paston Grammar School*, pp. 203–4.

[115] Stephens, 'Yorkshire schools', unpub. Ph.D. thesis, Univ. of Leeds, 1975. Stephens argues that of over 1500 schoolmasters he found for the period 1600–1700, the records indicate only one location for almost 98%.

[116] See, for example, Mulcaster, *Positions*, esp. p. 22; Sadoleto, *On Education*, pp. 81–2; Ascham, *Scholemaster*, p. 138.   [117] Simon, *Education and Society*, p. 365.

[118] Ascham, *Scholemaster*, ed. Giles, pp. 97–8, 112–13; Lupton, *London and Countrey*, p. 117; DeMolen, 'Richard Mulcaster and the profession of teaching', *Journal of the History of Ideas*, 35, p. 123.

to moderate the penchant for beating students. Though the crest of Louth school depicted a master with birch uplifted, Giles James was fired as master of Bedford Grammar School in 1629 for a combination of negligence and cruelty.[119] Few would abolish the rod, but the spirit of educationalists seems to have favoured the tempering of its use.[120]

Details of punishments and recreations in puritan writings and schools followed the humanist pattern.[121] Recreation was important, but had to be carefully guarded, not only because certain types of play were obviously unwise and immoral, but also because too much recreation could develop in the child a less serious attitude towards instruction and duty.[122] Recreation, of course, was never to interfere with the duties of the sabbath.[123] Liberty, as William Gouge stressed, could prove the greatest enemy to proper learning.[124] One afternoon per week of games seems to have been the norm. At Leicester, Thursday afternoon was to be set aside for honest recreation: shooting was recommended, but swimming, playing in the street, visiting alehouses, and raiding orchards were specifically forbidden.[125] Thomas Granger, while commending use of 'delightfull fables' for youngsters, insisted that children not be suffered to bring toys from home to the school; no distractions from the educational process were to be tolerated.[126] The restraint of the wilfulness of youth was thus carried on from the household. Recreation was to become part of classroom activity as much as relief from it.

As in the household, puritans called for the tempering, though by no means the abolition, of punishment. Beatings could prove counterproductive to both social hierarchy and Christian commitment. Thomas Becon argued that the rod should be used only with extremely stubborn children; it was his opinion that contemporary masters already employed it overmuch.[127] John Stockwood was deeply worried that 'cruel and butcherly beatyng' would likely produce hatred not only of schooling, but also of any instruction in godliness, a grave danger for the master to consider. John Brinsley, while noting that God had indeed sanctified the rod to save children from hell, argued that it should be used only as a last resort.[128] The vast literature leaves the impression – it

---

[119] *V.C.H. Bedford*, ii, pp. 163–4.

[120] See the very detailed statement by Archbishop Harsnet for Chigwell school, concerning a maximum of three hits with the rod, and the prohibition of any blows to the head (Stott, *Chigwell School*, p. 157).

[121] Northbrooke, *Dicing, Dauncing*, pp. 30–1; Harris, *True Blessedness*, p. 244; Granger, *Syntagma Grammaticum*, sig. B5ᵛ; Greenham, *Workes*, p. 278; Downame, *Guide to Godlinesse*, pp. 262, 267.

[122] Northbrooke, *Dicing, Dauncing*, p. 23.

[123] For an example of this very common proposition, see Dod & Cleaver, *Ten Commandements*, p. '143' (sic, for 153].　　[124] Gouge, *Domesticall Duties*, pp. 529, 527–8.

[125] Cross, *Free Grammar School of Leicester*, p. 20. Almost exactly the same phrasing was used at Ashby-de-la-Zouch (Fox, *Ashby*, p. 130).

[126] Granger, *Syntagma Grammaticum*, sigs. B6ᵛ–7, A5ʳ–ᵛ.　　[127] Becon, *Catechism*, p. 384.

[128] Stockwood, *Sermon at Paules Crosse*, p. 89; Brinsley, *Ludus Literarius*, p. 290.

cannot be much more – that those who had actually taught children (this category includes Becon, Stockwood, and Brinsley) tended to be less harsh in their attitude towards punishment. Puritan statutes, however, frequently make no specific mention of the type of correction, beyond the appointment of monitors.[129] Nor is it clear that puritans espoused any special view of the end of term exercise known as 'barring-out', which allowed students some regimented eruption against authority, but which seems to have been a regional practice.[130] Discipline and recreation were thus to combine in the puritan scheme to allow seemly pleasure guided by a will turned to the accept-ance of the social hierarchy (in the immediate person of the schoolmaster) and the necessity of a life of application to godliness. Success could be measured by the infrequency of corporal punishment. The child who controlled his own will in school, like the adult in his religious search, was becoming a suitable member of an hierarchical society.

IV

Against this background of statutory plans and general comments, it may also be useful to consider two detailed puritan expositions. Fear of revived Romanism was the basis of the proposal addressed to the Council in 1581 by Thomas Norton, the Elizabethan lawyer, M.P., playwright, and notorious anti-papist.[131] For Norton, the puritan preference for edification before struc-tural order (of the existing type) was a remedy to be applied directly to England's schools. Though Norton was willing in these 'Devices' to reform schools through episcopal pressure, he was also ready to deprive those bishops who failed in such an important task. Norton suggested that those bishops who did not quickly submit reports of their investigations to the Council were to suffer sequestration and loss of revenue to the queen until they demonstrated their dedication to reform and subservience to the Council. Bishops were to make immediate and far more thorough inquiry of all schoolmasters, both public and private, in their respective dioceses. Those teachers who could not demonstrate especial zeal in religion (beyond the usual oaths of loyalty and religion) were to be detained until the Privy Council determined their future. Bishops were also to inquire concerning texts and prayers used by scholars for religious instruction. The scholars themselves were to be asked to provide information on this delicate topic; evidently Norton was unwilling to trust ill-affected schoolmasters to answer openly. Zealous J.P.s were also to conduct an

[129] As, for example, at Ashby (Fox, *Ashby*, pp. 129, 130).
[130] See the enlightening paper by Keith Thomas, *Rule and Misrule in the Schools of Early Modern England, passim.*
[131] P.R.O. S.P. 12/177. The section of Norton's plan on the reform of schools covers fols. 171–3ᵛ. See below for Norton's comments on the universities and the Inns.

investigation in order to circumvent the dilatoriness of the bishops. A further
check on the bishops' commitment to forward protestantism was the requirement that each year they submit signed certificates concerning religious
beliefs from all schoolmasters. Norton's interest also extended to texts. As the
translator of the authorized catechism, Norton perhaps took an especial
interest in seeing that it was used in its English, Latin and Greek versions. He
also acknowledged the importance of the standardization of the Latin grammar
text under Henry VIII, and urged the same policy for Greek instruction.[132]

In order to ensure the continued supply of divinity students for the universities, the chief schools were to be attached to particular colleges, half of
whose vacant places they would then fill with divinity students.[133] To
counteract the influence of the Jesuits, all schoolboys aged sixteen were to
profess their religious conformity.[134] Norton also suggested that the Council
attempt to secure more information about the methods used by the Jesuits in
their seminaries, though whether this information was to serve as matter for
imitation in protestant schools is not fully clear.[135] To encourage a good
educational base in the countryside, Norton proposed that any M.A. willing to
teach school (either publicly or privately) should be allowed an absence from
his college of at least three years, with no loss of college stipend or allowances,
an obvious financial incentive to the combating of ungodliness at a lower
level.[136] On the other hand, no one expelled from the university for religious
reasons was to be allowed to hold a benefice or to teach school.[137] Norton also
turned his close attention to the religious commitment of the schoolmasters of
the queen's wards and to the education of the sons of 'men of value', where
popery was especially feared. All future grants of wardship were to be dependent upon a bond guaranteeing the raising of the child in true religion, and
children of the upper classes were to be placed, at the expense of their parents,
under the care of tutors and teachers known to be reliable.

Despite his earlier suspicion of the fervency of the bishops, it was to the
episcopacy that Norton looked to found godly seminaries in the country for
the well-born. Bishops were to entreat their suitably qualified chaplains to
become teachers, and to hire only servants who were themselves examples of
the benefits of gentlemanly education. As a further indication of the
functional closeness of teaching and preaching, he wished the church to restrict benefices worth more than £10 annually to ministers with teaching

---

[132] *Ibid.*, fols. 171^{r-v}, 173.   [133] *Ibid.*, fol. 172.
[134] This age limit would have engaged only the boys in the top form or two of grammar schools in such a
    profession of protestantism. Oaths were not normally tendered to children under 16 years of age.
    Perhaps Norton hoped that the lesson might percolate to the lower forms (*ibid.*, fol. 172^v).
[135] *Ibid.*, fol. 163^v.   [136] *Ibid.*, fol. 163.
[137] This provision would doubtless have endangered the puritans while Whitgift was leader of the church,
    but the clause should be read in the context of Norton's overall plan (*ibid.*, fol. 163^v).

experience.[138] His plea, similar to the effort of 1559, that the queen should institute royal visitations in matters ecclesiastical every seven years was a final statement of the need to keep abreast of the changing attitudes and reactions within both church and country.[139] Norton's aim, while others were concerned with subject matter, was directed to the purging of a still-infected system, and to the placement of godly teachers at all levels of the programme. Although the suggestions of the 'Devices' were not made the subject of any grand governmental plan of reform, many of Norton's desires found their way into administration policy towards papists, especially in time of national crisis.

John Brinsley was a 1588 M.A. of puritan Christ's College. A minister, and schoolmaster in the puritan school at Ashby, he demonstrated his commitment to classical and humanist learning by publishing translations.[140] His own approach – an amalgam of puritan fervency and pedagogical experience – was to create 'delightfull' seminaries of all schools, capable of sending boys to the universities and Inns of Court. Brinsley referred to learning as the 'chiefest glory of a Nation', and argued that the arts were the only true way to 'human perfection'.[141]

Brinsley included humanist views of the connexion of 'virtue' to education, though greater stress was given to texts by classical authors, in both the original and the English translation.[142] Noteworthy, however, were his emphatic support for the rhetoric of Ramus, in the very popular version by Charles Butler, and his choice of John Udall's amended English translation of a continental Hebrew grammar.[143] He wrote his own companion to Lily's grammar, which he hoped would simplify the education of younger children.[144] His recommended course of studies, he argued, would aid England in producing people more highly skilled (and more easily trained) in rhetoric, logic, philosophy and theology.[145] His emphasis on disputations, though confined to points of grammar, would have ensured early training for future casuists and polemicists.[146] The inclusion, too, of Hebrew in the curriculum, along with Greek and Latin, must be seen as intentional early

---

[138] *Ibid.*, fols. 172^v–3.
[139] Norton also suggested that a comprehensive plan by Alexander Nowell, concerning the standardization of routine within all of England's schools, would make a useful model for reform (*ibid.*, fol. 173^{r-v}).
[140] Of Aesop, Corderius' *Dialogues*, Cicero's *Offices*, and Ovid's *Metamorphoses*, as well as Virgil's *Eclogues*, (Baldwin, *Small Latine*, I & II, *passim*). [141] Brinsley, *Ludus Literarius*, sigs. ¶3, §.
[142] His list of texts includes Cicero, Virgil, Horace, the Latin and Greek Testaments, the Hebrew (Old) Testament, Terence, Juvenal, Ovid, Cato, Aesop, Corderius, Homer, and Lily's grammar (*Consolation*, pp. 52–8, 61ff.; *Ludus Literarius*, Ch. 8). He also recommended Stockwood on grammar (*Consolation*, p. 70). [143] Brinsley, *Consolation*, pp. 61–78.
[144] Brinsley, *Posing of the Parts*, sig. A3. [145] Brinsley, *Consolation*, pp. 10–11, 13.
[146] Brinsley, *Ludus Literarius*, pp. 205–10.

training in the trilingual ideal necessary for serious scriptural study, though this would certainly have strained the resources of the 'country Schooles' for which Brinsley supposedly wrote.[147] He perhaps showed greater awareness of the future apprenticeship of many pupils when he stressed the need also for more basic crafts, including skilled instruction in handwriting and in numeracy. For the latter he recommended Recorde's arithmetic and a spell in the 'cyphering school'.[148] But, though he was obviously aware of the growing urban need for more specialized education, Brinsley still sought to place the 'secular' skill in a religious context; he complained that innumeracy meant that pupils, while in church, could not scan their Bibles to find the texts mentioned by the preacher.[149]

Brinsley's approach to socialization was based on creating a bond between teacher and pupils. The first lesson was proper respect and obedience for the schoolmaster, who would then treat his charges in sympathetic fashion, 'using moderate correction, abhoring cruelty . . .'.[150] Since the schoolmaster represented the moral force of authority, any kind of corporal punishment had to be scrupulously fair; the children were likely to judge all authority in light of their verdict on their own teacher.[151] Absolutely incorrigible children, however, were to be removed from the school, as a threat not only to the master's discipline, but also by their wilfulness to the satisfactory socialization of the other pupils.[152]

Brinsley believed that in issuing his educational ideas he was simply fulfilling his specific calling; he could not, he noted, 'ever [have] stood before the Lord' if he had not 'sought the discharge of this my debt to the uttermost farthing'.[153] His interest was to elucidate a popularized system of education, based chiefly on Sturm, Erasmus, and Melanchthon.[154] He therefore suggested that education, as a form of play, should begin before the age of five, when children were more pliant and easily fascinated. They could also finish their training earlier (and within their parents' lifetime and supervision). This early start would also relieve the present burden of elementary instruction, which too often fell upon grammar masters. To this end of facilitating early edu-

[147] On Brinsley's methods of learning and teaching Hebrew, see *Ludus Literarius*, pp. 244–52; on Greek, ibid., pp. 222–43.   [148] *Ibid.*, pp. 27–40, 26.
[149] *Ibid.*, p. 25. Cressy found that in London, only 17% of people licensed to teach school (1580–1640) offered arithmetic ('Education and Literacy', unpub. Ph.D. thesis, Univ. of Cambridge, 1973, p. 173). This may have helped to prompt the great number of 'independent' teachers in the capital.
[150] Brinsley, *True Watch*, pp. 72–3.
[151] Brinsley, *Ludus Literarius*, pp. 275–8   [152] *Ibid.*, pp. 277–92, 295–6.
[153] Brinsley, *Consolation*, pp. 17–18, 19. See also Philoponus' comment (*Ludus Literarius*, p. 88) that he wished to make the best use of his knowledge, that is, 'communicate it to every one to whom it may doe good . . .'.
[154] He also mentioned the teaching of Touey, Coote, and Richardson as his sources (Brinsley, *Consolation*, pp. 17–18, 22, 24, 29–31, 42–4).

cation Brinsley further recommended the founding of reading schools, but recognized that this might prove impractical.[155]

Brinsley also recognized that only a small proportion of boys went on to university, and that therefore the grammar school had to serve a dual purpose. He specifically acknowledged that most boys would need correct and refined English more than any other subject. He also noted that he stressed the vernacular in response to complaints from parents that their children had been studying for six or seven years and still could not read English (let alone Latin) adequately, and so were not fit for any trade or apprenticeship.[156] The suggestion that young boys practise their English by reading a chapter of the Bible at home every day may only acknowledge the fact that the Bible was the most common book.[157] However, Brinsley's emphasis that this practice would enable these lads to 'shew their love to the Lord, and his Word, and their desire to have the Word dwell plentifully in their houses' reveals the puritan pedagogue's overriding desire to pervade common learning with the thrust of experiential faith.[158] Brinsley saw increased dedication to schooling and to expansion of the uses of the vernacular in the context of the Pauline drive to evangelize the world with the godly message. It was the education of children in forward godliness that 'doth make [scholars] truely blessed, and sanctifie all other their studies . . .'.[159]

God had thus ordained schools 'to be a principall meanes to reduce a barbarous people to civillitie, and thereby to prepare them the better to receive the glorious Gospell of Iesus Christ . . .'.[160] Brinsley insisted that greater purity of purpose in protestant schools would have meant that 'every where long ago, all Popery and Atheisme would have been rooted out'.[161] Children were therefore to read the Word in their homes every day, and in school they were each week to write themes on subjects 'Morall or Politicall'.[162] Brinsley's plan also called for students to pray twice each day, and spend an additional fifteen minutes each evening on Eusebius Paget's history of the Bible, so that not a single day should pass without godly gain.[163] Brinsley recommended the Biblical translations of both Erasmus and (especially) Theodore Beza, who was both more 'religiously' correct and who 'more fully

---

[155] Brinsley, *Ludus Literarius*, pp. 9–14.

[156] Brinsley, *Ludus Literarius*, pp. 22, 83, 106–7; *Consolation*, pp. 76–7.

[157] Since we have very little knowledge concerning the social composition of the student body of grammar schools – only a few lists of pupils are extant – it is difficult to know the ability of parents to pay for texts. Even knowledge of parental wealth would not, of course, reveal their *willingness* to spend larger sums on the process of education. Our understanding of this problem will likely always have to be impressionistic. It is therefore worthwhile to note that it was a matter which troubled contemporaries. At Market Bosworth, the number of books used was evidently limited because 'the school standeth much upon poor men's children whose parents are not able to buy them many books', (quoted in Simon, 'Town estates and schools', p. 19).   [158] Brinsley, *Ludus Literarius*, p. 24.

[159] *Ibid.*, p. 253.   [160] Brinsley, *Consolation*, sig. *3ᵛ, p. 5.   [161] *Ibid.*, p. 44.

[162] Brinsley, *Ludus Literarius*, pp. 24, 174–5, 185.   [163] *Ibid.*, p. 258.

[expressed] the sense and drift of the Holy Ghost'.[164] He also praised
Corderius' *Colloquies* as a useful practical basis of godly knowledge,[165] and
further recommended epitomes of the Bible by Shaw and Martinius.[166] Daily
catechizing was a necessary preparation to the compulsory attendance at the
Sunday sermon.[167] He suggested use of William Perkins' popular catechism as
a supplement to the authorized catechism of Alexander Nowell.[168] Instruction
in Greek and Hebrew in the higher forms, studied out of the New and Old
Testaments, was meant to impart religious as well as linguistic knowledge.

Religious training in schools, however, as in society generally, was to be
centred on a critical analysis of sermons, an indication of the strength of the
schoolmaster–minister axis.[169] Notes were to be taken of the sermon, the
highest forms in the school being responsible for the exact substance, bases,
and arguments of the preacher's exposition, as well as its application. Exact
quotations were to be noted if possible; verse and chapter to be remembered if
the former task superseded ability. Lower forms were to memorize five or six
points, and then to note them down after they had left the church. The sermon
was to serve as the basis of the following week's lessons, including translations
to and from Latin. By the end of the week, students should know the sermon
well enough to be able to repeat it without notes.[170] This concentration from
an early age on direct knowledge of the Scriptures, and on the sermon as the
crucial intellectual experience of the week, may have been intended to produce a number of attitudinal changes. The first was the creation of a body of
church-goers who would listen attentively to the sermon: we have already
noted contemporary complaints about the ignorance and restlessness of
audiences. Secondly, these protestants would have been capable of challenging their minister were he to cite texts incorrectly, or provide unsuitable
exegesis. As well, analysis of the sermon provided a continuing reinforcement
in the lessons of logic and rhetoric; it is significant that the Ramist Brinsley
thought that this close conjunction of sermon and school would work only if
the sermons 'be plainly and orderly delivered . . . .'.[171] Fourthly, the regimen
was to be uniform for all members of society. While it socialized the whole
school to the centrality in Reformed society of godly protestantism, it also
perhaps produced not only a lifelong habit of sermon attendance, but also a

---

[164] *Ibid.*, p. 262   [165] *Ibid.*, p. 257.   [166] Brinsley, *Consolation*, pp. 78–9.
[167] Brinsley, *Ludus Literarius*, pp. 254–5.   [168] Brinsley, *Consolation*, p. 79.
[169] Brinsley, *Ludus Literarius*, pp. 253–4. See also below, pp. 212–19.
[170] *Ibid.*, pp. 254–8; *Consolation*, p. 56. Joan Simon has concluded, partly on the basis of R.A. Marchant's
arguments, that Brinsley's plan of having students help one another 'reduces puritan ideas on church
government to the school level' (*Education and Society*, p. 381). But a greater impulse may have been the
context. Schools commonly had five or six forms with, usually, one or two teachers. At any given time,
many pupils must have been working without the direct attention of a teacher. This situation would
likely by itself have led to a certain cooperative approach to learning among students.
[171] Brinsley, *Consolation*, p. 56.

suitable view of the high status of the godly minister. And, finally, it 'socialized' learning itself to the puritan view of the proper hierarchy of knowledge. The development of the intellect in Brinsley's scheme was an encouragement not of discovery or of 'free-thinking', but rather of an increasing ability, as one climbed the ranks of the classes, to absorb and reproduce the lessons emanating from the godly pulpit. For Brinsley, then, the school was not to serve as merely an enclave of classical learning; but to stress his concessions to vernacular learning too highly is to miss the point. *All* learning was to be an adjunct of godly socialization.

As a point of comparison with the puritan balance between humane learning and godly instruction, we may briefly note the radical response. Henry Barrow insisted that schools were not places of learning to serve only the social or economic purposes of their graduates. Teachers and students were to exist under the control of the gathered saints,[172] to ensure that the 'artes and sciences which are thus taught or studied, be not vayne, curious, or unlawful, but necessarie and godlie'.[173] School expansion was to be financed by the nationalization of the resources of deans and chapters.[174] It is not clear whether Barrow favoured complete independence in the matter of congregational control of educational facilities. He did not elucidate, for example, on the questions of standardized texts, masters' qualifications, and precise curriculum. Some compromise with a superior governing body might have been a practical necessity, simply so that different congregations could produce fairly similar results in profane or practical subjects.

Schools were to become foundations 'of all godlie learning to garnish the church and commonwealth . . .'.[175] He allowed practical arts and languages since utilitarian to secular vocations, but the use of the regimen of 'the most heathenish and profane authors, lascivious poets, etc.' allowed by the established church aroused his ire.[176] Many of the models of grammar, rhetoric, and logic were written by heathens or by Renaissance adherents of the Roman church. Barrow therefore deemed it safer to advise only the study of the Bible, and that in English. In this he was acting in a continuing radical tradition; somewhat earlier the separatist schoolmaster Robert Harrison (the associate of Robert Browne) evidently had had qualms about teaching heathen authors to Christian children.[177] Thus, although the radicals issued few detailed curricula, it was evident that all was bad save that which was

[172] Barrow, *Pollution of Universitie-Learning*, pp. 7–8.
[173] Barrow, *Plaine Refutation*, p. 223, in *Writings of Henry Barrow 1590–91*, ed. Carlson.
[174] Barrow, *Pollution*, p. 12. [175] Barrow, *Plaine Refutation*, pp. 223–4.
[176] *Ibid.*, pp. 213–14. See also Barrow, *Brief Discoverie*, p. 344, in *Writings of Henry Barrow, 1587–1590*, ed. Carlson.
[177] Barrow, *Brief Discoverie*, p. 346; Barrow, *Pollution*, p. 6. C.U.L. MS. Ee.II.34, No. 152, vol. 128, on Harrison. See also below, p. 202.

positively godly. It was a black-and-white world in which to recognize neutrality was to compromise with the agents of Antichrist.

Puritans, then, had no wish to condemn those instruments which, when
suitably guarded, served them so well. And so they revealed with regard to
schools the same paradoxical attitudes that they had displayed towards learning in general. At first glance, they do not perhaps seem to have called for
great change in England's schools. There was seldom, in puritan considerations of schooling, the direct challenge to the authority of the ancients, save
in spiritual matters, which 'modernists' such as Mulcaster offered. With the
exception of Brinsley, puritans did not prove to be noteworthy theorists or
system builders. They operated rather on what may be called an *ad hoc* basis,
adjusting rather than radically altering the pre-university levels of English
education to accord with the overriding principle of godly instruction. Here,
too, was the synthesizing of the immediate and the contemplative levels of
puritan existence. Their greatest contribution to educational literature and
practice was the tremendous emphasis on permeating all schools and school
experience generally with godliness. So while they contributed relatively few
academic texts (apart from Ramist adaptations), they did offer a host of
catechisms and a stress on the use of sermons as the basis of classroom lessons,
thereby cementing the relationship of schoolmaster and minister. Here again,
they were less interested in advancing or restricting humane learning than in
ensuring its proper reception in a godly milieu.

10

SCHOOLMASTERS

I

Concern with the reform of schools was not confined to curriculum and text-books. The main educational thrust of church–state control was not so much at the schools themselves, over which there could be little legal control,[1] as at the schoolmasters. The inspection and licensing of teachers by the church began in earnest under Mary, and was continued by Elizabeth. Thus, after 1562, schoolmasters had to subscribe to the Thirty-Nine Articles of religion and the royal supremacy.[2] Control, however, was erratic, and tended chiefly to the elimination of papist influence. Few authorities were as conscientious as Bishop Overton of Coventry and Lichfield, who in 1584 decreed that recalcitrance in religion was due to 'intolerable corruption in schoolmasters', and so cancelled all the teaching licences in the diocese pending re-examination of the teachers.[3] As part of the national offensive against the old religion, schoolmasters who taught in England without a licence were made liable for up to a year in prison; their employers could be fined £10 per month.[4] The canons of 1571 and 1604 required teachers to attend Sunday church service with their pupils. As a further measure of control, curates were supposed to be given preference in the granting of teaching licences. Nonetheless, church control of schoolmasters seems at times to have been a chimera. Though perhaps economically motivated, the regularity with which schoolmasters appeared at visitations without licences, or simply ignored the summons and suffered nothing worse than a warning, or very occasionally a temporary suspension, is ample testimony to the common feeling that the church adminis-

---

[1] There were irregular attempts by ther state to control schools. In 1562, for example, the power to amend the statutes of a school founded in Mary's reign was delegated to the High Commission (Simon, *Education and Society*, p. 307).

[2] Orme, *English Schools*, pp. 285–6; Simon, 'Reformation and English education', *Past and Present*, 11, p. 62; O'Day, *Education and Society*, p. 27.

[3] Tate, 'Sources for the history of English grammar schools', *British Journal of Educational Studies*, 2, p. 74.

[4] Brown, *Elizabethan Schooldays*, p. 26. O'Day notes that a licence cost 10s., and 3d. fee for exhibition at a visitation (*Education and Society*, p. 28).

tration was losing its coercive authority in educational matters.[5] The leniency
with which the authorities generally treated offending schoolmasters may well
indicate also their plain understanding that English education would suffer
disastrously if they inhibited from teaching every master who lacked a licence.
The church therefore customarily concentrated only on those perceived as
enemies of the administration. In July 1573, for example, Bishop Parkhurst
strenuously objected to the appointment of Robert Harrison, M.A. of Corpus
Christi, Cambridge, as schoolmaster of Aylsham, on the grounds of his youth
and his evident opposition to the ceremonies of the church. Parkhurst was also
worried by Harrison's supposed refusal to use heathen authors in the school;
in 1574 the Brownist schoolmaster was removed from Aylsham.[6] John
Brinsley was likewise ejected from the mastership of Ashby-de-la-Zouche
school for his puritan opinions, and Eusabius Paget's school in London –
which opened without episcopal sanction – was closed by High Commission.[7]
The mechanisms of control, however, were obviously retributive rather than
preventive, and did little, especially in the case of peripatetic schoolmasters, to
stem the distribution of dissenting opinions.

While church and state sought more efficient modes of regulation, there
was also a universal interest in improving the standards of the schoolmasters.
Thomas Elyot, typifying the humanist thrust, complained: 'Lorde god, howe
many good and clene wittes of children be nowe a dayes perisshed by ignorant
schole maistres. How little substancial doctrine is apprehended by the
fewenesse of good gramariens?'[8] The Elizabethan humanist schoolmaster
Richard Mulcaster insisted on trilingual ability in the best masters, and at least
some academic standing and interest in pupils as the mark of all England's
teachers.[9] Evidently building on an idea of Vives, Mulcaster proposed the reorientation of university colleges towards particular professions; one college
was to be set aside for the training of a greater number of teachers, who could
then reach a greater proportion of the populace.[10] At the grass-roots level,
Mulcaster and other humanists recommended conferences of teachers with
parents and neighbours to discuss problems of education.[11] This unusual

[5] On licensing generally, see Tate, 'Episcopal licensing of schoolmasters', *Church Quarterly Review*, 157,
esp. pp. 426–7, 428, 432. On the costs of licensing (and for some criticisms of Tate), see Jenkins, 'A
note', *ibid.*, 159, pp. 78–9. The general comment on the lack of demonstrated authority is based on a
search of the Lincoln Episcopal Visitation Books.   [6]   C.U.L. MS Ee.II.34, No. 152, fol. 128.
[7] Wood, *Reformation*, p. 334.
[8] Quoted in Orme, *English Schools*, p. 162. See also Lupton, *London and Countrey*, pp. 115–22; Granger,
Syntagma Grammaticum, sig. A5.   [9]   Mulcaster, *Positions*, pp. 235–6.
[10] This was not wholly an original idea: Godshouse had been founded at Cambridge in 1439 by William
Bingham to correct a dearth of schoolmasters. *V.C.H. Cambridge*, III, pp. 429–30. See Orme, *Schools*, pp.
221–2 on the limitations of Godshouse. DeMolen, 'Richard Mulcaster and the profession of teaching',
Journal of the History of Ideas, 35, pp. 124–5.
[11] Mulcaster, *Positions*, pp. 235, 239ff.; Kempe, *Education of Children*, pp. 213, 220; Watson, *English Grammar Schools*, pp. 156–7; Charlton, 'Professions', *University of Birmingham Journal*, 12, p. 37.

reformer did not stand completely alone; numerous other more limited attempts were made to alert the public to the correlation of low salaries and poor teaching, and generally to raise the public perception of school-masters.[12]

The most common aspiration shared by school founders was the raising of the academic qualifications of the schoolmasters. Statutes of endowed schools came commonly to require B.A.s of both master and usher, and to suggest an M.A. for the master if at all possible.[13] A dispute over the succession of schoolmasters at Shrewsbury also emphasized the rising expectations of the vocation: one candidate was noted to be very learned in the Fathers, Schoolmen, Councils, and history, while the other, it was suggested, lacked sufficient Greek to be worthy of the headmastership of such a notable school.[14] Whether employer insistence or a surplus of graduates was the chief impetus to such change is not clear, but Cressy has demonstrated, for the diocese of London at least, that the resultant change in endowed schools was marked. In the 1580s, 27% of teachers in this diocese were university graduates; already in the 1590s this had risen to 35% graduates, with an additional 31% *literati*, that is with some experience of higher education. The percentage of graduates rose in every decade, culminating with 59% with degrees in the 1630s. The figure for the *literati* was more erratic, but for the 1610s, 1620s, and 1630s, the joint total of graduates and *literati* was over 80%, peaking at 89% in the 1630s. For the diocese of Norwich the pattern was similar, though the figures were understandably not as impressive, and revealed greater fluctuations over time. Nontheless, the peak was reached at the same time – in 1636 with 58% graduates.[15]

But we should not forget the other extreme of certain elementary schoolmasters who perhaps conveyed to their pupils almost as much academic skill as they possessed. The transitory nature of, and almost casual approach to, elementary education are illustrated by the recollection of Roger Lowe of Lancashire concerning a neighbour: 'Humphrey Harrison came to shop and stayd with me a great while and att last moved me to instruct his son in teaching hime to endite letters and to cast account up, which I promised I would doe.'[16] Mulcaster argued that primary teachers should be the best, and

---

[12] See, for example, Lyly, *Euphues*, fols. 52ᵛ–3; Fenton, *Christian Pollicie*, pp. 235–41, 198ff.

[13] See, for example, Parry, *Founding of Exeter School*, p. 104; Tate, *History of . . . Alnwick*, p. 82; Clark, *Foundation Deeds of Felsted*, pp. 15–16; Gray & Potter, *Ipswich School*, p. 40; Stocks, *Blackburn Grammar School*, pp. 72–3. See also Carlisle, *Endowed Grammar Schools, passim.*

[14] *C.S.P.D. 1637–1638*, pp. 337–8.

[15] Cressy, 'Education and literacy in London and East Anglia 1580–1700', unpub. Ph.D. thesis, Univ. of Cambridge, 1973, Ch. 5. See also Spufford, *Contrasting Communities*, p. 189; Simon, 'Leicestershire schools', *British Journal of Educational Studies*, 3, p. 45; Simon, *Education and Society*, p. 376 n. 2; Feyerharm, 'Status of schoolmasters', *History of Education*, 5, esp. pp. 104–5.

[16] *Diary of Roger Lowe*, ed. Sachse, p. 53.

recommended that they should be especially trained,[17] but he was perhaps too hopeful for the age. Rebecca Lanham, who was licensed to teach in South Walsham, incredibly marked rather than signed her subscription.[18] Elementary teachers seem generally to have been the most ill-prepared and the least 'professional' of educators. Small wonder when they were the lowest paid. In Norwich they included, in 1570, 'An Bucke of the age of 46 years, wydowe, souster [sauce-maker] . . .'.[19] While they were absent from grammar schools, women evidently quite commonly taught younger children.[20] In grammar schools, ushers, those overworked and underpaid assistants – the curates of the educational system – came in for especial criticism for their poor learning.[21]

It was the ideas of the humanists, and the technology of the printing press, that provided the momentum on which puritans grafted their own ideas. Nonetheless, as befitted a movement which aimed at certain changes, puritans tended to emphasize what remained to be done. So Thomas Granger, in the grammar he outlined for classroom use, blamed 'doubtfulness' (uncertain knowledge) and 'confusion' (unclear teaching) as the two principal causes of lack of progress in schools.[22] John Brinsley commented that university preparation was so deficient in the 'country schools' that college tutors had to act the part of schoolmasters and instill basic knowledge.[23]

Puritan school statutes contributed to the contemporary demand for graduate teachers by requiring degrees.[24] The statutes of Wakefield, for example, called for the 'placing of a fit teacher, from whom as the Root, the Schollars are to draw the Sap and Juice of Religion, Learning, and good Nurture . . .' This meant an M.A., and a man 'painfull in his own Studies . . .'[25] A surge of university graduates in our period might well have meant that employers who offered reasonable terms could afford to be selective in their choice of a new schoolmaster. Occasionally new teachers were even put to the test before being formally hired. William Bentley replied in 1588 to Colchester that he was very willing that 'my ability to teache prose, verse, latine and greeke be tryed accordinge to the orders of your schoole'. Francis

[17] DeMolen, 'Richard Mulcaster and the profession of teaching', p. 124; Mulcaster, *Positions*, p. 235. See also Coote, quoted in Watson, *English Grammar Schools*, p. 156.
[18] Carter, ed., *Norwich Subscription Books*, facing p. 8.
[19] Hudson & Tingey, eds., *Records of the City of Norwich*, II, p. 339.
[20] See the citations of Rachel Gill and Abigail Tyler, for example, for teaching without proper church approval (in the form of licences): Lincoln Record Office Vj 30, fol. 208ᵛ.
[21] See, for example, Lupton, *London and Countrey*, pp. 119–22.
[22] Granger, *Syntagma Grammaticum*, 'Epistle', sig. A3ʳ⁻ᵛ.
[23] Brinsley, *Consolation*, pp. 8–9; *Ludus Literarius*, pp. 1–8.
[24] See, for example, the statutes at Oakham and Uppingham; Heath; Otley; and Harrow. Respectively: Bingham, *Our Founder*, pp. 42–3; Cox, *History of Grammar School at Heath*, pp. 13, 50; Padgett, ed., *Chronicles of Otley*, p. 42; Bod. Lib. MS Tanner 121, fol. 2.   [25] B.L. MS Sloane 2204, fol. 29.

Cockman, appointed schoolmaster at Heath in 1629, had previously indicated his willingness 'to attend the divine dispensation: and to abide any fair tryall for your aprobation and your satisfaction . . .' At Wigston Magna, where the vicar taught school with a young scholar just down from the university as his assistant, there is a record for 1632 of the grant of one shilling to Mr Wattes, an unsuccessful candidate 'who offered himself to teach school with us'.[26] The notion of expense money for interviews, paid for by a comparatively poorly financed school, is rather interesting in a time when there was supposedly a great dearth of jobs and consequently, one would suppose, candidates willing to pay their own costs. From a survey of the statutes of a number of schools, it is difficult, however, to conclude whether puritan statute writers required higher academic standards of their schoolmasters than did contemporaries generally.

As in the case of ministers, so did educational writers and founders of schools also require good reputation in their schoolmasters. Candidates for teaching posts were commonly expected to produce letters of reference from colleges, former employers, or church officials; these generally attested to the man's academic ability, his 'conversation' and his religious fervency, or at least conformity (depending on the writer and perhaps also on the potential employer). Thomas Becon attempted to set both the standard for teachers and the obligation of state authority in protestant minds when he insisted that fervency and good civil conduct be combined:

a Christian magistrate must diligently provide, that such as shall be chosen and appointed schoolmasters be men of gravity, wisdom, knowledge, learning, of an honest and godly conversation, of an approved life, of uncorupt manners, diligent and painful in their office, favourers of true and pure religion, earnest lovers of Gods word, haters of idolatry and superstition . . .[27]

William Gouge noted that schoolmasters could be unsatisfactory because unskilful, covetous, negligent, or lacking in piety.[28] Thomas Morrice emphasized the practical utility of employing a schoolmaster who, in addition to the usual characteristics of 'sound beliefe, honest life, and civill conversation', was also an 'auncient man rather than a young . . .'. The older man would of course possess greater experience in 'methodicall teaching, and trayning up of children', but perhaps even more important was the possible difficulty with a younger teacher, who was 'commonly more proner to lewde

[26] Essex Record Office Morant MS D/Y 2/4, p. 97; Cox, *Grammar School at Heath*, p. 24; Simon, 'Town estates and schools', p. 21.   [27] Becon, *Catechism with Other Pieces*, p. 306.
[28] Gouge, *Domesticall Duties*, pp. 587–8.

lust, more apt to give badde example to his Scholler, more inconsiderate, of lesse discretion and experience, than an ancient man'.[29]

'Conversation' linked to academic ability was usually a point of some emphasis in letters of reference. William Bentley produced a certificate signed by ten fellows of Emmanuel, which attested, in addition to his stature as 'a man of such knowledge both in the hebrue greek and lattin tongues, and in other good artes', also to his 'honest conversation and good government meet for the trayninge upp of youthe . . .'.[30] Such comments, likely known by the writers of testimonials to be necessary, perhaps became something of a standard form (comparable to the brief 'Calvinist' introductions to most wills of the period). Another letter for Bentley, this one from ten fellows of Clare Hall, used virtually the same phrases to denote his academic stature and good conversation, referring to his 'skilfulnes both in the hebrue greek and lattin tongues, and in the artes . . .'.[31]

At Ashby-de-la-Zouche, the school at which John Brinsley was master from 1599 to 1617, the 1575 statutes explained that 'honest conversation' meant that the teacher 'shall be neither Adulterer, fforincator, Drunkard, Neither Game player, Noe swearer, or Blasphemer, neither ffaulty in any Grevious Crimes . . .'[32] At other puritan foundations, such as Wakefield, the prescription was more circumspect, requiring of the master simply that he be known to be of good conduct.[33] But at this school the author of the statues, Jeremy Gibson, laid such emphasis on the school as a seminary, that he may well have felt it unnecessary to spell out in further detail the requisite private characteristics of the teacher.[34]

But academic standards and 'good manners', while crucial, did not alone qualify a schoolmaster in the eyes of the godly. Since a youngster might spend most of his waking hours for several years in the custody of the same instructor, it was imperative that the teacher be equipped to instill not only literacy, grammar, and manners, but also godliness. This association of teaching with religion was of course the staple of the age. Powerful agents of the government pressed for godly reform. Burghley, for example, that occasional ally of the puritans, told the governors of the school at Bury St

---

[29] Morrice, *Apologie for Schoolemaster*, sig. B.6. Age could of course also be a drawback. Before the reorganization of the statutes of Wolverhampton school by the Merchant Taylors in 1617, a petition to one of the assistants of the company (dated 30 Sept. 1609) noted that many parents had recently removed their sons from school. 'Wee doe impute the cause to be in the Schole maister', they contended, and intimated that only his removal would save the school. The complaint concerned not only the schoolmaster's lack of discretion, but also, as it turned out, the 'great ymperfeccon in his hearing' (Mander, *History of Wolverhampton Grammar School*, p. 65).

[30] E.R.O. Morant MS D/Y 2/4, p. 113. The signatories included Nathaniel Gilby. For several examples of testimonials, see *H.M.C. Eighth Rep., App., Pt I*, Vol. XVI, p. 439.

[31] E.R.O. Morant MS D/Y 2/4, p. 131; for another letter to the same effect, *ibid.*, p. 143.

[32] Fox, *Ashby*, Appendix IV, p. 128.   [33] B.L. MS Sloane 2204, fol. 29.

[34] Peacock, *History of Wakefield*, p. 75.

Edmunds in 1581 that 'soundnes in religion . . . maners and conversacon, as were requisite for the good instruction & educacon of the youthe by doctryne and example' were the proper attributes of a schoolmaster.[35] But at the conservative end of the spectrum there was also the fear of enthusiasm. Elizabeth herself, as she was wary of too many fervent preachers, also deplored the possibility that education might be used to spread what she considered to be radical religion.[36] This fear extended to the end of our period. Dr Edward Martin, President of Queens', Cambridge, and Laud's ex-chaplain, similarly exclaimed in 1636/7 that there was 'no so obnoxious a pestilence to Church and Kingdom as a Puritan schoolmaster'.[37]

For the puritans, as with lax ministers, so with schoolmasters, passive religion was not enough. As they demanded the burning flame within their ministers, so they strove to secure godly schoolmasters for England's youth. John Stockwood excoriated those schoolmasters who thought humane learning and manners were the parameters of necessary instruction; the teacher, he argued, was also in duty bound to see that children were 'as well instructed unto salvation, as furthered in prophane learning'.[38] William Gouge argued quite simply that lack of piety was reason enough for dismissal.[39] Especially in the statutes of the puritan grammar schools, where a practical basis for godly instruction was being laid, does this fervour come to light. The example of Wakefield is again illustrative. The school's Elizabethan charter required simply a 'meete man for knowledge religion and liffe . . .'.[40] Jeremy Gibson's puritan statutes elaborated with the demand that he also be known as 'an Enemy to Popish Superstition, a Lover, and forward Embracer of Gods Truth . . .'.[41] But even public reputation was not enough. In an age of subscriptions and oaths, Gibson did not hesitate to require one more of the schoolmaster, this to his godly dedication.[42] At Heath, in Yorkshire, the master similarly had to be 'a man fearing God, zealous of the truth . . . diligent to train up his scholars not only in other learning and moral virtue, but also in the principles of Christian religion and farther understanding of the Holy Scriptures'; the usher was to be able to assist him as 'a man sound in religion . . .'[43] At Prescot, in Lancashire, the vicar considered the local gentlemen unfit, because of their backwardness in religion, to choose a suitable schoolmaster,

---

[35] Quoted in Cressy, 'Education and literacy', p. 147.
[36] Collinson, *Elizabethan Puritan Movement*, p. 85.
[37] *C.S.P.D. 1636–1637*, p. 429.
[38] Stockwood, *Sermon at Paules Crosse*, pp. 88–9. See also Greenham, *Two Learned and Godly Sermons*, sigs. A3, A3ᵛ.   [39] Gouge, *Domesticall Duties*, p. 588.   [40] Peacock, *Wakefield*, p. 13.
[41] B.L. MS Sloane 2204, fol. 29.
[42] The oath read: 'I doe in heart abhor all Popish Superstition . . . And I doe receive and reverence as the undoubted Word of God, the Books of the canonicall Scripture, comprised in the Old and New Testaments and the Truth in them contained . . .' (*ibid.*, fol. 29ᵛ).
[43] Cox, *Grammar School at Heath*, p. 50. See also the regulations for Oakham and Uppingham (Bingham, *Our Founder*, pp. 42–3).

since such a choice was 'meerly spirituall, and therefore requierethe men of
true religion, of sound conversation and good conscience . . .'.[44] To puritans, a
man could not effectively teach godliness unless he himself was godly. On the
other hand, where we might expect stress on religion from non-puritan
founders, we often do not find it. At Archbishop Harsnet's school in Chigwell,
the master was to be simply 'neither Papist nor Puritan . . .'.[45] Even Grindal, at
St Bees, left no special instructions concerning the master's godliness. It was,
then, the *degree* of stress on godly knowledge and on the repentant personal
life, presumably as an early stage of preparation for conversion, that
distinguished the recorded intentions of puritan school founders/statute
writers from non-puritans.

It must therefore remain a source of some puzzlement that puritans – so
very obviously concerned with the production of godly and learned
schoolmasters – did not advocate colleges or academies for their professional
training, in the manner of Richard Mulcaster's suggestion. Occasionally a
schoolmaster is discovered at a prophesying, though such attendance probably
testifies more to a concern for a future ministerial career than to designs for
the classroom. Here, puritan pressure again likely influenced the administration.
In 1583, for example, an order was issued by the Bishop of Chester and eight
preachers named by the Privy Council requiring all schoolmasters (among
others) to attend the exercises then being organized for the diocese.[46] But in
general puritans seem to have relied upon connexions with colleges and also
testimonials and suggestions from particular individuals to spread the
influence of the godly brotherhood to teaching, too. A degree and support
from a respected acquaintance became the passport to a teaching post. Typical
was the case of Thomas Wotton. Feeling himself incapable, because of his
own ignorance, of nominating a new master at Sandwich school, he wrote to
Laurence Humphrey, President of Magdalen College, asking him to suggest
someone who was simply a 'knowen, zelous christian man'.[47]

II

It was a common complaint in the late sixteenth and early seventeenth
centuries, and one in which puritans joined, that teachers were not accorded
status commensurate with their growing importance. Gone, perhaps, were the
days of widespread insensitivity to education, but Roger Ascham still
complained that more attention and greater salaries were paid to horse-

---

[44] Bailey, 'Prescot grammar school', *Trans. Hist. Soc. Lancs. & Cheshire*, 86, p. 11.
[45] Stott, *History of Chigwell School*, p. 152.   [46] Collinson, *Elizabethan Puritan Movement*, p. 211.
[47] *Thomas Wotton's Letter-Book*, ed. Eland, pp. 1–2.

trainers than to tutors.[48] In similar fashion, John Brinsley reminded schoolmasters not to be discouraged by the unthankfulness of parents, but also suggested that they make sure that they received their pay every quarter![49] Samuel Wright condemned the low status of teachers as arising 'through the malice of Satin . . .'.[50] Thomas Gataker reminded teachers that King David had thought it 'no scorne to play the part of a Scholemaster . . . Whence observe we, that Teaching even of children is no base profession . . .'[51] Others fondly rehearsed for their readers the great status of ancient schoolmasters.[52] Even public teachers may well have been regarded as lowly servants, given the statutes of Alford grammar school, which sought to protect its masters, and perhaps even raise their status, by providing them with the power to expel or refuse to admit 'all such as shall falsely and scandalously report anything of the schoolmaster . . .'. No one except the governors should presume to 'taunt and check [him], or to intermeddle with anything pertaining to his duty . . .'.[53] Even at the end of our period, a letter could complain that 'to bee a Schoolemaster is accounted a very inferiour employment. Whence it comes to passe, that many most fitt for this excellent worke abhorre the thought thereof . . .'[54]

It is very difficult to ascertain the degree to which the status of schoolmasters was dependent on salary, since an average worth is almost impossible to calculate.[55] Teachers frequently received entrance fees from an unknown number of boys, and occasionally also were given subsidized lodgings. Latin masters might generally expect an annual salary around £20 in the late sixteenth century, and something approaching £30 by the end of our period. Rogers has recently suggested, on the basis of a study of schoolmasters in Cheshire and Lancashire, that while prices rose about fivefold in the period

---

[48] Ascham, *Scholemaster*, p. 104. For the same analogy, see Cleland, *Institution of a Young Noble Man*, p. 29. Puritans reiterated this complaint (Granger, *Syntagma Grammaticum*, sig. B8ᵛ, and Woodward, *Childes Patrimony*, p. 158, who made the same point with the different criticism that parents spent more time selecting their child's clothes than they did his master).

[49] Brinsley, *Ludus Literarius*, p. 306.   [50] Wright, *Godly and Learned Sermons*, p. 264.

[51] Gataker, *Davids Instructer*, p. 16; also pp. 17–18 for his opinion that the callings which God had especially commended were 'commonly most disgraced and contemned in the World'.

[52] See esp. Morrice, *Apologie for Schoolemasters*, sigs. Bᵛff., C5ᵛ–8ᵛ, D, D2ᵛ, D3.

[53] Even the governors could not fire the schoolmaster until he had been condemned by two magistrates, one of whom the schoolmaster could choose (Brown, *Elizabethan Schooldays*, p. 129; Watson, *English Grammar Schools*, p. 134; Stowe, *English Grammar Schools*, p. 82).

[54] B.L. MS Sloane 649, fol. 57ᵛ.

[55] But note, generally, Robert Burton's 'scale' of employments:

> A Merchants gaine is great that goes to Sea,
>   A Souldier embossed all in gold:
> A Flatterer lies fox'd in brave array,
>   A Scholler only ragged to behold.

(Burton, *Anatomy of Melancholy*, p. 175).

1540–1640, schoolmasters' salaries rose only about threefold. The occupation was evidently under increasing financial pressure.[56] There seems little reason to suspect that puritan founders paid exceptionally high wages to schoolmasters. Their generosity here evidently did not match that towards lectureships, for which salaries occasionally rose to three figures. The scale provided in the will of John Rayney (proved April 1633) is typical. A citizen and draper of London, he left £40 a year for a lecturer at St Michael Cornhill, London, and £30 a year for a lecturer at Worsborough, Yorkshire, the site of his birth, but only £13 6s. 8d. a year for a schoolmaster in Worsborough.[57] For teachers operating outside the confines and reasonably assured salaries of endowed schools, all would have depended on what the teacher thought the market could bear in the way of fees. As well, masters in endowed schools could receive additional income from private tutoring, or from teaching subjects of skills – notably writing – which were not part of their contractual obligation.

For founders, one of the more troublesome questions concerning the role of the schoolmaster was whether he could also be a minister. In practice, this duality of roles seems to have been quite common. Some puritans who maintained ministerial seminaries in their homes also accepted younger pupils for non-professional, but obviously godly, instruction.[58] Nonetheless, the question caused much concern and difference of opinion. Much has been made by historians of education of the process of 'secularization' dating from the fifteenth century.[59] Attempts by founders and controlling companies to limit the involvement of the church's administration in schools seems, however, to have been a drive against an impure bureaucracy rather than a universal statement against the close connexion of church and education. Occasionally, as at Exeter, there was the stipulation that preaching required the prior approval of the Council.[60] But there were even provisions in puritan schools, such as

[56] Simon places schoolmasters' salaries at the middle of the sixteenth century, at around £10, but says that
      day fees and 'gratuities', as well as perquisites of the office (such as, frequently, lodgings) made this only
      a base figure. As early as 1531 Vives had proposed a system of state salaries for schoolmasters
      (DeMolen, 'Richard Mulcaster', p. 122). There were occasional exceptions to paying higher wages to
      those teaching more advanced studies. In the 1570s at St Olave's School, Southwark, the writing master
      was to be paid (according to a school memorandum) the same as the grammar master, since he (the for-
      mer) had so many more pupils (Simon, *Education and Society*, pp. 371, 374). Harsnet at Chigwell allowed
      the unusual distribution of £20 for the Latin master and £25 for the English master (Stott, *History of
      Chigwell School*, pp. 146, 161).
[57] Wallis, 'Worsborough grammar school', *Yorks. Arch. Journal*, 39, p. 150. In 1633, it was reported that
      the schoolmaster was paid 3s. 4d. per year for each grammar student, and 2s. 6d. per year for each
      'petty' student (*ibid.*, p. 151).   [58] On seminaries see below, Ch. 13.
[59] The first prohibition of a ministerial schoolmaster of which I am aware occurred at Sevenoaks school,
      Kent, in 1432. See esp. McMahon, *Education*, pp. 100–9 and *passim*; Simon, *Education and Society, passim*;
      Cross, *Church and People*, in which secularization is a major theme.
[60] Parry, *Exeter School*, pp. 104–5; B.L. MS Sloane 2204, fol. 29. For some local examples of the combin-
      ation of the two occupations, see Chalmers, 'Puritanism in Leicestershire', p. 276, and Smith,
      'Educational development in Lichfield and Coventry', pp. 137–8.

Wakefield, that the candidate appointed as schoolmaster not be 'called either to a Pastorall Charge, or hired to serve as Preacher, Minister, or Curate, in the Church . . . '.[61] The separation of the two tasks of preaching and teaching in a puritan school likely had nothing to do with the desire to 'free' education from clerical control. The objection (as in the argument against allowing masters of colleges to hold benefices) was rather based on fear of the dilution of either of such important tasks. There was, however, no hard-and-fast puritan opinion on this question. At Harrow the founder, John Lyon, who also left a sum to endow thirty sermons a year, required that the schoolmaster, if qualified, and *if it would not interfere with his teaching*, be given the first chance of delivering the godly sermons.[62] The puritan statutes of the free school at Otley took the opposite path from those of Wakefield in requiring not only that the master be a preacher, but that he preach at least every month.[63]

Many ministers, even before they ventured from college to countryside, had served in the twin capacities of tutor and preacher in the college. The combination of the two offices was therefore not a completely new experience. The various solutions offered by puritan writers and statutes, however, leave one unclear as to the comparable weight of the two factors of theory and pragmatism. Puritans may have concluded that, because of the similarity of purpose, theoretically the minister–schoolmaster link lay outside the prohibition they usually placed on ministers holding a second vocation. At least for those who believed in a presbyterian polity,however, this would seem to contravene the distinction of the church offices of doctor and pastor. In pragmatic terms, puritans may have placed the driving need for both ministers and schoolmasters above any qualms over the union of distinct vocations; indeed, it was undoubtedly better to have a godly minister than a reprobate teaching school. Furthermore, the union of functions might well provide continuity of approach and interpretation from childhood to adult membership in church and community.

But, whether clerical or lay, teachers were perceived as the lynchpin between training at the knee in the household and adult exhortation from the pulpit. Schoolmasters and children were soon seen to be bound by a special covenant which resembled that between children and their fathers.[64] The value of a close relationship between parents and the teacher was emphasized by early humanists and reiterated by the Elizabethan Mulcaster.[65] William Gouge considered teaching to be primarily an extension of parenthood; the master was therefore to be responsible to the 'Church and Commonwealth' as well as to the children.[66] He condemned those who 'cared not to what

---

[61] B.L. MS Sloane 2204, fol. 29.   [62] Bod. Lib. MS Tanner 121, fol. 2ᵛ.

[63] Padgett, ed., *Chronicles of Otley*, p. 17.

[64] See, for example, Gataker, *Davids Instructer*, p. 8; Sorocold, *Supplication for Saints*, pp. 288–9.

[65] Charlton, *Education*, pp. 202–3.

[66] Gouge, *Domesticall Duties*, p. 587. See also F. Bunny, *Guide unto Godlinesse*, p. 143; Gataker, *Davids Instructer*, p. 16.

schoolmaster they put their children, be he profane, or popish, or unlearned, especially if he be a kinsman, or one of their friends.'[67] The schoolmaster was thus both head of the household and proto-minister to those in his charge, and was therefore commonly included in the protection offered to superiors under the fifth commandment.[68] Indeed, the schoolmaster served as one of the more common allusions of godly metaphors: Edward Dering, for example, talked of Jesus as the schoolmaster of the godly; the papists, naturally, studied under the Antichrist.[69]

Thomas Granger, puritan author of both sermons and school texts, explained that it was also the function of the schoolmaster to provide early direction. Implicit was the assumption that such malleable students would have arrived with their wills already broken. Children could be drawn to follow any pathway because they were so pliable.[70] One of the first duties of the teacher, Granger insisted, was 'to drawe them from this varietie and mutabilitie, to a certain uniformitie, and constancie . . .'.[71] Yet puritans reflected experience as well as theory. Granger was enough of an empiricist about children to recognize their 'fickle, and restless' natures, which, encouraged by parental neglect, could easily stand in the way of successful indoctrination.[72] Reflecting, too, the Ramist emphasis on the agreement of art (in this case pedagogical concepts) with the external world, Granger stressed that the schoolmaster was limited in his effectiveness by the constraints of nature on the pupil.[73]

This bond of master and minister amounted in puritan ideas to a godly alliance.

And yet who come neerer to God then the Ministers of his word? Or who come neerer to Ministers then Schole-masters do? What is their Schole but a private Church? if it be ordered as it ought. If Christian Families be so, Christian Scholes much more. Or what are they themselves, (if they be at least what they should be) but private Catechists, but private Preachers?[74]

Thomas Becon had already defined 'the office and duty of a good and godly school-master, [as] first of all, and above all things, to instil into the minds of the younge christian children true persuasions of God, and of his holy religion . . .'.[75] Thomas Granger noted a parallel problem in that the two vocations often faced the same difficulty of convincing audiences that the message in question was directed to each attendant in particular.[76] William

---

[67] Gouge, *Domesticall Duties*, p. 543.   [68] See, for example, Brinsley, *True Watch*, pp. 72–3.
[69] Dering, *XXVII Lectures*, sigs. L.i^v, M.iiii and *passim*.
[70] Granger, *Syntagma Grammaticum*, sig. B6^v.   [71] *Ibid.*, sig. B6^v.   [72] *Ibid.*, sig. A4^v.
[73] *Ibid.*, sig. A7^v.   [74] Gataker, *Davids Instructer*, p. 18.
[75] Becon, *Catechism with Other Pieces*, p. 378; also pp. 378–83.
[76] Granger, *Syntagma Logicum*, sig. B8.

Perkins insisted that a schoolmaster was bound not only to be a passive receptacle of the faith 'in the assembly, when hee heareth the word, and receiveth the Sacraments'; he also had to be a proselytizer 'in the office of teaching'.[77] It is significant of the importance of schoolmasters in the puritan scheme for the reform of society that Perkins should use this example to illustrate the universal necessity of superimposing a general calling upon specific vocation.

At the heart of this perceived alliance of minister and teacher stood the abhorrence of popery. Great emphasis was therefore placed on expelling all papists from teaching positions.[78] John Brinsley, always illustrative of puritan educational directions, argued that schoolmasters had to be brothers-in-arms to the godly clergy in this final struggle. He therefore emphasized the office of the teacher 'next [only] unto the worke and charge of the holy Ministery, which we also are to helpe to furnish . . .'. At Ashby school, Brinsley may well have fulfilled his own expectations of a godly schoolmaster. William Lilly, one of Brinsley's pupils, later remembered him as of great scholarly ability, 'very severe in his life and conversation [and] . . . in religion he was a strict Puritan . . .'.[79] Schoolmasters were obviously instruments of academic knowledge, but in their vocation they were also to serve as slightly subordinate members of the special caste which would lead the nation to godly reform.

Schoolmasters similarly figure large in puritan hagiography concerning the working towards conversion. Samuel Clarke noted that Arthur Hildersam's schoolmaster had been the 'first blessed instrument that God was pleased to make use of to work in him a liking and relish of the Reformed Religion'.[80] Simonds D'Ewes offered the same point, though from a critical stance, denouncing his former teacher who, though a good Latinist, had had 'no regard to the souls of his scholars, though he were a minister . . .'. D'Ewes especially criticized him for not making greater classroom use of his sermons.[81] Even if the godly schoolmaster could not hope to work conversion in all his charges, he could at least start the process and join the household–church effort to keep them to the path of external obedience to God's commands. This was the legacy which the puritan Richard Norwood, surveyor of Bermuda, remembered about his early education:

During this time [*c.* 1600, when he was ten] the Lord was pleased by means of my

[77] Perkins, *Workes*, I, p. 759.
[78] See, for example, the petition from the Commons to King James (C.U.L. MS Gg.I.29(F), Pt II, No. 50, fol. 37) and Rushworth, *Historical Collections*, I, p. 186 for comment. See also a note of 1591 (?) on Lancashire and Cheshire, which listed the allowance of ungodly schoolmasters (who were not even examined) next to a complaint concerning the influx of seminary priests (P.R.O. S.P. 12/240/138).   [79] Brinsley, *Consolation*, p. 44; Fox, *Ashby*, 27.
[80] Clarke, *Lives of Thirty-two Divines*, p. 115. See also Gataker, *Davids Instructer*, p. 7.
[81] D'Ewes, *Autobiography*, ed. Halliwell, I, p. 62.

parents, school-dame, schoolmasters and sermons, to plant in my heart some seeds of religion and the fear of God, which though no fruits of regeneration, yet through the blessing of God they were special preservatives to keep me for many years from divers enormous sins whereof I was in danger and wherein in likelihood I should have perished.[82]

Puritan school statutes testified to this same fervent concern that the schoolmaster implant early the seeds of godliness. At base, these could be merely a more emphatic version of the norm of the age. The orders issued in 1599 by the Brewers Company of London for Richard Platt's school at Aldenham (founded 1596) insisted that the master's prime task was to 'have a speciall care to implante the seedes of vertue, pietie, and true Religion in his schollers myndes'.[83] But they could also aim at a new godly form of socialization. The most illuminating puritan statutes of the period, Jeremy Gibson's for Wakefield, required that the schoolmaster, though a layman, was to act 'as it were [as] a Minister, and Preacher of the same truth to his Schollers under him'. He was specifically required to use the sermon as the basis of the following Monday's lessons.[84] The alliance was further consolidated by making the schoolmaster the watchdog as well as the propagandist of godliness: boys who did not attend church, or who 'upon admonicion and correction cannot be drawn to frequent it with Reverence' were to be suspended.[85]

Disputes over teachers and schools also testify to the importance of the connexion. In the early 1580s trouble at Kilkhampton, Cornwall, led to High Commission action against David Blake, the local schoolmaster. He was accused of ignoring the order of the Bishop of Exeter to cease teaching. It was said that Blake and Eusabius Paget, the nonconformist rector of Kilkhampton (and a 'man well known to this Courte'), had built a new schoolhouse which they called a 'reformed College'. If this were not proof enough of the closeness of the vocational relationship, Blake, a layman, was also accused of preaching publicly and expounding the Scriptures.[86] Similarly, at Easton in Leicestershire, Francis Whinnell, though only a layman, and unlicensed, served as both schoolmaster and preacher. In 1627 he was charged with encouraging his students to take notes at sermons, which he would then get them, in school, to compare with his own notes. That Whinnell evidently also conducted a 'conventicle', at which sermons were repeated and expounded, did nothing to endear him to the authorities.[87] At Prescot in Lancashire, an Elizabethan dis-

[82] Norwood, *Journal of Richard Norwood*, ed. Craven & Hayward, p. 5.
[83] Since Platt remained a member of the company until his death in 1600, it would seem reasonable to suppose that the orders reflected his personal views (Beevor, Evans, & Savory, *History and Register of Aldenham School*, pp. xv, xvi, xvii, xx).   [84] B.L. MS Sloane 2204, fols. 29–30.
[85] B.L. MS Lansdowne 988, fol. 61.   [86] L.P.L. Carte Misc. XII/15.
[87] When he left Easton in 1627, certain parishioners evidently 'gadded' to hear him in neighbouring Great Bowden (Chalmers, 'Puritanism in Leicestershire', unpub. M.A. thesis, Univ. of Leeds, 1962, pp. 272–3.

pute of the 1580s and 1590s over the school resulted in a letter from the incumbent vicar, Thomas Mead, M.A. of King's College and a puritan, to Roger Goad, the puritan Provost of King's, which owned the impropriation. Mead pleaded for continuation of the school with the argument that catechizing and godly instruction of the youth would be the main help in removing popish superstition, with which the area was infested. He reminded Goad that reformation would come more quickly 'wen the minister and the scholmaster are one hand at the elbow of the other . . .' and concluded that it was with this understanding that schools had been established near churches. A letter of similar purpose to the Earl of Derby, the leading figure in Lancashire, argued that 'the scholmaster dothe prepare substance for the minister to worke upon, to make therof a spirituall building unto God'.[88] Where there was already a puritan minister, the chances of furthering local reformation by also hiring a forward schoolmaster were likely increased.

At Cranbrook, Kent, in 1575 a controversy erupted between Richard Fletcher, the non-puritan incumbent minister on the one hand, and Thomas Good, the local schoolmaster and John Strowd, a deprived puritan minister from the West Country, on the other. Strowd, employed by Fletcher as a curate, had evidently become a rival for the affections of the congregation. When Good defended Strowd, Fletcher's son, Richard, minister at Rye, Sussex, and later Bishop of London, replied by denouncing the right of a mere schoolmaster, whom he lumped with artificers, to 'meddle' with the duties of a separate calling.[89] He accused Strowd, in terms that puritans used against radicals, of coming 'from his occupacion broughte up at the feete of some mechanicall master unapproved unfurnyshed excepte that he be with the margente of an englishe bible . . .'.[90] Good, in reply, defended his own teaching and Strowd's continued right to preach. A bitter dispute followed, which culminated in an admonition to Good in archdeacon's court for neglect of his teaching and the inhibition of Strowd from preaching.[91] For our interest the important point is that even amid a controversy which might tell against his own position, the puritan schoolmaster strove to protect the godly minister. Though this was the duty of all members of the community, it was especially noteworthy when a person with the social visibility of a schoolmaster openly took sides in an ecclesiastical dispute.

The public association of the two vocations also became clear at Beverley Minster. In noting the puritan habit of repeating sermons to schoolchildren, I cited the example of John Garthwaite, M.A. of Christ's, headmaster of

---

[88] Bailey, ed., *Prescot Court Leet and Other Records*, p. 300; Bailey, 'Prescot grammar school', *Trans. Hist. Soc. Lancs. & Cheshire*, 86, pp. 3–4, 10.

[89] Morrice MSS, Vol. B, II, fols. 6–8ᵛ. Fletcher specifically argued that Good's pupils were not fulfilling their educational potential. [90] *Ibid.*, fol. 10. The reference was to the Geneva Bible.

[91] *Ibid.*, fols. 11, 16ff. (I have amended this paragraph from the hardcover edition in light of Collinson, 'Cranbrook and the Fletchers', *Reformation Principle and Practice*, ed. P. N. Brooks, esp. pp. 187–94.)

Beverley Minster since 1614, and an ordained minister himself (1617). In 1631 in Chancery Court, Richard Rhodes, the puritan lecturer of Beverley Minster, admitted that the scholars came to his house on Sundays to repeat the day's sermon, which they had already written out. Rhodes simply went over the main points with them again. The minister was thus singling out the intellectual elite of the next generation (which probably included the offspring of the socio-economic elite) for additional effort towards a particular vision of godliness. The possible effect of such indoctrination was not lost on his judges. The Court held that such classes were not illegal, but indeed were suspicious. Rhodes was dismissed with an order to cease such meetings.[92] Throughout the Laudian period – though the overall effect on educational opportunity remains to be calculated – puritan schoolmasters were caught in the net of 'Thorough', commonly when they were found to be using the wrong catechism.[93]

But while investigation on religious grounds might have been more scrupulous in the 1630s, it is important to note that all interested parties seem always to have comprehended how crucial was the role of the schoolmaster. Struggles to unite desk and pulpit in the battle for godliness were symptomatic of the puritan drive throughout the late sixteenth and early seventeenth centuries. In Colchester, for example, difficulty over the appointment of schoolmasters tested the godly forces in the 1580s. After George Northey, the puritan preacher of the town, was suspended in 1583 for non-subscribing, the Colchester bailiffs complained to Francis Walsingham, a former recorder of the town.[94] The challenge to the area's developing godliness, however, also threatened the professional success of the projected schoolmaster, Nicholas Coulte. Emphasizing that he had not yet decided to come to Colchester, he wrote in part to seek assurances that 'there is an ordinary publike sanctifyed ministery [since this] is one speciall point not the leaste to be regarded'.[95] A further dispute broke out in 1588, upon Samuel Harsnet's decision to quit his post as schoolmaster, 'chosing rather to folowe his studies at Cambridg, than ye painfull trade of teaching'.[96] The choice of successor lay between Mark Sadlington, supported by Harsnet and Francis Walsingham, and William Bentley, who had wider support, including that of several Cambridge colleges. Walsingham, a man himself forward in religion, noted that he had heard good reports of Sadlington's learning and 'sinceritie in religion', and offered his future services to the town – a tempting offer – if it would appoint Sadlington.[97] In favour of William Bentley, schoolmaster at Dedham, came

[92] Marchant, *Puritans and Church Courts*, pp. 248, 271.
[93] For several examples, see Cliffe, *Puritan Gentry*, p. 81.   [94] E.R.O. Morant MS D/Y 2/6, p. 89.
[95] *Ibid.*, D/Y 2/7, p. 165.   [96] *Ibid.*, D/Y 2/4, p. 149.
[97] *Ibid.*, D/Y 2/9, p. 269. Nor did Harsnet, who had taught at Colchester for two years, forget the town; as Archbishop of York, he granted Colchester a library (*ibid.*, D/Y 2/10,. pp. 21, 175).

letters from a great variety of sources – from Thomas, Baron Darcie, who also offered a favour in return; from Bentley's own schoolmaster; from the fellows of Clare Hall; from John Knewstub; from the suspended George Northey; from Emmanuel College, which letter would doubtless count highly with the godly faction; and finally, from Roger Goad, William Whitaker, Laurence Chaderton, and Andrew Downes.[98] The dispute grew testy: accusations of insufficient learning and superior godliness were traded back and forth. Puritans likely ranged themselves on Bentley's side for two reasons. The first was that he was seen to be qualified – he was an M.A. and recent fellow of Clare Hall, and an experienced teacher. But secondly Bentley comprehended the godly purpose of education. In a letter to the Corporation of Colchester, Bentley noted the 'greate weight' of such an appointment, especially as his view of the students was that 'beinge now tender plantes [they] may hereafter growe to be fruitefull trees in the lordes orchyarde'.[99] With the victory of Bentley, the godly forces demonstrated by wide and forceful participation the emphasis that they placed on the appointment of a known godly man to the mastership of a school of some consequence.

What distinguished the puritan concept of the schoolmaster, then, was not any greater or lesser emphasis on his learning, but rather a concentration on his godly purity. And herein lay the source of some confusion. It is well known that many ministers taught school for a few years while awaiting vacant benefices.[100] The attitude that teaching was less a vocation than a temporary occupation may well have been most prevalent among graduates, who could easily find a church living in the first half of our period. Puritans also seem to have viewed teaching posts as refuges for deprived or persecuted ministers. John Ball noted to his fellow nonconformist ministers that if he ever had to leave England, he could always earn a living teaching school.[101] As well, a post as a domestic chaplain to a gentleman, which would probably involve teaching any children of the family, would provide employment while also protecting the puritan minister from either the necessity of performing loathsome ceremonies or the threat of suspension and deprivation.

But a post as a schoolmaster was not only a way of filling time and stomach before a benefice or lectureship became available; schools also served as vocational seminaries in which the master could practise his public speaking and hone his godly arguments. Catechizing schoolchildren must also have

[98] *Ibid.*, D/Y 2/4, *passim.*   [99] *Ibid.*, p. 97.
[100] Feyerharm noted that the shift from teaching to a benefice often took place within five years ('Status of schoolmaster', esp. p. 105). See also Spufford, *Contrasting Communities*, p. 186; Wood, *Reformation*, p. 327; Marchant, *Puritans and Church Courts*, p. 38; Richardson, *English Preachers*, p. 6; O'Day, *English Clergy*, p. 224. This process continued in New England (Smith, 'Teacher in puritan culture', *Harvard Educational Review*, 36, p. 398).
[101] Clarke, *Lives of Thirty-two divines*, p. 150. For examples of puritan private schools and tutors, see Cliffe, *Puritan Gentry*, pp. 77–9.

been good practice for later dealing with backward adults. Some puritan ministers may therefore have entered schools before taking upon themselves the heavy obligation of a lectureship or cure of souls out of a spirit of insufficiency. Occasionally, teaching school was seen by a downcast puritan as something of a 'demotion'. John Field, the presbyterian organizer, wrote to Anthony Gilby in 1571/2 complaining that the efforts of the church authorities in putting him from his living had forced him to teach children rather than a congregation.[102] Such discontent, however, was far more likely to emanate from despair at a perception of being deprived of one's true calling than from conclusions concerning teaching *per se*. On the other hand, it seems unlikely that many of the ministers who did turn to teaching as a temporary occupation would have remained once the better-paying opportunity presented itself.[103] Though this requires further research, the lack of strict differentiation between the two vocations, and the view that the prime purpose of schooling was religious indoctrination, may have meant that teaching, for puritans at least, could not readily emerge as a 'profession' distinct from the ministry. Doubtless, status deprivation also slowed this development, as, too, would the necessarily common practice among teachers of maintaining another occupation, generally as a craftsman or farmer, a habit which drew criticism but, evidently, seldom funds to obviate the need.[104]

Puritans thus saw the schoolmaster as they also perceived the tutor and the godly minister – as an individual upon whom the forward development of England depended. The laxity of control by the administration at the school level meant that to a greater degree than in church or university puritans could attempt to actualize their attitudes. This, as we saw in the previous chapter, did not involve a radical reorientation of curriculum or texts, but rather only a greater stress on the teaching of fervent religion. With schoolmasters, too, puritans reflected the contemporary greater emphasis on academic qualifications and virtuous 'conversation'. Where they differed sharply was in insisting that 'vocational' skills be accompanied by a burning godliness that would be imprinted on the next generation of adults. The schoolmaster was therefore portrayed as the crucial link between correct early household instruction and efficacious ministering to adults. To the end of selecting only godly teachers, puritan statutes imposed religious oaths and an unusually heavy regimen of religious instruction upon sucessful candidates. Finally, the godly teacher was to labour hand-in-hand with the minister. The teacher was to take the scriptural lessons of the preacher and combine them with his own pedagogical skills

[102] C.U.L. MS Baker 32.23, p. 447.
[103] Feyerharm, 'Status of schoolmaster', esp. pp. 105–8. Feyerharm demonstrates that longevity of service correlated directly with salary in a sample of teachers in Norwich.
[104] *Ibid.*, p. 106. Some schools, however, forbade their masters to hold any other occupation. See, for example, St Albans (Carlisle, *Endowed Grammar Schools*, p. 516).

so that the household lessons of repetition and reinforcement would not be lost in the youthful years. And where there was no forward minister, the godly schoolmaster, assisted by purified texts and his own training under a puritan college tutor, could venture alone into the wilderness, so that, while much of the present generation might effectively be lost, the next could continue the progress to Jerusalem.

11

THE REFORM OF
HIGHER EDUCATION

I

The traditional function of the university in Western Europe had been the education of the clergy. The early Reformation contained little suggestion, in either argument or practice, that this primary function would be altered. Indeed, more than ever before, the universities became the havens of the reformers' hopes for the next generation of godly proselytizers. The urgency and complexity of the educational task facing the reformers was enhanced at the beginning of our period by the common argument that the ignorant propagation of unreformed doctrine could slow the building of a godly society, and might well lead to a formal resurrection of popery.[1] The educational state of the English clergy as Elizabeth ascended the throne fully justified the grave concern of the reformers. Supplications from the countryside complained that too many ministers were 'utterlie without learning'; learned reformers added their complaints from the universities.[2] Nor did they fabricate the problem; only a small proportion of the nation's ministers held degrees.[3] During our period, the ministry became generally university-educated. By the seventeenth century there was a common expectation that a new minister would hold a degree. This change was fostered by pressure from the administration, rising standards of lay education, and the increasingly professional nature of the universities themselves.[4] Nonetheless, the improvement took time and

---

[1] The theme that ignorance and popery went together was extremely common. See, for example, Gilby, *Pleasaunt Dialogue*, sig. N2^v.

[2] Morrice MSS, Vol. B, I, pp. 185, 143–4, 149, 191–2; *ibid.*, Vol. A, OLP., fol. 101^{r-v}; *C.S.P.D. 1598–1601*, p. 362; *C.S.P.D. 1591–1594*, p. 158; *Abstract of Certain Acts*, pp. 90–1; Gilby, *A Pleasaunt Dialogue*, sig. D3^v; Chaderton, *Excellent and Godly Sermon*, sig. C.iii.

[3] In the archdeaconry of Lincoln–Stow in 1576 only 14.1% of the clergy were graduates; in Leicester 14.8% held degrees. Even in London in 1560 only 47% of incumbents were graduates. In the diocese of Worcester in the same year, a mere 19% had a degree (Foster, *State of Clergy*, pp. 453–4; Seaver, *Puritan Lectureships*, p. 130; Hill, *Economic Problems*, p. 207, citing the figures of D.M. Barratt). See also O'Day, *English Clergy*, pp. 28, 132; Purvis, 'Literacy of later Tudor clergy in Yorkshire', in Cuming, ed., *Studies in Church History*, 5, esp. pp. 156ff. For contemporary analysis, see the puritan county surveys, excerpted in Peel, *Seconde Parte of a Register*, II, pp. 88–174.

[4] O'Day, *English Clergy*, pp. 139, 142–3. For specific figures on the rate of improvement of clerical education, see the sources cited in the previous footnote.

220

much effort, and not all the evidence from the provinces was encouraging, even after years of attempted reform. The continuation of puritan cries concerning ministerial standards cannot be ascribed solely to reckless polemic when defenders of the system also brought forth such damning testimony.[5]

At the beginning of Elizabeth's reign both church and state attempted to coerce unfit ministers into schools and universities. Though the goal was a graduate ministry, a more immediate aid was needed by many of the ministers currently serving England's ten thousand parishes. The employment of lectors could ease the burden only temporarily. To build for the future bishops issued extensive plans for private and communal ministerial study and also for testing. The most thorough plan was issued by Whitgift himself in 1585; even this was expanded by Convocation in 1586/7.[6] This effort continued in the seventeenth century, and was enlarged to include facilities for research in divinity. Most prominent was the abortive plan of Matthew Sutcliffe, Dean of Exeter, to found a protestant divinity college at Chelsea in 1610.[7]

In tracts, too, the forces of the administration urged improvement. Richard Cosin, in replying to the presbyterians, argued that the best-learned ministers in an archdeaconry should voluntarily help the less-learned to improve their knowledge of Scripture.[8] John Bridges also welcomed the improvements, but took a more cautious line, arguing that reformers should support the attempts of the administration to raise standards by internal reform.[9] These plans of the episcopal hierarchy were attacked by radical contemporaries as a pitiful attempt directed primarily to the end of silencing criticism. Illustrative of this clash was an episcopal suggestion that it be unlawful to appoint non-preachers to church livings. This, however, involved an immense legal stumbling block; the plan necessitated giving bishops legal powers to reject an 'insufficient' candidate and to dismiss any *quaere impedit* brought in such a case.[10] This would have meant a shift in local power from the nobility and gentry to the bishops; as a political possibility for passage through Parliament, the plan was stillborn. Such impractical suggestions, as well as tardiness in introducing reforms, drew

[5] For examples of bishops, in the late sixteenth and early seventeenth centuries, reporting the deplorable level of their clergy's education, see *C.S.P.D. 1598–1601*, p. 362; *C.S.P.D. 1611–1618*, p. 2; Greaves, *Society and Religion*, pp. 78, 80.

[6] For accounts of this pressure, see especially Collinson, 'Puritan classical movement', unpub. Ph.D. thesis, Univ. of London, 1957, pp. 244–60; O'Day, *English Clergy*, esp. pp. 72–4. For details of specific attempts at reform, see also Frere, *Visitation Articles and Injunctions*, III, pp. 2, 12–13, 31, 36–8, 39–43, 63; Parry, *Founding of Exeter School*, p. 11; Foster, *State of the Church*, I, pp. xix–xxi; Raine, ed., *Injunctions . . . of Richard Barnes*, pp. 20, 70, 78; Marchant, *Puritans and Church Courts*, pp. 17–18; Gee & Hardy, eds., *Documents Illustrative of English Church History*, p. 483; L.P.L. Whitgift's Register, I, fol. 131r–v.

[7] Jordan, *Charities of London*, p. 254. [8] Cosin, *Answer to Abstract*, sigs. C.iiv–iii.

[9] Bridges, *Defence*, esp. pp. 481, 486ff., 493, 1272–3.

[10] B.L. MS Add. 28,571, fols. 187–92 (undated), 'The Bps: proceedings and opinions touching those thinges which were committed to theire consideration'. See O'Day, *English Clergy*, pp. 79ff., for the legal problems involved in the action of *quaere impedit*.

criticism to the effect that the episcopal effort was a sham, intended to make bishops 'seeme to desire a learned Ministerie, as well as these reformers'.[11] Francis Knollys, too, though a less virulent commentator, nonetheless reminded Burghley of 'how vyolent the Archebysshoppe [Whitgift] hathe often bene agaynst the request of the parlement' for learned ministers.[12] Harsh penalties for infringement of minor clerical regulations suggested to reformers that for the hierarchy, conformity came before learned preaching in a minister.[13]

Parliament and Council also involved themselves in the reform of the clergy; as lay institutions they were less defensive about the condition of the church, and less loath to pressure the church's administration.[14] Petitions and bills abounded under Elizabeth, but, despite the occasional approval of both Commons and Lords, the intransigence of the queen meant that none became law.[15] To many, Elizabeth must have seemed more a Laodicea than a Gloriana. As well, private puritan plans for the provision of learned ministers were frequently issued during the sitting of Parliament; even if not formally directed to Parliament as petitions, they necessitated action by that body for the fulfilment of their proposed reforms.[16]

It must have seemed obvious to puritans, therefore, that they would have to develop a system of ministerial in-service training. The main puritan effort came in the form of prophesyings, and the later exercises which reached their zenith in England under James I.[17] In England prophesyings were, quite simply, regular gatherings of the clergy under learned moderators in which the best-learned ministers expounded on a given text and conferred among themselves.[18] Unlearned ministers were required to attend for the purpose of instruction; they were given a measure of Scripture to study and were later examined on it. At Northampton, for example, every second Saturday morning, from nine until eleven o'clock, in the presence of the congregation, the ministers spoke in turn on the interpretation of a text. Following this, the

---

[11] Udall, *State of Church*, p. 361. See also Gifford, *Dialogue*, Epistle.

[12] B.L. MS Lansdowne 64, No. 32, fol. 86.

[13] On this point, see the persuasive argument by Coolidge, *Pauline Renaissance*, esp. Ch. 2.

[14] See, for example, P.R.O. S.P. 12/282/71 (undated, but Elizabethan). A similar bill (dated 1604 in *C.S.P.D.*) resides as P.R.O. S.P. 14/8/66.

[15] See, for example, Bod. Lib. MS Tanner 78, No. 41, fols. 84–6ᵛ; *C.S.P.D. 1547–1580*, p. 284; Morrice MSS, Vol. A, OLP., fols. 156ᵛ–8.

[16] See, for example, 'A meane for the establishinge of a learned and sufficient ministrye' (1586) and 'Articles of reformation of the mynisterie' (1586), both in Peel, *Seconde Parte of a Register*, pp. 198–202.

[17] The best account of prophesyings in Collinson, *Elizabethan Puritan Movement*, esp. pp. 168–76. See also O'Day, *English Clergy*, pp. 72–4, 167. For briefer mentions, see Richardson, *Puritanism in North-West England*, pp. 65–70; Marchant, *Puritans and Church Courts*, pp. 17–18, 30–1, 134–5, 169; Haigh, *Reformation and Resistance*, pp. 240, 300–2, 325; Hughes, *Reformation in England*, III, pp. 182–6.

[18] On occasion, prophesyings could also aid expatriate ministers to join the English search for superior interpretation. John Cowper, the exiled Scottish minister, is known to have attended the exercise at Saltash, Cornwall (Cameron & Rait, eds., *The Warrender Papers*, I. pp. 203–5).

ministers withdrew for further discussion in private. They were bound to adhere closely to the text, and had to have prior approval in order to speak at all.[19] By application of this common pattern learning was conjoined to godly knowledge and due order, in preference to enthusiasm.[20] All conversation (with very minor exceptions) was to be in English. Laymen were sometimes admitted, but only very rarely allowed to speak. Prophesyings were thus small conventions of people with a similar calling who regarded themselves as a community separate from the greater society in which they worked. The purpose of the exercise was twofold: first, the raising of the educational standards of the non-graduate clergy, and, secondly, the protestantization of ministers who, graduate or not, might be lagging behind the reformed ideas of the founders of the exercise. As ordinands became better educated, however, the exercises tended to become more the functions of equals than were the purely instructional seminars of the 1560s and 1570s.[21] The widespread existence of the later exercises – the diocese of Chester contained fourteen in 1584, and Lincolnshire six in 1614[22] – supports the thesis of their continued importance. In the early seventeenth century, too, combination lectures often served the function of prophesyings while they provided sermons in poor or outlying parishes.[23]

All the evidence points to the conclusion that prophesyings began as instruments of puritan religious and educational policy, emphasized by godly ministers and laymen alike.[24] Puritans constantly petitioned, on the basis of educational value, to establish or continue such assemblies.[25] They also fre-

---

[19] P.R.O. S.P. 12/78/38 fol. 243[r–v]; B.L. MS Lansdowne 64, No. 16, fol. 51[r–v], describing 'Articles' of 1590 against the ministers of Northamptonshire and Warwickshire for holding *classes* and synods. See also Serjeantson, *History of the Church of All Saints, Northampton*, pp. 104–8.

[20] See the 'Order of the Prophesie at Norwich in Anno 1575', reprinted in Browne, *History of Congregationalism*, pp. 18–20; C.U.L. MS Ff.v.14, No. 8, fols. 85–7, 'Rules and orders . . . in Buckynghamshyre touchinge the exercyse of theym selves . . .', which also required speakers to 'register' beforehand, and to stick closely to the text at hand.

[21] On this point, see Collinson, 'Lectures by combination', p. 212.

[22] Richardson, *Puritanism*, pp. 65–6; Collinson, *Elizabethan Puritan Movement*, p. 481. See also B.L. MS Add. 8.199, a letter of 7 June 1717 from Ralph Thoresby to John Strype, which mentions that the Lincoln exercise was supported by 74 lecturers. J. A. Newton noted 47 or 48 preachers involved in the early seventeenth-century exercise at Halifax ('Puritanism in the diocese of York', pp. 218–19). For other locations, and the continuity of effort towards providing prophesyings/exercises, see Collinson, 'Lectures by combination', esp. pp. 195–8.

[23] Collinson, 'Lectures by combination', esp. pp. 185–7.

[24] See, for example, the letter of 10 June 1576 from Grindal to Burghley (B.L. MS Lansdowne 23, No. 4, fol. 7); Morrice MSS, Vol. A, OLP., fol. 154; *ibid.*, Vol. B, I, pp. 188, 436; Collinson, *Elizabethan Puritan Movement*, pp. 173, 174; Richardson, *Puritanism*, pp. 65–6; Seaver, *Puritan Lectureships*, pp. 86, 103. On the role of a godly layman – the third Earl of Huntingdon – in fostering exercises, see Cross, *Puritan Earl*, pp. 226–7, 260.

[25] B.L. MS Add. 48,066, fols. 2[v]–3; Barton, ed., *Registrum Vagum of Anthony Harison*, pt I, pp. 100–1; P.R.O. S.P. 15/12/27.

quently expressed the hope that the bishops would join in.[26] They would no doubt have been glad of the air of responsibility and respectability the episcopal presence would have lent. This applied, too, to the puritan desire to be seen as favouring social order by involving important laymen at least in the formation of exercises.[27] Frequently, however, this involvement, lay and ecclesiastical, was restricted to agreement to the regulations previously drawn up by puritan ministers.[28] The prime concern of authorities was commonly that the exercises not challenge proper authority.[29] In its cooperative ventures to train its own members, the church had always to guard against the radical fervency which could spill over into conventicles and challenge structures as well as reform ignorance.[30] Bishops therefore offered a mixed response to Grindal's inquiry concerning prophesyings, which prefaced his refusal to comply with Elizabeth's order for their suppression in the southern province.[31] Grindal's own refusal to support Elizabeth followed his contribution of a series of articles for the 'better running' of prophesyings.[32]

[26] B.L. MS Add. 27,632, fol. 49; B.L. MS Lansdowne 72, fols. 137ᵛ–8; C.U.L. MS Dd.ix.14(c), fols. 46ᵛ–9; H.M.C. Cal. MSS. Salisbury, ii, p. 196; D'Ewes, Journals, p. 358; Cade, Saint Paules Agonie, sig. A4ᵛ; Letters of Thomas Wood, ed. Collinson, esp. pp. 1, 18; Frere & Douglas, eds., Puritan Manifestoes, pp. 149–51.

[27] See, for example, B.L. MS Lansdowne 82, No. 53, a plea from Lincolnshire to (?) Burghley, regarding the practices of 'nonconformable' ministers, which emphasizes that a conference held at Louth operated under the auspices of Lord Clinton and the deputy lieutenant.

[28] This was certainly the case in the very detailed plan for the exercise in Lancashire, drawn up by the puritan Christopher Goodman, approved by the Privy Council, and issued under the authority also of the bishop: Gonville & Caius MS 197/103, pp. 175–84. For an explanation of the details, which were not unusual, but also of the numbers of ministers involved, which bespoke a real push for improvement, see Collinson, Elizabethan Puritan Movement, pp. 210–11. On this general point of administrative acquiescence, see also Marchant, Puritans and Church Courts, pp. 17–18, 29, 134, 169; Peck, Desiderata Curiosa, i, iii, p. 102; Wood, Reformation, pp. 316–17; Haigh, Reformation and Resistance, pp. 301–2; Richardson, Puritanism, p. 65; B.L. MS Lansdowne 27, No. 12, fol. 20; B.L. MS Add. 29, 546, fol. 42.

[29] Samuel Harsnet worried over the difficulties that could arise from dealing in these exercises with any form of contentious matter (Discovery of Fraudulent, pp. 270–1). Burghley himself wrote to the Aldermen of Stamford on 2 July 1580 forbidding a planned fast because it was an innovation of a group of puritan ministers (B.L. MS Lansdowne 102, No. 100, fol. 185). Edmund Hopwood commented of the Cheshire exercises that 'all fanatical and schismatical preachers, that are cashiered in other counties, resort into this corner of Lancashire . . .' (HMC 14th. Rep., App., Pt. iv, MSS of Lord Kenyon, p. 15).

[30] C.S.P.D. 1547–1580, p. 308, for a letter from the Council to Bishop Grindal (1568), requiring the suppression of conventicles in London, and B.L. MS Lansdowne 82, No. 53, a complaint from Lincolnshire against the severity of one Anderson, a judge of the Assizes, for his dealings against puritans; the report denied the presence of any 'Presbiteries' and said that the one known Brownist had fled.

[31] For Grindal's letter to the queen, see B.L. MS Add. 29,546, fols. 36–40ᵛ. The relevant letters from the bishops to Grindal, mostly dated early and mid-July, 1576, are preserved in the Laud–Selden–Fairhurst Collection of MSS in Lambeth Palace. 8 of the 12 bishops who expressed a firm opinion argued that such exercises were very helpful to the clergy. See also Collinson, Elizabethan Puritan Movement, pp. 171–4, 180, 192.

[32] Grindal's suggestions maintained the ministerial exposition of Scripture and the subsequent private discussions, and again limited the role of the congregation to listening (B.L. MS Lansdowne 109, No. 2, fol. 3). See also Grindal's letters in B.L. MS Lansdowne 15, No. 41, fol. 79 and B.L. MS Lansdowne 23, No. 4, fol. 7.

The precisians stressed the role exercises could play in establishing discipline, settling questions of doctrine and selecting new ministers. Exercises could help populace and serving ministers, just as they had aided those in the universities.[33] The education of ministers was not to be a finite stage in preparation, or even an hierarchical plan, but rather a cooperative, ongoing venture.[34] The presbyterian *Directory of Church-Government* similarly called for each new student to attend assemblies and give a demonstration of his abilities, with other students acting as critics, and a learned minister present as moderator. Again, only those chosen by a church were to be allowed to speak.[35] The professional separation of clergy from laity was maintained by the exclusion of laymen, 'saving in some partes, where a scholemaster, two, or thre desirous to traine themselves to the ministerie joined in with us'.[36] Given these safeguards, puritans reacted angrily to the slander of 'conventicle'-making. Josias Nichols raised the spectre of paranoia on the part of the administration. He noted that 'the people were become conventiclers [in their opponents' minds] if they met together to sing a Psalme, or to talke of Gods word'. John Winthrop called for a strict legal definition of a 'conventicle' so that people could not be caught unaware.[37]

Nor were the exercises seen as a temporary measure designed solely to relieve the religious and political burdens caused by an ignorant clergy. Rather, these sessions would always be in demand as opportunities for the future elucidation of interpretation of Scripture even among learned clergy. Here the example of the Dedham *classis* is illustrative. It was formed as a prophesying, the group of approximately nineteen people[38] (of whom eighteen were graduates) agreeing on the usual form of a moderator, a pre-announced question and a regular meeting time.[39] For the sake of secrecy as well as solidarity, no one was to be 'broughte in as one of the company, without the generall consente of the whole'. Members also agreed not to divulge the opinions of the sessions without prior approval. The sessions were intended partly for the general improvement of the members; admonition was to be given to any member 'tutchinge their mynistery, doctryne, or liffe' where necessary. At each session, an appointed speaker interpreted a portion of Scripture, and the others commented on the interpretation. The aim was to

---

33 B.L. MS Add. 27,632, fols. 47ᵛ, 49; B.L. MS Lansdowne 109, No. 11, fol. 11; Morrice MSS, Vol. B, I, pp. 187–8.   34 Cartwright, *Second Admonition*, esp. pp. 14, 27, 60, 63.

35 *Directory of Church-Government*, sigs. B3ᵛ, C. See, similarly, I.T.L. MS Petyt 538, fol. 71, for Thomas Lever's recommendations; Morrice MSS, Vol. B, II, fol. 52ᵛ, for John Udall's comments.

36 B.L. MS Lansdowne 72, No. 49, fol. 138. The authorities evidently had no objection to the presence of schoolmasters, many of whom, of course, were in orders anyway: see, for example, Gonville & Caius MS 197/103, the 1584 'Orders and Rules' for the exercise in Lancashire.

37 Nichols, *Plea of the Innocent*, p. 35; *Winthrop Papers*, I, p. 297, dated 1623/4, during the last Parliament of James I.

38 Usher, *Presbyterian Movement*, 'Minute book of the Dedham classis', p. 27. There were 19 signatories, but attendance varied, and not all of the original members remained in the area.

39 Between 1582 and 1589 the group held 80 meetings.

encourage lively application of scholarly skills to the questions of practical divinity as they arose in both pulpit explanations and private counselling of parishioners.[40] Prophesyings and exercises also permitted the consolidation of friendships either bred in the university or formulated out of sharing the same professional burden.[41] They likely were catalytic in bringing other preachers to greater effort, wider reading, and thus more acceptable modern interpretation.[42] They may also have served to raise the expectations of their congregations. But as educational institutions in the narrower sense, these gatherings can have done little to raise the standards of those who knew little Latin and no Greek; they were, rather, very necessary schools of practical divinity. For the goal of a ministry learned in the humane arts, puritans still perforce had to turn to the universities.

II

But even as puritans looked to Oxford and Cambridge to fulfil this traditional role, the universities themselves were reaching the culmination of one era of important change, and were about to enter another period of serious modification. In order to comprehend more fully the puritan thrust, we need first to set the context in which puritans were immersed and then, later in this chapter, to survey puritan suggestions for general reform. The following two chapters will detail specific puritan adaptations of English higher education.

Much of the early impetus for change lay in the diverse purposes, social composition, and curriculum of the new humanist-inspired colleges.[43] These, in general, reflected increased interest in both improved ministerial candidates and better-educated members of the lay econo-political elite.[44] John Fisher's statutes for St John's, Cambridge, typify the early approach that religion was the highest goal of a 'good' life. Fisher made provision for the teaching of philosophy, the arts, Greek, Hebrew, arithmetic, geometry, perspective, and cosmography; Arabic and Chaldaic also received official sanction, though they may not in fact have been taught. All the fellows were required to enter the priesthood; a quarter of them had to preach publicly in

40 Usher, *Presbyterian Movement*, pp. 25, 26, 30.
41 Collinson, 'Lectures by combination', *passim*; O'Day, *English Clergy*, esp. pp. 72–4, 166–70.
42 Collinson notes the use, for example, of the Tremellius Bible and the best of the 'modern' divines by preachers in Suffolk ('Lectures by combination', pp. 210–11). On the general importance of prophesyings, see *ibid.*, p. 200; Collinson, *Elizabethan Puritan Movement*, p. 51. On lectures, see Sheils, 'Religion in provincial towns', pp. 156–7.
43 At Oxford, Corpus Christi (1517), Cardinal (1525), Trinity (1555) and St John's (1557); at Cambridge, Christ's (1506), St John's (1511), and Trinity (1546).
44 McConica, 'Scholars and commoners', esp. pp. 153–6, in Stone, ed., *University in Society*, I; Mallet, *Oxford*, II, esp. pp. 22, 158, both concerning Richard Fox's Corpus, Thomas White's St John's and Thomas Pope's Trinity.

English. Trinity College, Cambridge, built upon this base of reformed learning by attempting to combine the humanist and protestant impulses. Scripture was exalted as the highest authority of the faith. With the exception of two each in medicine and civil law, the fellows were required to study divinity; a quarter of them were to be preachers. Every day, after breakfast, the preachers would in turn expound the Biblical verses which had been read during the meal.[45]

The humanist influence also led to curriculum change at the university level. The 1570 statutes for Cambridge commanded dedication to rhetoric in the first year, logic in the second and third years, and philosophy in the fourth year of the B.A. The required authors also reflected humanist tastes.[46] Nor were the old subjects of the trivium and quadrivium kept entirely separate. Sir Henry Savile insisted that advanced undergraduates attend the lectures in geometry which he founded in 1619. The Laudian statutes at Oxford also added Greek to the undergraduate curriculum. Though there were some variations between Oxford and Cambridge, a successful M.A. candidate necessarily studied logic, rhetoric, Greek, natural and moral philosophy, metaphysics, history, geometry, astronomy, Hebrew, and (at Oxford) Arabic.[47]

Collectively, at the two universities, chairs were endowed in history, geometry, anatomy, natural philosophy, moral philosophy, astronomy, and Arabic.[48] More 'modern' interests, too, infiltrated these designs. Savile insisted upon the practical and modern in his endowment of a professorship of astronomy, especially concerning geography and 'those parts of navigation depending on mathematics'. Camden, too, reflecting perhaps not only his own interest in portraying the Jacobean age as a period of decline post-Gloriana, but also the different proclivities of a changing student body, insis-

---

[45] Mullinger argues that Trinity (founded 1546, first statutes 1552) was the best example of the change from 'mediaeval' to 'modern' concepts of learning (Mullinger, *Cambridge*, II, pp. 81, 139–42).

[46] The lecturer in logic was required to teach either Aristotle or Cicero, the lecturer in medicine either Galen or Hippocrates. Rhetoric was to be examined from Quintilian, Hermogenes or Cicero (*Statutes of Queen Elizabeth for the University of Cambridge*, p. 5). Jardine, 'Place of dialectic teaching', *Studies in the Renaissance*, 21, esp. pp. 60–1, suggests that a basic list of texts for a late sixteenth-century B.A. might include a dialectic manual (probably Melanchthon or Agricola); Aristotle's *Ethics and Politics*; a Greek grammar and lexicon; an elementary arithmetic book (probably Recorde or Baker); Cicero's letters, orations, offices; Ovid's *Metamorphoses*; Erasmus' *de copia, Adagia*, or *Apophthegmata*; Valla's *Elegentiae*; a Greek New Testament; Terence; Virgil; Horace; Quintilian; Plutarch; Plato; Caesar's commentaries; Aesop's fables; Livy or Sallust. Of course, this list was highly variable. Ramus, in one of the commentary editions, made a strong appearance in the late sixteenth century. See also Jardine, 'Humanism and the sixteenth century arts course', *History of Education*, 4, esp. pp. 16–17. For a more personal list, see the account of Simonds D'Ewes, cited in Marsden, *College Life*, pp. 64–5.

[47] Curtis, *Oxford and Cambridge*, pp. 87–8, 91–2. On Arabic at Oxford, see the letter of 1639 from Thomas Graves to Laud (*C.S.P.D. 1639–40*, p. 73.)

[48] Curtis, *Oxford and Cambridge*, pp. 116–17; O'Day, *Education and Society*, pp. 110–11, notes that most of the lectures were not intended for undergraduates.

ted on civil rather than ecclesiastical history in his endowment (1622). Fulke
Greville, Lord Brooke, required a scholar of cosmography and chronology as
well as Latin and Greek, and hoped to attract a man with personal experience
of foreign parts, capable in modern languages, and with a background in
public affairs. His choice of Isaac Dorislaus, and his recommendation of
Tacitus' *Annales* as the text, reflects a parallel concern with the growing power
of an inadequate monarch.[49]

The arts curriculum (which included the M.A.) soon assumed a status not
only as a preparation to the professional degrees, but also as an independent
course which would train the young men of the next generation in the application, as well as in the contemplation, of (political) ethics.[50] If we consider that
Oxford and Cambridge, along with London, were the nation's intellectual
centres, and that all new works of scholarship would soon find their way there,
students could probably indulge virtually any intellectual interest they
developed. The influx of modern languages, the expanding interest in
mathematics, an increasingly common ability to play a musical instrument,
and perhaps also 'science' in Laudian Oxford, all indicate that the formal
undergraduate curriculum did not denote the limits of university learning.[51]

Nonetheless the form, and to a large degree the content, of university
education remained scholastic; indeed, in the second half of our period,
Oxford and Cambridge experienced an increasingly scholastic bent, albeit
humanist-influenced with regard to classical authors and the stress on Greek.[52]
Here the effect of the Reformation was rather to intensify than to dilute the
application of logical structures to both academic and everyday questions.
Students plodded their way through lectures, disputations, and declamations
much as had generations before them.[53] Some of the greatest academic battles
– for example, that involving Ramus and Aristotle – were over modifications
of traditional learning, rather than over the introduction of new systems of
thought. As Curtis has aptly summed up, education 'in the arts still tended to
be primarily moral, literary, speculative, and authoritative rather than historical, scientific, and empirical'.[54] Even the hints of improved mathematics and
botany at Oxford, for example, remained isolated ventures as yet still
overwhelmed by the traditional curriculum.

Although the Reformation did not turn the univerities into seminaries,

[49] Sharpe, 'Foundation of history chairs', *History of Universities*, 2, esp. pp. 133–7, 139–45.
[50] Curtis, *Oxford and Cambridge*, pp. 122–3; Sharpe, 'Foundation of history chairs', pp. 145–6.
[51] Tyacke, 'Science and religion', in Pennington & Thomas, eds., *Puritans and Revolutionaries*, esp. pp. 89–
93; Curtis, *Oxford and Cambridge*, esp. Ch. 4; Costello, *Scholastic Curriculum*, pp. 141–4.
[52] See, especially, Kearney, *Scholars and Gentlemen*, Ch. 5; Looney, 'Undergraduate education', *History of
Education*, 10, esp. p. 9–11; Schmitt, 'Philosophy and science in sixteenth-century universities: some
preliminary comments', in Murdoch & Sylla, eds., *The Cultural Context of Medieval Learning*, pp. 485–
530; Morgan, 'History of the universities', *Wiener Beiträge*, 5, *passim*, for a summary of the
literature.   [53] On scholastic forms, see Costello, *Scholastic Curriculum, passim*.
[54] Curtis, *Oxford and Cambridge*. p. 115. Charlton, *Education*, p. 160, cites the comment from Samuel Ward
that maths texts were 'Greek, I mean unintelligible, to all the fellows'.

religion was ever present. While students at neither Oxford nor Cambridge were required by statute to attend the lectures of the divinity professors, they were commanded to attend the catechetical lectures in their colleges.[55] Students were also bound to attend sermons. Religion pervaded the texts of the languages, and of course the questions of the philosophies. Tutors, too, were increasingly expected to guide the moral and religious growth of their charges. As well, religious controversies were frequently hottest in the universities, which served as incubators for the growing polemic against Antichrist. Theology remained the 'queen of sciences' in an academic sense, and a career in the ministry still the single most likely post for a university graduate. The universities thus continued for their students the course of religious socialization developed in the country's schools.

Recent scholarship has revealed dramatic changes in the social composition of sixteenth-century Oxford and Cambridge. Learning became a social and vocational necessity for the well-born. Lacking their own academies, sons of gentry and of well-off merchants flocked to the universities and within a generation of Elizabeth's accession were joined by an increasing number of sons of ministers.[56] Figures from the colleges vary, but there was an undeniable increase in the proportion of better-off students.[57] The degree to which the upper-class entrants may have been displacing those from the lower echelons of society is still unclear, partly because status claims were changeable in college and university records, and partly because the university expansion has not been fully tested against growth in general population.[58] Nevertheless, by the end of our period, in the peak enrolments of the 1630s, the universities were each year producing some six hundred educated laymen who were not entering either the church or the secular professions.[59] With these students,

---

[55] For an Elizabethan order to this effect, see Peile, *Christ's College*, p. 90; Curtis, *Oxford and Cambridge*, p. 185.

[56] Tyler, 'Status of Elizabethan parochial clergy', in Cuming, ed., *Studies in Church History*, 4, esp. p. 85; Green, 'Career prospects', *Past and Present*, 90, *passim*; Cressy, 'Social composition of Caius', *Past and Present*, 47, p. 114; Tyler found that clerical sons accounted for 16% of entrants ('Children of disobedience', p. 114).

[57] Stone, 'Educational revolution', p. 60; Cressy, 'Social composition of Caius', *Past and Present*, 47, p. 114; O'Day, *Education and Society*, pp. 100–1, 105.

[58] On this question, see O'Day, *Education and Society*, p. 100; McConica, 'Scholars and commoners', pp. 175–6; Tyler, 'Children of Disobedience', pp. 96ff., 114. Stone has noted that at least 2½% of eligible-age males were entering a university in the 1630s ('Educational revolution', *Past and Present*, 28, p. 57). The question of whether there was an 'educational revolution' in solely quantitative terms is, despite much work (especially by Stone), still not altogether clear. The number of university entrants was at a peak in the 1630s; however, the population of England also rose rapidly in the century before 1640. If we compare the decadal increases in population with the decadal increases in university enrolment, it would seem that the 1580s possibly witnessed the highest proportion of the population in attendance at Oxford and Cambridge. On the question of numbers attending the universities, see, most recently, Stone, 'Size and composition of Oxford student body', in Stone, ed., *The University in Society*, i, pp. 3–110. See also Stone, 'Educational revolution' esp. pp. 47–67. But see also the caveat by E. Russell, 'Influx of commoners', *E.H.R.*, 365, pp. 721–45. For population figures see Wrigley & Schofield, *Population History of England*, Appendix 3.   [59] Stone, 'Educational revolution', pp. 56–7.

whose aim was not a career in the ministry, puritan educationalists also had to come to grips.

Potentially an even more grievous threat to the purifying of the universities was the increasing imposition of state authority. Upon her accession, Elizabeth advised the chancellors of Oxford and Cambridge to encourage true religion,[60] but throughout her reign stress was rather on muting the religious disturbances at the centres of learning.[61] Pressure to conform rose and fell periodically, though there seems to have been an increasing effort to silence any 'oppositionist' voices in the universities after 1590.[62] William Prynne argued that Charles' proclamation of 1629 against promoting or criticizing Arminianism was intended more to muzzle puritan opposition in countryside and university than to interfere with the church's own Laudian strengths.[63] The Laudian statutes further subordinated Oxford to the principle of order and outside authority in an effort to consolidate the innovations of the church. All three monarchs of our period, then, attempted to avoid the 'disorder' that had plagued so many continental universities by rigorously controlling any religious 'deviance'.

As well as occasional monarchical regulation, the universities had to bear the closer integration of their own officers with the structures of power.[64] The government brought increasing pressure to bear on the heads of colleges, who at both universities increased their authority under Elizabeth at the expense of the regent masters. The increasing royal power exercised through the regius professorships and influence in elections of heads and fellows exacerbated the problem.[65] Though the administration was never monolithic in its aims, at times – the 1580s and 1630s are obvious examples – the universities became the focus of the drive to extirpate nonconformity from the church, and therefore also became centres of puritan resistance.

Combined with this threat of 'political corruption', puritans also had to face the problem of increasing moral disorder posed by the 'lay' undergraduates. This was evidently a continuing problem throughout our

[60] Curtis, *Oxford and Cambridge*, esp. pp. 167–70.
[61] The case of Thomas Cartwright bears this out (Pearson, *Thomas Cartwright, passim*; *C.S.P.D. 1547–1580*, esp. pp. 262, 263, 381, 382, 383, 388, 493). For another case, see Andrew Perne's letter to Cecil in 1575 on the recent disturbances at St John's, Cambridge (*ibid.*, p. 493). See also Porter, *Reformation and Reaction, passim*; Curtis, *Oxford and Cambridge*, p. 194.
[62] For various examples, see Cooper, *Annals of Cambridge*, III, pp. 8–12, 129–31; *C.S.P.D. 1603–1610*, p. 210; P.R.O. SP 14/89/60 and 61; B.L. MS Lansdowne 157, No. 33, fol. 128; Heywood & Wright, eds., *Cambridge University Transactions*, II, pp. 269–70, 273–7.
[63] Prynne, *Canterburies Doome*, pp. 160–1.
[64] Chancellors of Cambridge such as William and Robert Cecil concurrently held high offices of state, and of the six archbishops of Canterbury between 1558 and 1640, five had controlled a college, and three had occupied the post of Vice-Chancellor (V. Morgan, 'History of the English universities', *Wiener Beiträge*, 5, p. 161).
[65] *Ibid.*, pp. 160–2; Conant, 'Advancement of learning', *Proceedings of the Mass. Hist. Soc.*, 66, p. 7.

period. Early in the seventeenth century the puritan Sebastian Benefield complained that innocent undergraduates soon became marked by the contagion of immorality: 'their manners are lost; the tokens of their modesty and sobrietie are no more to be seene'.[66] Complaints seem to have increased shortly before the Revolution. It may have been not only the hostility of official Laudianism, but also the heaviest ever influx of students in the 1620s and 1630s that produced such despair at the condition of the universities. Indeed, in this criticism puritans were at one with establishment reformers such as Laud himself, who attempted to instil moral rectitude as well as religious conformity into Oxford students and dons.[67] Because of their serious moral corruption, William Prynne advocated the parliamentary reform of Oxford and Cambridge – an interesting portent – as early as 1628.[68] Opinions of moral laxity flowed from various sources. Thomas Crosfield, for example, remembered playing cards with the Provost and fellows of Queen's, Oxford, and commented that it had been common practice not to attend university sermons.[69] Visitors from the provinces registered shock at the rampant licentiousness. 'Prodigiously profane' was the description offered by Robert Woodford, Steward of Northampton, on a visit to Oxford in 1639. Similarly, Thomas Richardson of Warwickshire was accused of calling the universities 'sinks of sin and pits of iniquity'.[70] Repulsion at the perception of increasing laxity was one of the primary reasons which Forth Winthrop gave as justification for the great emigration:

The Fountaines of Learning and Religion are soe corrupted as (besides the unsupportable charge of there education) most children (even the best witts and of faierest hopes) are perverted, corrupted, and utterlie overthrowne by the multitude of evill examples and the licentious government of those Seminaries, where men straine at knatts, and swallowe camells, use all severity for mainetaynance of cappes, and other accomplymentes, but suffer al ruffianlike fashions, and disorder in manners to passe uncontrolled.[71]

The new swelling of numbers, though it offered great opportunities for puritan educational influence, was seen to come at the immediate price of lowering the standards of morality.

---

[66] Benefield, *Eight Sermons Preached in Oxford*, p. 17.
[67] For Oxford, see Mallet, *Oxford*, II, pp. 333–4; Sharpe, 'Archbishop Laud and the University of Oxford', in Lloyd-Jones, Pearl & Worden, eds., *History and Imagination*, pp. 146–64. For Cambridge, note the Royal Ordinances of 1630, the Academic Injunctions issued on the occasion of the royal visit in Mar. 1632/3, and the Injunctions issued by the vice-chancellor and heads in 1636 (Mullinger, *Cambridge*, III, p. 107). [68] Prynne, *Briefe Survay*, Epistle, sig. A.2. [69] *Diary of Crosfield*, ed. Boas, p. 11.
[70] *H.M.C. Ninth Rep., App. Pt II*, p. 498. Woodford would seem to have been a puritan; the entry in his diary for 28 Nov. 1639 (*ibid.*, p. 499) refers to Burton and Prynne as 'those holy living martyrs . . .'. On Richardson, *C.S.P.D. 1638–1639*, p. 213. [71] *Winthrop Papers*, II, p. 139.

III

The desperate need for a learned ministry, and the changing social basis of the universities, were clearly reflected in puritan schemes for the reform of Oxford and Cambridge. Generally, the puritan approach was to accept the basic curriculum, though to modify texts and subjects; to work within existing structures, though to introduce activities which would *in practice* demonstrate the aphorism that learning was but a handmaid to divinity; and to accept the changes in social composition of the colleges, while making every effort to inculcate even in non-degree-takers the fervent spirit of forward religion. The very battles in which puritans engaged for control of colleges and against restrictive authority brought them more closely into the circle of existing structures.

This present study, as I have sought to make clear, does not seek to analyse the puritan effect on the various levels of English education. Rather, our interest here lies in the elucidation of intellectual attitudes. The internal struggles of the colleges thus do not form a central part of our study. Nonetheless, the conflicts within the universities between the administration's imperative for order before further reform and the puritan enthusiasm for purification of knowlege and procedures produced a host of skirmishes which pertain to our interest. The clash of views was evident early in Laurence Humphrey's mastership of Magdalen College, which he turned into the puritan seminary of Oxford. It was also present in the struggle to save Thomas Cartwright of Cambridge from expulsion. It arose in dramatic form in the various episodes of the Elizabethan struggle for control of St John's College, Cambridge, and for power in Christ's, that early centre for Cambridge puritans.[72] It was present, too, in the tumult over Bainbrigg and Johnson, in the criticisms of Emmanuel and Sidney Sussex, and in the reason for the secrecy of the election of John Preston at Emmanuel. In the grudging retreat before the 'novel' religion and the imposition of new heads in the 1630s, it can be illustrated from a number of sources.[73]

Despite arguments from opponents that puritan success would 'cut of a great part of the study & profession of al good letters, both in divinity and humanity',[74] there can be no doubt that puritans favoured the strengthening of a reformed Oxford and Cambridge. Over the course of the period 1560–1640 puritans established themselves as a force at a good number of colleges. Even at the end of our period Magdalen Hall, New Inn Hall, Brasenose, Exeter, and

---

[72] But on the great importance attached to obtaining suitable heads of colleges, see, for example, Udall, *State of Church*, p. 359, in *A Parte of a Register*.

[73] See, for example, the correspondence of Samuel Ward and James Ussher (Mullinger, *Cambridge*, III, pp. 113–14; *Whole Works of James Ussher*, ed. Elrington, xv, p. 346.

[74] Bridges, *Defence*, p. 42.

Lincoln at Oxford remained attractive centres for puritan gentlemen, while Christ's, Emmanuel, Sidney Sussex, and St Catharine's Hall retained their puritan reputations at Cambridge.[75] Other colleges such as Magdalen at Oxford and St John's at Cambridge, had fallen by the wayside from a puritan point of view, but had made important contributions as early houses of godly learning. The attraction depended less, as we shall see, on any structural modifications than on godly personnel – masters and fellows to serve as tutors.[76]

Proof of puritan support does not depend, however, solely on the attendance of the sons of puritan gentlemen, who might well have felt compelled to attend a college even without benefit of puritan tutorship. Of more concern here is the record of the published attitudes of puritans concerning the function of the universities in building a Reformed nation. Dudley Fenner suggested appropriating part of the bishops' income to support higher education, one of the 'sinowes of the common wealth'.[77] And, in replying to Bridges' tirade against the presbyterians, Fenner specifically claimed that the recommended division of the clergy into doctors and pastors in fact encouraged a *greater* measures of learning in the clergy, and thus was an encouragement to the universities.[78] Richard Greenham, positively fulsome in his description, referred to the universities as the 'Epitomes of the Common-wealth . . . the eyes of the Common-wealth . . . They be the polished Saphires to garnish the house of the Lord.'[79] Admiration alone was not sufficient; puritans therefore insisted that it was the duty of the magistrate to 'erect schooles and colledges: finde and maintaine teachers and readers that the youth may be taught . . .'.[80] These reformed institutes, as Walter Travers made clear, were to serve as 'the meanes to preserve and make perfit all other noble artes and sciences and especially divinitie'; they should 'bothe kindle Religion [now] being putt out/ and also enflame and encrease yt being kindled . . .'.[81] Especially was this important since, as we noted, a degree was frequently taken to be the basic admission requirement for the ministry.[82] Henry Smith thus advised congregations to dispense with their own examination of prospective ministers, and instead simply rely on contacts in the universities to provide them.[83]

From the time of the Edwardian reformation, reformers had called for the purification of learning and purpose at Oxford and Cambridge. Already in

---

[75] Cliffe, *Puritan Gentry*, esp. pp. 85–92, 98–103. [76] On the role of tutors, see below, Ch. 13.

[77] Fenner, *Defence of Godlie Ministers*, p. 130. [78] *Ibid.*, p. 127.

[79] Greenham, *Workes*, p. 734. Compare, however, the more euphoric (and euphonic) language of Henry Peacham, quoted in Curtis, *Oxford and Cambridge*, p. 261.

[80] Travers, *Full and Plain Declaration*, pp. 100–1. See also Anon., *Complaint of Commonaltie*, p. 223, in *A Parte of a Register*; Turner, *Huntyng of Romyshe Vuolfe*, sigs. E.vi°–vii; Latimer, *Sermons*, p. 269; Cartwright, *Replye to Answere*, sig. N.ij°.

[81] Travers, *Full and Plain Declaration*, pp. 145, 146, 142–3.

[82] See, for example, *Abstract, of Certain Acts*, pp. 30, 71–2. [83] Smith, *Sermons*, p. 1014.

1550 Thomas Lever had complained of the recent degradation of institutionalized learning, and had emphasized that Edward VI was angered because the Reformation had not yet raised the level of university scholarship.[84] From the beginning of fervent English protestantism, then, religion and scholarship were symbiotically linked. Symptomatic of this union were the occasional purges of popish influence in the universities.[85] However, the irregularity of pressure towards godly reform caused puritans such as Bernard Gilpin to complain that a paucity of ministerial students meant that 'there is entering into England more blind ignorance, superstition, and infidelity, than ever was under the Romish bishops'.[86] Tracts and petitions constantly criticized Oxford and Cambridge for not rededicating themselves, as puritans insisted, 'to the sound building of themselves up in such things as their souls apparently stand in need of . . .'.[87] Cartwright remonstrated that divinity programmes followed the 'heathenish tradition of prophane scholes/ which rather seke by suche title to advance learning as they say/then by their learning to advantage the church of God'.[88] The administration was also frequently accused of barring the way to the proper union of mind and spirit by its allowance of unrestricted humane learning and by its purging of the godly learned from the universities for minor breaches of order.[89]

It is in this vein of the general puritan purpose of purification of the universities that we should see the long-term complaint, most vocal in the Elizabethan period, against those who refused to practise the ministry in the countryside but would 'tarry in theyr Colledge'.[90] As one solution, Cartwright proposed a stronger symbiosis between country and academy: at the expense of the colleges, serving ministers were to enter the universities for periods of further training.[91] But, against these complaints, Whitgift contended that ministers did not customarily remain at the universities, but stressed the advantages of such a measure, for then 'should not yong, factious, unruly and undiscrete persons, so greately trouble with their contentions and sects, bothe universities, and the whole realme also'. Any who stayed at the universities were therefore 'greatly to be commended' for ensuring the institutions' continued order and academic quality.[92] For puritans, this was rather dereliction

[84] Lever, *Sermon at Pauls Crosse*, sigs. D.viii^v, E.iii.
[85] See, for example, the list of complaints against Richard Swale, fellow of Caius, and the general complaints of popery at early Elizabethan Caius (C.U.L. MS Baker A.17, copied from B.L. MS Lansdowne 36.47).   [86] Gilpin, *Godly Sermon*, p. 37.   [87] Byfield, *Marrow of Oracles of God*, p. 454.
[88] Cartwright, *Second Admonition*, pp. 14–17; see also Travers, *Full and Plain Declaration*, p. 144.
[89] On the mixture of 'good' and 'corruption' in the universities, Greenham, *Workes*, p. 722.
[90] Field and Wilcox, *Admonition to Parliament*, sig. C.vi.   [91] Cartwright, *Second Admonition*, p. 63.
[92] Whitgift, *Answere to Certen Libel*, p. 223. See also Strype, *Life and Acts of Whitgift*, p. 50, 'Book of Articles offered to Parliament in 1580', for a similar episcopal statement that maintaining learned preachers in the universities was good for the realm. See, similarly, Cosin, *Answer to Abstract*, sig. I.v^v.

of God's calling.[93] Puritans, of course, were insistent that learned ministers should continue to serve as tutors and lecturers at Oxford and Cambridge, but such roles should for most of them be only a stage in their careers.

Those who remained over-long at the universities not only denied the church their assistance, but also blocked the advance of younger students. John Beacon, a civilian who led the Cambridge University Senate struggle against the imposition of the 1570 statutes, wrote to Burghley complaining that the queen had failed to live up to her promise of 1560 to promote worthy students of divinity. As a remedy, he suggested that the universities be compelled to send the queen lists of their prospects for the ministry.[94] Samuel Wright in 1612 condemned ministers who would preach only in the universities or at Paul's Cross, where a sizeable audience, and a probable printing, awaited a sermon.[95] William Perkins reminded ministers that 'the end we aime at, is not humane nor carnall; our purpose is to save souls . . .'. He therefore advised them to apply themselves to learning while at the university, but not to linger 'too long in their *speculative* courses: . . . when they are competently furnished with learning, & other qualities befitting that calling: let them shewe themselves willing & ready to yeild their service to the Church . . .'[96] He especially condemned those who 'think it sufficient to live there and send out other men, and give testimonies and Letters of commendations to other men, but themselves stirre not'.[97]

As we saw above in our examination of puritan attitudes towards learning and the recommended content of future ministers' education, puritan concern was more to purify knowledge than to rebuild it on completely new intellectual foundations. The chief thrust was against the perpetuation in a Christian commonwealth of institutions which, while inculcating thorough knowledge of Aristotle, could leave graduates 'insufficient & unlerned . . . without any maner of competent abilitie to expound the word of god, without divinitie, without science, without art . . . & in a great part without pietie and religion'.[98] With the undergraduate curriculum – especially as it was expanding to include Greek and 'purified logic', and also given the greater liberty of tutors to teach what they pleased – puritans did not find great fault.[99] Even the protestant–Ramist revolt against scholastic logic culminated in blends with

---

[93] A 1581 list of the preachers resident in the several colleges of Cambridge announced the presence of 132 such men, with Trinity (28), St John's (19) and Queens' (19) leading the way (B.L. MS Lansdowne 33, No. 44, fol. 86).   [94] Cooper, *Annals of Cambridge*, II, pp. 435–7.
[95] Wright, *Divers Godly Sermons*, p. 266.   [96] Perkins, *Workes*, III, pp. 442, 461; also p. 434.
[97] *Ibid.*, p. 461.
[98] Travers, *Defence of Ecclesiastical Discipline*, pp. 132–3. See also Field, *Godly Prayers and Meditations*, fol. 57ᵛ; Norden, *A Pensive Mans Practise*, fols. 51ᵛ–2.
[99] Curtis, *Oxford and Cambridge*, pp. 96–107, stresses the increasing ease with which the formal, statutory requirements could be at least partially circumvented.

Aristotle's system, as in Keckermann's 1614 logic from Geneva, which proved so popular at puritan Harvard.[100] Given the puritans' own university training and the proven utility of Oxford and Cambridge in providing learned preachers, their structural thrust became limited to adjustments, and to the transposition of proven schemes from the countryside. It may have been because they were so careful to maintain strict controls on their use of carnal learning that they remained uncreative in scholarship compared to either the humanists or the Baconians.

With the 'graduate' programme in theology, too, they seem to have been less troubled than one might have expected. Certainly puritans, and especially presbyterians, did object to the degree of 'doctor' because that title rightly belonged to a specific teaching office in the church rather than to a level of achievement in humane learning.[101] Thus Laurence Chaderton took his D.D. only under pressure from James I, and then only at the age of approximately seventy-seven. He had no such objections to the B.D., which he had taken thirty-four years earlier. Furthermore, a degree in theology may have seemed necessary only for those who would instruct future clerics at the universities. There may have been some fear that men with B.D.s and D.D.s would forget, after such an extended stay in the university, how to instruct the uneducated in the ordinary affairs of practical godliness if they ever took up a country living. The curriculum for degrees in theology was in many ways not objectionable, though puritans strongly suggested greater emphasis on scriptural exegesis and casuistical divinity. Adverse comments were directed rather at those who spent too much time with commentaries, or who regarded the direct examination of Scripture as of secondary importance. Given that candidates for theology degrees could reasonably easily avoid further examination,[102] and that the course of instruction was in any case the most 'protestant' part of the university curriculum, puritans by and large found no purpose in direct challenges to the structure of the theology course.

Puritan effort, especially in the early period, concentrated therefore on the production of learned ministers by the universities. In 1584 a petition to Parliament called for the establishment of endowed research in divinity to produce a body of protestant theological learning.[103] But, as it turned out, this

[100] Miller, *New England Mind*, esp. pp. 100-4; Miller & Johnson, *Puritans*, esp. pp. 25-7.
[101] Cartwright, *Second Admonition*, pp. 15-17; Cartwright, *Replye to Answere*, sig. Aa.iij. Whitgift suggested that Cartwright's objections stemmed from the experience of having been rejected for a higher degree (*Defence of Answer*, p. 470, in *Works*, III (Parker Society, vol. 49)). See also the case of Thomas Aldrich, who refused to proceed B.D. in 1573, thus touching off a dispute concerning authority at Corpus Christi, Cambridge (Porter, *Reformation and Reaction*, pp. 149ff.).
[102] Curtis, *Oxford and Cambridge*, esp. p. 164 on Cambridge.
[103] Mullinger, *Cambridge*, II, pp. 306ff. See also Strype, *Whitgift*, III, p. 49. Whitgift, who had defended learned ministers at the universities, evidently thought that such a plan would interfere with sending learned ministers out into the country!

had to be developed piecemeal from continental knowledge and puritan experience. Of more immediate impact was the attempt to pressure the administration to ensure that an adequate supply of preaching ministers would venture forth each year from the universities. Thus a 1586 puritan plan argued that in short time Cambridge could yield to the parishes 140 'meete men' and Oxford 194; if the situation at the universities were further reformed, 'non-residents being removed, bad heads displaced, and the younge fruit cherished, it would yield great plenty in short time".[104] The proposed 'Articles of reformation of the mynisterie', also of 1586, went further than a mere count of the expected university harvest. The universities were to be required to tell the Council each year just how many ministers they had provided; if the individual colleges did not supply their quota, the heads were to be answerable for the deficiency.[105] Thus did puritan effort quickly become incorporated in the existing institutions.

To this same end of yielding suitable ministers, puritans attempted to develop the use of prophesyings in the universities. This may well have amounted to their greatest structural innovation. The argument in 1586 that new ministers should be products of 'sufficient exercise in one of the Universities, or of the exercise of prophecying' is suggestive, but did not decree a format.[106] Laurence Chaderton argued that the preparation of students for the ministry had to go beyond academic scholarship. Ministers had to be able both to 'teache sound Doctrine by the interpretation of the Word' and to 'confute all contrarye errours by unanswerable arguments and reasons . . .'. He therefore proposed a 'mutuall conference of such as being very studious and of such good towardnes in learning' intended the ministry. The conference was to be very much a Biblical study group, which would be able to complete discussion of the text 'in two yeres or there abowts'.[107] Parallel to this course of mutual edification, Chaderton suggested a series of disputations which would determine especially the differences between protestants and papists and other heretics, and also settle any differences among the students.

There is some evidence that such groups existed, though no formal university requirement to this end was effected. John Carter, the future puritan minister, while still an undergraduate at Clare Hall, joined a circle which closely resembled Chaderton's plan.[108] A group, which included Chaderton himself, Lancelot Andrewes, Ezekiel Culverwell, John Knewstub, and 'divers others', met for the purpose of learned study of the Word.

---

[104] Peel, ed., *Seconde Parte of a Register*, II, pp. 198–9, 'A meane for the establishinge of a learned and sufficient ministrye'. [105] *Ibid.*, p. 435.
[106] *Ibid.*, p. 200. [107] Morrice MSS, Vol. A, OLP., fol. 191.
[108] Since Chaderton's plan is undated (and, though the ascription seems correct, also unsigned), we do not know whether Chaderton sketched his scheme on the basis of his experience in such a group as this, or whether the group activity was the actualization of the ideal.

At their meetings they had constant Exercises; first, They began with prayers, & then applied themselves to the Study of the Scriptures; one was for the *Original Languages*, anothers task was for the *Grammatical* Interpretation; anothers for the *Logical Analysis*; anothers for the true sense and meaning of the Text; another gathered the Doctrines, and thus they carried on their several imployments, till at last they went out, like Apollos, eloquent men, and mighty in the Scriptures: and the Lord was with them; so that they brought in a very great Harvest into Gods Barn.[109]

Thus could the 'arts' of Carter's formal studies be brought immediately into juxtaposition with vocational preparation for a proselytizing ministry. Chaderton also met with the influential William Whitaker and William Fulke for the purpose of examination of Scripture, though whether this was an on-going arrangement is not clear.[110] At Emmanuel, the presbyterian Chaderton made such a formal gathering compulsory in an effort to coordinate proselytizing activities in college and countryside by uniting the highest levels of humane scholarship with the necessities of practical divinity.[111]

IV

As well as brief criticisms of the structure and curriculum of the universities, puritans occasionally offered extended arguments for their reform. An examination of two such proposals will serve to cast the previous comments in a more specific light. The anonymous *Learned Discourse*, one of the principal tracts of Elizabethan presbyterianism, proposed an immediate return to a theological orientation for the universities. The first duty of 'doctors', the learned exegetes in the presbyterian scheme, was to use the universities to train the next generation of ministers.[112] The author claimed that a fully learned ministry could have been a reality had the universities concentrated from the beginning of the reign on their proper task.[113] Tradition and present law were not to stand in the way of such a mission. If necessary reform should not stop short of

thrusting out these unprofitable heades of Colledges, and other drone bees, which either are unable or unwilling to set forward the study of divinity in their severall houses, & . . . placing diligent and learned governors & students in their places, & by other good means reforming universities . . .[114]

This immediately served to warn the universities that they were above neither reproach nor coerced reform from without. Serving ministers whose learning was deemed insufficient were to be granted a stipend if they were willing to study and if they demonstrated any 'towardnes to become schollers in

---

[109] Clarke, *Ten Eminent Divines*, pp. 2–3.   [110] Lake, *Moderate Puritans*, p. 37.
[111] See below, pp. 251–2.   [112] *Learned Discourse*, pp. 16, 18–19, 37.
[113] *Ibid.*, pp. 38, 39, 41, 57, 128.   [114] *Ibid.*, pp. 54–5.

divinity'. But those who refused the extra burden were to be sent 'whence they came, to get their livinges with sweate of their brows . . .'.[115] Colleges. and the ministry were thus to be brought even closer together in Reformed society.

But though the *Discourse* excoriated current university orientation, it did not offer an alternative structure to effect the advocated reforms. Though the study of the Word was obviously to receive greater stress, there was no suggestion as to whether this would necessitate the addition of new subjects to the undergraduate curriculum (perhaps replacing other studies), or only the purification of standard subjects. Nor did the author suggest a controlling agency, list preferred texts or determine who was to judge who was fit to remain – as either teacher or student – in the reformed halls of learning, or whence replacements were to come for ejected masters. Certainly the *Discourse* was not intended primarily as a critique of England's universities, nor as a manual for educational reform. But in these omissions the *Discourse* reflected not only the limits of imagination and constructiveness in puritan thought, but also, in effect, the willingness of puritans to employ structures which had been perverted but which could still by reform be brought to serve a devout purpose.

More detailed, and perhaps more interesting because of their source, are the 'Devices' of Thomas Norton, which we have already encountered. The 'Devices' are of great importance for revealing not only a fervent drive to extirpate all vestiges of Romanism from England's educational institutions, but also a more organizational approach by a lay puritan outside the universities. Norton directed his appeal to the Council as the executive branch of government, which could act swiftly within the context of existing legislation.[116] New parliamentary statutes would have involved not only time, but doubtless also much eventual compromise with the defenders of university privileges. As a purgative for institutions which still produced converts to the Jesuit seminaries, Norton recommended a royal visitation, before which even the ancient rights of the universities could not stand.[117] Motivated by the fear of revivified popery, which he saw evidenced by the papal bull against Elizabeth and by rebellion in Ireland and northern England, Norton was concerned to determine the 'zeale of everie [one] to true relligion' and secondly 'their sufficiencie and their industrie in their places to further it'. The visitors were therefore to apply a stronger annual test than the oft-abused oath of allegiance. It is perhaps significant that Norton worded this requirement so

---

[115] *Ibid.*   [116] P.R.O. S.P. 12/177, fols. 158–9.

[117] In light of the modern debate over the respective condition of the two universities, it is interesting to note that Norton was especially concerned about Oxford (*ibid.*, fol. 159^{r-v}). Norton suggested that the visitation be led by Henry Knollys and John Hammond; Hammond already had experience of examining Jesuits (*D.N.B.*).

that the oath was to be to the *doctrine* of the English church, with which puritans were in agreement, rather than to the 'doctrines and practices'. The religious oath, he felt, would serve to root out all papists, who would lie about their political disloyalty, but not about a question of faith. Heads of colleges, required to be not merely 'no impugners of true relligion' but also 'well knowen to be notoriously zealous as persons to be specially trusted', would require an even higher standard of testing.[118]

This purifying zeal was not to cease after the initial visitation. The manner of teaching godly knowledge, for which Norton recommended the use of Nowell's Latin or Greek catechism, was also to be a matter of scrutiny. Norton suggested periodic tests of religious knowledge for the tutors, a point on which, interestingly, he was not specifically followed by other puritans, perhaps because they did not foresee being able to control such tests. Failure was to merit expulsion from the university. As a final mark of dedication, the heads of colleges were not to be allowed to hold benefices. Masters would thus be neither distracted from college business nor forced to overlook their ministerial responsibility by lapsing into non-residence.[119]

Having argued that learning 'in all tongues' was necessary to the church, Norton also wished to ensure that those colleges dedicated by statute to divinity fulfilled their legal obligation. Evidently aware that well-off students neither stayed for a degree nor entered the ministry, he decreed that any rich person filling a place originally destined for a poor youth would either have to study divinity himself or bear the expense of supporting another student in divinity. As a purgative of personal vice, he also demanded a general reduction in the level of fine apparel, a mark of dangerous vanity.[120] Norton also required the return of impropriations held by colleges. However, a tie was to remain, in that fellows of the respective colleges, if preachers, were to be preferred to vacancies before other candidates. To this end, too, he advised the strict implementation of any college statutes regarding undelayed entry into the ministry after completion of the divinity course.

Despite the seeming rigour of Norton's proposals, what remains striking is the lack of alteration of the basic structure. For the sake of religion and political stability, Norton wanted only devout protestants at Oxford and Cambridge, and he was willing to subject them to the pressure of oaths and tests to ensure it. But nowhere did he question the specific curriculum, or the chains of command which operated in the universities. The emphasis was rather on the godliness of the individual – head, tutor, pupil, 'censor', 'opposer'. In this, Norton clearly reflected puritan approaches to reform at all levels of institutions which they did not yet control.

[118] P.R.O. S.P. 12/177, fols. 159ᵛ, 160ᵛ, 161.   [119] *Ibid.*, fols. 161ᵛ–2.
[120] *Ibid.*, fol. 162ᵛ. As a model for a purer community, he recommended the reforms introduced by Thomas Sampson, Dean of Christ Church, Oxford.

V

While puritans sought a mixture of scriptural study and extended instruction in purified humane learning as the basis of their ministry, more radical minds sought more thorough reform of the content and purposes of the universities. A brief glimpse at the proposals should assist in the process of placing puritans more accurately in the spectrum of reform. Already in 1583 a proclamation had denounced the 'seditious, scismaticall, and erronious' works of Robert Browne and Robert Harrison.[121] Not only did they specifically condemn the Cambridge curriculum for its dependence upon 'those trifling bookes of Aristotle and of all that vaine Philosophie';[122] they also sought to decentralize learning, to universalize it by offering it in the vernacular, and (thus) to remove all associations of status.

Browne's printed works offer little in the way of constructive criticism, but the lottery of the historical record may well here tell against Browne. He wrote to his distant relative Lord Burghley on 15 April 1590, evidently offering him, in addition to the general comments of the letter itself, an accompanying treatise on the reformation of England's chief institutions of learning.[123] Browne argued in the letter that he had 'justly altered the arts & the rules and termes of Art, by evidence of the word', which he felt 'expressly sett downe, all necessarie & general rules of the arts & all learning', a point on which puritans seemed much less clear. Browne added that his scheme would teach more in one year than university scholars at present learned in ten. But, more important, learning would finally accord with Scripture rather than with the false and superfluous wisdom of the Schoolmen. He attempted to make it plain to Burghley that he was opposed not to the arts, but merely to the present falsifying of them'. Still possessed of the zeal that had once made him anathema to the administration, he offered to debate any opposition, promising if he could have a public forum to act 'in all quietnes also, not medling to condemne or controule any learned man or anie kind of profession'.[124] Perhaps it was his interest in reforming education that, in part, led Browne to conformity.

But if Browne fell by the wayside,[125] Henry Barrow continued the assault on the training of England's ministers. Though he was perhaps the most radical Elizabethan critic, Barrow insisted that he would happily allow 'any art or

---

[121] Quoted in Arber, *Transcript of the Registers of the Company of Stationers*, ı, p. 502.

[122] Browne, *Treatise upon the 23. of Matthewe*, p. 181.

[123] If this treatise ever existed, it has seemingly not survived. I know of no contemporary comment on it. Browne did refer to earlier suggestions sent to Burghley, which had evidently been shown to the bishops, 'but are ether neglected or through greater busines forgotten' (B.L. MS Lansdowne 64, No. 34, fol. 89). [124] *Ibid.*

[125] Barrow had harsh words for Browne, whom he regarded as a turncoat. Browne, he said, 'hath left the reliefe of Sion, to live upon the spoiles of Babylon' (*Platform*, sig. I7ᵛ).

science that is consonant to the word of God'.[126] He specifically approved schools 'to teach the tongues or any laudable or necessarie art'; indeed, he wished to extend facility in such matters to 'the whole church', primarily to ensure the end of a vain and dominant 'popish' clergy, which hid the plainness of Christ from the people.[127] At the same time, those studies which clashed with the pure Word – 'the curious and heathen artes, prophane and vaine bablings and oppositions of science falsely so caled' – were to be eliminated from the curriculum.[128] His vehemence against the basis of Latin and Greek, learned from heathen poets and philosophers, and School logic and rhetoric surpassed even Browne's criticisms.[129] Barrow saw the universities solely as narrow seminaries; lay students would have to go elsewhere. The curriculum was currently 'profane, curious, unfit for a Christian, much more for a Minister of the Church', at least partly because it relied on memorization of the (ungodly) human interpretations of the past. In an examination by the Council in 1588, Barrow answered the Bishop of London's accusations that he was unlearned with the retort that, despite his D.D., it was really Aylmer who was 'voyd of all true learning . . .'.[130] His chief objections to universities concerned those very aspects for which the puritans strongly defended them – the professionalization of theological knowledge and its subsequent restricted dissemination to the popular auditory.[131]

The final aspect of his critique was a consideration of whether the universities, like the monasteries before them, had become so corrupt that they were beyond redemption, and so should be abolished. At one time, as replacements for the universities, he proposed that institutes of 'the tongues and other godlie artes' should be established wherever there was a true Christian church or, more realistically, 'at the least in everie citie of the land'.[132] Teachers and scholars were therefore all to be kept 'under the holy government and censures of *Christ* in his Church . . .'.[133] But on this final point of destroying the monopoly of the universities Barrow temporized. In a letter to Burghley, written with John Greenwood, Barrow specifically allowed the continuation of the universities if they were adequately purged.[134]

Shortly before the Revolution, Samuel How, cobbler and Baptist, again challenged the inclusion of traditional humane learning in the education of

---

[126] Barrow, *Brief Discoverie*, p. 539, in *Writings of Henry Barrow 1587–1590*, ed. Carlson; see also Barrow, *Pollution*, pp. 7, 11.   [127] Barrow, *Brief Discoverie*, p. 539.   [128] *Ibid.*
[129] *Ibid.*, pp. 343–4; Barrow, *Pollution*, pp. 2, 3.
[130] Barrow, *Pollution*, p. 3; also pp. 1, 5. See also Barrow, *Plaine Refutation*, p. 213, in *Writings of Henry Barrow 1590–91*, ed. Carlson; Barrow, *Brief Summe*, p. 139, in *Writings of Henry Barrow 1587–1590*, ed. Carlson; B.L. MS Harley 7041, No. 23, p. 307. There is an especially strong diatribe against school divinity in Barrow, *Brief Discoverie*, pp. 344–5ff.   [131] Barrow, *Brief Discoverie*, p. 539.
[132] Barrow, *Plaine Refutation*, p. 223; Barrow, *Pollution*, p. 7.   [133] Barrow, *Pollution*, pp. 7–8.
[134] Barrow, *Platform*, sig. I. For further criticisms in this vein, though with nuances of their own, see Johnson & Ainsworth, *Apologie for True Christians*, pp. 77–8.

ministers. He thus added to an Elizabethan tradition which was still in circulation[135] How felt that the fundamental protestant idea of justification by faith alone had been so completely corrupted by accumulated layers of ministerial dependence on humane learning that it was necessary to re-establish, a century after the Reformation, its basic truth. How, like Barrow, did not condemn humane learning; on the contrary he argued that in its proper place it was a great aid in repairing the decay of man which came from sin. It was thus most suitable for statesmen, lawyers, physicians, and gentlemen. [136] Nonetheless, a godly unlearned man should be chosen for the ministry in preference to an equally godly learned man, since human 'additions' to God's grace were very likely to prove distractions – an extreme, but not unknown, argument.[137] Foreign languages were permitted since they were needed for translation of Scripture, but How was careful to point out that the translator did not have more understanding of God, solely because of his formal knowledge, than did the reader of the English translation.[138] Two other attacks which How launched at the coterie of the universities presaged the virulence of the Revolution. He revived the old criticism of such titles as 'doctor' as creating an elite based on the false criterion of humane learning rather than on godliness or the rightful class-structure, and he condemned university men for ignoring Jesus' admonition to the Apostles that they should earn their living with their hands.[139] With this opinion, which became widespread in the Revolution, How stood in diametrical opposition to university puritan views of a ministerial caste and to those local groups which had earlier petitioned for 'pure' ministers who had not soiled their hands with base callings.

That the radicals had already undergone the shock and abuse entailed in separating from one establishment – the church – may explain in part their lack of reticence to attack the universities. Given the increasing ties of ministry and university, they likely felt that in separating from the church they had already implicitly condemned the theological contribution of the universities. They may also have thought that they were simply invoking the reasonable conclusions of Reformed beliefs. Learning was to be utilitarian; it should have no separate existence as 'intellectualism', for that would be to turn method into end, and to forsake the 'handmaid' basis which made humane learning acceptable to the godly.

[135] The works of Marprelate and of Browne were evidently still available in the 1630s (*C.S.P.D. 1637*, pp. 257–8, June 1636, a petition from Nicholas Darton, the vicar of Kilsby, Northampton, to the effect that some of his parishioners were reading the 'scurrilous' pamphlets of these men).

[136] How, *Sufficiency of the Spirits Teaching*, p. 31.

[137] *Ibid.*, pp. 25, 15, 23. For the same point made in 1628 by Thomas Edwards (later author of *Gangraena*) see Heywood & Wright, eds., *Cambridge University Transactions*, II, pp. 361–3. For Anne Hutchinson's similar view, see Kearney, *Scholars and Gentlemen*, p. 114.

[138] How, *Sufficiency of the Spirits Teaching*, pp. 17–18.   [139] *Ibid.*, p. 34.

Puritans thus did not occupy the extreme of the spectrum of educational opinion. To their 'left' throughout our period stood those radicals who insisted on purging from ministerial instruction all forms of humane learning which had not been directly approved by Scripture. Puritans, on the other hand (as we saw earlier) permitted the broader framework for learning based on what did not contravene scriptural, and especially Pauline, guidelines. Scripture, however, was less applicable in drawing up statutes for further structural reform, or even for prescribing a contemporary curriculum. Given this lack of authoritative blueprint, puritans were able to recognize great advantages in Oxford and Cambridge. The universities could equip future ministers with generally the kinds of learning of which puritans approved. In addition, the statutory structure of instruction had become so malleable that students at any level could largely circumvent harmful influences. The increasing importance of college teaching meant that the battles for godly learning could be fought on a smaller scale, in a more pragmatic way. The opportunities which the influx of students from wealthy and influential families brought for future alliances in countryside, Parliament, and even college itself outweighed the losses incurred on the statutory and administrative fronts. The continuing impurities of university learning reflected the half-reformed church, from which puritans refused to separate while calling for immediate and massive reform, and instituting new structures such as prophesyings and lectureships. At the universities, then, as in the church, puritans found it necessary to erect purified examples of old forms.

12

>>>

THE INSTITUTIONALIZATION
OF REFORM

I

General reform of the English universities was never more than a remote possibility. Even had the puritans captured Parliament, the church would have objected; even had the church, in a spirit of enthusiasm, agreed, there was at no time in our period a monarch willing to see the precise faction gain the upper hand over Oxford and Cambridge. Puritans perforce looked away from the cumbersome legal machinery of the universities, and towards the individual colleges – self-governing bodies which, within the bounds of their charters, enjoyed immense liberty. Smaller, frequently representative of a geographic area, and already possessing a certain internal unity, the colleges proved to be the chief battleground of educational reform.

As in their criticism of the English church, puritans looked to the continent for models of reform of higher education too. Calvin himself made humanist classical learning the basis of his academy in Geneva,[1] but the academy also involved students in a full course of religious instruction: prayers, vernacular psalm-singing, repetition of the creed and commandments, attendance at Wednesday and Sunday sermons and Saturday afternoon catechizing, and readings from the Greek New Testament. In addition, communion was taken quarterly in the school, with an accompanying address by a minister. There was also a weekly prophesying under the guidance of the ministers, and a monthly theological disputation. Students were also bound to subscribe to the Calvinist 'confession'. Instruction in arts and the languages (including Aramaic and Syriac) was accompanied by the powerful presence of Calvin and Beza as the first two professors of theology.[2] Though Richard Bancroft spoke disparagingly in 1593 of the academy as 'beeing as it were a Grammar Schoole in comparison of our universities',[3] it became under Beza an intellectual cen-

---

[1] Harbison, *Christian Scholar*, pp. 144–6; Mackinnon, *Calvin and the Reformation*, p. 174, for the full curriculum of the academy. Calvin possibly modelled his enterprise on Sturm's school, at which he had taught while in exile from Geneva.
[2] Mackinnon, *Calvin and the Reformation*, pp. 174–7; McNeill, *History and Character of Calvinism*, pp. 193–5.   [3] Mullinger, *Cambridge*, II, p. 285 n. 2.

Godly Learning

tre for European, though only infrequently English, protestants.[4] At the same
time, the academy remained a stronghold of Aristotelianism and of Ciceronian
rhetoric; from the beginning, Calvinist learning was scholastic.[5] Dedicated to
purer Scriptures and to fighting Romanism, and yet rigidly connected to
traditional knowledge and to traditional approaches to knowledge, it became
a reformed mediaeval institute rather than the precursor of a 'modernist'
approach.

In Holland, too, the struggle for protestantism (and also independence)
produced an effort to reform the structure and content of university learning.
The University of Leiden, founded in 1575, attracted famous scholars in history, theology, philosophy, logic, and ethics, but also offered instruction in
optics, mathematics, anatomy, botany and geography.[6] The shock-wave of the
Synod of Dort gave more power to those who wished to redirect learning
towards William the Silent's original ends: 'ut studii theologici prima et
summa haberetur ratio'. From about 1625, theology students took courses in
New Testament Greek given by the University Professor of Greek.There was
thus, in the period of crisis, an attempt at a closer association of learning and
religious purpose, as the humanist thrust declined into a less brilliant protestant scholasticism.[7]

The Reformed impulse in Scotland took a rather different course in the late
sixteenth century. St Mary's College of St Andrews already represented the
institutionalization of a humanist curriculum, but at Marischal College (founded 1593) Andrew Melville introduced a more protestant thrust. Melville was
a strong advocate of Ramism, but perhaps more important was his emphasis on
the oriental languages as the basis of scriptural study. The course was designed
as the achievement of the trilingual ideal, with both Greek and Hebrew
introduced in the first year.[8] Combined with this academic incursion came
Melville's critique of the power of the aristocracy in Scottish church and
society, in favour of the middle-class urban godly.[9] The universities in
Scotland were located in the major economic centres. Thus in Scotland

[4]   One of the complaints against the administration of the Elizabethan church was that, while practitioners
      of medicine and law, educated abroad, were welcomed in England for their knowledge and skill, those
      educated overseas in the doctrines of Christ were forced to subscribe also to the English church's
      regulations. See, for example, *Copie of Letter to Londoner*, pp. 170–1, in *A Parte of a Register*.
[5]   Scheurleer & Meyjes, eds., *Leiden University*, p. 137. Peter Ramus delivered a course of lectures on logic
      and rhetoric, much to Beza's annoyance, and indeed Arminius, who studied under Beza (1582–7) was
      expelled from Geneva for tutoring in Ramist philosophy rather than for deviant theological opinions.
      Arminius evidently later returned to Geneva, finished his studies and even procured a testimonial
      from Beza.
[6]   Scheurleer & Meyjes, eds., *Leiden University*, pp. 9ff., 18; Morison, *Founding of Harvard College*, pp. 141–
      2.   [7]   Scheurleer & Meyjes, eds., *Leiden University*, esp. pp. 65ff.
[8]   Morison, *Founding of Harvard College*, pp. 133–4; Cameron, 'Renaissance tradition in Scotland', in
      Baker, ed., *Studies in Church History*, 14, esp. pp. 256–8; Henderson, *Founding of Marischal College*, pp.
      14–15.   [9]   Kearney, *Scholars and Gentlemen*, pp. 54–5.

Ramism became associated not only with academic innovation, but also with radical social reform.[10]

Religious instruction was formally based on a Sunday morning reading from the Greek New Testament, and an afternoon examination on the same lesson. In keeping with the presbyterian thrust, students were also required to attend a prophesying. While scholarship was thus not neglected, regular inspections of the College were to concentrate 'above all things' on religion. In very similar fashion to Thomas Norton's proposals for the imposition of individual discipline upon fellows and students alike, members of Marischal were bound to 'make a profession of faith, that Confession, namely, which, taken and transcribed from the Word of God, has been put forth and published in the Parliament of the realm; and this shall be done once at least every year'.[11] To add to the force of this purpose, in 1616/17 Patrick Copland, a graduate of the college, and a preacher for the East India Company, endowed a professorship of divinity for the college.[12] As with so much Reformed educational thought, the drive here was not to alter radically the undergraduate arts curriculum, but rather to direct it more effectively towards the twin purposes of serving commonwealth and (especially) church. The much stronger political connexions complicated the issue in Scotland, but, at bottom, the thrust which overtook Geneva and Leiden reached Scotland, too: the utilization of higher education in the cause of purifying the national church and proselytizing the countryside.

II

Mildmay's acorn, planted in Cambridge in 1584, has consistently been treated by historians as a house of nonconformity; such also was the verdict of contemporary opinion. In the 1630s, William Laud argued the necessity of cleansing Emmanuel; this was only the culmination of a half-century of criticism.[13]

[10] Kearney (*ibid.*, pp. 59–60) suggests that Whitgift and Bancroft opposed the English Ramists because of the Scottish example, and founded much of their polemic on the fear that similar events could take place in England if the Ramists were not extirpated from the universities. However, in his association of Ramism with the desire for radical reform, I think Professor Kearney goes too far. It warps the stand of William Perkins to include him in a 'list of the most radical Cambridge puritans' (*ibid.*, p. 61). Nor were English university puritans associated with an urban-based revolt against the power of the landed forces; on this, see the social composition of Emmanuel College, below, pp. 253–4.

[11] *Fasti Academiae Mariscallanae Aberdonensis*, I, pp. 66, 73, 74.   [12] *Ibid.*, pp. 159–84.

[13] Tyler, 'The children of disobedience', unpub. Ph.D. thesis, Univ. of California at Berkeley, 1976, p. 4; B.L. MS Harley 7033, fols. 161ff.

See, for example, Richard Corbett's annoyance that Emmanuel had not troubled herself with finery on the occasion of King James' visit to Cambridge in 1615:

> But the pure house of Emmanuel   An hypocrite, or painted thing;
> Would not be like proud Jezebel,   But, that the ways might all prove fair,
> Nor show herself before the King   Conceiv'd a tedious mile of prayer.

Quoted in Shuckburgh, *Emmanuel*, p. 37.

An analysis from the reign of James I noted that Emmanuel alone of the Cambridge colleges did not use the Book of Common Prayer, preferring 'a private course therein at their pleasure both sonday and workeday'. Emmanuel still did not use the surplice, and followed a different form of communion, admitting all members of the college rather than just ministers and deacons, as was usual. The college chapel, which remained unconsecrated, faced northwards where all other chapels looked east. The allowing of a married master (Chaderton) was unique among Cambridge colleges. Even in public habits such as wearing gowns and caps Emmanuel followed different rules.[14] But this is to note only a mild outward nonconformity, and to beg the question of the more important ways in which Emmanuel was a 'puritan' institution.

The puritan experimental faith in the power of education to lead to repentance and conversion was never more gracefuly phrased than in Mildmay's plea in his 1585 statutes that schools ought to be 'opened like fountains, that, arising out of the Paradise of God, they may as with a river of gold water all regions of our land . . . with a faith of purest doctrine and with a life of most holy discipline'. Mildmay recounted that it was a Christian tradition to train the young in arts and Scripture, so that they in turn could instruct others.[15] Lest there be any doubt concerning the vocational course which this entailed, Mildmay emphasized

that in establishing this College we have set before us this one aim of rendering as many persons as possible fit for the sacred ministry of the Word and the sacraments; so that from this seminary the Church of England might have men who it may call forth to instruct the people and undertake the duty of pastors . . . Be it known therefore to any Fellows or Scholars who intrude themselves into the College for any other purpose than to devote themselves to sacred Theology and in due time to labour in preaching the Word, that they render our hope vain . . .[16]

Though Mildmay could not have improved upon his choice of Chaderton – powerful godly preacher, educated in learned as well as modern languages, a strong Ramist, early public opponent of Baro, of presbyterian but not vitriolic opinion[17] – he was also intent on laying down qualifications in the statutes for future guidance. Masters were required to be English by birth, at least thirty years of age with sixteen years of study at Cambridge behind them, at least eight of which had to be in theology. They were to be ministers, public preachers, and practised in college 'lecturing', and known as detesters of 'Popery, heresy, and all superstitions and errors . . .'. The importance of the Master was to be impressed upon the college members in the sermon, commu-

14 I.T.L. MS Petyt 538/38, fol. 93: 'A breife of some differences in statutes and customes of Emmanuell Coll: in Camb: from all other foundations there'; B.L. MS Harley 7033, fols. 98ʳ⁻ᵛ, 164ᵛ.
15 Stubbings, ed., *Statutes of Mildmay . . . Emmanuel College*, 'Preface'.
16 Ibid., Ch. 21.   17 Dillingham, *Laurence Chaderton*, ed. Shuckburgh, esp. pp. 5–6.

nion and reading of statutes (and in the oath to obey them) which were to precede the secret ballot for the office.[18] Mildmay hoped that one of the fellows
of the college could be promoted, but if no one was qualified, then a search
should be made first at Christ's College, then in the whole university.[19] The
new Master was required to take an oath which offered an opening to the
institutionalizing of nonconformity:

I will set the authority of Scripture before the judgment of even the best of men . . .; I
will refute all opinions that be contrary to the Word of God, and that I will in the
cause of religion always set what is true before what is customary, what is written
before what is not written.[20]

Fellows were similarly bound to be English, of M.A. or at least advanced
B.A. standing, and chosen preferably from the scholars of the college; consideration was also to be given to those in financial need. The common custom
of a geographical preference was maintained, primacy of place being given to
Essex and Northampton.[21] The fellows were to be over twenty-one years old,
skilled in the three tongues, and knowledgeable in rhetoric, logic and 'physic'.
But there was a higher qualification in keeping with the more serious purposes: 'above all they shall be professors of pure religion, contrary to Popery
and other heresies, and such as have conformed their life and manners
thereunto'. Mildmay did not want unknown quantities as fellows; no one was
eligible for election until he had spent at least six years in the university.[22] As
well, prospective fellows were to be tested '(if need be) in Theology and the
true knowledge of God',[23] and were required to take an oath against popery
and in support of Mildmay's statutes.[24]

In offering a daily routine for the members of his college, Mildmay
rehearsed the typical prohibitions against frequenting taverns, entertaining
women in college, venturing outside the college in the evening, playing cards
or dice, and so one.[25] But it was in positively guiding the confluence of discipline, humane learning, and fervency that he sought to build an innovative
seminary. All students were to be placed in the care of a tutor (the master or a
fellow), who was responsible for morals, academic instruction, and personal
guidance, including religion.[26] The particular texts to be used by the college
lecturers Mildmay left to the expertise of the master and dean. If lecturers

---

[18] Stubbings, ed., *Statutes of Mildmay . . . Emmanuel College*, Ch. 9.
[19] *Ibid.* Christ's was both Chaderton's old college and an early centre of puritan activity at Cambridge;
Perkins was a Christ's man, for example.   [20] *Ibid.*, Ch. 11.
[21] Essex and Northampton were indeed counties in which puritans had strong bases, but Mullinger offers
the far more sensible explanation for this attachment, that Essex was the county of Mildmay's birth, and
Northampton his seat in Parliament (*Cambridge*, II, p. 312).
[22] Stubbings, ed., *Statutes of Mildmay . . . Emmanuel College*, Ch. 17.   [23] *Ibid.*, Ch. 18.
[24] *Ibid.*, Ch. 19.   [25] *Ibid.*, Ch. 22, on the conduct of fellows, Chs. 28 and 31, on students.
[26] *Ibid.*, Ch. 27. The close bond of tutors and pupils was encouraged by the common regulation that pupils
sleep in their tutor's chamber. On tutors, see below, pp. 282–92.

wished to expound an academic topic of their own choosing, they were enjoined to select from the works of Plato, Aristotle, or Cicero – the embodiment of solid scholarship. The head lecturer was also to serve as the moderator of the disputations and other scholastic exercises in which Mildmay followed contemporary university form.[27] By the end of the century Emmanuel undergraduates studied Greek, Ramus' *Logic* and Aristotle's *Organon*, *Ethics*, *Politics* and *Physics*, and, if time permitted, also Phrygius' *Natural Philosophy*.[28] Scholars, who were to be skilled in Greek, rhetoric, and logic,[29] were bound to attend all college lectures and, Mildmay insisted, also exercises in the public schools, 'according to the custom of the University'.[30]

Scholars were also to proceed to degrees as soon as the university statutes permitted; no one was to remain as a scholar more than a year after becoming eligible for the M.A.[31] Mildmay's purpose, after all, was to train men for the pastoral ministry. To this same end Mildmay in 1587/8 added a clause, *de mora sociorum*, which made clear that fellows were not to think that they had been granted a permanent home at Emmanuel. Mildmay thus institutionalized a common puritan objection that neither church nor state benefited from cloistered lives of academic contemplation. Master and fellows were to proceed to the doctorate in divinity as quickly as university statutes allowed. The master was to hold office permanently, but fellows could keep their tenure for only one year after becoming D.D., though certain extensions were allowed.[32] Fellows were, however, then to be considered for any vacant benefices to which the college held the right of appointment.[33]

It was in formulating regulations for the religious studies and practices of the college that Mildmay was most specific. All the fellows, scholars and other residents were to attend the public prayers in the college; the master was to deliver a sermon and administer communion at least every term, but preferably more frequently.[34] To make the search for true religion active rather than merely passive, Mildmay also decreed that each week the fellows were to

[27] *Ibid.*, Ch. 29.   [28] Shuckburgh, *Emmanuel*, p. 31.
[29] Stubbings, ed., *Statutes of Mildmay . . . Emmanuel College*, Ch. 32.   [30] *Ibid.*, Ch. 34.
[31] *Ibid.*, Ch. 35.
[32] The year's extension for fellows was not to include time served as Vice-Chancellor, Regius Professor of Divinity, or Lady Margaret Professor of Divinity. There was later an attempt to have this statute overthrown. In 1627 the fellows petitioned King Charles who, against the opposition of both Chaderton and Preston, set it aside. It was reintroduced by Parliament in 1641 (Shuckburgh, *Emmanuel*, pp. 62–5, 66). A 1627 letter from ten Emmanuel fellows to the Duke of Buckingham, arguing for repeal, put forward the contention, not perhaps to be expected from a 'puritan' college, that the statute had been designed to correct 'the scarcitie of sufficient Preachers'; this was no longer necessary, given that the church was 'now replenished with manie able men' (C.U.L. MS Baker 27.4, pp. 67–8; *ibid.*, pp. 69–71, for Charles' conditional suspension of the statute). See also C.U.L. MS Baker 30.25, pp. 415–16, for the reasons for Chaderton's opposition to the suspension.
[33] This provision, however, also meant that Emmanuel graduates tended to migrate to other colleges, where they were offered life tenure (Tyler, 'Children of disobedience', pp. 161–2).
[34] Stubbings, *Statutes of Mildmay . . . Emmanuel College*, Ch. 20.

hold a disputation in theology. This exercise was to be supplemented by the master and fellows engaging in 'such more fruitful manner of exercises as they shall decide to be most convenient for the promotion of the study of Theology and for the training of ministers of the Word'.[35] In order to lead this thrust, the four most senior fellows were always required to be ministers.[36] Mildmay also provided for a dean or catechist, who was to moderate the theology disputation and to note absences from divine service, a most serious offence. His duty on Saturdays was to expound for an hour on a particular topic of Christianity; he also had full power to examine the religious understanding of the scholars and undergraduates, whose knowledge was to be supplemented by the reading of the Bible by the scholars at every meal.[37]

Further college orders, adopted in 1588, required the master and fellows to meet periodically for a 'mutuall conference or communication of giftes'.[38] The resulting conclusions of this scholarly Biblicism were to be passed on by the tutors to their pupils.[39] Chaderton was himself involved with various aspects of the presbyterian movement, including secret meetings at St John's, Cambridge, to discuss the 'discipline'. His suggestion for a prophesying at Emmanuel therefore combined a theoretical view of the necessity of eventually restructuring the church with practical vocational training for those ministers who had to go immediately to the countryside. Chaderton was evidently particularly concerned to establish by scholarly means scriptural roots for contemporary ecclesiastical practices.[40] Especially important in light of our earlier discussion of the more abstract approach of puritans to 'learning' is that this blueprint for godly educational *practice* was based on a short analysis of the proselytizing efforts of Paul, who is thus again identified as the puritan model for existence at the immediate level.[41]

Under the Emmanuel plan, interpretation of a text was offered by 'two or three' speakers; judgement was then passed by the rest of the assembly. Since in this latter age the gift of direct revelation 'is ceased', no blame was to be attached to personal shortcomings. Presbyterians rather emphasized the supremacy of 'the whole company of Prophets' to the individual. Great emphasis was thus placed on the pooling of talents for mutual edification.[42] The group was to meet at seven p.m. on days on which there had been an exercise, in order to consider the opinions propounded. Senior members were

---

[35] *Ibid.*, Ch. 21.
[36] *Ibid.* Indeed, any fellow in line for promotion to the senior post who refused to become a minister was to be stripped of his fellowship.   [37] *Ibid.*, Chs. 14, 21, 35.
[38] Emma. MS Col. 14.1, pp. 3–8, entitled 'A mutuall conference or communication of giftes among Students in Divinity confirmed by the Canonicall Scriptures'.
[39] *Ibid.*   [40] Lake, *Moderate Puritans*, pp. 26, 43–4, 45.
[41] Especially is the stress on Paul's attempts to get the Corinthians 'to diligent use of the gift of Prophecy'. The Pauline references are to I Corinthians 14.29; I Thessalonians 5.21; Colossians 3.16; I Corinthians 12.7,25; I Corinthians 3.10. Emma. MS Col. 14.1, pp. 3–8.   [42] *Ibid.*, pp. 3–4, 5, 7.

always to speak first, and the 'rest in order'. Chaderton (if he was, as we may suspect, the prime mover) did not intend these sessions merely to give approval to received opinion; he well understood that keen young minds – learned and fervent – might well disagree. After all had spoken, the master, or senior fellow present, was to pronounce the judgement of the group.

It would seem that the chief speaker of the exercise would not be present during the drawing up of criticism, since no one was to 'reveale unto the party censured, who it was that found fault with him; because the judgement is the judgement of all & not of any one alone.' Any speaker so censured was to reform his opinion, or at least to cease publishing it until God more clearly revealed the truth of the matter. Public disagreement and disharmony were thus to be avoided. And so that the leaders of Emmanuel could not be accused of fomenting dissension within the wider church, all agreed that 'no man which is not of the company bee made privy to that whiche is done amongest us'.[43] For further secrecy, in which lay safety, in 1595 the fellows agreed 'for the better avoyding of publicke contradiction' that anyone speaking on a contentious religious question should submit his opinions beforehand to the community, which would effectively have the power to silence individual opinion. In addition, the fellows agreed to avoid any personal criticism in the exercise; for future concord, all prospective M.A.s were also to agree to this clause before they would be admitted.[44] By such means did the forward members of the society seek to guarantee a vision of uniformity to outsiders, and also to prevent the internal splits which had so rent other colleges.

The different form of church service, the neglect of surplices, sitting at communion, the irregular construction of the chapel – none of these argued an overt anti-episcopal atmosphere at Emmanuel, though men such as Chaderton certainly preferred presbyterianism.[45] Rather, the members of the college aimed at a scholarly testament to 'living religion'; in such did their distinction from their contemporaries lie. Though there is no hard evidence of direct instruction in the 'covenant' at Emmanuel in the Elizabethan period, it is highly likely that after the 1590s Emmanuel tutors exercised their pupils in its structures and popular ramifications. It is also hardly to be believed that John Preston would have been chosen second master only for his teaching ability and supposed political connexions if the fellows had not approved of his theology. Preston was one of the leading covenanters in England. In Preston's time, too, Anthony Tuckney delivered a catechism in the college chapel which reflected the importance of this doctrine in the training of godly students:

[43] *Ibid.*, p. 7.   [44] *Ibid.*, p. 11; this constitutes a separate 'Memorandum' headed 'Commonplacing'.
[45] For discussion of Chaderton's presbyterian opinions (and the ascription to him of a strongly presbyterian sermon on Romans 12.3–8), see Lake, *Moderate Puritans*, pp. 26–35.

Quest. How many covenants are there. Ans. the old which is the covenante of workes and the new which is the covenant of grace. Quest. what is the tenor of the covenant of workes. Ans. doe this & live. Q. what is the tenor of the covenante of grace. Ans. believe and be saved.[46]

Tyler has also noted that the sermons of Richard Holdsworth, Master of Emmanuel, 'reflect the common-law legalistic quality characteristic of much of covenant thought . . .'.[47] The same message as poured out from so many tracts and pulpits was thus delivered as a matter of policy before the gathered company of Emmanuel.

Despite the statutes' stress on religion and training for the ministry, Emmanuel did not turn out exactly as Mildmay had planned. Emmanuel remained a comparatively poor college with very few fellows. Nonetheless, it rapidly attracted a host of students, and over the period 1596–1645 Emmanuel admitted more members than even St John's. Indeed, during the 1620s, Emmanuel was the largest house in the university.[48] Not all these hundreds, however, came to study the humane arts, imbibe the gospel and return to their counties as ministerial proselytizers. Though inter-college migration attracted extra plebeians to Emmanuel,[49] Mildmay's college appealed especially to the well-born, and particularly to the ranks of the lower gentry. Emmanuel likely offered a distinct home for the 'politically and socially important ranks', who were already suffering 'profound disenchantment' with the church settlement and with Stuart innovations.[50] This emphasis on the well-born was reflected in the low incidence of degree-taking by Emmanuel students generally, and especially by the college's esquires/gentlemen.[51] The social composition is further reflected in a statistic that would surely have sorrowed Mildmay. While the ministry remained the most common post-university occupation, a smaller percentage of students entered the ministry from Emmanuel than from a number of other Cambridge colleges. This may have been due, in part, to Emmanuel's social composition; the high-born only infrequently chose the ministry as a career.[52] A certain discouragement to becoming a minister may

---

[46] Emma. MS III.i.13, dated 1628.

[47] Tyler, 'Children of disobedience', p. 256; also pp. 255–6, for other evidence of teaching of the covenant at Emmanuel.

[48] *Ibid.*, pp. 40, 43–4; Kearney, *Scholars and Gentlemen*, pp. 56–7. As a mark of Emmanuel's poor financial attractions, we may note that in December 1640 a committee of the House of Commons under Sir Henry Mildmay, grandson of the founder, concluded that the limit of £4 per year on scholarships and £10 per year on Fellows' salaries, rendered them 'contemptible'. B.L. MS Harley 7033, fol. 102[r–v]; Twigg, 'University of Cambridge', unpublished Ph.D. thesis, Univ. of Cambridge, 1983, pp. 35–6.

[49] Tyler, 'Children of disobedience', pp. 180–1; the comparative basis is St John's, King's, and Jesus.   [50] *Ibid.*, pp. 245, 147, 199; Cliffe, *Puritan Gentry*, esp. pp. 96–7.

[51] Tyler, 'Children of disobedience', pp. 322, 162.

[52] Only 11.8% of gentle youths at Emmanuel (17.2% in the other three colleges) entered the ministry (*ibid.*, p. 163).

have affected Emmanuel students because so few of them rose to the upper levels of the ecclesiastical hierarchy.[53]

At first sight, the two factors of well-born students and lower incidence of ministerial entrants among students would seem to have defeated Mildmay's intention of educating young men (and especially the poor) only for the ministry. And yet, paradoxically, this social composition may indeed have ensured the nonconformist impact of Emmanuel. First, Emmanuel's sizars still evidently aimed for a degree: 77.5% proceeded at least B.A., a figure which fitted in with other colleges; 83.6% of plebeian students at Emmanuel took a degree.[54] In terms of traditional class orientation towards degrees, and the attractiveness of the formal study of theology, Emmanuel did not lag behind. Secondly, Emmanuel seems to have been able to build a particular, faithful following. There was a strong bond between clerics who had attended Cambridge and the choice of Emmanuel; this paid off for Mildmay's plan in the next generation.[55] At the same time, reflecting the nonconformist reputation of Emmanuel, the higher clergy chose other colleges for their sons.[56] Those who were struggling in their vocation to bring godliness to the countryside evidently knew that Emmanuel especially would encourage clerical sons to continue God's work.

One might have supposed that political pressure, moral corruption, and the increasing lay quotient might have driven puritans to abandon universities in favour of private seminaries. On the other side of the religious dialectic, by 1626 thirty-six seminaries had been founded in response to the Council of Trent's direction.[57] Prophesyings may have served as a partial substitute for more formal seminaries, especially as any such puritan foundation would have come under immediate suspicion, if not outright attack. But perhaps most important was the realization of the utility of the close alliance with young gentlemen and merchants (and possibly their parents) that would be built in the universities. One should not forget the economic problems of a young, poorly endowed, popular college; esquires and gentlemen could more than pay their way. Similarly, Emmanuel seems to have attracted the upper crust of the 'plebeian' entrants, especially the sons of well-to-do merchants who would enter as fellow-commoners and pensioners.[58] Emmanuel evidently became the most consistent choice for educational charity of the London mercantile elite; Wolstan Dixie, for example, sometime Sheriff and Lord Mayor of the capital, granted the college £1250 and endowed a Greek and Hebrew lectureship.[59] Emmanuel thus combined three crucial social groups: the lower

---

[53]   *Ibid.*, p. 222, noting also that Emmanuel graduates became lecturers in disproportionate numbers.
[54]   *Ibid.*, pp. 323, 203.   [55]   *Ibid.*, pp. 172–3, 176.   [56]   *Ibid.*, pp. 171, 153–4.
[57]   Morgan, 'Approaches to the history of the English universities', p. 143 n. 15.
[58]   Tyler, 'Children of disobedience', p. 189.
[59]   Jordan, *Charities of London*, p. 264. Jordan also lists several other large donations to the college.

gentry, the upper bourgeoisie and clerical offspring. The former two groups proved crucial to godly reform by providing patronage and then protecting ministers, and also by proselytizing their own households.[60] A study of the lay students at Emmanuel and their later dealings with puritan ministers may well reveal the creation of the same sort of bonding as Haller found among the 'brotherhood' of ministers.[61] By training all together in humane arts, non-conformist church practices, and covenant theology, Emmanuel produced an influential body of godly alumni. This unified form of education also had the advantage of requiring the broader training of 'clerical' students, who perhaps more quickly learned the nature of the problems for future casuistry, and who were also thus prevented from developing monkish attitudes. By not becoming a seminary in the narrower sense of the word, Emmanuel became a greater one for the society as a whole.

III

Though Emmanuel was the first, and remained the foremost, attempt to institutionalize reformed education, the impulse spread elsewhere in our period. A decade after Mildmay penned his original statutes, the Countess of Sussex bequeathed £5000 for the foundation of a new college, or, failing that, for the embellishment of Clare Hall. Her executors, seeking to found another seminary for the training of a godly ministry, in large measure copied the statutes of Emmanuel in establishing Sidney Sussex College, though there were certain modifications.[62] The godly thrust, however, was maintained. So the office of college catechist included presiding, in term, at a weekly theological disputation, spending an hour on Sunday afternoon expounding some article of Christian faith, and examining the Christian knowledge of all the scholars, pensioners, and servants dwelling in the college. The college's prime purpose of training suitably qualified candidates for the ministry required the master to preach in the chapel at least at the beginning of each term. Students were also required to attend public prayers in the chapel and to be frequent attenders of university sermons. Candidates for fellowships were examined on their knowledge of Latin, Greek, rhetoric, logic, theology, and Hebrew; if successful, they engaged, as fellows, in the weekly disputations in theology.[63]

The required course of undergraduate studies showed no great variance from that imbibed elsewhere. But as at Emmanuel, the inclusion of a clause *de*

---

[60] See esp. Cliffe, *Puritan Gentry*, pp. 96–7, and Ch. 9.   [61] Haller, *Rise of Puritanism*, Ch. 2.

[62] For example, the master was to be chosen from Trinity if no suitable Sidney candidates were available; the master also had greater power at Sidney than at Emmanuel (Mullinger, *Cambridge*, II, p. 362).

[63] Edwards, *Sidney Sussex*, pp. 29, 30, 33–4, 37. Sidney, however, like Emmanuel, remained poor. In 1612 it was suggested that the college could afford only 7 fellows rather than the 10 originally mentioned (Mullinger, *Cambridge*, II, pp. 359–60).

mora sociorum in collegio attempted to force fellows into the practice of the ministry; all fellows were to take orders within three years of their election, and were to leave the college within seven years of attaining eligibility for the D.D.[64] However, pressure from the fellows (as later at Emmanuel) led to the rescinding of this statute in 1614. In a letter of 1629 to Charles, Laud described Sidney Sussex as one of the 'Nurseries of Puritanism'. But though Sidney remained by reputation a forward college to opponents of the puritan spirit, it was unable to maintain the virtually complete independence and drive of Emmanuel. James Montagu, first master, and later a bishop, even prescribed the wearing of the surplice, an important outward mark of conformity.[65] Nonetheless, under the long mastership of Samuel Ward, even through the Laudian ascendancy, Sidney continued to provide a home for Calvinist 'orthodoxy', advice for puritan preachers, and a bulwark against innovations. But it always remained a more quiet centre of nonconformity and existed perpetually in the shadow of the reputation of Emmanuel.

The establishment of Trinity College, Dublin (1591), was supposed to serve the needs for higher education of both English colonists and Irish natives, who 'heretofore used to travaile into ffrance, Italy and Spaine to gett learning in such forreigne universities, whereby they have been infected with poperie and other ill qualities, and soe became evill subjects'.[66] From the beginning the small college of only four fellows, modelled on Cambridge, attempted to combine the arts with the forward protestant urge to more edifying scriptural interpretation: 'On Saturdays in the afternoon, each tutor read a divinity lecture in Latin to his pupils, dictating it (as they did all other their lectures) so deliberately that they might easily write after them, to their great benefit and advantage.' This method, for many of the pupils, must have seemed the continuation and perfection of the traditional Sunday spent in church with other pupils, struggling to make notes on a sermon delivered for the general edification of the whole congregation. As well, however, it should perhaps be suggested that this process might have testified to a shortage of books.[67]

Despite the statutory requirement of the usual arts course, Trinity lagged behind the English universities and, before the end of our period 'does not appear to have been a very effective place of learning . . .'.[68] That the college

---

[64] Edwards, *Sidney Sussex College*, p. 35.
[65] Cliffe, *Puritan Gentry*, p. 98; Tyler, 'Children of disobedience', pp. 3–4, 6.
[66] Dixon, *Trinity College*, p. 7, quoting the warrant from Elizabeth for the founding of the college.
[67] *Ibid.*, p. 20, quoting the report by the chaplain of Henry Ussher, Archdeacon of Dublin (later Archbishop of Armagh) and the man who obtained the charter for Trinity. See also Kearney, *Scholars and Gentlemen*, p. 69; McDowell & Webb, 'Courses and teaching in Trinity College', *Hermathena*, 69, p. 10.
[68] Morison, *Founding of Harvard College*, p. 124; Stubbs, *University of Dublin*, p. 21. The lack of adequate instruction in Hebrew is also noted in McDowell & Webb, 'Courses and teaching in Trinity College', p. 11.

maintained a schoolmaster is further testimony to this lower level of scholarship.[69] Despite Archbishop Abbot's claim in 1613 that some of the college statutes were 'flat puritannical', and his suggestion in 1616 that the college surrender its charter in order to receive another one,[70] it was rather the leadership of the college than its structures or courses which brought it early notice. The succession of the first three provosts – Adam Loftus, Walter Travers, and Henry Alvey – indicates an increasingly radical puritan direction for the college, which was assisted by the policy of inviting learned men from Cambridge to come over as either dons or parish ministers. Assisting this thrust further was the very strong influence of Ramist teaching, especially under the famed logician William Temple, the fourth provost (and the first to be a layman). He, too, worked to bring the college closer in line with the Reformed model of a seminary. He established the post of Professor of Theological Controversies, later called the Regius Professorship, to which the puritan Joshua Hoyle was the first named.[71] He also appointed two deans, a bursar and a librarian, increased the number of fellows from four to sixteen, and instituted the office of catechist, which had served to such advantage in many colleges. Upon Temple's death, the appointment fell to William Bedell, sometime fellow of Emmanuel and minister.[72] Bedell proved a happy choice from the point of view of the godly cause, as he instituted a catechizing session on Sundays after dinner. True to the Pauline impulse, Bedell also aimed at the conversion of the Irish by producing ministers who could preach in the vernacular. He evidently organized diocesan synods and conferences of ministers, and also, before ordaining anyone – he was later a bishop – always closely examined the candidate with the help of two or three other ministers, in keeping with old puritan plans for a consensus of practising ministers concerning the quality of entrants.[73] He also established a scheme for translating the Old Testament into Irish.[74] To the end of fulfilling vocation, he instituted a policy that fellows should leave the college after studying divinity for seven years, thus bringing Mildmay's regulation to bear on this Irish outpost of intended godliness.[75]

The election of William Chappel as provost in 1633, following the relatively brief rule of Robert Ussher, brought the Ramist influence to its height. Chappell was later the author of a Ramist manual on preaching. He

---

[69]   Stubbs, *University of Dublin*, p. 21.   [70]   Dixon, *Trinity College*, p. 29.

[71]   *Ibid.*, pp. 27–8. Hoyle was later a member of the Westminster Assembly of Divines, and from 1648 to his death in 1654 served as Regius Professor of Divinity in Oxford. On the policy of attracting Cambridge scholars, see Mahaffey, *Epoch in Irish History*, pp. 139–40.

[72]   Thus the first five provosts were all Cambridge men. Richard Sibbes was offered the job after Temple's death, but evidently preferred England and the master's post at St Catharine's, Cambridge (Mahaffey, *Epoch in Irish History*, pp. 193–4).

[73]   Bod. Lib. MS Tanner 278, No. 2, fols. 32, 32ᵛ; Mahaffey, *Epoch in Irish History*, pp. 203–4.

[74]   Bod. Lib. MS Tanner 278, No. 2, fol. 40.
       Dixon, *Trinity College*, pp. 33–5. The latter point, on the connexion in purpose of Mildmay and Bedell, is noted by Morison, *Founding of Harvard College*, p. 356 n. 3.

served by Laud's appointment, though on the advice of the strongly Calvinist
Archbishop of Armagh, James Ussher; he was provost when the Laudian
statutes were imposed in 1637.[76] Chappell was something of a paradox – a
Ramist with a contemporary reputation which ranged from puritan to high
churchman.[77] The late 1630s at Trinity, as in Oxford and Cambridge, proved
to be a low point for the precise forces. Chappell was evidently not the man to
lead a godly seminary in resistance against religious 'innovation'. Trinity
therefore ended our period as one of those puritan seminaries in need of
revivification.

IV

Before the end of our period, the puritan educational impulse had been carried
to New England; within a generation of the first landings, the puritan exiles
had commanded the erection of a system of schools and had founded a new
college (1636). Even before structure and endowment had been worked out,
puritans were suggesting extraordinary methods of ensuring the existence of
higher learning in the colony. An early suggestion from Emmanuel Downing
to John Winthrop illustrates the degree to which methods in church and
education were intertwined in puritan minds:

The name of a Colledge in your plantation would much advantadge yt considering the
present distast against our universityes. you need not stay till you have Colledges to
lodge schollars, for if you could but make a Combination of some few able men,
ministers, or others to read certeyne lectures, and that yt were knowne here amongst
honest men, you would soone have students, hence, and Incouradgement to proceed
further therein; what great burthen would yt be to a Minister for the present (till you
have meanes and be better supplyed with schollars) once a week for a moneth in evrie
quarter to reade a logick, greke or hebrew lecture or the like[78]

The combination lecture had brought the godly light to so many dark parishes
of England; now it was to be appropriated, by lay teachers as well, to spread
the logic and trilingual knowledge indispensable to the perpetuation of a
godly community.

  S. E. Morison argued that Harvard was founded for the 'advancement of
learning', though in a strongly Christian vein.[79] Morison stressed the fervency

---

[76] *D.N.B.*, s.v. 'William Chappell'.
[77] Parliament later proceeded against Chappell, but his preaching manual is in the style of Perkins and
     Bernard. For a variety of opinions on Chappell, see *D.N.B.*; Miller, *New England Mind, passim*; Dixon,
     Trinity College, pp. 36–7; Morison, *Founding of Harvard College*, pp. 112–13; Kearney, *Scholars and
     Gentlemen*, p. 95; Fletcher, *Intellectual Development, passim*; Mahaffey, *Epoch in Irish History*, pp.
     230–1.   [78] *Winthrop Papers*, III, p. 370.
[79] Morison, *Founding of Harvard College*, esp. pp. 247–51; Morison, *Harvard in the Seventeenth Century*. For
     an early criticism, see Hudson, 'Morison myth', *Church History*, 8, pp. 148–59.

of the early colonists, and acknowledged that Henry Dunster, 'no less than Augustine and Aquinas, accounted pride of knowledge a deadly sin'.[80] The crucial sentence describing purpose is extracted from 'New England's First Fruits', a promotional pamphlet of 1643 designed to encourage English donations. 'One of the next things we longed for, and looked after, was to advance *Learning* and perpetuate it to Posterity; dreading to leave an illiterate Ministry to the Churches, when our present Ministers shall lie in the Dust.'[81] Morison read these as separate clauses and, therefore, as separate purposes.[82] He did not see the vibrant puritan dialectic between godliness and humane learning which was epitomized in the puritan approach to education, and which was reflected even in the early statutes of Harvard.

Another, tangential problem has arisen from the belief that puritans could bring into existence in New England what they could but hope for in the more hostile English environment.[83] The concern with what puritans 'would have done' had they faced no opposition can easily be turned the other way. Puritans arrived in New England to find what they regarded as social and cultural desolation. They had no institutional means of perpetuating their learning other than by sending all youths back to England – a virtually impossible task – or by founding schools. That they founded certain institutions is perhaps testimony not necessarily so much to what was at the 'core of puritan belief' as simply to what was regarded as the basis of an acceptable social fabric. In New England puritans had to provide for both future ministers and the learned lay occupations.

Harvard, like Emmanuel before it, did not become a narrow seminary; only about 40–50% of its students entered the ministry.[84] Since the first generation of emigrants to New England included a high proportion of ministers, it is perhaps not surprising that Harvard turned out slightly more graduates who did not enter the ministry. The restricted job market for ministers in New England must also have been a factor. Puritans, as we have seen, did not favour

---

[80] Morison, *Founding*, p. 251. See also Miller, *New England Mind*, pp. 75–6, for a tempering of Morison's interpretation.   [81] Morison, *Founding of Harvard College*, Appendix D, p. 432.

[82] Morison argued (*ibid.*, p. 419) that the semi-colon after 'Posterity' was crucial; changing it to a comma, he observed, altered the meaning of the sentence. This stand is highly questionable. He noted (*ibid.*, p. 419) that he had corrected certain printer's errors in the text, such as the irregular numbering of the pages, and also certain grammatical errors. But, 'I have altered no punctuation' (*ibid.*, p. 419), though why the assumption was made that a printer who could number consecutive pages 6–15–8–9–18–19–12–13–22–15 should get the punctuation perfect, is not explained. It could well be observed that the placing of a semi-colon after 'Posterity' renders the rest of the sentence ungrammatical; a comma there would make the sentence grammatically correct. Either, then, this is a printer's error, or the puritans (as all readers of their tracts know) did not conform to our grammatical usage. It is, in either case, a very dubious basis on which to place such emphasis.   [83] Miller, *New England Mind*, p. 75.

[84] Morison says 40%; Smith, 'Teacher in puritan culture', *Harvard Educational Review*, 36, pp. 396–7, says 50%.

a society in which only the ministers possessed the arts.[85] Indeed, it had become a clear function of protestant education that undergraduate 'lay' and 'clerical' students be educated side by side. In all likelihood, the object of 'New England's First Fruits' was to point out that the college functioned largely in Oxbridge form, and to the same (though purified) purposes. Though by the 1630s virtually all new ministers were graduates, a polemical pamphlet destined for an England in which the balance of power was as yet uncertain must have sought to ensure that New Englanders could not be accused, as were early puritans, of abandoning the heritage of the universities for the wilderness of enthusiasm. The authors[86] therefore noted the presence of a grammar school by the college to train youngsters in *Academicall Learning*, the training in 'tongues and Arts' and 'the principles of Divinity and Christianity' to the students' great 'progresse in Learning and godlinesse also', the familiar regimen of scholastic exercises, the use of classical authors, the system of tutors, the importance placed on catechizing, and the usual course of studies, which also formally added Hebrew and 'the Easterne tongues' to the undergraduate curriculum. Great emphasis was placed on godliness; the authors noted that students could be expelled for transgressing the laws of God as well as those of the college.[87]

The absence of a standardized school system meant that early Harvard not only maintained its own schoolmaster, but also entered boys at an early age and with low academic standards.[88] By 1650 the college had to insist also on a testament from the pupil's schoolmaster concerning his 'obedience & submission to all Godly School-discipline & of his studiousness & diligence . . .'. It had learned 'by experience' that it was 'prejudicial to the promotion of Learning & good manners' to admit negligent and overly young students.[89] The requirements for a Harvard B.A. were raised in the regulations of 1655. Now, in addition to four years' residence, each student had to demonstrate that

upon proofe [he] is able to read extempore the Pentateuch, and the New Testament into Latin out of the Originall Tongues, & being Skilled in Logicke, & Competently principled in Naturall and Morall philosophy & the Mathematicks, & also of honest Life & Conversation, & at any publicke Act hath publicke approbation of the Overseers & President of the Colledge . . .[90]

[85] To this point, see the letter of 12 Aug. 1629 from Robert Ryece to his friend John Winthrop, suggesting reasons for *not* emigrating to New England. One of them was 'How harde wyll it bee for one broughte up amonge boockes and learned men to lyve in a barbarous place where is no learnynge and lesse cyvillytie' (*Winthrop Papers*, II, p. 106).
[86] The pamphlet is anonymous, but Morison argues that the authors were Hugh Peter and Thomas Weld (*Founding of Harvard College*, pp. 303–4).   [87] 'New Englands first fruits', in *ibid.*, pp. 433–6.
[88] *Ibid.*, p. 433.
[89] 'The lawes . . . of Harvard College [1650], *Collections*, Publications of the Colonial Society of Massachusetts, 15, pp. 28–9.
[90] 'Lawes of the College . . . 1655', *Collections*, Public. Col. Soc. Mass., xxxi, p. 334.

The arts course thus remained essentially conservative. Ramus was well known at Harvard, but he did not reign alone. Indeed, the texts owned by students reflect a devotion to Alsted, Burgersdicius, Calvin, Keckermann, and Aristotle – in sum, the common protestant scholastic thrust of Reformed universities.[91] The requisite botany course, for example, was Aristotelian, studied probably through Keckermann; chemistry was not added until 1687.[92] As well, the Aristotelian position (again transmitted through Keckermann) that ethics and theology were distinct seems to have been favoured at early Harvard over Ames' argument that proper ethics could not exist outside the concept of true religion.[93]

The 'religious demography' of the early colony might well have been expected to affect radically the nature of its higher education. New England enjoyed a higher proportion of godly ministers than England. As well, the colony was to a much higher degree presumed to contain the 'godly'. Finally, Harvard was free from the oppressive university restrictions which colleges at Oxford and Cambridge could not fully circumvent in their practices. To a large degree, then, New England enjoyed the circumstantial liberty to establish a new form of godly learning. The conservatism of the structure and scholastic curriculum of Harvard must therefore reinforce the conclusion that puritans were interested not in the 'advancement of learning', but rather only in the proper employment of what was already known to greater scriptural understanding.

Students at Harvard, as in England, were in the charge of a tutor. It must be expected that those who entered the college with no intention of the ministry, and therefore a lesser intention of proceeding to a degree, would have had their course tailored more to the humane arts. The maintaining of the social hierarchy at Harvard – all 'fellow-commoners' were to donate silver plate of a minimum value of £3 – is a further indication that there was no expectation that the college would become a narrow seminary. The M.A. course, as in England, remained an arts degree. Normally this degree at Harvard was attractive to future ministers, and candidates spent much time reading theology. But the slackness of regulations governing subject, and especially the absence of a mandatory residence rule, meant that these students were left very much to their own devices.[94]

Despite the emphasis on the arts, it has been argued that at Harvard the 'religious exercises and the study of the Bible formed the center of the scheme, the other subjects were such as aided the student first, to interpret the Bible correctly for himself; and second, to expound to others, and to defend

---

[91]   Norton, 'Harvard text-books', *Transactions 1930–1933*, Public. Col. Soc. Mass., xxviii, *passim*.
[92]   Morison, *Harvard in the Seventeenth Century*, p. 235.   [93]   *Ibid.*, pp. 260–1.
[94]   'Lawes of the College . . . 1655', *passim*.

(in public debate if need be) his interpretation'. Beyond personal assurance and ministerial training, it was hoped that those who used humane learning for 'secular' purposes would at least proceed from a godly bias. Norton noted that the curriculum and exercises aspired to this godly goal through a sixfold division: the practice of piety; the study and analysis of the Bible; instruction in the principles of divinity; the mastery of the languages needed to read Scripture in the 'original'; auxiliary studies necessary to provide correct interpretation of the Bible; and, finally, the studies and exercises required for effective exposition of an interpretation.[95]

To the first end of inculcating piety, the 1655 laws required each student to attend chapel twice daily, and, in turn, to repeat a sermon in hall. On Saturday evenings, students were to give an account of 'their profitting by the Sermons preached the weeke past'. That this was required of *all* undergraduates reinforces the view of Harvard as a seminary in the wider sense of Emmanuel. On Sunday students were to attend the services of the local church.[96] 'Conversation' was held to be crucial; the customary rules against student 'vices' were included in the laws, with severe penalties for offences. Especially harshly punished, however, were the missing of religious exercises and also blasphemy or profaning the Lord's Day, which latter two called for expulsion *ipso facto*.[97]

For the second part of the scheme – analysis of the Bible – students were to read the Bible twice a day and be prepared to give a demonstration of comprehension 'both in *Theoreticall* observations of the Language, and *Logick*, and in *Practicall* and spirituall truths, as his Tutor shall require . . .'. The Old Testament was to be read at morning prayer, and the New at evening prayer. Students were to translate the Old Testament from Hebrew into Greek, and the New from English into Greek, and then were to listen while the text in question was analysed logically, an important lesson for future preachers and godly magistrates alike. Thus was skill in scriptural knowledge and the humane arts provided at the same time and, also important, seen to be provided for the same purpose.

The third aspect, divinity, included catechizing and commonplaces on Saturday mornings, study of the Bible in the original tongues, and the study of systematic theology, using especially William Ames.[98] From the beginning, Harvard students were fully exercised in the covenant, as the frequency in booklists of Ames, Preston, Sibbes, and Downame attests.[99] More advanced authors, such as Calvin, Zanchius, Martyr, and Voetius were studied for the

95 Norton, 'Harvard text-books', p. 367–9.   96 *Ibid.*, pp. 369–73.
97 'Lawes of the College . . . 1655', pp. 335, 338.
98 Norton, 'Harvard text-books', pp. 371, 384–5.
99 Miller also notes the frequent use at Harvard of continental authors on the covenant (*New England Mind*, p. 504).

M.A.[100] The required fortnightly commonplace in divinity also meant an opportunity to absorb the godly application of learning. The tongues included Greek, Hebrew, Syriac, and Aramaic, the last three really of scant use except for the study of Scripture.[101] The fifth group – Norton's 'auxiliary studies' – comprised logic, physics, botany, metaphysics, politics, history, arithmetic and astronomy. The final task – exposition and defence of scriptural interpretation – required a detailed study of rhetoric, the scholastic exercises of declamations and disputations, the repetition of sermons, and the systematic discussion of a point of divinity in the form of a short sermon. The centrality of the religious impulse in Harvard's curriculum represented the culmination of puritan efforts, stretching from Emmanuel, which demonstrated the puritan commitment to the traditional institutional apparatus. That the regimen of learning and godliness conformed so closely to that of Mildmay's seminary near the Cam is testament to the preponderance of Emmanuel men in early New England.

From all the puritan institutions emerged a similar picture which manifested the usual puritan combination of a Pauline drive to build a purer society and a keen eye for exploiting the immediate context to best advantage. Thus the stress in the curriculum on advanced humane learning, of the best classics with recent improvements (such as Ramus), was tempered and guided by subjects (such as Hebrew and the oriental languages) and practices (commonplaces, prophesyings, sermon repetitions) which would ensure that learning never escape its purposeful role in the pursuit of godliness. This served as the actualization of the historic compromise worked out by the puritans as the best English exemplars of the Reformed movement.

V

The opportunities for higher education included one other attempt to balance professional training for a career with the social training and developing of connexions which a well-born young man would need. Increasingly, law, like other studies, became book-based, though, as at the university, aural means of learning continued to be important. In the sixteenth century the Inns of Court were dramatically affected by the same influx that so changed the universities.[102] The greater numbers, which peaked in the middle of James' reign,

---

[100] Hall, *Faithful Shepherd*, p. 178.

[101] Morison himself regarded the inclusion of Hebrew at the undergraduate level as the most 'distinctive feature' of the Harvard curriculum (*Harvard in the Seventeenth Century*, p. 200). But see above on Marischal College and Trinity College Dublin.

[102] The annual rate of admission quadrupled between 1500 and 1600. On admissions generally, see Knafla, 'Matriculation revolution', pp. 232–64, in Slavin, ed., *Tudor Men and Institutions*. Prest, *Inns of Court*, pp. 5–7, argues that the upward trend began not with the Elizabethan period, but rather under Henry VIII. This parallels Elizabeth Russell's argument concerning the expansion of the universities (see above, p. 229). See also Cliffe, *Puritan Gentry*, pp. 108–9.

did not reflect only a thirst for legal knowledge. Only a small proportion planned to stay for the very lengthy course that would enable them to practise law; indeed, the average stay was only two years. Even the 'commentaries' on the law were likely too difficult for the young gentleman who avoided the 'learning exercises' altogether. The appearance of books on law among the popular literature of the day should not lead to the conclusion of a gentry competent in the intricacies of law, any more than the scores of works on religion meant that the same group (as a whole) was competent in theology.[103]

The Inns were distinguished from the universities not only by the narrowness of the official curriculum and teaching methods, but also by the much higher social standing of their entrants.[104] Much of the restriction was due to higher fees and the absence of scholarships.[105] Neither studying law, nor staying the full course, these students were sent to the Inns by the same social pressure which had driven many of them to the university for several terms. College provided the veneer of a scholarly (but provincial) education; the Inn may originally have been expected to instil enough of a smattering of law for the county role expected of the landowner. Possession of legal knowledge also came to be seen as a prerequisite for the gentleman's special duty to the commonwealth. But, as the educational and cultural opportunities of London expanded, an Inn became a marvellous place for a young gentleman to be trained in the worldliness which was increasingly expected of him.[106] Indeed, the Inns themselves provided masques, revels, dancing, and gambling. Even puritans such as Simonds D'Ewes learned dancing and fencing while at an Inn.[107] The Inns also served as literary centres for England's intellectual circles. William Crashawe, the puritan lecturer of the Temple from 1605 to 1613, claimed that the Inns were the most scholarly setting in England after the universities. Students are known to have engaged in geography, history, mathematics, astronomy, anatomy, and foreign languages, but the 'cultural and intellectual norms tended to be aristocratic, literary and non-utilitarian', with overlays of court fashion and previous scholastic instruction.[108] For parents wary of the expense or the infection of a 'grand tour' for their son, a sojourn in an Inn might well prove a reasonable substitute. Inns also provided

[103] Prest, *Inns of Court*, pp. 11, 23, 145–56, esp. 151–3.
[104] For the period 1570–1639, Stone noted that at least 81% of entrants were sons of county gentry and of clergy; another almost 12% were 'urban gentry'. Prest noted at least 88.4% of entrants as gentlemen or higher, that is, 47.8% gentlemen and 40.6% sons of peers/esquires (Stone, 'Educational revolution', p. 59; Prest, *Inns of Court*, p. 30). In addition, a very significant 75.1% of clearly defined entrants were the only or eldest son (Prest, *Inns of Court*, pp. 31–32). This class base of the Inns was frequently commented on (usually favourably) by contemporaries; see, for example, Buck, *Third Universitie*, p. 1073.
[105] Prest, *Inns of Court*, Ch. 1.
[106] O'Day notes that in the period 1590–1639 only 2138 out of 12,163 students were called to the Bar (*Education and Society*, p. 163).   [107] Prest, *Inns of Court*, pp. 153–4.   [108] *Ibid.*, pp. 158–9, 167.

students with a spectrum of associates of similar social class. As our period progressed, the Inns produced economic and political connexions of telling importance.[109] As well, the common law, for those who did desire a vocational training, provided the career with the greatest promise of success based on either talent or patronage.

The attractiveness of converting to godliness the socio-economic cream of England's youth was evident at the Inns as it was also present at the universities, and perhaps especially at Emmanuel.[110] The puritan attempt to reform the church through Parliament stood to benefit greatly from an influential presence at the Inns. Tied to this was the fear that Romanist missionaries would be successful in producing papist lawyers and Romanist gentlemen who would protect priests in the countryside. The threat posed by popery at the Inns was doubtless of small significance after the 1570s, but the chance to extirpate subversives continued to be attractive to puritan ministers such as William Crashawe, who suggested that the Inns be made centres of anti-popery.[111] Finally, though this can be exaggerated, given that lawyers were evidently not considered by contemporaries to be a particularly puritan group,[112] traditional anti-clericalism seems to have merged with hostility to the prerogative courts' challenge to the supremacy of common law. The possibility that a group which thrived on argument would appreciate the plain rhetoric of puritan sermons reinforced the puritan impulse to strengthen this 'incomplete and temporary alliance.'[113] Legal backing could prove most helpful to those ministers who challenged the authority of High Commission. Moreover, the similarity between the language of legal contracts and that of the developing covenant theology may well have offered potential for like thinking between lawyers and puritan ministers.

In Elizabeth's reign there were only two formal checks on the religion of the Inns: the required taking of the Oath of Allegiance, and the mandatory attendance at divine service, though the Inns themselves in 1583 imposed on their members the additional obligation to take communion annually or face expulsion.[114] Nonetheless, the importance of protestantizing the Inns (Gray's especially was seen as a problem) was recognized by government and church in the middle of the reign.[115] Various schemes of the Council and of the

---

[109] In the 1563 House of Commons, 26% of M.P.s had attended an Inn; in 1584, 36%; in 1593, 43%; and in 1640–2, fully 55% of the Members had experience of an Inn (Stone, 'Educational revolution', p. 63; Prest, *Inns of Court, passim*).

[110] A higher proportion of Emmanuel students proceeded to an Inn, though the reason for this remains unclear, beyond the social attraction for the well-born (Tyler, 'Children of disobedience', p. 108). Perhaps surprisingly, a higher percentage of the Emmanuel entrants (compared to those from King's, Jesus and St John's) stayed the course and eventually practised law (*ibid.*, p. 164).

[111] Crashawe, *Sermon, passim*.

[112] Prest, *Inns of Court*, pp. 211–14. But see also Eusden, *Puritans, Lawyers, and Politics, passim*.

[113] Prest, *Inns of Court*, esp. pp. 209–14.   [114] *Ibid.*, pp. 181–2.   [115] *Ibid.*, pp. 11, 38, 53, 176.

Bishops of London involved surveying the Inns and promoting the appointment of preachers there.[116] In 1569 Grindal expressed to Cecil a hope that papists could be excluded from the bar, if not actually from the Inns themselves.[117] In 1585 Burghley, too, evidently proposed a visitation of the Inns to expel recusants, perhaps following Thomas Norton's suggestions.[118] Four of the first five preachers appointed at the Inns – Chaderton, Travers, William Clarke and Thomas Crooke – were vocal puritans.[119] But this cooperative forward policy did not long survive Whitgift's elevation to Canterbury and his emphasis on order above edification. The effective victory of Hooker over Travers at the Temple confirmed this shift. Stuart policy, which was rather to leave the Inns alone than to delve into private religious practices, consolidated this change. It was left to the House of Commons to continue the harassment of suspected popery in the Inns.[120] From the mid-1580s, the scattered appointments of lecturers at the Inns reveals no certain policy or emphatic religious strain on the part of the members. Gray's, Lincoln's, and the Temple church all had puritan preachers at one time or another, but all also had non-puritans, or even 'Arminians'.[121] The Inns seem therefore to have gone through stages of more and less protestant fervency, bending on occcasion before outside pressure, but not bowing completely.

Perhaps somewhat strange, however, is the paucity of puritan specific criticism of the Inns. Positive general comments were frequent. William Covell, writing in 1595, noted that the Inns served to help establish England's reputation for learning, especially by complementing the function of the universities.[122] In 1617, Richard Bernard reminded the Inns that common law was the natural enemy of the papists; he therefore urged the members to be diligent in their studies so that 'due iustice may be executed upon Priests, Iesuites, and other traiterous spirits . . .'.[123] At the same time, the Inns were occasionally also seen as a threat to the development of a proper, protestant ministry. In 1579 John Stockwood complained that numerous papists were hiding in the Inns.[124] William Day proposed in a Paul's Cross sermon of 1566 that the number of places at the Inns should be restricted. Thus would those

[116] See, for example, P.R.O. S.P. 12/45/10.
[117] Strype, *Life and Acts of Grindal*, pp. 137–8. In 1569 some members of the Inns were in fact subjected to episcopal examination concerning their church attendance and reading of papist literature; several of them were committed to the Fleet (*ibid.*, p. 152).
[118] Prest comments that 'no action seems to have followed' (*Inns of Court*, p. 188 n. 22).
[119] Appointments were evidently made cooperatively by church, Council, and Inns (*ibid.*, pp. 190–2).
[120] *Ibid.*, p. 183.
[121] Lincoln's Inn had the important puritans William Charke, Gataker, Preston, Edward Reynolds, and Joseph Caryl, and yet from 1616 to 1622 the lecturer there was John Donne. At Gray's Inn, the long-serving covenant theologian Richard Sibbes died in 1635; he was succeeded by the 'Arminian' Hannibal Potter (*ibid.*, pp. 189, 202).   [122] Covell, *Polimanteia*, sigs. P3ff., Rff.
[123] Bernard, *Ray of Knowledge*, sigs. A5–7.   [124] Stockwood, *Very Fruiteful Sermon*, fol. 28^{r-v}.

desiring some educated future be forced into the ministry.[125] Given the expanding function of the Inns as institutes of social training for the well-born, it was not a proposal with any chance of implementation. Such general asides represented the force of the external puritan approach to the Inns. The failings of the Inns as teaching institutions, and the extremely complicated and technical nature of the legal knowledge, may have accounted for this. In an age of the popularization of all forms of knowledge, law remained curiously aloof. Even such attempts at simplification as Abraham Fraunce's *Lawiers Logike* were designed for students at the Inns rather than for general readership.

Even within the Inns, the puritan lectures seem not to have addressed themselves to questions of curriculum. Rather, they attempted to provide a godly context for the members, in which purer living and proper religious practice would help direct their professional activities to more godly ends. Thus Richard Alvey, Master of the Temple from 1562, imposed a modest reform of ecclesiastical discipline in 1582 by the imposition of a system of overseers to record absence from church service. The plan, which included private admonition for recalcitrant members, was likely designed by the presbyterian Walter Travers.[126] In the main puritan sermons at the Inns seem to have been characterized by the concerns voiced from country pulpits too.[127] Foremost among these, especially in the seventeenth century, was the question of assurance via membership in the covenant. Given the presence of both Sibbes and Preston at Inns, one may again suggest the receptivity of lawyers to theology phrased contractually.

As ever, the puritan preachers concentrated on the development of connexions. Though students at the Inns were generally older than their university counterparts, and the preachers did not have the advantage of standing over them as tutors, nonetheless bonds were fashioned (or continued) in this context. The movement of preachers such as John Preston between the universities and the Inns may have persuaded parents to send their son to a particular Inn. Furthermore, fears concerning the dissolute life of the Inns may have been lessened somewhat for godly parents who knew that their son could at least receive the comfort and guidance of a forward preacher. The students themselves likely established a network of the reformist-minded. The presence in the Inns of many members of the puritan Providence Island Company, for example, served as a focus for gatherings and political discussions. The contribution of the Inns was therefore far greater as a meeting place and breeding

---

[125] Day was later Bishop of Winchester, but at the time of this sermon he was an opponent of the ceremonialism which remained in the English church (O'Day, 'Clerical patronage', unpub. Ph.D. thesis, Univ. of London, 1972, p. 233). John Stockwood, the puritan preacher and schoolmaster, joined in this opinion (Prest, *Inns of Court*, p. 26).

[126] Fisher, 'Reformation of clergy at Inns of Court', *Past and Present*, 38, p. 91.

[127] See, for example, Gataker, *Discours Apologetical*, p. 37.

ground for political lay puritan feelings than as an exercise in purely educational or ecclesiological reform.[128]

At the same time, the puritan presence was not strong enough to curb young gentlemen in their pursuit of pleasure. The preachers may well have appreciated that it was strategically wiser to build quietly for the future than noisily to alienate one's future patrons and protectors. There were some successes. At Lincoln's Inn, committees were established in 1600 and again in 1611 to oversee the religion of the House. Gataker himself transferred the Wednesday morning sermon to Sunday afternoon to reduce the amount of business conducted on the sabbath. Christmases were restricted in their splendour; professional actors were barred; and gaming was prohibited in hall on Saturday nights (1627). The new chapel at Lincoln's Inn (1623) evidently soon became a 'focal centre of London puritanism . . .'.[129]

But the thrust had limitations. The recollections of William Prynne, himself a former student of Lincoln's Inn, serve to reveal the intransigence of many of the benchers concerning reform of customs. Though at one time he referred to Lincoln's Inn as a 'famous Nurserie both of Law and Piety',[130] Prynne, while only a 'Puny Barrester', had attempted to stop the habit of holding 'Revels, Dancing, Dicing and Musick . . . every Saturday night' until the early hours of the morning. This caused the sabbath to be 'much prophaned' by the revellers, who 'slept out the Forenoon Sermons and other divine Exercises for the most part, either in their Beds or at Church, if they resorted to it . . .' Prynne claimed that he had organized a group of pious benchers against these profanities. But while they were able to restrict the hours of the revelling, the majority of the benchers pleaded 'long prescription, custome, and unwillingness: to displease the Revellers and young Students, for their continuance . . .'.[131] The Inns, then, remained an enigma: professionally beyond the competence of puritan academics to reform; structurally not given to the close supervision which might bring young men into the godly fold; 'conversationally' overpowered by the courtly training and amusing recreations of London.

The only plan in our period for the direct reform of the Inns came from Thomas Norton, the puritan lawyer and M.P.[132] His position as remembrancer to the Lord Mayor of London made him an intermediary between the City and the Privy Council; he was on especially close terms with both Hatton and

[128] On the circle of lay puritans at the Inns, see Prest, *Inns of Court*, pp. 207–9; Eusden, *Puritans, Lawyers, and Politics, passim*.   [129] Prest, *Inns of Court*, p. 205.   [130] Prynne, *Histrio-Mastix*, sig. *.
[131] Prynne, *Briefe Polemicall Dissertation*, sig. A2. Prest argues that the revels reflected a falling away from Calvinist values at the Inns by those members brought up under James I (Prest, *Inns of Court*, p. 112).
[132] Norton entered the Middle Temple in 1555. He later plied his legal knowledge as counsel to the Stationers' Co. and to the Merchant Taylors Co. (Graves, 'Thomas Norton', *Historical Journal*, 23, pp. 18, 26).

Walsingham (themselves both members of an Inn). The thrust of Norton's plan, here as also with his comments on schools and the universities, was the extirpation of popery. Norton wanted the Council to instruct the judges and the senior benchers that only known protestants were to be admitted, and that all others were to be expelled. As a test, all members of the Inns were to attend divine service, partake of communion twice each term, and also swear to the Articles of Religion. Refusal was to bring expulsion after a respite of a month for reflection. Similarly, those who did not attend communion were to be excluded from 'commons' until the seniors had determined that it was not disaffection with the established church and faith that had caused the absence. As well, offenders were to be barred from all courts until the matter of their religion had been settled satisfactorily. All preferments in the Inns, including promotion to the office of serjeant, were to be awarded to those who were 'knowen sound in religion'. Recognizing that the Inns lacked the powerful protestantizing force of godly tutors, Norton suggested that the senior members were to give special assistance to those who were especially 'zealous in religion' so that England would soon be blessed not merely with a protestant legal profession, but with a host of 'forward' lawyers. To reach this goal, Norton insisted that preaching be maintained where it existed, and that lectures be established in the other Inns.[133] As well, the members of the Inns of Chancery were to resort to the sermons in the Inns of Court or in their parish churches. In a way similar to that in which he had relied heavily (though certainly not exclusively) on episcopal action at the school level, Norton expected Aylmer, Bishop of London, to oversee this provision of new lectures.[134]

Norton concluded with a section on the ways in which lawyers could make the laws governing religion more effective. Again this was to be a synthesis of learning and enthusiasm involving 'certaine of the best learned in lawe and known zealous.' Godly legal interpretations and precedents were to be sent directly to J.P.s in all shires for their application. By thus manipulating legal opinion at the Inns, Norton hoped also to control the channels of legal communication and judicial practice in the counties. Ill-affected lawyers were to be subject to some (unspecified) penalty so that they would not become wealthy from the law while the godly dedicated themselves to the service of the commonwealth. Private wealth, Norton feared, would allow the recusants

---

[133] P.R.O. S.P. 12/177, fols. 174–5.
[134] Indeed, Norton was very complimentary to Aylmer, referring to his 'wisdome, zeale, and industrie', and remarking that 'I would every bushoppe in England had taken paine and done their parts for relligion proportionately as he hath done' (*ibid.*, fol. 175). Prest notes that Aylmer had supported the introduction of fervent ministers into the Inns after his elevation to London in 1577. Though he began to curb the puritans in 1581, his attack did not gain real effect until Whitgift's promotion to Canterbury in 1583 (*Inns of Court*, p. 193).

to 'mainteine perilous seducers' in their houses, and to continue their other subversive practices. All courts, too, were to be reformed at least to the level of purification Norton had decreed for the Inns themselves. Especially important, given their number and the function of their office, was the careful choice of religiously well-affected J.P.s.[135]

The section on the purification of the Inns, the final stage in Norton's thorough plan for the cleansing of all levels of education, was, however, the least explicit. There is no suggestion of texts, as (briefly) in his programme for schools, nor is there the concentration on the teaching offices, as with schoolmasters and tutors, even though Norton must from his own experience have been well aware of the shortcomings of the teaching structures at the Inns. Nor did Norton attempt to curb gentlemanly recreations. In some additional comments written probably in 1584 while he was in the Tower for over-harsh criticisms of the bishops,[136] Norton stressed that no one should be permitted to continue in residence at the Inns who was not studying the law, languages, or 'some other gentlemanlie activitie'. This final allowance of riding, dancing, fencing, and so on, and the insistence that these skills be used in Christian manner for the service of the commonwealth, reflected Norton's pragmatic approach to dealing with the gentry.[137] Norton was content to combine the social training of youth with a measure of academic study and as close supervision of the religion of these youths as the structures of the Inns permitted.

The strangely muted puritan approach to the Inns, and the absence of any call for, or attempt to found, a new Inn, requires some explanation. In the first place, puritan educationalists likely considered the specific knowledge of the law to be 'morally neutral'. It was rather the application of the law and the religious training of the lawyers that concerned puritans, and Norton addressed both of these difficulties in his scheme. The presence at the Inns of notable puritan preachers likely reflects (as well as the lure of promotion, better salary, and high profile) an understanding of the social importance of the membership of the Inns. The sermons delivered at the Inns illustrate the preachers' comprehension that the younger men in the audience were (for the most part) already adults who now were to be addressed rather as a congregation of important citizens than wholly as pupils. Secondly, as an increasing proportion of the entrants came from a university, the Inns methodically became places of a more protestant, if not wholly forward, membership. College tutors and university sermons had prepared these students for a

---

[135] P.R.O. S.P. 12/177, fols. 175ᵛ, 176.

[136] Graves, 'Thomas Norton', p. 33. Norton was released upon the intervention of Walsingham and Hatton.

[137] Prest suggests that this placed Norton in the tradition of Laurence Humphrey (*Inns of Court*, p. 170). On Humphrey, see below, pp. 278–9.

measure of independence. Hence Norton's insistence on both the maintenance of preachers and the enrolment in some form of training by the members; the Inns were not to become merely a club for the dissolute. Thirdly,
puritans were not ever able to gain control of any of the Inns to the degree that
they controlled (even if usually only for a limited time) some of the colleges at
Oxford and Cambridge. In addition the approach at the Inns had to be more
circumspect because of the lack of teaching capacity in the Inns, a function
which puritans had frequently united with preaching at the universities.

    This undistinguished record at the Inns leads, in turn, to the conclusion that
the strength of the puritan impulse in England may well have emanated not so
much from preaching alone as from the close *teaching* connexions which
puritan schoolmasters and college tutors built up with their pupils. Though
hagiographical and pastoral literature maintained the strong image that the
interpreted Word from the pulpit was crucial, it must also be remembered
that puritan preachers themselves recalled how barren the soil could prove in
country congregations. The frequency of conversion recorded in the university precincts may well, as the preparationists insisted, have followed upon a
lengthy course of external observance and study. For this, it was the ministers
qua tutors (as much as *qua* pastoral guides) who were responsible. At the Inns,
this function was lacking, and the puritan cause diminished correspondingly.
In the end, then, to breed the new godly, the puritan preachers needed the
ongoing close relationship provided by the educational structures of school
and college. This may also help to explain the absence of any attempt to
establish a network of formal seminaries whose sole function was to train
ministers. The changing context of the universities – that is, their somewhat
altered social composition – thrust upon puritans a golden opportunity which
they were quick to seize: the advantage of forming an alliance with the important lay youths who within a few years would be running county society.
Herein lay the more rapid and more widespread godly reform of England; not
from the pulpit alone, but from the bench, the household, and even Parliament, England would be turned to godliness. Thus did the puritan impulses
blend to produce a wider seminary for the whole nation in the context of a
traditional educational institution. Below this level of the institutional
framework, puritans also sought to cement the individual bond.

13

THE INDIVIDUALIZATION
OF REFORM

I

The progression of grammar school, college, and Inn was not, however, the only course of advanced learning open to the gentry and mercantile elite. Our period also witnessed the development of alternative sources of education. The response to scholarly needs, especially in London, was both quick and immense. No longer did an adult need to feel limited because he had not attended Oxford or Cambridge; tutors in London would instruct him in the trivium and quadrivium. But far more important in the development of London as a cultural and economic centre was the vast array of 'practical subjects' available from private schools and tutors. Mathematics for the counting house; geography and navigation for the seafaring merchant; riding, dancing, and the military arts for the young gentleman; poetry and painting for the cultured circle; law and physic for the future professional – as well as a host of other studies – could be found with ease in the capital.[1] The art of writing – seldom taught sufficiently in schools – and foreign languages for merchants and gentleman travellers seem to have undergone a special vogue.[2] Print and translation also enabled vocational learning to cross both national and religious boundaries. The emphasis on the experiential wisdom gained from the practice of a craft helped to break down the old (Platonic) disdain for technical knowledge.[3] So Richard Hakluyt's proposal for navigational lecturers was actualized by Sir Thomas Smith in 1588 with the endowment of a lecture to concentrate on the use of mathematics in military affairs, and by the later inclusion of navigational matters.[4] London had scientific lectures at Leadenhall Chapel, cosmography lectures at Blackfriars, and courses in hydrography and navigation at Deptford. Much of the learning was organized in schools; some of them even offered qualifications. London also contained the beginnings of research groups, for example the Society of Antiquaries

---

[1]   Buck, *Third Universitie*, p. 1062, for a lengthy list of subjects available in London.
[2]   Charlton, *Education*, pp. 267–9ff.   [3]   *Ibid.*, esp. pp. 272–3, 279.
[4]   *Ibid.*, pp. 281–2. So important were they considered to be that the Privy Council ordered their continuation after the expiry of the initial two-year term.

(from the 1580s), whose membership was overwhelmingly from the aristocracy.[5]

Above all other institutions of learning in London not dedicated to the 'professions' stood Gresham College. Opened in 1596 it provided, in accordance with Sir Thomas Gresham's will, seven lecturers, who were to expound on the liberal sciences: divinity, civil law, physic, rhetoric, astronomy, geometry and music.[6] Emphasis was always to be on the practical. Though there are no records of who actually attended the lectures, the stipulation that Latin lectures were to be repeated in English suggests a non-university-trained auditory. Some present may have been teachers themselves, so the knowledge may have been quickly disseminated to an even larger audience. The absence of entrance qualifications and matriculation procedures, and also of degrees, made Gresham an informal centre of learning which did not present barriers to the interested bourgeois.[7]

The attempt to link in a direct manner puritans, merchants and Baconian empirical knowledge has not been successful.[8] Puritan support of vernacular reading ability for religious reasons likely helped to develop a readership which sought knowledge also for vocational and recreational reasons. The puritan emphasis on fulfilling one's calling as a means both of obtaining earthly reward and of satisfying one's duty to God probably also acted as a catalyst. At Gresham College, Henry Gellibrand and Samuel Foster, both puritans, served consecutively as professors of astronomy.[9] Gellibrand, as well as issuing a trigonometry text, spent much of his time in the naval yards at Deptford, working on the very troublesome prolem of compass variations. The puritan Henry Briggs, who later served as Savilian professor of astronomy (at Oxford), was hired as the first Gresham professor of geometry.[10] The succession of appointees as professor of divinity before the Revolution included a number of puritans (Wotton, Gray, possibly Holdsworth), a non-puritan Calvinist (Dakins), a man whose livings were later sequested by the Commons (Osbolston), and an Arminian (Brooke).[11] In this mixture, Gresham College was like the universities – representative of the diversity of the English church, dependent on various sources of pressure and influence for appointments, and not designed for the success of any particular grouping or faction,

[5] Simon, *Education and Society*, pp. 389, 390.
[6] Buck, *Third Universitie*, p. 1078; Charlton, *Education*, pp. 283–4; Simon, *Education and Society*, p. 388. The 7 lecturers were each to receive £50 per year.
[7] Adamson, 'Early history of Gresham College', unpub. Ph.D. thesis, Univ. of Cambridge, 1974, pp. 41–3, 45–6, 47.
[8] See especially Hill, *Intellectual Origins*, Ch. 3; Webster, *Great Instauration*, esp. Ch. 1; Simon, *Education and Society*, Ch. 15.
[9] Gellibrand lost his post because he would not kneel at communion (Adamson, 'Early history of Gresham College', pp. 87–8). He was reinstated in 1641.
[10] Charlton, *Education*, p. 286. *D.N.B.*, s.v. 'Henry Briggs'.
[11] Adamson, 'Early History of Gresham College', pp. 47–91.

though used by all. No longer can it be held that Gresham was a puritan foundation.[12]

A direct connexion between puritan attitudes and the development of the practical learning of London is impossible to establish quantitatively, and in any case would not have been exclusive. Merchants and common lawyers may have been impressed by the parallels between puritan arguments concerning the covenant and divine sovereignty and their own increasing concern with legal contract and the sovereignty of law. It may well have been also that the puritan emphasis on an individual, experiential approach to true religion gave a psychological boost to the growing mercantile demand for practical knowledge in all fields. As we have seen, 'practice' became the key word emphasized in the vernacular literature for vocation and godliness alike. Those who came from more godly households were perhaps more likely to be attuned to absorbing knowledge from the printed page, and might well have been more attractive to masters who needed apprentices already adept at familiarizing themselves with a more knowledgeable world and with the increasing specialization of learning. Print and protestantism may therefore have been linked not only in their own world of information and reflection, but in the way that as a unit they harmonized with social hierarchy and changing economic patterns.

At the same time, while London's central supply of such practical education distinguished it from the traditional pattern of the universities, we should be careful not to erect a dichotomy where none existed. Grammar schools endowed by London-made money as a generality bear no different stamp from other such institutions. There is no discernible effort in these schools as a group to introduce radical alterations tending towards vocational rather than academic learning. London developed her 'third' system of education because economic events demanded it. But this growth of the practical should not be interpreted as a condemnation of the traditional grammar school curriculum within its own prescribed limits. Puritans, for their part, generally seem to have been content to encourage this new practical learning *because* it was tied so closely to vocational interests and therefore to the maintenance of hierarchy and the fulfilment of calling, and also because it therefore presented no challenge to the direction of traditional learning towards the ministry and the training of the social elite. Indeed, through indoctrination of masters, such practical education could well serve to propagate the godly message to many boys who would have spent scant time under a godly grammar school master.

[12] Of Briggs in particular, Adamson argued that his 'infatuation with his subject' was distinguished from his personal religion so that 'it is perhaps more accurate to describe him as a puritan and scientist than as a puritan scientist' (Adamson, 'Early history of Gresham College', p. 133).

II

The sixteenth and early seventeenth centuries also witnessed detailed suggestions for, and some new attempts at, especial training of the peerage and upper gentry as a prelude to their newly requisite more active role in the public governing of society. Education was thus both economic self-interest and defence against social climbers from below.[13] The early humanist stress on the development in combination of learning and manners (a position assumed, too, by protestants) led also to the hiring of private tutors who could supply skills not provided in the almost purely academic atmosphere of the grammar schools and universities.

It was the omissions in the institutional curricula that in part prompted the plethora of commentaries on the proper education of the 'gentleman',[14] frequently modelled on Castiglione's *Courtier*. Though certain proposals aimed specifically at the removal of the insufficiently well-born,[15] most seem simply to have presumed that the 'gentle' alone would receive the recommended training. Following Cleland's imprecation that an 'ignorant Lord Living at home shall be a scourge unto his farmers, a torment to his familie, a mocking stocke to his neighbours, a shame to his friends, & a slander to his Parents',[16] these works recommended instruction variously in modern languages, Latin and Greek, music, dancing, drawing, astronomy, natural philosophy, cosmography, geography, history, geometry, arithmetic, logic, and rhetoric.[17] On certain subjects, such as astrology, manuals for gentlemen, like the age, were split, some finding understanding of heavenly motion useful, others despising the study as immoral and irreligious. All commentators, in stressing the military role of the governing class, recommended training in weapons, military movements and fortifications, and riding.[18] Though the well-born were no longer a professional military class in England, traditionalism, the obvious class-separation which military outfitting and expertise brought, and troubled contemporary international politics combined to render such train-

---

[13] See, for an example of a contemporary humanist, Mulcaster, *Positions*, p. 146. On the dramatic change this involved, see Hexter, 'Education of the aristocracy', in his *Reappraisals in History*, pp. 49–52.

[14] For examples of the early aspects of this genre, see Eby & Arrowood, *History and Philosophy of Education*, p. 797; Orme, *English Schools*, p. 34.

[15] See, for example, the list of 'Considerations' submitted to Parliament at the beginning of Elizabeth's reign, which suggested (among other socio-economic restrictions) abolishing the right of yeomen's sons to enter the Inns, and retaining a good proportion of the 'free places' in the universities for sons of poor gentlemen (Simon, *Education and Society*, pp. 334–5).

[16] Cleland, *Institution of Young Noble Man*, p. 138.

[17] See, for example, the wide curriculum recommended by Humphrey Gilbert, *Queen Elizabethes Achademy*, pp. 10, 6–8.

[18] Greaves, 'Sprigg and the Cromwellian revolution', *Huntington Library Quarterly*, 34, pp. 108–9.

ing advisable. Writers also stressed the importance of recreation for the young aristocracy; as in schools, emphasis was on activities connected to physical (hence, military) prowess such as wrestling, archery, riding, and even sports such as tennis. Games, however, were dangerous, since they could easily become obsessions rather than forms of relaxation.

Much of the advice in our period was concerned with the training of a protestant society. Humphrey Gilbert's scheme for an academy therefore proclaimed the need to avoid 'evil religion'.[19] Philip Sidney became a symbol not only of Renaissance ideals and the development of English arts, but also especially, by his own contacts with leading protestants such as Walsingham, of a strongly Calvinist gentleman who understood his duty to God as well as to the commonwealth.[20] By the end of Elizabeth's reign, the protestant strain of this educational proposal had sunk in. As well, the immense popularity of Bacon's essays demonstrated the degree to which English concepts of 'gentle' education had developed beyond the limitations of early humanist thought. Especially was this the time to scour English history to develop a fervent patriotism; no longer would the study of ancient history in order to produce a sense of duty to the state suffice. Also noteworthy was the increasing emphasis placed on Christian 'goodness' rather than secular 'greatness'.[21] It is a mark, too, of the dominance of the 'practical' in this form of educational advice that students were told to turn not only to treatises on statecraft, but also to historians (ancient and recent) who portrayed the *actual* running of a state.[22]

A more immediate experience which authors of aristocratic education came to praise was the inclusion of travel in a young man's training. Travel no longer meant only war or pilgrimage, but rather a European tour through which knowledge of languages, geography, customs, manners, economics, and politics would help the youth to appraise English society and serve it better.[23] On occasion the travellers attended foreign academies where they engaged in courtly practices; at other times they studied privately with protestant tutors of repute or simply gathered experience by private observation. Objections were, however, commonly raised to travelling for the purpose of either study or recreation. There were, of course, physical dangers associated with travel, but it was more the moral and political perils that commentators lamented. Ascham, Mulcaster, and Joseph Hall were among those who voiced serious reservations concerning travel to Italy, centre of both popery and the contemporary degradation of personal morals.[24]

---

[19] Gilbert, *Queen Elizabethes Achademy*, p. 1.   [20] Simon, *Education and Society*, pp. 347–8.

[21] Ustick, 'Changing ideals', *Modern Philology*, 30, pp. 155, 159, argues that this was most common in the early seventeenth century, in such tracts as Richard Brathwait's *English Gentleman*, (1630).

[22] Charlton, *Education*, pp. 246–50.

[23] See, for example, Morrice, *Apologie for Schoolemasters*, sig. D6ᵛff.

[24] Charlton, *Education*, pp. 224ff.

In general the puritan contribution to this genre of educational literature was limited.[25] The question of travel provides a useful illustration. While puritan ministers presented the strongest argument against travel for purely personal reasons, puritan laymen do not seem to have been completely convinced that England was the only safe soil for the godly well-born.[26] Though they adapted to the presence of the socio-economic elite in the universities, puritans were less forthcoming concerning the specific and separate education of this class. We may suggest certain explanations for this. The particular functions of the well-born were by no means irrelevant in puritan eyes, but puritans stressed the early intermixing of the social classes via education. The private household could too easily hide recusants or even Jesuit education. Public education served to make the upper classes aware of their responsibilities to the cause of learning; especially at the universities it served to bring the well-born into contact with great numbers of otherwise probably remote plebeians. These plebeians were frequently the future ministers of England. Alliances formed here could serve the puritan cause to a far greater degree than could even the correct private and secluded household education of a gentleman or noble. Thus the anonymous parliamentary 'Plot for Reformation' included the suggestion that wardship could still be useful. The paper protested against the ruination of the young rich by inferior education, and proposed that those who had the aptitude should continue their schooling into the universities. Others were to attend court and be taught the usual gentlemanly qualities.[27] At the same time, this plan was made more socially comprehensive by the suggestion that the nation, by appropriating a quarter of the church's goods, could also afford to train the poor – some in the arts, some in trades, and many in agriculture and various forms of service.[28]

Individual accounts also testify to the service which a broad education could offer to experiential godliness. Simonds D'Ewes, part of the invasion of London, studied Latin, Hebrew, Syriac, French, Greek, and, notably, the writing of English prose with Henry Reynolds and, surprisingly, with his even more learned daughter.[29] This last skill enabled D'Ewes to 'take notes in writing at sermons' which distinguished him from 'the brute creatures that were in the church with me, never regarding or observing any part of Divine service'.[30] The letters contained in the Winthrop Papers similarly testify to the growing interest in scholarship, as they list exchanges of books and, on occasion, searches unsuccessful even in London for some rare works.[31] John Bruen of Chester was known to be so careful in instructing servants and children in

---

[25] On the more general attitudes of puritans towards this class, see Walzer, *Revolution of the Saints*, esp. Ch. 7.   [26] Greaves, *Society and Religion*, pp. 369–72.
[27] B.L. MS Add. 48,066, fols. 3–4ᵛ: 'Howe youth maybe well brought uppe and made profytable members of the Commen Wealth'.   [28] *Ibid.*, fol. 4.   [29] D'Ewes, *Autobiography*, I, pp. 63, 94–5.
[30] *Ibid.*, p. 95.   [31] See, for example, *Winthrop Papers*, I, pp. 311, 386.

godliness and humane learning, an abundance of which he had from his own training at Oxford, that his house became a centre for children of the gentry in Chester.[32] Lord John Harington, first Baron of Exton, combined a knowledge of foreign languages and a serious interest in navigation and military skills with his godly household routine and his academic learning.[33] Puritans thus did take note of the necessary components of upper-class education, and of the responsibility to pass along such learning.

At the same time, there were few puritan tracts devoted wholly to the education of the very well-born. The main two date from 1559 (English edition 1563) and 1616, far enough apart possibly to reflect changes in the degree of humanist influence and the development of pressure for more pactical knowledge. In *The Nobles* Laurence Humphrey, Regius Professor of Divinity at Oxford and President of Magdalen College, addressed the 'christian noblesse' – not just the peerage, but all those of the upper classes who possessed 'nobility', which he defined as a quality rather than merely a pedigree. In view of the cataclysm in Germany in the 1520s, and the spread of Anabaptism since, Humphrey began by arguing forcefully against the abolition of the nobles as a social class; on earth hierarchy always had been, and should be, the rule.[34]

Humphrey emphasized, by citing Plato and Aristotle, that there should not be any idle nobles engaged only in recreation and consumption. Both the ancients – on whom Humphrey rested heavily – and Scripture demanded an occupation for all men.[35] True nobility, for Humphrey, therefore consisted in the careful fulfilment of three duties: to God, to one's household and neighbours, and to oneself. Especially did Humphrey stress the first, requiring not only that true nobles study the Scripture and confess their faith, but also that they lead the prince to godly religion. Nobles might even have to defend religion against backward prelates.[36] Though Humphrey was in general opposed to a frequent call to arms for political reasons, the fight against idolatry in defence of the Gospel was a profound duty of the true Christian noble.[37] It pained Humphrey that, even when nobles did read, they turned not to Scripture, but to 'humane thinges, not devine, love toyes not fruteful lessons, Venus games not weyghtie studyes tendyng to encrease of godlynes, dignytie, or true and sounde commodity'. It was the same complaint as prompted the purification drives in schools and colleges. Of duties to others, Humphrey emphasized especially the need for generosity towards the learned. Nobles

[32] Clarke, *Marrow*, pp. 84, 90. For other examples, see Cliffe, *Puritan Gentry*, pp. 77–8, 191.
[33] Clarke, *Marrow*, pp. 58–9.   [34] Humphrey, *Nobles*, sigs. b.vi ff., c.iii^v ff., c.vii^{v}ff.
[35] *Ibid.*, sig. h.viii^{v}ff.
[36] *Ibid.*, sig. m.vii^{r-v}. Indeed, he was insistent that prelates should not be considered 'nobles', since this would be to combine, and therefore confuse, two vocations. A bishop was properly 'a teacher and preacher of God' (*ibid.*, sigs. f.iv, g.vi^{v}ff.).   [37] *Ibid.*, sigs. n.iii^{v}ff.

were to resume their (supposed) old role of being the 'protectours and nurses of learnynge, learned, and students'.[38] They were even, he suggested, to make donations to libraries to further the spread of knowledge.

The key to Humphrey's training of a true noble was the use of learning in service to the commonwealth, which he felt was not adequately esteemed by this class.[39] As a remedy Humphrey proposed a reading course for nobles. He noted that he had attempted to imitate the best leassons of the ancients rather than simply impose his own opinions, but his contemporary university experience and his protestant fervour permeate the plan. Humphrey emphasized that the hiring of a master 'of reasonable yeares, fauteles life, and learning' was crucial, as was close cooperation between parents and tutor.[40] The course of studies – a blend of ancients, humanists, and protestants – represented an early example of the type of learning later recommended for the well-born students at Oxford and Cambridge. Nobles were to become accomplished in Greek, Latin, Hebrew, logic (from Aristotle), rhetoric (from Erasmus), ethics, manners, philosophy, mathematics, arithmetic, geometry, geography, history and travel.[41] As well, they were to study the model texts on nobility by Erasmus, Sturm, Philo, Jerome, Plutarch, and others.

The course remained theoretical rather than empirical: Aristotle was the chief source of knowledge about foreign countries. Particularly interesting as illustrative of the Christian (and especially puritan) dilemma of the proper mixture of the classics with Scripture was Humphrey's blend in his recommendation for ethics: Isocrates, Demonicus, Nicolaus, and Epictetus with Deuteronomy, Ecclesiastes, Proverbs, Psalms, and Joshua. Similarly, he blended Xenophon, Aristotle, and St Paul for philosophy, and Plutarch, Appian, Thucydides, Caesar, Livy, and Justinian with Joseph and the books of Genesis, Exodus, Judges, and Kings for history. Humphrey, however (as William Prynne would later emphasize in *Histrio-Mastix*), was not enamoured of all 'learning'. He was very wary about astrology, which could too easily be erected as an alternative authority to the Lord's Providence. He also feared morally corrupting influences such as Terence, though he finally allowed him, interestingly enough, because of Cicero's approval. It may have been the dominance of ancient writers in the humanist view, and the insecurity about erecting a wholeheartedly Christian curriculum that caused Humphrey to pass over (as he specifically noted) the Christian writers. He also refrained, beyond mentioning the primacy of Calvin's *Institutes*, from commenting on a choice of catechism or on protestant works on Christianity. Perhaps Humphrey felt that, as yet, there was not a suitable vernacular godly literature to recommend. The next eighty years of puritan effort were dedicated to filling that gap.

---

[38] *Ibid.*, sig. x.v^v.   [39] *Ibid.*, sig. x.ii ff.   [40] *Ibid.*, sig. y.ii^v.
[41] The full contents of the various texts of Humphrey's recommended reading course have been printed in Baldwin, *Shakspere's Small Latine*, I, pp. 316–19.

A second puritan tract which specifically addressed the question of the education of the upper classes was the anonymous *Office of Christian Parents* (1616). The author dealt with the various stages of childhood, emphasizing throughout the parents' responsibility to teach the proper nature of both civil and spiritual existence to their offspring.[42] Addressed to those of gentle status, the tract made clear the obligation of the well-born to serve the commonwealth, and the necessity of learning, especially in eldest sons: 'otherwise they are fit to follow nothing, but an horse, an hawke, an whoore, and an hound, and all other the wicked works of darknes'.[43] It is the section of the *Office* pertaining to ages fourteen to twenty-eight that is of greatest application here. The author rehearsed the customary lack of interest in developing girls' intellectual interests: they were guided to 'service' in the home, the avoidance of lust, and quiet waiting for an 'honest gentleman' for a suitable marriage.[44] For boys the *Office* stressed the common choices – university, Inns of Court, a military career, the ministry, or travel – but also suggested that apprenticeship, even for the well-born, was a respectable alternative.[45] The author advised that the parent search carefully for a competent and Christian master, and then not interfere in the relationship. Indeed, this emphasis on a godly overseer was stressed regardless of the course taken by the lad.[46] Nonetheless, the parent was not to neglect his son, who was to resort frequently to his father to deliver a report on his activities. The caution concerning the 'Atheisme, and Poperie' of England's institutions of higher learning, and the worry over the quality of tutors there, reflect the common move from private to public education for the well-born.

The course of studies recommended by the *Office* for the youth before he left home (for higher education or a career) included Greek, Latin, Hebrew, handwriting, French, Italian, singing, arithmetic, geometry, geography, and some logic and rhetoric, as well as a thorough grounding in history and religion.[47] Beyond this academic instruction, if the lad stayed at home he was to be drilled in the arts of a gentleman suitable for a service to the commonwealth: religion, law, and military affairs. This was the combination of practice with learning so important to the age. War, for example, was a 'delightful study, containing many pleasant things, and namely the knowledge of historie, Arithmetike, Geometry, Geography, etc. which are pleasant in study, profitable in use, comely for a gentleman . . .'.[48] Even knowledge of a manual trade (gained at a younger age) could prove useful.[49] The intermixture of the classical heritage with Christian duty is reflected by the author's immediate reliance

---

[42] *Office of Christian Parents*, p. 45.   [43] *Ibid.*, p. 97.   [44] *Ibid.*, pp. 138–40ff.
[45] At the same time, the author cautioned those of lesser birth not to think their apprentice sons were gentlemen, and so equip them with fine clothes and a sword (*ibid.*, pp. 151, 143).
[46] *Ibid.*, pp. 147, 153.   [47] *Ibid.*, p. 152.   [48] *Ibid.*, p. 163 (printed as '183').
[49] *Ibid.*, pp. 75–6, 96.

on Xenophon in delineating duties to one's society.[50] Proper training also included a regimen of decent recreations. As usual, 'manly feats' such as hawking and hunting received approbation; both servants and sons were to abandon 'effeminate delights' such as dicing, dancing, fine apparel, over-rich food, and excessive revelry. The growing puritan stress on these aspects of 'conversation' (perhaps in reaction to a perceived greater decadence in the early seventeenth century) is reflected in the stricter pose which the *Office* adopted as compared to Humphrey.

Where Humphrey had simply insisted on the Christian nature of nobles' education without really delineating a course, the *Office* insisted on a full regimen of religious instruction even for young adults. Virtually sixty years after the re-establishment of protestantism in England, and further removed from the heyday of humanism, the *Office* was clearer about the comparable value of the two approaches to learning:

Christians, which are taught and have learned Christ, according as the truth is in Christ Iesus, doe by many degrees excell all Philosophers and wisemen of the world whatsoever: for their learning was naturall, earthly, and sensuall; but the learning of Christians, is supernaturall, heavenly, and spirituall.[51]

Thus 'all other learning is but losse and drosse in comparison thereof; for the holy Scriptures containe the perfect doctrine of faith unto salvation, and of charity unto honestie and godlinesse of life'.[52] A short catechism of knowledge of the Scriptures was inserted into the text, along with the insistence that youths should learn the histories of the Scriptures by continued private reading and family instruction. That this instruction might be received in the proper spirit, the author also included a prayer against disobedience for the edification of young gentlemen.[53] The tract concluded by pointing out that the youth who relied on good companions, the lessons of the Word, and the comfort and assistance of prayer would be better equipped to meet the challenge of a Christian existence. As well, young men should pattern their lives after certain Biblical figures: Joshua, whom he termed 'valiant'; Peter, the 'zealous'; and the usual puritan model, Paul, the 'resolute'.[54]

Throughout the puritan approach to the training of the well-born, there are certain continuous themes. Most obvious is the residue of humanist influence, chiefly the dedication of a life of service to the commonwealth, with the Aristotelian theme that the well-born stood as the balance between the extremities of monarchical and democratic polities – a crucial lesson for the early seventeenth century. Within the context of a leading social, economic, and political role, the aristocracy, for puritans, was also to serve as the bulwark against resurgent Romanism, to succour the ministers of the Word, and to lead

---

[50] *Ibid.*, p. 156; also pp. 162–3, 157, on service to the commonwealth.   [51] *Ibid.*, p. 14.
[52] *Ibid.*, p. 171.   [53] *Ibid.*, pp. 170–1, 177ff.   [54] *Ibid.*, pp. 220ff.

repentance and conversion by the extremely important example of their own lives. Against debauchery and courtly pastimes, puritan gentlemen were to provide the bedrock of an alternative style of life that, in our period, no one else had the social prestige and influence to commence. That the volume of puritan literature for the very well-born was comparatively restricted does not bespeak a lack of puritan interest in the leaders of their age. It may rather reveal the degree to which puritans were keenly aware of, and promoted (as the social composition of Emmanuel reveals), the influx of the well-born into the institutions of public higher learning.

III

Despite supporting and participating in the education offered generally by the 'third univerisitie' and specifically to the privileged classes, puritans continued to dedicate their greatest efforts to the two universities. The growth of colleges at both Oxford and Cambridge in the sixteenth century brought radical changes to the nature of undergraduate life and education. Where the 'university' had been a large, rambling collection of people into and out of which students could drift leaving no official record, the college soon became a tightly knit community of fellows and students, the more so as virtually all students ate, studied, and slept within the college walls. Increasingly, too, the college fellows acted as the main teachers. The responsibility of the tutors not only to educate their charges academically, but also to clothe them, suggest times of recreation, buy books for them, pay outstanding bills and bring them forward in religion, meant that for several years the tutor acted very much *in loco parentis*. Indeed, the relationship between tutor and pupil may quickly have become the real foundation of university education.[55]

Foremost among the teaching duties of a tutor was the inculcation of a body of academic learning. It was generally the tutor who would decide which basic texts to use, what 'extra' reading to assign, which side of an academic dispute to emphasize, and which interpretation to press into his students' minds.[56] Provided he did not openly transgress university or ecclesiastical boundaries, the tutor, whose status at Cambridge was confirmed by the 1570 statutes, could direct his pupils as he saw fit. Typical of the three-cornered relationship of father, son and tutor were letters from college to home reporting on academic progress and beseeching further funds. Thus Brian Twyne, later one of the editors of Laud's statutes for Oxford, wrote to his father in 1597, noting that he had learned some Hebrew and had avoided (in accordance with his

[55] For contemporary examples of the multiplicity of roles the tutor had to serve, see the letters from Thomas Mill of Oxford to his father Edward Mill of Gray's Inn (P.R.O. S.P. 46/21/82 and S.P. 46/21/85). See also Venn, *Early Collegiate Life*, pp. 207, 226–7.
[56] On this question generally, see O'Day, *Education and Society*, esp. pp. 113–18.

father's wishes) spending all his time on divinity, and reporting on his achievements and his needs: 'Mr Allen doth read unto me and hath doone a great while Natural Philosophie and I have not Aristotle his phisickes'. This lack he desired his father to rectify, in both Greek and Latin editions, with translation and commentaries.[57]

Illustrative of the role of the tutor was the career of Joseph Mead of Christ's. Mead seems to have recognized a division in his undergraduate pupils between 'lay' and 'clerical', that is, between those intending, respectively, secular and ministerial careers. In general, the latter proceeded to a degree, while the former left before attaining a qualification.[58] Mead was no puritan, and his wide intellectual interests may make him atypical of Oxbridge tutors. Nonetheless, his recommendations of what his students should buy likely correlated to a degree with both scholastic and 'market' demand.[59] Lay and clerical students shared an academic base of logic, religion, Latin, and Greek; from here clerical students moved on generally to Hebrew, ethics, physics, geometry, and metaphysics, while lay students furthered their Latin proficiency and turned to arithmetic, history, and geography. In religious instruction, the breakdown of book purchases is especially indicative of future career; the degree-takers (clericals) emphasized theology texts, while non-degree-takers purchased devotional works and Scripture.[60] Though there is no concrete evidence, the suggestion has also been made that such variations in book purchases may have reflected separate tutorials for 'lay' and 'clerical' students after the first year.[61]

A caveat has more recently been added to this interpretation, stressing that purchase was not the only method of obtaining books; students borrowed from each other and from their tutors, and, if well-off, could probably gain access to college and university libraries. The poorer the student, too, the less likely he was to have any money for academic expenditures beyond those necessary to see him through his course; in all likelihood, he would first buy the standard texts for his degree studies.[62] Nonetheless, it seems sensible to presume that students bought those books which were of greatest importance to them. The

---

[57] Bod. Lib. MS Greek Miscellaneous D.2, fols. 47v–8.
[58] Looney, 'Undergraduate education at early Stuart Cambridge', *History of Education*, 10, pp. 11–12, for the argument, which seems convincing, concerning this correlation, which Looney calls 'clearly not precise, but . . . sufficiently strong to be usable'.
[59] *D.N.B.*, s.v. 'Joseph Mead'. The subject breakdown of the books Mead recommended for purchase was: logic 14.7%, ethics 5.3%, rhetoric 1.4%, physics 9.0%, metaphysics 4.2%, Latin 15.2%, Greek 12.2%, Hebrew 4.9%, religion 13.0%, mathematics, including astronomy and optics, 2.7%, geography, including cosmography and 'travel', 3.3%, history 9.3%, and a potpourri of manners, music, modern languages, and contemporary affairs 4.8% (Looney, 'Undergraduate education at early Stuart Cambridge', *History of Education*, 10, p. 12, based on the account books of Mead while a tutor at Christ's College). The purchases cover the years 1613 to 1638 (effectively only to 1634); they record about 200 different titles (1600 books) for about 100 students (*ibid.*, p. 11).   [60] *Ibid.*, pp. 13, 14–15.
[61] *Ibid.*, p. 14.   [62] O'Day, *Education and Society*, pp. 115, 124–5.

great discrepancies between lay and clerical students, especially with regard to mathematics and religious works, would seem to yield a tentative conclusion that status and expected future occupation or social role influenced the core of studies important enough to the individual for him to purchase books in that area.

This suggested division of pupils by expected future career, and the increasing interest in expanding curriculum to include more modern subjects, is borne out by a number of detailed plans of advice written by tutors for their pupils. The best known is the Cambridge 'Directions for a Student in the Universitie', traditionally ascribed to Richard Holdsworth.[63] The 'Directions' further reveal contemporary awareness of a changing student body by including a reading course for those who 'come to the University not with the intention to make Scholarship their profession, but only to gett such learning as may serve for delight and ornament and such as the want whereof would speake a defect in breeding rather then Scholarship'.[64] The author was obviously at pains to maintain a base of scholastic learning while also emphasizing the variety of newer learning available. Therefore the 'Directions' were divided into a morning programme, which pretty well followed the traditional university prescripts, and an afternoon course of humanist studies. For the non-degree students the author suggested readings in natural philosophy, modern history, classical history and literature (much of it, it should be noted, in English translation), post-classical Latin literature, English literature, modern languages, travel and geography, practical morality and divinity, manners and courtesy, and heraldry.[65] Tutors, with the freedom to recommend books as soon as they were published, could much more easily stay abreast of new intellectual directions than could statutes. Both Mead and the 'Directions' recommended very recent works. Tutors also had to be aware of contemporary academic and religious issues if they were to maintain a reputation, and thus a following (and an income).[66] Nonetheless, the recommendations of the 'Directions' and of similar tutors' guidelines, were frequently conservative in the types of knowledge to which they directed their pupils.[67]

Since fellow-commoners especially sought extra-curricular modern studies, tutors could also supply contacts for instruction in subjects in which

---

[63] I have followed Kearney (*Scholars and Gentlemen*, p. 103) in the treatment of this document. Kearney calls into serious question Holdsworth's authorship, and conclusively dates the 'Directions' to the late 1640s. They therefore lie outside our period of study (1560–1640), and have accordingly been treated only briefly.

[64] 'Directions', p. 647, in Fletcher, *Intellectual Development*, Appendix II. Fletcher prints the whole document, pp. 622–55.   [65] The categories are devised by Curtis, *Oxford and Cambridge*, pp. 131–2.

[66] Morgan, 'History of English universities', p. 158.

[67] For discussion of the 'conservative' content of the 'Directions', see esp. Hill, *Intellectual Origins*, pp. 307–9; Kearney, *Scholars and Gentlemen*, pp. 103–5.

they themselves were not skilled. A letter from Bassingbourne Gawdy to his
father, just after the end of our period, recounted a desire to study
mathematics, but explained that this would involve an extra charge, because 'I
beleeve my Tutor is not skilled in it, and there is a man in towne who makes it
his whole profession and hath teached very many.'[68] The presence of
freelance instructors in the university towns, whose prime source of income
might have been educating well-born pupils in modern subjects in which their
scholastically trained college tutors did not feel competent, deserves further
investigation as a link in the process by which the universities adapted to the
pressure for a more modern curriculum.

We have noted the emphasis placed at Emmanuel on attracting not only
students who would be likely to enter the ministry, but also those who would
prove influential in lay society. Individual puritan tutors, too, pursued this
policy. John Preston, Dean of Queens' College, Lecturer of Lincoln's Inn, and
second Master of Emmanuel provides a good example. Preston's popularity
evidently rose so high that he was 'accounted the only Tutor' or, perhaps
rather unkindly, 'the greatest *Pupil-monger* in *England* . . .'.[69] Preston was willing to take pupils, so it was reported, only on two conditions: that they were of
staid, sober carriage, and that they were elder brothers, hence probably the
more influential members of the next generation.[70] Preston's policy of concentrating on the well-born, whose academic interests might have lain
elsewhere, was presumably intended to ensure that college was at least partly a
godly experience for them too.

For the well-born themselves, knowledge of the tutor under whom their
son would serve was reassuring as they changed from private tutors to public
higher education. When the Earl of Northampton sent his son to Queens',
with the request that the boy have two tutors so that one might always be with
him, Samuel Fairclough, a future godly light, wrote in Latin to the earl seeking
the post. The letter impressed a number of the fellows, including Preston, who
'discerned *especially* the seriousness, sobriety, and a seeming Piety that *breathed*
in every line . . .'.[71] Matching a godly tutor with a noble's offspring was a useful success for the cause of future purification. Indeed Preston, in serving as
one of Charles' chaplains, and in seeking the favour of the Duke of
Buckingham, was at the extreme of puritan involvement with the well-born
and the powerful.

Parents also wanted to be sure that tutors were reliable. A letter from John

[68] Quoted in Venn, *Early Collegiate Life*, p. 212; the letter is dated 1655 from Christ's College, Cambridge. [69] Fuller, *Worthies*, p. 291; Clarke, *32 Lives*, p. 82.
[70] *Diary of H. Slingsby*, ed. Parsons, p. 318. When he was at Queen's, Oxford, Preston admitted 16 fellow-commoners in one year (O'Day, *Education and Society*, p. 92).
[71] Clarke, *Eminent Persons*, pp. 155–7.

Ireton to Anthony Gilby, dated 1572, illustrates this quest. Gilby's son (and another lad), reported Ireton, had been placed in Christ's College

with such Tutors, as I doubt not, will faithfully discharge their duties in overseeinge & instructinge them. Mr. [Laurence] Chaderton taketh none of his tuition, but traveled [i.e., travailed] what he cold [sic] for the best placinge of them. Your Sonnes Tutor is one Mr. Dickinson a Lancashire man, a yonge man verie godlie & lerned, one that hathe great staye of himselfe, & able to trayne him up in the knowledge of the tongs, & this yeare is the Logycke Reader in the Scholes.[72]

Parents and patrons frequently would not commit all responsibility to the tutor, however. Henry Slingsby's father wrote to his son in 1619 to let him know that he expected a full account of the education he was paying for from the renowned John Preston: 'If Mr. Preston be at Cambridge & not come to London, tell him I expecte to heare some what frome him . . .'[73] John Winthrop corresponded with his son's Cambridge tutor concerning both expenses and the progress of the young man's education.[74] Even as well-established a man as Laurence Chaderton, Master of Emmanuel when he received a letter from Edward Zouche in 1600, might be offered specific instructions of intent. Zouche, himself educated at Trinity by Whitgift, sent Chaderton one Peter Painsacke, with the admonition to guide him to the ministry. He noted that he had chosen Chaderton 'having regarde and perswading my selfe of your zeale to Godes Church', and continued that Chaderton was to mix instruction in godly existence with a little further training in the arts.[75] Here, then, was a prominent noble writing to a godly master of a puritan foundation, outlining what he expected of higher education. Such continued interest – Zouche wrote again later in the year – must have strengthened the bonds which connected patron and tutor as soon as they realized that they shared a mutual attempt to bring higher education to a pattern of godliness.

In order to derive greatest advantage from the university, whether for clerical or lay career, it was crucial to the godly that they find a tutor of acceptable religious persuasion who would also encourage godly knowledge and practices in his charges. Herbert Palmer exemplified the mould. At Queens', Cambridge, he insisted that all students attend public worship and that everyone in the college, including servants, be instructed in religion. He increased the number of sermons in the college, counselled those whose 'conversation' was open to radical improvement, and made the fellows conduct prayers and repetitions of sermons every night with their pupils.[76]

[72]   C.U.L. MS Baker 32.23, pp. 437–8.
[73]   *Diary of H. Slingsby*, ed. Parsons, p. 311. Slingsby turned out to be a royalist; he was executed in 1658.   [74]   *Winthrop Papers*, I, *passim*.   [75]   B.L. MS Egerton 2812, fol. 28r–v.
[76]   Clarke, *General Martyrologie*, p. 197. For other examples, see Clarke, *Eminent Persons*, p. 174, on Edmund Staunton, the puritan fellow and later President of Corpus Christi, Oxford; Clarke, *Ten Eminent Divines*, pp. 2–3, on John Carter.

For such dedication to godliness, pupils frequently praised their former tutors. Simonds D'Ewes recalled the useful training in godliness that he had received from Richard Holdsworth.[77] The minister/physician Matthew Robinson recollected that his tutor, Zachary Cawdry of St John's, Cambridge, was 'so famed then for loyalty, learning and ingenuity, and after so noted in Cheshire [as a minister] for his singular zeal piety and moderation'.[78] It seems a requisite part of the puritan hagiography that the saint be, as Samuel Clarke recorded of his own mentor, Thomas Hooker, 'one of the choicest Tutors in the University . . .'.[79] Of John Cotton, for example, it was recorded that 'by his School-stratagems he won the hearts of his Pupils both to himself, and to a desire of Learning: they were each to other as the Prophets, and the sons of the Prophets: his Pupils were honourers, and lovers of him: and he was a Tutor, a Friend, and a Father unto them'.[80] In the puritan scheme tutors, of course, always had to remember the proper limits of humane learning. Thus of Thomas Cawton his biographer recorded that 'he had learned how to possess learning rather than be possessed of it, and that by ballasting his mind, lest knowledge should puff him up'.[81]

The example of Robert Harris illustrates the differences in puritan eyes between acceptable and useless tutors. Educated at Magdalen Hall, Oxford, Harris first suffered under an unnamed tutor who provided little help with either learning or godliness. When removed to the tutorship of Mr Goffe, however, Harris at once prospered. Goffe required Harris to 'joyn in reading the Scriptures, Repetition of Sermons and Prayers; which new course he [Harris] being unaccustomed to, was somewhat troubled at . . .'. Godly tutorship also metamorphosed into communal education. While Goffe continued to teach philosophy to Harris, he did so on condition that Harris teach him Greek. They studied Hebrew together, and read Calvin's *Institutes* in turn. Harris, himself a tutor later, continued the godly counsel of young preachers, recommending to them knowledge of the texts in the original languages, but also the sage interpretations of contemporary puritan writers, including Baynes, Ames, Sibbes, Ball, Capel, Preston, Hildersam, and Whately.[82] Thus was the flow of godly instruction continued through the generations of tutors, constantly bringing new students in sight of the covenant, and creating in them religion, where before was only indifference.

Most useful, of course, was the combination of scholarship, influence, and godliness in the single agent in the university. Thomas Cawton was unfortunate to be placed under John Goodwin at Queens'; luckily, 'he sucked in none of his evil Principles, which even then he endeavoured to infuse into his Pupils . . .' Cawton himself, in his own turn as a tutor, was especially sensitive

---

[77] D'Ewes, *Autobiography*, I, p. 107.   [78] *Autobiography of Matthew Robinson*, ed. Mayor, p. 16.
[79] Clarke, *Lives of Sundry Eminent Persons*, p. 3.   [80] Clarke, *Ten Eminent Divines*, p. 57.
[81] *Life and Death of Cawton*, p. 6.   [82] Clarke, *Ten Eminent Divines*, pp. 275, 276, 313–14.

to those in the college who 'drew away new-come Students from their books and studies to their ungodly company, and so made them debauched like themselves, they were not content to go to Hell alone . . .'. Cawton in fact served as a picket for the godly cause at Cambridge:

Particular and especiall notice was taken of one thing for which he was eminent and exemplary, which was this, that when any young youths came to the University either from his own Country, or else where, such as he knew, or was informed were well educated under godly Parents, or a godly Ministry, he would be sure to get acquaintance with them at their first coming to the University, before they were ingaged, intangled, or infected with bad company and would bring them into the company of some pious Schollers . . .[83]

The career of Roger Goad is especially illustrative. Educated at Eton and King's, a former master of Guildford school, and an M.A., Goad was Provost of King's from 1570 to 1610. Accused of financial mis-management and of harboring 'drones and dunses' by some younger members of the college, Goad set out a lengthy defence of his actions. Though written for pragmatic reasons, it serves as an academic parallel to the more familiar puritan spiritual autobiographies. Goad noted that he had continued the regular lectures and disputations, appointed two of the younger M.A.s to read philosophy lectures to the B.A.s and 'young ffellowes', helped to furnish the new library, provided a daily Greek lecture, and secured a Frenchman to read a Hebrew lecture in chapel for students in divinity (perhaps further evidence of the poor state of English Hebrew scholarship). In addition, he had read his own divinity lecture three mornings a week in chapel, had catechized the whole college and exhorted the members to read Scripture, and had overseen the rise in the number of ministers in the college from four to 'a score'.[84] The individual godly agents, moving within the formal structures of the institution, and adding to, rather than dismembering, the existing curriculum, could, as with the single ministers in the countryside, adjust the path of learning to more godly service by their individual effort and their collective action within the college.

Occasionally, however, the extreme closeness of tutor–pupil relationships could, compounded by more flagrant offences, catch the eye of the university and ecclesiastical authorities. A sermon preached at Christ Church in London brought a list of articles exhibited against Hugh Broughton. Included among the items, presumably to demonstrate Broughton's adamant nature against full conformity, was a clause which noted that 'his scholars do hold, that none doe teache trulye, but these that do folowe his course . . .'.[85] Within the college, tutors possessed great latitude. But when they attempted to institutionalize their deviance, they brought their whole cause into the light of administrative

[83] *Life and Death of Cawton*, pp. 3, 11, 10.
[84] B.L. MS Lansdowne 23, Nos. 40, 41. [85] Bod. Lib. MS Tanner 79, No. 45.

investigation. John Oxenbridge was a puritan tutor of Magdalen College, Oxford who in 1634 fell foul of the increasing pressure for conformity. In order to improve the 'government' of the college, Oxenbridge persuaded his students to subscribe to 'certain articles'. Though these are seemingly no longer extant, we learn from his replies to an investigation by the Vice-Chancellor of the University that Oxenbridge had drafted this 'Sacramentum Academicum' in London, and that four or five students had signed it, with two others orally agreeing to the rules.[86] He admitted that he had indeed 'dehorted my schollers' from reading anything tending 'to lasciviousnesse or Atheisme', but beyond that insisted that he had followed university practices. His admission that he had specifically 'expresst my approbation of their reading Classical Authours rather than novell ones'[87] may reflect the view that there was perhaps less to fear in the ancients, who would automatically be recognized as non-Christian, than in some recent writers, who could more effectively challenge puritan interpretation.

But it was Oxenbridge's particular religious instruction of his pupils that most interested the authorities. Oxenbridge insisted that he had professed only true religion, and specifically denied having forbidden his group to hear certain people at St Mary's. The course of religious instruction he offered reflected earlier puritan schemes, but also revealed the low quality of undergraduate scholarship:

The bookes which I ordinarily and generally have for the grounds of religion prescribed to my schollers are Junius his Bible with notes for study, and without for common prayers, Rogers his treatises, psalme booke, and a Catechisme which is ordinarily called Balls Catechisme, but the epistle imports more authors then one, the fittenesse of the allegations and the logicall disposition more then usuall in such writings have commended it to me. Many allso did beginne at once to translate and analize Calvins Institutions, but scarce have made any progresse in it, for it proves too hard or large for them who streightned in time and understanding especially in serious matters, so that of late I have not sette any to this worke. They are allso provided with some that write on the sacrament as Bradshaw, Pemble, etc.[88]

From the scores of catechisms, he had selected the offering of John Ball, a leading exponent of the covenant. Whether Oxenbridge's select few intended the ministry is unknown, but, even if they became heads of households rather than of congregations, they would carry forth a certain comprehension of the heavenly contract. Oxenbridge's written covenant with his pupils, while perhaps unique in the extant puritan evidence, was only the extreme of the recognized centrality of the bond between tutor and pupil. That the authorities, too, realized the importance of the challenge is to be inferred from

---

[86] P.R.O. S.P. 16/266/43, fol. 227. One of the students, named Bigge, was the chief informant in the case.   [87] *Ibid.*, fol. 229.   [88] *Ibid.*

Oxenbridge's expulsion from the university and the transfer of his pupils to other tutors 'freest from Faction'.[89]

Illustrative of both the magnitude and the diversity of the bond that remained between tutors and ex-pupils and college friends is the voluminous correspondence of Samuel Ward. Though Ward had probably abandoned his puritan traits before he became Master of Sidney Sussex, he retained both his Calvinism (at a time of its diminution in the universities) and his reputation as a scholar and adviser. Numerous letters requested university favours of Ward. Joseph Davenant wanted a good word with the Master and fellows of Trinity Hall, to which his nephew Thomas Fuller wished to transfer.[90] Frances Taylor, about to send his eldest son to Cambridge, confided that he was already (in June) looking for a suitable tutor. He had heard good reports of Mr Booth in Corpus Christi and requested that Ward act as go-between. Given that the son had already 'perfected' his Hebrew grammar, the father likely already saw the lad as a future divine. Here, then, the network was expected to work at a secondary level, 'once-removed' as it were. Taylor did not seek Ward's tutelage for his son, but only his good offices. Toby Matthew asked Ward to find his son a place at Sidney 'where he maie be both the sooner & better educated by a religious & carefull Tutor . . .'.[91] A few months later, Ward had evidently accomplished the task, for Matthew wrote again thanking him for 'providing so good a Tutor for my Josias, as Mr. Garbutt is . . .'.[92] The network continued over time, too. This same Richard Garbutt, some six years later, wrote to Ward from Newcastle, where he was then a lecturer, to ask advice on certain theological questions.[93]

William Bedell asked for some 'direction for the course of his studies' for his son, a minister.[94] Bedell, a fellow of Emmanuel, also helped to organize a circle of ministers which preached in places around Cambridge; Thomas Gataker, for one, was a member of this 'combination'.[95] This extra-university purpose of the network is illustrated even more clearly by a letter of 1608/9 from Samuel Crake in Essex to Ward, informing him of an available lectureship recently founded in Basingstoke in Hampshire, and requesting someone suitable.[96] Robert Jenison, another ex-pupil of Ward, similarly asked for a suggestion of someone to fill the important and vacant lectureship in Newcastle.[97] The puritan Thomas Gataker also frequently sought Ward's opinions, and even sent him one of his new works for comment.[98] At the same time, pupils also progressed past their tutors. Thus the ex-pupil Thomas Whitfield wrote to Ward questioning Ward's propriety in holding several

[89] *The Second Volume of the Remains of . . . William Laud . . . written by Himself . . .*, ed. Wharton, p. 70.
[90] Bod. Lib. MS Tanner 67, fol. 147.   [91] *Ibid.*, 80, No. 74, fol. 168.
[92] *Ibid.*, 290, No. 8, fol. 11.   [93] *Ibid.*, 72, No. 80, fol. 167.   [94] *Ibid.*, 70, fol. 74r–v.
[95] *Ibid.*, 75, fol. 129. This was the William Bedell who was later Provost of Trinity College, Dublin. The international 'brotherhood' thus preceded the New England connexion.   [96] *Ibid.*, 75, fol. 318.
[97] *Ibid.*, 73, fol. 136r–v.   [98] *Ibid.*, 72, fol. 294r–v; *ibid.*, 290, fol. 78.

livings, when so 'many of the worthyes of our church, such as Greenham, Perkens, Rogers & others . . . have contented themselves with a fourth part of your allowance'.[99]

Gentlemen sought at Oxford and Cambridge perhaps not only their own further education, but also the connexions which would provide them with a future supply of educated 'servants' such as chaplains, lawyers, and suitable appointees for benefices and other offices. They perhaps viewed the universities as an expansion of household education or as an alternative to the specialized academies proposed by Starkey, Gilbert, Nicholas Bacon, and William Cecil, among others.[100] There was a potential conflict of aims here. The better-born, not seeking degrees, doubtless were a threat to influence their tutors away from the course puritans deemed necessary for future ministers. From the other side, teaching provided the tutor not only with much-needed income, but, more important for his probable career, with training in comforting, teaching, and developing members of a community. The tutors themselves were thus also training their casuistical skills even as they brought forward the next generation.

Especially important were the increasing personal contacts which allowed parents an opportuntiy to appraise the academic and religious capacities of their son's tutor.[101] These included the regular delivery and collection of the son at the beginning and end of each term; the Great Commencement; intermittent occasions such as tutors fleeing the plague with their students, either to a country estate owned by the college, or to the home of one of the pupils; fairs near the university, as at Stourbridge; and visits to the country during the long vacation, at which tutors could not only meet parents, but perhaps also deliver impressive sermons and thus win country livings for themselves. Many puritan divines found their first employment after college as domestic chaplains in the homes of puritan gentlemen. This, too, occasioned correspondence between gentlemen and ministers in the colleges, tightened the bond of cleric and godly layman, and extended the mutual interest in perpetuating a strong puritan presence at Oxford and Cambridge. Without these safe houses, which offered succour and a sense of accomplishment, as well as protection, the periodic attacks of the administration on public dissent would probably have been far more successful. As well, service in such a home frequently brought the reward of promotion to a benefice in the patronage of the householder.[102]

Beyond these personal meetings, an extensive correspondence developed between fathers and tutors. In addition to information concerning the pupil's

[99] *Ibid.*, 72, fol. 170^{r-v}.
[100] McConica, 'Scholars and commoners', pp. 179–80; Cliffe, *Puritan Gentry*, pp. 11–12, 95, 135–8, 158–60, 163–5, 187–9, 191.
[101] This paragraph is based on Morgan, 'Cambridge and the country', esp. pp. 225–34, in Stone, ed., *University in Society*, i.
[102] For examples of such patronage, see esp. Cliffe, *Puritan Gentry*, pp. 165–7 and Ch. 9, *passim*.

educational progress, tutors were also likely to offer news of recent political, social, theological, even cultural, events. Tutors, already receiving funds for the upkeep of their pupils, were also likely to be asked to send books into the country homes of pupils' fathers. Finally, the tutors themselves were independent sources of intercourse with the counties. They might well choose to correspond with their own native areas, or with past comrades and pupils in new regions, or even with their old college once they had left. There was also the possibility that college members on a scholarship would have to make a pilgrimage every so often to the donor's parish to deliver a sermon.

One further point concerning the importance of the spread of information perhaps deserves some emphasis. As more young lads from a particular area attended the universities, a stock of local, communal knowledge would become available at market day, court sessions, sermons, and social gatherings, concerning not only which colleges were advantageous (whether for wealth, discipline, or connexions) but also which tutors were most prized, so that a father could possibly learn from the experiences of his neighbours. Indeed, the influence of the 'network' may have complemented traditional geographical patterns of affiliation with a particular college. It would seem, for example, that Yorkshire puritans sent their sons in disproportionate numbers to Emmanuel, Sidney Sussex, and Christ's – all colleges of puritan reputation.[103] At the same time, given that tutors left the university for ministerial appointments, it was important to stay abreast of new reputations, and of the inter-college migration of fellows.[104] Puritans, struggling to build alliances with the influential laity, and constantly battling to resist administration attempts at further regulation, encouraged the growing power and independence of the tutor. In an age of declining Calvinism and renewed efforts at uniformity (especially under the Laudian regime), and corresponding lessening of puritan weight in the university governing bodies, puritans found that the office of tutor became crucial to the perpetuation of godliness at Oxford and Cambridge. Beyond this, from their first coming up to their later careers, godly students could expect the assistance of their college tutors who, through their protégés, could extend godliness to the countryside even while they (or some of them) remained in the colleges. Indeed, this constantly expanding network of the Pauline thrust must have served to soothe the consciences of those who thought themselves forward, but who, like the Emmanuel fellows who petitioned against *de mora sociorum*, could not bring themselves to abandon the cloisters. The dialectic of enthusiasm and learning had thus found another point of synthesis.

[103] Stephens, 'Yorkshire schools and schoolmasters, 1600–1700', unpub. Ph.D. thesis, Univ. of Leeds, 1975, p. 27. For other regional affiliations, see Cliffe, *Puritan Gentry*, p. 92.
[104] The average length of tenure for tutors at Oxford and Cambridge is not yet known. Wilson Smith suggests that it was three years for Harvard tutors in the period 1650–4 ('Teacher in puritan culture', *Harvard Educational Review*, 36, p. 400, n. 24).

IV

At the beginning of Elizabeth's reign, the church had so many vacancies, and the educational level of the serving ministers was so low, that to rush newly learned clerics to congregations seemed the most important response. But as the emergency lessened, puritans started to emphasize the need for a stage between academic learning and the preaching of the Word which would turn learned graduates into worthy ministers before they met their congregations. There is little contemporary comment on why household 'seminaries' were deemed necessary, but we may perhaps make certain suggestions. First, while they continued to press for university education in ministers, puritans may well have decided by the early seventeenth century that the first level of producing an academic base had been reached, and that now they could afford to divert some of their effort to more purely vocational training, that is, to offering a few years' training in a small group which emphasized casuistry and preaching, in which very little formal practice was available at the universities.

Secondly, the universities suffered increased repression of Reformed opinions after the 1590s. Puritans may well have decided that a degree was no longer a sufficient test of a candidate's readiness for the ministry; there would now have to be an extra instructional process. The changing social composition of the universities, with their greater laicization, may also have suggested the need for a 'cleansing' period. The idea of formal seminaries may have been ruled out because such institutions would have had some difficulty in reproducing the practical problems which ministers would face in their parishes. Thirdly, there may simply have been a desire to expand the parameters of the godly household, which already included catechizing, Scripture-reading, and conferences of relatives and servants, to include educated young men who could add to the knowledge of the circle while honing their own public skills. Finally, the impact of covenant theology, with its central notion of a contract between the individual and God, may have heightened the ministers' awareness of the need for specialized pastoral training.

Reformed ministers of various persuasions had long understood the necessity of specialized vocational training. Andrew Gerardus insisted on correcting the sermons written by his students, and on listening to their delivery *in private* before they came to a public pulpit. He also instituted a form of examination of the students' knowledge in divinity, something that puritans emphasized was sorely lacking in the English church.[105] John Whitgift, while archbishop, evidently maintained a number of young men in his household for vocational training.[106] Among non-puritans in our period, however, this

---

[105] Orthius, *Life of Hyperius*, sig. Bb.viii. See also the similar suggestion by P. Gerard, *Preparation to Ministerie*, pp. 256ff. [106] Walker, *Peterhouse*, p. 91.

aspect of ministerial development received comparatively little emphasis.[107] We might recall here an allied attempt to make available to ministers further instruction after they had left the university. In 1624 Thomas White, D.D and Canon of Windsor, likely not a puritan, left £3000 to found Sion College in London. This was not White's first venture into educational charity; he had also founded a chair in moral philosophy at Oxford, and had endowed five exhibitions at his old college, Magdalen.[108] The new college was intended to serve the needs of all the clergy of greater London, and to reduce differences of opinion within the established church. To this end, a library was later provided for the ministers' use. Each year the clergy were to elect a president and two deans to run what amounted to a 'society' rather than a seminary of inhabitants with a specific routine. The college failed to become a centre of research and dispute to match the universities. Nonetheless, it did attract much support, some of it from puritans. Walter Travers, for example, left the college £50 in his will to endow the further education of ministers by providing ten shillings per quarter for the cleric who preached 'in Latin *ad clerum*'.[109]

Pressure had grown among puritans, even in the Elizabethan era, to have new ministers tested before they assumed in full responsibilities of a cure of souls. The presbyterian *Directory of Church-government*, which required each church to provide for some poor scholars to study divinity, 'especially for the expounding of holy Scripture', also insisted that students practise their preaching in front of a minister and other students, who would then criticize the sermon.[110] Richard Greenham argued for a delay in entering the ministry 'until after a continual publique teaching by come convenient tyme and some requisite trials of the people . . .'.[111] Greenham was, in fact, intent upon presenting young ministers with what amounted to a practical course in casuistry. He was evidently troubled by the rapid education and the 'preposterous zeal and hasty runing of yong men into the ministry', which gave them no time to learn their own faults, and which, he believed, clashed with the practices of the early church, still an important standard.[112] Greenham's participation was not limited to theoretical advice; he was often approached by the godly to 'traine up some younger men to [the ministry], and communicate his experience with them'.[113] Robert Browne, the Elizabethan radical, was among those who studied and trained with Greenham.[114]

[107] On the limitations of the non-puritans, see O'Day, *English Clergy*, Ch. 10 and esp. p. 142.
[108] The historian of Sion College argues of White that 'there is no firm ground for classing him as a Puritan . . .' (Pearce, *Sion College and Library*, p. 1). See also Jordan, *Charities of London*, pp. 254–5.
[109] Pearce, *Sion College*, pp. 1, 177.　　[110] Lorimer, ed., *Directory of Church-government*, sig. B3ᵛ.
[111] John Rylands Library, Eng. MS 524, fol. 2, Arthur Hildersam's record of Richard Greenham's casuistry.　　[112] *Ibid.*, fol. 54ʳ⁻ᵛ.
[113] Greenham, *Workes*, 'To the Reader' [by Henry Holland], sig. A5. Clarke, *General Martyrologie*, especially praised Greenham's ability to soothe troubled consciences.
[114] Browne, *True and Short Declaration*, p. 398, in *Writings of Harrison and Browne*, ed. Peel & Carlson.

William Bradshaw resided with a gentleman's family, conducting private exercises with them while also preaching on Sundays. It is worth noting that at first he preached in the gentleman's chapel, graduating to the parish church only when 'called' by the overflowing audience at the first site.[115] Such prior training, not taken at the expense of a whole congregation, proved an indispensable opportunity to improve those skills upon which the successful propagation of the Word depended. William Perkins, in the same era, also entertained many ministers, 'who did resort unto him from everywhere' for advice on the practice of godly ministry.[116] The members of the Dedham *classis* started what may have been the first organized scheme for pastoral postgraduate training. At one of their meetings, they agreed to take divinity students who were already sufficient in humane learning and turn them into able ministers.[117]

It was, however, in the early seventeenth century that examples of such apprenticeship became most evident. So Robert Harris studied the Scriptures – in the original tongues – with godly John Dod, whom he succeeded when Dod was suspended for nonconformity. Clarke tells us that, after Dod had moved to safer territory in Northamptonshire, 'God was pleased to supply [Harris'] want by the resort of sundry young Students from Oxford to Hanwell, so that . . . his house was a little Academy . . .'.[118] In London, Charles Offspring ran a famous seminary at St Antholin's which provided lectures on four of the weekdays, and promoted junior members through the ranks of preaching until they were ready to fill the job offers that came in to Offspring's agency.[119] Patrons evidently regarded membership in such a seminary as proof of both proper conviction and sufficient skill. Thus, though our period had started with a puritan clamour for equipping ministers with a degree and then rushing them to the pulpit, by then end of our time Jonathan Mitchell could comment (1663) that a Harvard student who joined the ministry with only a B.A. was considered 'raw' and unready.[120]

Those who frequented such establishments came to see them as the vocational conclusion of their scholarly education. Samuel Winter studied under John Preston at Queens', and attained 'a great measure of knowledge, both in the *Tongues* and *Arts*, and also in *Divinity*'. It would seem that Winter was thus eminently qualified to go forth to the ministry. It is therefore highly significant that, even after receiving his M.A., Winter was 'as yet unwilling to enter upon that great and dreadful work of the Ministry', and so went to live

[115] Clarke, *General Martyrologie*, p. 44. Puritan ministers who had been suspended or deprived also repaired to the houses of puritan laymen. But since the motivation was more often refuge than training or education, such cases have not been considered here. For an example, see P.R.O. S.P. 14/10A/81, the case of Melanchthon Jewell, a deprived puritan minister of Essex.

[116] Knappen, ed., *Two Elizabethan Puritan Diaries*, p. 130 (from the diary of Samuel Ward).

[117] Usher, ed., *Presbyterian Movement*, p. 93.   [118] Clarke, *Ten Eminent Divines*, p. 282.

[119] Calder, 'St Antholin's', *Church Quarterly Review*, 160, esp. pp. 52ff.

[120] Morison, *Harvard in the Seventeenth Century*, I, p. 274.

with John Cotton in Boston.[121] One of those who joined Herbert Palmer's household at Ashwell in Hertfordshire was Thomas Cawton, who moved the twelve miles from Cambridge to assist Palmer in his ministry, and to learn the difference, as his biographer tells us, between knowledge and the essence of divinity. Even after this experience, however, Cawton did not feel fully secure in his profession, and so he put in another four years in the household of Sir William Armin, where he expounded the Scriptures, catechized the family, and also preached for nearby ministers, so as 'not to let the gift of preaching rest, and so rust . . .'. Only then would he accept his own living, in Essex.[122] The frequency of such incidents reduces the likelihood of an individual psychological barrier to acceptance of what puritans understood to be a gruelling and exacting burden.[123]

The seminaries, offering young graduates frequent opportunities to preach (out of the eye of the church authorities) and to be helpfully evaluated, likely contributed heavily to the perpetuation and wide propagation of the puritan 'plain style'. John Yates, who became one of the leading English exponents of the Ramist notion of 'technometria', studied under the Ramist Laurence Chaderton at Emmanuel. His greatest Ramist mentor, however, was the very influential Alexander Richardson, to whose academy in Barking, Essex, Yates repaired. His company included William Ames, Thomas Hooker, and Charles Chauncey, a triad of great intellectual, godly, and organizational power, especially in the New World.[124]

While these godly teaching households never achieved any formal status, they seem to have become a fundamental part of the puritan educational apparatus. In a sense the seminaries represented the achievement of the Elizabethan radical demand for the decentralization of higher education, and the separation of ministerial training from the concerns of humane learning. A sample picture of one of these seminaries may be gleaned from Clarke's account of Richard Blackerby's establishment. After his nonconformity had cost him his living in Norfolk, Blackerby lectured in neighbouring parishes and towns, and opened his house to the offspring of pious gentry, tradesmen and yeomen, whom he instructed in religion and learning.[125] He also afforded his postgraduate charges a chance to preach; doubtless his local connexions

---

[121] Clarke, *Eminent Persons*, pp. 97, 95.   [122] *Life and Death of Cawton*, p. 13–16.
[123] For the very similar story of Samuel Fairclough, see Clarke, *Eminent Persons*, p. 159.
[124] Sprunger 'John Yates of Norfolk', esp. pp. 699–701.
[125] Clarke, *Eminent Persons*, pp. 58, 81. See also Shipps, 'Lay patronage of East Anglian puritan clerics', unpub. Ph.D. thesis, Yale Univ. 1971, p. 75. n. 25, for information on the puritan graduates of Blackerby's seminary. They included Samuel Fairclough, Nicholas Bernard, Samuel Stone, and Jonas Proost, minister of various Dutch congregations in England. Other forms of godly connexion, too, were built in these seminaries: Fairclough married Blackerby's eldest daughter, Sarah (*ibid.*, p. 78). Shipps also suggests that Stephen Marshall, located nearby at Clare, Suffolk, might have been associated with Blackerby's seminary (*ibid.*, pp. 75–6).

helped to gain invitations for the ministerial novices. Samuel Fairclough, for example, while at Blackerby's, was able to study divinity for four days a week and humane learning for two, and also test his preaching ability at nearby villages.[126] The model curriculum evidently revolved around Blackerby, who taught Hebrew (which was in poor condition at the universities), scriptural exegesis, and divinity; that is, he 'gave them excellent advice for Learning, Doctrine, and Life . . .'.[127]

Though these households were intended primarily for ministers, puritans did not forget the advantages of a well-tuned state. Blackerby therefore evidently prepared some junior members of his gathered circle for university, the post-university members for the ministry, and 'others for other Callings' so that 'many grew to be excellent persons in Church and State . . .'.[128] Similarly, Herbert Palmer continued his reputation of being a careful tutor at Queens' into his ministry at Ashwell. He boarded sons of the gentry and nobility who were sent to him for a 'better education in Religion' as well as in the learning for which he hired a schoolmaster.[129] After he had settled as the minister of Rotherhithe, near London, Thomas Gataker founded his own informal academy. It not only served as 'one of the best Schooles for a young Student to learn Divinity in', but also reflected the puritan interest in influential laymen by catering for sons of gentlemen, and especially for foreigners. The pastoral circumstances ensured that Gataker's students learned 'as Paul was [taught] at the feet of Gamaliel'.[130] Lay and clerical were thus intertwined even at the highest level of puritan-directed education. The experience in catechizing and educating young children also provided a background for the teaching jobs which were not unusual interludes in ministerial careers, and which helped to solidify the bonds between ministers and schoolmasters.

These seminaries also served as models for the future households of their postgraduate students. John Cotton of Boston set a very strict pattern in his family duties; every morning and evening he engaged the household in readings and prayers and also expounded doctrine. He corrected the errors of his children and servants by applying Scripture to their particular situation. As

---

[126] Clarke, *Eminent Persons*, pp. 160–2. For further details on the career of Samuel Fairclough, see Shipps, 'Lay patronage of East Anglian puritan clerics', esp. pp. 74–9.

[127] Clarke, *Eminent Persons*, pp. 58, 159. Blackerby also kept diaries in Greek, English and Latin; all of them, says Clarke, perished in a fire (*ibid.*, p. 63). For similar centres of instruction, see Clarke's sketch of John Ball's seminary (*General Martyrologie*, pp. 147, 149) and John Angier's account of John Cotton's household (*Life*, p. 9).

[128] Clarke, *Eminent Persons*, p. 58. Bernard Gilpin had similarly boarded 24 young scholars in his home; every Sunday he offered them religious instruction.

[129] Clarke, *General Martyrologie*, pp. 185, 190. See also, for other examples, *ibid.*, p. 65 (Richard Stock); Clarke, *Marrow*, p. 90 (John Bruen); Angier, *Life*, p. 65; Clarke, *Eminent Persons*, p. 58 (Thomas Taylor); Clarke, *Ten Eminent Divines*, pp. 101–2 (William Gouge); Fuller, *Abel Redivivus*, pp. 588–9 (Robert Bolton); Featley *et al.*, *House of Mourning*, p. 409 (John Moulson); Bod. Lib. MS Tanner 278, fol. 22ᵛ (William Bedell). [130] Clarke, *Ten Eminent Divines*, pp. 132, 145–6.

was the custom in godly households, Cotton's observance of the sabbath began on Saturday evening. He catechized children and servants and spent the rest of the evening, and all day Sunday (with the exception of time spent in public duties), in private study. On Sunday evening he repeated his sermon to the family, and after supper sang a psalm, and then ended the day in further prayer and study.[131] This seminary was thus a fount of case-divinity for attendant scholars. At these seminaries students also formed close bonds which added to the strength of the university 'brotherhood'. John Angier, for example, remembered John Cotton's household as the source of his lasting friendships with Anthony Tuckney, Thomas Hill, and Samuel Winter.[132] The milieu of such visible godliness had its intended effect. Clarke's pages are full of the conversions of learned young men who came from the universities ungodly, but who left private seminaries as the shining lights of the Lord.[133]

This was not, as can be imagined, the sort of training that would likely produce malleable servants of an administration moving away from the English Calvinist tradition. It was not long, therefore, before the administration sought ways to curtail these centres of independent thought. Illustrative is the case of Thomas Hooker, Emmanuel-bred puritan and later pastor in Massachusetts and Connecticut. Samuel Collins, the minister of Braintree, reported with anguish the great size of Hooker's audience at his Chelmsford lecture; Collins also noted the evident support for Hooker's message. In a time of economic depression, and amid the view of 'my Lord of London as a man indevouring to suppress good preaching & advance Popery', the authorities had extra cause to fear the political influence of the sermons of a man 'altogether unconformable'. Collins reported that students had almost forsaken their usual course of studies in favour of propagating Hooker's opinions; he also recorded the formative influence of such a leader on the seminarians: 'he is their Oracle in cases of Conscience & pointes of Devinity & their principall library'.[134] Hooker was hounded by Laud after 1629 from both his lectureship and his later schoolmaster's job in Essex.[135] Collins, however, perceived that the influence of a good teacher could outlive his school; even if Hooker were removed from the lectureship, Collins argued, 'His Genius will still haunte all the pulpits in the Countrey where any of his schollers may be admitted to preach . . . .'.[136] The followers were thought to be more fanatical than their leader. Such alumni from Hooker's circle as

---

[131] *Ibid.*, pp. 68–9. For very similar portraits, see also *ibid.*, pp. 7–8 (about John Carter's household); *Ibid.*, pp. 145–6 (Thomas Gataker); Clarke, *General Martyrologie*, p. 126 (Thomas Taylor); *ibid.*, pp. 188, 190–1 (Herbert Palmer); Bod. Lib. MS Tanner 278, esp. fol. 23^{r-v} (William Bedell).

[132] Angier, *Life*, esp. p. 9.

[133] Most of the examples contained in the preceding notes from Clarke contain such incidents. See also Powell, *Life and Death*, pp. 2–3; Goodwin, *Workes*, v, pp. v–vii.

[134] P.R.O. S.P. 16/142/113.   [135] *D.N.B.*, s.v. 'Thomas Hooker'.   [136] P.R.O. S.P. 16/142/113.

Jeremiah Burroughes, John Beadle, and Nathaniel Rogers did little to prove Collins wrong.[137]

Shipps has suggested that the seminaries became centres of 'opposition' thought in the 1630s. The seminaries were indeed unlike prophesyings or combination lectures in that they operated in private residences, frequently of deprived or suspended ministers who thus had a personal animosity to the administration and perhaps the structure of the established church. The equality of ministers in the deliberations may have fostered congregationalist tendencies. It is, however, difficult to generalize about fully decentralized and independent facilities. But that most seminaries ceased to exist in the 1630s upon the death of their founders, is at least a mark of the lack of oppositional *organization*.

Stronger attractions to seminaries may well have been the opportunity to study in preparation for M.A. exams,[138] and feelings of professional insecurity, as in the case of Winter and Fairclough. In some university graduates there was probably a fear of the gulf that distinguished their scholarship from the knowledge and casuistical needs of the rank and file of most country congregations. The mass of Christians could hardly have been an uplifting sight – in terms of education as well as morals – for the new godly preacher. At the godly households ministers must have struggled simply to learn how to *communicate* with their parishioners. A year or two listening to an experienced minister, combined with the chance to practise one's own vocational talents, must have appealed to those who were not yet emotionally strong enough to overcome the natural self-doubt of their own readiness and worthiness for such a crucial task. The members doubtless resolved to counter the deviant innovative theology of the administration. In following this course, the seminaries did perhaps drift apart from the thrust of the universities.

The added stress placed on the individual in these puritan homes may have contributed to a loosening of the authority of the church. The argument may be made that such individualism was antithetical to the structure of the established church. But the operation of that church, ever since the Reformation, had been loose enough for these seminaries to fit easily into the mould of an Elizabethan Richard Greenham or a Jacobean John Dod, both typical puritan figures – occasionally in trouble with the authorities, but generally working within the pattern of the Church of England. It may therefore be more helpful to see these seminaries as institutions which promoted 'resistance' to the Laudian attack on orthodoxy, rather than as an 'opposition', which has over-formalized connotations. Seminaries were created not as bold steps for political ecclesiological reform – one might compare the scheme of the feoffees for impropriations to gain control of parish livings – but rather as the final stage in the long and increasingly refined educational process of producing a puritan ministry which balanced fervency and humane learning in its preparation for the further edification of the church.

Indeed, this was the final stage in that immensely long process of retraining will and reason which we have traced from the mother's breast to the homes of practising ministers. The production of godly men and women was crucial to the erection of a New Jerusalem, but at the forefront, as puritan literature kept emphasizing, came the proper education of the ministerial vanguard. The household seminaries provided the conditioning for existential Being, as the universities had offered the essence of theology. Only together could these two provide the coalition of fervency and knowledge required for the thorough reconstruction of Christian existence.

At all stages of this development – through household, school, college, and (for some of those entering the ministry) seminary – puritans thus emphasized re-forming the character and social outlook of the individual Christian. In this chapter I have attempted to demonstrate that at the highest level of institutional education, as lower down, puritans stressed the importance of turning the individual instructor towards a regimen of godly learning. It is regrettably not clear whether this emphasis emanated more from the theoretical position that it would take godly men to build a godly society (that is, that the acts of the individual are of greater effect upon his social institutions than *vice versa*), or simply from a recognition that, for all their well-placed connexions, they did not have the power to redraft England's institutions, even had they wished to attempt such a task. On the side of the former interpretation can be placed the centrality in puritan thought of the covenant and, in turn, its own crux of the experience of conversion. Despite the best efforts of institutions, went the argument of practical divinity, the individual would be changed – born anew – only after his recognition of his direct bond with the Lord. In favour of the latter idea is the bountiful evidence, some of which has been presented here, that puritans shaped the public presentation of their ideas with a very keen sense of the nuances of the immediate context. The issue can perhaps not be finally decided, but it can at least be said that modification of the social institutions of education through the remodelling of the individual was ever the core of the puritan plan for the gradual realization of that New Jerusalem which they so dearly cherished.

CONCLUSION

I

At the core of the puritan struggle for meaning in the darkness of this fallen world, humane learning could provide only flickering illuminations. It provided the skills and the knowledge necessary for the comprehension of the greater light. But the full brightness, as countless puritan sermonizers made clear, was available only to those who could leave behind the false propositions of human reason. Only by casting off the chains forged by overreliance on reason, and by entering the higher sphere of enthusiasm, could puritans come to a comprehension of their own Being. Imbued as their experiences and modes of thinking were by scholarship, they accepted humane learning as a base. The realization by these dwellers at the highest level of understanding that, in their vocation as ministers, they would have to return to the caves – the 'dark corners of the land' – and express themselves to the unbelieving, still chained to the shadows of myths, popish superstition, and rank irreligion, also caused them not to abandon humane learning, but rather to probe and modify it in the search for an expression which could transmit the light to the darkness. It was, indeed, the degree to which they rejected the extremes of both pure enthusiasm and the supremacy of rational interpretation over the molten core of faith that provided them with their own distinctive *via media*.

The puritan social thrust throughout the eighty years before the Revolution had been to lay the bases for a new society of disciplined godliness. Though at first social control would have to be exercised primarily through the reformed agencies of church and state, the long-term success of the proposed transformation had to rest on the internalization of this new discipline. The puritan aim was not simply to impose a body of Reformed theology upon the bishops and the universities, but rather to build the New Jerusalem by transforming the individual members of English society. While this of course necessitated a suitable explanation to human reason, far more important in constructing the bases of massive change was the capturing of the individual will. The path to salvation was now to be seen and publicly explained as an individual contract which each petitioner had to assume. The parental, ministerial, and schoolmasterly task was to turn the reason and the will of each generation towards a *desire* for salvation. The continuing dedication to the search for external perfection in society and in humanity, and yet the firm realization that it was not there, could never be there, provided the ultimate level of the absurd in the puritan existential struggle.

If the preliminary to entry into the covenant was a course of preparation, then godly education had to start as soon as possible in life. Parents became in a very real sense the vanguard of the ministerial army: catechizing, reading, praying, instructing their children in acceptable patterns of Christian behaviour. Similarly, schoolmasters were to provide their students – whether petties or upper-school grammar students – not just with the matter of humane learning, but with a visible example of godliness and with a godly atmosphere in which to develop their own intellect and will. Schoolmasters were therefore to be examined as closely on their conversation and dedication to building the New Jerusalem as on their academic stature. Committed godliness was a greater variable; therefore testimonials, interviews, close supervision, and (school) statutory requirements, sometimes even including oaths to especial godliness, were invoked in an attempt to ensure acceptable practices. Schoolmasters were expected to coordinate their activities with those of the local minister if he was a godly force, or even to replace his effect in the community if he was retrograde. Adults were thus bound to provide, through enforced study, attendance at church, catechizing, school lessons and sermon repetitions, the passing along of godly consciousness to the next generation. That is, while recognizing that their theology did not allow salvation based on earthly performance, puritans staunchly 'argued', by their actions, that somehow the existential struggle might perchance have a more favourable conclusion if the environment were improved. Only godly men and concerted action could change context; and only modified context could act upon the condition of the human will. The two blended to produce a cycle of godly social attitudes. '

This leads into the question of the degree to which the pre-1640 puritans can legitimately be described as 'radical' and as the intellectual forerunners of the revolutionaries of the 1640s. To a large degree their influence must have inhered in their emphasis on the individualization of salvation and the necessity of a ministry which would stress the free interpretation of Scripture before any constraint of human law. The puritan assertion that assurance depended on godly conversation and the performance of good works came to be a staple of the arduous progress which covenant theology required of stalwart Christians. By silencing contentious preachers, and by aborting public discussion of such central theological ideas as predestination, the Laudian administration severely hampered the fulfilling of the duties of vocation by the godly ministers. For the previous seventy years, puritan ministers had hammered at congregations the idea that the duty of the laity was to carry out the requirements propounded by this special caste. If the religious imperative ran as deep in a section of the gentry and upper bourgeoisie as letters and diaries would seem to indicate, then the Laudian interference with the close relationship of preacher and people may well have provided the intellectual bedrock needed for members of such classes to start contemplating not merely the avoidance of unacceptable 'mannerisms' of a 'halfly-reformed' church, but rather the beginnings of an organized opposition to the institutional power wielded by the incumbent church and state.

It is perhaps indicative of the degree to which England was still a 'psychologically decentralized' nation – that is, an area in which the term 'countrey' still commonly meant 'county' – that this opposition was first evident in any 'organized' form as the attempted protection of local institutions such as afternoon sermons and combination lectures. Parliament was already a profoundly important institution, but it was occasional and, as yet, convoked and dismissed at the monarch's will. It was in the several 'countreys' of the land that puritan gentry and ministers could relatively safely and effectively oppose the commands of King and High Commission. In the period of the Caroline repression, it is not surprising that opponents sought to defend their local institutions first.

For our concern here, it is important to note that education was a local interest. Protection of ministers by gentlemen meant the perpetuation of godly instruction. This was true of pulpit, household, and school. But the sense of local defence spawned by the intellectual attitudes propagated by puritan ministers went a crucial step further. Given the statutory geographical bias of many colleges, given the known connexions of schools and colleges, and given the close relations of tutors and gentlemen, it seems clear that the universities were regarded not as national institutions, but rather as extensions of local life. Protection of godliness in Oxford and Cambridge was not continued as a national challenge to the structure of church or state, but as a necessary guarantee of the flow of godly instructors and mediators to the 'countrey'.

The struggle, then, in the forthcoming 'puritan revolution', was not so much over the perceived national implications of any grand puritan statements on the proper structure of a godly polity as over the defence of life in the countryside, which had been deeply affected by the puritan covenant and its effects on the practice of religion and on the institutions of education. Mildmay had said that Scripture should be set above the judgement of even the best of men, though, in most cases, puritans meant 'judgement' only in the sense of scholarly interpretation. The political implications of this belief, when attached to the individualism of covenant theology, must go far towards explaining the strong religious component of the intellectual origins of the English Revolution.

But this is to question what listeners made of a sermon, or what readers construed from a text, a very different problem from that broached here. Here we have been interested in portraying the intentions of the puritan writers and sermonizers – the content of the message they intended to issue to the English people, and specifically the directions in which they urged England to develop. The reaction of the 'followers' has been of only secondary interest. Suffice it to note that the political thrust of lay puritan individualism should not be taken as directly illustrative of the socio-political doctrine emanating from puritan pulpits. Historians such as Hill and Walzer have rightly stressed certain revolutionary implications of pre-1640 puritan thought, but they have understated the essentially conservative *intentions* of the puritan message.

The puritans themselves – that mainstream which was Chaderton, Perkins, Dod, Gouge, Preston, Sibbes, Gataker – called always for a halt: a halt to commercial exploitation, in favour of communal well-being; a halt to foreign policy based on termporary advantage, in favour of alliances of the international brotherhood of the godly against the resurgent Antichrist; a halt to novelty in the church in the 1630s, in favour of 'old protestantism'. The puritans always looked backwards for their future. The future held only the end of the present and the reintroduction, at the millennium, of a purer past. Much of this conservative approach was grounded upon attitudes inculcated in schools and colleges by godly schoolmasters and tutors.

The belief that learned godliness should be pervasive and should help to lead to a new society did not imply an absence or rejection of class-consciousness on the part of pre-revolutionary puritan ministers. Puritans insisted that the Almighty had provided a social, economic, and political hierarchy on earth as a necessity for a fallen context; levelling was no part of puritan policy. At the same time, puritans saw society as a functionally inter-dependent commonwealth. All had to fulfil the demands of a specific vocation. Rank therefore had its duties as well as its privileges. The conjunction in puritan thought of firm support for the earthly hierarchy and the imperative to proselytize (dependent, in practice, on patronage and protection) allowed ministers to ally themselves with individual members of the socio-economic elite who would otherwise have been beyond their social reach. The attraction of a religion which supported earthly privilege, and which may well have been interpreted as allowing the highest ranks the best opportunity (through 'good works') to demonstrate both privately and publicly their own assurance, quickly bound many of the gentry to the puritan thrust. Against the background of an increasingly well-educated gentry it was, in part, the tenuous combination of learning and enthusiasm in religion that provided pre-revolutionary puritan ministers with their tremendous influence at this level.

The question has arisen, too, of the degree to which puritans should be seen as 'modern' because of their emphasis on the rational. I hope that I have demonstrated the ways in which puritans sought restrictions on unbridled reason. The early seventeenth century, despite its intellectual changes, was not yet the 'age of the *philosophes*' with a grudging nod to a functionless deity. Puritans instead consciously aimed at the unity of reason and faith, with the former continuing its traditional subordinate role. While puritans supported the use of reason for earthly purposes, we have their abundant word for it that the 'freeing' of reason into a weapon which could be used to restrict, hamper, and criticize formal religion was anathema to them.

When this strange dialectic of reason and faith was worked out in the Restoration to the advantage of learning as a component in an increasingly 'professional' occupation, a stern price had to be paid. During the Revolution the full rebellion of enthusiasm against formal learning condemned, at its extreme, even printed Scripture for the restrictions it placed on the individual spirit. This threat to the customary synthesis caused 'traditional' puritans to decry the non-rational force more solemnly than before and to subordinate it until, in the safer air of the 1660s, when the radicals had been purged, they could reintroduce it as a non-revolutionary component of their own thought. With the lower orders, the forsaking of enthusiasm may well have led to a more pronounced alienation from the socially controlled learning of the post-1660 period, and to increased anticlericalism as ministers became attached not so much to old imagined status as chosen men of God as to a new perceived status as products of the cleansed universities, that is, as gentlemen.

Puritans are thus to be seen as a series of dichotomies, a collection of contrasting emphases which they could not fully synthesize by 1640 and which thereafter tore apart the surface unity which they had moulded in the decades since the accession of Elizabeth. The puritan emphasis on the primacy of personal religious experience clashed with insistence upon the dominance of ministerial interpretation of God's role in human affairs; the emphasis on everyday experience stood against Ramist refinement of the traditional syllogistic approach to the use of reason; again, emphasis on ordinary experience had to co-exist with a pronounced reluctance to study God through his works in Nature; emphasis on the individuality of assurance conflicted with the standardized message of the all-important printed Word; finally – the core of this present work – there was the great dialectic between reason and enthusiasm in the lives of the faithful.

II

Puritans did not venture far from the traditional academic routine. The structures of educational institutions, and the content as affected by Renaissance urgings, seemed to satisfy their need for an academic base. There can certainly be no doubt of the very limited effect of puritans in adding to the legacy of the Renaissance, or in developing the human intellect in the Baconian sense of the 'advancement of learning'. Modern scholars would therefore at first sight seem right to denigrate the contribution of the puritans to the history of education. At the same time we must comprehend that the puritans' 'failure' did not lie in their inability to develop a 'modern mind'. As Quentin Skinner has noted, 'it cannot (logically) be a correct appraisal of any agent's action to say that he failed to do something unless it is first clear that he did have, and even could have had, the intention to try to perform *that* action.'[1] I have argued here that the puritans' thrust was wholly towards a community of faith consisting of enthusiasm tempered by reason (rather than the other way around). Indeed, any attempt to delineate a 'puritan intellect' separate from the imperative of the search for salvation would seem destined to commit a great historical inaccuracy. A novel theory of learning or education lay outside the necessities of a puritan blueprint for the future. Puritans were far more concerned to build a practical divinity on top of the (modified) Calvinism which provided their theological base. Their great strength – in both church and university – lay in the progressive development of a mode of Christian *existence* in a fallen world nearing the apocalypse.

I have preferred here to assess puritans not as an evolutionary link between mediaeval and modern man, but rather as an existential reaction to the problems of their own particular context, as an attempt to establish a new essence in a generally hostile environment. Central to this development came the design of education as a medium for spiritual growth through the harnessing of man's non-rational aspects. Puritans sought to erect in practice an England which resembled the early Christian communities in the Mediterranean for which Paul had struggled so valiantly. In Paul they found the perfect historical parallel for their own existential quest for a way to balance, if not fully blend, enthusiasm and humane learning. Paul himself had laboured in the shining world of Graeco-Roman learning into which a new fervency of the heart had been injected. His central problem, it seemed to puritans, had been to blaze a suitably socialized Christian trail for this context – something between hermetic escapism and the full fusion of Greek philosophy with a religious ethic.

If the puritans' response to reason was modelled on Pauline wariness, their attitude towards educational institutions was also based on a Pauline view of practical necessity. Humanist learning was seen as immensely valuable because it could be blended with the enthusiasm of faith to produce a more logical interpretation of Scripture and an intellectual side of protestantism more secure against the assaults of the Roman Antichrist. This did not mean that puritans sought merely to perpetuate a mediaeval outlook regarding the coordination of reason and faith. Scholasticism was seen not as a corpus of

[1] Skinner, 'Meaning and understanding in the history of ideas', p. 29.

religious knowledge, but rather as an intellectual method, to be redefined and modified.

Thus puritans sought to imitate the atmosphere of the early church, in which the legacy of the intellect existed as source material, as illustration, as analogy, but in which also the fierce flame of a new vigorous faith burned brightly. To regard puritans as wishing merely to restrain the intellectual 'excesses' of the Renaissance is to underestimate their vision. The puritan imperative also demanded the resurrection in each individual, and in the church as community, of the fervency of Paul fighting in a hostile world. Puritans thus saw themselves as the true Christian heirs of Paul's warning against allowing learning to puff men up: vainglory was the surest roadblock on the godly path. But within their own circle, among their own comrades, they could freely employ their own learning in its proper, adjunctive role. And against those who cursed learning as a whore puritans thus always insisted upon it as a prerequisite to scriptural scholarship.

As there were difficulties with the current structure and order of the English church, so were there serious anomalies, from a Reformed point of view, in England's schools and universities. But, very much as the English church proved fertile soil for puritan infiltration at the ground level, so, too, did the educational system both permit the training of purified citizens and ministers, and allow the modification of content and method of instruction. At all levels, puritans were able to fashion necessary changes in an *ad hoc* fashion. Concerning learning and education, puritans had the lessons of Geneva and of a developing protestant scholasticism to guide them. Yet there was never a rigid plan. As they developed the bonds of the 'spiritual brotherhood' and, more formally, the combination lecture and the *classis* in the countryside, so in new colleges such as Emmanuel and Sidney Sussex they established different parameters for godly behaviour and godly study. In neither case did puritans challenge the accepted structure.

The 'reform' of the universities in the Revolution produced little lasting progress towards the purification and eventual godliness of all knowledge because, evidently, too many people saw too many other ends to pursue. Puritans in our period did not have the power to control society, but their criticisms of popular culture – both the 'magic' of the old ways and the corrupted print of the new – provided forewarning of the opposition they would stir when outward conformity to their view of godliness was no longer wholly voluntary. The puritan emphasis on creating readers in a population not wholly 'reborn' produced a desire for knowledge that easily outran the puritans' ability to censor and control. The promotion of classical learning in what they envisaged as the safer confines of Emmanuel produced not only a generation of godly emigrés for Massachusetts, but neo-Platonism and latitudinarianism as well.

The puritan educational thrust is therefore still to be classified as one of the failures of history – one of the all-encompassing cultural schemes which struggled to impose itself, and yet failed, in the end, because of popular rejection. To a growing degree, the contemporary emphasis on secular, human knowledge seems to have regarded an ageless Christian approach to education as outdated and inadequate. In the second half of the seventeenth century, as the impact of Hobbes, Locke, and Newton illustrates, men were seeking knowledge of a new fixity in their lives and in the world around them. The puritan approach to human existence, which had decreed that the objective universe could provide no meaning, no longer satisfied increasingly significant proportions of the nation's intelligentsia, which now searched instead for explanations capable of empirical verification. Newton's quest for the Number of the Beast, though an important facet of his own existence, was nonetheless comparatively an aberration at the end of the seventeenth century, whereas John Napier's similar search in the 1610s had blended well with the intellectual thrust of his age. Puritans were cast adrift from what became the intellectual mainstream also because they did not apply themselves very much to the demand for vocational learning. Charges of pedantry arose against schoolmasters and scholars because their specialized knowledge was increasingly out of tune with the rising demand for learning that was practical.

Patrick Collinson has recently argued that puritan attitudes did not express so much an 'individualism', as a 'stereotyped. programmed corporateness'. That is, puritans struggled not for anarchy but rather for the existence of a tightly knit community of the godly within the greater mass of the reprobate.[2] This, indeed, reflects the portrait I have painted here of puritan educational attitudes. The godly evidently recognized not only the crucial importance of cementing their own faith and purer conversation in the present generation (as Collinson illustrates), but also the absolute necessity of perpetuating the growing purification through cleansing the structures of learning, and of purging learning itself of hostile influences. There would have been little point in pursuing only the former of these aims. Puritan groupings therefore served as well to exchange information concerning schoolmasters, colleges, and tutors. The degree to which this network served as a source of useful information is noted in the reputation of Emmanuel and in the memoirs of individuals concerning their schoolmasters and the selection of tutors. The close connexion between college and country – that is, between puritan tutor and puritan gentleman – was intended to provide a structural base for the generational continuity of the godly community. Though the soteriology of the puritans indeed made the individual an island in the universe, the social

[2] Collinson, *Religion of Protestants*, pp. 251, 268ff.; Collinson, *Godly People*, pp. 548–9.

relations deemed necessary for the construction of the New Jerusalem required a close coordination of voluntary effort among the godly.

In this sense, puritan influence may well have proved pervasive in our period. I noted in the Introduction that my concern was with the puritans' own thought rather than with the effects of that thought. Other studies will have to determine the degree to which grammar schools really built changed minds in the late sixteenth and seventeenth centuries. But of the importance of education within the puritan scheme itself there can be no doubt. The godly schoolmaster was the full comrade of the minister, enrolling minds in the arduous course of preparation, even if he seldom effected conversion. Where this close relationship of religion and teaching existed, puritans could score notable successes. But where it was absent – as at the Inns of Court – puritan ministers had a much more difficult time converting their audience to a purer conversation. In this very important sense, then, 'teaching' in the formal educational institutions and seminaries became a central aspect of puritan practical divinity. It provided both the learning that could perceive the knowledge contained in the Scriptures and also the incipient search for personal reformation that preceded membership in the covenant.

Puritans thus contributed to the final flowering of a tradition of attempting to blend faith and reason, enthusiasm and learning, into a *Christian* balance, something which had been the chief intellectual enterprise of Western Europe for the previous millennium-and-a-half. They were doomed in that their age foreshadowed not the New Jerusalem, but the birth of the immensely stronger light of human reason. Against the enormous intellectual attraction of Descartes' anthropocentric *cogito ergo sum*, which made God contingent on man's rational consciousness, and offered man intellectual (and, by extension, physical) dominion over the beasts, the self-questioning rigour of puritan thought could not stand. For the next two hundred and fifty years Cartesian philosophy and the evident successes of reason drove the Western world to heights of human self-glorification. This is not to deny the periodic eruptions of Christian enthusiasm. But only in our century – in the illumination cast by Nietzsche, Freud, Heidegger, and the nineteenth- and twentieth-century Russian and French existential writers, and in the shadows of unparalleled destruction –has the search for meaning beyond reason really become once again a dominant theme among secular as well as religious members of society.

Puritans sought, then, not man's intellectual dominion in a rational universe, but rather a subordination of human reason to the demands of an enthusiastic faith. In the first era of mass communication through the printed word, when vernacular knowledge of any sort was available for a few pennies, the blending of man's rational and non-rational elements was no mean cultural contribution. The dominant intellectual thrust of succeeding generations found it unpalatable, and sought contentment through denying the force of the irrational in man. But to many, for several generations, the puritan answers proved challenging, powerful, unsettling at times, but, finally, an inspiration to the spirit and therefore fundamentally satisfying amidst existence in a meaningless world.

BIBLIOGRAPHY

MANUSCRIPTS

Cambridge:
Emmanuel College
  MS III.i.13.VIII
  Emma. Archives Box 8
  Emma MS Col. 14.1
Gonville & Caius College
  MS 53/30
  MS 197/103
St John's College
  MS 347
  MS 408
  MS 413
University Library
  MS Baker A.17
  MS Baker B.8
  MS Baker D.10
  MS Baker 26.6
  MS Baker 27.4
  MS Baker 27.8
  MS Baker 27.20
  MS Baker 29.13
  MS Baker 30.7
  MS Baker 30.25
  MS Baker 32.6
  MS Baker 32.23
  MS Baker 38.9
  MS Dd.II.32
  MS Dd.IX.14(c)
  MS Dd.XI.73
  MS Ee.II.34, Nos. 114, 152, 194, 201, 207
  MS Ff.XIV.8
  MS Gg.I.29(F), Pt II, NO. 50
  MS Gg.IV, Pt II, No. 13

311

MS Mm.v.1(C), No. 10
MS Mm.vi.49(C), No. 28
Cambridge University Archives: Guard Book 6(i)

Chelmsford
Essex Record Office
  MS D/Y 2/4 Morant MS
  MS D/Y 2/6 Morant MS
  MS D/Y 2/7 Morant MS
  MS D/Y 2/8 Morant MS
  MS D/Y 2/9 Morant MS
  MS D/Y 2/10 Morant MS
  Q/Rsr. 2/70

London
British Library
  Additional MS 8.199
  Additional MS 8.201
  Additional MS 9.255
  Additional MS 33
  Additional MS 58
  Additional MS 4293, No. 21
  Additional MS 25,480
  Additional MS 27,632
  Additional MS 28,571
  Additional MS 29,546
  Additional MS 38,492
  Additional MS 48,023
  Additional MS 48,064
  Additional MS 48,066
  Additional Charter 27,701
  MS Birch 4275
  MS Egerton 2713
  MS Harley 419, No. 48
  MS Harley 4774
  MS Harley 6848
  MS Harley 6849
  MS Harley 7033, No. 23
  MS Harley 7041, No. 23
  MS Lansdowne 11, No. 93
  MS Lansdowne 12, No. 86
  MS Lansdowne 15, Nos. 41, 49, 68
  MS Lansdowne 17, No. 43
  MS Lansdowne 21, No. 2

MS Lansdowne 23, Nos. 4, 40
MS Lansdowne 25, Nos. 29, 50
MS Lansdowne 27, No. 12
MS Lansdowne 30, No. 46
MS Lansdowne 33, No. 44
MS Lansdowne 43, Nos. 9, 45, 48
MS Lansdowne 61, Nos. 26, 34, 63, 74
MS Lansdowne 63, No. 91
MS Lansdowne 64, Nos. 13, 15, 16, 32, 34
MS Lansdowne 65, No. 65
MS Lansdowne 68, Nos. 41, 48
MS Lansdowne 72, No. 49
MS Lansdowne 82, No. 53
MS Lansdowne 89, No. 17
MS Lansdowne 102, Nos. 86, 100
MS Lansdowne 109, Nos. 2, 3, 10, 11
MS Lansdowne 120, No. 3
MS Lansdowne 157, Nos. 33, 74
MS Lansdowne 973
MS Sloane 271
MS Sloane 649
MS Sloane 2204
Dr Williams's Library
  Modern MS 24.7
  Modern MS 24.8
  Morrice MSS
Inner Temple Library
  MS Petyt 538, vol. 38
Lambeth Palace Library
  Carte Misc. XII/15
  Carte Misc. XII/16
  MS 2007
  Whitgift's Register
Public Record Office
  Various P.C.C. Wills
  c/93/7/4: Charity Commissioners' Inquiries
  Sta Cha 5/49/34
  S.P. 12/41/67
  S.P. 12/45/10
  S.P. 12/78/38
  S.P. 12/176/68
  S.P. 12/177
  S.P. 12/234/35
  S.P. 12/240/138
  S.P. 12/282/71

S.P. 14/6/18
S.P. 14/8/66
S.P. 14/10A/81
S.P. 14/11/21
S.P. 14/89/60
S.P. 14/89/61
S.P. 14/129/58
S.P. 14/131/70
S.P. 14/132/85
S.P. 15/9/77
S.P. 15/9/78
S.P. 15/11/23
S.P. 15/12/27
S.P. 15/29/73
S.P. 16/142/113
S.P. 16/193/91
S.P. 16/202/3
S.P. 16/236/7
S.P. 16/266/43
S.P. 16/271/82
S.P. 16/280/33
S.P. 16/346/67
S.P. 16/351/39
S.P. 16/371/63
S.P. 16/372/44
S.P. 16/386/89

Manchester:
John Rylands Library
  Eng. MS 524
  Eng. MS 874

Oxford:
Bodleian Library
  MS Greek Miscellaneous D.2
  MS Rawlinson D. 273
  MS Tanner 68, Nos. 2, 7
  MS Tanner 70, Nos. 7, 31, 35
  MS Tanner 73
  MS Tanner 75, No. 21
  MS Tanner 78, No. 41
  MS Tanner 88, No. 1(g)
  MS Tanner 94, No. 3
  MS Tanner 121, No. 1
  MS Tanner 126, No. 27

MS Tanner 278
MS Tanner 279, No. 37
MS Tanner 280, No. 27
MS Tanner 290, Nos. 8, 32, 47
MS Tanner 301, No. 8
MS Tanner 447, No. 1
MS Tanner 465, No. 49
Exeter College
    MS 166

PRIMARY SOURCES PRINTED BEFORE 1700

(Note: place or date of publication has been omitted where not stated on the title-page.)

An Abridgement of That Booke which the Ministers of Lincolne Diocesse Delivered to his Maiestie upon the first of December 1605 . . . An Apologie for Themselves and Their Brethren That Refuse the Subscription and Conformitie which is required. London, 1617.
An Abstract, Of Certain Acts of parliament . . . for the peaceable government of the Church . . . 1584.
Adams, Thomas, *The Workes of Thomas Adams.* London, 1630.
Agrippa, Henry Cornelius. *Of the Vanitie and uncertaintie of Artes and Sciences: Englished by Iames Sandford Gent.* London, 1575.
Ainsworth, Henry. *Annotations Upon the Five Bookes of Moses, the Booke of the Psalmes, and the Song of Songs, or Canticles.* London, 1627.
    An Apologie or Defence of Such True Christians as are commonly . . . called Brownists . . . 1604.
    A True Confession Of the Faith . . . Amsterdam, 1596
Airay, Henry. *Lectures Upon The Whole Epistle of St Paul to the Philippians . . .* London, 1618.
Aldam, Thomas, et. al. *A Brief Discovery Of a threefold estate of Antichrist . . .* London, 1653.
Alison, Richard. *A Plaine Confutation of a Treatise of Brownisme . . .* London, 1590.
Allen, Robert. *The Odorifferous Garden of Charitie.* London, 1603.
Ames, William. *Conscience with the Power and Cases Thereof.* 1639.
    The Marrow of Sacred Divinity London, 1642.
Andrewes, Bartimeus. *Certaine Verie worthie, godly and profitable Sermons, upon the fifth Chapiter of the Songs of Solomon.* London, 1583.
    A very short and pithie Catechisme. London, 1586
Angier, John. *A Narrative of the Holy Life, and Happy Death of . . . John Angier, Many years Pastor of the Church of Christ at Denton, near Manchester in Lancashire . . .* London, 1685.
Ar, A. *The Practise of Princes.* 1630.

Articles delivered unto maister Edwarde Diringe [sic], with his aunswers thereunto: pp. 73–80 in *A Parte of a Register*. London, 1593

Askew, Egeon. *Brotherly Reconcilement . . . With An Apologie of the use of Fathers, and Secular learning in Sermons*. London, 1605.

The aunswere to the complaint . . .; pp. 131–2 in *A Parte of a Register*. London, 1593.

Averell, W. *A Dyall for dainty Darlings, rockt in the cradle of Securitie . . .* London, 1584.

Aylmer, John. *An Harborowe for faithfull and trewe subjects . . .* London, 1559.

Ayrault, Pierre. *A Discourse for Parents honour and Authoritie. Written respectively to reclaime a young man that was a counterfeit Jesuite . . . [transl.] By John Budden Doctor of the Lawes, and his Maiesties Professor in the Universitie of Oxford*. London, 1616.

Bacon, Francis. *Essays . . .* London, 1597.

> *The Twoo Bookes of Francis Bacon. Of the proficience and aduancement of Learning, divine and humane*. London, 1605.

Baldwin, William. *A treatise of Morall Phylosophye, Contayning the sayinges of the wyse*. London, 1547.

Bale, John. *A dialoge or communycacyon . . .* London, 1549.

Ball, John. *Short Questions And Answers, Explaining the Common Catechisme in the Booke of Common Prayer*. London, 1639.

> *A Short Treatise Contayning all the Principall Grounds of Christian Religion. By way of Questions and Answers, very profitable for all men, but especially for Householders*. London, 1633.

> *A Treatise of the Covenant of Grace*. London, 1645.

Bancroft, Richard. *Dangerous Positions and Proceedings, Published and Practised . . . Under Pretence of Reformation. And for the Presbyterian Discipline*. London, 1593.

> *A Survay of the Pretended Holy Discipline*. London, 1593.

Barckley, Sir Richard. *A Discourse of the Felicitie of Man: Or His Summum Bonum*. London, 1598.

Barker, Peter. *A Learned and Familiar Exposition upon the Ten Commandements . . .* London, 1633.

Barrow, Henry. *Mr. Henry Barrowes Platform. Which may serve as a Preparative to purge away Prelatisme: with some other parts of Poperie . . .* London, 1611.

> *The Pollution of Universitie-Learning, Or, Sciences (Falsly so called) . . .* London, 1642.

Baxter, Richard. *A Christian Directory: Or, a Summ of Practical Theologie, and Cases of Conscience . . .* London, 1673.

> *A Holy Commonwealth, Or Political Aphorisms*. London, 1659.

Bayly, Lewis. *The Practice of Pietie: Directing a Christian how to Walke that he may please God*. London, 1632.

Baynes, Paul. *Briefe Directions unto a Godly Life . . .* London, 1618.

> *A Helpe To true Happinesse: Or, A briefe and learned Exposition of the maine and fundamental points of Christian Religion*. London, 1635.

Beard, Thomas. *The Theatre of Gods Judgements: Revised, and augmented*. London, 1631.

Becon, Thomas. *The Sicke Mans Salve. Wherin the Faithful Christians may learn both how to behave them selves paciently and thankfully in the time of sicknesse, and also vertuously to dispose their temporall goods, and finally to prepare them selves gladly and godly to die.* London, 1561.

Benefield, Sebastian. *Eight Sermons Publikely Preached In the University of Oxford . . . Begunne in the yeare 1595 . . .* Oxford, 1614.

Bernard, Richard. *Christian Advertisements and Counsels of Peace. Also disswasions from the Separatists schisme, commonly called Brownisme . . .* London, 1608.

The Common Catechisme . . . London, 1634.

The Faithfull Shepheard . . . Wherein is . . . set forth the excellencie and necessitie of the Ministerie . . . London, 1607.

The Faithfull Shepheard . . . Wholly Transposed and Made Anew . . . London, 1621.

The Ready Way to Good Works, Or, A Treatise of Charitie . . . London, 1635.

The Shepheards Practice. London, 1621.

The Bible and Holy Scriptures Conteyned In The Old And Newe Testament. Geneva, 1560; London, 1599.

Bird, Samuel. *The Lectures of Samuel Bird of Ipswidge upon the II. chapter of the Epistle unto the Hebrewes, and upon the 38. Psalme.* Cambridge, 1598.

Blundeville, Thomas. *The Arte of Logicke . . .* London, 1619.

Bolton, Edward. *The Cities Advocate, In this Case or Question of Honor and Armes, Whether Apprentiship extinguisheth Gentry? . . .* London, 1629.

Bolton, Robert. *A Cordiall for Christians in the Time of Affliction . . .* London, 1640.

A Discourse about the State of True Happinesse . . . Sermons . . . London, 1614.

Mr. Boltons Last & Learned Worke of the Foure last Things . . . Together with the Life and Death of the Author, Published by E[dward] B[agshaw]. London, 1632.

The Saints Sure and Perpetuall Guide. Or, A Treatise Concerning the Word . . . London, 1634.

Some General Directions For A Comfortable Walking with God . . . London, 1626.

The Workes . . . London, 1641.

Bownde, Nicholas. *The Doctrine Of The Sabbath . . .* London, 1595.

The Holy Exercise of Fasting . . . Cambridge, 1604.

Bradford, John. *Godly meditations uppon the ten commaundementes.* London, 1567.

Bradshaw, William. *A Briefe Forme of Examination . . .* [appended to *Direction for the Weaker Sort . . .*] London, 1609.

English Puritanisme Containeuing the maine opinions of the rigidest sort of those called puritanes. (?) Amsterdam, 1605.

A Protestation Of the Kings Supremacie . . . (?) Amsterdam, 1605.

& Digges, Thomas. *Humble Motives for Association To Maintaine Religion Established. . .* London, 1601.

Brathwait, Richard. *The English Gentleman: Containing Sundry excellent Rules of exquisite Observations, tending to Direction of every Gentleman, of selecter ranke and qualitie . . .* London, 1630.

The English Gentlewoman . . . London, 1641.

The Schollers Medley, Or, An Intermixt Discourse Upon Historicall And Poeticall relations. A Subject of it selfe well meriting the approbation of the Iudicious, who best know how to confirme their knowledge . . . And no lesse profitable to such as desire to better their immaturity of knowledge by Morall Readings. Distinguished into severall heads for the direction of the Reader . . . London, 1614.

Bredwell, Stephen. *The Raising of the Foundations of Brownisme* . . . London, 1588.

Brentius, John. *A Right Godly and learned discourse upon the booke of Ester* . . . [transl.] Iohn Stockwood, Schoolemaster of Tunbridge. London, 1584.

Bridges, John. *A Defence Of The Government Established In The Church of Englande For Ecclesiastical Matters . . . aunswere unto a Treatise called, The Learned Discourse* . . . London, 1587.

A Briefe and plain declaration, concerning the desires of all those faithfull Ministers, that have and do seeke for the Discipline and reformation of the Church of Englande . . . [*Learned Discourse*]. London, 1584.

Brinsley, John, the Elder. *The Posing of the Parts* . . . London, 1612.

The Trve Watch, and Rvle of Life. London, 1611.

Brinsley, John, the Younger. *The Preachers Charge and the Peoples Duty.* London, 1631.

Broughton, Hugh. *An Epistle To The Learned Nobilitie of England. Touching translating the Bible* . . . Middelburg, 1597.

Letters to Queen Elizabeth. ?1591.

A Petition To the King. For Authority And Allowance to expound the Apocalyps in Hebrew and Greek . . . Middelburg, 1611.

A Petition To The King To Hasten Allowance for Ebrew Institution of Ebrewes. 1608.

Principall Positions for groundes of the holy bible. 1609.

A Require of Agreement To the groundes of Divinitie studie: wherin great Scholers falling, & being caught of Iewes, disgrace the Gospel & trap them to destruction. Middleburg, 1611.

Sundry workes . . . London, 1591.

Two Epistles Unto Great Men of Britaine . . . London, 1606.

Browne, Gregorie. *An Introduction to Pietie and Humanitie: containing, . . . A Short Catechisme . . . Secondly, Certaine Briefe and Effectuall rules for life and conversation. Penned Specially for the use of the poore children of Christs Hospitall in London* . . . London, 1613.

Browne, Robert. *A Booke which Sheweth the life and manners of all true Christians* . . . Middelburg, 1582.

A Treatise of reformation without tarying for anie, and of the wickednesse of those Preachers which will not reforme till the Magistrate commaunde or compell them. Middelburg, 1582.

A Treatise upon the 23. of Matthewe. Middelburg, 1582.

The Brownists Synagogue Or A Late Discovery Of their Conventicles, Assemblies; and places of meeting . . . 1641.

Brucioli, Antonio. *A Commentary upon the Canticle of Canticles* . . . London, 1598.

Bruts, G. M. *The Necessarie, Fit, And Convenient Education of a yong Gentlewoman* . . . translated into English by W. P. London, 1598.

Bryan, John. *The Vertuous Daughter. A Sermon Preached* . . . 1636. London, 1636.

Buck, Sir George. *The Third Universitie of England* . . . London . . . London, 1631.

Bulkeley, Peter. *The Gospel-Covenant; Or The Covenant of Grace Opened . . . Preached in Concord in New England* . . . London, 1646.

Bunny, Edmund. *A Short Summe of Christian Religion* . . . London, 1576.

Bunny, Francis. *A Guide unto Godlinesse: Or A Plaine and familiar Explanation of the ten Commandements . . . Fittest for the instruction of the simple and ignorant people.* London, 1617.

Burgess, Anthony. *The Difficulty of, And the Encouragements to A Reformation. A Sermon Preached . . . House of Commons . . . Septem. 27, 1643.* London, 1643.

Burroughes, Jeremiah. *The Excellency Of A Gracious Spirit* . . . London, 1638.

Burton, Henry. *A Plea to An Appeale: Traversed Dialogue wise.* London, 1626.

Burton, Robert. *The Anatomy of Melancholy* . . . Oxford, 1624.

Burton, William. *Certaine Questions and Answeres, concerning the knowledge of God . . . [and] the right use of the law of God* . . . London, 1591.

Davids Thanksgiving for the Arraignement of the Man of Earth . . . London, 1598.

The Rowsing of the Sluggard, in Seven Sermons. London, 1598.

Byfield, Nicholas. *Directions for the private reading of the Scriptures* . . . London, 1618.

The Marrow of Oracles of God, or Divers Treatises . . . London, 1628.

The Principles Or, The Patterne of wholesome Words . . . London, 1627.

The Signes Or An Essay Concerning the assurance of Gods love, and mans salvation . . . London, 1641.

C, B. *Puritanisme the Mother, Sinne The Daughter. Or a Treatise, wherein is demonstrated from Twenty severall Doctrines, and Positions of Puritanisme; That the Fayth and Religion of the Puritans, doth forcibly induce its Professours to the perpetrating of Sinne, and doth warrant the committing of the same.* St Omer, 1633.

Cade, Anthony. *Saint Paules Agonie. A Sermon Preached at Leicester at the Ordinary Monthly Lecture* . . . London, 1618.

Calamy, Edmund. *Englands Looking-Glasse* . . . London, 1642.

Capel, Richard. *Tentations: Their Nature, Danger, Cure. To Which is added a Briefe dispute as touching Restitution in the case of Usury.* London, 1635.

Carpenter, John. *Contemplations For the institution of children in the Christian Religion.* London, 1601.

Cartwright, Thomas. *A Replye To An answere made of M. Doctor Whitgifte, Agaynste The Admonition to the Parliament.* London.

A second Admonition to the Parliament. London, 1572.

A Treatise of Christian Religion . . . London, 1616.

Cawdray, Robert. *A Treasurie Or Store-Hovse of Similies* . . . London, 1600.

Cecil, William. *Precepts, Or, Directions for the well ordering and carriage of a mans life* . . . London, 1637.

Certaine Questions, Arguments, and Objections . . . Popishe apparell . . . : pp. 37–55, in A Parte of a register. London, 1593.

Chaderton, Laurence. *An Excellent and Godly Sermon, most needfull for this time, wherein we live in all securitie and sinne, to the great dishonour of God, and contempt of his holy word. Preached at Paules Crosse the xxvi. daye of October, An. 1578* . . . London.

A Fruitfull Sermon, upon the 3. 4. 5. 6. 7 and 8 verses, of the 12. Chapiter of the Epistle of St. Paul to the Romans . . . London, 1584.

320 *Godly Learning*

Chamberlain, Robert. *Nocturnall Lucubrations: Or Meditations Divine and Morall* . . . London, 1638

Chapman, E. *A Catechisme with a Prayer annexed, meete for all Christian families.* London, 1583.

Chappell, William. *The Preacher, Or the Art and Method of Preaching* . . . London, 1656.

Chauncey, Charles. *Gods Mercy Shewed To His People In Giving Them A Faithful Ministry And Schooles of Learning For The Continual Supplyes Thereof . . . Sermon . . . Cambridge* . . . Cambridge, Massachusetts, 1655.

A Christian Letter of certaine English Protestants, unfained favourers of the present state of Religion, authorised and professed in England: unto . . . Mr. R. Hoo. requiring resolution in certaine matters of doctrine . . . Middelburg, 1599.

Clarke, John. *Holy Incense For the Censers of the Saints. Or, A method of Prayer, with matter, and formes in selected Sentences of sacred Scripture* . . . London, 1634.

Holy Oyle For The Lampes Of The Sanctuarie: Or, Scripture-Phrases Alphabetically disposed . . . London, 1630.

Clarke, Samuel. *A Collection of the lives of Ten Eminent Divines, Famous in their Generations for Learning, Prudence, Piety, and painfulness in the work of the Ministry* . . . London, 1662.

A General Martyrologie, . . . Whereunto is Added the Lives of Thirty Two English Divines . . . London, 1677 (orig. 1651).

The Lives of Sundry Eminent Persons in this Later Age . . . London, 1683.

The Lives of Thirty-two English Divines . . . London, 1660.

The Marrow of Ecclesiastical History . . . London, 1675 (orig. 1650).

Cleaver, Robert. *A Briefe Explanation Of The Whole Booke of the Proverbs of Salomon.* London, 1615.

A Godlie Forme of Householde Government: For the Ordering of Private Families, according to the direction of Gods word. London, 1612.

The Patrimony of Christian Children: Or, A Defence of Infants. London, 1624.

A Plaine and Familiar Exposition of the First and Second Chapters of the Proverbs of Salomon. London, 1614.

Comenius, J. A. *A Reformation of Schooles.* London, 1642.

The complaint presented to . . . private counsell, by the godlie Ministers . . .: pp. 128–31 in *A Parte of a Register.* London, 1593.

Cooper, Thomas. *Admonition to People of England.* London, 1589.

Certaine Sermons wherein is contained the Defense of the Gospell nowe preached . . . London, 1580.

Coote, Edmund. *The English schoole-maister.* London, 1596

Copie of a Letrer [sic] . . .: pp. 132–200 in *A Parte of a Register.* London, 1593.

Corderoy, Jeremy. *A Short Dialogue between a Gallant, A Scholler of Oxforde, and a Church-Papist; wherein is proved that good works are necessary to salvation.* Oxford, 1604.

Cosin, Richard. *An Answer to the first and principall Treatises of a certeine factious libell* . . . London, 1584.

Cotton, Clement. *The Christian Concordance: Containing the Most materiall words in the New Testament* . . . London, 1622.

Cotton, John. *The Covenant of Gods free Grace* . . . London, 1645.

The New Covenant, Or, A Treatise, unfolding the order and manner of the giving and receiving of the Covenant of Grace to the Elect . . . London, 1654.

Covell, William. *A Modest and reasonable examination, of some things in use in the Church of England* . . . London, 1604.

Polimanteia, Or, The meanes lawfull and unlawfull, to Iudge of the Fall of A Common-Wealth . . . London, 1595.

Crashawe, William. *Romish Forgeries and Falsifications* . . . London, 1606.

A Sermon Preached in London . . . *Febr. 21, 1609.* London, 1610.

The crie of the poore for the death of the Right Honourable Earle of Huntingdon . . . London, 1596.

Crooke, Samuel. *The Guide Unto True Blessednesse. Or, A Body of the Doctrine of the Scriptures, directing man to the saving knowledge of God.* London, 1614.

The Ministeriall Husbandry and Building. Preached at the Triennial Visitation at Bath. London, 1615.

Crosse, Henry. *The Schoole of Pollicie: Or The araignement of State-abuses* . . . London, 1605.

Vertues Common-wealth: Or The High-Way to Honour . . . London, 1603.

Crowley, Robert. *An informacion and Peticion agaynst the oppressours of the pore Commons of this Realme, compiled and Imprinted for this onely purpose that amongest them that have to doe in the Parliamente, some godlye mynded men, may hereat take occacion to speake more in the matter than the Authore was able to write.* London.

A Sermon made in the Chappel at the Gylde Halle in London, the xxix day of September, 1574 . . . London, 1575.

A setting open of the subtyle Sophistrie of Thomas Watson Doctor of Divinitie . . . London, 1569.

Cyvile and uncyvile life. A discourse very profitable, pleasant, and fit to bee read of all Nobilitie and Gentlemen . . . London, 1579.

Daneau, Lambert. *The Wonderfull Woorkmanship of the World.* London, 1578.

Davenport, John. *An Apologeticall Reply To a booke Called An Answer to the unjust complaint of W.B.* . . . Rotterdam, 1636.

Denison, Stephen. *The New Creature. A Sermon Preached at Pauls Cross. January 17, 1619.* London, 1619.

Dent, Arthur. *A Pastime for Parents: Or A recreation, to passe away the time* . . . London, 1606.

The Plaine Mans Path-way to Heaven. London, 1601.

A Sermon of Repentaunce . . . *preached* . . . *1581, the 7. of March.* London, 1583.

Dering, Edward. *A Briefe and necessarie Catechisme or Instruction very needfull to be known of al Housholders. Whereby they may teach and instruct theyr familie in such poynts of Christian Religion as is most meete.* London, 1597.

Godlie Private Praiers, for Householders to meditate uppon, and to saye in their Families . . . London, 1576.

A sermon preached before the Queenes Maiesty . . . *1569.* London, 1586.

XXVII Lectures, or readings, upon part of the Epistle written to the Hebrues. London, 1576.

A Dialogue Concerning the strife of our Churche: Wherein are aunswered divers of those uniust accusations, wherewith the godly preachers and professors of the Gospell, are falsly charged . . . London, 1584.

A Dialogue. Wherin Is Plainly Laide Open, the tyrannicall dealing of L. Bishopps against Gods chldren . . . Rochelle.

Dillingham, Francis. *Christian Oeconomy. Or Houshold Government . . . London, 1609.*

A Godly and Learned Sermon Concerning the Magistrates dutie and death, preached at the Court . . . Cambridge, 1605.

The Doctrine of the Bible: Or, Rules of Discipline: Briefly Gathered through the whole course of the Scripture, by way of Questions and Answers. London, 1616.

Dod, John & Cleaver, Robert. *A Plaine and Familiar Exposition of the Ninth and Tenth Chapters of the Proverbs of Salomon. London, 1608.*

A Plaine and Familiar Exposition of the Eleventh and Twelfth Chapters of the Proverbs of Salomon. London, 1608.

A Plaine and Familiar Exposition of the Thirteenth and Fourteenth Chapters of the Proverbs of Salomon. London, 1609.

A Plaine and Familiar Exposition of the Ten Commandements. London, 1609.

Dod, John & Hinde, William. *Bathshebaes Instructions to her Sonne Lemuel: Containing a fruitfull and plaine Exposition of the last Chapter of the Proverbs . . . London, 1614.*

Dove, John. *An Advertisement To The English Seminaries, and Jesuites . . . London, 1610.*

Downame, John. *The Christian Warfare . . . London, 1612.*

A Guide to Godliness Or a Treatise of a Christian Life . . . London, 1629.

The Plea of the Poore, Or A Treatise of Beneficence and Almes-Deeds . . . London, 1616.

The Summe of Sacred Divinitie . . . London.

Downe, John. *Two Treatises 1. Concerning the force and efficacy of Reading 2. Christs prayer for his Church. Oxford, 1633.*

Drant, Thomas. *Three godly and learned Sermons, very necessarie to be read and regarded of all men. London, 1584.*

Dyke, Jeremiah. *A Caveat for Archippus. A Sermon . . . London . . . Septemb. 23 1618. London, 1619.*

A Sermon Dedicatory. London, 1623.

E., G. *The Christian Schoole-Maister, Or A Dialogue Betweene the Maister and the Scholler. London, 1613.*

An Ease For Overseers of the poore . . . Cambridge, 1601.

Egerton, Stephen. *A Briefe Methode of Catechizing . . . London, 1615.*

Estey, George. *Certaine Godly and learned Expositions upon divers parts of Scripture . . . London, 1603.*

Evans, William. *A Translation of the Booke of Nature, into the Use of Grace. Performed and Principally intended for the Benefit of those who plead ignorance, or that they are not Book-learned, or that they want teachers . . . Oxford, 1633.*

D'Ewes, Simonds. *The Journals of All the Parliaments During the Reign of Queen Elizabeth, Both of the House of Lords and House of Commons. London, 1682.*

Fairclough, Samuel. *The Saints worthinesse and The worlds worthlesnesse . . . A Sermon preached at the Funerall of . . . Sr. Nathaniel Barnardiston . . .* London, 1653.

Featley, Daniel. *Cygnea Cantio: Or, Learned Decisions, And Most Prudent And Pious Directions For Students In Divinitie; Delivered by our late Soverayne of Happie Memorie, King James . . .* London, 1629.

et. al. θρηγοικος *The House of Mourning . . . Delivered in XLVII Sermons Preached at the Funeralls of divers Faithfull servants of Christ.* London, 1640.

Felltham, Owen. *Resolves: Divine, Moral, Political.* London, 1661.

Fen, Humphrey. *The Last Will And Testament, With the Profession of the Faith of Humfrey Fen, sometimes Pastor of one of the Churches of Coventry . . .* London, 1641.

Fenner, Dudley. *The Artes Of Logike And Rethorike, plainlie set foorth in the English tounge, easie to be learned and practised . . .* Middelburg, 1584.

Certaine godly and learned treatises . . . Edinburgh, 1592.

A Counter-Poyson, Modestly written for the time, to make aunswere to the obiections and reproches, wherewith the aunswerer to the Abstract, would disgrace the holy Discipline of Christ. London, ?1584.

A Defence Of the godlie Ministers, against the slaunders of D. Bridges, contained in his answere to the Preface before the Discourse of Ecclesiastical governement, with a Declaration of the Bishops proceeding against them. Middelburg, 1587.

A Defence Of The Reasons of the Counter-Poyson, for maintenance of the Eldership, against an aunswere made to them by Doctor Copequor . . . 1584 . . . Middelburg, 1586.

A Short and profitable Treatise, of lawfull and unlawfull Recreations . . . Middelburg, (?)1587.

Fenton, Geoffrey. *A forme of Christian pollicie . . .* London, 1574.

Ferne, John. *The Blazon of Gentrie . . .* London, 1586.

Ferrarius, Johannes. *A Woorke of J . . . F . . . M . . ., touchynge the good orderynge of a common weale . . . Englished by William Bavende.* London, 1559.

Field, John. *A Caveat for Parsons Howlet . . . necessarie for him and all the rest of that darke broode, and uncleane cage of papistes . . .* London, 1581.

Godly Prayers and Meditations . . . London, 1601.

& Wilcox, Thomas. *An Admonition to the Parliament.* London, 1572.

Certaine Articles, collected and taken . . . by the Byshops out of . . . an Admonition to the Parliament/wyth an Answere to the same . . . London, 1572.

Fleming, Abraham. *The Footepath to Felicitie, Which everie Christian must walke in, before he can come to the land of Canaan.* London, 1581.

The Schoole of Skill, or, The rule of a reformed life. The first sententious sequence of the A, B, C, delivering divers doctrines of vertue and vice to be folowed and avoided. London, 1581.

Floyd, Thomas. *The Picture of a perfit Common wealth.* London, 1600.

Fly. An Almanack . . . London, 1660.

Fox, George. *The Lambs Officer . . .* London, 1659.

A Visitation of Love unto all People . . . London, 1659.

A friendly caveat to Bishop Sands . . .: pp. 371–81 in *A Parte of a Register.* London, 1593.

Fulke, William. *A Goodly Gallerye With A Most Pleasaunt Prospect, into the garden of naturall contemplation . . .* London, 1563.

Fuller, Thomas. *Abel Redivivus: or, The Dead yet Speaking. The Lives and Deaths of the*

Modern Dvines. London, 1651.

The History of the Worthies of England. London, 1662.

The Holy State. Cambridge, 1642.

Furio, Federigo. *A very briefe and profitable Treatise declaring howe many counsells, and what maner of Counselers a Prince that will governe well ought to have . . .* [transl. Thomas Blundeville, from the Italian version by A. d'Ulloa]. London, 1570.

Gaetani, Enrico. *Instructions for young gentlemen*. London, 1633.

Gainsford, Thomas. *The Glory of England . . .* London, 1618.

The Rich Cabinet Furnished with varietie of Excellent discriptions . . . London, 1616.

Gataker, Thomas. *Abrahams Decease. A Meditation on Genesis 25.8. Delivered at the Funerall of that Worthy Servant of Christ, Mr. Richard Stock . . .* London, 1627.

Christian Constancy Crowned by Christ. A Funerall Sermon on Apocalyps. 2.10 . . . London, 1624.

The Christian Mans Care. A Sermon on Matth. 6.33. Together with a Short Catechisme for the Simpler Sort. London, 1624.

Davids Instructer. A Sermon Preached at the Visitation of the Free-Schole at Tunbridge in Kent, by the Wardens of the Worshipfull companie of Skinners . . . London, 1620.

The Decease of Lazarus Christ's Friend. A Funerall Sermon on John. Chap. 11. Vers. 11 . . . London, 1640.

Discours Apologetical . . . London, 1654.

Gods Parley with Princes: with an Appeale from Them to Him. The Summe of two Sermons . . . Preached at Sergeants-Inne in Fleet-Streete. London, 1620.

A Good Wife Gods Gift: And, A Wife Indeed. Two Marriage Sermons. London, 1623.

Saint Stevens Last Will And Testament. A Funerall Sermon On Acts 7. Ver. 59 . . . London, 1638.

Two Funerall Sermons . . . London, 1620.

Gellibrand, Henry. *An Institution Trigonometricall . . .* London, 1635.

Gerard, Peter. *A Preparation To The Most Holie Ministerie . . .* London, 1593.

Gerardus [a.k.a. Hyperius], Andrew. *The Practise of Preaching, . . . Conteyning an excellent Method how to frame Divine Sermons; & to interpret the holy Scriptures according to the capacitie of the vulgar people . . . Englished by John Ludham . . . 1577*. London, 1577.

Gifford, George. *A Catechisme conteining the summe of Christian Religion, giving a most excellent light to all those that seek to enter the path-way to salvation . . .* London, 1582.

A Dialogue betweene a Papist and a Protestant, applied to the capacitie of the unlearned. London, 1582.

A Plaine Declaration that our Brownists be full Donatists . . . Also a replie to Master Greenwood touching read prayer . . . London, 1590.

A Sermon on the Parable of the Sower . . . London, 1582.

A short Reply unto the last printed books of Henry Barrow and John Greenwood, the chiefe ringleaders of our Donatists in England . . . London, 1591.

A Short Treatise against the Donatists of England, whome we call Brownists . . .

London, 1590.

Gilby, Anthony. *A pleasaunt dialogue, betweene a souldier of Barwicke and an English chaplaine.* 1581.

Gilpin, Bernard. *A Godly Sermon preached in the Court at Greenwich the firste Sonday after the Epiphanie, . . . 1552 . . .* London, 1581.

A Goodly Dialogue betweene knowledge and Symplicitie. London.

Goodman, Christopher. *How Superior Powers Oght To Be Obeyd Of Their subiects: and Wherin they may lawfully by Gods Worde be disobeyed and resisted . . .* Geneva, 1558.

Goodman, Godfrey. *The Creatures Praysing God: Or, The Religion of dumbe Creatures.* London, 1622.

Goodwin, Thomas. *A Glimpse of Syons Glory: Or, The Churches Beautie specified . . .* London, 1641.

The Vanity of Thoughts Discovered: With Their Danger And Cure. London, 1637.

Gouge, William. *Gods Three Arrowes: Plague, Famine, Sword . . .* London, 1631.

A Learned And Very Useful Commentary on the Whole Epistle to the Hebrewes . . . 2 vols. London, 1655.

Of Domesticall Duties. Eight Treatises. VI. Duties of Parents. London, 1622.

A short Catechisme, wherein are briefly laid downe the fundamental Principles of Christian Religion. London, 1615.

Granger, Thomas. *The Application of Scripture. Or, The maner how to use the Word to most edifying.* London, 1616.

A Familiar Exposition or Commentarie on Ecclesiastes. Wherein the worlds vanity, and the true felicitie are plainely deciphered. London, 1621.

Syntagma Grammaticum, Or An easie, and methodicall explanation of Lillies Grammar . . . London, 1626.

Syntagma Logicum. Or, The Divine Logike. Serving especially for the use of Divines in the practise of preaching, and for the further helpe of iudicious Hearers, and generally for all. London, 1620.

The Tree of Good and Evill: Or A Profitable and Familiar Exposition of the Commandements . . . London, 1616.

Gratarolus, Gulielmus. *The Castel of Memorie: wherein is conteyned the restoring, augmenting, and conservinge of the Memorie and Remembrance . . . Englyshed by William Fulwood.* London, 1563.

Greene, John. *A Refutation of the Apology for Actors . . .* London, 1615.

Greenham, Richard. *Two Learned and Godly Sermons . . .* London, 1595.

The Workes of the Reverend Richard Greenham . . . ed. Henry Holland. London, 1612.

Greenwood, John. *An Answere To George Giffords Pretended Defence Of Read Praiers and devised Litourgies . . .* Dort, 1590.

Guilde, William. *A Yong Mans Inquisition, Or Triall.* London, 1608.

Guy, Nicholas. *Pieties Pillar: Or, A Sermon Preached at the Funerall of Mistresse Elizabeth Gouge . . . With a true Narrative of her Life and Death.* London, 1626.

Gybson, Thomas. *A Fruitful sermon, preached at Occham . . . 1583.* London, 1584.

Hake, Edward. *A Touchstone for this time present, expressly declaring such ruines, enormities, and abuses as trouble the Churche of God and our Christian common wealth at this daye. Whereunto is annexed a perfect rule to be observed of all Parents and Schole-Maisters, in the trayning up of their Schollers and Children in learning.* London, 1574.

Hall, Joseph. *Epistles.* London, 1608.

Salomons Divine Arts, Of 1. Ethickes, 2. Politickes, 3. Oeconomicks . . . London, 1609.

The Works of Joseph Hall . . . London, 1625.

Harmar, Samuel. *Vox Populi . . .* London, 1642.

Harris, Robert. *Gods Goodnes and Mercie . . . Preached at Pauls Crosse . . . 1622.* London, 1626.

Samuels Funerall. Or A Sermon Preached at the Funerall of Sir Anthonie Cope Knight and Baronet. London, 1618.

The Way to True Blessednesse. In xxiv Sermons on the Beatitudes, in Workes. London, 1635.

The Way to True Happinesse. Delivered in xxiv. Sermons upon the Beatitudes. London, 1632.

Harsnet, Samuel. *A Discovery Of The Fraudulent practises of John Darrel Bacheler of Artes, in his proceedings Concerning The Pretended Possession and dispossession of William Somers at Nottingham . . .* London, 1599.

Hastings, Francis. *An Apologie or Defence of the watchword . . .* London, 1600.

A Watchword to all religious and true hearted English-men. London, 1598.

Helwys, Thomas. *Objections: Answered by way of Dialogue, wherein is proved . . . That no man ought to be persecuted for his religion, so he testifie his allegeance by the Oath, appointed by Law.* 1615.

Hemmingsen, Niel. *The Epistle of the Blessed Apostle Sainte Paule . . . to the Ephesians . . .* London, 1580.

The Preacher, or Methode of preaching . . . London, 1574.

Heywood, John. *Woorkes.* London, 1562.

Hieron, Samuel. *A Defence of the Ministers Reasons, For Refusall of Subscription To The Booke of Common prayer, and of Conformitie . . .* 1607.

A Helpe unto Devotion, in Sermons. London, 1624.

The Preachers Plea: Or, A Treatise in forme of a plaine Dialogue, making knowne the worth and necessity of that which we call Preaching . . ., in Sermons. London, 1624.

The Workes. Vol. II. London, 1624.

Hildersam, Arthur. *CLII Lectures upon Psalm LI.* London, 1635.

A Treatise Of the Ministery of the Church of England . . . 1595.

Hill, Robert. *A Direction to Live Well.* London, 1613.

The Pathway To Prayer And Pietie . . . London, 1613.

Hill, Thomas. *The Schoole of Skil . . .* London, 1599.

Holme, John. *The Burthen of the Ministerie . . . Verie Profitable To Be read of every faithfull subiect, and of all that desire to be taught in the waie of truth.* London, 1592.

Hooker, Thomas. *A Comment Upon Christ's last Prayer In the Seventeenth of John . . .* London, 1656.

Foure Learned and Godly Treatises . . . London, 1638.

The Soules Preparation For Christ . . . London, 1632.

The Soules Vocation Or Effectual Calling to Christ. London, 1638.

How, Samuel. *The Sufficiency of the Spirits Teaching Without Humane Learning. Or a Treatise tending to prove Humane Learning to be no help to the Spirituall Understanding of the Word of God.* London, 1655.

Howson, John. *A Sermon preached at Paules Crosse the 4. of December. 1597 . . .* London, 1597.

Huarte, Juan. *The Examination of Mens Wits . . .* London, 1594.

The humble petition of the Communaltie to their most renowmed [sic] and gracious Soveraigne, the Ladie Elizabeth . . .: pp. 304–22 in *A Parte of a Register.* London, 1593.

Humphrey, Laurence. *The Nobles: or of Nobilitye.* London, 1563.

Hutton, Thomas. *Reasons for Refusal of Subscription to the booke of Common praier . . . [by] certaine Ministers of Devon and Cornwall . . . with an Amswere [sic] . . . by Thomas Hutton . . .* Oxford, 1605.

Ingelend, Thomas. *A pretie and Mery new Enterlude: called the Disobedient Child.* London.

The Institucion of a gentleman. London, 1555.

Jackson, Abraham. *The Pious Prentice, Or, The Prentices Piety . . .* London, 1640.

Jacob, Henry. *Reasons Taken Out Of Gods Word And The Best Humane Testimonies Proving A Necessitie of Reforming Our Churches in England . . .* London, 1624.

Joceline, Elizabeth. *The Mothers Legacie . . .* London, 1624.

Johnson, Francis & Ainsworth, Henry. *An Apologie or Defence Of Such True Christians As are commonly (but uniustly) called Brownists . . .* 1604.

Johnson, Robert. *Essaies, Or Rather imperfect Offers.* London, 1607.

King, John. *Lectures Upon Jonas, Delivered At Yorke . . . 1594.* Oxford, 1597.

Kingsmill, Andrew. *A Most Excellent and comfortable Treatise, for all such as are any maner of way either troubled in minde or afflicted in bodie . . .* London 1577.

Knewstub, John. *A Sermon preached at Paules Crosse the Fryday before Easter . . . 1579.* London, 1579.

The Lamentable Complaint of the Commonaltie . . . to the high Court of Parliament for a learned Ministerie . . .: pp. 201–76 in *A Parte of a Register.* London, 1593.

Lawne, Christopher. *Brownisme Turned The In-side out-ward . . .* London, 1613.

Leigh, Dorothy. *The Mothers Blessing: Or, The godly Counsaile of a Gentle-woman, not long since deceased . . . Contayning many good exhortations, and godly admonitions, profitable for all Parents, to leave as a legacy to their Children.* London, 1618.

le Roy, Louis. *Of the Interchangeable Course, or Variety of Things in the Whole World; and the Concurrence of Armes and Learning thorough the first and famousest Nations . . . Translated into English by R. Ashley.* London, 1594.

Lever, Thomas. *A Sermon preached at Pauls Crosse, the xiiii. day of December . . .* London, 1550.

Ley, John. *A patterne of Pietie. Or The Religious life and death of that Grave and gracious Matron, Mrs. Jane Ratcliffe Widow and Citizen of Chester.* London, 1640.

The Life and Death of that Holy and Reverend Man of God Mr. Thomas Cawton. London, 1662.

A Light for the Ignorant Or A Treatise shewing, that in the new Testament, is set forth three Kingly States or Governments . . . Amsterdam, 1638.

Lilburne, John. *An Answer to Nine Arguments.* London, 1644.

The Legall Fundamentall Liberties of the People of England . . . London, 1649.

Ling, Nicholas. *Politeuphia Wits Common wealth.* London, 1597.

Lupton, Donald. *London and the Countrey . . .* London, 1632

Lyly, John. *Euphues. The Anatomy of Wyt. Very pleasant for all Gentlemen to reade . . .* London, 1578.

Lyster, John. *A Rule how to bring up children.* London, 1588.

MacIlmaine, Roland (transl.). *The Logike of the most Excellent Philosopher P. Ramus Martyr . . .* London, 1581.

Markham, Gervase. *The English Hovse-wife, Containing the inward and outward Vertues which ought to be in a compleate Woman . . .* London, 1637.

   The Gentlemans Academie. Or, The Booke of S. Albans . . . compiled by Juliana Barnes, in . . . 1486 And now reduced into a better method by G. M. London, 1595.

Marprelate, Martin. *Hay any worke for Cooper.* 1589.

Martyn, William. *Youths Instruction.* London, 1612.

Mason, Francis. *The Authoritie Of The Church in making Canons and Constitutions concerning things indifferent, And the obedience thereto required . . . Delivered in a Sermon . . . 1605 . . .* London, 1607.

Mayer, John. *A Patterne for Women . . .* London, 1619.

More, John. *A Lively Anatomie Of Death: Wherein you may see from whence it came, what it is by nature and what by Christ . . .* London, 1596.

   Three Godly And Fruitfull Sermons . . . Cambridge, 1594.

Morrice, Thomas. *An Apologie for Schoolemasters . . .* London, 1619.

Mulcaster, Richard. *Positions wherein those primitive circumstances be examined, which are necessarie for the training up of children, either for skill in their booke, or health in their bodie.* London, 1581.

Nenna, John. *Nennio, Or A Treatise of Nobility . . . Done into English by William Jones Gent.* London, 1595.

Newnham, John. *Newnams Night-Crowe . . . Wherein is remembred that kindeley and provident regard which Fathers ought to have towards their Sonnes.* London, 1590.

Nichols, Josias. *An Order of Houshold Instruction . . .* London, 1596.

   The Plea of the Innocent: Wherein is averred; That the Ministers & people falslie termed Puritans, are iniuriouslie slaundered for enemies or troublers of the State . . . 1602.

Niclas, Henry. *Introductio. An Introduction to the holy Understanding of the Glasse of Righteousnes . . .* Amsterdam.

Nixon, Anthony. *The Dignitie of Man, Both in the Perfections of His Soule and Bodie. Shewing as well the Faculties in the disposition of the one: as the Senses and Organs, in the composition of the other.* London, 1612.

Norden, John. *A pensive mans practise: Very profitable for all personnes, wherein are conteyned very devout and necessary prayers for sundry godlie purposes.* London, 1584.

   A Progresse of Pietie. Or The harbour of Heavenly harts ease, to recreate the afflicted Soules of all such as are shut up in anye inward or outward affliction. London, 1596.

Northbrooke, John. *Spiritus Est Vicarius Christi In Terra. The Poore Mans Garden.* London, 1573.

   A Treatise wherein Dicing, Dauncing, Vaine playes or Enterludes with other idle pastimes . . . are reproved . . . London, 1571.

Nowell, Alexander. *A Catechisme, or first Instruction and Learning of Christian Religion.*

Translated out of Latine into Englishe [by T. Norton]. London, 1570.

The Office of Christian Parents: Shewing how children are to be governed throughout all ages and times of their life . . . Cambridge, 1616.

Ormerod, Oliver. *The Picture of a Puritane: Or. A relation of the opinions, qualities, and practises of the Anabaptists in Germanie, and of the Puritanes in England* . . . London, 1605.

P., B. *The Prentises Practise in Godlinesse, and his true freedome* . . . London, 1613.

Parker, Henry & Ley, John. *A Discourse Concerning Puritans* . . . London, 1641.

Parr, Richard. *The Life Of . . . James Usher . . . With a Collection of Three Hundred Letters.* London, 1686.

A Parte of a Register, contayinge sundrie memorable matters . . . Edinburgh, 1593.

Peacham, Henry. *The Compleat Gentleman* . . . London, 1634.

Pemble, William. *Five Godly, And Profitable Sermons* . . . Oxford, 1628.

A Plea for Grace . . . London, 1629.

Salomons Recantation And Repentance: Or, The Booke of Ecclesiastes briefly and fully explained. London, 1628.

Penry, John. *A defence of that which hath bin written in the questions of the ignorant ministerie, and the communicating with them.* London, 1588.

An exhortation unto the Governours and people of her Maiesties countrie of Wales, to labour earnestly to have the preaching of the Gospell planted among them. Oxford, 1587.

A Treatise wherein Is Manifestlie Proved, That Reformation And Those that sincerely favour the same, are unjustly charged to be enemies, unto hir Maiestie, and the state . . . Edinburgh, 1590.

Perkins, William. *The Arte of Prophecying. Or a Treatise Concerning The Sacred And Onely True Manner And Methode Of Preaching.* Cambridge, 1609.

An Exposition of the Lord's Prayer: In the way of Catechising serving for ignorant people . . . London, 1595.

The Foundation of Christian Religion: Gathered into sixe Principles. And it is to be learned of ignorant people, that they may be fit to heare Sermons with Profit, and to receive the Lordes Supper with comfort . . . London, 1595.

How to Live, and that Well: in all Estates and Times . . ., in *Workes*, Vol. I. Cambridge, 1608.

A Treatise of the Vocations, Or, Callings of men . . . Cambridge, 1603.

A Treatise tending unto a declaration whether a man be in the estate of damnation or in the estate of grace: and if he be in the first, how he may in time come out of it: if in the second, how he maie discerne it, and perservere in the same to the end. London.

Two Treatises. I Of the nature and practise of repentance. II Of the combat of the flesh and spirit. Cambridge, 1595.

A Warning against the Idolatrie of the last times. And An instruction touching Religious or Divine Worship, in Workes, Vol. I. Cambridge, 1608.

The Workes . . ., 3 vols. London, 1626–31.

A petition made to the Convocation house in the yeare 1586. by the godly Ministers tending to reconciliation . . .: pp. 323–33 in *A Parte of a Register.* London, 1593.

Philips, Edward. *Certaine Godly And Learned Sermons* . . . London, 1605.

Piety, and painfulness in the work of the Ministry . . . London, 1662.

Powel, Gabriel. *A Consideration of the Deprived and Silenced Ministers Arguments, for their Restitution to the use and libertie of their Ministerie* . . . London, 1606.

The Resolved Christian. London, 1600.

Preston, John. *The Breastplate of Faith and Love.* London, 1630.

The Doctrine of the Saints Infirmities . . . London, 1637.

Four Godly and Learned Treatises. London, 1633.

A Profitable Sermon Preached at Lincolnes Inne, On Gen. XXII, XIV . . . London, 1635.

Remaines Of That Reverend and Learned Divine, John Preston . . . London, 1634.

The Saints Daily Exercise. A Treatise concerning the whole dutie of prayer . . . London, 1629.

The Saints Qualification . . . London, 1633.

Sermons Preached Before His Maiestie, and upon other speciall occasions . . . London, 1634.

Sinnes Overthrow: Or, A Godly and Learned Treatise of Mortification . . . London, 1635.

Primaudaye, Peter de la. *The French Academie* . . . *(transl. S. B.).* London, 1586.

Pritchard, Thomas. *The Schoole of honest and vertuous lyfe: Profitable and necessary for all estates and degrees, to be trayned in: but (cheefely) for all the pettie Schollers* . . . *bee they men or Women* . . . London, 1579.

Prynne, William. *A Briefe Survay and Censure of Mr. Cozens his Couzening Devotions* . . . London, 1628.

Canterburies Doome. Or The First Part of a Compleat History of The . . . *Tryall* . . . *of William Laud* . . . London, 1646.

The Church of Englands Old Antithesis To New Arminianisme . . . London, 1629.

God, No Imposter, nor Deluder . . . London, 1629.

Histrio-Mastix. The Players Scourge . . . London, 1633.

Pyrrye, C. *The praise and Dispraise of Women* . . . London, 1569.

Rainolds, *An Excellent Oration of that late famously learned John Rainolds, D. D. and Lecturer of the Greek tongue in Oxford. Very usefull for all such as affect the studies of Logick and Philosophie, and admire profane Learning. Translated out of Latine by J. L. [John Leycaster] Schoolmaster.* London, 1638.

A Letter of Dr. Reinolds to his friend, concerning his advice for the studie of Divinitie. London, 1613.

The Prophesie of Haggai . . . London, 1649.

The Summe Of The Conference Betweene Iohn Rainoldes And Iohn Hart: Touching The Head And The Faith Of The Church . . . London, 1584.

Rich, Barnabe. *The Excellency of good women* . . . London, 1613.

Richardson, Alexander. *The Logicians School-Master: Or, A Comment upon Ramus Logicke.* London, 1629.

Richardson, Charles. *A Workeman, That Needeth Not To Be Ashamed: Or The faithfull Steward of Godshouse. A Sermon describing the duety of a godly Minister, both in his Doctrine and in his Life.* London, 1616

Robinson, John. *A Justification Of Separation from the Church of England. Against Mr. Richard Bernard his invective, Intituled; The Separatist schisme.* 1610.

Rogers, Richard. *Certaine Sermons* . . . London, 1612.

    The Practice of Christianitie. Or, An Epitome of seven Treatises . . . London, 1618.

    Seven Treatises, Containing Such Direction As Is Gathered Out Of The Holie Scriptures, leading and guiding to true happines . . .and may be called the practise of Christianitie . . . London, 1603.

    et. al., A Garden of Spirituall Flowers. Planted by Ri. Ro. Will. Per. R. Gree. M.M. and Geo. Web. London, 1625

Rogers, Thomas. *The Faith, Doctrine, and religion, professed, & protected in the Realme of England,* . . . *Expressed in 39 Articles* . . . Cambridge, 1607.

Romei, Count Hannibal. *The Courtiers Academie . . . 7. Of precedence of Letters or Armes . . . translated into English by I.K.* London, 1598.

Rous, Francis. *The Arte of Happines* . . . London, 1619.

    The Diseases of the Time, Attended by their Remedies. London, 1622.

    The Heavenly Academie . . . London, 1638.

    Meditations of Instruction, of Exhortation, of Reprofe . . . London, 1616.

Ryves, Thomas. *The Poor Vicars Plea. Declaring, that a competence of meanes is due to them out of the Tithes of their severall Parishes, notwithstanding the Impropriations.* London, 1620.

Salter, Thomas. *A Mirrhor mete for all Mothers* . . . London, 1579.

Sampson, Thomas. *A Briefe collection of the Church, and of certayne Ceremonies thereof . . .* London, 1581.

Scott, Thomas. *The Belgicke Pismire* . . . London, 1622.

Scott, William. *An Essay of Drapery* . . . London, 1635.

Scudder, Henry. *The Christians Daily Walke in holy Securitie and Peace . . . First intended for private use; now (through importunitie) published for the common good.* London, 1637.

Serres, Jean. *A Godlie and Learned Commentarie upon the excellent book of Solomon, commonly called Ecclesiastes, or the Preacher . . . newly turned into English by John Stockwood* . . . London, 1585.

Shelford, Robert. *Five Pious And Learned Discourses . . . 2. A Sermon preferring holy Charity before Faith, Hope, and Knowledge* . . . Cambridge, 1635.

    Lectures Or Readings upon the 6. verse of the 22. Chapter of the Proverbs, concerning the vertuous education of Youth . . . London, 1606.

Sherrard, R. *The Country-Man With His Houshold* . . . London, 1620.

A short Catechisme for Housholders with praiers to the same adioyning. London, 1614.

A Short Dialogue Proving That The Ceremonyes, And Some Other Corruptions now in question, are defended, by none other Arguments then such as the Papists have heretofore used . . . 1605.

Shute, Nathaniel. *Corona Charitatis, The Crowne of Charitie* . . . London, 1626.

Sibbes, Richard. *The Christians Portion, or, The Charter of a Christian* . . . London, 1638.

    The Excellencie Of The Gospell above the Law. Wherein the Liberty of the Sonnes of God is shewed. With the Image of their Graces here, and Glory hereafter . . . London, 1639.

    Light From Heaven, Discovering The Fountaine Opened. Angels Acclamations. Churches

Riches. Rich Povertie. In four Treatises . . . London, 1638.

Sixe Demaunds (from an unlearned Protestant, to a learned Papist) . . . London, 1609.

Smith, Henry. *The affinitie of the Faithfull* in, *Three Sermons made by Maister Henry Smith.* London, 1599.

    The Christians Sacrifice. London, 1591.

    Gods Arrow Against Atheists. London, 1604.

    The Lawiers Question. The Answere to the Lawiers Question. The Censure of Christ upon the Answere. London, 1595.

    The Paterne of True Prayer. London, 1592.

    The Poore-Mans Teares. Opened in a Sermon preached by Henrie Smith. Treating of Almes deeds: and releeving the poore. London, 1592.

    The Sermons of Master Henrie Smith . . . London, 1592.

    The Sinfull Mans Search: Or Seeking Of God . . . London, 1592.

    Thirteene Sermons Upon Severall Textes of Scripture. Containing Necessarie and profitable doctrine, as well for the reformation of our lives, as for the comfort of troubled consciences in all distresses. London, 1592.

    The Trumpet of the Soule Sounding to Iudgement . . . London, 1632.

Smith, Samuel. *Davids Repentance.* London, 1614.

Some, Robert. *Godly Treatise containing and deciding certaine questions, moved of late in London and other places, touching the Ministerie, Sacraments, and Church* . . . London, 1588.

Sorocold, Thomas. *Supplication of Saints. A Booke of Prayers and Prayses.* London, 1639.

Spencer, Thomas. *The Art of Logick, Delivered in the Precepts of Aristotle and Ramus* . . . London, 1638.

S., S. *A Briefe instruction for all Families, to be brought up in the knowledge of their duetie to God, and one to another: and to be taught in the hope of salvation in Christe Jesus.* London, 1583.

Stafford, Anthony. *Meditations, and Resolutions, Moral, Divine, Politicall . . . Written for the instruction and bettering of Youth; but, especially of the better and more Noble.* London, 1612.

Stafford, William. *A Compendious or briefe examination of certayne ordinary complaints* . . . London, 1581.

Stockwood, John. *A Plaine And Easie Laying open of the meaning and understanding of the Rules of Construction in the English Accidence, appointed by authoritie to be taught in all Schooles of hir Maiesties dominions* . . . London, 1590.

    A Sermon Preached at Paules Crosse on Bartholmew day . . . *1578* . . . London, 1578.

    A very fruiteful Sermon preached at Paules Crosse the tenth of May last . . . London, 1579.

Stoughton, William. *An Assertion For true Christian Church-Policie* . . . Middelburg, 1604.

Stubbes, Philip. *The Anatomie of Abuses* . . . London, 1581.

    A Christall Glasse For Christian Women. Containing A most excellent discourse of the Godly life and Christian death of Mistresse Katherine Stubbes . . . London, 1612.

Studley, Peter. *The Looking-Glasse of Schisme* . . . London, 1634.

Sturm, John. *A ritch Storehouse or Treasurie for Nobilitye and Gentlemen* . . . London, 1570.

A Supplication of The Family of Love . . . Examined, and found to be derogatorie in an hie degree . . . Cambridge, 1606.

Sutcliffe, Matthew. *A Treatise Of Ecclesiasticall Discipline: Wherein that confused forme of government, which certeine under false pretence, and title of Reformation, and true discipline do strive to bring into the Church of England, is examined and confuted* . . . London, 1591.

Sutton, Christopher. *Learn to Live* . . . London, 1602.

Sydenham, Humphrey. *The Athenian Babler. A Sermon Preached At St. Maries In Oxford, the 9. of July, 1626* . . . London, 1627.

Taylor, Thomas. *Christs Combate And Conquest: Or, The Lyon of the tribe of Judah* . . . Cambridge, 1618.

  A Commentarie upon the Epistle of S. Paul written to Titus . . . London, 1612.

  Davids Learning, Or The Way To True Happinesse: In a Commentarie upon the XXXII Psalme . . . London, 1618.

  The Principles of Christian Practice. Containing the Institution of a Christian Man . . . London, 1635.

  The Progresse Of Saints To Full Holinesse . . . London, 1631.

  The Works . . . London, 1653.

Temple, William. *A Logicall Analysis of Twentie Select Psalmes.* London, 1605.

Terry, John. *The Triall of Truth: Containing A Plaine And Short Discovery of the chiefest pointes of the great Antichrist, and of his adherentes the false Teachers and Heretikes of these last times.* Oxford, 1600.

Travers, Walter. *A Defence of the Ecclesiasticall Discipline ordayned of God to be used in his Church. Against a Replie of Master Bridges* . . . 1588.

  A full and plaine declaration of Ecclesiasticall Discipline owt off the word off God/and off the declininge off the churche off England from the same [transl. T. Cartwright]. Zurich, 1574.

Tuke, Thomas. *The Picture Of a true Protestant: Or, Gods House and Husbandry: wherein is declared the duty and dignitie of all Gods children, both Ministers and People.* London, 1609.

Turner, William. *The Huntyng of the Romyshe Vuolfe* . . . Zurich, 1554.

Udall, John. *Certaine Sermons, Taken Out Of Several Places Of Scripture.* London, 1596.

  The state of the Church of England . . .: pp. 333–65 in *A Parte of a Register.* London, 1593.

The unlawfull Practices of Prelates, against godly Ministers . . .: pp. 280–303 in *A Parte of a Register.* London, 1593.

Ursinus, Zacharius. *The Summe of Christian Religion . . . Translated into English by Henrie Parrie* . . . Oxford, 1587.

A viewe of Antichrist, his lawes and ceremonies, in our English Church unreformed: pp. 56–72 in *A Parte of a Register.* London, 1593.

Ward, Samuel. *A Coal from the Altar, to Kindle the holy fire of Zeale* . . . London, 1615.

Watson, Christopher. *Briefe Principles of religion, for the exercise of youth.* London,

1581.

Webbe, George. *Gods Controversie with England. Or A Description of the Fearefull and lamentable estate which this Land at this present is in.* London, 1609.

West, William. *Symbolaeographia* . . . London, 1590.

Whately, William. *The New Birth: Or, a Treatise of Regeneration* . . . London, 1618.

A Pithie, Short, And Methodicall opening of the Ten Commandments. London, 1622.

The Poore Mans Advocate, Or, A Treatise of Liberality to the needy . . . London, 1637.

Whetstones, George. *A Mirour for Magestrates of Cyties* . . . London, 1584.

Wiburn, Percival. *A Checke or reproofe of M. Howlets untimely shreeching [sic] in her Maiesties eares* . . . London, 1581.

Widdowes, Giles. *The Schismatical Puritan* . . . Oxford, 1630.

Widley, G. *The Doctrine of the Sabbath* . . . London, 1604.

Wilcox, Thomas. *Large Letters. Three in number, containing much necessarie matter, for the instruction and comfort of such, as are distressed in conscience by feeling of sinne, and feare of Gods wrath.* London, 1589.

A Right Godly And learned Exposition, upon the whole Booke of Psalmes: Wherein is set forth the true Division, Sence, and Doctrine contained in every Psalme: for the great furtheraunce and necessarie instruction of every Christian Reader . . . London, 1586.

A Short, Yet Sound Commentarie: written on that woorthie worke called; The Proverbes of Salomon: and now published for the profite of Gods people. London, 1589.

The Unfouldyng of sundry untruths and absurde propositions, lately propounded by one I.B. a greate favourer of the horrible Heresie of the Libertines . . . London, 1581.

Wilkins, John. *Ecclesiastes, Or, A Discourse concerning the Gift of Preaching as it fals under the rules of Art.* London, 1647.

Wilson, Thomas. *The Arte of Rhetorique* . . . London, 1553.

A Sermon Preached . . . *to the Corporation of Blacksmiths.* London, 1610.

Woodward, Hezekiah. *A Childes Patrimony.* London, 1640.

A Light to Grammar, And All other Arts and Sciences . . . London, 1641.

Vestibulum Or, A Manuduction towards a Faire Edifice by their Hands, who are designed to open the way thereunto. London, 1640.

Wotton, Anthony. *Runne from Rome. Or, A Treatise Shewing the necessitie of Separating from the Church of Rome.* London, 1624.

Wright, Samuel. *Divers Godly and Learned Sermons Of A Reverend And Faithfull Servant of God* . . . London, 1612.

Yates, John. *A Modell of Divinitie, Catechistically Composed* . . . London, 1622.

Zwingli, Ulrich. *A Short pathwaye to the ryghte and true understanding of the holye & sacred Scriptures: set fourth by* . . . *Huldrich Zwinglius, and now translated out of Laten, into Englysshe by Ihon Veron* . . . Worcester, 1550.

MODERN EDITIONS OF PRIMARY SOURCES

The ABC Both in Latyn & Englyshe: Being A facsimile reprint of the earliest extant English Reading Book, ed. E. S. Schuckburgh. London, 1889.

Ascham, Roger. *The Scholemaster* [1570], in *The Whole Works of Roger Ascham*, ed. Rev. Dr. Giles, Vol. III. London, 1864.

Assheton, Nicholas. *The Journal of Nicholas Assheton* . . ., Chetham Society, xiv, Manchester, 1848.

Bacon, Francis. *Works*, ed. J. Spedding, R. L. Ellis, & D. D. Heath, 14 vols. London, 1857–74.

Bancroft, Richard. *Tracts ascribed to Richard Bancroft* . . ., ed. A. Peel. Cambridge, 1953.

Barrow, Henry. *A Brief Discoverie of the False Church* [1590], in *The Writings of Henry Barrow 1587–1590*, ed. L. H. Carlson. London, 1962.

A Brief Summe of the Causes of Our Separation . . ., in *The Writings of Henry Barrow 1587–1590*, ed. L. H. Carlson. London, 1962.

A Plaine Refutation . . ., in *The Writings of Henry Barrow 1590–91*, ed. L. H. Carlson. London, 1966.

Becon, Thomas. *The Catechism . . . With Other Pieces Written by him in the Reign of King Edward the Sixth*. Cambridge , 1844.

The Early Works. . . Being the Treatises Published by him in the Reign of King Henry VIII. Cambridge, 1843.

A Booke of the Forme of Common Prayers, administration of the Sacraments: &c. agreeable to Gods Worde, and the use of the reformed churches, in *Fragmenta Liturgica*, Vol. I. Bath, 1884.

Bradford, William. *History of the Plimoth Plantation*, ed. John A. Doyle. London, 1896.

Breton, Nicholas. *The Court and Country* . . . [1618], in *Complaint and Reform in England 1436–1714*, ed. W. H. Dunham, Jr & Stanley Pargellis. New York, 1938.

Brinsley, John. *A Consolation for our Grammar Schooles* [1622], intro. Thomas Clark Pollock. New York, 1943.

Ludus Literarius or the Grammar Schoole [1612], ed. E. T. Campagnac, Liverpool & London, 1917.

Browne, Robert. *A True and Short Declaration* . . . [?1583], in *The Writings of Robert Harrison and Robert Browne*, ed. A. Peel & L. H. Carlson. London, 1953.

Burghall, Edward. 'Providence Improved': pp. 1–22 & 226–36 in *Memorials of the Civil War in Cheshire*, ed. J. Hall, The Record Society. London, 1889.

Calvin, John. *Institutes of the Christian Religion* [1561 English], ed. John T. McNeill, 2 vols. London, 1961.

Cartwright, Thomas. *Cartwrightiana*, ed. Albert Peel & L. H. Carlson. London, 1951.

Cleland, James. *The Institution of a Young Noble Man* [1607], intro. Max Molyneux. New York, 1948.

Clement, Frances. *The Petie Schole with An English Orthographie* . . . [1587], ed. R. D. Pepper. Gainesville, Florida, 1966.

Comenius, J. A. *The Great Didactic of John Amos Comenius*, ed. M. W. Keatinge. 2 vols. London, 1896.

Crosfield, Thomas. *The Diary of Thomas Crosfield M.A., B.D. Fellow of Queen's College, Oxford* . . ., ed. F. S. Boas. London, 1935.

D'Ewes, Simonds. *The Autobiography and Correspondence of Sir Simonds D'Ewes* . . ., ed. James O. Halliwell, 2 vols. London, 1845.

A Directory of Church-government . . . [1644], ed. P. Lorimer. London, 1872.

Elyot, Sir Thomas. *The Book named the Governor* [1531]. London, 1966.

Erasmus, Desiderius. *de duplici copia verborum ac rerum commentarii duo*, transl. B. I. Knott: pp. 279–659 in *Collected Works of Erasmus*, ed. C. R. Thompson, Vol. 24. Toronto, 1978.

    de ratione studii ac legendi interpretandique auctores ('On the method of study', transl. Brian McGregor): pp. 661–91 in *Collected Works of Erasmus*, ed. C. R. Thompson, Vol. 24. Toronto, 1978.

    Desiderius Erasmus: concerning the Aim and Method of Education, ed. W. H. Woodward. Cambridge, 1904.

    The Paraclesis: pp. 92–106 in *Desiderius Erasmus: Christian Humanism and the Reformation* . . ., ed. John C. Olin. New York, 1965.

Fenner, Dudley. *The Artes of Logike and Rethorike* . . ., (1584): pp. 143–80 in *Four Tudor Books*, ed. R. D. Pepper. Gainesville, Florida, 1966.

Fuller, Thomas. *The Church History of Britain* . . ., ed. J. S. Brewer, Vol. V. Oxford, 1845.

Gilbert Humphrey. *Queene Elizabethes Achademy*, ed. F. J. Furnivall, *Early English Text Society*, extra ser., viii, London, 1869.

Goodwin, Thomas. *The Works of Thomas Goodwin D. D. Sometime President of Magdalen College in Oxford* . . . *To which is Prefix'd An Account of Author's LIFE from his own Memoirs*, Vol. 5. London, 1704.

Harrison, Anthony. *The Registrum Vagum of Anthony Harison: part I*, ed. Thomas F. Barton, Norfolk Record Society. Norwich, 1963.

Hoby, Margaret. *Diary of Lady Margaret Hoby 1599–1605*, ed. Dorothy Meads. London, 1903.

Hooker, Richard. *The Works of . . . Mr. Richard Hooker* . . ., ed. John Keble, 3 vols. Oxford, 1888.

Kempe, William. *The education of children in learning: declared by the dignitie, utilitie, and method thereof* [1588], ed. R. D. Pepper. Gainesville, Florida, 1966.

Knox, John. *John Knox's Geneva Service Book 1556* . . ., ed. William D. Maxwell. Edinburgh & London, 1931.

Latimer, Hugh. *Sermons*. Cambridge, 1844.

    Sermons and Remains. Cambridge, 1845.

Lawne, Christopher. *Brownisme Turned The In-side out-ward. Being A Paralell Betweene The Profession And Practise of the Brownists Religion* [1613]. Amsterdam, 1968.

'The Life of Master John Shaw', *The Publications of the Surtees Society*, 115, pp. 119–62 & 358–444.

Martindale, Adam. *Life, by himself*, ed. R. Parkinson. Chetham Society, iv. Manchester, 1845.

Muggleton, Lodowick. *The Acts of the Witnesses of the Spirit* . . . London, 1699.

New England's First Fruits . . . [1643], repr. as Appendix 'D' in S. E. Morison, *The Founding of Harvard College*. Cambridge, Massachusetts, 1935.

Norwood, Richard. *The Journal of Richard Norwood*, ed. W. F. Craven & W. P. Hayward. New York, 1945.

Osborne, Francis. *Works*, 9th edn. London, 1689.

Pace, Richard. *de fructu qui ex doctrina percipitur (The Benefit of a Liberal Education)*, ed. Frank Manley & Richard S. Sylvester. New York, 1967.

Percy, Henry, 9th Earl of Northumberland. *Advice to his Son*, ed. G. B. Harrison. London, 1930.

Perkins, William. *The Work of William Perkins*, intro. & ed. Ian Breward. Appleford, 1970.

Plutarch. *The Education or bringinge up of children/translated oute of Plutarche by syr Thomas Eliot Knyght.* New York & Amsterdam, 1969.

Robinson, John. *The Works of John Robinson . . .*, ed. Robert Ashton. London, 1851.

Robinson, Matthew. *Autobiography* ed. J. E. B. Mayor. Cambridge, 1856.

Rogers, Edward. *Some Account of the Life and Opinions of a Fifth-Monarchy Man. Chiefly Extracted from the Writings of John Rogers, Preacher.* London, 1867.

Rous, John. *Diary of John Rous, Incumbent of Santon Downham, Suffolk, from 1625 to 1642*, ed. Mary A. E. Green, Camden Society, lxvi. London, 1856.

Sadoleto. *Sadoleto on Education. A Translation of the De Pueris Recte Instituendis.* London, 1916.

Sibbes, Richard. *The Complete Works of Richard Sibbes, D. D.* Edinburgh & London, 1872–4.

Slingsby, Henry. *The Diary of Sir Henry Slingsby . . . and Extracts from Family Correspondence and Papers . . .*, ed. Daniel Parsons. London, 1836.

Smyth, John. *The Works of John Smyth*, ed. W. T. Whitley. Cambridge, 1915.

Ussher, James. *The Whole Works of James Ussher . . .*, ed. C. R. Elrington. Dublin, 1847–64.

Vives, Juan Luis, *de subventione pauperum*: pp. 1–31 in *Some Early Tracts on Poor Relief*, ed. F. R. Salter. London, 1926.

   On Education, A Translation of the De Tradendis Disciplinis of Juan Luis Vives . . ., intro. Foster Watson. Cambridge, 1913.

Weigall, Rachel. 'An Elizabethan gentlewoman. The journal of Lady Mildmay, circa 1570–1617', *The Quarterly Review*, 215 (1911), 119–38.

Weston, William. *The Autobiography of an Elizabethan*, transl. Philip Caraman. London, 1955.

Whitelocke, James. *Liber Famelicus of Sir James Whitelocke, A Judge of the Court of King's Bench in the Reigns of James I. and Charles I . . .*, ed. John Bruce. Camden Society, lxx. London, 1858.

Whitgift, John. *The Works of John Whitgift, D.D. . . .*, ed. John Ayre, Vols. I & III. London, 1851 & 1853.

Winthrop Papers: Vol. I: 1498–1628, The Massachusetts Historical Society. Boston, Massachusetts, 1929.

Winthrop Papers: Vol. II: 1623–1630. The Massachusetts Historical Society. Boston, Massachussetts, 1931.

Wood, Thomas. *Letters of Thomas Wood, Puritan, 1566–1577*, ed. Patrick Collinson, *Bulletin of the Institute of Historical Research*, Special Supplement No. 5 (Nov. 1960).

Woodford, Robert. *The Diary of Robert Woodford, Steward of Northampton, 9th Report of* the *Royal Commission on Historical Manuscripts, Appendix, Pt* II. London, 1884.

Wotton, Thomas. *Thomas Wotton's Letter-Book 1574–1586*, ed. G. Eland. London, 1960.

Zwingli, Ulrich & Bullinger, Henry. *Zwingli and Bullinger: Selected Translations . . .*, ed. G. W. Bromily. London, 1953.

CALENDARS & COLLECTIONS OF DOCUMENTS

Acts and Proceedings of the General Assemblies of the Kirk of Scotland . . ., Vol I. Edinburgh, 1839.

Anderson, P. J. (ed.). *Fasti Academiae Mariscallanae Aberdonensis*, I. Aberdeen, 1889.

Arber, Edward. *A Transcript of the Registers of the Company of Stationers of London, 1554–1640 A.D.*, 5 vols. London, 1875–94.

Bailey, F. A. (ed.). *A Selection from the Prescot Court Leet and Other Records 1447–1600.* 1937.

Barnes, Richard. *The Injunctions and Other Ecclesiastical Proceedings of Richard Barnes, Bishop of Durham, from 1575 to 1587*, ed. J. Raine, Surtees Society, Vol. 22. Durham, 1850.

Bolton, Robert (transl.). *A Translation of the Charter and Statutes of Trinity-College, Dublin . . .* Dublin, 1749.

Calendar of State Papers, Domestic Series, 1547–1640, 28 vols. London, 1856–73.

Cardwell, Edward. *Documentary Annals of the Reformed Church of England; . . . from the year 1546 to the year 1716 . . .*, 2 vols. Oxford, 1839.

  Synodalia: A Collection of Articles of Religion, Canons, and Proceedings of Convocations . . ., Vol. I. Oxford, 1842.

Carlisle, N. *A concise description of the endowed grammar schools in England and Wales*, 2 vols. London, 1818.

Carter, E. H. (ed.). *The Norwich Subscription Books . . . 1637–1800.* London, 1937.

Cooper, Charles Henry. *Annals of Cambridge, Vol. II: 1546–1602* and *Vol. III: 1603–1688.* Cambridge, 1843 & 1845.

  Athenae Cantabrigienses, 2 vols. Cambridge, 1858–61.

Davies, G. (ed.). *Autobiography of Thomas Raymond and Memoirs of the Family of Guise of Elmore, Gloucestershire.* Camden Society, 3rd ser., xxviii. London, 1917.

Davis, C. H. *The English Church Canons of 1604 . . .* London, 1869.

Ellis, Henry (ed.). *Original Letters . . .* London, 1843.

England, Parliament. *Fourth Report from the Select Committee on Education.* London, 1818.

Foster, C. W. *The State of the Church in the Reigns of Elizabeth and James I as illustrated by documents relating to the Diocese of Lincoln, Vol. I.* Lincoln Record Society, 23. Lincoln, 1926.

  (ed.). *Lincoln Episcopal Records in the Time of Thomas Cooper, S.T.P., Bishop of Lincoln, A.D. 1571 to A.D. 1584.* Lincoln Record Society, 2. Lincoln, 1912.

Foster, Joseph (ed.). *Alumni Oxonienses: The Members of the University of Oxford, 1500–1714 . . .*, 4 vols. Oxford, 1891–2.

Frere, W. H. (ed.). *Visitation Articles and Injunctions of the Period of the Reformation*, 3 vols. London, 1910.

Frere, W. H. & Douglas, C. E. (eds.). *Puritan Manifestoes: A Study of the Origin of the Puritan Revolt* . . . London, 1954 (orig. 1907).

Gee, Henry & Hardy, William John (eds.). *Documents Illustrative of English Church History*. London, 1896.

Gibson, Edmund. *Codex Juris Ecclesiastici Anglicani*, 2 vols. Oxford, 1701.

Hawley, A. (ed.). *A Translation of the Foundation Grant of Oakham and Uppingham Schools 1587*. London, 1929.

Heywood, James (ed.). *Early Cambridge University and College Statutes* . . . London, 1855.

& Wright, Thomas (eds). *Cambridge University Transactions During the Puritan Controversies of the 16th and 17th Centuries*, Vol. II. London, 1854.

Historical Manuscripts Commission. *Calendar of Manuscripts: Salisbury: Pts. II, VI, X, XI*. London & Dublin, 1888–1906.

Eighth Report: Report and Appendix. Part I. London, 1881.

14th Report: Appendix, Part IV: The Manuscripts of Lord Kenyon. London, 1894.

Report on the Manuscripts of the late R. R. Hastings . . ., Vol. II. London, 1930.

Report on the Manuscripts of Lord Montagu of Beaulieu. London, 1900.

Report on Manuscripts in Various Collections, Vol. III. London, 1904.

Twelfth Report: Appendix IV: the Manuscripts of the Duke of Rutland. London, 1888.

Hudson, William & Tingey, John C. (eds.). *The Records of the City of Norwich*, Vol. II. Norwich & London, 1910.

Kennedy, W. P. M. *Elizabethan Episcopal Administration* . . ., Vol. III. London, 1924.

Kidd, B. J. (ed.). *Documents Illustrative of the Continental Reformation*. Oxford, 1911.

Knappen, M. M. (ed.). *Two Elizabethan Puritan Diaries by Richard Rogers and Samuel Ward*. Chicago, Illinois, 1933.

'The lawes liberties & orders of Harvard Colledge . . . in the yeares 1642, 1643, 1644, 1645 & 1646 . . .': pp. 24–9 in *Collections*, Publications of the Colonial Society of Massachusetts, xv. Boston, Massachusetts, 1925.

'The lawes of the colledge published publiquely before the students of Harvard Colledge May 4, 1655: pp. 327–40 in *Collections*, Publications of the Colonial Society of Massachusetts, xxxi. Boston, Massachusetts, 1935.

Leach, A. F. (ed.). *Early Yorkshire Schools, vol. II*, The Yorkshire Archaeological Society Record Series, xxxiii. Leeds, 1903.

Educational Charters and Documents, 598 to 1909. Cambridge, 1911.

Leishmann, J. B. (ed.). *The Three Parnassus Plays (1598–1601)*. London, 1949.

Lowe, Roger. *The Diary of Roger Lowe of Ashton-in-Makerfield, Lancashire 1663–74*, ed. William L. Sachse. London, 1938.

McKerrow, R. B. (ed.). *A Dictionary of Printers and Booksellers in England, Scotland and Ireland, and of Foreign Printers of English Books 1557–1640*. London, 1910.

'The manifolde Enormities of the Ecclesiasticall state in the most partes of the Countie of Lancaster; and many of them in som partes also of Cheshire . . .': pp. 1–13 in *Chetham Miscellanies*, Vol. V Manchester, 1902.

More, P. E. & Cross, F. L. (eds.). *Anglicanism: The Thought and Practice of the Church of*

England Illustrated from the Religious Literature of the Seventeenth Century. London, 1935.

Padgett, L. (ed.) *Chronicles of the Free Grammar School of Prince Henry at Otley.* Otley, 1923.

Parker, Matthew. *Correspondence of Matthew Parker, D.D. Archbishop of Canterbury. Comprising Letters . . . from A.D. 1535, to . . . A.D. 1575,* ed. J. Bruce & T. T. Perrowne. Parker Society, xxxi. Cambridge, 1853.

Peck, Francis. *Desiderata Curiosa: Or A Collection of Divers Scarce And Curious Pieces Relating Chiefly to Matters of English History . . .* London, 1779.

Peel, Albert, (ed.). *The Seconde Parte of a Register: being a calendar of manuscripts under that title . . . now in Dr. Williams's Library, London,* 2 vols. Cambridge, 1915.

Pollard, A. W. & Redgrave, G. R. *A Short-Title Catalogue of Books Printed in England, Scotland & Ireland And of English Books Printed Abroad 1475–1640.* London, 1926.

Porter, H. C. (ed.). *Puritanism in Tudor England.* London, 1970.

'President Dunster's quadriennium memoir, 1654': pp. 291–300 in *Collections,* Publications of the Colonial Society of Massachusetts, xxxi. Boston, Massachusetts, 1935.

Prothero, G. W. (ed.). *Select Statutes and Other Constitutional Documents Illustrative of the Reigns of Elizabeth and James I.* Oxford, 1894.

Rushworth, John. *Historical Collections of private passages of State . . .* London, 1659.

Saunders, H. W. (ed.). *The Official Papers of Sir Nathaniel Bacon of Stiffkey, Norfolk As Justice of the Peace 1580–1620.* Camden Society, 3rd ser., xxvi. London, 1915.

Southern, A. C. (ed.). *An Elizabethan Recusant House, comprising The Life of the Lady Magdalen Viscountess Montagu (1538–1608)* [by Richard Smith, Bishop of Chalcedon]. London & Glasgow, n.d.

The Statutes of Queen Elizabeth for the University of Cambridge (1570). London, 1838.

Stephen, Leslie & Lee, Sidney (eds.). *The Dictionary of National Biography . . .,* 22 vols. Oxford, 1937–8.

Stocks, George Alfred (ed.). *The Records of Blackburn Grammar School,* Part I. Chetham Society, lxvi. Manchester, 1909.

Stocks, Helen (ed.). *Records of the Borough of Leicester . . . 1603–1688.* Cambridge, 1923.

Stocks, J. E. & Bragg, W. B. (eds.). *Market Harborough Parish Records 1531 to 1837.* London, 1926.

Stubbings, F. H. *Statutes of Sir Walter Mildmay . . . Emmanuel College.* Cambridge, 1983.

Thompson, A. H. (ed.). 'The chantry certificates for Leicestershire returned under the Act of 37 Henry VIII, cap. iv . . .', *Architectural and Archaeological Societies' Reports,* 30 (1910).

Trinterud, Leonard J. (ed.). *Elizabethan Puritanism.* New York, 1971.

Turnbull, G. H. *Hartlib, Dury and Comenius: gleanings from Hartlib's papers.* Liverpool, 1947.

Usher, Roland G. (ed.). *The Presbyterian Movement in the Reign of Queen Elizabeth as*

Illustrated by the Minute Book of the Dedham Classis 1582–1589. Royal Historical Society, 3rd ser., viii. London, 1905.

Venn, John & Venn, J. A. *Alumni Cantabrigienses . . . Part I from the Earliest Times to 1751*, 4 vols. Cambridge, 1922–7.

Wallis, P. J. *Histories of Old Schools. A revised List for England and Wales*. Newcastle-upon-Tyne, 1966.

Ward, G. R. M. (transl.). *Oxford University Statutes, Vol. I. The Caroline Code . . .* London, 1845.

Wilkins, David. *Concilia Magnae Britanniae . . .*, Vol. IV. London, 1734.

Wing, Donald. *Short-Title Catalogue of Books Printed in England, Scotland, Ireland, Wales, and British America And of English Books Printed in Other Countries 1641–1700*, 3 vols. New York, 1945–51.

Wood, Anthony a. *Athenae Oxonienses . . .*, 4 vols. London, 1813–20.

Wright, Louis B. (ed.). *Advice to a son: precepts of Lord Burghley, Sir Walter Raleigh, and Francis Osborne*. Ithaca, N.Y., 1962.

SECONDARY SOURCES

Allen, Don Cameron. *Doubt's Boundless Sea: Skepticism and Faith in the Renaissance*. Baltimore, Maryland, 1964.

Anders, H. 'The Elizabethan ABC with the Catechism', *The Library*, 4th ser., 16 (1935–6), 32–48.

Aries, Philippe. *Centuries of Childhood.: A Social History of Family Life*. New York, 1962.

Armstrong, Brian. *Calvinism and the Amyraut Heresy . . .* Madison, Wisconsin, 1969.

Aston, Margaret. 'Lollardy and literacy', *History*, 62 (1977), 347–71.

Austen-Leigh, Augustus. *King's College*. London, 1899.

Axtell, James. *The School upon a Hill: Education and Society in Colonial New England*. New York, 1976.

Babbage, Stuart Barton, *Puritanism and Richard Bancroft*. London, 1962.

Bailey, F. A. 'Prescot grammar school in Elizabethan times: a sidelight on the Reformation', *Transactions of the Historic Society of Lancashire and Cheshire*, 86 (1935), 1–20.

Bailyn, Bernard. *Education in the Forming of American Society . . .* New York, 1960.

Baker, Herschel. *The Dignity of Man: Studies in the Persistence of An Idea*. Cambridge, Massachusetts, 1947.

Baldwin, T. W. *William Shakspere's Small Latine & Lesse Greeke*, 2 vols. Urbana, Illinois, 1944.

Bamborough, J. B. *The Little World of Man*. London, 1952.

Baron, Hans. 'Secularization of wisdom and political humanism in the Renaissance', *Journal of the History of Ideas*, 21 (1960), 131–50.

Beevor, E., Evans, R. J. & Savory, T. H. *The History and Register of Aldenham School*. Worcester, 1948 (orig. 1938).

Berry, Boyd M. 'The first English pediatricians and Tudor attitudes towards childhoood', *Journal of the History of Ideas*, 35 (1974), 561–77.

Bingham, C. R. *Our Founder: Some Account of Archdeacon Johnson . . . With An Appendix Containing the [Uppingham School] Statutes of 1625.* Uppingham, 1884.

Blench, J. W. *Preaching in England in the late Fifteenth and Sixteenth Centuries: A Study of English Sermons 1450–c. 1600.* Oxford, 1964.

Bolgar, R. R. *The Classical Heritage and its Beneficiaries.* Cambridge, 1973 (orig. 1954).

'Classical reading in Renaissance schools', *The Durham Research Review*, 2 (1955), 18–26.

'Humanist education and its contribution to the Renaissance': pp. 1–19 in *The Changing Curriculum.* London, 1971.

Boyd, William & Shuffrey, W. A. *Littondale: Past and Present.* Leeds, 1893.

Brauer, Jerald C. 'Reflections on the nature of English Puritanism', *Church History*, 23 (1954), 99–108.

Bredvold, Louis I. 'The religious thought of Donne in relation to medieval and later traditions': pp. 191–232 in *Studies in Shakespeare, Milton and Donne*, University of Michigan Publications, i. New York, 1925.

Breward, I. 'The significance of William Perkins', *The Journal of Religious History*, 4, No. 2 (Dec. 1966), 113–28.

(ed.) *The Work of William Perkins.* Appleford, 1970.

Brigden, Susan. 'Youth and the English Reformation', *Past and Present*, 95 (1982), 37–67.

Brook, Benjamin. *The Lives of the Puritans . . .,* 3 vols. London, 1813.

Brooks, F. W. 'The social position of the parson in the sixteenth century', *The Journal of the British Archaeological Association*, 3rd ser., 10 (1945–7), 23–37.

Brown, J. Howard. *Elizabethan Schooldays: An Account of the English Grammar Schools in the second half of the Sixteenth Century.* Oxford, 1933.

Brown, W. Adams. 'Covenant theology', in *Encyclopaedia of Religion and Ethics*, ed. James Hastings, Vol. IV. Edinburgh, 1911.

Browne, John. *History of Congregationalism and Memorials of the Churches in Norfolk and Suffolk.* London, 1877.

Brushfield, T. N. 'The financial diary of a citizen of Exeter, 1631–43', *Reports and Transactions of the Devonshire Association for the Advancement of Science, Literature, and Art*, 33 (1901), 187–269.

Bush, Douglas. *The Renaissance and English Humanism.* Toronto, 1939.

Calder, Isabel M. 'A seventeenth century attempt to purify the Anglican Church', *The American Historical Review*, 52, No. 4 (July, 1948), 760–75.

Cameron, James K. 'The Renaissance tradition in the reformed church of Scotland': pp. 251–69 in *Studies in Church History*, 14, ed. Derek Baker. Oxford, 1977.

Capp, B. S. 'Will formularies', *Local Population Studies*, 14 (1975), 49–50.

Carlisle, Nicholas. *A Concise Description of the Endowed Grammar Schools in England and Wales.* London, 1818.

Caspari, Fritz. *Humanism and the Social Order in Tudor England.* New York, 1968.

Charlton, Kenneth. *Education in Renaissance England.* London, 1965.

'Liberal education and the Inns of Court in the sixteenth century'. *British Journal of Educational Studies*, 9 (1960–1), pp. 25–38.

'The professions in sixteenth century England', *University of Birmingham Historical Journal*, 12, No. 1 (1969), 20–41.

Christianson, Paul. 'Reformers and the Church of England', *Journal of Ecclesiastical History*, 31 (1980), 463–82.

Clark, Peter. 'The ownership of books in England, 1560–1640: the example of some Kentish townsfolk': pp. 95–111 in *Schooling and Society: Studies in the History of Education*, ed. L. Stone. Baltimore, Maryland, 1976

Cliffe, J. T. *The Puritan Gentry: The Great Puritan Families of Early Stuart England.* London, 1984.

Collinson, Patrick. 'The beginnings of English Sabbatarianism', pp. 207–21 in C. W. Dugmore & Charles Duggan (eds.), *Studies in Church History*, 1. London & Edinburgh, 1964.

'A comment: concerning the name puritan', *Journal of Ecclesiastical History*, 31, 483–88.

The Elizabethan Puritan Movement. London, 1967.

'Episcopacy and reform in England in the later sixteenth century': pp. 91–125 in *Studies in Church History*, 3, ed. G. J. Cuming. Leiden, 1966.

Godly People: Essays on English Protestantism and Puritanism. London, 1983.

'Lectures by combination: structures and characteristics of church life in 17th-century England', *Bulletin of the Institute of Historical Research*, 48 (1975), 182–213.

' "A magazine of religious patterns": an Erasmian topic transposed in English Protestantism': pp. 223–49 in *Renaissance and Renewal in Christian History, Studies in Church History*, 14, ed. Derek Baker. Oxford, 1977.

A Mirror of Elizabethan Puritanism: The Life and Letters of 'Godly Master Dering'. London, 1964.

The Religion of Protestants: The Church in English Society 1559–1625. Oxford, 1982.

'The role of women in the English Reformation illustrated by the life and friendships of Anne Locke': pp. 258–72 in *Studies in Church History*, 2, ed. G. J. Cuming. London, 1965.

Conant, James B. 'The advancement of learning during the Puritan Commonwealth', *Proceedings of the Massachusetts Historical Society*, 66 (1936–41), 3–31.

Coolidge, John S. *The Pauline Renaissance in England.* Oxford, 1970.

Cornwall, Julian. 'Evidence of population mobility in the seventeenth century', *Bulletin of the Institute of Historical Research*, 11 (1967), 143–52.

Costello, William T. *The Scholastic Curriculum at Early Seventeenth-Century Cambridge.* Cambridge, Massachusetts, 1958.

Cox, Thomas. *A Popular History of the Grammar School of Queen Elizabeth, at Heath, near Halifax.* Halifax, 1879.

Craig, Hardin, Jr. 'The Geneva Bible as a political document', *The Pacific Historical Review*, (1938), 40–9.

Cremin, Lawrence A. *American Education: the Colonial Experience 1607–1783.* New York, 1970.

Cressy, David. 'Levels of illiteracy in England, 1530–1730', *The Historical Journal*, 20

(1977), 1–23.

Literacy and the Social Order: Reading and Writing in Tudor and Stuart England. Cambridge, 1980.

'Literacy in seventeenth-century England: more evidence', *The Journal of Inter-disciplinary History*, 8 (1977–8), 141–50.

'School and college admission ages', *History of Education*, 8 (1979), 167–77.

'The social composition of Caius College, Cambridge 1580–1640'. *Past & Present*, 47 (1970), 113–15.

Cross, M. Claire. *Church and People 1450–1660: The Triumph of the Laity in the English Church.* Glasgow, 1976.

'An example of lay intervention in the Elizabethan church': pp. 273–82 in *Studies in Church History, 2,* ed. G. J. Cuming. London, 1965.

The Free Grammar School of Leicester, University College of Leicester, Department of English Local History: Occasional Papers, iv (Leicester, 1953).

The Puritan Earl: The Life of Henry Hastings Third Earl of Huntingdon 1536–1595. London, 1966.

'The Third Earl of Huntingdon and Elizabethan Leicestershire', *The Leicestershire Archaeological and Historical Society, Transactions*, 36 (1960), 6–21.

Curtis, Mark H. 'The alienated intellectuals of early Stuart England', *Past and Present*, 23 (1962), 25–43.

'Education and apprenticeship': pp. 53–72 in *Shakespeare in His Own Age*, ed. Allardyce Nicoll, Shakespeare Survey, xvii (Cambridge, 1964).

Oxford and Cambridge in Transition 1558–1642: An Essay on Changing Relationships between the English Universities and English Society. Oxford, 1959.

Danner, Dan G. 'Anthony Gilby: puritan in exile – a biographical approach', *Church History*, 40 (1971), 412–22.

Davies, Godfrey. 'English political sermons, 1603–40', *Huntington Library Quarterly*, 3 No. 1 (Oct. 1939), 1–22.

Davies, Horton. *Worship and Theology in England*, Vols. I & II. Princeton, New Jersey, 1970 & 1975.

The Worship of the English Puritans. Glasgow, 1948.

Davies, Kathleen. 'Continuity and change in literary advice on marriage': pp. 58–80 in *Marriage and Society*, ed. R. B. Outhwaite. London, 1981.

De Jong, Peter Y. *The Covenant Idea in New England Theology 1620–1847.* Grand Rapids, Michigan, 1945.

deMause, Lloyd. 'The evolution of childhood': pp. 1–73 in *The History of Childhood*, ed L. deMause. London, 1976.

DeMolen, Richard L. 'Richard Mulcaster and the profession of teaching in sixteenth-century England', *Journal of the History of Ideas*, 35 (1974), 121–9.

'Richard Mulcaster's philosophy of education', *The Journal of Medieval and Renaissance Studies*, 2 (1972), 69–91.

Dixon, W. MacNeile. *Trinity College, Dublin.* London, 1902.

Eby, Frederick & Arrowood, Charles Flinn. *The History and Philosophy of Education Ancient and Medieval.* New York, 1942.

Edwards, G. M. *Sidney Sussex College.* London, 1899.

Eisenstein, Elizabeth. *The Printing Press as an Agent of Change*. Cambridge, 1979.
  'Some conjectures about the impact of printing on Western society and thought: a preliminary report', *Journal of Modern History*, 40 (1968), 1–56.

Ellis, Charles. *Carre's Grammar School, Sleaford 1604–1954*. Sleaford, 1954.

Emerson, Everett H. 'Calvin and covenant theology', *Church History*, 25 (1956), 136–44.

Eusden, John D. *Puritans, Lawyers, and Politics in Early Seventeenth-Century England*. New Haven, Connecticut, 1958.

Feyerharm, William R. 'The status of the schoolmaster and the continuity of education in Elizabethan East Anglia' *History of Education*, 5 (1976), 103–15.

Fink, D. P. J. *Queen Mary's Grammar School 1554–1954*. Walsall, 1954.

Fisch, Harold. 'The Puritans and the reform of prose-style', *E.L.H. A Journal of English Literary History* 19 (1952), 229–48.

Fisher, R. M. 'The reformation of clergy at the Inns of Court 1530–1580', *Sixteenth Century Journal*, 12 (1981), 69–92.

Fleming, Sandford. *Children & Puritanism: The Place of Children in the Life and Thought of the New England Churches 1620–1847*. New Haven, Connecticut, 1933.

Fletcher, A. J. 'The expansion of education in Berkshire and Oxfordshire, 1500–1670', *British Journal of Educational Studies*, 15 (1967), 51–9.

Fletcher, Harris Francis. *The Intellectual Development of John Milton Vol. II: The Cambridge University Period 1625–32*. Urbana, Illinois, 1961.

Forder, C. R. *A History of the Paston Grammar School, North Walsham, Norfolk*. North Walsham, 1934.

Fox, Levi. *A Country Grammar School: A History of Ashby-de-la-Zouch through four centuries 1567 to 1967*. Oxford, 1967.

Gardiner, Dorothy. *English Girlhood at School*. London, 1929.

George, Charles H. & George, Katherine. *The Protestant Mind of the English Reformation 1570–1640*. Princeton, New Jersey, 1961.

Gerrish, B. A. *Grace and Reason: A Study in the Theology of Luther*. Oxford, 1962.
  'Priesthood and ministry in the theology of Luther', *Church History*, 34 (1965), 404–22.

Gilson, Etienne. *Reason and Revelation in the Middle Ages*. New York, 1966.

Ginzburg, Carlo. 'High and low: the theme of forbidden knowledge in the sixteenth and seventeenth centuries', *Past and Present*, 73 (1976), 28–41.

Graff, Harvey. *The Literacy Myth*. New York, 1979.

Graves, M. A. R. 'Thomas Norton the parliament man: an Elizabethan M.P., 1559–1581', *The Historical Journal*, 23 (1980), 17–35.

Gray, I. E. & Potter, W. E. *Ipswich School 1400–1950*. Ipswich, 1950.

Greaves, Richard L. 'The early Quakers as advocates of educational reform', *Quaker History*, 58 (1969), 22–30.
  'The ordination controversy and the spirit of reform in puritan England', *Journal of Ecclesiastical History*, 21 (1970), 225–41.
  'The origins and early development of English covenant thought', *The Historian: A Journal of History*, 31 (1968), 21–35.
  'Puritanism and science: the anatomy of a controversy', *Journal of the History of Ideas*,

30 (1969), 345–68.

The Puritan Revolution and Educational Thought. New Brunswick, New Jersey, 1969.

'The role of women in early English nonconformity', *Church History*, 52 (1983), 299–311.

Society and Religion in Elizabethan England. Minneapolis, Minnesota, 1981.

Green, Ian. 'Career prospects and clerical conformity in the early Stuart church', *Past and Present*, 90 (1981), 71–115.

Green, V. H. H. *Religion at Oxford and Cambridge.* London, 1964.

Greven, Philip. *The Protestant Temperament: Patterns of Child-Rearing, Religious Experience, and the Self in Early America.* New York, 1977.

Grislis, Egil. 'The hermeneutical problem in Richard Hooker': pp. 159–206 in *Studies in Richard Hooker*, ed. W. Speed Hill. Cleveland & London, 1972.

Haigh, Christopher. 'Puritan evangelism in the reign of Elizabeth I', *The English Historical Review*, 92 (1977), 30–58.

Reformation and Resistance in Tudor Lancashire. Cambridge, 1975.

Hall, Basil. 'Calvin against the Calvinists', *Proceedings of the Huguenot Society of London*, 20 (1958–64), 284–301.

'Puritanism: the problem of definition': pp. 283–96 in *Studies in Church History*, 2, ed. G. J. Cuming. London, 1965.

'The trilingual college of San Ildefonso and the making of the complutensian polyglot Bible': pp. 114–46 in *Studies in Church History*, ed. G. J. Cuming. Leiden, 1969.

Hall, David D. 'Education and the social order in colonial America', *Reviews in American History*, 3 (1975), 178–83.

The Faithful Shepherd: A History of the New England Ministry in the Seventeenth Century. New York, 1974.

'Understanding the puritans': pp. 330–49 in *The State of American History*, ed. H. J. Bass. Chicago, Illinois, 1970.

'The world of print and collective mentality in seventeenth-century New England': pp. 166–80 in *New Directions in American Intellectual History*, ed. John Higham & Paul K. Conkin. Baltimore, Maryland, 1979.

Haller, William. *Foxe's Book of Martyrs and the Elect Nation.* London, 1963.

The Rise of Puritanism Or, The Way to the New Jerusalem . . . New York, 1957 (orig. 1938).

Harbison, E. Harris. *The Christian Scholar in the Age of the Reformation.* New York, 1956.

Hart, Arthur Tindal. *The Country Clergy: In Elizabethan & Stuart Times 1558–1660.* London, 1958.

Haydn, Hiram. *The Counter-Renaissance.* New York, 1950.

Hazlitt, W. Carew. *Schools, School-Books and Schoolmasters: A Contribution to the History of Educational Development in Great Britain.* London, 1888.

Heal, Felicity & O'Day, Rosemary. *Church and Society in England: Henry VIII to James I.* London, 1977.

Henderson, G. D. *The Founding of Marischal College, Aberdeen.* Aberdeen, 1947.

Herr, Alan Fager. *The Elizabethan Sermon: A Survey and a Bibliography.* Philadelphia,

Pennsylvania, 1940.

Hexter, J. H. 'The education of the aristocracy in the Renaissance', in *Reappraisals in History*. New York & Evanston, Illinois, 1963.

Hill, Christopher. *Economic Problems of the Church from Archbishop Whitgift to the Long Parliament*. Oxford, 1956.

God's Englishman: Oliver Cromwell and the English Revolution. Harmondsworth, 1973.

Intellectual Origins of the English Revolution. London, 1972 (orig. 1965).

'Plebeian irreligion in 17th century England': pp. 46–61 in *Studien über die Revolution*, ed. Manfred Kossok. Berlin, 1971.

'The radical critics at Oxford and Cambridge in the 1650s': pp. 107–32 in *Universities in Politics: Case Studies from the Late Middle Ages and Early Modern Period*, ed. John W. Baldwin & Richard A. Goldthwaite. Baltimore, Maryland, 1972.

' "Reason" and "reasonableness" in seventeenth-century England', *The British Journal of Sociology*, 20, No. 3 (1969), 235–52.

Society and Puritanism in Pre-Revolutionary England. London, 1969 (orig. 1964).

The World Turned Upside Down: Radical Ideas during the English Revolution. London, 1972.

The History and Description of Ashby-de-la-Zouch. London & Ashby, 1852.

Holden, William P. *Anti-Puritan Satire 1572–1642*. New Haven, 1954.

Houlbrooke, Ralph. 'The protestant episcopate 1547–1603: the pastoral contribution': pp. 78–98 in *Church and Society in England: Henry VIII to James I*, ed. F. Heal & R. O'Day. London, 1977.

Howell, W. S. *Logic and Rhetoric in England, 1500–1700*. Princeton, New Jersey, 1956.

'Ramus and English rhetoric: 1574–1681', *The Quarterly Journal of Speech*, 37 (1951), 299–310.

Hudson, Winthrop S. 'The Morison myth concerning the founding of Harvard College', *Church History*, 8 (1939), 148–59.

Huehns, Gertrude. *Antinomianism in English History: with special reference to the period 1640–1660*. London, 1951.

Hughes, Philip. *The Reformation in England*. London, 1963 (orig. 1950).

Hutchinson, Lucy. *Memoirs of the Life of Colonel Hutchinson*. London, 1968, orig. 1806.

Illick, Joseph E. 'Child-rearing in seventeenth-century England and America': pp. 303–50 in *The History of Childhood*, ed. L. deMause. London, 1976.

Ives, E. W. 'Social change and the law', *The English Revolution 1600–1660*, ed. E. W. Ives. London, 1968.

Jardine, Lisa. 'Humanism and the sixteenth century Cambridge arts course', *History of Education*, 4 (1975), 16–31.

'The place of dialectic teaching in sixteenth-century Cambridge', *Studies in the Renaissance*, 21 (1974), 31–62.

Jarman, T. L. 'Education', *Life Under the Stuarts*, intro. J. E. Morpurgo. London, 1950.

Jenkins, Gladys. 'A note on "The episcopal licensing of schoolmasters in England" ',

Church Quarterly Review, 159 (1958), 78–81.

Johansson, Egil. *The History of Literacy in Sweden, In comparison with some other countries.* Educational Reports, xii. Umeå, 1977.

Johnson, J. H. 'Chelmsford grammar school', *The Essex Review*, 54 (1945), 45–61, 100–6.

Johnson, James T. 'English puritan thought on the ends of marriage', *Church History*, 38 (1969), 429–36.

Jones, Richard Foster. *Ancients and Moderns: A Study of the Background of the Battle of the Books.* Washington University Studies New Ser. Language and Literature, vi. St Louis, Missouri, 1936.

'The humanistic defence of learning in the mid-seventeenth century': pp. 71–92 in *Reason and the Imagination: Studies in the History of Ideas 1600–1800*, ed. J. A. Mazzeo. London, 1962.

The Triumph of the English Language. Stanford, California, 1953.

Jones, William B. 'Hawarden grammar school', *Journal of the Flintshire Historical Society* (1916–17), 63–83.

Jordan, W. K. *The Charities of London 1480–1660: The Aspirations and the Achievements of the Urban Society.* London, 1960.

The Charities of Rural England 1480–1660 . . . London, 1961.

Philanthropy in England 1480–1660. London, 1959.

Kay, Margaret M. *The History of Rivington and Blackrod Grammar School.* Manchester, 1966.

Kearney, Hugh. *Scholars and Gentlemen: Universities and Society in Pre-Industrial Britain 1500–1700.* London, 1970.

Kelso, Ruth. *Doctrine for a Lady of the Renaissance.* Urbana, Illinois. 1956.

Kendall, R. T. *Calvin and English Calvinism to 1649.* Oxford, 1979.

Kennedy, W. P. M. *Elizabethan Episcopal Administration: An Essay in Sociology and Politics*, 3 vols. London, 1924.

Kirby, Ethyn W. 'The lay feoffees: a study in militant puritanism', *The Journal of Modern History*, 14 (1942), 1–25.

Knafla, Louis A. 'The matriculation revolution and education at the Inns of Court in Renaissance England': pp. 232–64 in *Tudor Men and Institutions: Studies in English Law and Government*, ed. A. J. Slavin. Baton Rouge, Louisiana, 1972.

Knappen, M. M. *Tudor Puritanism: A Chapter in the History of Idealism.* Chicago, Illinois, 1970 (orig. 1939).

Kocher, Paul H. *Science and Religion in Elizabethan England.* New York, 1969 (orig. 1953).

Kristeller, Paul Oskar. *Renaissance Thought: The Classic, Scholastic, and Humanistic Strains.* New York, 1961.

Kussmaul, Ann. *Servants in Husbandry in Early Modern England.* Cambridge, 1981.

Laborde, E. D. *Harrow School Yesterday and Today.* London, 1948.

Lake, Peter. 'Mathew Hutton – a puritan bishop?', *History*, 64 (1979), 182–204.

Moderate Puritans and the Elizabethan Church. Cambridge, 1982.

'Puritan identities', *The Journal of Ecclesiastical History*, 35 (1984), 112–23.

Lawson, John. *A Town Grammar School through Six Centuries.* London, 1963.

Leach, A. F. *English Schools at the Reformation 1546–8.* Westminster, 1896.

Lee, P. A. 'Some English academies: an experiment in the education of Renaissance gentlemen', *History of Education Quarterly*, 10 (1970), 273–86.

Lempriere, William. *A History of the Girls' School of Christ's Hospital, London, Hoddesdon and Hertford*. Cambridge, 1924.

Lester, D. N. R. *The History of Batley Grammar School 1612–1962*. Batley, n.d.

Lewalski, Barbara. 'Milton on learning and the learned minister controversy', *The Huntington Library Quarterly*, 24 (1961), 267–81.

Lievsay, John L. 'Silver-tongued Smith', *Huntington Library Quarterly*, 11 (1947–8), 13–36.

Linder, Robert D. 'Pierre Viret's ideas and attitudes concerning humanism and education', *Church History*, 34 (1965), 25–35.

Little, David. *Religion, Order, and Law: A Study in Pre-Revolutionary England*. Oxford, 1970.

Lockridge, Kenneth A. *Literacy in Colonial New England . . .* New York, 1974.

Logan, F. Donald. 'The origins of the so-called regius professorships: an aspect of the Renaissance in Oxford and Cambridge': pp. 271–8 in *Studies in Church History*, 14, ed. D. Baker, London, 1977.

Looney, Jefferson. 'Undergraduate education at early Stuart Cambridge', *History of Education*, 10 (1980), 9–19.

Lovejoy, Arthur O. *The Great Chain of Being: A Study of the History of an Idea*. Cambridge, Massachusetts, 1936.

Lunsingh Scheurleer, Th. H. & Meyjes, G. H. M. P. (eds.) *Leiden University in the Seventeenth Century: An Exchange of Learning*. Leiden, 1975.

Luoma, John K. 'Who owns the Fathers? Hooker and Cartwright on the authority of the primitive Church', *The Sixteenth Century Journal*, 8 (1977), 45–59.

MacCaffrey, Wallace T. *Exeter, 1540–1640: The Growth of an English Country Town*. Cambridge, 1958.

McConica, James. *English Humanists and Reformation Politics*. Oxford, 1965.
    'Humanism and Aristotle in Tudor Oxford', *English Historical Review*, 94 (1979), 291–317.
    'Scholars and commoners in Renaissance Oxford': pp. 151–81 in *The University in Society*, ed. L. Stone, Vol I. Princeton, New Jersey, 1974.

McDowell, R. B. & Webb, D. A. 'Courses and teaching in Trinity College, Dublin, during the first 200 years', *Hermathena*, (1947), 9–30.

McGee, J. Sears. *The Godly Man in Stuart England: Anglicans, Puritans, and the Two Tables, 1620–1670*. New Haven, Connecticut, & London, 1976.

McGiffert, Arthur C. *Protestant Thought Before Kant*. London, 1911.

MacKinnon, James. *Calvin and the Reformation*. London, 1936.

Maclear, J. F. 'Popular anticlericalism in the puritan revolution', *Journal of the History of Ideas*, 17, No. 4 (1956), 443–70.

Maclure, Millar. *The Paul's Cross Sermons 1534–1642*. Toronto, 1958.

McMahon, Clara P. *Education in Fifteenth Century England*. New York, 1968.

McNeill, John T. *The History and Character of Calvinism*. New York, 1954.

Mahaffey, John P. *An Epoch in Irish History: Trinity College, Dublin . . . 1591–1660*. Port Washington, Wisconsin, 1970.

Mallet, C. E. *A History of the University of Oxford, Vol. II: The Sixteenth and Seventeenth*

Centuries. London, 1924.

Mander, G. P. *The History of the Wolverhampton Grammar School*. Wolverhampton, 1913.

Manning, Roger B. 'The crisis of episcopal authority during the reign of Elizabeth I', *The Journal of British Studies*, 11 (1971), 1–25.

Marchant, Ronald A. *The Puritans and the Church Courts in the Diocese of York, 1560–1642*. London, 1960.

Marsden, George M. 'Perry Miller's rehabilitation of the puritans: a critique', *Church History*, 39 (1970), 91–105.

Martin, Alfred von. *Sociology of the Renaissance*. New York, 1963.

Mather, Cotton. *Magnalia Christi Americana*, Vol I. Edinburgh, 1853.

Merton, Robert K. 'Science, technology and society in seventeenth century England', *Osiris*, 4 (1938), 360–632.

Michaelson, Robert S. 'Changes in the Puritan concept of calling or vocation', *The New England Quarterly*, 26 (1953), 315–36.

Miller, Perry. *The New England Mind: The Seventeenth Century*. Cambridge, Massachusetts, 1954 (orig. 1939).

   Orthodoxy in Massachusetts, 1630–1650. A Genetic Study. Cambridge, Massachusetts, 1933.

   ' "Preparation for salvation" in seventeenth-century New England', *Journal of the History of Ideas*, 4 (1943), 253–86.

   & Johnson, Thomas H. (eds.). *The Puritans*. New York, 1938.

Mitchell, W. Fraser. *English Pulpit Oratory from Andrewes to Tillotson: A Study of its Literary Aspects*. London, 1932.

Møller, Jens G. 'The beginnings of puritan covenant theology', *The Journal of Ecclesiastical History*, 14 (1963), 46–67.

Morgan, Edmund S. *The Puritan Family: Religion & Domestic Relations in Seventeenth-Century New England*, rev. edn. New York, 1966 (orig. 1944).

   Visible Saints: The History of a Puritan Idea. Ithaca, New York, 1971 (orig. 1963).

Morgan, Irvonwy. *The Godly Preachers of the Elizabethan Church*. London, 1965.

Morgan, John. 'Puritanism and science: a reinterpretation', *The Historical Journal*, 22 (1979), 535–60.

Morgan, Victor. 'Approaches to the history of the English universities in the sixteenth and seventeenth centuries', *Wiener Beiträge*, 5, 138–64.

   'Cambridge University and "the country" 1560–1640', pp. 183–245 in *The University in Society*, ed. L. Stone, I. Princeton, New Jersey, 1974.

Morison, Samuel Eliot. *The Founding of Harvard College*. Cambridge, Massachusetts, 1935.

   Harvard College in the Seventeenth Century: Part I. Cambridge, Massachusetts, 1936.

   The Intellectual Life of Colonial New England. New York, 1956.

   The Puritan Pronaos: Studies in the Intellectual Life of New England in the Seventeenth Century. New York, 1936.

Müller, Gustav E. 'Calvin's *Institutes of the Christian Religion* as an illustration of Christian thinking', *Journal of the History of Ideas*, 4 (1943), 287–300.

Mullinger, J. B. *The University of Cambridge*, Vols. II & III. Cambridge, 1884 & 1911.

Murray, Athol L. *Sebright School, Wolverley: A History.* Cambridge, 1954.

Nauert, Charles G. *Agrippa and the Crisis of Renaissance Thought.* Urbana, Illinois, 1965.

Neale, J. E. *Elizabeth I and her Parliaments 1584–1601.* London, 1957.

Nelson, N. E. *Peter Ramus and the Confusion of Logic, Rhetoric, and Poetry,* University of Michigan Contributions in Modern Philology, ii. Ann Arbor, Michigan, 1947.

New, John F. H. *Anglican and Puritan: The Basis of their Opposition 1558–1640.* London, 1964.

Noble, Mary E. *A History of the Parish of Bampton.* Kendal, 1901.

Norton, Arthur O. 'Harvard text-books and reference books of the seventeenth century': pp. 361–438 in *Transactions 1930–1933,* Publications of the Colonial Society of Massachusetts, xxviii. Boston, Massachusetts, 1933.

Nuttall, Geoffrey F. *The Holy Spirit in Puritan Faith and Experience.* Oxford, 1946.

O'Day, Rosemary. *Education and Society 1500–1800.* London, 1982.

  The English Clergy: The Emergence and Consolidation of a Profession 1558–1642. Leicester, 1979.

  'The reformation of the ministry, 1558–1642': pp. 55–75 in *Continuity and Change: Personnel and Administration of the Church of England,* ed. R. O'Day & F. Heal. Leicester, 1976.

Olsen, V. Norskov. *John Foxe and the Elizabethan Church.* Berkeley, Los Angeles, & London, 1973.

Ong, Walter J. *Ramus: Method, and the Decay of Dialogue . . .* Cambridge, Massachusetts, 1958.

Orme, Nicholas. *English Schools in the Middle Ages.* London, 1973.

Owst, G. R. *Preaching in Medieval England . . . c. 1350–1450.* Cambridge, 1926.

Parkyn, Robert. 'Devotional treatises': pp. 59–88 in *Tudor Treatises,* ed. A. G. Dickens, Yorkshire Archaeological Society Record Series, cxxv. Wakefield, 1959.

Parry, H. L. *The Founding of Exeter School.* Exeter & London, 1913.

Peacock, George. *Observations on the Statutes of the University of Cambridge.* London, 1841.

Peacock, M. H. *History of the Free Grammar School of Queen Elizabeth at Wakefield . . .* Wakefield, 1892.

Pearce, E. H. *Sion College and Library.* Cambridge 1913.

Pearson, A. F. Scott. *Thomas Cartwright and Elizabethan Puritanism.* Cambridge, 1925.

Peile, John. *Christ's College.* London, 1900.

Pepper, R. D. (ed.) *Four Tudor Books on Education . . .* Gainesville, Florida, 1966.

Petegorsky, David. *Left-Wing Democracy in the English Civil Wars: A Study of the Social Philosophy of Gerrard Winstanley.* London, 1940.

Pettit, Norman. *The Heart Prepared: Grace and Conversion in Puritan Spiritual Life.* New Haven, Connecticut, & London, 1966.

Pinchbeck, I. 'The State and the child in sixteenth century England', *The British Journal of Sociology,* 7, No. 4 (1956), 273–85; 8, No. 1 (1957), 59–74.

Porter, H. C. *Reformation and Reaction in Tudor Cambridge.* Cambridge, 1958.

Powell, Chilton Latham. *English Domestic Relations 1487–1653: A Study of Matrimony and Family Life in Theory and Practice as revealed by the Literature, Law, and History of the Period.* New York, 1917.

Prest, Wilfrid R. *The Inns of Court under Elizabeth I and the Early Stuarts.* London, 1972.

'Legal education of the gentry at the Inns of Court, 1560–1640', *Past & Present*, 38 (1967), 20–39.

Preston, Arthur E. *The Church and Parish of St. Nicholas, Abingdon: The Early Grammar School . . .* London, 1929.

Price, F. D. 'The abuses of excommunication and the decline of ecclesiastical discipline under Queen Elizabeth', *The English Historical Review*, 57, No. 225 (1942), 106–15.

Purvis, J. S. 'The literacy of the later Tudor clergy in Yorkshire', pp. 147–65, *Studies in Church History*, 5, ed. G. J. Cuming. Leiden, 1969.

Quintana, Ricardo. 'Note on English educational opinion during the seventeenth century', *Studies in Philology* 27 (1930), 265–92.

Reinitz, Richard. 'Perry Miller and recent American historiography', *Bulletin of the British Association for American Studies*, 8 (1964), 27–35.

Rice, Eugene F., Jr. *The Renaissance Idea of Wisdom.* Cambridge, Massachusetts, 1958.

Richardson, R. C. *Puritanism in North-West England: A Regional Study of the Diocese of Chester to 1642.* Manchester, 1972.

Rogers, C. D. 'Education in Lancashire and Cheshire, 1640–1660', *Transactions of the Historic Society of Lancashire and Cheshire*, 123 (1972), 39–56.

Rohr, John von. 'Covenant and assurance in early English puritanism'. *Church History*, 34 (1965), 195–203.

Russell, Conrad. 'Arguments for religious unity in England, 1530–1650', *The Journal of Ecclesiastical History*, 18 (1967), 201–26.

Russell, Elizabeth. 'The influx of commoners into the University of Oxford before 1581: an optical illusion?', *The English Historical Review*, 365 (1977), 721–45.

Schlatter, R. B. 'The higher learning in puritan England', *Historical Magazine of the Protestant Episcopal Church*, 23 (1954), 167–87.

Schmitt, Charles B. 'Towards a reassessment of Renaissance Aristotelianism', *History of Science*, 11 (1973), 159–93.

Schnucker, Robert V. 'Elizabethan birth control and puritan attitudes', *The Journal of Interdisciplinary History*, 5 (1975), 655–67.

'The English puritans and pregnancy, delivery and breast feeding', *History of Childhood Quarterly*, 1 (1974), 637–58.

Schochet, Gordon J. 'II. Patriarchalism, politics and mass attitudes in Stuart England', *The Historical Journal*, 12 (1969), 413–41.

Schofield, R. S. 'The measurement of literacy in pre-industrial England': pp. 311–25 in *Literacy in Traditional Societies*, ed. Jack Goody. Cambridge, 1968.

Schultz, Howard. *Milton and Forbidden Knowledge.* New York, 1955.

'The teaching of handwriting in Tudor and Stuart times', *Huntington Library Quarterly*, 6 (1942–3), 381–425.

Seaver, Paul S. *The Puritan Lectureships: The Politics of Religious Dissent 1560–1662.* Stanford, California, 1977.

Serjeantson, R. M. *A History of the Church of All Saints, Northampton.* Northampton, 1901.

Sharpe, Kevin. 'Archbishop Laud and the University of Oxford': pp. 146–64 in *History and Imagination: Essays in honour of H. R. Trevor-Roper*, ed. H. Lloyd-Jones, V. Pearl, & B. Worden. London, 1981.

Sheils, W. J. 'Religion in provincial towns: innovation and tradition': pp. 156–76 in *Church and Society in England: Henry VIII to James I*, ed. F. Heal & R. O'Day. London, 1977.

Shipps, Kenneth. 'The "political puritan" ', *Church History*, 45 (1976), 196–205.

Short, K. R. M. 'A theory of common education in Elizabethan puritanism', *The Journal of Ecclesiastical History*, 23, No. 1 (1972), 31–48.

Shuckburgh, E. S. *Emmanuel College.* London, 1904.

Laurence Chaderton, D. D. . . . translated from a Latin memoir of Dr. Dillingham . . . Cambridge, 1884.

Simon, Brian. 'Leicestershire schools 1625–40', *British Journal of Educational Studies*, 3 (1954–55), 42–58

Simon, Joan. 'The Comenian educational reformers 1640–1660 and the Royal Society of London', *Acta Comenia*, 2, No. 26 (1970), 165–78.

Education and Society in Tudor England. Cambridge, 1967.

'The Reformation and English education', *Past & Present*, 11 (1957), 48–65.

'The social origins of Cambridge students 1603–1640', *Past & Present*, 26 (1963), 58–67.

'Town estates and schools in the sixteenth and early seventeenth centuries': pp. 3–26 in *Education in Leicestershire 1540–1940: A Regional Study.* Leicester, 1968.

Simpson, Alan. *Puritanism in Old and New England.* Chicago, Illinois, 1955.

Skinner, Quentin. 'Meaning and understanding in the history of ideas', *History and Theory*, 8 (1969), 3–53.

Sloane, William. *Children's Books in England & America in the Seventeenth Century.* New York, 1955.

Smith, Alan. 'Samuel Ogden – a 17th-century Derbyshire schoolmaster', *The Derbyshire Archaeological Journal*, 94 (1974), 32–4.

Smith, Dwight C. 'Robert Browne, Independent', *Church History*, 6 (1937), 289–349.

Smith, Steven R. 'The London apprentices as seventeenth-century adolescents', *Past & Present*, 61 (1973), 149–61.

'Religion and the conception of youth in seventeenth-century England', *History of Childhood Quarterly*, 2 (1974–5), 493–516.

Smith, Wilson. 'The teacher in puritan culture', *Harvard Educational Review*, 36 (1966), 394–411.

Sprunger, Keith L. 'John Yates of Norfolk: the radical puritan preacher as Ramist philosopher', *Journal of the History of Ideas*, 37 (1976), 697–706.

'Technometria: a prologue to puritan theology', *Journal of the History of Ideas*, 29 (1968), 115–22.

Spufford, Margaret. *Contrasting Communities: English Villagers in the Sixteenth and*

Seventeenth Centuries. Cambridge, 1974.

'First steps in literacy: the reading and writing experiences of the humblest seventeenth-century spiritual autobiographers', *Social History*, 4 (1979), 407–35.

'The schooling of the peasantry in Cambridgeshire, 1575–1700': pp. 112–47 in *Land, Church, and People*, ed. Joan Thirsk. Reading, 1970.

Small Books and Pleasant Histories: Popular Fiction and Its Readership in Seventeenth-Century England. London, 1981.

Stearns, Raymond P. 'Assessing the New England mind', *Church History*, 10 (1941), 246–62.

Stephens, W. B. 'Illiteracy and schooling in the provincial towns, 1640–1870: a comparative approach': pp. 27–47 in *Urban Education in the Nineteenth Century*, ed. D. A. Reader). New York, 1978.

Stone, Lawrence. *The Crisis of the Aristocracy 1558–1641*. Oxford, 1966 (orig. 1965).

'The educational revolution in England, 1560–1640', *Past & Present*, 28 (1964), 41–80.

The Family, Sex and Marriage In England 1500–1800. New York, 1977.

'Literacy and education in England 1640–1900', *Past & Present*, 42 (1969), 69–139.

'Literacy in seventeenth-century England', *The Journal of Interdisciplinary History*, 8 (1978), 799–800.

'The rise of the nuclear family in early modern England: the patriarchal stage': pp. 13–57 in *The Family in History*, ed. C. E. Rosenberg. Philadelphia, Pennsylvania, 1975.

'The size and composition of the Oxford student body 1580–1909': pp. 3–110 in *The University in Society*, ed. L. Stone, Vol. I. Princeton, New Jersey, 1974.

Stott, G. *A History of Chigwell School*. Ipswich, 1960.

Stout, Harry S. 'University men in New England 1620–1660: a demographic analysis', *The Journal of Interdisciplinary History*, 4 (1974), 375–400.

Stowe, A. Monroe. *English Grammar Schools in the Reign of Queen Elizabeth*. New York, 1908.

Strauss, Gerald. *Luther's House of Learning: Indoctrination of the Young in the German Reformation*. Baltimore, Maryland, 1978.

Strype, John. *Annals of the Reformation and Establishment of Religion . . . in the Church of England . . .*, 4 vols. London, 1725–31 (orig. 1709).

The History of the life and Acts of . . . E. Grindal . . . London, 1710.

The Life and Acts of John Whitgift, D.D., 3 vols. Oxford, 1822 (orig. 1718).

Stubbs, John William. *The History of the University of Dublin . . .* Dublin, 1889.

Sykes, Norman. 'Richard Hooker': pp. 63–89 in *The Social & Policial Ideas of Some Great Thinkers of the Sixteenth & Seventeenth Centuries . . .*, ed. F. J. C. Hearnshaw. London, 1926.

Tate, George. *The History of the Borough, Castle, and Barony of Alnwick*, 2 vols. Alnwick, 1868–9.

Tate, W. E. 'The episcopal licensing of schoolmasters in England', *Church Quarterly Review*, 157 (1956), 426–32.

'Sources for the history of English grammar schools', *British Journal of Educational Studies*, 1, (1950–1), 164–75; 2 (1951–2), 67–81.

Thomas, Keith. *Rule and Misrule in the Schools of Early Modern England*. Reading, 1976.

'Women and the civil war sects', *Past & Present*, 13 (1958), 42–62.

Thompson, Pishey. 'The Johnson family', *The New England Historical and Genealogical Register*, 8 (1854), 358–62.

Tillyard, E. M. *The Elizabethan World Picture*. Harmondsworth, 1963 (orig. 1943).

Todd, Margo. 'Humanists, puritans, and the spiritual household', *Church History*, 49 (1980), 18–34.

Trevelyan, G. M. 'Undergraduate life under the Protectorate', *The Cambridge Review*, 64, No. 1575 (1943), 328–30.

Trinterud, Leonard J. 'The origins of puritanism', *Church History*, 20 (1951), 37–57.

Troeltsch, Ernst. *The Social Teaching of the Christian Churches*, 2 vols. London, 1931 (orig. 1913).

Tuck, J. P. 'The use of English in Latin teaching in England in the sixteenth century', *The Durham Research Review*, 1, No. 1 (1950), 22–30.

Tyacke, Nicholas. 'Puritanism, Arminianism and Counter-Revolution': pp. 119–43 in *The Origins of the English Civil War*, ed. Conrad Russell. London, 1973.

'Science and religion at Oxford before the Civil War': pp. 73–93 in *Puritans and Revolutionaries*, ed. D. Pennington & K. Thomas. Oxford, 1978.

Tyler, Philip. 'The status of the Elizabethan parochial clergy': pp. 76–97 in *Studies in Church History*, 4, ed. G. J. Cuming. Leiden, 1967.

Usher, Roland G. *The Reconstruction of the English Church*, 2 vols. London & New York, 1910.

Ustick, W. Lee. 'Changing ideals of aristocratic character and conduct in seventeenth-century England', *Modern Philology*, 30 (1932–3), 147–66.

Vann, Richard T. 'Literacy in seventeenth-century England: some hearth-tax evidence', *The Journal of Interdisciplinary History*, 5 (1974), 287–93.

Venn, John. *Early Collegiate Life*. Cambridge, 1913.

The Victoria History of the Counties of England.

Walker, Thomas Alfred. *Peterhouse*. London, 1906.

Wall, Richard. 'The age at leaving home', *Journal of Family History*, 3 (1978), 181–202.

(ed). *Family Forms in Historic Europe*. Cambridge, 1983.

Wallis, P. J. 'Worsborough grammar school', *The Yorkshire Archaeological Journal*, 39 (1958), 147–63.

Walzer, Michael. *The Revolution of the Saints: A Study in the Origins of Radical Politics*. London, 1966.

'Revolutionary uses of repression', pp. 122–36 in *Essays in theory and history*, ed. Melvin Richter. Cambridge, Massachusetts, 1970.

Watkins, Owen. *The Puritan Experience*. London, 1972.

Watson, Foster. 'The curriculum and text books of English schools in the first half of the seventeenth century', *Transactions of the Bibliographical Society*, 6 (1900–2), 159–267.

The English Grammar Schools to 1660: Their Curriculum and Practice. London, 1968 (orig. 1908).

'The State and education during the Commonwealth', *The English Historical Review*, 15 (1900), 58–72.

Webster, Charles. *The Great Instauration: Science, Medicine and Reform 1626–1660*. London, 1975.

West, W. Morris S. 'John Hooper and the origins of puritanism', *The Baptist Quarterly*, 15 (1954), 346–8.

Wolff, Cynthia Griffin. 'Literary reflections of the puritan character', *Journal of the History of Ideas*, 29 (1968), 13–32.

Wood, Norman. *The Reformation and English Education: A Study of the Influence of Religious Uniformity on English Education in the Sixteenth Century*. London 1931.

Wright, Louis B. *Middle-Class Culture in Elizabethan England*. Chapel Hill, North Carolina, 1935.

Wrigley, E. A. & Schofield, R. S. *The Population History of England 1541–1871: A Reconstruction*. Cambridge, Massachusetts, 1982.

Yarborough, Anne. 'Apprentices as adolescents in sixteenth century Bristol', *Journal of Social History*, 13 (1979), 57–86.

Zaret, David. 'Ideology and organization in puritanism', *Archives européennes de Sociologie*, 21 (1980), 83–115.

Ziff, Larzer. *The Career of John Cotton: Puritanism and the American Experience*. Princeton, New Jersey, 1962.

UNPRINTED WORKS: UNPUBLISHED THESES
(Ph.D. unless otherwise noted)

Adamson, Ian. 'The foundation and early history of Gresham College London, 1596–1704'. Cambridge, 1974.

Bauckham, Richard John. 'The career and thought of Dr William Fulke (1537–1589)'. Cambridge, 1973.

Chalmers, C. D. 'Puritanism in Leicestershire, 1558–1633'. Leeds (M.A.), 1962.

Christophers, R. A. 'Social and educational background of the Surrey clergy, 1520–1620'. London, 1975.

Collinson, Patrick. 'The Puritan classical movement in the reign of Elizabeth I'. London, 1957.

Cressy, David. 'Education and literacy in London and East Anglia 1580–1700'. Cambridge, 1973.

Cross, M. Claire. 'The career of Henry Hastings, Third Earl of Huntingdon, 1536–1595'. Cambridge, 1559.

Foreman, Henry. 'The early separatists, the Baptists and education 1580–1700 (with special reference to the education of the clergy)'. Leeds, 1976.

Houston, R. A. 'Aspects of society in Scotland and North-East England, c1550–c1750: social structure, literacy and geographical mobility'. Cambridge, 1981.

Lake, Peter. 'Laurence Chaderton and the Cambridge moderate puritan tradition, 1570–1604'. Cambridge, 1978.

McKee, William Wakefield. 'The idea of covenant in early English puritanism (1580–1643)'. Yale, 1948.

Newton, R. A. 'Puritanism in the Diocese of York (excluding Nottinghamshire) 1603–1640'. London, 1955.

O'Day, Rosemary. 'Clerical patronage and recruitment in England in the Elizabethan and early Stuart periods with special reference to the Diocese of Coventry and Lichfield'. London, 1972.

Rogers, C. D. 'The development of a teaching profession in England 1547–1700'. Manchester, 1975.

Schwarz, Marc Lewis. 'The religious thought of the protestant laity in England 1590–1640'. U.C.L.A., 1965.

Shipps, Kenneth W. 'Lay patronage of East Anglian puritan clerics in pre-revolutionary England'. Yale, 1971.

Smith, Alan. 'A study of educational development in the Diocese of Lichfield and Coventry in the seventeenth century'. Leicester, 1972.

Stephens, J. E. 'Yorkshire schools and schoolmasters, 1600–1700: aspects of the control of education'. Leeds, 1975.

Twigg, J. D. 'The University of Cambridge and the English Revolution, 1625–1688'. Cambridge, 1983.

Tyler, Richard. 'The children of disobedience: the social composition of Emmanuel College, Cambridge, 1596–1645'. Berkeley, California, 1976.

Wrighton, K. E. 'The puritan reformation of manners with special reference to the counties of Lancashire and Essex 1640–1660'. Cambridge, 1974.

UNPUBLISHED MANUSCRIPTS

Schofield, R. S. 'Some dimensions of illiteracy in England, 1600–1800'.

INDEX

Sherman, Ursula, 167
Sherrington, Grace, 166
Sibbes, Richard, 29–30, 83, 102, 117, 129, 262, 267, 287, 304
Sidney, Philip, 276
Sidney, Frances, Countess of Sussex, 255
Sion College, 294
Skinner, Quentin, 5, 306
Slingsby, Henry, 286
Smith, Anne, 152
Smith, Henry, 71, 152, 233
Smith, Robert, 185
Smith, Sir Thomas, 272
social order, puritans on, 82–3, 83–4, 86, 92–4, 146–7, 151, 165–70, 216, 265, 303–4
Society of Antiquaries, 272
Socrates, 48
South Walsham, 204
Spencer, Thomas, 110
Stanley, Henry, Earl of Derby, 215
Starkey, Thomas, 291
Stock, Richard, 119–20
Stockton, Elianor, 28
Stockwood, John, 128, 158, 159, 174, 179, 182, 187, 192, 207, 266
Strowd, John, 215
Studley, Peter, 14
Sturm, John, 178, 179, 196, 279
Sutcliffe, Matthew, 221
Sweden, 185

Talon, Omer, 108, 183
Taylor, Frances, 290
Taylor, Thomas, 36, 70, 130–1, 157, 158, 170
Temple, William, 257
temporary faith, 24
Tertullian, 41, 115
theology, 112–17, 229, 235, 236–7, 288, 297
Thomism (*see also* Aquinas, Thomas), 50, 52, 62, 63
Thornton, Lucy, 39
Throckmorton, Job, 12
Travers, Walter, 98, 110, 127, 233, 235, 257, 266, 267, 294
Trinity College, Dublin, 70, 256–8
Tuckney, Anthony, 252–3, 298
Tuke, Thomas, 87

tutors (*see also* Cambridge, Oxford), 233, 240, 249, 261, 271, 282–92, 296, 297, 308–9
Twyne, Brian, 282–3
Tyndale, William, 178

Udall, John, 37, 76, 126–7, 195
understanding, *see* reason
universities (*see also* Cambridge, Oxford, tutors)
  continental models, 245–7
  curriculum, 226–9, 249–50, 261–2
  'immorality' at, 230–1
  puritan attitudes towards, 232–4
  puritan emphasis on religion at, 248–53, 255–9, 260–3
  Learned Discourse on, 238–9
  Thomas Norton on, 239–40
  radicals on, 241–4
  social composition of, 229–30, 253–4
  suggestions for reform of, 233–8
Ussher, James, Archbishop of Armagh, 258
Ussher, Robert, 257

Valla, Lorenzo, 66
vanity, *see* learning
Villiers, George, Duke of Buckingham, 285
visitations, 201–2
Vives, Juan Luis, 42, 113, 178, 182, 184, 202
vocation, 56, 89–94, 146–50

Walsingham, Sir Francis, 216, 269, 276
Ward, Samuel, 71, 256, 290
wardship, 277
Whately, William, 37, 117, 157, 287
Whinnell, Francis, 214
Whitaker, William, 117, 217, 238
White, Thomas, Canon of Windsor, 293–4
Whitfield, Thomas, 290
Whitgift, John, Archbishop of Canterbury, 67, 68, 74, 84, 102, 221, 234, 266, 286, 293
Widdowes, Giles, 12
Wigston Hospital, Leicester, 191
Wilcox, Thomas, 12
will, 23, 46–7, 129–30, 146, 148, 212, 301
Wilson, Thomas, 132, 183
Winter, Samuel, 295, 298, 299